D0782164

Natural Language Understanding

James Allen
University of Rochester

The Benjamin/Cummings Publishing Company, Inc.

Redwood City, California • Menlo Park, California • Reading, Massachusetts
New York • Don Mills, Ontario • Wokingham, U.K. • Amsterdam • Bonn
Sydney • Singapore • Tokyo • Madrid • San Juan

Acquisitions Editor: J. Carter Shanklin
Executive Editor: Dan Joraanstad
Editorial Assistant: Melissa Standen
Cover Designer: Yvo Riezebos Design
Technical Assistant: Peg Meeker

Production Editor: Ray Kanarr
Copy Editor: Barbara Conway
Proofreader: Joe Ruddick
Design Consultant: Michael Rogondino

Macintosh is a trademark of Apple Computer, Inc. Word is a trademark of Microsoft, Inc. Canvas is a trademark of Deneba Software.

Camera-ready copy for this book was prepared on a Macintosh with Microsoft Word and Canvas.

The programs and the applications presented in this book have been included for their instructional value. They have been tested with care but are not guaranteed for any particular purpose. The publisher does not offer any warranties or representations, nor does it accept any liabilities with respect to the programs or applications.

Library of Congress Cataloging-in-Publication Data

```
Allen, James.
    Natural language understanding / James Allen. -- 2nd ed.
       p.    cm.
    Includes bibliographical references and index.
    ISBN 0-8053-0334-0
    1. Programming languages (Electronic computers)--Semantics.
 2. Language and logic.  3. Artificial intelligence.   I. Title.
 QA76.7.A44   1994
 006.3'6--dc20                                             94-18218
                                                              CIP
```

1 2 3 4 5 6 7 8 9 10 – MA – 98 97 96 95 94

The Benjamin/Cummings Publishing Company, Inc.
390 Bridge Parkway
Redwood City, CA 94065

Brief Contents

Contents

(∘—optional topic)

v

Chapter 15
Using World Knowledge

Chapter 16
Discourse Structure

Chapter 17
Defining a Conversational Agent

Preface

The primary goal of this book is to provide a comprehensive, in-depth description of the theories and techniques used in the field of natural language understanding. To do this in a single book requires eliminating the idiosyncratic complexities of particular approaches and identifying the underlying concepts of the field as a whole. It also requires developing a small number of notations that can be used to describe a wide range of techniques. It is not possible to capture the range of specific notations that are used in the literature, and attempting to do so would mask the important ideas rather than illuminate them. This book also attempts to make as few assumptions about the background of the reader as possible. All issues and techniques are described in plain English whenever possible. As a result, any reader having some familiarity with the basic notions of programming will be able to understand the principal ideas and techniques used. There is enough detail in this book, however, to allow a sophisticated programmer to produce working systems for natural language understanding.

The book is intended both as textbook and as a general reference source for those interested in natural language processing. As a text, it can be used both in under-graduate and graduate courses in computer science or computational linguistics. As a reference source, it can be used by researchers in areas related to natural language, by developers building natural language systems, and by individuals who are simply interested in how computers can process language.

Work in natural language understanding requires background in a wide range of areas, most importantly computer science, linguistics, logic, psycholinguistics, and the philosophy of language. As very few people have all this background, this book intro-duces whatever background material is required, as needed. For those who have no familiarity with symbolic programming or logical formalisms, two appendices are provided that describe enough of the basic ideas to enable nonprogrammers to read the book. Background in linguistics and other areas is introduced as needed throughout the book.

The book is organized by problem area rather than by technique. This allows the overlap in different approaches to be presented once, and facilitates the comparison of the different techniques. For example, rather than having a chapter on context-free grammars, one on transition network grammars, and another on logic programming techniques, these three techniques are discussed in many chapters, each focusing on a specific set of problems. There is a chapter on basic parsing techniques, then another on using features, and another on handling movement phenomena in language. Each chapter lays out its problem, and then discusses how the problem is addressed in each approach. This way, the similarities and differences between the approaches can be clearly identified.

Why a Second Edition?

I have taught a course based on the first edition regularly since it first appeared. Given developments in the field, I began to find it lacking in some areas. In other areas the book had the right content, but not the right emphasis. Another motivation came from what I saw as a potential split in the field with the introduction of statistically-based techniques and corpus-based research. Claims have been made as to how the new techniques make the old obsolete. But on examining the issues carefully, it was clear to me that the old and new approaches are complementary, and neither is a substitute for the other. This second edition attempts to demonstrate this by including new material on statistical methods, with an emphasis on how they interact with traditional schemes.

Another motivation was to improve the pedagogical aspects of the book. While the original edition was intended for use by students and researchers at different levels of background and with different needs, its organization sometimes made this difficult. The second edition addresses this problem in several ways, as described below in the section on using this book. As a result, it should be accessible to students with little background—say, undergraduates in a computer science program with little linguistics background, or undergraduates in a linguistics program with only a basic course in programming—yet also comprehensive enough for more advanced graduate-level courses, and for use as a general reference text for researchers in the field.

There are many other changes throughout the book, reflecting how the field has changed since the first edition, or at least reflecting how my views have changed. Much of this is a change in emphasis. The sections on syntax, for instance, now use feature-based context-free grammars as the primary formalism for developing the ideas, rather than augmented transition networks. This better reflects current work in the field, and also allows for a better integration of insights from linguistics. Transition network formalisms are still covered in detail, however, as they underlie much work in the field. The sections on semantics have also changed substantially, focusing more on underlying principles and issues rather than specific computational techniques. The logical form language was updated to cover more complex sentences, and the primary method of semantic interpretation is a compositional rule-by-rule analysis. This allows for both a better discussion of the underlying problems in semantic interpretation and a better integration of insights from linguistics. New material has also been added on domain-specific semantic interpretation techniques that have been an active focus in practical systems in the last few years. The material on contextual processing and discourse has generally been rewritten and updated to reflect new work and my better understanding of the principles underlying the techniques in the literature.

The other significant change is the development of software to accompany the book. Most of the principal examples and algorithms have been implemented and tested. This code is available so that students can run the examples to get a better understanding of the algorithms. It also provides a strong base from which students can extend algorithms and develop new grammars for assignments. The code also helps to clarify and simplify the discussion of the algorithms in the book, both because they can be more precise, being based on running programs, and because implementation details can be omitted from the text and still be available to the student in the code.

How to Use This Book

To cover the entire book in detail would require a two-semester sequence at the undergraduate level. As a graduate seminar, it is possible to move more quickly and cover most of the book in a single semester. The most common use of this book, however, is as an undergraduate-level course for a single semester. The book is designed to make this possible, and to allow the instructor to choose the areas on which to focus. There are several mechanisms to help customize the book to your needs. First, each chapter is divided into core material and optional material. Optional sections are marked with an open dot (o). In general, if you are using a chapter, all of the core material should be covered. The optional material can be selected as best fits the design of your course. Additional optional material is included in boxes. Material in boxes is never required, but can be used to push a little deeper in some areas.

The chapters themselves have the general dependencies shown in the figure on the next page. This means that the student should cover the core material in the earlier chapters to best understand the later chapters. In certain cases, material in a section may require knowledge of a technique discussed earlier but not indicated in the dependencies shown here. For example, one of the techniques discussed in Chapter 11 uses some partial parsing techniques described in Chapter 6. In such a case, the earlier section will need to be covered even though the chapter as a whole is skipped.

Readers familiar with the first edition will notice that the two final chapters, dealing with question answering and generation, are not present in the second edition. In keeping with the organization by topic rather than technique, the material from these chapters has been integrated into other chapters. Sections dealing with generation appear as each topic area is discussed. For example, a head-driven realization algorithm is described in Chapter 9 on linking syntax and semantics, and the procedural semantics technique used in database query systems appears in Chapter 13 on knowledge representation techniques.

Software

The software accompanying this book is available via anonymous ftp from bc.aw.com in the subdirectory "bc/allen." All software is written in standard COMMON LISP, and should run with any COMMON LISP system. To retrieve the software, ftp to bc.aw.com by typing

    ftp bc.aw.com

and log in as "anonymous." Change to the directory for this book by typing

    cd bc/allen

Before retrieving the files, it is a good idea to look at the "readme" file to see if changes have been made since this book went to press. To retrieve this file, type

    get README

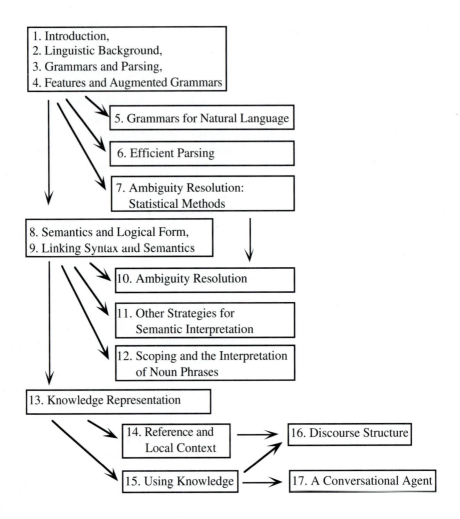

Quit ftp to log off and read the file. (Although the file can be read online, it is courteous not to tie up the login for reading.) Log back on when you are ready to download. You can also get a listing of filenames available using either the conventional UNIX "ls" command or the DOS "dir" command. Assuming that you are in the proper subdirectory, these commands require no arguments:

dir or ls

Using ftp and then de-archiving files can get complicated. Instructions vary as to whether you are downloading Macintosh, DOS, or UNIX files. More instructions are included in the README file. If you are new to using ftp, it is best to consult your favorite UNIX guide or wizard.

References

This book contains extensive references to literature in this field, so that the particular details of the techniques described here can easily be found. In addition, references are provided to other key papers that deal with issues beyond the scope of the book to help identify sources for research projects. References are chosen based on their general availability. Thus I have tried to confine citations to journal articles, books, and major conferences, avoiding technical reports and unpublished notes that are hard to find ten years after the fact. In general, most work in the field is published first in technical reports; more accessible publications often do not appear until many years after the ideas were introduced. Thus the year of publication in the references is not a reliable indicator of the time when the work was done, or when it started to influence other work in the field. While I've tried to provide a wide range of sources and to give credit to the ideas described in this book, I know I have omitted key papers that I will regret immensely when I remember them. To these authors, I extend my apologies.

Acknowledgments

This book would not have been completed except for a sabbatical from the University of Rochester, and for the continual support of the Computer Science Department over the last three years. I was provided with the extra resources needed to complete the project without question, and I am very grateful. I also must thank Peggy Meeker for her efforts in editing and preparing endless drafts as well as the final pages you see here. Peggy has had amazing patience and good humor through countless revisions, and has enforced a consistency of notation and grammatical style that appears to be foreign to my natural way of writing!

I have been fortunate to have a wide range of reviewers on various drafts, both those working for the publisher and many other friends who have taken much time to read and comment on drafts. The list is long, and each one has devoted such effort that listing their names hardly seems sufficient. But here goes. Many thanks to Glenn Blank, Eugene Charniak, Michelle Degraff, George Ferguson, Mary Harper, Peter Heeman, Chung-Hee Hwang, Susan McRoy, Brad Miller, Johanna Moore, Lynn Peterson, Victor Raskin, Len Schubert, Mark Steedman, Mike Tanenhaus, David Traum, and the students in CSC 447 who used the book in the Spring of 1994. The book is significantly different and improved from the early drafts because of all the honest and critical feedback I received.

Finally, I must thank my wife, Judith Hook, for putting up with all this for a second time after experiencing the trauma of doing the first edition. Pushing the book to completion became an obsession that occupied me day and night for nearly a year. Thanks to Judi, and to Jeffrey, Daniel, and Michael, for putting up with me during this time and keeping an appropriate sense of humor about it.

James F. Allen
Rochester, New York

CHAPTER

Introduction to Natural Language Understanding

1.1 The Study of Language

1.2 Applications of Natural Language Understanding

1.3 Evaluating Language Understanding Systems

1.4 The Different Levels of Language Analysis

1.5 Representations and Understanding

1.6 The Organization of Natural Language Understanding Systems

This chapter describes the field of natural language understanding and introduces some basic distinctions. Section 1.1 discusses how natural language understanding research fits into the study of language in general. Section 1.2 discusses some applications of natural language understanding systems and considers what it means for a system to understand language. Section 1.3 describes how you might evaluate whether a system understands language. Section 1.4 introduces a few basic distinctions that are made when studying language, and Section 1.5 discusses how computational systems often realize these distinctions. Finally, Section 1.6 discusses how natural language systems are generally organized, and introduces the particular organization assumed throughout this book.

1.1 The Study of Language

Language is one of the fundamental aspects of human behavior and is a crucial component of our lives. In written form it serves as a long-term record of knowledge from one generation to the next. In spoken form it serves as our primary means of coordinating our day-to-day behavior with others. This book describes research about how language comprehension and production work. The goal of this research is to create computational models of language in enough detail that you could write computer programs to perform various tasks involving natural language. The ultimate goal is to be able to specify models that approach human performance in the linguistic tasks of reading, writing, hearing, and speaking. This book, however, is not concerned with problems related to the specific medium used, whether handwriting, keyboard input, or speech. Rather, it is concerned with the processes of comprehending and using language once the words are recognized. Computational models are useful both for scientific purposes—for exploring the nature of linguistic communication—and for practical purposes—for enabling effective human-machine communication.

Language is studied in several different academic disciplines. Each discipline defines its own set of problems and has its own methods for addressing them. The linguist, for instance, studies the structure of language itself, considering questions such as why certain combinations of words form sentences but others do not, and why a sentence can have some meanings but not others. The psycholinguist, on the other hand, studies the processes of human language production and comprehension, considering questions such as how people identify the appropriate structure of a sentence and when they decide on the appropriate meaning for words. The philosopher considers how words can mean anything at all and how they identify objects in the world. Philosophers also consider what it means to have beliefs, goals, and intentions, and how these cognitive capabilities relate to language. The goal of the computational linguist is to develop a computational theory of language, using the notions of algorithms and data structures from computer science. Of course, to build a computational model, you must take advantage of what is known from all the other disciplines. Figure 1.1 summarizes these different approaches to studying language.

Discipline	Typical Problems	Tools
Linguists	How do words form phrases and sentences? What constrains the possible meanings for a sentence?	Intuitions about well-formedness and meaning; mathematical models of structure (for example, formal language theory, model theoretic semantics)
Psycholinguists	How do people identify the structure of sentences? How are word meanings identified? When does understanding take place?	Experimental techniques based on measuring human performance; statistical analysis of observations
Philosophers	What is meaning, and how do words and sentences acquire it? How do words identify objects in the world?	Natural language argumentation using intuition about counter-examples; mathematical models (for example, logic and model theory)
Computational Linguists	How is the structure of sentences identified? How can knowledge and reasoning be modeled? How can language be used to accomplish specific tasks?	Algorithms, data structures; formal models of representation and reasoning; AI techniques (search and representation methods)

Figure 1.1   The major disciplines studying language

As previously mentioned, there are two motivations for developing computational models. The scientific motivation is to obtain a better understanding of how language works. It recognizes that any one of the other traditional disciplines does not have the tools to completely address the problem of how language comprehension and production work. Even if you combine all the approaches, a comprehensive theory would be too complex to be studied using traditional methods. But we may be able to realize such complex theories as computer programs and then test them by observing how well they perform. By seeing where they fail, we can incrementally improve them. Computational models may provide very specific predictions about human behavior that can then be explored by the psycholinguist. By continuing in this process, we may eventually acquire a deep understanding of how human language processing occurs. To realize such a dream will take the combined efforts of linguists, psycholinguists, philosophers, and computer scientists. This common goal has motivated a new area of interdisciplinary research often called cognitive science.

The practical, or technological, motivation is that natural language processing capabilities would revolutionize the way computers are used. Since most of human knowledge is recorded in linguistic form, computers that could understand natural language could access all this information. In addition, natural language interfaces to computers would allow complex systems to be accessible to

---

BOX 1.1 Boxes and Optional Sections

This book uses several techniques to allow you to identify what material is central and what is optional. In addition, optional material is sometimes classified as advanced, indicating that you may need additional background not covered in this book to fully appreciate the text. Boxes, like this one, always contain optional material, either providing more detail on a particular approach discussed in the main text or discussing additional issues that are related to the text. Sections and subsections may be marked as optional by means of an open dot (○) before the heading. Optional sections provide more breadth and depth to chapters, but are not necessary for understanding material in later chapters. Depending on your interests and focus, you can choose among the optional sections to fill out the core material presented in the regular sections. In addition, there are dependencies between the chapters, so that entire chapters can be skipped if the material does not address your interests. The chapter dependencies are not marked explicitly in the text, but a chart of dependencies is given in the preface.

---

everyone. Such systems would be considerably more flexible and intelligent than is possible with current computer technology. For technological purposes it does not matter if the model used reflects the way humans process language. It only matters that it works.

This book takes a middle ground between the scientific and technological goals. On the one hand, this reflects a belief that natural language is so complex that an *ad hoc* approach without a well-specified underlying theory will not be successful. Thus the technological goal cannot be realized without using sophisticated underlying theories on the level of those being developed by linguists, psycholinguists, and philosophers. On the other hand, the present state of knowledge about natural language processing is so preliminary that attempting to build a cognitively correct model is not feasible. Rather, we are still attempting to construct any model that appears to work.

The goal of this book is to describe work that aims to produce linguistically motivated computational models of language understanding and production that can be shown to perform well in specific example domains. While the book focuses on computational aspects of language processing, considerable space is spent introducing the relevant background knowledge from the other disciplines that motivates and justifies the computational approaches taken. It assumes only a basic knowledge of programming, although the student with some background in linguistics, artificial intelligence (AI), and logic will appreciate additional subtleties in the development.

1.2 Applications of Natural Language Understanding

A good way to define natural language research is to consider the different applications that researchers work on. As you consider these examples, it will also be a good opportunity to consider what it would mean to say that a computer system understands natural language. The applications can be divided into two major classes: text-based applications and dialogue-based applications.

Text-based applications involve the processing of written text, such as books, newspapers, reports, manuals, e-mail messages, and so on. These are all reading-based tasks. Text-based natural language research is ongoing in applications such as

- finding appropriate documents on certain topics from a database of texts (for example, finding relevant books in a library)
- extracting information from messages or articles on certain topics (for example, building a database of all stock transactions described in the news on a given day)
- translating documents from one language to another (for example, producing automobile repair manuals in many different languages)
- summarizing texts for certain purposes (for example, producing a 3-page summary of a 1000-page government report)

Not all systems that perform such tasks must be using natural language understanding techniques in the way we mean in this book. For example, consider the task of finding newspaper articles on a certain topic in a large database. Many techniques have been developed that classify documents by the presence of certain keywords in the text. You can then retrieve articles on a certain topic by looking for articles that contain the keywords associated with that topic. Articles on law, for instance, might contain the words *lawyer, court, sue, affidavit*, and so on, while articles on stock transactions might contain words such as *stocks, takeover, leveraged buyout, options,* and so on. Such a system could retrieve articles on any topic that has been predefined by a set of keywords. Clearly, we would not say that this system is understanding the text; rather, it is using a simple matching technique. While such techniques may produce useful applications, they are inherently limited. It is very unlikely, for example, that they could be extended to handle complex retrieval tasks that are easily expressed in natural language, such as the query *Find me all articles on leveraged buyouts involving more than 100 million dollars that were attempted but failed during 1986 and 1990.* To handle such queries, the system would have to be able to extract enough information from each article in the database to determine whether the article meets the criteria defined by the query; that is, it would have to build a representation of the information in the articles and then use the representation to do the retrievals. This identifies a crucial characteristic of an understanding system: it must compute some representation of the information that can be used for later inference.

Consider another example. Some machine translation systems have been built that are based on pattern matching; that is, a sequence of words in one language is associated with a sequence of words in another language. The translation is accomplished by finding the best set of patterns that match the input and producing the associated output in the other language. This technique can produce reasonable results in some cases but sometimes produces completely wrong translations because of its inability to use an understanding of content to disambiguate word senses and sentence meanings appropriately. In contrast, other machine translation systems operate by producing a representation of the meaning of each sentence in one language, and then producing a sentence in the other language that realizes the same meaning. This latter approach, because it involves the computation of a representation of meaning, is using natural language understanding techniques.

One very attractive domain for text-based research is story understanding. In this task the system processes a story and then must answer questions about it. This is similar to the type of reading comprehension tests used in schools and provides a very rich method for evaluating the depth of understanding the system is able to achieve.

Dialogue-based applications involve human-machine communication. Most naturally this involves spoken language, but it also includes interaction using keyboards. Typical potential applications include

- question-answering systems, where natural language is used to query a database (for example, a query system to a personnel database)
- automated customer service over the telephone (for example, to perform banking transactions or order items from a catalogue)
- tutoring systems, where the machine interacts with a student (for example, an automated mathematics tutoring system)
- spoken language control of a machine (for example, voice control of a VCR or computer)
- general cooperative problem-solving systems (for example, a system that helps a person plan and schedule freight shipments)

Some of the problems faced by dialogue systems are quite different than in text-based systems. First, the language used is very different, and the system needs to participate actively in order to maintain a natural, smooth-flowing dialogue. Dialogue requires the use of acknowledgments to verify that things are understood, and an ability to both recognize and generate clarification sub-dialogues when something is not clearly understood. Even with these differences, however, the basic processing techniques are fundamentally the same.

It is important to distinguish the problems of speech recognition from the problems of language understanding. A speech recognition system need not involve any language understanding. For instance, voice-controlled computers and VCRs are entering the market now. These do not involve natural language understanding in any general way. Rather, the words recognized are used as commands, much like the commands you send to a VCR using a remote control. Speech recognition is concerned only with identifying the words spoken from a given speech signal, not with understanding how words are used to communicate. To be an understanding system, the speech recognizer would need to feed its input to a natural language understanding system, producing what is often called a spoken language understanding system.

With few exceptions, all the techniques discussed in this book are equally relevant for text-based and dialogue-based language understanding, and apply equally well whether the input is text, keyboard, or speech. The key characteristic of any understanding system is that it represents the meaning of sentences in some representation language that can be used later for further processing.

1.3 Evaluating Language Understanding Systems

As you can see, what counts as understanding might vary from application to application. If this is so, how can you tell if a system works? One obvious way to evaluate a system is to run the program and see how well it performs the task it was designed to do. If the program is meant to answer questions about a database of facts, you might ask it questions to see how good it is at producing the correct answers. If the system is designed to participate in simple conversations on a certain topic, you might try conversing with it. This is called **black box evaluation** because it evaluates system performance without looking inside to see how it works. While ultimately this method of evaluation may be the best test of a system's capabilities, it is problematic in the early stages of research because early evaluation results can be misleading. Sometimes the techniques that produce the best results in the short term will not lead to the best results in the long term. For instance, if the overall performance of all known systems in a given application is uniformly low, few conclusions can be drawn. The fact that one system was correct 50 percent of the time while another was correct only 40 percent of the time says nothing about the long-term viability of either approach. Only when the success rates become high, making a practical application feasible, can much significance be given to overall system performance measures.

An alternative method of evaluation is to identify various subcomponents of a system and then evaluate each one with appropriate tests. This is called **glass box evaluation** because you look inside at the structure of the system. The problem with glass box evaluation is that it requires some consensus on what the various components of a natural language system should be. Achieving such a consensus is an area of considerable activity at the present.

Despite the difficulties, evaluations are of crucial importance to the field, as very little can be concluded from examining a few examples that a particular system can handle. If you cannot interact freely with the program yourself but must depend on transcripts of others' interactions, you can easily be mislead into overestimating a program's abilities. It is very hard for people not to attribute much more intelligence to the program than is actually present.

Consider a concrete example—the ELIZA program that was developed in the mid-1960s at MIT. This program must be one of the most popular AI

User:	ELIZA:
Men are all alike.	In what way?
They're always bugging us about something or other.	Can you think of a specific example?
Well, my boyfriend made me come here.	Your boyfriend made you come here.
He says I'm depressed much of the time.	I am sorry to hear you are depressed.
It's true, I am unhappy.	Do you think coming here will help you not to be unhappy?
I need some help; that much seems certain.	What would it mean to you if you got some help?
Perhaps I could learn to get along with my mother.	Tell me more about your family.
My mother takes care of me.	Who else in your family takes care of you?
My father.	Your father.
You are like my father in some ways.	What resemblance do you see?

Figure 1.2 A dialogue with ELIZA

programs of all time, and versions of it exist for most machines, including most personal computers. ELIZA was never claimed to embody a theory of language comprehension and production, but it serves as an excellent example as its behavior initially seems impressive. The system plays the role of a therapist and, to obtain the best results, the user should correspondingly play the role of a patient. Figure 1.2 presents a transcript of this system in operation. Given this transcript, or even playing with the system yourself for a few minutes, ELIZA's performance certainly seems impressive.

Here is a simple description of how ELIZA works. There is a database of particular words that are called **keywords**. For each keyword, the system stores an integer, a pattern to match against the input, and a specification of the output. The algorithm is as follows: Given a sentence S, find a keyword in S whose pattern matches S. If there is more than one keyword, pick the one with the highest integer value. Use the output specification that is associated with this keyword to generate the next sentence. If there are no keywords, generate an innocuous continuation statement, such as *Tell me more* or *Go on*.

Figure 1.3 shows a fragment of a database of keywords. In this database a pattern consists of words and variables. The prefix ? before a letter indicates a variable, which can match any sequence of words. For example, the pattern

?X are you ?Y

would match the sentence *Why are you looking at me?*, where the variable ?X matches *Why* and ?Y matches *looking at me*. The output specification may also use the same variables. In this case, ELIZA inserts the words that match the variables in the input into the output after making some minor changes in the

Word	Rank	Pattern	Outputs
alike	10	?X	In what way?
			What resemblance do you see?
are	3	?X are you ?Y	Would you prefer it if I weren't ?Y?
	3	?X are ?Y	What if they were not ?Y?
always	5	?X	Can you think of a specific example?
			When?
			Really, always?
what	2	?X	Why do you ask?
			Does that interest you?

Figure 1.3 Sample data from ELIZA

pronouns (for example, replacing *me* with *you*). Thus, for the pattern above, if the output specification is

Would you prefer it if I weren't ?Y?

the rule would generate a response *Would you prefer it if I weren't looking at you?* When the database lists multiple output specifications for a given pattern, ELIZA selects a different one each time a keyword rule is used, thereby preventing unnatural repetition in the conversation. Using these rules, you can see how ELIZA produced the first two exchanges in the conversation in Figure 1.2. ELIZA generated the first response from the first output of the keyword *alike* and the second response from the first output of the keyword *always*.

This description covers all of the essential points of the program. You will probably agree that the program does not understand the conversation it is participating in. Rather, it is a collection of tricks. Why then does ELIZA appear to function so well? There are several reasons. Perhaps the most important reason is that, when people hear or read a sequence of words that they understand as a sentence, they attribute meaning to the sentence and assume that the person (or machine) that produced the sentence actually intended that meaning. People are extremely good at distinguishing word meanings and interpreting sentences to fit the context. Thus ELIZA appears to be intelligent because you use your own intelligence to make sense of what it says.

Other crucial characteristics of the conversational setting also aid in sustaining the illusion of intelligence. For instance, the system does not need any world knowledge because it never has to make a claim, support an argument, or answer a question. Rather, it simply asks a series of questions. Except in a patient-therapist situation, this would be unacceptable. ELIZA evades all direct questions by responding with another question, such as *Why do you ask?* There is no way to force the program to say something concrete about any topic.

Even in such a restricted situation, however, it is relatively easy to demonstrate that the program does not understand. It sometimes produces completely off-the-wall responses. For instance, if you say *Necessity is the mother of invention,* it might respond with *Tell me more about your family,* based on its pattern for the word *mother.* In addition, since ELIZA has no knowledge about the structure of language, it accepts gibberish just as readily as valid sentences. If you enter *Green the adzabak are the a ran four,* ELIZA will respond with something like *What if they were not the a ran four?* Also, as a conversation progresses, it becomes obvious that the program does not retain any of the content in the conversation. It begins to ask questions that are inappropriate in light of earlier exchanges, and its responses in general begin to show a lack of focus. Of course, if you are not able to play with the program and must depend only on transcripts of conversations by others, you would have no way of detecting these flaws, unless they are explicitly mentioned.

Suppose you need to build a natural language program for a certain application in only six months. If you start to construct a general model of language understanding, it will not be completed in that time frame and so will perform miserably on the tests. An ELIZA-like system, however, could easily produce behavior like that previously discussed with less than a few months of programming and will appear to far outperform the other system in testing. The differences will be especially marked if the test data only includes typical domain interactions that are not designed to test the limits of the system. Thus, if we take short-term performance as our only criteria of progress, everyone will build and fine-tune ELIZA-style systems, and the field will not progress past the limitations of the simple approach.

To avoid this problem, either we have to accept certain theoretical assumptions about the architecture of natural language systems and develop specific evaluation measures for different components, or we have to discount overall evaluation results until some reasonably high level of performance is obtained. Only then will cross-system comparisons begin to reflect the potential for long-term success in the field.

1.4 The Different Levels of Language Analysis

A natural language system must use considerable knowledge about the structure of the language itself, including what the words are, how words combine to form sentences, what the words mean, how word meanings contribute to sentence meanings, and so on. However, we cannot completely account for linguistic behavior without also taking into account another aspect of what makes humans intelligent—their general world knowledge and their reasoning abilities. For example, to answer questions or to participate in a conversation, a person not only must know a lot about the structure of the language being used, but also must know about the world in general and the conversational setting in particular.

The following are some of the different forms of knowledge relevant for natural language understanding:

Phonetic and phonological knowledge—concerns how words are related to the sounds that realize them. Such knowledge is crucial for speech-based systems and is discussed in more detail in Appendix C.

Morphological knowledge—concerns how words are constructed from more basic meaning units called **morphemes**. A morpheme is the primitive unit of meaning in a language (for example, the meaning of the word *friendly* is derivable from the meaning of the noun *friend* and the suffix *-ly,* which transforms a noun into an adjective).

Syntactic knowledge—concerns how words can be put together to form correct sentences and determines what structural role each word plays in the sentence and what phrases are subparts of what other phrases.

Semantic knowledge—concerns what words mean and how these meanings combine in sentences to form sentence meanings. This is the study of context-independent meaning—the meaning a sentence has regardless of the context in which it is used.

Pragmatic knowledge—concerns how sentences are used in different situations and how use affects the interpretation of the sentence.

Discourse knowledge—concerns how the immediately preceding sentences affect the interpretation of the next sentence. This information is especially important for interpreting pronouns and for interpreting the temporal aspects of the information conveyed.

World knowledge—includes the general knowledge about the structure of the world that language users must have in order to, for example, maintain a conversation. It includes what each language user must know about the other user's beliefs and goals.

These definitions are imprecise and are more characteristics of knowledge than actual distinct classes of knowledge. Any particular fact might include aspects from several different levels, and an algorithm might need to draw from several different levels simultaneously. For teaching purposes, however, this book is organized into three parts, each describing a set of techniques that naturally cluster together. Part I focuses on syntactic and morphological processing, Part II focuses on semantic processing, and Part III focuses on contextual effects in general, including pragmatics, discourse, and world knowledge.

BOX 1.2 Syntax, Semantics, and Pragmatics

The following examples may help you understand the distinction between syntax, semantics, and pragmatics. Consider each example as a candidate for the initial sentence of this book, which you know discusses natural language processing:

1. Language is one of the fundamental aspects of human behavior and is a crucial component of our lives.
2. Green frogs have large noses.
3. Green ideas have large noses.
4. Large have green ideas nose.

Sentence 1 appears to be a reasonable start (I hope!). It agrees with all that is known about syntax, semantics, and pragmatics. Each of the other sentences violates one or more of these levels. Sentence 2 is well-formed syntactically and semantically, but not pragmatically. It fares poorly as the first sentence of the book because the reader would find no reason for using it. But however bad sentence 2 would be as a start, sentence 3 is much worse. Not only is it obviously pragmatically ill-formed, it is also semantically ill-formed. To see this, consider that you and I could argue about whether sentence 2 is true or not, but we cannot do so with sentence 3. I cannot affirm or deny sentence 3 in coherent conversation. However, the sentence does have some structure, for we can discuss what is wrong with it: Ideas cannot be green and, even if they could, they certainly cannot have large noses. Sentence 4 is even worse. In fact, it is unintelligible, even though it contains the same words as sentence 3. It does not even have enough structure to allow you to say what is wrong with it. Thus it is syntactically ill-formed. Incidentally, there are cases in which a sentence may be pragmatically well-formed but not syntactically well-formed. For example, if I ask you where you are going and you reply "I go store," the response would be understandable even though it is syntactically ill-formed. Thus it is at least pragmatically well-formed and may even be semantically well-formed.

1.5 Representations and Understanding

As previously stated, a crucial component of understanding involves computing a representation of the meaning of sentences and texts. Without defining the notion of representation, however, this assertion has little content. For instance, why not simply use the sentence itself as a representation of its meaning? One reason is that most words have multiple meanings, which we will call **senses**. The word *cook*, for example, has a sense as a verb and a sense as a noun; *dish* has multiple senses as a noun as well as a sense as a verb; and *still* has senses as a noun, verb, adjective, and adverb. This ambiguity would inhibit the system from making the appropriate inferences needed to model understanding. The disambiguation problem appears much easier than it actually is because people do not generally notice ambiguity. While a person does not seem to consider each of the possible senses of a word when understanding a sentence, a program must explicitly consider them one by one.

To represent meaning, we must have a more precise language. The tools to do this come from mathematics and logic and involve the use of formally specified representation languages. Formal languages are specified from very simple building blocks. The most fundamental is the notion of an atomic symbol, which is distinguishable from any other atomic symbol simply based on how it is written. Useful representation languages have the following two properties:

- The representation must be precise and unambiguous. You should be able to express every distinct reading of a sentence as a distinct formula in the representation.
- The representation should capture the intuitive structure of the natural language sentences that it represents. For example, sentences that appear to be structurally similar should have similar structural representations, and the meanings of two sentences that are paraphrases of each other should be closely related to each other.

Several different representations will be used that correspond to some of the levels of analysis discussed in the last section. In particular, we will develop formal languages for expressing syntactic structure, for context-independent word and sentence meanings, and for expressing general world knowledge.

Syntax: Representing Sentence Structure

The syntactic structure of a sentence indicates the way that words in the sentence are related to each other. This structure indicates how the words are grouped together into phrases, what words modify what other words, and what words are of central importance in the sentence. In addition, this structure may identify the types of relationships that exist between phrases and can store other information about the particular sentence structure that may be needed for later processing. For example, consider the following sentences:

1. John sold the book to Mary.
2. The book was sold to Mary by John.

These sentences share certain structural properties. In each, the noun phrases are *John, Mary,* and *the book,* and the act described is some selling action. In other respects, these sentences are significantly different. For instance, even though both sentences are always either true or false in the exact same situations, you could only give sentence 1 as an answer to the question *What did John do for Mary?* Sentence 2 is a much better continuation of a sentence beginning with the phrase *After it fell in the river,* as sentences 3 and 4 show. Following the standard convention in linguistics, this book will use an asterisk (*) before any example of an ill-formed or questionable sentence.

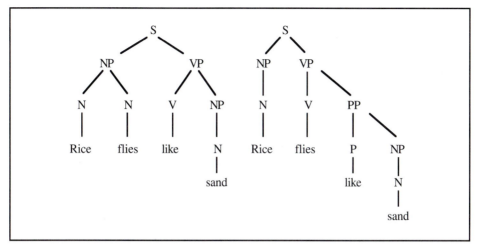

Figure 1.4 Two structural representations of *Rice flies like sand.*

3.   *After it fell in the river, John sold Mary the book.
4.   After it fell in the river, the book was sold to Mary by John.

Many other structural properties can be revealed by considering sentences that are not well-formed. Sentence 5 is ill-formed because the subject and the verb do not agree in number (the subject is singular and the verb is plural), while 6 is ill-formed because the verb *put* requires some modifier that describes where John put the object.

5.   *John are in the corner.
6.   *John put the book.

Making judgments on grammaticality is not a goal in natural language understanding. In fact, a robust system should be able to understand ill-formed sentences whenever possible. This might suggest that agreement checks can be ignored, but this is not so. Agreement checks are essential for eliminating potential ambiguities. Consider sentences 7 and 8, which are identical except for the number feature of the main verb, yet represent two quite distinct interpretations.

7.   Flying planes are dangerous.
8.   Flying planes is dangerous.

If you did not check subject-verb agreement, these two sentences would be indistinguishable and ambiguous. You could find similar examples for every syntactic feature that this book introduces and uses.

Most syntactic representations of language are based on the notion of context-free grammars, which represent sentence structure in terms of what phrases are subparts of other phrases. This information is often presented in a tree form, such as the one shown in Figure 1.4, which shows two different structures for the sentence *Rice flies like sand.* In the first reading, the sentence is formed from a noun phrase (NP) describing a type of fly, rice flies, and a verb phrase (VP) that asserts that these flies like sand. In the second structure, the sentence is formed from a noun phrase describing a type of substance, rice, and a verb phrase stating that this substance flies like sand (say, if you throw it). The two structures also give further details on the structure of the noun phrase and verb phrase and identify the part of speech for each word. In particular, the word *like* is a verb (V) in the first reading and a preposition (P) in the second.

The Logical Form

The structure of a sentence doesn't reflect its meaning, however. For example, the NP *the catch* can have different meanings depending on whether the speaker is talking about a baseball game or a fishing expedition. Both these interpretations have the same syntactic structure, and the different meanings arise from an ambiguity concerning the sense of the word *catch*. Once the correct sense is identified, say the fishing sense, there still is a problem in determining what fish are being referred to. The intended meaning of a sentence depends on the situation in which the sentence is produced. Rather than combining all these problems, this book will consider each one separately. The division is between context-independent meaning and context-dependent meaning. The fact that *catch* may refer to a baseball move or the results of a fishing expedition is knowledge about English and is independent of the situation in which the word is used. On the other hand, the fact that a particular noun phrase *the catch* refers to what Jack caught when fishing yesterday is contextually dependent. The representation of the context-independent meaning of a sentence is called its **logical form.**

The logical form encodes possible word senses and identifies the semantic relationships between the words and phrases. Many of these relationships are often captured using an abstract set of semantic relationships between the verb and its NPs. In particular, in both sentences 1 and 2 previously given, the action described is a selling event, where *John* is the seller, *the book* is the object being sold, and *Mary* is the buyer. These roles are instances of the abstract semantic roles AGENT, THEME, and TO-POSS (for final possessor), respectively.

Once the semantic relationships are determined, some word senses may be impossible and thus eliminated from consideration. Consider the sentence

9.   Jack invited Mary to the Halloween ball.

The word *ball,* which by itself is ambiguous between the plaything that bounces and the formal dance event, can only take the latter sense in sentence 9, because the verb *invite* only makes sense with this interpretation. One of the key tasks in semantic interpretation is to consider what combinations of the individual word meanings can combine to create coherent sentence meanings. Exploiting such interconnections between word meanings can greatly reduce the number of possible word senses for each word in a given sentence.

The Final Meaning Representation

The final representation needed is a general knowledge representation (KR), which the system uses to represent and reason about its application domain. This is the language in which all the specific knowledge based on the application is represented. The goal of contextual interpretation is to take a representation of the structure of a sentence and its logical form, and to map this into some expression in the KR that allows the system to perform the appropriate task in the domain. In a question-answering application, a question might map to a database query, in a story-understanding application, a sentence might map into a set of expressions that represent the situation that the sentence describes.

For the most part, we will assume that the first-order predicate calculus (FOPC) is the final representation language because it is relatively well known, well studied, and is precisely defined. While some inadequacies of FOPC will be examined later, these inadequacies are not relevant for most of the issues to be discussed.

1.6 The Organization of Natural Language Understanding Systems

This book is organized around the three levels of representation just discussed: syntactic structure, logical form, and the final meaning representation. Separating the problems in this way will allow you to study each problem in depth without worrying about other complications. Actual systems are usually organized slightly differently, however. In particular, Figure 1.5 shows the organization that this book assumes.

As you can see, there are interpretation processes that map from one repre-sentation to the other. For instance, the process that maps a sentence to its syntactic structure and logical form is called the **parser**. It uses knowledge about word and word meanings (the **lexicon**) and a set of rules defining the legal struc-tures (the **grammar**) in order to assign a syntactic structure and a logical form to an input sentence. An alternative organization could perform syntactic processing first and then perform semantic interpretation on the resulting structures. Combining the two, however, has considerable advantages because it leads to a reduction in the number of possible interpretations, since every proposed inter-pretation must simultaneously be syntactically and semantically well formed. For example, consider the following two sentences:

10.   Visiting relatives can be trying.
11.   Visiting museums can be trying.

These two sentences have identical syntactic structure, so both are syntactically ambiguous. In sentence 10, the subject might be relatives who are visiting you or

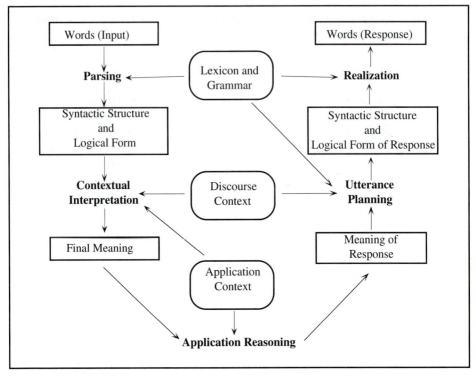

Figure 1.5   The flow of information

the event of you visiting relatives. Both of these alternatives are semantically valid, and you would need to determine the appropriate sense by using the contextual mechanism. However, sentence 11 has only one possible semantic interpretation, since museums are not objects that can visit other people; rather they must be visited. In a system with separate syntactic and semantic processing, there would be two syntactic interpretations of sentence 11, one of which the semantic interpreter would eliminate later. If syntactic and semantic processing are combined, however, the system will be able to detect the semantic anomaly as soon as it interprets the phrase *visiting museums,* and thus will never build the incorrect syntactic structure in the first place. While the savings here seem small, in a realistic application a reasonable sentence may have hundreds of possible syntactic structures, many of which are semantically anomalous.

Continuing through Figure 1.5, the process that transforms the syntactic structure and logical form into a final meaning representation is called contextual processing. This process includes issues such as identifying the objects referred to by noun phrases such as definite descriptions (for example, *the man*) and pronouns, the analysis of the temporal aspects of the new information conveyed by the sentence, the identification of the speaker's intention (for example, whether *Can you lift that rock* is a yes/no question or a request), as well as all the inferential processing required to interpret the sentence appropriately within the application domain. It uses knowledge of the discourse context (determined by the sentences that preceded the current one) and knowledge of the application to produce a final representation.

The system would then perform whatever reasoning tasks are appropriate for the application. When this requires a response to the user, the meaning that must be expressed is passed to the generation component of the system. It uses knowledge of the discourse context, plus information on the grammar and lexicon, to plan the form of an utterance, which then is mapped into words by a realization process. Of course, if this were a spoken language application, the words would not be the final input and output, but rather would be the output of a speech recognizer and the input to a speech synthesizer, as appropriate.

While this text focuses primarily on language understanding, notice that the same levels of knowledge are also used for the generation task as well. For instance, knowledge of syntactic structure is encoded in the grammar. This grammar can be used either to identify the structure of a given sentence or to realize a structure as a sequence of words. A grammar that supports both pro-cesses is called a **bidirectional grammar**. While most researchers agree that bidirectional grammars are the preferred model, in actual practice grammars are often tailored for the understanding task or the generation task. This occurs because different issues are important for each task, and generally any given researcher focuses just on the problems related to their specific task. But even when the actual grammars differ between understanding and generation, the grammatical formalisms used remain the same.

Summary

This book describes computational theories of natural language understanding. The principal characteristic of understanding systems is that they compute representations of the meanings of sentences and use these representations in reasoning tasks. Three principal levels of representation were introduced that correspond to the three main subparts of this book. Syntactic processing is con-cerned with the structural properties of sentences; semantic processing computes a logical form that represents the context-independent meaning of the sentence; and contextual processing connects language to the application domain.

Related Work and Further Readings

A good idea of work in the field can be obtained by reading two articles in Shapiro (1992), under the headings "Computational Linguistics" and "Natural Language Understanding." There are also articles on specialized subareas such as machine translation, natural language interfaces, natural language generation, and so on. Longer surveys on certain areas are also available. Slocum (1985) gives a survey of machine translation, and Perrault and Grosz (1986) give a survey of natural language interfaces.

You can find a description of the ELIZA program that includes the transcript of the dialogue in Figure 1.2 in Weizenbaum (1966). The basic technique of using template matching was developed further in the PARRY system, as described in the paper by Colby in Schank and Colby (1973). That same book also contains descriptions of early natural language systems, including those by Winograd and by Schank. Another important early system is the LUNAR system, an overview of which can be found in Woods (1977). For another perspective on the AI approach to natural language, refer to the introduction in Winograd (1983).

Exercises for Chapter 1

1.   (*easy*) Define a set of data rules for ELIZA that would generate the first seven exchanges in the conversation in Figure 1.2.

2.   (*easy*) Discover all of the possible meanings of the following sentences by giving a paraphrase of each interpretation. For each sentence, identify whether the different meanings arise from structural ambiguity, semantic ambiguity, or pragmatic ambiguity.

   a.   Time flies like an arrow.
   b.   He drew one card.
   c.   Mr. Spock was charged with illegal alien recruitment.
   d.   He crushed the key to my heart.

3.   (*easy*) Classify these sentences along each of the following dimensions, given that the person uttering the sentence is responding to a complaint that the car is too cold: (i) syntactically correct or not; (ii) semantically correct or not; (iii) pragmatically correct or not.

   a.   The heater are on.
   b.   The tires are brand new.
   c.   Too many windows eat the stew.

4.   (*medium*) Implement an ELIZA program that can use the rules that you developed in Exercise 1 and run it for that dialogue. Without adding any more rules, what does your program do on the next few utterances in the conversation in Figure 1.2? How does the program do if you run it in a different context—say, a casual conversation at a bar?

PART I
Syntactic Processing

As discussed in the introduction, this book divides the task of understanding sentences into three stages. Part I of the book discusses the first stage, syntactic processing. The goal of syntactic processing is to determine the structural components of sentences. It determines, for instance, how a sentence is broken down into phrases, how those phrases are broken down into sub-phrases, and so on, all the way down to the actual structure of the words used. These structural relationships are crucial for determining the meaning of sentences using the techniques described in Parts II and III.

There are two major issues discussed in Part I. The first issue concerns the formalism that is used to specify what sentences are possible in a language. This information is specified by a set of rules called a grammar. We will be concerned both with the general issue of what constitutes good formalisms for writing grammars for natural languages, and with the specific issue of what grammatical rules provide a good account of English syntax. The second issue concerns how to determine the structure of a given sentence once you know the grammar for the language. This process is called parsing. There are many different algorithms for parsing, and this book will consider a sampling of the techniques that are most influential in the field.

Chapter 2 provides a basic background to English syntax for the reader who has not studied linguistics. It introduces the key concepts and distinctions that are common to virtually all syntactic theories. Chapter 3 introduces several formalisms that are in common use for specifying grammars and describes the basic parsing algorithms in detail. Chapter 4 introduces the idea of features, which extend the basic grammatical formalisms and allow many aspects of natural languages to be captured concisely. Chapter 5 then describes some of the more difficult aspects of natural languages, especially the treatment of questions, relative clauses, and other forms of movement phenomena. It shows how the feature systems can be extended so that they can handle these complex sentences. Chapter 6 discusses issues relating to ambiguity resolution. Some techniques are aimed at developing more efficient representations for storing multiple interpretations, while others are aimed at using local information to choose between alternative interpretations while the parsing is in progress. Finally, Chapter 7 discusses a relatively new area of research that uses statistical information derived from analyzing large databases of sentences. This information can be used to identify the most likely classes for ambiguous words and the most likely structural analyses for structurally ambiguous sentences.

CHAPTER

2

Linguistic Background: An Outline of English Syntax

2.1   Words

2.2   The Elements of Simple Noun Phrases

2.3   Verb Phrases and Simple Sentences

2.4   Noun Phrases Revisited

2.5   Adjective Phrases

2.6   Adverbial Phrases

This chapter provides background material on the basic structure of English syntax for those who have not taken any linguistics courses. It reviews the major phrase categories and identifies their most important subparts. Along the way all the basic word categories used in the book are introduced. While the only structures discussed are those for English, much of what is said applies to nearly all other European languages as well. The reader who has some background in linguistics can quickly skim this chapter, as it does not address any computational issues. You will probably want to use this chapter as a reference source as you work through the rest of the chapters in Part I.

Section 2.1 describes issues related to words and word classes. Section 2.2 describes simple noun phrases, which are then used in Section 2.3 to describe simple verb phrases. Section 2.4 considers complex noun phrases that include embedded sentences such as relative clauses. The remaining sections briefly cover other types of phrases: adjective phrases in Section 2.5 and adverbial phrases in Section 2.6.

2.1 Words

At first glance the most basic unit of linguistic structure appears to be the word. The word, though, is far from the fundamental element of study in linguistics; it is already the result of a complex set of more primitive parts. The study of **morphology** concerns the construction of words from more basic components corresponding roughly to meaning units. There are two basic ways that new words are formed, traditionally classified as **inflectional** forms and **derivational** forms. Inflectional forms use a **root** form of a word and typically add a **suffix** so that the word appears in the appropriate form given the sentence. Verbs are the best examples of this in English. Each verb has a basic form that then is typically changed depending on the subject and the tense of the sentence. For example, the verb *sigh* will take suffixes such as *-s*, *-ing*, and *-ed* to create the verb forms *sighs*, *sighing*, and *sighed*, respectively. These new words are all verbs and share the same basic meaning. Derivational morphology involves the derivation of new words from other forms. The new words may be in completely different categories from their subparts. For example, the noun *friend* is made into the adjective *friendly* by adding the suffix *-ly*. A more complex derivation would allow you to derive the noun *friendliness* from the adjective form. There are many interesting issues concerned with how words are derived and how the choice of word form is affected by the syntactic structure of the sentence that constrains it.

Traditionally, linguists classify words into different categories based on their uses. Two related areas of evidence are used to divide words into categories. The first area concerns the word's contribution to the meaning of the phrase that contains it, and the second area concerns the actual syntactic structures in which the word may play a role. For example, you might posit the class **noun** as those words that can be used to identify the basic type of object, concept, or place being discussed, and **adjective** as those words that further qualify the object, concept, or place. Thus *green* would be an adjective and *book* a noun, as shown in the phrases *the green book* and *green books*. But things are not so simple: *green* might play the role of a noun, as in *That green is lighter than the other*, and *book* might play the role of a modifier, as in *the book worm*. In fact, most nouns seem to be able to be used as a modifier in some situations. Perhaps the classes should be combined, since they overlap a great deal. But other forms of evidence exist. Consider what words could complete the sentence *It's so . . . .* You might say *It's so green, It's so hot, It's so true,* and so on. Note that although *book* can be a modifier in *the book worm*, you cannot say **It's so book* about anything. Thus there are two classes of modifiers: adjective modifiers and noun modifiers.

Consider again the case where adjectives can be used as nouns, as in *the green*. Not all adjectives can be used in such a way. For example, the noun phrase *the hot* can be used, given a context where there are hot and cold plates, in a sentence such as *The hot are on the table.* But this refers to the hot plates; it cannot refer to hotness in the way the phrase *the green* refers to green. With this evidence you could subdivide adjectives into two subclasses—those that can also be used to describe a concept or quality directly, and those that cannot. Alternatively, however, you can simply say that *green* is ambiguous between being an adjective or a noun and, therefore, falls in both classes. Since *green* can behave like any other noun, the second solution seems the most direct.

Using similar arguments, we can identify four main classes of words in English that contribute to the meaning of sentences. These classes are nouns, adjectives, verbs, and adverbs. Sentences are built out of phrases centered on these four word classes. Of course, there are many other classes of words that are necessary to form sentences, such as articles, pronouns, prepositions, particles, quantifiers, conjunctions, and so on. But these classes are fixed in the sense that new words in these classes are rarely introduced into the language. New nouns, verbs, adjectives and adverbs, on the other hand, are regularly introduced into the language as it evolves. As a result, these classes are called the **open class words**, and the others are called the **closed class words**.

A word in any of the four open classes may be used to form the basis of a phrase. This word is called the **head** of the phrase and indicates the type of thing, activity, or quality that the phrase describes. For example, with noun phrases, the head word indicates the general classes of objects being described. The phrases

> the dog
> the mangy dog
> the mangy dog at the pound

are all noun phrases that describe an object in the class of dogs. The first describes a member from the class of all dogs, the second an object from the class of mangy dogs, and the third an object from the class of mangy dogs that are at the pound. The word *dog* is the head of each of these phrases.

Noun Phrases

The **president** *of the company*
His **desire** *to succeed*
Several **challenges** *from the opposing team*

Verb Phrases

looked *up the chimney*
believed *that the world was flat*
ate *the pizza*

Adjective Phrases

easy *to assemble*
happy *that he'd won the prize*
angry *as a hippo*

Adverbial Phrases

rapidly *like a bat*
intermittently *throughout the day*
inside *the house*

Figure 2.1   Examples of heads and complements

Similarly, the adjective phrases

hungry
very hungry
hungry as a horse

all describe the quality of hunger. In each case the word *hungry* is the head.

In some cases a phrase may consist of a single head. For example, the word *sand* can be a noun phrase, *hungry* can be an adjective phrase, and *walked* can be a verb phrase. In many other cases the head requires additional phrases following it to express the desired meaning. For example, the verb *put* cannot form a verb phrase in isolation; thus the following words do not form a meaningful sentence:

*Jack put.

To be meaningful, the verb *put* must be followed by a noun phrase and a phrase describing a location, as in the verb phrase *put the dog in the house.* The phrase or set of phrases needed to complete the meaning of such a head is called the **complement** of the head. In the preceding phrase *put* is the head and *the dog in the house* is the complement. Heads of all the major classes may require complements. Figure 2.1 gives some examples of phrases, with the head indicated by boldface and the complements by italics. In the remainder of this chapter, we will look at these different types of phrases in more detail and see how they are structured and how they contribute to the meaning of sentences.

2.2   The Elements of Simple Noun Phrases

Noun phrases (NPs) are used to refer to things: objects, places, concepts, events, qualities, and so on. The simplest NP consists of a single pronoun: *he, she, they, you, me, it, I,* and so on. Pronouns can refer to physical objects, as in the sentence

It hid under the rug.

to events, as in the sentence

Once I opened the door, I regretted *it* for months.

and to qualities, as in the sentence

He was so angry, but he didn't show *it*.

Pronouns do not take any modifiers except in rare forms, as in the sentence

He who hesitates is lost.

Another basic form of noun phrase consists of a **name** or **proper noun**, such as *John* or *Rochester*. These nouns appear in capitalized form in carefully written English. Names may also consist of multiple words, as in the *New York Times* and *Stratford-on-Avon*.

Excluding pronouns and proper names, the head of a noun phrase is usually a common noun. Nouns divide into two main classes:

> **count nouns**—nouns that describe specific objects or sets of objects.
> **mass nouns**—nouns that describe composites or substances.

Count nouns acquired their name because they can be counted. There may be one *dog* or many *dogs*, one *book* or several *books*, one *crowd* or several *crowds*. If a single count noun is used to describe a whole class of objects, it must be in its plural form. Thus you can say *Dogs are friendly* but not **Dog is friendly*.

Mass nouns cannot be counted. There may be *some water, some wheat*, or *some sand*. If you try to count with a mass noun, you change the meaning. For example, *some wheat* refers to a portion of some quantity of wheat, whereas *one wheat* is a single type of wheat rather than a single grain of wheat. A mass noun can be used to describe a whole class of material without using a plural form. Thus you say *Water is necessary for life*, not **Waters are necessary for life*.

In addition to a head, a noun phrase may contain **specifiers** and **qualifiers** preceding the head. The qualifiers further describe the general class of objects identified by the head, while the specifiers indicate how many such objects are being described, as well as how the objects being described relate to the speaker and hearer. Specifiers are constructed out of **ordinals** (such as *first* and *second*), **cardinals** (such as *one* and *two*), and **determiners**. Determiners can be subdivided into the following general classes:

> **articles**—the words *the, a,* and *an*.
> **demonstratives**—words such as *this, that, these,* and *those*.
> **possessives**—noun phrases followed by the suffix *'s*, such as *John's* and *the fat man's,* as well as possessive pronouns, such as *her, my,* and *whose*.
> **wh-determiners**—words used in questions, such as *which* and *what*.
> **quantifying determiners**—words such as *some, every, most, no, any, both,* and *half*.

Number	First Person	Second Person	Third Person
singular	I	you	he (masculine) she (feminine) it (neuter)
plural	we	you	they

Figure 2.2 Pronoun system (as subject)

Number	First Person	Second Person	Third Person
singular	my	your	his, her, its
plural	our	your	their

Figure 2.3 Pronoun system (possessives)

A simple noun phrase may have at most one determiner, one ordinal, and one cardinal. It is possible to have all three, as in *the first three contestants.* An exception to this rule exists with a few quantifying determiners such as *many, few, several,* and *little.* These words can be preceded by an article, yielding noun phrases such as *the few songs we knew.* Using this evidence, you could subcategorize the quantifying determiners into those that allow this and those that don't, but the present coarse categorization is fine for our purposes at this time.

The qualifiers in a noun phrase occur after the specifiers (if any) and before the head. They consist of adjectives and nouns being used as modifiers. The following are more precise definitions:

adjectives—words that attribute qualities to objects yet do not refer to the qualities themselves (for example, *angry* is an adjective that attributes the quality of anger to something).

noun modifiers—mass or count nouns used to modify another noun, as in *the cook book* or *the ceiling paint can.*

Before moving on to other structures, consider the different inflectional forms that nouns take and how they are realized in English. Two forms of nouns—the singular and plural forms—have already been mentioned. Pronouns take forms based on **person** (first, second, and third) and **gender** (masculine, feminine, and neuter). Each of these distinctions reflects a systematic analysis that is almost wholly explicit in some languages, such as Latin, while implicit in others. In French, for example, nouns are classified by their gender. In English many of these distinctions are not explicitly marked except in a few cases. The pronouns provide the best example of this. They distinguish **number**, **person**, **gender,** and **case** (that is, whether they are used as possessive, subject, or object), as shown in Figures 2.2 through 2.4.

Number	First Person	Second Person	Third Person
singular	me	you	him her it
plural	us	you	them

Figure 2.4 Pronoun system (as object)

Mood	Example
declarative (or assertion)	The cat is sleeping.
yes/no question	Is the cat sleeping?
wh-question	What is sleeping? or Which cat is sleeping?
imperative (or command)	Shoot the cat!

Figure 2.5 Basic moods of sentences

Form	Examples	Example Uses
base	hit, cry, go, be	*Hit* the ball! I want to *go*.
simple present	hit, cries, go, am	The dog *cries* every day. I *am* thirsty.
simple past	hit, cried, went, was	I *was* thirsty. I *went* to the store.
present participle	hitting, crying, going, being	I'm *going* to the store. *Being* the last in line aggravates me.
past participle	hit, cried, gone, been	I've *been* there before. The cake was *gone*.

Figure 2.6 The five verb forms

2.3 Verb Phrases and Simple Sentences

While an NP is used to refer to things, a sentence (S) is used to assert, query, or command. You may assert that some sentence is true, ask whether a sentence is true, or command someone to do something described in the sentence. The way a sentence is used is called its **mood**. Figure 2.5 shows four basic sentence moods.

A simple declarative sentence consists of an NP, the subject, followed by a verb phrase (VP), the predicate. A simple VP may consist of some adverbial modifiers followed by the head verb and its complements. Every verb must appear in one of the five possible forms shown in Figure 2.6.

Tense	The Verb Sequence	Example
simple present	simple present	He walks to the store.
simple past	simple past	He walked to the store.
simple future	*will* + infinitive	He will walk to the store.
present perfect	*have* in present + past participle	He has walked to the store.
future perfect	*will* + *have* in infinitive + past participle	I will have walked to the store.
past perfect (or pluperfect)	*have* in past + past participle	I had walked to the store.

Figure 2.7 The basic tenses

Tense	Structure	Example
present progressive	*be* in present + present participle	He is walking.
past progressive	*be* in past + present participle	He was walking.
future progressive	*will* + *be* in infinitive + present participle	He will be walking.
present perfect progressive	*have* in present + *be* in past participle + present participle	He has been walking.
future perfect progressive	*will* + *have* in present + *be* as past participle + present participle	He will have been walking.
past perfect progressive	*have* in past + *be* in past participle + present participle	He had been walking.

Figure 2.8 The progressive tenses

Verbs can be divided into several different classes: the **auxiliary verbs**, such as *be, do,* and *have;* the **modal verbs**, such as *will, can,* and *could;* and the **main verbs**, such as *eat, ran,* and *believe.* The auxiliary and modal verbs usually take a verb phrase as a complement, which produces a sequence of verbs, each the head of its own verb phrase. These sequences are used to form sentences with different tenses.

The **tense system** identifies when the proposition described in the sentence is said to be true. The tense system is complex; only the basic forms are outlined in Figure 2.7. In addition, verbs may be in the **progressive tense.** Corresponding to the tenses listed in Figure 2.7 are the progressive tenses shown in Figure 2.8.

	First	**Second**	**Third**
Singular	I *am*	you *are*	he *is*
	I *walk*	you *walk*	she *walks*
Plural	we *are*	you *are*	they *are*
	we *walk*	you *walk*	they *walk*

Figure 2.9   Person/number forms of verbs

Each progressive tense is formed by the normal tense construction of the verb *be* followed by a present participle.

Verb groups also encode person and number information in the first word in the verb group. The person and number must agree with the noun phrase that is the subject of the verb phrase. Some verbs distinguish nearly all the possibilities, but most verbs distinguish only the third person singular (by adding an -*s* suffix). Some examples are shown in Figure 2.9.

Transitivity and Passives

The last verb in a verb sequence is called the **main verb**, and is drawn from the open class of verbs. Depending on the verb, a wide variety of complement struc- tures are allowed. For example, certain verbs may stand alone with no comple- ment. These are called **intransitive** verbs and include examples such as *laugh* (for example, *Jack laughed*) and *run* (for example, *He will have been running*). Another common complement form requires a noun phrase to follow the verb. These are called **transitive** verbs and include verbs such as *find* (for example, *Jack found a key*). Notice that *find* cannot be intransitive (for example, **Jack found* is not a reasonable sentence), whereas *laugh* cannot be transitive (for example, **Jack laughed a key* is not a reasonable sentence). A verb like *run,* on the other hand, can be transitive or intransitive, but the meaning of the verb is different in each case (for example, *Jack ran* vs. *Jack ran the machine*).

Transitive verbs allow another form of verb group called the **passive** form, which is constructed using a *be* auxiliary followed by the past participle. In the passive form the noun phrase that would usually be in the object position is used in the subject position, as can be seen by the examples in Figure 2.10. Note that tense is still carried by the initial verb in the verb group. Also, even though the first noun phrase semantically seems to be the object of the verb in passive sentences, it is syntactically the subject. This can be seen by checking the pronoun forms. For example, *I was hit* is correct, not **Me was hit.* Furthermore, the tense and number agreement is between the verb and the syntactic subject. Thus you say *I was hit by them,* not **I were hit by them.*

Some verbs allow two noun phrases to follow them in a sentence; for example, *Jack gave Sue a book* or *Jack found me a key.* In such sentences the

Active Sentence	Related Passive Sentence
Jack saw the ball.	The ball was seen by Jack.
I will find the clue.	The clue will be found by me.
Jack hit me.	I was hit by Jack.

Figure 2.10 Active sentences with corresponding passive sentences

second NP corresponds to the object NP outlined earlier and is sometimes called the **direct object**. The other NP is called the **indirect object**. Generally, such sentences have an equivalent sentence where the indirect object appears with a preposition, as in *Jack gave a book to Sue* or *Jack found a key for me*.

Particles

Some verb forms are constructed from a verb and an additional word called a **particle**. Particles generally overlap with the class of prepositions considered in the next section. Some examples are *up, out, over,* and *in*. With verbs such as *look, take,* or *put*, you can construct many different verbs by combining the verb with a particle (for example, *look up, look out, look over,* and so on). In some sentences the difference between a particle and a preposition results in two different readings for the same sentence. For example, *look over the paper* would mean reading the paper, if you consider *over* a particle (the verb is *look over*). In contrast, the same sentence would mean looking at something else behind or above the paper, if you consider *over* a preposition (the verb is *look*).

You can make a sharp distinction between particles and prepositions when the object of the verb is a pronoun. With a verb-particle sentence, the pronoun must precede the particle, as in *I looked it up*. With the prepositional reading, the pronoun follows the preposition, as in *I looked up it*. Particles also may follow the object NP. Thus you can say *I gave up the game to Mary* or *I gave the game up to Mary*. This is not allowed with prepositions; for example, you cannot say **I climbed the ladder up*.

Clausal Complements

Many verbs allow clauses as complements. Clauses share most of the same properties of sentences and may have a subject, indicate tense, and occur in passivized forms. One common clause form consists of a sentence form preceded by the complementizer *that*, as in *that Jack ate the pizza*. This clause will be identified by the expression S[that], indicating a special subclass of S structures. This clause may appear as the complement of the verb *know*, as in *Sam knows that Jack ate the pizza*. The passive is possible, as in *Sam knows that the pizza was eaten by Jack*.

Another clause type involves the infinitive form of the verb. The VP[inf] clause is simply a VP starting in the infinitive form, as in the complement of the verb *wish* in *Jack wishes to eat the pizza.* An infinitive sentence S[inf] form is also possible where the subject is indicated by a *for* phrase, as in *Jack wishes for Sam to eat the pizza.*

Another important class of clauses are sentences with complementizers that are wh-words, such as *who, what, where, why, whether,* and *how many.* These question clauses, S[WH], can be used as a complement of verbs such as *know,* as in *Sam knows whether we went to the party* and *The police know who committed the crime.*

Prepositional Phrase Complements

Many verbs require complements that involve a specific prepositional phrase (PP). The verb *give* takes a complement consisting of an NP and a PP with the preposition *to,* as in *Jack gave the book to the library.* No other preposition can be used. Consider

*Jack gave the book from the library. (OK only if *from the library* modifies book.)

In contrast, a verb like *put* can take any PP that describes a location, as in

Jack put the book in the box.
Jack put the book inside the box.
Jack put the book by the door.

To account for this, we allow complement specifications that indicate prepositional phrases with particular prepositions. Thus the verb *give* would have a complement of the form NP+PP[to]. Similarly the verb *decide* would have a complement form NP+PP[about], and the verb *blame* would have a complement form NP+PP[on], as in *Jack blamed the accident on the police.*

Verbs such as *put,* which take any phrase that can describe a location (complement NP+Location), are also common in English. While locations are typically prepositional phrases, they also can be noun phrases, such as *home,* or particles, such as *back* or *here.* A distinction can be made between phrases that describe locations and phrases that describe a path of motion, although many location phrases can be interpreted either way. The distinction can be made in some cases, though. For instance, prepositional phrases beginning with *to* generally indicate a path of motion. Thus they cannot be used with a verb such as *put* that requires a location (for example, **I put the ball to the box*). This distinction will be explored further in Chapter 4.

Figure 2.11 summarizes many of the verb complement structures found in English. A full list would contain over 40 different forms. Note that while the examples typically use a different verb for each form, most verbs will allow several different complement structures.

Verb	Complement Structure	Example
laugh	Empty (intransitive)	Jack laughed.
find	NP (transitive)	Jack found a key.
give	NP+NP (bitransitive)	Jack gave Sue the paper.
give	NP+PP[to]	Jack gave the book to the library.
reside	Location phrase	Jack resides in Rochester
put	NP+Location phrase	Jack put the book inside.
speak	PP[with]+PP[about]	Jack spoke with Sue about the book.
try	VP[to]	Jack tried to apologize.
tell	NP+VP[to]	Jack told the man to go.
wish	S[to]	Jack wished for the man to go.
keep	VP[ing]	Jack keeps hoping for the best.
catch	NP+VP[ing]	Jack caught Sam looking in his desk.
watch	NP+VP[base]	Jack watched Sam eat the pizza.
regret	S[that]	Jack regretted that he'd eaten the whole thing.
tell	NP+S[that]	Jack told Sue that he was sorry.
seem	ADJP	Jack seems unhappy in his new job.
think	NP+ADJP	Jack thinks Sue is happy in her job.
know	S[WH]	Jack knows where the money is.

Figure 2.11 Some common verb complement structures in English

2.4 Noun Phrases Revisited

Section 2.2 introduced simple noun phrases. This section considers more complex forms in which NPs contain sentences or verb phrases as subcomponents.

All the examples in Section 2.2 had heads that took the null complement. Many nouns, however, may take complements. Many of these fall into the class of complements that require a specific prepositional phrase. For example, the noun *love* has a complement form PP[of], as in *their love of France,* the noun *reliance* has the complement form PP[on], as in *his reliance on handouts,* and the noun *familiarity* has the complement form PP[with], as in *a familiarity with computers.*

Many nouns, such as *desire, reluctance,* and *research,* take an infinitive VP form as a complement, as in the noun phrases *his desire to release the guinea pig, a reluctance to open the case again,* and *the doctor's research to find a cure for cancer.* These nouns, in fact, can also take the S[inf] form, as in *my hope for John to open the case again.*

Noun phrases can also be built out of clauses, which were introduced in the last section as the complements for verbs. For example, a *that* clause (S[that]) can be used as the subject of a sentence, as in the sentence *That George had the ring was surprising.* Infinitive forms of verb phrases (VP[inf]) and sentences (S[inf]) can also function as noun phrases, as in the sentences *To own a car would be delightful* and *For us to complete a project on time would be unprecedented.* In addition, the **gerundive** forms (VP[ing] and S[ing]) can also function as noun phrases, as in the sentences *Giving up the game was unfortunate* and *John's giving up the game caused a riot.*

Relative clauses involve sentence forms used as modifiers in noun phrases. These clauses are often introduced by **relative pronouns** such as *who, which, that,* and so on, as in

The man *who gave Bill the money* . . .
The rug *that George gave to Ernest* . . .
The man *whom George gave the money to* . . .

In each of these relative clauses, the embedded sentence is the same structure as a regular sentence except that one noun phrase is missing. If this missing NP is filled in with the NP that the sentence modifies, the result is a complete sentence that captures the same meaning as what was conveyed by the relative clause. The missing NPs in the preceding three sentences occur in the subject position, in the object position, and as object to a preposition, respectively. Deleting the relative pronoun and filling in the missing NP in each produces the following:

The man gave Bill the money.
George gave *the rug* to Ernest.
George gave the money to *the man.*

As was true earlier, relative clauses can be modified in the same ways as regular sentences. In particular, passive forms of the preceding sentences would be as follows:

Bill was given the money by the man.
The rug was given to Ernest by George.
The money was given to the man by George.

Correspondingly, these sentences could have relative clauses in the passive form as follows:

The man *Bill was given the money by* . . .
The rug *that was given to Ernest by George* . . .
The man whom *the money was given to by George* . . .

Notice that some relative clauses need not be introduced by a relative pronoun. Often the relative pronoun can be omitted, producing what is called a **base relative clause**, as in the NP *the man George gave the money to.* Yet another form deletes the relative pronoun and an auxiliary *be* form, creating a **reduced relative clause**, as in the NP *the man given the money,* which means the same as the NP *the man who was given the money.*

2.5 Adjective Phrases

You have already seen simple adjective phrases (ADJPs) consisting of a single adjective in several examples. More complex adjective phrases are also possible, as adjectives may take many of the same complement forms that occur with verbs. This includes specific prepositional phrases, as with the adjective *pleased,* which takes the complement form PP[with] (for example, *Jack was pleased with the prize*), or *angry* with the complement form PP[at] (for example, *Jack was angry at the committee*). *Angry* also may take an S[that] complement form, as in *Jack was angry that he was left behind.* Other adjectives take infinitive forms, such as the adjective *willing* with the complement form VP[inf], as in *Jack seemed willing to lead the chorus.*

These more complex adjective phrases are most commonly found as the complements of verbs such as *be* or *seem,* or following the head in a noun phrase. They generally cannot be used as modifiers preceding the heads of noun phrases (for example, consider **the angry at the committee man* vs. *the angry man* vs. *the man angry at the committee*).

Adjective phrases may also take a degree modifier preceding the head, as in the adjective phrase *very angry* or *somewhat fond of Mary.* More complex degree modifications are possible, as in *far too heavy* and *much more desperate.* Finally, certain constructs have degree modifiers that involve their own complement forms, as in *too stupid to come in out of the rain, so boring that everyone fell asleep,* and *as slow as a dead horse.*

2.6 Adverbial Phrases

You have already seen adverbs in use in several constructs, such as indicators of degree (for example, *very, rather, too*), and in location phrases (for example, *here, everywhere*). Other forms of adverbs indicate the manner in which something is done (for example, *slowly, hesitantly*), the time of something (for example, *now, yesterday*), or the frequency of something (for example, *frequently, rarely, never*).

Adverbs may occur in several different positions in sentences: in the sentence initial position (for example, ***Then,*** *Jack will open the drawer*), in the verb sequence (for example, *Jack **then** will open the drawer, Jack will **then** open the drawer*), and in the sentence final position (for example, *Jack opened the drawer **then***). The exact restrictions on what adverb can go where, however, is quite idiosyncratic to the particular adverb.

In addition to these adverbs, adverbial modifiers can be constructed out of a wide range of constructs, such as prepositional phrases indicating, among other things, location (for example, *in the box*) or manner (for example, *in great haste*); noun phrases indicating, among other things, frequency (for example, *every day*); or clauses indicating, among other things, the time (for example, *when the bomb exploded*). Such adverbial phrases, however, usually cannot occur except in the sentence initial or sentence final position. For example, we can say *Every day*

John opens his drawer or *John opens his drawer every day,* but not **John every day opens his drawer.*

Because of the wide range of forms, it generally is more useful to consider adverbial phrases (ADVPs) by function rather than syntactic form. Thus we can consider manner, temporal, duration, location, degree, and frequency adverbial phrases each as its own form. We considered the location and degree forms earlier, so here we will consider some of the others.

Temporal adverbials occur in a wide range of forms: adverbial particles (for example, *now*), noun phrases (for example, *today, yesterday*), prepositional phrases (for example, *at noon, during the fight*), and clauses (for example, *when the clock struck noon, before the fight started*).

Frequency adverbials also can occur in a wide range of forms: particles (for example, *often*), noun phrases (for example, *every day*), prepositional phrases (for example, *at every party*), and clauses (for example, *every time that John comes for a visit*).

Duration adverbials appear most commonly as prepositional phrases (for example, *for three hours, about 20 feet*) and clauses (for example, *until the moon turns blue*).

Manner adverbials occur in a wide range of forms, including particles (for example, *slowly*), noun phrases (for example, *this way*), prepositional phrases (for example, *in great haste*), and clauses (for example, *by holding the embers at the end of a stick*).

In the analyses that follow, adverbials will most commonly occur as modifiers of the action or state described in a sentence. As such, an issue arises as to how to distinguish verb complements from adverbials. One distinction is that adverbial phrases are always optional. Thus you should be able to delete the adverbial and still have a sentence with approximately the same meaning (missing, obviously, the contribution of the adverbial). Consider the sentences

Jack put the box by the door.
Jack ate the pizza by the door.

In the first sentence the prepositional phrase is clearly a complement, since deleting it to produce **Jack put the box* results in a nonsensical utterance. On the other hand, deleting the phrase from the second sentence has only a minor effect: *Jack ate the pizza* is just a less general assertion about the same situation described by *Jack ate the pizza by the door.*

Summary

The major phrase structures of English have been introduced—namely, noun phrases, sentences, prepositional phrases, adjective phrases, and adverbial phrases. These will serve as the building blocks for the syntactic structures introduced in the following chapters.

Related Work and Further Readings

An excellent overview of English syntax is found in Baker (1989). The most comprehensive sources are books that attempt to describe the entire structure of English, such as Huddleston (1988), Quirk et al. (1972), and Leech and Svartvik (1975).

Exercises for Chapter 2

1. (*easy*) The text described several different example tests for distinguishing word classes. For example, nouns can occur in sentences of the form *I saw the X,* whereas adjectives can occur in sentences of the form *It's so X*. Give some additional tests to distinguish these forms and to distinguish between count nouns and mass nouns. State whether each of the following words can be used as an adjective, count noun, or mass noun. If the word is ambiguous, give all its possible uses.

   milk, house, liquid, green, group, concept, airborne

2. (*easy*) Identify every major phrase (noun, verb, adjective, or adverbial phrases) in the following sentences. For each, indicate the head of the phrase and any complements of the head. Be sure to distinguish between complements and optional modifiers.

   The man played his fiddle in the street.
   The people dissatisfied with the verdict left the courtroom.

3. (*easy*) A very useful test for determining the syntactic role of words and phrases is the conjunction test. Conjunctions, such as *and* and *or,* tend to join together two phrases of the same type. For instance, you can conjoin nouns, as in *the man and woman*; noun phrases, as in *the angry men and the large dogs*; and adjective phrases, as in *the cow, angry and confused, broke the gate*. In each of the following sentences, identify the type of phrase being conjoined, and underline each phrase.

   He was tired and hungrier than a herd of elephants.
   We have never walked home or to the store from here.
   The dog returned quickly and dropped the stick.

4. (*easy*) Explain in detail, using the terminology of this chapter, why each of the following sentences is ill formed. In particular, state what rule (given in this chapter) has been violated.

   a. He barked the wrong tree up.
   b. She turned waters into wine.
   c. Don't take many all the cookies!
   d. I feel floor today.
   e. They all laughed the boy.

5. (*easy*) Classify the following verbs as being intransitive, transitive, or bitransitive (that is, it takes a two-NP complement). If the verb can be used in more than one of these forms, give each possible classification. Give an example sentence for each form to demonstrate your analysis.

   a. cry
   b. sing
   c. donate
   d. put

6. (*easy*) Using the verb *to be,* give example sentences that use the six basic tenses listed in Figure 2.7 and the six progressive tenses listed in Figure 2.8.

7. (*easy*) Using the verb *donate,* give examples of the passive form for each of the six basic tenses listed in Figure 2.7.

8. (*easy*) Classify the following verbs by specifying what different complement structures they allow, using the forms defined in Figure 2.11.

   give, know, assume, insert

   Give an example of an additional complement structure that is allowed by one of these verbs but not listed in the figure.

9. (*easy*) Find five verbs not discussed in this chapter that take an indirect object and, for each one, give a paraphrase of the same sentence using a prepositional phrase instead of the indirect object. Try for as wide a range as possible. Can you find one that cannot be paraphrased using either the preposition *to* or *for*?

10. (*medium*) Wh-questions are questions that use a class of words that includes *what, where, who, when, whose, which,* and *how.* For each of these words, give the syntactic categories (for example, verb, noun, noun group, adjective, quantifier, prepositional phrase, and so on) in which the words can be used. Justify each classification with some examples that demonstrate it. Use both positive and negative arguments as necessary (such as "it is one of these because . . .," or "it can't be one of these even though it looks like it might, because . . .").

Grammars and Parsing

3.1 Grammars and Sentence Structure

3.2 What Makes a Good Grammar

3.3 A Top-Down Parser

3.4 A Bottom-Up Chart Parser

3.5 Transition Network Grammars

○ 3.6 Top-Down Chart Parsing

○ 3.7 Finite State Models and Morphological Processing

○ 3.8 Grammars and Logic Programming

To examine how the syntactic structure of a sentence can be computed, you must consider two things: the **grammar**, which is a formal specification of the structures allowable in the language, and the **parsing technique**, which is the method of analyzing a sentence to determine its structure according to the grammar. This chapter examines different ways to specify simple grammars and considers some fundamental parsing techniques. Chapter 4 then describes the methods for constructing syntactic representations that are useful for later semantic interpretation.

The discussion begins by introducing a notation for describing the structure of natural language and describing some naive parsing techniques for that grammar. The second section describes some characteristics of a good grammar. The third section then considers a simple parsing technique and introduces the idea of parsing as a search process. The fourth section describes a method for building efficient parsers using a structure called a chart. The fifth section then describes an alternative representation of grammars based on transition networks. The remaining sections deal with optional and advanced issues. Section 3.6 describes a top-down chart parser that combines the advantages of top-down and bottom-up approaches. Section 3.7 introduces the notion of finite state transducers and discusses their use in morphological processing. Section 3.8 shows how to encode context-free grammars as assertions in PROLOG, introducing the notion of logic grammars.

3.1 Grammars and Sentence Structure

This section considers methods of describing the structure of sentences and explores ways of characterizing all the legal structures in a language. The most common way of representing how a sentence is broken into its major subparts, and how those subparts are broken up in turn, is as a **tree**. The tree representation for the sentence *John ate the cat* is shown in Figure 3.1. This illustration can be read as follows: The sentence (S) consists of an initial noun phrase (NP) and a verb phrase (VP). The initial noun phrase is made of the simple NAME *John*. The verb phrase is composed of a verb (V) *ate* and an NP, which consists of an article (ART) *the* and a common noun (N) *cat.* In list notation this same structure could be represented as

```
(S  (NP  (NAME John))
    (VP  (V ate)
         (NP  (ART the)
              (N cat))))
```

Since trees play such an important role throughout this book, some terminology needs to be introduced. Trees are a special form of graph, which are structures consisting of labeled **nodes** (for example, the nodes are labeled S, NP, and so on in Figure 3.1) connected by **links**. They are called trees because they resemble upside-down trees, and much of the terminology is derived from this analogy with actual trees. The node at the top is called the **root** of the tree, while

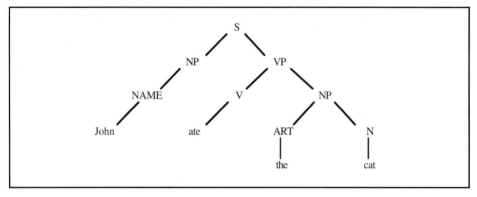

Figure 3.1 A tree representation of *John ate the cat*

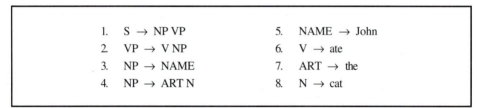

1.	S → NP VP	5.	NAME → John
2.	VP → V NP	6.	V → ate
3.	NP → NAME	7.	ART → the
4.	NP → ART N	8.	N → cat

Grammar 3.2 A simple grammar

the nodes at the bottom are called the **leaves**. We say a link points from a **parent** node to a **child** node. The node labeled S in Figure 3.1 is the parent node of the nodes labeled NP and VP, and the node labeled NP is in turn the parent node of the node labeled NAME. While every child node has a unique parent, a parent may point to many child nodes. An **ancestor** of a node N is defined as N's parent, or the parent of its parent, and so on. A node is **dominated** by its ancestor nodes. The root node dominates all other nodes in the tree.

To construct a tree structure for a sentence, you must know what structures are legal for English. A set of **rewrite rules** describes what tree structures are allowable. These rules say that a certain symbol may be expanded in the tree by a sequence of other symbols. A set of rules that would allow the tree structure in Figure 3.1 is shown as Grammar 3.2. Rule 1 says that an S may consist of an NP followed by a VP. Rule 2 says that a VP may consist of a V followed by an NP. Rules 3 and 4 say that an NP may consist of a NAME or may consist of an ART followed by an N. Rules 5–8 define possible words for the categories. Grammars consisting entirely of rules with a single symbol on the left-hand side, called the **mother**, are called **context-free grammars** (CFGs). CFGs are a very important class of grammars for two reasons: The formalism is powerful enough to describe most of the structure in natural languages, yet it is restricted enough so that efficient parsers can be built to analyze sentences. Symbols that cannot be further decomposed in a grammar, namely the words in the preceding example, are called **terminal symbols**. The other symbols, such as NP, VP, and S, are called

nonterminal symbols. The grammatical symbols such as N and V that describe word categories are called **lexical symbols**. Of course, many words will be listed under multiple categories. For example, *can* would be listed under V and N.

Grammars have a special symbol called the start symbol. In this book, the start symbol will always be S. A grammar is said to **derive** a sentence if there is a sequence of rules that allow you to rewrite the start symbol into the sentence. For instance, Grammar 3.2 derives the sentence *John ate the cat*. This can be seen by showing the sequence of rewrites starting from the S symbol, as follows:

S
$\Rightarrow$ NP VP	(rewriting S)
$\Rightarrow$ NAME VP	(rewriting NP)
$\Rightarrow$ John VP	(rewriting NAME)
$\Rightarrow$ John V NP	(rewriting VP)
$\Rightarrow$ John ate NP	(rewriting V)
$\Rightarrow$ John ate ART N	(rewriting NP)
$\Rightarrow$ John ate the N	(rewriting ART)
$\Rightarrow$ John ate the cat	(rewriting N)

Two important processes are based on derivations. The first is **sentence generation**, which uses derivations to construct legal sentences. A simple generator could be implemented by randomly choosing rewrite rules, starting from the S symbol, until you have a sequence of words. The preceding example shows that the sentence *John ate the cat* can be generated from the grammar. The second process based on derivations is **parsing**, which identifies the structure of sentences given a grammar. There are two basic methods of searching. A **top-down strategy** starts with the S symbol and then searches through different ways to rewrite the symbols until the input sentence is generated, or until all possibilities have been explored. The preceding example demonstrates that *John ate the cat* is a legal sentence by showing the derivation that could be found by this process.

In a **bottom-up strategy**, you start with the words in the sentence and use the rewrite rules backward to reduce the sequence of symbols until it consists solely of S. The left-hand side of each rule is used to rewrite the symbol on the right-hand side. A possible bottom-up parse of the sentence *John ate the cat* is

$\Rightarrow$ NAME ate the cat	(rewriting John)
$\Rightarrow$ NAME V the cat	(rewriting ate)
$\Rightarrow$ NAME V ART cat	(rewriting the)
$\Rightarrow$ NAME V ART N	(rewriting cat)
$\Rightarrow$ NP V ART N	(rewriting NAME)
$\Rightarrow$ NP V NP	(rewriting ART N)
$\Rightarrow$ NP VP	(rewriting V NP)
$\Rightarrow$ S	(rewriting NP VP)

A tree representation, such as Figure 3.1, can be viewed as a record of the CFG rules that account for the structure of the sentence. In other words, if you kept a record of the parsing process, working either top-down or bottom-up, it would be something similar to the parse tree representation.

3.2 What Makes a Good Grammar

In constructing a grammar for a language, you are interested in **generality**, the range of sentences the grammar analyzes correctly; **selectivity**, the range of non-sentences it identifies as problematic; and **understandability**, the simplicity of the grammar itself.

In small grammars, such as those that describe only a few types of sentences, one structural analysis of a sentence may appear as understandable as another, and little can be said as to why one is superior to the other. As you attempt to extend a grammar to cover a wide range of sentences, however, you often find that one analysis is easily extendable while the other requires complex modification. The analysis that retains its simplicity and generality as it is extended is more desirable.

Unfortunately, here you will be working mostly with small grammars and so will have only a few opportunities to evaluate an analysis as it is extended. You can attempt to make your solutions generalizable, however, by keeping in mind certain properties that any solution should have. In particular, pay close attention to the way the sentence is divided into its subparts, called **constituents**. Besides using your intuition, you can apply a few specific tests, discussed here.

Anytime you decide that a group of words forms a particular constituent, try to construct a new sentence that involves that group of words in a conjunction with another group of words classified as the same type of constituent. This is a good test because for the most part only constituents of the same type can be conjoined. The sentences in Figure 3.3, for example, are acceptable, but the following sentences are not:

*I ate a hamburger and on the stove.
*I ate a cold hot dog and well burned.
*I ate the hot dog slowly and a hamburger.

To summarize, if the proposed constituent doesn't conjoin in some sentence with a constituent of the same class, it is probably incorrect.

Another test involves inserting the proposed constituent into other sentences that take the same category of constituent. For example, if you say that *John's hitting of Mary* is an NP in *John's hitting of Mary alarmed Sue,* then it should be usable as an NP in other sentences as well. In fact this is true—the NP can be the object of a verb, as in *I cannot explain John's hitting of Mary* as well as in the passive form of the initial sentence *Sue was alarmed by John's hitting of Mary.* Given this evidence, you can conclude that the proposed constituent appears to behave just like other NPs.

NP-NP: I ate *a hamburger* and *a hot dog.*

VP-VP: I will *eat the hamburger* and *throw away the hot dog.*

S-S: *I ate a hamburger* and *John ate a hot dog.*

PP-PP: I saw a hot dog *in the bag* and *on the stove.*

ADJP-ADJP: I ate a *cold* and *well burned* hot dog.

ADVP-ADVP: I ate the hot dog *slowly* and *very carefully.*

N-N: I ate a *hamburger* and *hot dog.*

V-V: I will *cook* and *burn* a hamburger.

AUX-AUX: I *can* and *will* eat the hot dog.

ADJ-ADJ: I ate the very *cold* and *burned* hot dog (that is, very cold and very burned).

Figure 3.3 Various forms of conjunctions

As another example of applying these principles, consider the two sentences *I looked up John's phone number* and *I looked up John's chimney.* Should these sentences have the identical structure? If so, you would presumably analyze both as subject-verb-complement sentences with the complement in both cases being a PP. That is, *up John's phone number* would be a PP.

When you try the conjunction test, you should become suspicious of this analysis. Conjoining *up John's phone number* with another PP, as in **I looked up John's phone number and in his cupboards*, is certainly bizarre. Note that *I looked up John's chimney and in his cupboards* is perfectly acceptable. Thus apparently the analysis of *up John's phone number* as a PP is incorrect.

Further evidence against the PP analysis is that *up John's phone number* does not seem usable as a PP in any sentences other than ones involving a few verbs such as *look* or *thought.* Even with the verb *look,* an alternative sentence such as **Up John's phone number, I looked* is quite implausible compared to *Up John's chimney, I looked.*

This type of test can be taken further by considering changing the PP in a manner that usually is allowed. In particular, you should be able to replace the NP *John's phone number* by the pronoun *it.* But the resulting sentence, *I looked up it,* could not be used with the same meaning as *I looked up John's phone number.* In fact, the only way to use a pronoun and retain the original meaning is to use *I looked it up,* corresponding to the form *I looked John's phone number up.*

Thus a different analysis is needed for each of the two sentences. If *up John's phone number* is not a PP, then two remaining analyses may be possible. The VP could be the complex verb *looked up* followed by an NP, or it could consist of three components: the V *looked,* a **particle** *up,* and an NP. Either of these is a better solution. What types of tests might you do to decide between them?

As you develop a grammar, each constituent is used in more and more different ways. As a result, you have a growing number of tests that can be performed to see if a new analysis is reasonable or not. Sometimes the analysis of a

BOX 3.1 Generative Capacity

Grammatical formalisms based on rewrite rules can be compared according to their **generative capacity**, which is the range of languages that each formalism can describe. This book is concerned with natural languages, but it turns out that no natural language can be characterized precisely enough to define generative capacity. Formal languages, however, allow a precise mathematical characterization.

Consider a formal language consisting of the symbols $a, b, c,$ and d (think of these as words). Then consider a language L1 that allows any sequence of letters in alphabetical order. For example, *abd, ad, bcd, b,* and *abcd* are all legal sentences. To describe this language, we can write a grammar in which the right-hand side of every rule consists of one terminal symbol possibly followed by one nonterminal. Such a grammar is called a **regular** grammar. For L1 the grammar would be

S $\rightarrow$ a S1	S $\rightarrow$ d	S1 $\rightarrow$ d	S3 $\rightarrow$ d
S $\rightarrow$ b S2	S1 $\rightarrow$ b S2	S2 $\rightarrow$ c S3	
S $\rightarrow$ c S3	S1 $\rightarrow$ c S3	S2 $\rightarrow$ d	

Consider another language, L2, that consists only of sentences that have a sequence of a's followed by an equal number of b's—that is, *ab, aabb, aaabbb,* and so on. You cannot write a regular grammar that can generate L2 exactly. A context-free grammar to generate L2, however, is simple:

$$S \rightarrow a b \qquad S \rightarrow a S b$$

Some languages cannot be generated by a CFG. One example is the language that consists of a sequence of a's, followed by the same number of b's, followed by the same number of c's—that is, *abc, aabbcc, aaabbbccc,* and so on. Similarly, no context-free grammar can generate the language that consists of any sequence of letters repeated in the same order twice, such as *abab, abcabc, acdabacdab,* and so on. There are more general grammatical systems that can generate such sequences, however. One important class is the **context-sensitive grammar**, which consists of rules of the form

$$\alpha A \beta \rightarrow \alpha \psi \beta$$

where A is a symbol, α and β are (possibly empty) sequences of symbols, and ψ is a nonempty sequence of symbols. Even more general are the **type 0** grammars, which allow arbitrary rewrite rules.

Work in formal language theory began with Chomsky (1956). Since the languages generated by regular grammars are a subset of those generated by context-free grammars, which in turn are a subset of those generated by context-sensitive grammars, which in turn are a subset of those generated by type 0 languages, they form a hierarchy of languages (called the **Chomsky Hierarchy**).

new form might force you to back up and modify the existing grammar. This backward step is unavoidable given the current state of linguistic knowledge. The important point to remember, though, is that when a new rule is proposed for a grammar, you must carefully consider its interaction with existing rules.

1.	S $\rightarrow$ NP VP	4.	VP $\rightarrow$ V
2.	NP $\rightarrow$ ART N	5.	VP $\rightarrow$ V NP
3.	NP $\rightarrow$ ART ADJ N		

Grammar 3.4

3.3 A Top-Down Parser

A parsing algorithm can be described as a procedure that searches through various ways of combining grammatical rules to find a combination that gene-rates a tree that could be the structure of the input sentence. To keep this initial formulation simple, we will not explicitly construct the tree. Rather, the algorithm will simply return a yes or no answer as to whether such a tree could be built. In other words, the algorithm will say whether a certain sentence is accepted by the grammar or not. This section considers a simple top-down pars-ing method in some detail and then relates this to work in artificial intelligence (AI) on search procedures.

A top-down parser starts with the S symbol and attempts to rewrite it into a sequence of terminal symbols that matches the classes of the words in the input sentence. The state of the parse at any given time can be represented as a list of symbols that are the result of operations applied so far, called the **symbol list.** For example, the parser starts in the state (S) and after applying the rule S $\rightarrow$ NP VP the symbol list will be (NP VP). If it then applies the rule NP $\rightarrow$ ART N, the symbol list will be (ART N VP), and so on.

The parser could continue in this fashion until the state consisted entirely of terminal symbols, and then it could check the input sentence to see if it matched. But this would be quite wasteful, for a mistake made early on (say, in choosing the rule that rewrites S) is not discovered until much later. A better algorithm checks the input as soon as it can. In addition, rather than having a separate rule to indicate the possible syntactic categories for each word, a structure called the **lexicon** is used to efficiently store the possible categories for each word. For now the lexicon will be very simple. A very small lexicon for use in the examples is

cried: V
dogs: N, V
the: ART

With a lexicon specified, a grammar, such as that shown as Grammar 3.4, need not contain any lexical rules.

Given these changes, a state of the parse is now defined by a pair: a symbol list similar to before and a number indicating the current position in the sentence. Positions fall between the words, with 1 being the position before the first word. For example, here is a sentence with its positions indicated:

$_1$ The $_2$ dogs $_3$ cried $_4$

A typical parse state would be

((N VP) 2)

indicating that the parser needs to find an N followed by a VP, starting at position two. New states are generated from old states depending on whether the first symbol is a lexical symbol or not. If it is a lexical symbol, like N in the preceding example, and if the next word can belong to that lexical category, then you can update the state by removing the first symbol and updating the position counter. In this case, since the word *dogs* is listed as an N in the lexicon, the next parser state would be

((VP) 3)

which means it needs to find a VP starting at position 3. If the first symbol is a nonterminal, like VP, then it is rewritten using a rule from the grammar. For example, using rule 4 in Grammar 3.4, the new state would be

((V) 3)

which means it needs to find a V starting at position 3. On the other hand, using rule 5, the new state would be

((V NP) 3)

A parsing algorithm that is guaranteed to find a parse if there is one must systematically explore every possible new state. One simple technique for this is called **backtracking**. Using this approach, rather than generating a single new state from the state ((VP) 3), you generate all possible new states. One of these is picked to be the next state and the rest are saved as backup states. If you ever reach a situation where the current state cannot lead to a solution, you simply pick a new current state from the list of backup states. Here is the algorithm in a little more detail.

A Simple Top-Down Parsing Algorithm

The algorithm manipulates a list of possible states, called the **possibilities list**. The first element of this list is the **current state**, which consists of a symbol list and a word position in the sentence, and the remaining elements of the search state are the **backup states**, each indicating an alternate symbol-list–word-position pair. For example, the possibilities list

(((N) 2) ((NAME) 1) ((ADJ N) 1))

indicates that the current state consists of the symbol list (N) at position 2, and that there are two possible backup states: one consisting of the symbol list (NAME) at position 1 and the other consisting of the symbol list (ADJ N) at position 1.

Step	Current State	Backup States	Comment
1.	((S) 1)		initial position
2.	((NP VP) 1)		rewriting S by rule 1
3.	((ART N VP) 1)		rewriting NP by rules 2 & 3
		((ART ADJ N VP) 1)	
4.	((N VP) 2)		matching ART with *the*
		((ART ADJ N VP) 1)	
5.	((VP) 3)		matching N with *dogs*
		((ART ADJ N VP) 1)	
6.	((V) 3)		rewriting VP by rules 5–8
		((V NP) 3)	
		((ART ADJ N VP) 1)	
7.			the parse succeeds as V is matched to *cried*, leaving an empty grammatical symbol list with an empty sentence

Figure 3.5 Top-down depth-first parse of $_1$ *The* $_2$ *dogs* $_3$ *cried* $_4$

The algorithm starts with the initial state ((S) 1) and no backup states.

1. Select the current state: Take the first state off the possibilities list and call it C. If the possibilities list is empty, then the algorithm fails (that is, no successful parse is possible).

2. If C consists of an empty symbol list and the word position is at the end of the sentence, then the algorithm succeeds.

3. Otherwise, generate the next possible states.

   3.1. If the first symbol on the symbol list of C is a lexical symbol, and the next word in the sentence can be in that class, then create a new state by removing the first symbol from the symbol list and updating the word position, and add it to the possibilities list.

   3.2. Otherwise, if the first symbol on the symbol list of C is a non-terminal, generate a new state for each rule in the grammar that can rewrite that nonterminal symbol and add them all to the possibilities list.

Consider an example. Using Grammar 3.4, Figure 3.5 shows a trace of the algorithm on the sentence *The dogs cried*. First, the initial S symbol is rewritten using rule 1 to produce a new current state of ((NP VP) 1) in step 2. The NP is then rewritten in turn, but since there are two possible rules for NP in the grammar, two possible states are generated: The new current state involves (ART N VP) at position 1, whereas the backup state involves (ART ADJ N VP) at position 1. In step 4 a word in category ART is found at position 1 of the sentence, and the new current state becomes (N VP). The backup state generated in step 3 remains untouched. The parse continues in this fashion to step 5, where two different rules can rewrite VP. The first rule generates the new current state, while the other rule is pushed onto the stack of backup states. The parse completes successfully in step 7, since the current state is empty and all the words in the input sentence have been accounted for.

Consider the same algorithm and grammar operating on the sentence

$_1$ The $_2$ old $_3$ man $_4$ cried $_5$

In this case assume that the word *old* is ambiguous between an ADJ and an N and that the word *man* is ambiguous between an N and a V (as in the sentence *The sailors man the boats*). Specifically, the lexicon is

the: ART
old: ADJ, N
man: N, V
cried: V

The parse proceeds as follows (see Figure 3.6). The initial S symbol is rewritten by rule 1 to produce the new current state of ((NP VP) 1). The NP is rewritten in turn, giving the new state of ((ART N VP) 1) with a backup state of ((ART ADJ N VP) 1). The parse continues, finding *the* as an ART to produce the state ((N VP) 2) and then *old* as an N to obtain the state ((VP) 3). There are now two ways to rewrite the VP, giving us a current state of ((V) 3) and the backup states of ((V NP) 3) and ((ART ADJ N) 1) from before. The word *man* can be parsed as a V, giving the state (( ) 4). Unfortunately, while the symbol list is empty, the word position is not at the end of the sentence, so no new state can be generated and a backup state must be used. In the next cycle, step 8, ((V NP) 3) is attempted. Again *man* is taken as a V and the new state ((NP) 4) generated. None of the rewrites of NP yield a successful parse. Finally, in step 12, the last backup state, ((ART ADJ N VP) 1), is tried and leads to a successful parse.

Parsing as a Search Procedure

You can think of parsing as a special case of a **search problem** as defined in AI. In particular, the top-down parser in this section was described in terms of the following generalized search procedure. The possibilities list is initially set to the start state of the parse. Then you repeat the following steps until you have success or failure:

1. Select the first state from the possibilities list (and remove it from the list).
2. Generate the new states by trying every possible option from the selected state (there may be none if we are on a bad path).
3. Add the states generated in step 2 to the possibilities list.

Step	Current State	Backup States	Comment
1.	((S) 1)		
2.	((NP VP) 1)		S rewritten to NP VP
3.	((ART N VP) 1)	((ART ADJ N VP) 1)	NP rewritten producing two new states
4.	((N VP) 2)	((ART ADJ N VP) 1)	
5.	((VP) 3)	((ART ADJ N VP) 1)	the backup state remains
6.	((V) 3)	((V NP) 3) ((ART ADJ N VP) 1)	
7.	(( ) 4)	((V NP) 3) ((ART ADJ N VP) 1)	
8.	((V NP) 3)	((ART ADJ N VP) 1)	the first backup is chosen
9.	((NP) 4)	((ART ADJ N VP) 1)	
10.	((ART N) 4)	((ART ADJ N) 4) ((ART ADJ N VP) 1)	looking for ART at 4 fails
11.	((ART ADJ N) 4)	((ART ADJ N VP) 1)	fails again
12.	((ART ADJ N VP) 1)		now exploring backup state saved in step 3
13.	((ADJ N VP) 2)		
14.	((N VP) 3)		
15.	((VP) 4)		
16.	((V) 4)	((V NP) 4)	
17.	(( ) 5)		success!

Figure 3.6 A top-down parse of $_1$ *The* $_2$ *old* $_3$ *man* $_4$ *cried* $_5$

For a **depth-first strategy**, the possibilities list is a stack. In other words, step 1 always takes the first element off the list, and step 3 always puts the new states on the front of the list, yielding a **last-in first-out** (LIFO) strategy.

In contrast, in a **breadth-first strategy** the possibilities list is manipulated as a queue. Step 3 adds the new positions onto the end of the list, rather than the beginning, yielding a **first-in first-out** (FIFO) strategy.

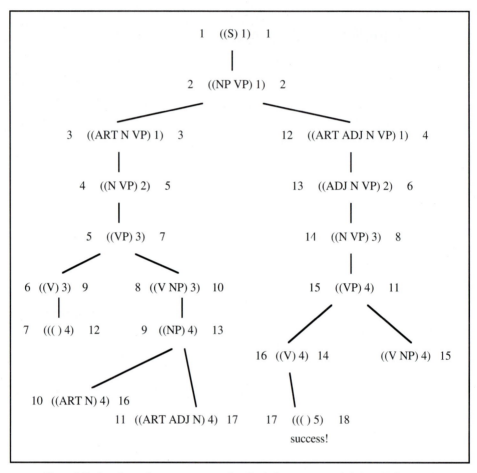

Figure 3.7 Search tree for two parse strategies (depth first strategy on left; breadth first on right)

We can compare these search strategies using a tree format, as in Figure 3.7, which shows the entire space of parser states for the last example. Each node in the tree represents a parser state, and the sons of a node are the possible moves from that state. The number beside each node records when the node was selected to be processed by the algorithm. On the left side is the order produced by the depth-first strategy, and on the right side is the order produced by the breadth-first strategy. Remember, the sentence being parsed is

1 The 2 old 3 man 4 cried 5

The main difference between depth-first and breadth-first searches in this simple example is the order in which the two possible interpretations of the first NP are examined. With the depth-first strategy, one interpretation is considered and expanded until it fails; only then is the second one considered. With the breadth-first strategy, both interpretations are considered alternately, each being expanded one step at a time. In this example, both depth-first and breadth-first searches found the solution but searched the space in a different order. A depth-first search often moves quickly to a solution but in other cases may spend considerable time pursuing futile paths. The breadth-first strategy explores each possible solution to a certain depth before moving on. In this particular example the depth-first strategy found the solution in one less step than the breadth-first. (The state in the bottom right-hand side of Figure 3.7 was not explored by the depth-first parse.)

In certain cases it is possible to put these simple search strategies into an infinite loop. For example, consider a left-recursive rule that could be a first account of the possessive in English (as in the NP *the man's coat*):

$$NP \rightarrow NP \text{ 's } N$$

With a naive depth-first strategy, a state starting with the nonterminal NP would be rewritten to a new state beginning with NP 's N. But this state also begins with an NP that could be rewritten in the same way. Unless an explicit check were incorporated into the parser, it would rewrite NPs forever! The breadth-first strategy does better with left-recursive rules, as it tries all other ways to rewrite the original NP before coming to the newly generated state with the new NP. But with an ungrammatical sentence it would not terminate because it would rewrite the NP forever while searching for a solution. For this reason, many systems prohibit left-recursive rules from the grammar.

Many parsers built today use the depth-first strategy because it tends to minimize the number of backup states needed and thus uses less memory and requires less bookkeeping.

3.4 A Bottom-Up Chart Parser

The main difference between top-down and bottom-up parsers is the way the grammar rules are used. For example, consider the rule

$$NP \rightarrow ART \text{ ADJ } N$$

In a top-down system you use the rule to find an NP by looking for the sequence ART ADJ N. In a bottom-up parser you use the rule to take a sequence ART ADJ N that you have found and identify it as an NP. The basic operation in bottom-up parsing then is to take a sequence of symbols and match it to the right-hand side of the rules. You could build a bottom-up parser simply by formulating this matching process as a search process. The state would simply consist of a symbol list, starting with the words in the sentence. Successor states could be generated by exploring all possible ways to

- rewrite a word by its possible lexical categories
- replace a sequence of symbols that matches the right-hand side of a grammar rule by its left-hand side symbol

1. $S \rightarrow NP\ VP$
2. $NP \rightarrow ART\ ADJ\ N$
3. $NP \rightarrow ART\ N$
4. $NP \rightarrow ADJ\ N$
5. $VP \rightarrow AUX\ VP$
6. $VP \rightarrow V\ NP$

Grammar 3.8 A simple context-free grammar

Unfortunately, such a simple implementation would be prohibitively expensive, as the parser would tend to try the same matches again and again, thus duplicating much of its work unnecessarily. To avoid this problem, a data structure called a **chart** is introduced that allows the parser to store the partial results of the matching it has done so far so that the work need not be reduplicated.

Matches are always considered from the point of view of one constituent, called the **key**. To find rules that match a string involving the key, look for rules that start with the key, or for rules that have already been started by earlier keys and require the present key either to complete the rule or to extend the rule. For instance, consider Grammar 3.8.

Assume you are parsing a sentence that starts with an ART. With this ART as the key, rules 2 and 3 are matched because they start with ART. To record this for analyzing the next key, you need to record that rules 2 and 3 could be continued at the point after the ART. You denote this fact by writing the rule with a dot ($\circ$), indicating what has been seen so far. Thus you record

2′. $NP \rightarrow ART \circ ADJ\ N$
3′. $NP \rightarrow ART \circ N$

If the next input key is an ADJ, then rule 4 may be started, and the modified rule 2′ may be extended to give

2″. $NP \rightarrow ART\ ADJ \circ N$

The chart maintains the record of all the constituents derived from the sentence so far in the parse. It also maintains the record of rules that have matched partially but are not complete. These are called the **active arcs**. For example, after seeing an initial ART followed by an ADJ in the preceding example, you would have the chart shown in Figure 3.9. You should interpret this figure as follows. There are two completed constituents on the chart: ART1 from position 1 to 2 and ADJ1 from position 2 to 3. There are four active arcs indicating possible constituents. These are indicated by the arrows and are interpreted as follows (from top to bottom). There is a potential NP starting at position 1, which needs an ADJ starting at position 2. There is another potential NP starting at position 1, which needs an N starting at position 2. There is a potential NP

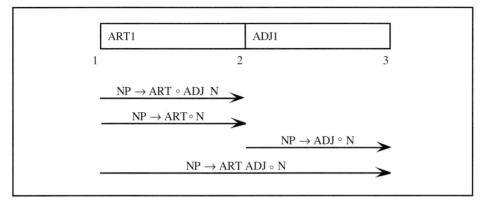

Figure 3.9 The chart after seeing an ADJ in position 2

To add a constituent C from position p_1 to p_2:

1. Insert C into the chart from position p_1 to p_2.

2. For any active arc of the form $X \rightarrow X_1 \dots \circ C \dots X_n$ from position p_0 to p_1, add a new active arc $X \rightarrow X_1 \dots C \circ \dots X_n$ from position p_0 to p_2.

3. For any active arc of the form $X \rightarrow X_1 \dots X_n \circ C$ from position p_0 to p_1, then add a new constituent of type X from p_0 to p_2 to the agenda.

Figure 3.10 The arc extension algorithm

starting at position 2 with an ADJ, which needs an N starting at position 3. Finally, there is a potential NP starting at position 1 with an ART and then an ADJ, which needs an N starting at position 3.

The basic operation of a chart-based parser involves combining an active arc with a completed constituent. The result is either a new completed constituent or a new active arc that is an extension of the original active arc. New completed constituents are maintained on a list called the **agenda** until they themselves are added to the chart. This process is defined more precisely by the arc extension algorithm shown in Figure 3.10. Given this algorithm, the bottom-up chart parsing algorithm is specified in Figure 3.11.

As with the top-down parsers, you may use a depth-first or breadth-first search strategy, depending on whether the agenda is implemented as a stack or a queue. Also, for a full breadth-first strategy, you would need to read in the entire input and add the interpretations of the words onto the agenda before starting the algorithm. Let us assume a depth-first search strategy for the following example.

Consider using the algorithm on the sentence *The large can can hold the water* using Grammar 3.8 with the following lexicon:

Do until there is no input left:

1. If the agenda is empty, look up the interpretations for the next word in the input and add them to the agenda.

2. Select a constituent from the agenda (let's call it constituent C from position p_1 to p_2).

3. For each rule in the grammar of form $X \to C\ X_1 \dots X_n$, add an active arc of form $X \to \circ\ C\ X_1 \dots X_n$ from position p_1 to p_2.

4. Add C to the chart using the arc extension algorithm above.

Figure 3.11   A bottom-up chart parsing algorithm

the: ART
large: ADJ
can: N, AUX, V
hold: N, V
water: N, V

To best understand the example, draw the chart as it is extended at each step of the algorithm. The agenda is initially empty, so the word *the* is read and a constituent ART1 placed on the agenda.

Entering ART1: (*the* from 1 to 2)
    Adds active arc NP $\to$ ART $\circ$ ADJ N from 1 to 2
    Adds active arc NP $\to$ ART $\circ$ N from 1 to 2

Both these active arcs were added by step 3 of the parsing algorithm and were derived from rules 2 and 3 in the grammar, respectively. Next the word *large* is read and a constituent ADJ1 is created.

Entering ADJ1: (*large* from 2 to 3)
    Adds arc NP $\to$ ADJ $\circ$ N from 2 to 3
    Adds arc NP $\to$ ART ADJ $\circ$ N from 1 to 3

The first arc was added in step 3 of the algorithm. The second arc added here is an extension of the first active arc that was added when ART1 was added to the chart using the arc extension algorithm (step 4).

The chart at this point has already been shown in Figure 3.9. Notice that active arcs are never removed from the chart. For example, when the arc NP $\to$ ART $\circ$ ADJ N from 1 to 2 was extended, producing the arc from 1 to 3, both arcs remained on the chart. This is necessary because the arcs could be used again in a different way by another interpretation.

For the next word, *can*, three constituents, N1, AUX1, and V1 are created for its three interpretations.

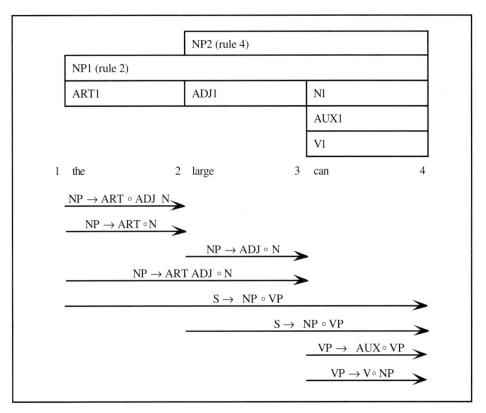

Figure 3.12 After parsing *the large can*

Entering N1: (*can* from 3 to 4)

No active arcs are added in step 2, but two are completed in step 4 by the arc extension algorithm, producing two NPs that are added to the agenda: The first, an NP from 1 to 4, is constructed from rule 2, while the second, an NP from 2 to 4, is constructed from rule 4. These NPs are now at the top of the agenda.

Entering NP1: an NP (*the large can* from 1 to 4)
    Adding active arc S → NP ∘ VP from 1 to 4
Entering NP2: an NP (*large can* from 2 to 4)
    Adding arc S → NP ∘ VP from 2 to 4
Entering AUX1: (*can* from 3 to 4)
    Adding arc VP → AUX ∘ VP from 3 to 4
Entering V1: (*can* from 3 to 4)
    Adding arc VP → V ∘ NP from 3 to 4

The chart is shown in Figure 3.12, which illustrates all the completed constituents (NP2, NP1, ART1, ADJ1, N1, AUX1, V1) and all the uncompleted active arcs entered so far. The next word is *can* again, and N2, AUX2, and V2 are created.

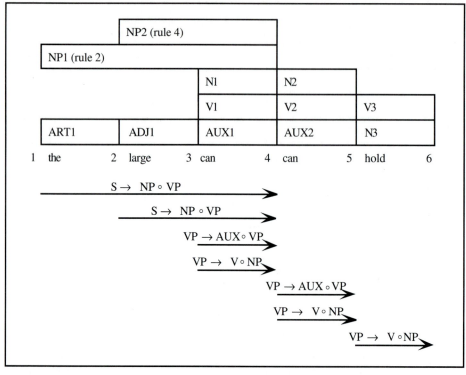

Figure 3.13 The chart after adding *hold*, omitting arcs generated for the first NP

Entering N2: (*can* from 4 to 5, the second *can*)
    Adds no active arcs
Entering AUX2: (*can* from 4 to 5)
    Adds arc VP → AUX ∘ VP from 4 to 5
Entering V2: (*can* from 4 to 5)
    Adds arc VP → V ∘ NP from 4 to 5

The next word is *hold*, and N3 and V3 are created.

Entering N3: (*hold* from 5 to 6)
    Adds no active arcs
Entering V3: (*hold* from 5 to 6)
    Adds arc VP → V ∘ NP from 5 to 6

The chart in Figure 3.13 shows all the completed constituents built so far, together with all the active arcs, except for those used in the first NP.

Entering ART2: (*the* from 6 to 7)
    Adding arc NP → ART ∘ ADJ N from 6 to 7
    Adding arc NP → ART ∘ N from 6 to 7

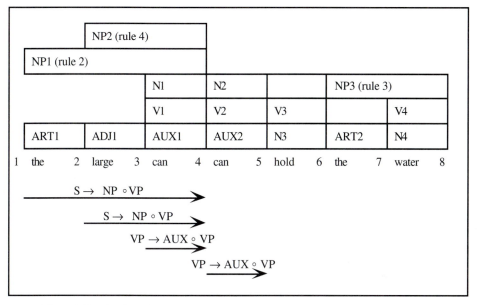

Figure 3.14 The chart after all the NPs are found, omitting all but the crucial active arcs

Entering N4: (*water* from 7 to 8)
No active arcs added in step 3
An NP, NP3, from 6 to 8 is pushed onto the agenda, by completing
arc NP $\rightarrow$ ART $\circ$ N from 6 to 7
Entering NP3: (*the water* from 6 to 8)
A VP, VP1, from 5 to 8 is pushed onto the agenda, by completing
VP $\rightarrow$ V $\circ$ NP from 5 to 6
Adds arc S $\rightarrow$ NP $\circ$ VP from 6 to 8

The chart at this stage is shown in Figure 3.14, but only the active arcs to be used in the remainder of the parse are shown.

Entering VP1: (*hold the water* from 5 to 8)
A VP, VP2, from 4 to 8 is pushed onto the agenda, by completing
VP $\rightarrow$ AUX $\circ$ VP from 4 to 5
Entering VP2: (*can hold the water* from 4 to 8)
An S, S1, is added from 1 to 8, by completing
arc S $\rightarrow$ NP $\circ$ VP from 1 to 4
A VP, VP3, is added from 3 to 8, by completing
arc VP $\rightarrow$ AUX $\circ$ VP from 3 to 4
An S, S2, is added from 2 to 8, by completing
arc S $\rightarrow$ NP $\circ$ VP from 2 to 4

Since you have derived an S covering the entire sentence, you can stop successfully. If you wanted to find all possible interpretations for the sentence,

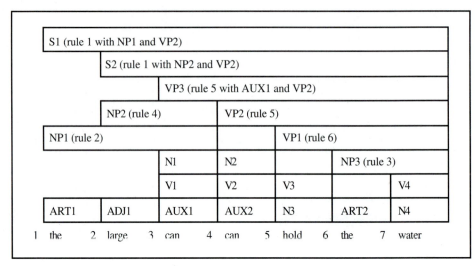

Figure 3.15 The final chart

you would continue parsing until the agenda became empty. The chart would then contain as many S structures covering the entire set of positions as there were different structural interpretations. In addition, this representation of the entire set of structures would be more efficient than a list of interpretations, because the different S structures might share common subparts represented in the chart only once. Figure 3.15 shows the final chart.

Efficiency Considerations

Chart-based parsers can be considerably more efficient than parsers that rely only on a search because the same constituent is never constructed more than once. For instance, a pure top-down or bottom-up search strategy could require up to C^n operations to parse a sentence of length n, where C is a constant that depends on the specific algorithm you use. Even if C is very small, this exponential complexity rapidly makes the algorithm unusable. A chart-based parser, on the other hand, in the worst case would build every possible constituent between every possible pair of positions. This allows us to show that it has a worst-case complexity of $K*n^3$, where n is the length of the sentence and K is a constant depending on the algorithm. Of course, a chart parser involves more work in each step, so K will be larger than C. To contrast the two approaches, assume that C is 10 and that K is a hundred times worse, 1000. Given a sentence of 12 words, the brute force search might take 10^{12} operations (that is, 1,000,000,000,000), whereas the chart parser would take $1000 * 12^3$ (that is, 1,728,000). Under these assumptions, the chart parser would be up to 500,000 times faster than the brute force search on some examples!

3.5 Transition Network Grammars

So far we have examined only one formalism for representing grammars, namely context-free rewrite rules. Here we consider another formalism that is useful in a wide range of applications. It is based on the notion of a **transition network** consisting of **nodes** and **labeled arcs**. One of the nodes is specified as the **initial state**, or **start state**. Consider the network named NP in Grammar 3.16, with the initial state labeled NP and each arc labeled with a word category. Starting at the initial state, you can traverse an arc if the current word in the sentence is in the category on the arc. If the arc is followed, the current word is updated to the next word. A phrase is a legal NP if there is a path from the node NP to a **pop arc** (an arc labeled pop) that accounts for every word in the phrase. This network recognizes the same set of sentences as the following context-free grammar:

$$NP \to ART\ NP1$$
$$NP1 \to ADJ\ NP1$$
$$NP1 \to N$$

Consider parsing the NP *a purple cow* with this network. Starting at the node NP, you can follow the arc labeled art, since the current word is an article—namely, *a.* From node NP1 you can follow the arc labeled adj using the adjective *purple,* and finally, again from NP1, you can follow the arc labeled noun using the noun *cow.* Since you have reached a pop arc, *a purple cow* is a legal NP.

Simple transition networks are often called **finite state machines** (FSMs). Finite state machines are equivalent in expressive power to regular grammars (see Box 3.2), and thus are not powerful enough to describe all languages that can be described by a CFG. To get the descriptive power of CFGs, you need a notion of recursion in the network grammar. A **recursive transition network** (RTN) is like a simple transition network, except that it allows arc labels to refer to other networks as well as word categories. Thus, given the NP network in Grammar 3.16, a network for simple English sentences can be expressed as shown in Grammar 3.17. Uppercase labels refer to networks. The arc from S to S1 can be followed only if the NP network can be successfully traversed to a pop arc. Although not shown in this example, RTNs allow true recursion—that is, a network might have an arc labeled with its own name.

Consider finding a path through the S network for the sentence *The purple cow ate the grass.* Starting at node S, to follow the arc labeled NP, you need to traverse the NP network. Starting at node NP, traverse the network as before for the input *the purple cow.* Following the pop arc in the NP network, return to the S network and traverse the arc to node S1. From node S1 you follow the arc labeled verb using the word *ate.* Finally, the arc labeled NP can be followed if you can traverse the NP network again. This time the remaining input consists of the words *the grass.* You follow the arc labeled art and then the arc labeled noun in the NP network; then take the pop arc from node NP2 and then another pop from node S3. Since you have traversed the network and used all the words in the sentence, *The purple cow ate the grass* is accepted as a legal sentence.

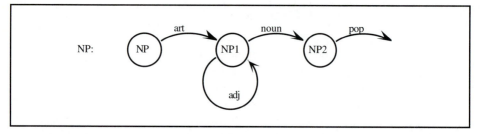

Grammar 3.16

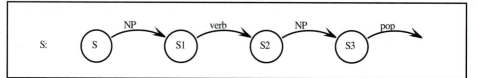

Grammar 3.17

Arc Type	Example	How Used
CAT	noun	succeeds only if current word is of the named category
WRD	of	succeeds only if current word is identical to the label
PUSH	NP	succeeds only if named network can be successfully traversed
JUMP	jump	always succeeds
POP	pop	succeeds and signals the successful end of the network

Figure 3.18 The arc labels for RTNs

In practice, RTN systems incorporate some additional arc types that are useful but not formally necessary. Figure 3.18 summarizes the arc types, together with the notation that will be used in this book to indicate these arc types. According to this terminology, arcs that are labeled with networks are called **push arcs**, and arcs labeled with word categories are called **cat arcs**. In addition, an arc that can always be followed is called a **jump arc**.

Top-Down Parsing with Recursive Transition Networks

An algorithm for parsing with RTNs can be developed along the same lines as the algorithms for parsing CFGs. The state of the parse at any moment can be represented by the following:

> **current position**—a pointer to the next word to be parsed.
> **current node**—the node at which you are located in the network.
> **return points**—a stack of nodes in other networks where you will continue if you **pop** from the current network.

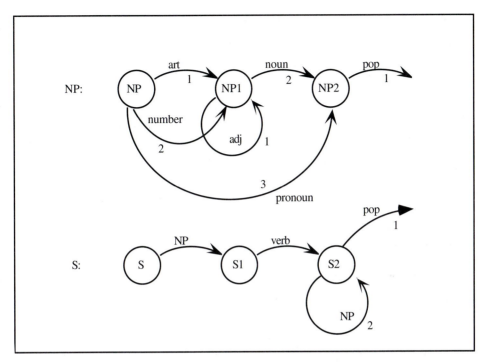

Grammar 3.19

First, consider an algorithm for searching an RTN that assumes that if you can follow an arc, it will be the correct one in the final parse. Say you are in the middle of a parse and know the three pieces of information just cited. You can leave the current node and traverse an arc in the following cases:

Case 1: **If** arc names word category and next word in sentence is in that category,
  Then (1) update *current position* to start at the next word;
  (2) update *current node* to the destination of the arc.
Case 2: **If** arc is a push arc to a network N,
  Then (1) add the destination of the arc onto *return points*;
  (2) update *current node* to the starting node in network N.
Case 3: **If** arc is a pop arc and *return points* list is not empty,
  Then (1) remove first return point and make it *current node*.
Case 4: **If** arc is a pop arc, *return points* list is empty and there are no words left,
  Then (1) parse completes successfully.

Grammar 3.19 shows a network grammar. The numbers on the arcs simply indicate the order in which arcs will be tried when more than one arc leaves a node.

Step	Current Node	Current Position	Return Points	Arc to be Followed	Comments
1.	(S,	1,	NIL)	S/1	initial position
2.	(NP,	1,	(S1))	NP/1	followed push arc to NP network, to return ultimately to S1
3.	(NP1,	2,	(S1))	NP1/1	followed arc NP1/1 (*the*)
4.	(NP1,	3,	(S1))	NP1/2	followed arc NP1/1 (*old*)
5.	(NP2,	4,	(S1))	NP2/2	followed arc NP1/2 (*man*) since NP1/1 is not applicable
6.	(S1,	4,	NIL)	S1/1	the pop arc gets us back to S1
7.	(S2,	5,	NIL)	S2/1	followed arc S2/1 (*cried*)
8.					parse succeeds on pop arc from S2

Figure 3.20 A trace of a top-down parse

Figure 3.20 demonstrates that the grammar accepts the sentence

₁ The ₂ old ₃ man ₄ cried ₅

by showing the sequence of parse states that can be generated by the algorithm. In the trace, each arc is identified by the name of the node that it leaves plus the number identifier. Thus arc S/1 is the arc labeled 1 leaving the S node. If you start at node S, the only possible arc to follow is the push arc NP. As specified in case 2 of the algorithm, the new parse state is computed by setting the current node to NP and putting node S1 on the return points list. From node NP, arc NP/1 is followed and, as specified in case 1 of the algorithm, the input is checked for a word in category art. Since this check succeeds, the arc is followed and the current position is updated (step 3). The parse continues in this manner to step 5, when a pop arc is followed, causing the current node to be reset to S1 (that is, the NP arc succeeded). The parse succeeds after finding a verb in step 6 and following the pop arc from the S network in step 7.

In this example the parse succeeded because the first arc that succeeded was ultimately the correct one in every case. However, with a sentence like *The green faded,* where *green* can be an adjective or a noun, this algorithm would fail because it would initially classify *green* as an adjective and then not find a noun following. To be able to recover from such failures, we save all possible backup states as we go along, just as we did with the CFG top-down parsing algorithm.

Consider this technique in operation on the following sentence:

₁ One ₂ saw ₃ the ₄ man ₅

The parser initially attempts to parse the sentence as beginning with the NP *one saw,* but after failing to find a verb, it backtracks and finds a successful parse starting with the NP *one.* The trace of the parse is shown in Figure 3.21, where at

Step	Current State	Arc to be Followed	Backup States
1.	(S, 1, NIL)	S/1	NIL
2.	(NP, 1, (S1))	NP/2 (& NP/3 for backup)	NIL
3.	(NP1, 2, (S1))	NP1/2	(NP2, 2, (S1))
4.	(NP2, 3, (S1))	NP2/1	(NP2, 2, (S1))
5.	(S1, 3, NIL)	no arc can be followed	(NP2, 2, (S1))
6.	(NP2, 2, (S1))	NP2/1	NIL
7.	(S1, 2, NIL)	S1/1	NIL
8.	(S2, 3, NIL)	S2/2	NIL
9.	(NP, 3, (S2))	NP/1	NIL
10.	(NP1, 4, (S2))	NP1/2	NIL
11.	(NP2, 5, (S2))	NP2/1	NIL
12.	(S2, 5, NIL)	S2/1	NIL
13.	parse succeeds		NIL

Figure 3.21 A top-down RTN parse with backtracking

each stage the current parse state is shown in the form of a triple (current node, current position, return points), together with possible states for backtracking. The figure also shows the arcs used to generate the new state and backup states.

This trace behaves identically to the previous example except in two places. In step 2, two arcs leaving node NP could accept the word *one*. Arc NP/2 classifies *one* as a number and produces the next current state. Arc NP/3 classifies it as a pronoun and produces a backup state. This backup state is actually used later in step 6 when it is found that none of the arcs leaving node S1 can accept the input word *the*.

Of course, in general, many more backup states are generated than in this simple example. In these cases there will be a list of possible backup states. Depending on how this list is organized, you can produce different orderings on when the states are examined.

An RTN parser can be constructed to use a chart-like structure to gain the advantages of chart parsing. In RTN systems, the chart is often called the **well-formed substring table** (WFST). Each time a pop is followed, the constituent is placed on the WFST, and every time a push is found, the WFST is checked before the subnetwork is invoked. If the chart contains constituent(s) of the type being pushed for, these are used and the subnetwork is not reinvoked. An RTN using a WFST has the same complexity as the chart parser described in the last section: $K*n^3$, where n is the length of the sentence.

3.6 Top-Down Chart Parsing

So far, you have seen a simple top-down method and a bottom-up chart-based method for parsing context-free grammars. Each of the approaches has its advantages and disadvantages. In this section a new parsing method is presented that actually captures the advantages of both. But first, consider the pluses and minuses of the approaches.

Top-down methods have the advantage of being highly predictive. A word might be ambiguous in isolation, but if some of those possible categories cannot be used in a legal sentence, then these categories may never even be considered. For example, consider Grammar 3.8 in a top-down parse of the sentence *The can holds the water,* where *can* may be an AUX, V, or N, as before.

The top-down parser would rewrite (S) to (NP VP) and then rewrite the NP to produce three possibilities, (ART ADJ N VP), (ART N VP), and (ADJ N VP). Taking the first, the parser checks if the first word, *the,* can be an ART, and then if the next word, *can,* can be an ADJ, which fails. Trying the next possibility, the parser checks *the* again, and then checks if *can* can be an N, which succeeds. The interpretations of *can* as an auxiliary and a main verb are never considered because no syntactic tree generated by the grammar would ever predict an AUX or V in this position. In contrast, the bottom-up parser would have considered all three interpretations of *can* from the start—that is, all three would be added to the chart and would combine with active arcs. Given this argument, the top-down approach seems more efficient.

On the other hand, consider the top-down parser in the example above needed to check that the word *the* was an ART twice, once for each rule. This reduplication of effort is very common in pure top-down approaches and becomes a serious problem, and large constituents may be rebuilt again and again as they are used in different rules. In contrast, the bottom-up parser only checks the input once, and only builds each constituent exactly once. So by this argument, the bottom-up approach appears more efficient.

You can gain the advantages of both by combining the methods. A small variation in the bottom-up chart algorithm yields a technique that is predictive like the top-down approaches yet avoids any reduplication of work as in the bottom-up approaches.

As before, the algorithm is driven by an agenda of completed constituents and the arc extension algorithm, which combines active arcs with constituents when they are added to the chart. While both use the technique of extending arcs with constituents, the difference is in how new arcs are generated from the grammar. In the bottom-up approach, new active arcs are generated whenever a completed constituent is added that could be the first constituent of the right-hand side of a rule. With the top-down approach, new active arcs are generated whenever a new active arc is added to the chart, as described in the top-down arc introduction algorithm shown in Figure 3.22. The parsing algorithm is then easily stated, as is also shown in Figure 3.22.

Consider this new algorithm operating with the same grammar on the same sentence as in Section 3.4, namely *The large can can hold the water.* In the initialization stage, an arc labeled $S \to \circ NP\ VP$ is added. Then, active arcs for each rule that can derive an NP are added: $NP \to \circ ART\ ADJ\ N$, $NP \to \circ ART\ N$,

Top-Down Arc Introduction Algorithm

To add an arc $S \rightarrow C_1 \ldots \circ C_i \ldots C_n$ ending at position j, do the following:

For each rule in the grammar of form $C_i \rightarrow X_1 \ldots X_k$, recursively add the new arc $C_i \rightarrow \circ X_1 \ldots X_k$ from position j to j.

Top-Down Chart Parsing Algorithm

Initialization: For every rule in the grammar of form $S \rightarrow X_1 \ldots X_k$, add an arc labeled $S \rightarrow \circ X_1 \ldots X_k$ using the arc introduction algorithm.

Parsing: Do until there is no input left:

1. If the agenda is empty, look up the interpretations of the next word and add them to the agenda.

2. Select a constituent from the agenda (call it constituent C).

3. Using the arc extension algorithm, combine C with every active arc on the chart. Any new constituents are added to the agenda.

4. For any active arcs created in step 3, add them to the chart using the top-down arc introduction algorithm.

Figure 3.22 The top-down arc introduction and chart parsing algorithms

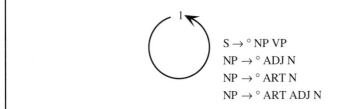

$S \rightarrow \circ NP\ VP$

$NP \rightarrow \circ ADJ\ N$

$NP \rightarrow \circ ART\ N$

$NP \rightarrow \circ ART\ ADJ\ N$

Figure 3.23 The initial chart

and $NP \rightarrow \circ ADJ\ N$ are all added from position 1 to 1. Thus the initialized chart is as shown in Figure 3.23. The trace of the parse is as follows:

Entering ART1 (*the*) from 1 to 2
    Two arcs can be extended by the arc extension algorithm
        $NP \rightarrow ART \circ N$ from 1 to 2
        $NP \rightarrow ART \circ ADJ\ N$ from 1 to 2
Entering ADJ1 (*large*) from 2 to 3
    One arc can be extended
        $NP \rightarrow ART\ ADJ \circ N$ from 1 to 3
Entering AUX1 (*can*) from 3 to 4
    No activity, constituent is ignored
Entering V1 (*can*) from 3 to 4
    No activity, constituent is ignored

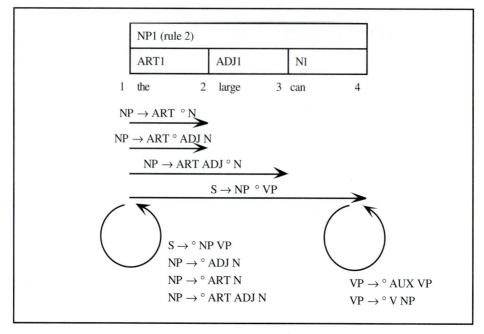

Figure 3.24 The chart after building the first NP

Entering N1 (*can*) from 3 to 4
  One arc extended and completed yielding
    NP1 from 1 to 4 (*the large can*)
Entering NP1 from 1 to 4
  One arc can be extended
    S → NP ∘ VP from 1 to 4
  Using the top-down rule (step 4), new active arcs are added for VP
    VP → ∘ AUX VP from 4 to 4
    VP → ∘ V NP from 4 to 4

At this stage, the chart is as shown in Figure 3.24. Compare this with Figure 3.10. It contains fewer completed constituents since only those that are allowed by the top-down filtering have been constructed.

The algorithm continues, adding the three interpretations of *can* as an AUX, V, and N. The AUX reading extends the VP → ∘ AUX VP arc at position 4 and adds active arcs for a new VP starting at position 5. The V reading extends the VP → ∘ V NP arc and adds active arcs for an NP starting at position 5. The N reading does not extend any arc and so is ignored. After the two readings of *hold* (as an N and V) are added, the chart is as shown in Figure 3.25. Again, compare with the corresponding chart for the bottom-up parser in Figure 3.13. The rest of the sentence is parsed similarly, and the final chart is shown in Figure 3.26. In comparing this to the final chart produced by the bottom-up parser (Figure 3.15), you see that the number of constituents generated has dropped from 21 to 13.

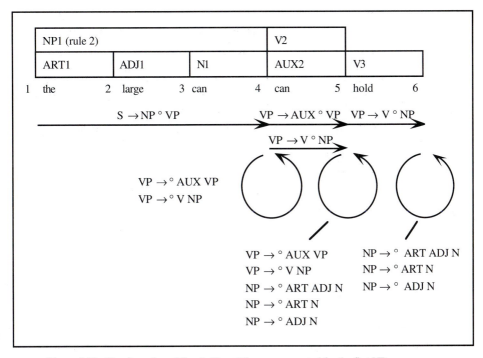

Figure 3.25 The chart after adding *hold*, omitting arcs generated for the first NP

Figure 3.26 The final chart for the top-down filtering algorithm

While it is not a big difference here with such a simple grammar, the difference can be dramatic with a sizable grammar.

It turns out in the worst-case analysis that the top-down chart parser is not more efficient that the pure bottom-up chart parser. Both have a worst-case complexity of $K*n^3$ for a sentence of length n. In practice, however, the top-down method is considerably more efficient for any reasonable grammar.

BOX 3.2 Generative Capacity of Transition Networks

Transition network systems can be classified by the types of languages they can describe. In fact, you can draw correspondences between various network systems and rewrite-rule systems. For instance, simple transition networks (that is, finite state machines) with no push arcs are expressively equivalent to regular grammars—that is, every language that can be described by a simple transition network can be described by a regular grammar, and vice versa. An FSM for the first language described in Box 3.1 is

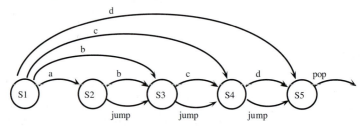

Recursive transition networks, on the other hand, are expressively equivalent to context-free grammars. Thus an RTN can be converted into a CFG and vice versa. A recursive transition network for the language consisting of a number of a's followed by an equal number of b's is

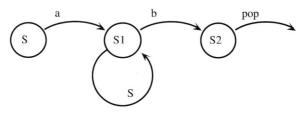

○ **3.7 Finite State Models and Morphological Processing**

Although in simple examples and small systems you can list all the words allowed by the system, large vocabulary systems face a serious problem in representing the lexicon. Not only are there a large number of words, but each word may combine with affixes to produce additional related words. One way to address this problem is to preprocess the input sentence into a sequence of morphemes. A word may consist of single morpheme, but often a word consists of a root form plus an affix. For instance, the word *eaten* consists of the root form *eat* and the suffix *-en*, which indicates the past participle form. Without any preprocessing, a lexicon would have to list all the forms of *eat*, including *eats, eating, ate,* and *eaten.* With preprocessing, there would be one morpheme *eat* that may combine with suffixes such as *-ing, -s,* and *-en,* and one entry for the irregular form *ate.* Thus the lexicon would only need to store two entries (*eat* and

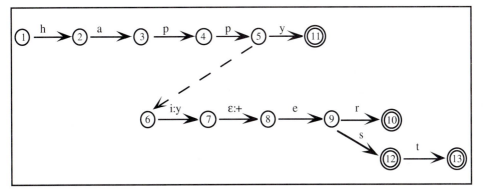

Figure 3.27 A simple FST for the forms of *happy*

ate) rather than four. Likewise the word *happiest* breaks down into the root form *happy* and the suffix -*est,* and thus does not need a separate entry in the lexicon. Of course, not all forms are allowed; for example, the word *seed* cannot be decomposed into a root form *se* (or *see*) and a suffix -*ed.* The lexicon would have to encode what forms are allowed with each root.

One of the most popular models is based on **finite state transducers (FSTs),** which are like finite state machines except that they produce an output given an input. An arc in an FST is labeled with a pair of symbols. For example, an arc labeled i:y could only be followed if the current input is the letter *i* and the output is the letter *y*. FSTs can be used to concisely represent the lexicon and to transform the surface form of words into a sequence of morphemes. Figure 3.27 shows a simple FST that defines the forms of the word *happy* and its derived forms. It transforms the word *happier* into the sequence *happy +er* and *happiest* into the sequence *happy +est.*

Arcs labeled by a single letter have that letter as both the input and the output. Nodes that are double circles indicate success states, that is, acceptable words. Consider processing the input word *happier* starting from state 1. The upper network accepts the first four letters, *happ,* and copies them to the output. From state 5 you could accept a *y* and have a complete word, or you could jump to state 6 to consider affixes. (The dashed link, indicating a jump, is not formally necessary but is useful for showing the break between the processing of the root form and the processing of the suffix.) For the word *happier,* you must jump to state 6. The next letter must be an *i,* which is transformed into a *y*. This is followed by a transition that uses no input (the empty symbol ε) and outputs a plus sign. From state 8, the input must be an *e,* and the output is also *e.* This must be followed by an *r* to get to state 10, which is encoded as a double circle indicating a possible end of word (that is, a success state for the FST). Thus this FST accepts the appropriate forms and outputs the desired sequence of morphemes.

The entire lexicon can be encoded as an FST that encodes all the legal input words and transforms them into morphemic sequences. The FSTs for the

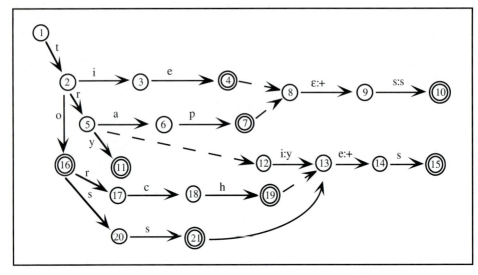

Figure 3.28　A fragment of an FST defining some nouns (singular and plural)

different suffixes need only be defined once, and all root forms that allow that suffix can point to the same node. Words that share a common prefix (such as *torch, toss,* and *to*) also can share the same nodes, greatly reducing the size of the network. The FST in Figure 3.28 accepts the following words, which all start with *t*: *tie* (state 4), *ties* (10), *trap* (7), *traps* (10), *try* (11), *tries* (15), *to* (16), *torch* (19), *torches* (15), *toss* (21), and *tosses* (15). In addition, it outputs the appropriate sequence of morphemes.

Note that you may pass through acceptable states along the way when processing a word. For instance, with the input *toss* you would pass through state 15, indicating that *to* is a word. This analysis is not useful, however, because if *to* was accepted then the letters *ss* would not be accounted for.

Using such an FST, an input sentence can be processed into a sequence of morphemes. Occasionally, a word will be ambiguous and have multiple different decompositions into morphemes. This is rare enough, however, that we will ignore this minor complication throughout the book.

○ 3.8 Grammars and Logic Programming

Another popular method of building a parser for CFGs is to encode the rules of the grammar directly in a logic programming language such as PROLOG. It turns out that the standard PROLOG interpretation algorithm uses exactly the same search strategy as the depth-first top-down parsing algorithm, so all that is needed is a way to reformulate context-free grammar rules as clauses in PROLOG. Consider the following CFG rule:

$$S \rightarrow NP\ VP$$

This rule can be reformulated as an axiom that says, "A sequence of words is a legal S if it begins with a legal NP that is followed by a legal VP." If you number each word in a sentence by its position, you can restate this rule as: "There is an S between position p1 and p3, if there is a position p2 such that there is an NP between p1 and p2 and a VP between p2 and p3." In PROLOG this would be the following axiom, where variables are indicated as atoms with an initial capitalized letter:

s(P1, P3) :– np(P1, P2), vp(P2, P3)

To set up the process, add axioms listing the words in the sentence by their position. For example, the sentence *John ate the cat* is described by

word(john, 1, 2)
word(ate, 2, 3)
word(the, 3, 4)
word(cat, 4, 5)

The lexicon is defined by a set of predicates such as the following:

isart(the)
isname(john)
isverb(ate)
isnoun(cat)

Ambiguous words would produce multiple assertions—one for each syntactic category to which they belong.

For each syntactic category, you can define a predicate that is true only if the word between the two specified positions is of that category, as follows:

n(I, O) :– word(Word, I, O), isnoun(Word)
art(I, O) :– word(Word, I, O), isart(Word)
v(I, O) :– word(Word, I, O), isverb(Word)
name(I, O) :– word(Word, I, O), isname(Word)

Using the axioms in Figure 3.29, you can prove that *John ate the cat* is a legal sentence by proving s(1, 5), as in Figure 3.30. In Figure 3.30, when there is a possibility of confusing different variables that have the same name, a prime (´) is appended to the variable name to make it unique. This proof trace is in the same format as the trace for the top-down CFG parser, as follows. The state of the proof at any time is the list of subgoals yet to be proven. Since the word positions are included in the goal description, no separate position column need be traced. The backup states are also lists of subgoals, maintained automatically by a system like PROLOG to implement backtracking. A typical trace of a proof in such a system shows only the current state at any time.

Because the standard PROLOG search strategy is the same as the depth-first top-down paring strategy, a parser built from PROLOG will have the same computational complexity, C^n, that is, the number of steps can be exponential in the

```
1.  s(P1, P3)  :−  np(P1, P2), vp(P2, P3)
2.  np(P1, P3) :−  art(P1, P2), n(P2, P3)
3.  np(P1, P3) :−  name(P1, P3)
4.  pp(P1, P3) :−  p(P1, P2), np(P2, P3)
5.  vp(P1, P2) :−  v(P1, P2)
6.  vp(P1, P3) :−  v(P1, P2), np(P2, P3)
7.  vp(P1, P3) :−  v(P1, P2), pp(P2, P3)
```

Figure 3.29 A PROLOG-based representation of Grammar 3.4

Step	Current State	Backup States	Comments
1.	s(1, 5)		
2.	np(1, P2) vp(P2, 5)		
3.	art(1, P2′) n(P2′, P2) vp(P2, 5)	name(1, P2) vp(P2, 5)	fails as no ART at position 1
4.	name(1, P2) vp(P2, 5)		
5.	vp(2, 5)		name(1, 2) proven
6.	v(2, 5)	v(2, P2) np(P2, 5) v(2, P2) pp(P2, 5)	fails as no verb spans positions 2 to 5
7.	v(2, P2) np(P2, 5)	v(2, P2) pp(P2, 5)	
8.	np(3, 5)	v(2, P2) pp(P2, 5)	v(2, 3) proven
9.	art(3, P2) n(P2, 5)	name(3, 5) v(2, P2) pp(P2, 5)	
10.	n(4, 5)	name(3, 5) v(2, P2) pp(P2, 5)	art(3, 4) proven
11.	√ proof succeeds	name(3, 5) v(2, P2) pp(P2, 5)	n(4, 5) proven

Figure 3.30 A trace of a PROLOG-based parse of *John ate the cat*

length of the input. Even with this worst-case analysis, PROLOG-based grammars can be quite efficient in practice. It is also possible to insert chart-like mechanisms to improve the efficiency of a grammar, although then the simple correspondence between context-free rules and PROLOG rules is lost. Some of these issues will be discussed in the next chapter.

It is worthwhile to try some simple grammars written in PROLOG to better understand top-down, depth-first search. By turning on the tracing facility, you can obtain a trace similar in content to that shown in Figure 3.30.

Summary

The two basic grammatical formalisms are context-free grammars (CFGs) and recursive transition networks (RTNs). A variety of parsing algorithms can be used for each. For instance, a simple top-down backtracking algorithm can be used for both formalisms and, in fact, the same algorithm can be used in the standard logic-programming-based grammars as well. The most efficient parsers use a chart-like structure to record every constituent built during a parse. By reusing this information later in the search, considerable work can be saved.

Related Work and Further Readings

There is a vast literature on syntactic formalisms and parsing algorithms. The notion of context-free grammars was introduced by Chomsky (1956) and has been studied extensively since in linguistics and in computer science. Some of this work will be discussed in detail later, as it is more relevant to the material in the following chapters.

Most of the parsing algorithms were developed in the mid-1960s in computer science, usually with the goal of analyzing programming languages rather than natural language. A classic reference for work in this area is Aho, Sethi, and Ullman (1986), or Aho and Ullman (1972), if the former is not available. The notion of a chart is described in Kay (1973; 1980) and has been adapted by many parsing systems since. The bottom-up chart parser described in this chapter is similar to the left-corner parsing algorithm in Aho and Ullman (1972), while the top-down chart parser is similar to that described by Earley (1970) and hence called the Earley algorithm.

Transition network grammars and parsers are described in Woods (1970; 1973) and parsers based on logic programming are described and compared with transition network systems in Pereira and Warren (1980). Winograd (1983) discusses most of the approaches described here from a slightly different perspective, which could be useful if a specific technique is difficult to understand. Gazdar and Mellish (1989a; 1989b) give detailed descriptions of implementations of parsers in LISP and in PROLOG. In addition, descriptions of transition network parsers can be found in many introductory AI texts, such as Rich and Knight (1992), Winston (1992), and Charniak and McDermott (1985). These books also contain descriptions of the search techniques underlying many of the parsing algorithms. Norvig (1992) is an excellent source on AI programming techniques.

The best sources for work on computational morphology are two books: Sproat (1992) and Ritchie et al. (1992). Much of the recent work on finite state models has been based on the KIMMO system (Koskenniemi, 1983). Rather than requiring the construction of a huge network, KIMMO uses a set of FSTs which are run in parallel; that is, all of them must simultaneously accept the input and agree on the output. Typically, these FSTs are expressed using an abstract language that allows general morphological rules to be expressed concisely. A compiler can then be used to generate the appropriate networks for the system.

Finite state models are useful for a wide range of processing tasks besides morphological analysis. Blank (1989), for instance, is developing a grammar for English using only finite state methods. Finite state grammars are also used extensively in speech recognition systems.

Exercises for Chapter 3

1. (*easy*)

   a. Express the following tree in the list notation in Section 3.1.

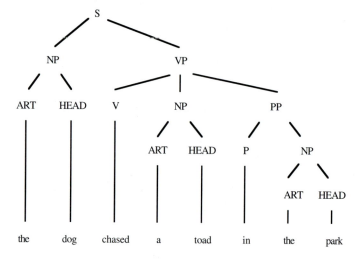

   b. Is there a tree structure that could not be expressed as a list structure? How about a list structure that could not be expressed as a tree?

2. (*easy*) Given the CFG in Grammar 3.4, define an appropriate lexicon and show a trace in the format of Figure 3.5 of a top-down CFG parse of the sentence *The man walked the old dog.*

3. (*easy*) Given the RTN in Grammar 3.19 and a lexicon in which *green* can be an adjective or a noun, show a trace in the format of Figure 3.21 of a top-down RTN parse of the sentence *The green faded.*

4. (*easy*) Given the PROLOG-based grammar defined in Figure 3.29, show a trace in the format of Figure 3.30 of the proof that the following is a legal sentence: *The cat ate John.*

5. (*medium*) Map the following context-free grammar into an equivalent recursive transition network that uses only three networks—an S, NP, and PP network. Make your networks as small as possible.

$$S \rightarrow NP\ VP \qquad NP2 \rightarrow ADJ\ NP2$$
$$VP \rightarrow V \qquad NP2 \rightarrow NP3\ PREPS$$
$$VP \rightarrow V\ NP \qquad NP3 \rightarrow N$$
$$VP \rightarrow V\ PP \qquad PREPS \rightarrow PP$$
$$NP \rightarrow ART\ NP2 \qquad PREPS \rightarrow PP\ PREPS$$
$$NP \rightarrow NP2 \qquad PP \rightarrow NP$$
$$NP2 \rightarrow N$$

6. (*medium*) Given the CFG in Exercise 5 and the following lexicon, construct a trace of a pure top-down parse and a pure bottom-up parse of the sentence *The herons fly in groups*. Make your traces as clear as possible, select the rules in the order given in Exercise 5, and indicate all parts of the search. The lexicon entries for each word are

the: ART
herons: N
fly: N V ADJ
in: P
groups: N V

7. (*medium*) Consider the following grammar:

$$S \rightarrow ADJS\ N$$
$$S \rightarrow N$$
$$ADJS \rightarrow ADJS\ ADJ$$
$$ADJS \rightarrow ADJ$$

Lexicon: ADJ: red, N: house

a. What happens to the top-down depth-first parser operating on this grammar trying to parse the input *red red*? In particular, state whether the parser succeeds, fails, or never stops.

b. How about a top-down breadth-first parser operating on the same input *red red*?

c. How about a top-down breadth-first parser operating on the input *red house*?

d. How about a bottom-up depth-first parser on *red house*?

e. For the cases where the parser fails to stop, give a grammar that is equivalent to the one shown in this exercise and that is parsed correctly. (Correct behavior includes failing on unacceptable phrases as well as succeeding on acceptable ones.)

f. With the new grammar in part (e), do all the preceding parsers now operate correctly on the two phrases *red red* and *red house*?

8. (*medium*) Consider the following CFG:

   S → NP V
   S → NP AUX V
   NP → ART N

   Trace one of the chart parsers in processing the sentence

   ₁ The ₂ man ₃ is ₄ laughing ₅

   with the lexicon entries:

   the: ART
   man: N
   is: AUX
   laughing: V

   Show every step of the parse, giving the parse stack, and drawing the chart each time a nonterminal constituent is added to the chart.

9. (*medium*) Consider the following CFG that generates sequences of letters:

   s → a x c
   s → b x c
   s → b x d
   s → b x e
   s → c x e
   x → f x
   x → g

   a. If you had to write a parser for this grammar, would it be better to use a pure top-down or a pure bottom-up approach? Why?

   b. Trace the parser of your choice operating on the input *bffge*.

10. (*medium*) Consider the following CFG and RTN:

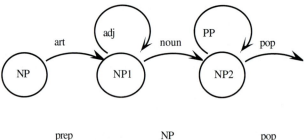

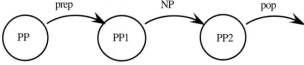

$$NP \rightarrow ART \ NP1$$
$$NP1 \rightarrow ADJ \ N \ PPS$$
$$PPS \rightarrow PP$$
$$PPS \rightarrow PP \ PPS$$
$$PP \rightarrow P \ NP$$

a. State two ways in which the languages described by these two grammars differ. For each, give a sample sentence that is recognized by one grammar but not the other and that demonstrates the difference.

b. Write a new CFG equivalent to the RTN shown here.

c. Write a new RTN equivalent to the CFG shown here.

11. (*hard*) Consider the following sentences:

List A	**List B**
i. Joe is reading the book.	*i.* *Joe has reading the book.
ii. Joe had won a letter.	*ii.* *Joe had win.
iii. Joe has to win.	*iii.* *Joe winning.
iv. Joe will have the letter.	*iv.* *Joe will had the letter.
v. The letter in the book was read.	*v.* *The book was win by Joe.
vi. The letter must have been in the book by Joe.	*vi.* *Joe will can be mad.
vii. The man could have had one.	*vii.* *The man can have having one.

a. Write a context-free grammar that accepts all the sentences in list A while rejecting the sentences in list B. You may find it useful to make reference to the grammatical forms of verbs discussed in Chapter 2.

b. Implement one of the chart-based parsing strategies and, using the grammar specified in part (a), demonstrate that your parser correctly accepts all the sentences in A and rejects those in B. You should maintain enough information in each entry on the chart so that you can reconstruct the parse tree for each possible interpretation. Make sure your method of recording the structure is well documented and clearly demonstrated.

c. List three (distinct) grammatical forms that would not be recognized by a parser implementing the grammar in part (a). Provide an example of your own for each of these grammatical forms.

Features and Augmented Grammars

Context-free grammars provide the basis for most of the computational parsing mechanisms developed to date, but as they have been described so far, they would be very inconvenient for capturing natural languages. This chapter describes an extension to the basic context-free mechanism that defines constituents by a set of **features**. This extension allows aspects of natural language such as agreement and subcategorization to be handled in an intuitive and concise way.

Section 4.1 introduces the notion of feature systems and the generalization of context-free grammars to allow features. Section 4.2 then describes some useful feature systems for English that are typical of those in use in various grammars. Section 4.3 explores some issues in defining the lexicon and shows how using features makes the task considerably simpler. Section 4.4 describes a sample context-free grammar using features and introduces some conventions that simplify the process. Section 4.5 describes how to extend a chart parser to handle a grammar with features. The remaining sections, which are optional, describe how features are used in other grammatical formalisms and explore some more advanced material. Section 4.6 introduces augmented transition networks, which are a generalization of recursive transition networks with features, and Section 4.7 describes definite clause grammars based on PROLOG. Section 4.8 describes generalized feature systems and unification grammars.

4.1 Feature Systems and Augmented Grammars

In natural languages there are often agreement restrictions between words and phrases. For example, the NP *a men* is not correct English because the article *a* indicates a single object while the noun *men* indicates a plural object; the noun phrase does not satisfy the **number agreement** restriction of English. There are many other forms of agreement, including subject-verb agreement, gender agreement for pronouns, restrictions between the head of a phrase and the form of its complement, and so on. To handle such phenomena conveniently, the grammatical formalism is extended to allow constituents to have **features**. For example, we might define a feature NUMBER that may take a **value** of either s (for singular) or p (for plural), and we then might write an augmented CFG rule such as

$$NP \rightarrow ART \ N \quad \text{only when NUMBER}_1 \text{ agrees with NUMBER}_2$$

This rule says that a legal noun phrase consists of an article followed by a noun, but only when the number feature of the first word agrees with the number feature of the second. This one rule is equivalent to two CFG rules that would use different terminal symbols for encoding singular and plural forms of all noun phrases, such as

$$NP\text{-SING} \rightarrow ART\text{-SING N-SING}$$
$$NP\text{-PLURAL} \rightarrow ART\text{-PLURAL N-PLURAL}$$

While the two approaches seem similar in ease-of-use in this one example, consider that all rules in the grammar that use an NP on the right-hand side would now need to be duplicated to include a rule for NP-SING and a rule for NP-PLURAL, effectively doubling the size of the grammar. And handling additional features, such as person agreement, would double the size of the grammar again and again. Using features, the size of the augmented grammar remains the same as the original one yet accounts for agreement constraints.

To accomplish this, a constituent is defined as a **feature structure**—a mapping from features to values that defines the relevant properties of the constituent. In the examples in this book, feature names in formulas will be written in boldface. For example, a feature structure for a constituent ART1 that represents a particular use of the word *a* might be written as follows:

ART1: (**CAT** ART
     ROOT a
     NUMBER s)

This says it is a constituent in the category ART that has as its root the word *a* and is singular. Usually an abbreviation is used that gives the CAT value more prominence and provides an intuitive tie back to simple context-free grammars. In this abbreviated form, constituent ART1 would be written as

ART1: (ART **ROOT** a **NUMBER** s)

Feature structures can be used to represent larger constituents as well. To do this, feature structures themselves can occur as values. Special features based on the integers—1, 2, 3, and so on—will stand for the first subconstituent, second subconstituent, and so on, as needed. With this, the representation of the NP constituent for the phrase *a fish* could be

NP1: (NP **NUMBER** s
      1 (ART **ROOT** a
             NUMBER s)
      2 (N **ROOT** fish
           NUMBER s))

Note that this can also be viewed as a representation of a parse tree shown in Figure 4.1, where the subconstituent features 1 and 2 correspond to the subconstituent links in the tree.

The rules in an augmented grammar are stated in terms of feature structures rather than simple categories. Variables are allowed as feature values so that a rule can apply to a wide range of situations. For example, a rule for simple noun phrases would be as follows:

(NP **NUMBER** ?n) → (ART **NUMBER** ?n) (N **NUMBER** ?n)

This says that an NP constituent can consist of two subconstituents, the first being an ART and the second being an N, in which the NUMBER feature in all three constituents is identical. According to this rule, constituent NP1 given previously is a legal constituent. On the other hand, the constituent

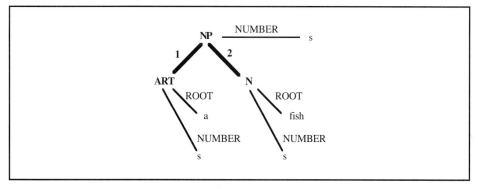

Figure 4.1 Viewing a feature structure as an extended parse tree

$$*(NP \quad \mathbf{1} \, (ART \, \mathbf{NUMBER} \, s)$$
$$\mathbf{2} \, (N \, \mathbf{NUMBER} \, s))$$

is not allowed by this rule because there is no NUMBER feature in the NP, and the constituent

$$*(NP \quad \mathbf{NUMBER} \, s$$
$$\mathbf{1} \, (ART \, \mathbf{NUMBER} \, s)$$
$$\mathbf{2} \, (N \, \mathbf{NUMBER} \, p))$$

is not allowed because the NUMBER feature of the N constituent is not identical to the other two NUMBER features.

Variables are also useful in specifying ambiguity in a constituent. For instance, the word *fish* is ambiguous between a singular and a plural reading. Thus the word might have two entries in the lexicon that differ only by the value of the NUMBER feature. Alternatively, we could define a single entry that uses a variable as the value of the NUMBER feature, that is,

$$(N \, \mathbf{ROOT} \, fish \, \mathbf{NUMBER} \, ?n)$$

This works because any value of the NUMBER feature is allowed for the word *fish*. In many cases, however, not just any value would work, but a range of values is possible. To handle these cases, we introduce **constrained variables**, which are variables that can only take a value out of a specified list. For example, the variable $?n\{s \, p\}$ would be a variable that can take the value s or the value p. Typically, when we write such variables, we will drop the variable name altogether and just list the possible values. Given this, the word *fish* might be represented by the constituent

$$(N \, \mathbf{ROOT} \, fish \, \mathbf{NUMBER} \, ?n\{s \, p\})$$

or more simply as

$$(N \, \mathbf{ROOT} \, fish \, \mathbf{NUMBER} \, \{s \, p\})$$

BOX 4.1 Formalizing Feature Structures

There is an active area of research in the formal properties of feature structures. This work views a feature system as a formal logic. A feature structure is defined as a partial function from features to feature values. For example, the feature structure

> ART1: (**CAT** ART
> **ROOT** a
> **NUMBER** s)

is treated as an abbreviation of the following statement in FOPC:

$$ART1(CAT) = ART \land ART1(ROOT) = a \land ART1(NUMBER) = s$$

Feature structures with disjunctive values map to disjunctions. The structure

> THE1: (**CAT** ART
> **ROOT** the
> **NUMBER** {s p})

would be represented as

$$THE1(CAT) = ART \land THE1(ROOT) = the$$
$$\land (THE1(NUMBER) = s \lor THE1(NUMBER) = p)$$

Given this, agreement between feature values can be defined as equality equations.

There is an interesting issue of whether an augmented context-free grammar can describe languages that cannot be described by a simple context-free grammar. The answer depends on the constraints on what can be a feature value. If the set of feature values is finite, then it would always be possible to create new constituent categories for every combination of features. Thus it is expressively equivalent to a context-free grammar. If the set of feature values is unconstrained, however, then such grammars have arbitrary computational power. In practice, even when the set of values is not explicitly restricted, this power is not used, and the standard parsing algorithms can be used on grammars that include features.

4.2   Some Basic Feature Systems for English

This section describes some basic feature systems that are commonly used in grammars of English and develops the particular set of features used throughout this book. Specifically, it considers number and person agreement, verb form features, and features required to handle subcategorization constraints. You should read this to become familiar with the features in general and then refer back to it later when you need a detailed specification of a particular feature.

Person and Number Features

In the previous section, you saw the number system in English: Words may be classified as to whether they can describe a single object or multiple objects. While number agreement restrictions occur in several different places in English, they are most importantly found in subject-verb agreement. But subjects and verbs must also agree on another dimension, namely with respect to the **person**. The possible values of this dimension are

First Person (1): The noun phrase refers to the speaker, or a group of people including the speaker (for example, *I, we, you, and I*).

Second Person (2): The noun phrase refers to the listener, or a group including the listener but not including the speaker (for example, *you, all of you*).

Third Person (3): The noun phrase refers to one or more objects, not including the speaker or hearer.

Since number and person features always co-occur, it is convenient to combine the two into a single feature, AGR, that has six possible values: first person singular (1s), second person singular (2s), third person singular (3s), and first, second and third person plural (1p, 2p, and 3p, respectively). For example, an instance of the word *is* can agree only with a third person singular subject, so its AGR feature would be 3s. An instance of the word *are*, however, may agree with second person singular or any of the plural forms, so its AGR feature would be a variable ranging over the values {2s 1p 2p 3p}.

Verb-Form Features and Verb Subcategorization

Another very important feature system in English involves the form of the verb. This feature is used in many situations, such as the analysis of auxiliaries and generally in the subcategorization restrictions of many head words. As described in Chapter 2, there are five basic forms of verbs. The feature system for verb forms will be slightly more complicated in order to conveniently capture certain phenomena. In particular, we will use the following feature values for the feature VFORM:

base—base form (for example, *go, be, say, decide*)
pres—simple present tense (for example, *go, goes, am, is, say, says, decide*)
past—simple past tense (for example, *went, was, said, decided*)
fin—finite (that is, a tensed form, equivalent to {pres past})
ing—present participle (for example, *going, being, saying, deciding*)
pastprt—past participle (for example, *gone, been, said, decided*)
inf—a special feature value that is used for infinitive forms with the word *to*

Value	Example Verb	Example
_none	laugh	Jack laughed.
_np	find	Jack found a key.
_np_np	give	Jack gave Sue the paper.
_vp:inf	want	Jack wants to fly.
_np_vp:inf	tell	Jack told the man to go.
_vp:ing	keep	Jack keeps hoping for the best.
_np_vp:ing	catch	Jack caught Sam looking at his desk.
_np_vp:base	watch	Jack watched Sam look at his desk.

Figure 4.2　The SUBCAT values for NP/VP combinations

To handle the interactions between words and their complements, an additional feature, SUBCAT, is used. Chapter 2 described some common verb subcategorization possibilities. Each one will correspond to a different value of the SUBCAT feature. Figure 4.2 shows some SUBCAT values for complements consisting of combinations of NPs and VPs. To help you remember the meaning of the feature values, they are formed by listing the main category of each part of the complement. If the category is restricted by a feature value, then the feature value follows the constituent separated by a colon. Thus the value _np_vp:inf will be used to indicate a complement that consists of an NP followed by a VP with VFORM value inf. Of course, this naming is just a convention to help the reader; you could give these values any arbitrary name, since their significance is determined solely by the grammar rules that involve the feature. For instance, the rule for verbs with a SUBCAT value of _np_vp:inf would be

> (VP) → (V **SUBCAT** _np_vp:inf)
> 　　　　(NP)
> 　　　　(VP **VFORM** inf)

This says that a VP can consist of a V with SUBCAT value _np_vp:inf, followed by an NP, followed by a VP with VFORM value inf. Clearly, this rule could be rewritten using any other unique symbol instead of _np_vp:inf, as long as the lexicon is changed to use this new value.

Many verbs have complement structures that require a prepositional phrase with a particular preposition, or one that plays a particular role. For example, the verb *give* allows a complement consisting of an NP followed by a PP using the preposition *to*, as in *Jack gave the money to the bank.* Other verbs, such as *put,* require a prepositional phrase that describes a location, using prepositions such as *in, inside, on,* and *by.* To express this within the feature system, we introduce a feature PFORM on prepositional phrases. A prepositional phrase with a PFORM value such as TO must have the preposition *to* as its head, and so on. A prepositional phrase with a PFORM value LOC must describe a location. Another useful PFORM value is MOT, used with verbs such as *walk,* which may take a

Value	Example Prepositions	Example
TO	to	I gave it to the bank.
LOC	in, on, by, inside, on top of	I put it on the desk.
MOT	to, from, along, ...	I walked to the store.

Figure 4.3 Some values of the PFORM feature for prepositional phrases

Value	Example Verb	Example
_np_pp:to	give	Jack gave the key to the man.
_pp:loc	be	Jack is at the store.
_np_pp:loc	put	Jack put the box in the corner.
_pp:mot	go	Jack went to the store.
_np_pp:mot	take	Jack took the hat to the party.
_adjp	be, seem	Jack is happy.
_np_adjp	keep	Jack kept the dinner hot.
_s:that	believe	Jack believed that the world was flat.
_s:for	hope	Jack hoped for the man to win the prize.

Figure 4.4 Additional SUBCAT values

prepositional phrase that describes some aspect of a path, as in *We walked to the store.* Prepositions that can create such phrases include *to, from,* and *along.* The LOC and MOT values might seem hard to distinguish, as certain prepositions might describe either a location or a path, but they are distinct. For example, while *Jack put the box {in on by} the corner* is fine, **Jack put the box {to from along} the corner* is ill-formed. Figure 4.3 summarizes the PFORM feature.

This feature can be used to restrict the complement forms for various verbs. Using the naming convention discussed previously, the SUBCAT value of a verb such as *put* would be _np_pp:loc, and the appropriate rule in the grammar would be

(VP) → (V **SUBCAT** _np_pp:loc)
      (NP)
      (PP **PFORM** LOC)

For embedded sentences, a complementizer is often needed and must be subcategorized for. Thus a COMP feature with possible values *for, that,* and *no-comp* will be useful. For example, the verb *tell* can subcategorize for an S that has the complementizer *that.* Thus one SUBCAT value of *tell* will be _s:that. Similarly, the verb *wish* subcategorizes for an S with the complementizer *for,* as in *We wished for the rain to stop.* Thus one value of the SUBCAT feature for *wish* is _s:for. Figure 4.4 lists some of these additional SUBCAT values and examples for a variety of verbs. In this section, all the examples with the

SUBCAT feature have involved verbs, but nouns, prepositions, and adjectives may also use the SUBCAT feature and subcategorize for their complements in the same way.

Binary Features

Certain features are binary in that a constituent either has or doesn't have the feature. In our formalization a binary feature is simply a feature whose value is restricted to be either + or –. For example, the INV feature is a binary feature that indicates whether or not an S structure has an inverted subject (as in a yes/no question). The S structure for the sentence *Jack laughed* will have an INV value –, whereas the S structure for the sentence *Did Jack laugh?* will have the INV value +. Often, the value is used as a prefix, and we would say that a structure has the feature +INV or –INV. Other binary features will be introduced as necessary throughout the development of the grammars.

The Default Value for Features

It will be useful on many occasions to allow a **default value** for features. Any-time a constituent is constructed that could have a feature, but a value is not specified, the feature takes the default value of –. This is especially useful for binary features but is used for nonbinary features as well; this usually ensures that any later agreement check on the feature will fail. The default value is inserted when the constituent is first constructed.

4.3 Morphological Analysis and the Lexicon

Before you can specify a grammar, you must define the lexicon. This section explores some issues in lexicon design and the need for a morphological analysis component.

The lexicon must contain information about all the different words that can be used, including all the relevant feature value restrictions. When a word is ambiguous, it may be described by multiple entries in the lexicon, one for each different use.

Because words tend to follow regular morphological patterns, however, many forms of words need not be explicitly included in the lexicon. Most English verbs, for example, use the same set of suffixes to indicate different forms: *-s* is added for third person singular present tense, *-ed* for past tense, *-ing* for the present participle, and so on. Without any morphological analysis, the lexicon would have to contain every one of these forms. For the verb *want* this would require six entries, for *want* (both in base and present form), *wants, wanting,* and *wanted* (both in past and past participle form).

In contrast, by using the methods described in Section 3.7 to strip suffixes there needs to be only one entry for *want.* The idea is to store the base form of the verb in the lexicon and use context-free rules to combine verbs with suffixes to derive the other entries. Consider the following rule for present tense verbs:

(V **ROOT** ?r **SUBCAT** ?s **VFORM** pres **AGR** 3s) →
    (V **ROOT** ?r **SUBCAT** ?s **VFORM** base) (+S)

where +S is a new lexical category that contains only the suffix morpheme *-s*. This rule, coupled with the lexicon entry

    want: (V **ROOT** want
           SUBCAT {_np _vp:inf _np_vp:inf}
           VFORM base)

would produce the following constituent given the input string *want -s*

    want: (V **ROOT** want
           SUBCAT {_np _vp:inf _np_vp:inf}
           VFORM pres
           AGR 3s)

Another rule would generate the constituents for the present tense form not in third person singular, which for most verbs is identical to the root form:

(V **ROOT** ?r **SUBCAT** ?s **VFORM** pres **AGR** {1s 2s 1p 2p 3p}) →
    (V **ROOT** ?r **SUBCAT** ?s **VFORM** base)

But this rule needs to be modified in order to avoid generating erroneous interpretations. Currently, it can transform any base form verb into a present tense form, which is clearly wrong for some irregular verbs. For instance, the base form *be* cannot be used as a present form (for example, **We be at the store*). To cover these cases, a feature is introduced to identify irregular forms. Specifically, verbs with the binary feature +IRREG-PRES have irregular present tense forms. Now the rule above can be stated correctly:

(V **ROOT** ?r **SUBCAT** ?s **VFORM** pres **AGR** {1s 2s 1p 2p 3p}) →
    (V **ROOT** ?r **SUBCAT** ?s **VFORM** base **IRREG-PRES** −)

Because of the default mechanism, the IRREG-PRES feature need only be specified on the irregular verbs. The regular verbs default to −, as desired. Similar binary features would be needed to flag irregular past forms (IRREG-PAST, such as *saw*), and to distinguish *-en* past participles from *-ed* past participles (EN-PASTPRT). These features restrict the application of the standard lexical rules, and the irregular forms are added explicitly to the lexicon. Grammar 4.5 gives a set of rules for deriving different verb and noun forms using these features.

Given a large set of features, the task of writing lexical entries appears very difficult. Most frameworks allow some mechanisms that help alleviate these problems. The first technique—allowing default values for features—has already been mentioned. With this capability, if an entry takes a default value for a given feature, then it need not be explicitly stated. Another commonly used technique is

Present Tense
1. (V **ROOT** ?r **SUBCAT** ?s **VFORM** pres **AGR** 3s) →
   (V **ROOT** ?r **SUBCAT** ?s **VFORM** base **IRREG-PRES** –) +S
2. (V **ROOT** ?r **SUBCAT** ?s **VFORM** pres **AGR** {1s 2s 1p 2p 3p}) →
   (V **ROOT** ?r **SUBCAT** ?s **VFORM** base **IRREG-PRES** –)

Past Tense
3. (V **ROOT** ?r **SUBCAT** ?s **VFORM** past **AGR** {1s 2s 3s 1p 2p 3p}) →
   (V **ROOT** ?r **SUBCAT** ?s **VFORM** base **IRREG-PAST** –) +ED

Past Participle
4. (V **ROOT** ?r **SUBCAT** ?s **VFORM** pastprt) →
   (V **ROOT** ?r **SUBCAT** ?s **VFORM** base **EN-PASTPRT** –) +ED
5. (V **ROOT** ?r **SUBCAT** ?s **VFORM** pastprt) →
   (V **ROOT** ?r **SUBCAT** ?s **VFORM** base **EN-PASTPRT** +) +EN

Present Participle
6. (V **ROOT** ?r **SUBCAT** ?s **VFORM** ing) →
   (V **ROOT** ?r **SUBCAT** ?s **VFORM** base) +ING

Plural Nouns
7. (N **ROOT** ?r **AGR** 3p) →
   (N **ROOT** ?r **AGR** 3s **IRREG-PL** –) +S

Grammar 4.5   Some lexical rules for common suffixes on verbs and nouns

to allow the lexicon writing to define clusters of features, and then indicate a cluster with a single symbol rather than listing them all. Later, additional techniques will be discussed that allow the inheritance of features in a feature hierarchy.

Figure 4.6 contains a small lexicon. It contains many of the words to be used in the examples that follow. It contains three entries for the word *saw*—as a noun, as a regular verb, and as the irregular past tense form of the verb *see*—as illustrated in the sentences

The saw was broken.
Jack wanted me to saw the board in half.
I saw Jack eat the pizza.

With an algorithm for stripping the suffixes and regularizing the spelling, as described in Section 3.7, the derived entries can be generated using any of the basic parsing algorithms on Grammar 4.5. With the lexicon in Figure 4.6 and Grammar 4.5, correct constituents for the following words can be derived: *been, being, cries, cried, crying, dogs, saws* (two interpretations), *sawed, sawing, seen, seeing, seeds, wants, wanting,* and *wanted.* For example, the word *cries* would be transformed into the sequence *cry +s*, and then rule 1 would produce the present tense entry from the base form in the lexicon.

```
a:       (CAT ART                saw:    (CAT N
         ROOT A1                          ROOT SAW1
         AGR 3s)                          AGR 3s)
be:      (CAT V                  saw:    (CAT V
         ROOT BE1                         ROOT SAW2
         VFORM base                       VFORM base
         IRREG-PRES +                     SUBCAT _np)
         IRREG-PAST +            saw:    (CAT V
         SUBCAT {_adjp _np})              ROOT SEE1
cry:     (CAT V                           VFORM past
         ROOT CRY1                        SUBCAT _np)
         VFORM base              see:    (CAT V
         SUBCAT _none)                    ROOT SEE1
dog:     (CAT N                           VFORM base
         ROOT DOG1                        SUBCAT _np
         AGR 3s)                          IRREG-PAST +
fish:    (CAT N                           EN-PASTPRT +)
         ROOT FISH1              seed:   (CAT N
         AGR {3s 3p}                      ROOT SEED1
         IRREG-PL +)                      AGR 3s)
happy:   (CAT ADJ               the:    (CAT ART
         SUBCAT _vp:inf)                  ROOT THE1
he:      (CAT PRO                         AGR {3s 3p})
         ROOT HE1               to:     (CAT TO)
         AGR 3s)                want:   (CAT V
is:      (CAT V                           ROOT WANT1
         ROOT BE1                         VFORM base
         VFORM pres                       SUBCAT {_np _vp:inf _np_vp:inf})
         SUBCAT {_adjp _np}     was:    (CAT V
         AGR 3s)                          ROOT BE1
Jack:    (CAT NAME                        VFORM past
         AGR 3s)                          AGR {1s 3s}
man:     (CAT N1                          SUBCAT {_adjp _np})
         ROOT MAN1              were:   (CAT V
         AGR 3s)                          ROOT BE
men:     (CAT N                           VFORM past
         ROOT MAN1                        AGR {2s 1p 2p 3p}
         AGR 3p)                          SUBCAT {_adjp _np})
```

Figure 4.6 A lexicon

Often a word will have multiple interpretations that use different entries and different lexical rules. The word *saws,* for instance, transformed into the sequence *saw +s,* can be a plural noun (via rule 7 and the first entry for *saw*), or the third person present form of the verb *saw* (via rule 1 and the second entry for *saw*). Note that rule 1 cannot apply to the third entry, as its VFORM is not base.

The success of this approach depends on being able to prohibit erroneous derivations, such as analyzing *seed* as the past tense of the verb *see.* This analysis will never be considered if the FST that strips suffixes is correctly designed. Specifically, the word *see* will not allow a transition to the states that allow the *-ed* suffix. But even if this were produced for some reason, the IRREG-PAST value + in the entry for *see* would prohibit rule 3 from applying.

4.4 A Simple Grammar Using Features

This section presents a simple grammar using the feature systems and lexicon developed in the earlier sections. It will handle sentences such as the following:

> The man cries.
> The men cry.
> The man saw the dogs.
> He wants the dog.
> He wants to be happy.
> He wants the man to see the dog.
> He is happy to be a dog.

It does not find the following acceptable:

> *The men cries.
> *The man cry.
> *The man saw to be happy.
> *He wants.
> *He wants the man saw the dog.

Before developing the grammar, some additional conventions are introduced that will be very useful throughout the book. It is very cumbersome to write grammatical rules that include all the necessary features. But there are certain regularities in the use of features that can be exploited to simplify the process of writing rules. For instance, many feature values are unique to a feature (for example, the value inf can only appear in the VFORM feature, and _np_vp:inf can only appear in the SUBCAT feature). Because of this, we can omit the feature name without introducing any ambiguity. Unique feature values will be listed using square parentheses. Thus (VP **SUBCAT** inf) will be abbreviated as VP[inf]. Since binary features do not have unique values, a special convention is introduced for them. For a binary feature B, the constituent C[+B] indicates the constituent (C **B** +).

Many features are constrained so that the value on the mother must be identical to the value on its head subconstituent. These are called **head features.** For instance, in all VP rules the VFORM and AGR values are the same in the VP and the head verb, as in the rule

BOX 4.2 Systemic Grammar

An important influence on the development of computational feature-based systems was **systemic grammar** (Halliday, 1985). This theory emphasizes the functional role of linguistic constructs as they affect communication. The grammar is organized as a set of choices about discourse function that determine the structure of the sentence. The choices are organized into hierarchical structures called **systems**. For example, the mood system would capture all the choices that affect the mood of the sentence. Part of this structure looks as follows:

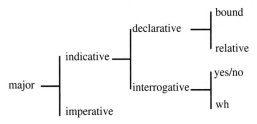

This structure indicates that once certain choices are made, others become relevant. For instance, if you decide that a sentence is in the declarative mood, then the choice between bound and relative becomes relevant. The choice between yes/no and wh, on the other hand, is not relevant to a declarative sentence.

Systemic grammar was used in Winograd (1973), and Winograd (1983) contains a good discussion of the formalism. In recent years it has mainly been used in natural language generation systems because it provides a good formalism for organizing the choices that need to be made while planning a sentence (for example, see Mann and Mathiesson (1985) and Patten (1988)).

(VP **VFORM** ?v **AGR** ?a) →
    (V **VFORM** ?v **AGR** ?a **SUBCAT** _np_vp:inf)
    (NP)
    (VP **VFORM** inf)

If the head features can be declared separately from the rules, the system can automatically add these features to the rules as needed. With VFORM and AGR declared as head features, the previous VP rule can be abbreviated as

    VP → (*V SUBCAT _np_vp:inf*) NP (VP **VFORM** inf)

The head constituent in a rule will be indicated in italics. Combining all the abbreviation conventions, the rule could be further simplified to

    VP → *V*[_np_vp:inf] NP VP[inf]

A simple grammar using these conventions is shown as Grammar 4.7. Except for rules 1 and 2, which must enforce number agreement, all the rest of the feature constraints can be captured using the conventions that have been

1. S[–inv] → (NP **AGR** ?a) (*VP*[{*pres past*}] ***AGR*** *?a*)
2. NP → (ART **AGR** ?a) (*N* ***AGR*** *?a*)
3. NP → *PRO*
4. VP → *V*[*_none*]
5. VP → *V*[*_np*] NP
6. VP → *V*[*_vp:inf*] VP[inf]
7. VP → *V*[*_np_vp:inf*] NP VP[inf]
8. VP → *V*[*_adjp*] ADJP
9. VP[inf] → *TO* VP[base]
10. ADJP → *ADJ*
11. ADJP → *ADJ*[*_vp:inf*] VP[inf]

Head features for S, VP: **VFORM**, **AGR**
Head features for NP: **AGR**

Grammar 4.7   A simple grammar in abbreviated form

1. (S **INV** – **VFORM** ?v{pres past} **AGR** ?a) →
   (NP **AGR** ?a) (*VP* ***VFORM*** *?v* {*pres past* } ***AGR*** *?a*)
2. (NP **AGR** ?a) → (ART **AGR** ?a) (*N* ***AGR*** *?a*)
3. (NP **AGR** ?a) → (*PRO* ***AGR*** *?a*)
4. (VP **AGR** ?a **VFORM** ?v) → (*V* ***SUBCAT*** *_none* ***AGR*** *?a* ***VFORM*** *?v*)
5. (VP **AGR** ?a **VFORM** ?v) → (*V* ***SUBCAT*** *_np* ***AGR*** *?a* ***VFORM*** *?v*) NP
6. (VP **AGR** ?a **VFORM** ?v) →
   (*V* ***SUBCAT*** *_vp:inf* ***AGR*** *?a* ***VFORM*** *?v*) (VP **VFORM** inf)
7. (VP **AGR** ?a **VFORM** ?v) →
   (*V* ***SUBCAT*** *_np_vp:inf* ***AGR*** *?a* ***VFORM*** *?v*) NP (VP **VFORM** inf)
8. (VP **AGR** ?a **VFORM** ?v) →
   (*V* ***SUBCAT*** *_adjp* ***AGR*** *?a* ***VFORM*** *?v*) ADJP
9. (VP **SUBCAT** inf **AGR** ?a **VFORM** inf) →
   (*TO* ***AGR*** *?a* ***VFORM*** *inf*) (VP **VFORM** base)
10. ADJP → *ADJ*
11. ADJP → *ADJ* (***SUBCAT*** *_inf*) (VP **VFORM** inf)

Grammar 4.8   The expanded grammar showing all features

introduced. The head features for each category are declared at the bottom of the
figure. This grammar is an abbreviation of Grammar 4.8. Consider how rule 1 in
Grammar 4.7 abbreviates rule 1 in Grammar 4.8. The abbreviated rule is

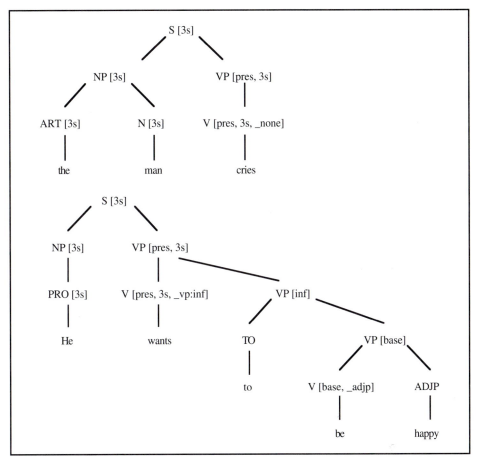

Figure 4.9 Two sample parse trees with feature values

S[–inv] → (NP **AGR** ?a) (*VP*[{ *pres past*}] *AGR ?a*)

The unique values can be expanded in the obvious way: the value [–inv] becomes (**INV** –) and the value [{pres past}] becomes (**VFORM** ?v{pres past}). The head features for S are AGR and VFORM, so these features must be added to the S and VP head. The resulting rule is

(S **INV** – **VFORM** ?v{pres past} **AGR** ?a) →
   (NP **AGR** ?a)
   (VP **VFORM** ?v{pres past} **AGR** ?a)

as shown in Grammar 4.8.

The abbreviated form is also very useful for summarizing parse trees. For instance, Figure 4.9 shows the parse trees for two of the previous sample sentences, demonstrating that each is an acceptable sentence.

Consider why each of the ill-formed sentences introduced at the beginning of this section are not accepted by Grammar 4.7. Both *The men cries and *The man cry are not acceptable because the number agreement restriction on rule 1 is not satisfied: The NP constituent for *the men* has the AGR value 3p, while the VP *cries* has the AGR value 3s. Thus rule 1 cannot apply. Similarly, *the man cry* is not accepted by the grammar since *the man* has AGR 3s and the VP *cry* has as its AGR value a variable ranging over {1s 2s 1p 2p 3p}. The phrase *the man saw to be happy* is not accepted because the verb *saw* has a SUBCAT value _np. Thus only rule 5 could be used to build a VP. But rule 5 requires an NP complement, and it is not possible for the words *to be happy* to be a legal NP.

The phrase *He wants* is not accepted since the verb *wants* has a SUBCAT value ranging over {_np _vp:inf _np_vp:inf}, and thus only rules 5, 6, and 7 could apply to build a VP. But all these rules require a nonempty complement of some kind. The phrase *He wants the man saw the dog* is not accepted for similar reasons, but this requires a little more analysis. Again, rules 5, 6, and 7 are possible with the verb *wants*. Rules 5 and 6 will not work, but rule 7 looks close, as it requires an NP and a VP[inf]. The phrase *the man* gives us the required NP, but *saw the dog* fails to be a VP[inf]. In particular, *saw the man* is a legal VP, but its VFORM feature will be past, not inf.

4.5 Parsing with Features

The parsing algorithms developed in Chapter 3 for context-free grammars can be extended to handle augmented context-free grammars. This involves generalizing the algorithm for matching rules to constituents. For instance, the chart-parsing algorithms developed in Chapter 3 all used an operation for extending active arcs with a new constituent. A constituent X could extend an arc of the form

$$C \to C1 \dots Ci \circ X \dots Cn$$

to produce a new arc of the form

$$C \to C1 \dots Ci\ X \circ \dots Cn$$

A similar operation can be used for grammars with features, but the parser may have to instantiate variables in the original arc before it can be extended by X. The key to defining this matching operation precisely is to remember the definition of grammar rules with features. A rule such as

1. (NP **AGR** ?a) $\to \circ$ (ART **AGR** ?a) (N **AGR** ?a)

says that an NP can be constructed out of an ART and an N if all three agree on the AGR feature. It does not place any restrictions on any other features that the NP, ART, or N may have. Thus, when matching constituents against this rule, the only thing that matters is the AGR feature. All other features in the constituent can be ignored. For instance, consider extending arc 1 with the constituent

2. (ART **ROOT** A **AGR** 3s)

To make arc 1 applicable, the variable ?a must be instantiated to 3s, producing

3.   (NP **AGR** 3s) $\rightarrow$ $\circ$ (ART **AGR** 3s) (N **AGR** 3s)

This arc can now be extended because every feature in the rule is in constituent 2:

4.   (NP **AGR** 3s) $\rightarrow$ (ART **AGR** 3s) $\circ$ (N **AGR** 3s)

Now, consider extending this arc with the constituent for the word *dog*:

5.   (N **ROOT** DOG1 **AGR** 3s)

This can be done because the AGR features agree. This completes the arc

6.   (NP **AGR** 3s) $\rightarrow$ (ART **AGR** 3s) (N **AGR** 3s) $\circ$

This means the parser has found a constituent of the form (NP **AGR** 3s).

This algorithm can be specified more precisely as follows: Given an arc A, where the constituent following the dot is called NEXT, and a new constituent X, which is being used to extend the arc,

     a.   Find an instantiation of the variables such that all the features specified in NEXT are found in X.

     b.   Create a new arc A', which is a copy of A except for the instantiations of the variables determined in step (a).

     c.   Update A' as usual in a chart parser.

For instance, let A be arc 1, and X be the ART constituent 2. Then NEXT will be (ART **AGR** ?a). In step a, NEXT is matched against X, and you find that ?a must be instantiated to 3s. In step b, a new copy of A is made, which is shown as arc 3. In step c, the arc is updated to produce the new arc shown as arc 4.

When constrained variables, such as ?a{3s 3p}, are involved, the matching proceeds in the same manner, but the variable binding must be one of the listed values. If a variable is used in a constituent, then one of its possible values must match the requirement in the rule. If both the rule and the constituent contain variables, the result is a variable ranging over the intersection of their allowed values. For instance, consider extending arc 1 with the constituent (ART **ROOT** the **AGR** ?v{3s 3p}), that is, the word *the*. To apply, the variable ?a would have to be instantiated to ?v{3s 3p}, producing the rule

(NP **AGR** ?v{3s 3p}) $\rightarrow$ (ART **AGR** ?v{3s 3p}) $\circ$ (N **AGR** ?v{3s 3p})

This arc could be extended by (N **ROOT** dog **AGR** 3s), because ?v{3s 3p} could be instantiated by the value 3s. The resulting arc would be identical to arc 6. The entry in the chart for *the* is not changed by this operation. It still has the value ?v{3s 3p}. The AGR feature is restricted to 3s only in the arc.

Another extension is useful for recording the structure of the parse. Subconstituent features (1, 2, and so on, depending on which subconstituent is being added) are automatically inserted by the parser each time an arc is extended. The values of these features name subconstituents already in the chart.

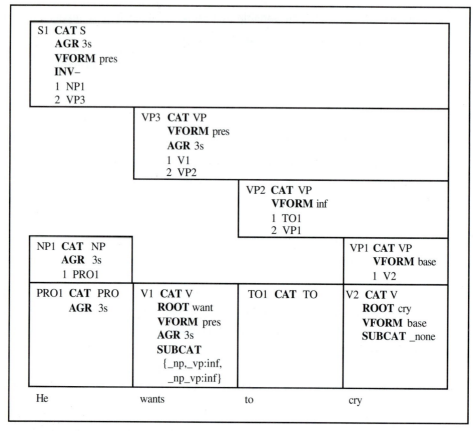

Figure 4.10 The chart for *He wants to cry.*

With this treatment, and assuming that the chart already contains two constituents, ART1 and N1, for the words *the* and *dog,* the constituent added to the chart for the phrase *the dog* would be

$$(NP \; \mathbf{AGR} \quad 3s$$
$$\mathbf{1} \qquad ART1$$
$$\mathbf{2} \qquad N1)$$

where ART1 = (ART **ROOT** the **AGR** {3s 3p}) and N1 = (N **ROOT** dog **AGR** {3s}). Note that the AGR feature of ART1 was not changed. Thus it could be used with other interpretations that require the value 3p if they are possible. Any of the chart-parsing algorithms described in Chapter 3 can now be used with an augmented grammar by using these extensions to extend arcs and build constituents. Consider an example. Figure 4.10 contains the final chart produced from parsing the sentence *He wants to cry* using Grammar 4.8. The rest of this section considers how some of the nonterminal symbols were constructed for the chart.

Constituent NP1 was constructed by rule 3, repeated here for convenience:

3.   (NP **AGR** ?a) → (PRO **AGR** ?a)

To match the constituent PRO1, the variable ?a must be instantiated to 3s. Thus the new constituent built is

NP1: (**CAT** NP
       AGR 3s
       1 PRO1)

Next consider constructing constituent VP1 using rule 4, namely

4.   (VP **AGR** ?a **VFORM** ?v) → (V **SUBCAT** _none **AGR** ?a **VFORM** ?v)

For the right-hand side to match constituent V2, the variable ?v must be instantiated to base. The AGR feature of V2 is not defined, so it defaults to –. The new constituent is

VP1: (**CAT** VP
       AGR –
       VFORM base
       1 V2)

Generally, default values are not shown in the chart. In a similar way, constituent VP2 is built from TO1 and VP1 using rule 9, VP3 is built from V1 and VP2 using rule 6, and S1 is built from NP1 and VP3 using rule 1.

4.6   Augmented Transition Networks

Features can also be added to a recursive transition network to produce an **augmented transition network** (ATN). Features in an ATN are traditionally called **registers**. Constituent structures are created by allowing each network to have a set of registers. Each time a new network is pushed, a new set of registers is created. As the network is traversed, these registers are set to values by **actions** associated with each arc. When the network is popped, the registers are assembled to form a constituent structure, with the CAT slot being the network name.

Grammar 4.11 is a simple NP network. The actions are listed in the table below the network. ATNs use a special mechanism to extract the result of following an arc. When a lexical arc, such as arc 1, is followed, the constituent built from the word in the input is put into a special variable named *. The action

DET := *

then assigns this constituent to the DET register. The second action on this arc,

AGR := **AGR**$_*$

assigns the AGR register of the network to the value of the AGR register of the new word (the constituent in *).

Agreement checks are specified in the **tests**. A test is an expression that **succeeds** if it returns a nonempty value and **fails** if it returns the empty set or nil.

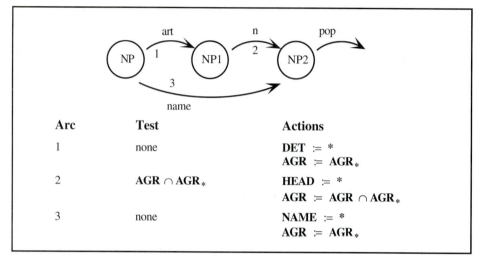

Arc	Test	Actions
1	none	$DET := *$ $AGR := AGR_*$
2	$AGR \cap AGR_*$	$HEAD := *$ $AGR := AGR \cap AGR_*$
3	none	$NAME := *$ $AGR := AGR_*$

Grammar 4.11 A simple NP network

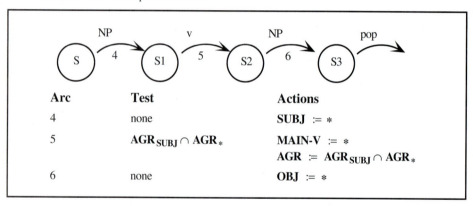

Arc	Test	Actions
4	none	$SUBJ := *$
5	$AGR_{SUBJ} \cap AGR_*$	$MAIN\text{-}V := *$ $AGR := AGR_{SUBJ} \cap AGR_*$
6	none	$OBJ := *$

Grammar 4.12 A simple S network

If a test fails, its arc is not traversed. The test on arc 2 indicates that the arc can be followed only if the AGR feature of the network has a non-null intersection with the AGR register of the new word (the noun constituent in *).

Features on push arcs are treated similarly. The constituent built by traversing the NP network is returned as the value *. Thus in Grammar 4.12, the action on the arc from S to S1,

$$SUBJ := *$$

would assign the constituent returned by the NP network to the register SUBJ. The test on arc 2 will succeed only if the AGR register of the constituent in the SUBJ register has a non-null intersection with the AGR register of the new constituent (the verb). This test enforces subject-verb agreement.

Trace of S Network

Step	Node	Position	Arc Followed	Registers Set
1.	S	1	arc 4 succeeds (for recursive call see trace below)	**SUBJ** ← (NP **DET** the **HEAD** dog **AGR** 3s)
5.	S1	3	arc 5 (checks if $3p \cap 3p$)	**MAIN-V** ← saw **AGR** ← 3p
6.	S2	4	arc 6 (for recursive call trace, see below)	**OBJ** ← (NP **NAME** Jack **AGR** 3s)
9.	S3	5	pop arc succeeds	returns (S **SUBJ** (NP **DET** the **HEAD** dog **AGR** 3s) **MAIN-V** saw **AGR** 3p **OBJ** (NP **NAME** Jack **AGR** 3s))

Trace of First NP Call: Arc 4

Step	Node	Position	Arc Followed	Registers Set
2.	NP	1	1	**DET** ← the **AGR** ← {3s 3p}
3.	NP1	2	2 (checks if {3s 3p} $\cap$ 3p)	**HEAD** ← dog
4.	NP2	3	pop	returns (NP **DET** the **HEAD** dog **AGR** 3s)

Trace of Second NP Call: Arc 6

Step	Node	Position	Arc Followed	Registers Set
7.	NP	4	3	**NAME** ← John **AGR** ← 3s
8.	NP2	5	pop	returns (NP **NAME** John **AGR** 3s)

Figure 4.13 Trace tests and actions used with $_1$ *The* $_2$ *dog* $_3$ *saw* $_4$ *Jack* $_5$

With the lexicon in Section 4.3, the ATN accepts the following sentences:

The dog cried.
The dogs saw Jack.
Jack saw the dogs.

Consider an example. A trace of a parse of the sentence *The dog saw Jack* is shown in Figure 4.13. It indicates the current node in the network, the current

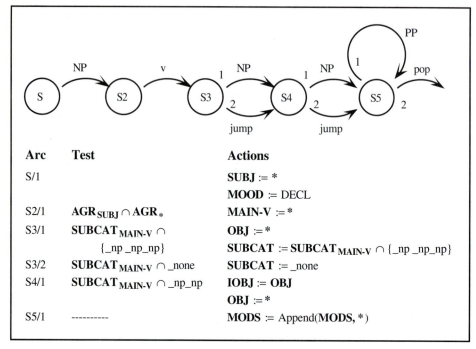

Arc	Test	Actions
S/1		$SUBJ := *$
		$MOOD := DECL$
S2/1	$AGR_{SUBJ} \cap AGR_*$	$MAIN\text{-}V := *$
S3/1	$SUBCAT_{MAIN\text{-}V} \cap$	$OBJ := *$
	$\{\_np \_np\_np\}$	$SUBCAT := SUBCAT_{MAIN\text{-}V} \cap \{\_np \_np\_np\}$
S3/2	$SUBCAT_{MAIN\text{-}V} \cap \_none$	$SUBCAT := \_none$
S4/1	$SUBCAT_{MAIN\text{-}V} \cap \_np\_np$	$IOBJ := OBJ$
		$OBJ := *$
S5/1	----------	$MODS := Append(MODS, *)$

Grammar 4.14 An S network for assertions

word position, the arc that is followed from the node, and the register manipulations that are performed for the successful parse. It starts in the S network but moves immediately to the NP network from the call on arc 4. The NP network checks for number agreement as it accepts the word sequence *The dog*. It constructs a noun phrase with the **AGR** feature plural. When the pop arc is followed, it completes arc 4 in the S network. The NP is assigned to the **SUBJ** register and then checked for agreement with the verb when arc 3 is followed. The NP *Jack* is accepted in another call to the NP network.

An ATN Grammar for Simple Declarative Sentences

Here is a more comprehensive example of the use of an ATN to describe some declarative sentences. The allowed sentence structure is an initial NP followed by a main verb, which may then be followed by a maximum of two NPs and many PPs, depending on the verb. Using the feature system extensively, you can create a grammar that accepts any of the preceding complement forms, leaving the actual verb-complement agreement to the feature restrictions. Grammar 4.14 shows the S network. Arcs are numbered using the conventions discussed in Chapter 3. For instance, the arc S3/1 is the arc labeled 1 leaving node S3. The NP network in Grammar 4.15 allows simple names, bare plural nouns, pronouns, and a simple sequence of a determiner followed by an adjective and a head noun.

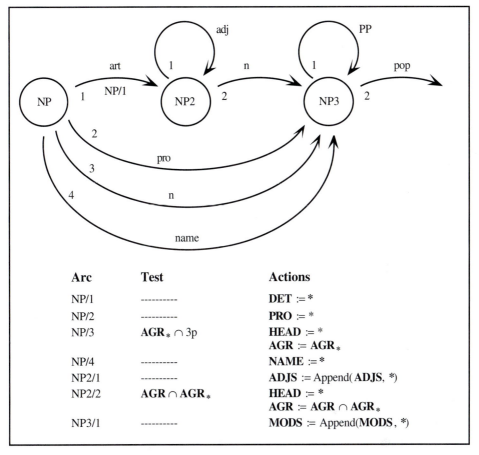

Arc	Test	Actions
NP/1	----------	**DET** := *
NP/2	----------	**PRO** := *
NP/3	$\mathbf{AGR}_* \cap 3p$	**HEAD** := *
		AGR := $\mathbf{AGR}_*$
NP/4	----------	**NAME** := *
NP2/1	----------	**ADJS** := Append(**ADJS**, *)
NP2/2	$\mathbf{AGR} \cap \mathbf{AGR}_*$	**HEAD** := *
		AGR := $\mathbf{AGR} \cap \mathbf{AGR}_*$
NP3/1	----------	**MODS** := Append(**MODS**, *)

Grammar 4.15 The NP network

Allowable noun complements include an optional number of prepositional phrases. The prepositional phrase network in Grammar 4.16 is straightforward. Examples of parsing sentences with this grammar are left for the exercises.

Presetting Registers

One further extension to the feature-manipulation facilities in ATNs involves the ability to preset registers in a network as that network is being called, much like parameter passing in a programming language. This facility, called the **SENDR** action in the original ATN systems, is useful to pass information to the network that aids in analyzing the new constituent.

Consider the class of verbs, including *want* and *pray,* that accept complements using the infinitive forms of verbs, which are introduced by the word *to.* According to the classification in Section 4.2, this includes the following:

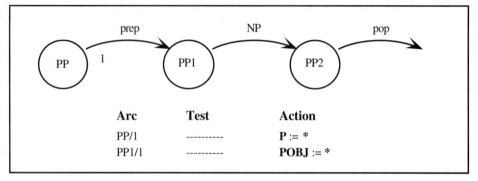

Arc	Test	Action
PP/1	----------	**P** := *
PP1/1	----------	**POBJ** := *

Grammar 4.16 The PP network

_vp:inf	Mary wants *to have a party.*
_np_vp:inf	Mary wants John *to have a party.*

In the context-free grammar developed earlier, such complements were treated as VPs with the VFORM value inf. To capture this same analysis in an ATN, you would need to be able to call a network corresponding to VPs but preset the VFORM register in that network to inf. Another common analysis of these constructs is to view the complements as a special form of sentence with an understood subject. In the first case it is Mary who would be the understood subject (that is, the host), while in the other case it is John. To capture this analysis, many ATN grammars preset the SUBJ register in the new S network when it is called.

4.7 Definite Clause Grammars

You can augment a logic grammar by adding extra arguments to each predicate to encode features. As a very simple example, you could modify the PROLOG rules to enforce number agreement by adding an extra argument for the number on every predicate for which the number feature is relevant. Thus you would have rules such as those shown in Grammar 4.17.

Consider parsing the noun phrase *the dog cried,* which would be captured by the assertions

    word(the, 1, 2) :–
    word(dog, 2, 3) :–

With these axioms, when the word *the* is parsed by rule 2 in Grammar 4.17, the number feature for the word is returned. You can see this in the following trace of the simple proof of

    np(1, Number, 3)

Using rule 1, you have the following subgoals:

```
1.    np(P1, Number, P3) :- art(P1, Number, P2), n(2, Number, P3)
2.    art(I, Number, O) :- word(Word, I, O), isart(Word, Number)
3.    isart(a, 3s) :-
4.    isart(the, 3s) :-
5.    isart(the, 3p) :-
6.    n(I, Number, O) :- word(Word, I, O), isnoun(Word, Number)
7.    isnoun(dog, 3s) :-
8.    isnoun(dogs, 3p) :-
```

Grammar 4.17

```
1.    s(P1, Number, s(Np, Vp), P3) :-
             np(P1, Number, Np, P2), vp(P2, Number, Vp, P3)
2.    np(P1, Number, np(Art, N), P3) :-
             art(P1, Number1, Art, P2), n(P2, Number2, N, P3)
3.    vp(P1, Number, vp(Verb), P2) :-
             v(P1, Verb, P2)
4.    art(I, Number, art(Word), O) :-
             word(Word, I, O), isart(Word, Number)
5.    n(I, Number, n(Word), O) :-
             word(Word, I, O), isnoun(Word, Number)
6.    v(I, Number, v(Word), O) :-
             word(Word, I, O), isverb(Word, Number)
```

Grammar 4.18

art(1, Number, P2)
n(P2, Number, 3)

The first subgoal succeeds by using rule 2 and proving

word(the, 1, 2) isart(the, 3s)

which binds the variables in rule 2 as follows:

Number ← 3s
P2 ← 2

Thus, the second subgoal now is

n(2, 3s, 3)

Using rule 6, this reduces to the subgoals word(Word, 2, 3) and isnoun(Word, 3s), which are established by the input and rule 7, respectively, with Word bound to dog. Thus the parse succeeds and the number agreement was enforced.

The grammar can also be extended to record the structure of the parse by adding another argument to the rules. For example, to construct a parse tree, you could use the rules shown in Grammar 4.18. These rules would allow you to prove the following on the sentence *The dog cried*:

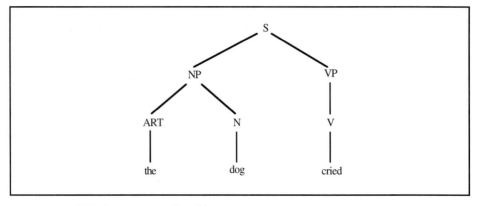

Figure 4.19 A tree representation of the structure

S(1, 3s, s(np(art(the), n(dog)), vp(v(cried))), 4)

In other words, between positions 1 and 4 there is a sentence with number feature 3s and the structure

s(np(art(the), n(dog)), vp(v(cried)))

which is a representation of the parse tree shown in Figure 4.19.

For specifying grammars, most logic-based grammar systems provide a more convenient format that is automatically converted into PROLOG clauses like those in Grammar 4.18. Since the word position arguments are on every predicate, they can be omitted and inserted by the system. Similarly, since all the predicates representing terminal symbols (for example, art, N, V) are defined systematically, the system can generate these rules automatically. These abbreviations are encoded in a format called **definite clause grammars** (DCGs).

For example, you could write Grammar 4.18 by specifying just three DCG rules. (The symbol $\rightarrow$ is traditionally used to signal DCG rules.)

s(Number, s(Np, Vp)) $\rightarrow$ np(N1, Np), vp(N2, Vp)
np(Number, np(Art, N)) $\rightarrow$ art(N1, Art), n(N2, N)
vp(Number, vp(Verb)) $\rightarrow$ v(Number, Verb)

The result is a formalism similar to the augmented context-free grammars described in Section 4.3. This similarity can be made even closer if a feature/value representation is used to represent structure. For instance, let us replace all the argument positions with a single argument that is a feature structure. The DCG equivalent to the first five rules in Grammar 4.7 would be as shown in Grammar 4.20, where square parentheses indicate lists in PROLOG. Notice that rule 1 will not succeed unless the S, NP, and VP all agree on the agr feature, because they have the same variable as a value.

Of course, this encoding will only work if every constituent specifies its feature values in the same order so that the feature lists unify. For example, if the

1. s([inv − agr Agr]) → np([agr Agr]), vp([agr Agr vform pres])
2. np([agr Agr2]) → art([agr Agr2]), n([agr Agr2])
3. np([agr Agr3]) → pro([agr Agr3])
4. vp([agr Agr4 vform Vf3]) →
   v([subcat _none agr Agr4 vform Vf3])
5. vp([agr Agr4 vform Vf3]) →
   v([subcat _np agr Agr4 vform Vf3]) np()

Grammar 4.20   A DCG version of Grammar 4.7

S features consist of inv, agr, inv, and vform, every rule using an S must specify all these features in the same order. In a realistic grammar this would be awkward, because there will be many possible features for each constituent, and each one must be listed in every occurrence. One way to solve this problem is to extend the program that converts DCG rules to PROLOG rules so that it adds in any unspecified features with variable values. This way the user need only specify the features that are important.

4.8   Generalized Feature Systems and Unification Grammars

You have seen that feature structures are very useful for generalizing the notion of context-free grammars and transition networks. In fact, feature structures can be generalized to the extent that they make the context-free grammar unnecessary. The entire grammar can be specified as a set of constraints between feature structures. Such systems are often called **unification grammars**. This section provides an introduction to the basic issues underlying such formalisms.

The key concept of a unification grammar is the **extension** relation between two feature structures. A feature structure F1 **extends**, or is more specific than, a feature structure F2 if every feature value in F1 is specified in F2. For example, the feature structure

> (**CAT** V
> **ROOT** cry)

extends the feature structure (**CAT** V), as its **CAT** value is V as required, and the **ROOT** feature is unconstrained in the latter feature structure. On the other hand, neither of the feature structures

> (**CAT** V   (**CAT** V
> **ROOT** cry)   **VFORM** pres)

extend the other, because both lack information required by the other. In particular, the first lacks the VFORM feature required by the second, and the second lacks the ROOT feature required by the first.

Two feature structures **unify** if there is a feature structure that is an extension of both. The **most general unifier** is the minimal feature structure that is an extension of both. The most general unifier of the above two feature structures is

> (**CAT** V
> **ROOT** cry
> **VFORM** pres)

Note that this is an extension of both original feature structures, and there is no smaller feature structure that is an extension of both. In contrast, the structures

> (**CAT** V   (**CAT** V
> **AGR** 3s)   **AGR** 3p)

do not unify. There can be no FS that is an extension of both because they specify contradictory AGR feature values.

This formalism can be extended to allow simple disjunctive values (for example, {3s 3p}) in the natural way. For example, (**AGR** 3s) extends (**AGR** {3s 3p}).

The notion of unification is all that is needed to specify a grammar, as all feature agreement checks and manipulations can be specified in terms of unification relationships. A rule such as S $\rightarrow$ NP VP in Grammar 4.7 could be expressed in a unification grammar as

> X0 $\rightarrow$ X1 X2 $\mathbf{CAT}_0 = S$
> $\mathbf{CAT}_1 = NP$
> $\mathbf{CAT}_2 = VP$
> $\mathbf{AGR}_0 = \mathbf{AGR}_1 = \mathbf{AGR}_2$
> $\mathbf{VFORM}_0 = \mathbf{VFORM}_2$

This says that a constituent X0 can be constructed out of a sequence of constituents X1 and X2 if the CAT of X0 is S, the CAT of X1 is NP, the CAT of X2 is VP, the AGR values of all three constituents are identical, and the VFORM values of constituents X0 and X2 are identical. If the CAT value is always specified, such rules can be abbreviated as follows:

> S $\rightarrow$ NP VP $\mathbf{AGR} = \mathbf{AGR}_1 = \mathbf{AGR}_2$
> $\mathbf{VFORM} = \mathbf{VFORM}_2$

where the CAT values are used in the rule. Also, the 0 subscript is omitted. Using these abbreviations, a subpart of Grammar 4.7 is rewritten as the unification grammar in Grammar 4.21. Since such grammars retain the structure of context-free rules, the standard parsing algorithms can be used on unification grammars. The next section shows how to interpret the feature equations to build the constituents.

1'. $S \rightarrow NP\ VP$ $\qquad AGR = AGR_1 = AGR_2$
$\qquad\qquad\qquad\qquad\qquad VFORM = VFORM_2$

2'. $NP \rightarrow ART\ N$ $\qquad AGR = AGR_1 = AGR_2$

8'. $VP \rightarrow V\ ADJP$ $\qquad SUBCAT_1 = \_adjp$
$\qquad\qquad\qquad\qquad\qquad VFORM = VFORM_1$
$\qquad\qquad\qquad\qquad\qquad AGR = AGR_1$

10'. $ADJP \rightarrow ADJ$

Grammar 4.21 A unification grammar

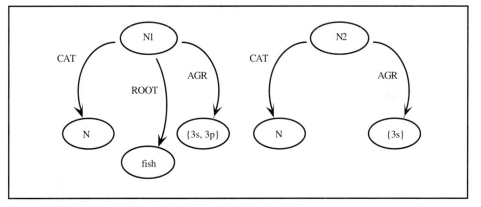

Figure 4.22 Two noun phrase DAGs

Formal Development: Feature Structures as DAGs

The unification-based formalism can be defined precisely by representing feature structures as directed acyclic graphs (DAGs). Each constituent and value is represented as a node, and the features are represented as labeled arcs. Representations of the following two constituents are shown in Figure 4.22:

N1: (**CAT** N $\qquad$ N2: (**CAT** N
   ROOT fish $\qquad\qquad$ **AGR** 3s)
   AGR {3s 3p})

The **sources** of a DAG are the nodes that have no incoming edges. Feature structure DAGs have a unique source node, called the **root node**. The DAG is said to be **rooted** by this node. The **sinks** of a DAG are nodes with no outgoing edges. The sinks of feature structures are labeled with an atomic feature or set of features (for example, {3s 3p}).

The unification of two feature structures is defined in terms of a graph-matching algorithm. This takes two rooted graphs and returns a new graph that is

To unify a DAG rooted at node N_i with a DAG rooted at node N_j:

1. If N_i equals N_j, then return N_i and succeed.
2. If both N_i and N_j are sink nodes, then if their labels have a non-null intersection, return a new node with the intersection as its label. Otherwise, the DAGs do not unify.
3. If N_i and N_j are not sinks, then create a new node N. For each arc labeled F leaving N_i to node NF_i,
   3a. If there is an arc labeled F leaving N_j to node NF_j, then recursively unify NF_i and NF_j. Build an arc labeled F from N to the result of the recursive call.
   3b. If there is no arc labeled F from N_j, build an arc labeled F from N to NF_i.
   3c. For each arc labeled F from N_j to node NF_j where there is no F arc leaving N_i, create a new arc labeled F from N to NF_j.

Figure 4.23 The graph unification algorithm

the unification of the two. The algorithm is shown in Figure 4.23. The result of applying this algorithm to nodes N1 and N2 in Figure 4.22 is the new constituent

> N3: (**CAT** N
>   **ROOT** fish
>   **AGR** 3s)

You should trace the algorithm on this example by hand to see how it works. This is a very simple case, as there is only one level of recursion. The initial call with the nodes N1 and N2 is handled in step 3, and each recursive call simply involves matching of sink nodes in step 2.

With this algorithm in hand, the algorithm for constructing a new constituent using the graph unification equations can be described. Once this is developed, you can build a parser using any standard parsing algorithm. The algorithm to build a new constituent of category C using a rule with feature equations of form $F_i = V$, where F_i indicates the F feature of the i'th subconstituent, is shown as Figure 4.24.

Consider an example. Assume the following two constituents shown in Figure 4.25 are defined already. In LISP notation, they are

> ART1: (**CAT** ART   N1: (**CAT** N
>   **ROOT** the   **ROOT** fish
>   **AGR** {3s 3p})   **AGR** {3s 3p})

The new NP will be built using rule 2' in Grammar 4.21. The equations are

> $CAT_0 = NP$
> $CAT_1 = ART$
> $CAT_2 = N$
> $AGR = AGR_1 = AGR_2$

The algorithm produces the constituent represented by the DAG in Figure 4.26.

Given a rule X0 → X1 ... Xn and set of feature equations of form $F_i = V$, where SC1, ..., SCn are the subconstituents corresponding to X1, ..., Xn, this algorithm builds a DAG that satisfies all the feature equations.

1. Create a node CC0 to be the root of the new feature structure.
2. Make a copy of each DAG rooted by SC_i (call the new root of each CC_i), and add an arc labeled i from CC0 to each CC_i.
3. For each feature equation of form $F_i = V$, where V is a value, follow the F link from node CCi to a node Ni, and unify Ni with V.
4. For each feature equation (of form $F_i = G_j$),
   4a. If there is an F link from CC_i, and a G link from CC_j, then
      i.   follow the F link to node N_i and the G link to N_j;
      ii. unify N_i and N_j, using the graph unification algorithm, to create new node X;
      iii. change all arcs pointing to either N_i or N_j to point to X;
   4b. If there is no F link from CC_i, but there is a G link from CC_j to node N_j, create an F link from CC_i to N_j;
   4c. If there is no G link from CC_j, but there is an F link from CC_i to N_i, create a G link from CC_j to N_i.

Figure 4.24 An algorithm to build a new constituent using feature equations

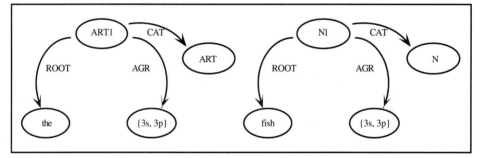

Figure 4.25 Lexical entries for *the* and *fish*

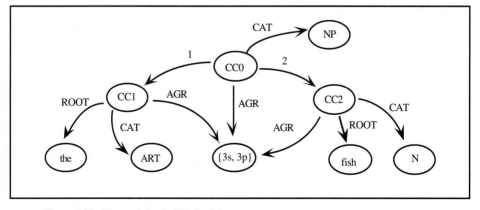

Figure 4.26 The graph for the NP *the fish*

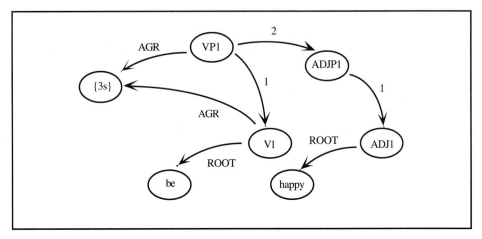

Figure 4.27 The analysis of the VP *is happy*

Continuing the example, assume that the VP *is happy* is analyzed similarly and is represented as in Figure 4.27. To simplify the graph, the CAT arcs are not shown. Figure 4.28 shows the analysis of *The fish is happy* constructed from rule 1 in Grammar 4.21. The value of the AGR slot is now the same node for S1, NP1, ART1, N1, VP1, and V1. Thus the value of the AGR feature of CC1, for instance, changed when the AGR features of NP1 and VP1 were unified.

So far, you have seen unification grammars used only to mimic the behavior of the augmented context-free grammars developed earlier. But the unification framework is considerably richer because there is no requirement that rules be based on syntactic categories. For example, there is a class of phrases in English called **predicative** phrases, which can occur in sentences of the form

NP be ___

This includes prepositional phrases (*He is in the house*), noun phrases (*He is a traitor*), and adjective phrases (*He is happy*). Grammars often include a binary feature, say PRED, that is true of phrases that can be used in this way. In a standard CFG you would need to specify a different rule for each category, as in

VP → (V **ROOT** be) (NP **PRED** +)
VP → (V **ROOT** be) (PP **PRED** +)
VP → (V **ROOT** be) (ADJP **PRED** +)

With the unification grammar framework, one rule handles all the categories, namely

$$X0 \rightarrow X1\ X2 \qquad \textbf{CAT}_0 = VP$$
$$\textbf{CAT}_1 = V$$
$$\textbf{ROOT}_1 = be$$
$$\textbf{PRED}_2 = +$$

in which any constituent X2 with the +PRED feature is allowed.

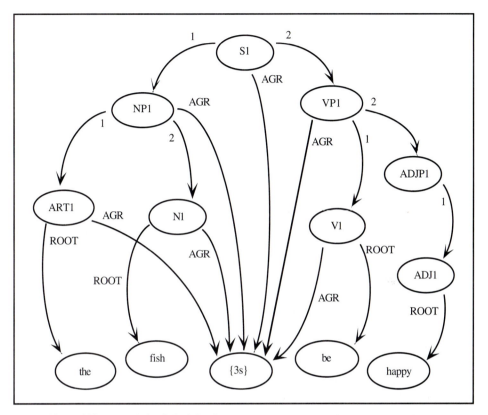

Figure 4.28 An analysis of *The fish is happy.*

Of course, if the categories of constituents are not specified, it is not so clear how to adapt the standard CFG parsing algorithms to unification grammar. It can be shown that as long as there is a finite subset of features such that at least one of the features is specified in every constituent, the unification grammar can be converted into a context-free grammar. This set of features is sometimes called the **context-free backbone** of the grammar.

Another powerful feature of unification grammars is that it allows much more information to be encoded in the lexicon. In fact, almost the entire grammar can be encoded in the lexicon, leaving very few rules in the grammar. Consider all the rules that were introduced earlier to deal with different verb subcategorizations. These could be condensed to a few rules: one for verbs that subcategorize for one subconstituent, another for verbs that subcategorize for two, and so on. The actual category restrictions on the complement structure would be encoded in the lexicon entry for the verb. For example, the verb *put* might have a lexicon entry as follows:

put: (**CAT** V **SUBCAT** (**FIRST** (**CAT** NP) **SECOND** (**CAT** PP **LOC** +)))

The general rule for verbs that subcategorize for two constituents would be

$$VP \rightarrow V\ X2\ X3 \qquad 2 = FIRST_{SUBCAT\,1}$$
$$3 = SECOND_{SUBCAT\,1}$$

This rule would accept any sequence V X2 X3, in which X2 unifies with the FIRST feature of the SUBCAT feature of X1 and X3 unifies with the SECOND feature of the SUBCAT feature of X1. If V is the verb *put*, this rule would require X2 to unify with (**CAT** NP) and X3 to unify with (**CAT** PP **LOC** +), as desired. Of course, this same rule would put completely different constraints on X2 and X3 for a verb like *want*, which would require X3 to unify with (**CAT** VP **VFORM** inf).

Such techniques can dramatically reduce the size of the grammar. For instance, a reasonable grammar would require at least 40 rules to handle verb subcategorizations. But no rule involves more than three subconstituents in the verb complement. Thus these 40 rules could be reduced to four in the unification grammar, including a rule for null complements. In addition, these same rules could be reused to handle all nouns and adjective subcategorizations, if you generalize the category restrictions on X1.

Summary

This chapter has extended the grammatical formalisms introduced in Chapter 3 by adding features to each constituent and augmenting the grammatical rules. Features are essential to enable the construction of wide-coverage grammars of natural language. A useful set of features for English was defined, and morpho-logical analysis techniques for mapping words to feature structures (that is, constituents) were developed. Several different forms of augmentation were examined. The first allowed context-free rules to specify feature agreement restrictions in addition to the basic category, producing augmented context-free grammars. The standard parsing algorithms described in Chapter 3 can be extended to handle such grammars. The second technique produced augmented transition networks, in which different procedural tests and actions could be defined on each arc to manipulate feature structures. The final method was based on the unification of feature structures and was used to develop unification grammars.

Related Work and Further Readings

Augmented CFGs have been used in computational models since the introduction of **attribute grammars** by Knuth (1968), who employed them for parsing programming languages. Since then many systems have utilized annotated rules of some form. Many early systems relied on arbitrary LISP code for annotations, although the types of operations commonly implemented were simple feature

BOX 4.3 Lexical Functional Grammar

A linguistic theory that has been influential in the development of computational formalisms is lexical functional grammar (Kaplan and Bresnan, 1982), usually abbreviated as LFG. LFG can be viewed as a type of unification grammar. A typical LFG rule is as follows:

$$S \rightarrow \quad NP \qquad\qquad VP$$
$$(\uparrow SUBJ) = \downarrow \quad \uparrow = \downarrow$$

The up arrow ($\uparrow$) indicates the constituent named on the left-hand side of the rule (the S constituent); the down arrow ($\downarrow$) indicates the constituent to which the annotation is attached. Thus this rule is equivalent to the following in the notation:

$$S \rightarrow NP\ VP \qquad \mathbf{SUBJ} = 1$$
$$\mathbf{0} = \mathbf{2}$$

Note the unification of the entire S and VP structure, making them the same constituent. Computationally, this can be viewed as an efficient way to transfer all the registers from the VP to the S, but it has linguistic implications as well, as discussed in Kaplan and Bresnan (1982). The effect is that any further modification to the S or VP structure will affect both, since they are now the same constituent.

LFGs encode most of their information in the lexicon. In particular, lexical entries may indicate which slots they will fill in the constituent that contains them. For example, the entries for *a, the,* and *bird* might be as follows:

$$a \qquad\quad ART \qquad (\uparrow SPEC) = INDEF$$
$$(\uparrow AGR) = (3s)$$
$$the \qquad ART \qquad (\uparrow SPEC) = DEF$$
$$bird \qquad N \qquad (\uparrow AGR) = (3s)$$
$$(\uparrow HEAD) = BIRD$$

The up-arrow annotations actually fill in slots in the NP structure. Using the rule

$$NP \rightarrow ART\ N$$

on the phrase *a bird* would result in the AGR feature of the NP being set to 3s when the word *a* is parsed, and then this value is unified with 3s to check number agreement when the noun *bird* is parsed. With the article *the,* no number agreement is checked, since the word *the* does not set the AGR feature of its NP.

tests and structure building along the lines of those discussed here. Examples of such systems are Sager (1981) and Robinson (1982).

The particular features used in this chapter and the techniques for augmenting rules are loosely based on work in the generalized phrase structure grammar (GPSG) tradition (Gazdar, Klein, Pullum, and Sag, 1985). GPSG introduces a finite set of feature values that can be attached to any grammatical symbol. These play much the same role as the annotations developed in this book except that there are no feature names. Rather, since all values are unique, they define both the feature type and the value simultaneously. For example, a plural noun phrase in the third person with gender female would be of the grammatical type

NP[PL,3,F]

Since the number of feature values is finite, the grammar is formally equivalent to a context-free grammar with a symbol for every combination of categories and features. One of the important contributions of GPSG, however, is the rich structure it imposes on the propagation of features. Rather than using explicit feature equation rules, GPSG relies on general principles of feature propagation that apply to all rules in the grammar. A good example of such a general principle is the **head feature convention**, which states that all the head features on the parent constituent must be identical to its head constituent. Another general principle enforces agreement restrictions between constituents. Some of the conventions introduced in this chapter to reduce the number of feature equations that must be defined by hand for each rule are motivated by these theoretical claims. An excellent survey of GPSG and LFG is found in Sells (1985).

The ATN framework described here is drawn from the work described in Woods (1970; 1973) and Kaplan (1973). A good survey of ATNs is Bates (1978). Logic programming approaches to natural language parsing originated in the early 1970s with work by Colmerauer (1978). This approach is perhaps best described in a paper by Pereira and Warren (1980) and in Pereira and Shieber (1987). Other interesting developments can be found in McCord (1980) and Pereira (1981). A good recent example is Alshawi (1992).

The discussion of unification grammars is based loosely on work by Kay (1982) and the PATR-II system (Shieber, 1984; 1986). There is a considerable amount of active research in this area. An excellent survey of the area is found in Shieber (1986). There is also a growing body of work on formalizing different forms of feature structures. Good examples are Rounds (1988), Shieber (1992), and Johnson (1991).

Exercises for Chapter 4

1. (*easy*) Using Grammar 4.7, draw the complete charts resulting from parsing the two sentences *The man cries* and *He wants to be happy,* whose final analyses are shown in Figure 4.9. You may use any parsing algorithm you want, but make sure that you state which one you are using and that the final chart contains every completed constituent built during the parse.

2. (*medium*) Define the minimal set of lexicon entries for the following verbs so that, using the morphological analysis algorithm, all standard forms of the verb are recognized and no illegal forms are inadvertently produced. Discuss any problems that arise and assumptions you make, and suggest modifications to the algorithms presented here if needed.

Base	Present Forms	Past	Past-Participle	Present-Participle
go	go, goes	went	gone	going
sing	sing, sings	sang	sung	singing
bid	bid, bids	bid	bidden	bidding

3. (*medium*) Extend the lexicon in Figure 4.6 and Grammar 4.7 so that the following two sentences are accepted:

> He was sad to see the dog cry.
> He saw the man saw the wood with the saw.

Justify your new rules by showing that they correctly handle a range of similar cases. Either implement and test your extended grammar using the supplied parser, or draw out the full chart that would be constructed for each sentence by a top-down chart parser.

4. (*medium*)

a. Write a grammar with features that will successfully allow the following phrases as noun phrases:

> three o'clock   quarter after eight
> ten minutes to six   seven thirty-five
> half past four

but will not permit the following:

> half to eight   three twenty o'clock
> ten forty-five after six

Specify the feature manipulations necessary so that once the parse is completed, two features, HOUR and MINUTES, are set in the NP constituent. If this requires an extension to the feature mechanism, carefully describe the extension you assume.

b. Choose two other forms of grammatical phrases accepted by the grammar. Find an acceptable phrase not accepted by your grammar. If any nongrammatical phrases are allowed, give one example.

5. (*medium*) English pronouns distinguish case. Thus *I* can be used as a subject, and *me* can be used as an object. Similarly, there is a difference between *he* and *him*, *we* and *us*, and *they* and *them*. The distinction is not made for the pronoun *you*. Specify an augmented context-free grammar and lexicon for simple subject-verb-object sentences that allows only appropriate pronouns in the subject and object positions and does number agreement between the subject and verb. Thus it should accept *I hit him*, but not *me love you*. Your grammar should account for all the pronouns mentioned in this question, but it need have only one verb entry and need cover no other noun phrases but pronouns.

6. (*medium*) Consider the following simple ATN:

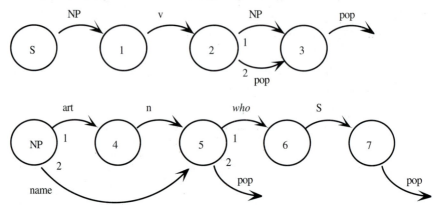

a. Specify some words by category and give four structurally different sentences accepted by this network.

b. Specify an augmentation for this network in the notation defined in this chapter so that sentences with the main verb *give* are allowed only if the subject is animate, and sentences with the main verb *be* may take either an animate or inanimate subject. Show a lexicon containing a few words that can be used to demonstrate the network's selectivity.

7. (*medium*) Using the following unification grammar, draw the DAGs for the two NP structures as they are when they are first constructed by the parser, and then give the DAG for the complete sentence (which will include all subconstituents of S as well) *The fish is a large one.* You may assume the lexicon in Figure 4.6, but define lexical entries for any words not covered there.

1.	S → NP VP	**INV** = −
		VFORM$_2$ = pres
		AGR = **AGR**$_1$ = **AGR**$_2$
2.	NP → ART N	**AGR** = **AGR**$_1$ = **AGR**$_2$
3.	NP → ART ADJ N	**AGR** = **AGR**$_1$ = **AGR**$_3$
4.	VP → V NP	**VFORM** = **VFORM**$_1$
		AGR = **AGR**$_1$ = **AGR**$_2$
		ROOT = BE1

CHAPTER

5

Grammars for Natural Language

5.1 Auxiliary Verbs and Verb Phrases

5.2 Movement Phenomena in Language

5.3 Handling Questions in Context-Free Grammars

5.4 Relative Clauses

5.5 The Hold Mechanism in ATNs

5.6 Gap Threading

Augmented context-free grammars provide a powerful formalism for capturing many generalities in natural language. This chapter considers several aspects of the structure of English and examines how feature systems can be used to handle them. Section 5.1 discusses auxiliary verbs and introduces features that capture the ordering and agreement constraints. Section 5.2 then discusses the general class of problems often characterized as movement phenomena. The rest of the chapter examines various approaches to handling movement. Section 5.3 discusses handling yes/no questions and wh-questions, and Section 5.4 discusses relative clauses. The remaining sections discuss alternative approaches. Section 5.5 discusses the use of the hold mechanism in ATNs and Section 5.6 discusses gap threading in logic grammars.

5.1 Auxiliary Verbs and Verb Phrases

English sentences typically contain a sequence of auxiliary verbs followed by a main verb, as in the following:

> I *can see* the house.
> I *will have seen* the house.
> I *was watching* the movie.
> I *should have been watching* the movie.

These may at first appear to be arbitrary sequences of verbs, including *have, be, do, can, will,* and so on, but in fact there is a rich structure. Consider how the auxiliaries constrain the verb that follows them. In particular, the auxiliary *have* must be followed by a past participle form (either another auxiliary or the main verb), and the auxiliary *be* must be followed by a present participle form, or, in the case of passive sentences, by the past participle form. The auxiliary *do* usually occurs alone but can accept a base form following it (*I did eat my carrots!*). Auxiliaries such as *can* and *must* must always be followed by a base form. In addition, the first auxiliary (or verb) in the sequence must agree with the subject in simple declarative sentences and be in a finite form (past or present). For example, **I going, *we be gone,* and **they am* are all unacceptable.

This section explores how to capture the structure of auxiliary forms using a combination of new rules and feature restrictions. The principal idea is that auxiliary verbs have subcategorization features that restrict their verb phrase complements. To develop this, a clear distinction is made between auxiliary and main verbs. While some auxiliary verbs have many of the properties of regular verbs, it is important to distinguish them. For example, auxiliary verbs can be placed before an adverbial *not* in a sentence, whereas a main verb cannot:

> I *am* not going!
> You *did* not try it.
> He *could* not have seen the car.

Auxiliary	COMPFORM	Construction	Example
modal	base	modal	can *see the house*
have	pastprt	perfect	have *seen the house*
be	ing	progressive	is *lifting the box*
be	pastprt	passive	was *seen by the crowd*

Figure 5.1 The COMPFORM restrictions for auxiliary verbs

In addition, only auxiliary verbs can precede the subject NP in yes/no questions:

Did you see the car?
Can I try it?
*Eat John the pizza?

In contrast, main verbs may appear as the sole verb in a sentence, and if made into a yes/no question require the addition of the auxiliary *do*:

I ate the pizza.	Did I eat the pizza?
The boy climbed in the window.	Did the boy climb in the window?
I have a pen.	Do I have a pen?

The primary auxiliaries are based on the root forms *be* and *have*. The other auxiliaries are called **modal** auxiliaries and generally appear only in the finite tense forms (simple present and past). These include the following verbs organized in pairs corresponding roughly to present and past verb forms *do* (*did*), *can* (*could*), *may* (*might*), *shall* (*should*), *will* (*would*), *must*, *need*, and *dare*. In addition, there are phrases that also serve a modal auxiliary function, such as *ought to, used to,* and *be going to.*

Notice that *have* and *be* can be either an auxiliary or a main verb by these tests. Because they behave quite differently, these words have different lexical entries as auxiliaries and main verbs to allow for different properties; for example, the auxiliary *have* requires a past-participle verb phrase to follow it, whereas the verb *have* requires an NP complement.

As mentioned earlier, the basic idea for handling auxiliaries is to treat them as verbs that take a VP as a complement. This VP may itself consist of another auxiliary verb and another VP, or be a VP headed by a main verb. Thus, extending Grammar 4.7 with the following rule covers much of the behavior:

VP → (*AUX* ***COMPFORM*** *?s*) (VP **VFORM** ?s)

The COMPFORM feature indicates the VFORM of the VP complement. The values of this feature for the auxiliaries are shown in Figure 5.1.

There are other restrictions on the auxiliary sequence. In particular, auxiliaries can appear only in the following order:

Modal +	have +	be (*progressive*) +	be (*passive*)
The song might	have	been	being played as they left.

To capture the ordering constraints, it might seem that you need eight special rules: one for each of the four auxiliary positions plus four that make each optional. But it turns out that some restrictions can fall out from the feature restrictions. For instance, since modal auxiliaries do not have participle forms, a modal auxiliary can never follow *have* or *be* in the auxiliary sequence. For example, the sentence

*He has might see the movie already.

violates the subcategorization restriction on *have*. You might also think that the auxiliary *have* can never appear in its participle forms, as it must either be first in the sequence (and be finite) or follow a modal and be an infinitive. But this is only true for simple matrix clauses. If you consider auxiliary sequences appearing in VP complements for certain verbs, such as *regret,* the participle forms of *have* as an auxiliary can be required, as in

I regret having been chosen to go.

As a result, the formulation based on subcategorization features over-generates. While it accepts any legal sequence of auxiliaries, it would also accept

*I must be having been singing.

This problem can be solved by adding new features that further restrict the complements of the auxiliary *be* so that they do not allow additional auxiliaries (except *be* again for the passive). A binary head feature MAIN could be introduced that is + for any main verb, and – for auxiliary verbs. This way we can restrict the VP complement for *be* as follows:

VP → *AUX*[*be*] VP[ing, +main]

The lexical entry for *be* would then have to be changed so that the original auxiliary rule does not apply. This could be done by setting its COMPFORM feature to –. The only remaining problem is how to allow the passive. There are several possible approaches. We could, for instance, treat the *be* in the passive construction as a main verb form rather than an auxiliary. Another way would be simply to add another rule allowing a complement in the passive form, using a new binary feature PASS, which is + only if the VP involves passive:

VP → *AUX*[*be*] VP[ing, +pass]

The passive rule would then be:

VP[+pass] → *AUX*[*be*] VP[pastprt, main]

While these new rules capture the ordering constraints well, for the sake of keeping examples short, we will generally use the first rule presented for handling auxiliaries throughout. While it overgenerates, it will not cause any problems for the points that are illustrated by the examples.

can: (**CAT** AUX
    MODAL +
    VFORM pres
    AGR {1s 2s 3s 1p 2p 3p}
    COMPFORM base)

could: (**CAT** AUX
    MODAL +
    VFORM {pres past}
    AGR {1s 2s 3s 1p 2p 3p}
    COMPFORM base)

do: (**CAT** AUX
    MODAL +
    VFORM pres
    AGR {1s 2s 1p 2p 3p}
    COMPFORM base)

did: (**CAT** AUX
    MODAL +
    VFORM past
    AGR {1s 2s 3s 1p 2p 3p}
    COMPFORM base)

be: (**CAT** AUX
    VFORM base
    ROOT be
    COMPFORM ing)

have: (**CAT** AUX
    VFORM base
    ROOT have
    COMPFORM pastprt)

Figure 5.2 Lexicon entries for some auxiliary verbs

A lexicon for some of the auxiliary verbs is shown in Figure 5.2. All the irregular forms would need to be defined as well.

o Passives

The rule for passives in the auxiliary sequence discussed in the previous section solves only one of the problems related to the passive construct. Most verbs that include an NP in their complement allow the passive form. This form involves using the normal "object position" NP as the first NP in the sentence and either omitting the NP usually in the subject position or putting it in a PP with the preposition *by*. For example, the active voice sentences

> I will hide my hat in the drawer.
> I hid my hat in the drawer.
> I was hiding my hat in the drawer.

can be rephrased as the following passive voice sentences:

> My hat will be hidden in the drawer.
> My hat was hidden in the drawer.
> My hat was being hidden in the drawer.

The complication here is that the VP in the passive construction is missing the object NP. One way to solve this problem would be to add a new grammatical rule for every verb subcategorization that is usable only for passive forms, namely all rules that allow an NP to follow the verb. A program can easily be written that would automatically generate such passive rules given a grammar. A

1. S[–inv] → (NP **AGR** ?a) (*VP* [*fin*] **AGR** *?a*)
2. VP → (*AUX* ***COMPFORM*** *?v*) (VP **VFORM** ?v)
3. VP → *AUX*[*be*] VP[ing, +main]
4. VP → *AUX*[*be*] VP[ing, +pass]
5. VP[+pass] → *AUX* [*be*] VP[pastprt, main, +passgap]
6. VP[–passgap, +main] → V[*_none*]
7. VP[–passgap, +main] → V[*_np*] NP
8. VP[+passgap, +main] → V[*_np*]
9. NP → (ART **AGR** ?a) (*N* **AGR** *?a*)
10. NP → *NAME*
11. NP → *PRO*

Head features for S, VP: AGR and VFORM
Head features for NP: AGR

Figure 5.3 A fragment handling auxiliaries including passives

new binary head feature, PASSGAP, is defined that is + only if the constituent is missing the object NP. As usual, this feature would default to – if it is not speci-fied in the left-hand side of a rule. The rule for a simple _np subcategorization in Grammar 4.5 would then be realized as two rules in the new grammar:

VP[–passgap] → V[*_np*] NP
VP[+passgap] → V[*_np*]

Since the PASSGAP feature defaults to –, the only way the PASSGAP feature can become + is by the use of passive rules. Similarly, VP rules with lexical heads but with no NP in their complement are –PASSGAP, because they cannot participate in the passive construction. Figure 5.3 shows a fragment of Grammar 4.5 extended to handle auxiliaries and passives. The rules are as developed above except for additional variables in each rule to pass features around appropriately.

Figure 5.4 shows the analysis of the active voice sentence *Jack can see the dog* and the passive sentence *Jack was seen.* Each analysis uses rule 1 for the S and rule 7 for the VP. The only difference is that the active sentence must use auxiliary rule 2 and NP rule 9, while the passive sentence must use auxiliary rule 5 and NP rule 8.

5.2 Movement Phenomena in Language

Many sentence structures appear to be simple variants of other sentence struc-tures. In some cases, simple words or phrases appear to be locally reordered; sentences are identical except that a phrase apparently is moved from its expected

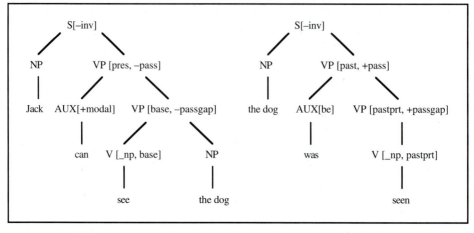

Figure 5.4 An active and a passive form sentence

position in a basic sentence. This section explores techniques for exploiting these generalities to cover questions in English.

As a starting example, consider the structure of yes/no questions and how they relate to their assertional counterpart. In particular, consider the following examples:

> Jack is giving Sue a back rub. He will run in the marathon next year.
> Is Jack giving Sue a back rub? Will he run in the marathon next year?

As you can readily see, yes/no questions appear identical in structure to their assertional counterparts except that the subject NPs and first auxiliaries have swapped positions. If there is no auxiliary in the assertional sentence, an auxiliary of root *do,* in the appropriate tense, is used:

> John went to the store. Henry goes to school every day.
> Did John go to the store? Does Henry go to school every day?

Taking a term from linguistics, this rearranging of the subject and the auxiliary is called **subject-aux inversion**.

Informally, you can think of deriving yes/no questions from assertions by moving the constituents in the manner just described. This is an example of **local** (or bounded) **movement**. The movement is considered local because the rearranging of the constituents is specified precisely within the scope of a limited number of rules. This contrasts with **unbounded movement,** which occurs in wh-questions. In cases of unbounded movement, constituents may be moved arbitrarily far from their original position.

For example, consider the wh-questions that are related to the assertion

> The fat man will angrily put the book in the corner.

If you are interested in who did the action, you might ask one of these questions:

> Which man will angrily put the book in the corner?
> Who will angrily put the book in the corner?

On the other hand, if you are interested in how it is done, you might ask one of the following questions:

> How will the fat man put the book in the corner?
> In what way will the fat man put the book in the corner?

If you are interested in other aspects, you might ask one of these questions:

> What will the fat man angrily put in the corner?
> Where will the fat man angrily put the book?
> In what corner will the fat man angrily put the book?
> What will the fat man angrily put the book in?

Each question has the same form as the original assertion, except that the part being questioned is removed and replaced by a wh-phrase at the beginning of the sentence. In addition, except when the part being queried is the subject NP, the subject and the auxiliary are apparently inverted, as in yes/no questions. This similarity with yes/no questions even holds for sentences without auxiliaries. In both cases, a *do* auxiliary is inserted:

> I found a bookcase.
> Did I find a bookcase?
> What *did* I find?

Thus you may be able to reuse much of a grammar for yes/no questions for wh-questions. A serious problem remains, however, concerning how to handle the fact that a constituent is missing from someplace later in the sentence. For example, consider the italicized VP in the sentence

> What will the fat man *angrily put in the corner*?

While this is an acceptable sentence, *angrily put in the corner* does not appear to be an acceptable VP because you cannot allow sentences such as **I angrily put in the corner.* Only in situations like wh-questions can such a VP be allowed, and then it is allowed only if the wh-constituent is of the right form to make a legal VP if it were inserted in the sentence. For example, *What will the fat man angrily put in the corner?* is acceptable, but **Where will the fat man angrily put in the corner?* is not.

If you constructed a special grammar for VPs in wh-questions, you would need a separate grammar for each form of VP and each form of missing constituent. This would create a significant expansion in the size of the grammar.

This chapter describes some techniques for handling such phenomena concisely. In general, they all use the same type of approach. The place where a subconstituent is missing is called the **gap**, and the constituent that is moved is called the **filler**. The techniques that follow all involve ways of allowing gaps in constituents when there is an appropriate filler available. Thus the analysis of the

VP in a sentence such as *What will the fat man angrily put in the corner?* is parsed as though it were *angrily put what in the corner,* and the VP in the sentence *What will the fat man angrily put the book in?* is parsed as though the VP were *angrily put the book in what.*

There is further evidence for the correctness of this analysis. In particular, all the well-formedness tests, like subject-verb agreement, the case of pronouns (who vs. whom), and verb transitivity, operate as though the wh-term were actually filling the gap. For example, you already saw how it handled verb transitivity. The question *What did you put in the cupboard?* is acceptable even though *put* is a transitive verb and thus requires an object. The object is a gap filled by the wh-term, satisfying the transitivity constraint. Furthermore, a sentence where the object is explicitly filled is unacceptable:

> *What did you put the bottle in the cupboard?

This sentence is unacceptable, just as any sentence with two objects for the verb *put* would be unacceptable. In effect it is equivalent to

> *You put what the bottle in the cupboard?

Thus the standard transitivity tests will work only if you assume the initial wh-term can be used to satisfy the constraint on the standard object NP position.

Many linguistic theories have been developed that are based on the intuition that a constituent can be moved from one location to another. As you explore these techniques further, you will see that significant generalizations can be made that greatly simplify the construction of a grammar. **Transformational grammar** (see Box 5.1) was based on this model. A context-free grammar generated a base sentence; then a set of transformations converted the resulting syntactic tree into a different tree by moving constituents. Augmented transition networks offered a new formalism that captured much of the behavior in a more computationally effective manner. A new structure called the **hold list** was introduced that allowed a constituent to be saved and used later in the parse by a new arc called the virtual (VIR) arc. This was the predominant computational mechanism for quite some time. In the early 1980s, however, new techniques were developed in linguistics that strongly influenced current computational systems.

The first technique was the introduction of **slash** categories, which are complex nonterminals of the form X/Y and stand for a constituent of type X with a subconstituent of type Y missing. Given a context-free grammar, there is a simple algorithm that can derive new rules for such complex constituents. With this in hand, grammar writers have a convenient notation for expressing the constraints arising from unbounded movement. Unfortunately, the size of the resulting grammar can be significantly larger than the original grammar. A better approach uses the feature system. Constituents are stored in a special feature called GAP and are passed from constituent to subconstituent to allow movement. In this analysis the constituent S/NP is shorthand for an S constituent with the GAP feature NP. The resulting system does not require expanding the size of

BOX 5.1 Movement in Linguistics

The term *movement* arose in transformational grammar (TG). TG posited two distinct levels of structural representation: **surface structure**, which corresponds to the actual sentence structure, and **deep structure**. A CFG generates the deep structure, and a set of **transformations** map the deep structure to the surface structure. For example, the deep structure of *Will the cat scratch John?* would be:

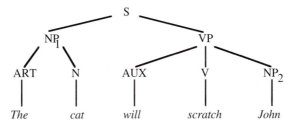

The yes/no question is then generated from this deep structure by a transformation expressed schematically as follows:

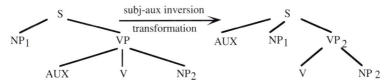

With this transformation the surface form will be

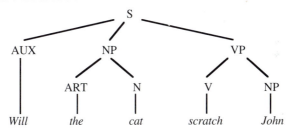

In early TG (Chomsky, 1965), transformations could do many operations on trees, including moving, adding, and deleting constituents. Besides subj-aux inversion, there were transformational accounts of passives, wh-questions, and embedded sentences. The modern descendants of TG do not use transformations in the same way. In **government-binding (GB) theory**, a single transformation rule, Move-α, allows any constituent to be moved anywhere! The focus is on developing constraints on movement that prohibit the generation of illegal surface structures.

the grammar significantly and appears to handle the phenomena quite well. The following sections discuss two different feature-based techniques for context-free grammars and the hold-list technique for ATNs in detail.

BOX 5.2 Different Types of Movement

While the discussion in this chapter will concentrate on wh-questions and thus will examine the movement of wh-terms extensively, the techniques discussed are also needed for other forms of movement as well. Here are some of the most common forms of movement discussed in the linguistics literature. For more details, see a textbook on linguistics, such as Baker (1989).

wh-movement—move a wh-term to the front of the sentence to form a wh-question

topicalization—move a constituent to the beginning of the sentence for emphasis, as in

I never liked this picture.
This picture, I never liked.

adverb preposing—move an adverb to the beginning of the sentence, as in

I will see you tomorrow.
Tomorrow, I will see you.

extraposition—move certain NP complements to the sentence final position, as in

A book discussing evolution was written.
A book was written discussing evolution.

As you consider strategies to handle movement, remember that constituents cannot be moved from any arbitrary position to the front to make a question. For example,

The man who was holding the two balloons will put the box in the corner.

is a well-formed sentence, but you cannot ask the following question, where the gap is indicated by a dash:

*What will the man who was holding   put the box in the corner?

This is an example of a general constraint on movement out of relative clauses.

5.3 Handling Questions in Context-Free Grammars

The goal is to extend a context-free grammar minimally so that it can handle questions. In other words, you want to reuse as much of the original grammar as possible. For yes/no questions, this is easily done. You can extend Grammar 4.7 with one rule that allows an auxiliary before the first NP and handles most examples:

S [+inv] → (*AUX AGR ?a SUBCAT ?v*) (NP **AGR** ?a) (VP **VFORM** ?v)

This enforces subject-verb agreement between the AUX and the subject NP, and ensures that the VP has the right VFORM to follow the AUX. This one rule is all that is needed to handle yes/no questions, and all of the original grammar for assertions can be used directly for yes/no questions.

As mentioned in Section 5.2, a special feature GAP is introduced to handle wh-questions. This feature is passed from mother to subconstituent until the appropriate place for the gap is found in the sentence. At that place, the appropriate constituent can be constructed using no input. This can be done by introducing additional rules with empty right-hand sides. For instance, you might have a rule such as

$$(NP\ \textbf{GAP} ((\textbf{CAT}\ NP)\ (\textbf{AGR}\ ?a))\ \textbf{AGR}\ ?a) \rightarrow \varepsilon$$

which builds an NP from no input if the NP sought has a GAP feature that is set to an NP. Furthermore, the AGR feature of this empty NP is set to the AGR feature of the feature that is the value of the GAP. Note that the GAP feature in the mother has another feature structure as its value. To help you identify the structure of such complex values, a smaller font size is used for feature structures acting as values.

You could now write a grammar that passed the GAP feature appropriately. This would be tedious, however, and would also not take advantage of some generalities that seem to hold for the propagation of the GAP feature. Specifically, there seem to be two general ways in which the GAP feature propagates, depending on whether the head constituent is a lexical or nonlexical category. If it is a nonlexical category, the GAP feature is passed from the mother to the head and not to any other subconstituents. For example, a typical S rule with the GAP feature would be

$$(S\ \textbf{GAP}\ ?g) \rightarrow (NP\ \textbf{GAP}\ -)\ (VP\ \textit{GAP}\ ?g)$$

The GAP can be in the VP, the head subconstituent, but not in the NP subject. For rules with lexical heads, the gap may move to any one of the nonlexical subconstituents. For example, the rule for verbs with a _np_vp:inf complement,

$$VP \rightarrow V[\_np\_vp{:}inf]\ NP\ PP$$

would result in two rules involving gaps:

$$(VP\ \textbf{GAP}\ ?g) \rightarrow V[\_np\_vp{:}inf]\ (NP\ \textbf{GAP}\ ?g)\ (PP\ \textbf{GAP}\ -)$$
$$(VP\ \textbf{GAP}\ ?g) \rightarrow V[\_np\_vp{:}inf]\ (NP\ \textbf{GAP}\ -)\ (PP\ \textbf{GAP}\ ?g)$$

In other words, the GAP may be in the NP or in the PP, but not both. Setting the GAP feature in all but one subconstituent to – guarantees that a gap can be used in only one place.

An algorithm for automatically adding GAP features to a grammar is shown in Figure 5.5. Note that it does not modify any rule that explicitly sets the GAP feature already, allowing the grammar designer to introduce rules that do not follow the conventions encoded in the algorithm. In particular, the rule for subject-aux inversion cannot allow the gap to propagate to the subject NP.

For each rule $Y \rightarrow X_1 \dots H_i \dots X_n$ with head constituent H_i

1. If the rule specifies a GAP feature in some constituent already, then skip.
2. If the head H_i is not a lexical category, then add a GAP feature to the head and the mother, and $-$GAP to the other subconstituents, producing a rule of form:

   $(Y \text{ } \textbf{GAP } ?g) \rightarrow (X_1 \text{ } \textbf{GAP } -) \dots (H_i \text{ } \textbf{GAP } ?g) \dots (X_n \text{ } \textbf{GAP } -)$
3. If the head H_i is a lexical category, then for each nonlexical subconstituent X_j, add a rule of the form:

   $(Y \text{ } \textbf{GAP } ?g) \rightarrow (X_1 \text{ } \textbf{GAP } -) \dots (X_j \text{ } \textbf{GAP } ?g) \dots (X_n \text{ } \textbf{GAP } -)$

Figure 5.5 An algorithm for adding GAP features to a grammar

Using this procedure, a new grammar can be created that handles gaps. All that is left to do is analyze where the fillers for the gaps come from. In wh-questions, the fillers are typically NPs or PPs at the start of the sentence and are identified by a new feature WH that identifies a class of phrases that can introduce questions. The WH feature is signaled by words such as *who, what, when, where, why,* and *how* (as in *how many* and *how carefully*). These words fall into several different grammatical categories, as can be seen by considering what type of phrases they replace. In particular, *who, whom,* and *what* can appear as pronouns and can be used to specify simple NPs:

> *Who* ate the pizza?
> *What* did you put the book in?

The words *what* and *which* may appear as determiners in noun phrases, as in

> *What* book did he steal?

Words such as *where* and *when* appear as prepositional phrases:

> *Where* did you put the book?

The word *how* acts as an adverbial modifier to adjective and adverbial phrases:

> *How* quickly did he run?

Finally, the word *whose* acts as a possessive pronoun:

> *Whose* book did you find?

The wh-words also can act in different roles. All of the previous examples show their use to introduce wh-questions, which will be indicated by the WH feature value Q. A subset of them can also be used to introduce relative clauses, which will be discussed in Section 5.4. These will also have the WH feature value R. To make the WH feature act appropriately, a grammar should satisfy the following constraint: If a phrase contains a subphrase that has the WH feature, then the larger phrase also has the same WH feature. This way, complex phrases

what:	(**CAT** PRO **WH** Q **AGR** {3s 3p})	when:	(**CAT** PP-WRD **WH** {Q R} **PFORM** TIME)	
what:	(**CAT** QDET **WH** Q **AGR** {3s 3p})	who:	(**CAT** PRO **WH** {Q R} **AGR** {3s 3p})	
which:	(**CAT** QDET **WH** Q **AGR** {3s 3p})	where:	(**CAT** PP-WRD **WH** {Q R} **PFORM** {LOC MOT})	
which:	(**CAT** PRO **WH** R **AGR** {3s 3p})	whose:	(**CAT** PRO **WH** {Q R} **POSS** + **AGR** {3s 3p})	

Figure 5.6 A lexicon for some of the wh-words

1. (NP **POSS** ?p **WH** ?w) → (*PRO POSS ?p WH ?w*)
2. (NP **WH** ?w) → (DET **WH** ?w **AGR** ?a) (*CNP AGR ?a*)
3. CNP → *N*
4. CNP → ADJ *N*
5. DET → *ART*
6. (DET **WH** ?w) → (*NP*[+*POSS*] *WH ?a*)
7. (DET **WH** ?w) → (*QDET WH ?w*)
8. (PP **WH** ?w) → *P* (NP **WH** ?w)
9. (PP **WH** ?w) → (*PP-WRD WH ?w*)

Head feature for NP, DET and CNP: AGR
Head feature for PP: PFORM

Grammar 5.7 A simple NP and PP grammar handling wh-words

containing a subconstituent with a WH word also can be used in questions. For example, the sentence

In what store did you buy the picture?

is a legal question since the initial PP *in what store* has the WH value Q because the NP *what store* has the WH value Q (because the determiner *what* has the WH value Q). With this constraint, the final S constituent will also have the WH value Q, which will be used to indicate that the sentence is a wh-question. Figure 5.6 gives some lexical entries for some wh-words. Note the introduction of new lexical categories: QDET for determiners that introduce wh-terms, and PP-WRD for words like *when* that act like prepositional phrases. Grammar 5.7 gives some rules for NPs and PPs that handle the WH feature appropriately.

10. (S[–inv] **WH** ?w) →
    (NP **WH** ?w **AGR** ?a)
    (*VP* [*fin*] *AGR ?a*)

11. (S[+inv] **WH** ?w **GAP** ?g) →
    (*AUX COMPFORM ?s AGR ?a*)
    (NP **WH** ?w **AGR** ?a **GAP** –)
    (VP **VFORM** ?s **GAP** ?g)

12. S → (NP[Q,–gap] **AGR** ?a) (*S*[*+inv*] *GAP* (*NP AGR ?a*))

13. S → (PP[Q,–gap] **PFORM** ?p) (*S*[*+inv*] *GAP* (*PP PFORM ?p*))

14. VP → (*AUX COMPFORM ?s*) (VP **VFORM** ?s)

15. VP → V[_*none*]

16. VP → V[_*np*] NP

17. VP → V[_*vp:inf*] VP[inf]

18. VP → V[_*np_vp:inf*] NP VP[inf]

19. VP[inf] → *TO* VP[base]

20. VP → V[_*np_pp:loc*] NP PP[loc]

Head features for S, VP: VFORM, AGR

Grammar 5.8   The unexpanded S grammar for wh-questions

With the WH feature defined and a mechanism for modifying a grammar to handle the GAP feature, most wh-questions can be handled by adding only two new rules to the grammar. Here are the rules for NP- and PP-based questions:

S → (NP[Q,–gap] **AGR** ?a) (S[+inv] **GAP** (NP **AGR** ?a))
S → (PP[Q,–gap] **PFORM** ?p) (S[+inv] **GAP** (PP **PFORM** ?p))

Both of these rules set the value of the GAP feature to a copy of the initial WH constituent so that it will be used to fill a gap in the S constituent. Since the S constituent must have the feature +INV, it must also contain a subject-aux inversion. Given the NP and PP rules in Grammar 5.7, Grammar 5.8 provides the S and VP rules to handle questions. Grammar 5.9 shows all the derived rules introduced by the procedure that adds the GAP features. Rules 11, 12, and 13 are not changed by the algorithm as they already specify the GAP feature.

Parsing with Gaps

A grammar that allows gaps creates some new complications for parsing algorithms. In particular, rules that have an empty right-hand side, such as

(NP **AGR** ?a **GAP** (NP **AGR** ?a)) → ε

10. (S[–inv] **WH** ?w **GAP** ?g) →
    (NP **WH** ?w **AGR** ?a)
    (*VP*[*fin*] *AGR ?a GAP ?g*)

11. (S[+inv] **WH** ?w **GAP** ?g) →
    (*AUX COMPFORM ?s AGR ?a*)
    (NP **WH** ?w **AGR** ?a **GAP** –)
    (VP **VFORM** ?s **GAP** ?g)

12. S → (NP[Q,–gap] **AGR** ?a) (*S*[*+inv*] *GAP* (*NP AGR ?a*))

13. S → (PP[Q,–gap] **PFORM** ?p) (*S*[*+inv*] *GAP* (*PP PFORM ?p*))

14. (VP **GAP** ?g) → (*AUX COMPFORM ?s*) (VP **VFORM** ?s **GAP** ?g)

15. VP → V[_*none*]

16. (VP **GAP** ?g) → V[_*np*] (NP **GAP** ?g)

17. (VP **GAP** ?g)→ V[_*vp:inf*] (VP[inf] **GAP** ?g)

18. (VP **GAP** ?g)→ V[_*np_vp:inf*] (NP **GAP** ?g) (VP[inf] **GAP** –)

18'. (VP **GAP** ?g)→ V[_*np_vp:inf*] (NP **GAP** –) (VP[inf] **GAP** ?g)

19. (VP[inf] **GAP** ?g) → *TO* (VP[base] **GAP** ?g)

20. (VP **GAP** ?g) → V[_*np_pp:loc*] (NP **GAP** ?g) (PP[loc] **GAP** –)

20'. ((VP **GAP** ?g) → V[_*np_pp:loc*] (NP **GAP** –) (PP[loc] **GAP** ?g)

Head features for S, VP: VFORM, AGR

Grammar 5.9 The S grammar for wh-questions with the GAP feature

may cause problems because they allow an empty NP constituent anywhere. In a bottom-up strategy, for instance, this rule could apply at any position (or many times at any position) to create NPs that use no input. A top-down strategy fares better, in that the rule would only be used when a gap is explicitly predicted. Instead of using such rules, however, the arc extension algorithm can be modified to handle gaps automatically. This technique works with any parsing strategy.

Consider what extensions are necessary. When a constituent has a GAP feature that matches the constituent itself, it must be realized by the empty constituent. This means that an arc whose next constituent is a gap can be extended immediately. For example, consider what happens if the following arc is suggested by the parser:

(VP **GAP** (NP **AGR** 3s))
    → V[_*np_pp:loc*] ∘ (NP **GAP** (NP **AGR** 3s)) PP[LOC]

The next constituent needed is an NP, but it also has a GAP feature that must be an NP. Thus the constituent must be empty. The parser inserts the constituent

(NP **AGR** 3s **EMPTY** +)

BOX 5.3 The Movement Constraints

In linguistics the principles that govern where gaps may occur are called **island constraints**. The term draws on the metaphor of constituent movement. An island is a constituent from which no subconstituent can move out (just as a person cannot walk off an island). Here are a few of the constraints that have been proposed.

The A over A Constraint—No constituent of category A can be moved out of a constituent of type A. This means you cannot have an NP gap within an NP, a PP gap within a PP, and so on, and provides justification for not allowing non-null constituents of the form NP/NP, PP/PP, and so on. This disallows sentences such as

*What book$_1$ did you meet the author of —$_1$?

Complex-NP Constraint—No constituent may be moved out of a relative clause or noun complement. This constraint disallows sentences like

*To whom$_1$ did the man who gave the book —$_1$ laughed?

where the PP *to whom* would have been part of the relative clause *who gave the book to whom* (as in *The man who gave the book to John laughed*).

Sentential Subject Constraint—No constituent can be moved out of a constituent serving as the subject of a sentence. This overlaps with the other constraints when the subject is an NP, but non-NP subjects are possible as well, as in the sentence *For me to learn these constraints is impossible.* This constraint eliminates the possibility of a question like

*What$_1$ is for me to learn —$_1$ impossible?

Wh-Island Constraint—No constituent can be moved from an embedded sentence with a wh-complementizer. For example, while *Did they wonder whether I took the book?* is an acceptable sentence, you cannot ask

*What$_1$ did they wonder whether I took —$_1$?

Coordinate Structure Constraint—A constituent cannot be moved out of a coordinate structure. For example, while *Did you see John and Sam?* is an acceptable sentence, you cannot ask

*Who$_1$ did you see John and —$_1$?

Note that these constraints apply to all forms of movement, not just wh-questions. For example, they constrain topicalization and adverb preposing as well.

to the chart, which can then extend the arc to produce the new arc

$$(VP\ \textbf{GAP}\ (NP\ \textbf{AGR}\ 3s))$$
$$\rightarrow V[\_np\_pp:loc]\ (NP\ \textbf{GAP}\ (NP\ \textbf{AGR}\ 3s)) \circ PP[LOC]$$

A more precise specification of the algorithm is given in Figure 5.10.

Whenever an arc of the form

X → ... ∘ (C **F1** V1 ... **Fn** Vn **GAP** (C **G1** ?vg1 ... **Gm** ?vgm)) ...

is suggested by the parser, and the constituent pattern that is the GAP feature, that is,

(C **G1** ?vg1 ... **Gm** ?vgm)

matches the constituent itself

(C **F1** V1 ... **Fn** Vn **GAP** (C **G1** VG1 ... **Gm** VGm))

then add a new constituent (C **G1** ?vg1 ... **Gm** ?vgm **EMPTY** +), with the variables bound as necessary, to the chart. Use this constituent to extend the original arc.

Figure 5.10 The algorithm to insert empty constituents as needed

Consider parsing *Which dogs did he see?* using the bottom-up strategy. Only the rules that contribute to the final analysis will be considered. Rule 7 in Grammar 5.7 applies to the constituent QDET1 (*which*) to build a constituent DET1, and rule 3 applies to the constituent N1 (*dogs*) to build a constituent CNP1, which then is combined with DET1 by rule 2 to build an NP constituent of the form

NP1: (NP   **AGR** 3p
            WH Q
            1 QDET1
            2 CNP1)

This NP introduces an arc based on rule 12 in Grammar 5.8. The next word, *did,* is an AUX constituent, which introduces an arc based on rule 11. The next word, *he,* is a PRO, which creates an NP, NP2, using rule 1, and extends the arc based on rule 1. The chart at this stage is shown in Figure 5.11.

The word *see* introduces a verb V1, which can extend rule 16. This adds the arc labeled

(VP **GAP** ?g) → V[_np] ∘ (NP **GAP** ?g)

Since the GAP value can match the required NP (because it is unconstrained), an empty NP is inserted in the chart with the form

EMPTY-NP1:   (NP **AGR** ?a **GAP** (NP **AGR** ?a)) EMPTY +)

This constituent can then be used to extend the VP arc, producing the constituent

VP1:   (VP   **VFORM** inf
             GAP (NP **AGR** ?a)
             1 V1
             2 EMPTY-NP1)

Now VP1 can extend the arc based on rule 11 to form the S structure:

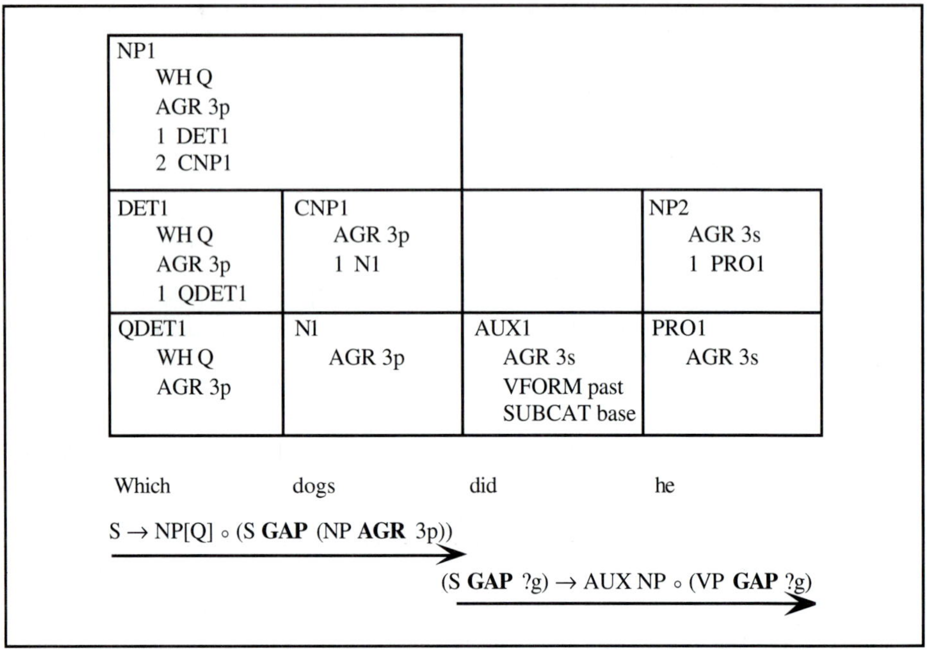

Figure 5.11   The chart after the word *he*

S1: (S   **GAP** (NP **AGR** ?a)
         INV +
         1 AUX1
         2 NP2
         3 VP1)

Finally, NP1 and S1 can combine using rule 12 to produce an S constituent. The final chart is shown in Figure 5.12.

Thus, by using the WH and GAP features appropriately and by extending the parser to insert empty constituents as needed to fill gaps, the original grammar for declarative assertions can be extended to handle yes/no questions and wh-questions with only three new rules. The success of this approach depends on getting the right constraints on the propagation of the GAP feature. For instance, in a rule a gap should only be passed from the mother to exactly one of the subconstituents. If this constraint were not enforced, many illegal sentences would be allowed. There are some cases where this constraint appears to be violated. They are discussed in Exercise 6.

With a bottom-up parsing strategy, many empty constituents are inserted by the parser, and many constants with gaps are added to the chart. Most of these are not used in any valid analysis of the sentence. The top-down strategy greatly reduces the number of empty constants proposed and results in a considerably smaller chart.

S2				
VFORM past 1 NP1 2 S1				

NP1		S1		
WH Q AGR 3p 1 DET1 2 CNP1		INV+ GAP (NP **AGR** 3p) VFORM past 1 AUX1 2 NP2 3 VP1		

DET1	CNP1		NP2	VP1
WH Q AGR 3p 1 QDET1	AGR 3p 1 N1		AGR 3s 1 PRO1	VFORM inf GAP (NP **AGR** 3p) 1 V1 2 EMPTY-NP1

QDET1	N1	AUX1	PRO1	
WH Q AGR 3p	AGR 3p	AGR 3s VFORM past SUBCAT base	AGR 3s	

Which	dogs	did	he	see

Figure 5.12   The final chart for *Which dogs did he see?*

○ 5.4 Relative Clauses

This section examines the structure of relative clauses. A relative clause can be introduced with a rule using a new category, REL:

CNP → *CNP* REL

A large class of relative clauses can be handled using the existing grammar for questions as they involve similar constructs of a wh-word followed by an S structure with a gap. The main difference is that only certain wh-words are allowed (*who, whom, which, when, where,* and *whose*) and the S structure is not inverted. The special class of wh-words for relative clauses is indicated using the WH feature value R. Figure 5.6 showed lexicon entries for some of these words.

Given this analysis, the following rules

REL → (NP **WH** R **AGR** ?a) (S[–inv, fin] **GAP** (NP **AGR** ?a))
REL → (PP **WH** R **PFORM** ?p) (S[–inv, fin] **GAP** (PP **PFORM** ?p))

handle relative clauses such as

The man *who we saw at the store*
The exam *in which you found the error*
The man *whose book you stole*

BOX 5.4 Feature Propagation in GPSG

GPSG (generalized phrase structure grammar) (Gazdar et al., 1985) formalizes all feature propagation in terms of a set of general principles. The GAP feature corresponds to the SLASH feature in GPSG. Their claim is that no special mechanism is needed to handle the SLASH feature beyond what is necessary for other features. In particular, the SLASH feature obeys two general GPSG principles. The head feature principle, already discussed, requires all head features to be shared between a head subconstituent and its mother constituent. The foot feature principle requires that if a foot feature appears in any subconstituent, it must be shared with the mother constituent. The constraints on the propagation of the SLASH feature result from it being both a head feature and a foot feature.

GPSG uses meta-rules to derive additional rules from a basic grammar. Meta-rules only apply to rules with lexical heads. One meta-rule accounts for gaps by taking an initial rule, for example,

VP → V NP

and producing a new rule

VP/NP → V NP[+NULL]

where VP/NP is a VP with the SLASH feature NP, and the feature +NULL indicates that the constituent is "phonologically null," that is, not stated or present in the sentence.

GPSG meta-rules are used for other phenomena as well. For example, one meta-rule generates rules for passive voice sentences from rules for active voice sentences, while another generates subject-aux inversion rules from noninverted S rules. Meta-rules play much the same role as transformations, but they are limited to act on only a single rule at a time, and that rule must have a lexical head, whereas transformations may operate on arbitrary trees. The passive meta-rule looks something like this:

VP → V[TRANSITIVE] NP X ⇒
VP[PASSGAP] → V X

Here the symbol X stands for any sequence of constituents. Thus this meta-rule says that if there is a rule for a VP consisting of a transitive verb, an NP, and possibly some other constituents, then there is another rule for a passive VP consisting of the same verb and constituents, except for the NP. As long as there is an upper limit to the number of symbols the variable X can match, you can show that the language described by the grammar expanded by all possible meta-rule applications remains a context-free language.

Because gaps don't propagate into the subject of a sentence, a new rule is needed to allow NPs like *The man who read the paper,* where the wh-word plays the role of subject. This can be covered by the rule

REL → NP[R] VP[fin]

In addition, there is a common class of relative clauses that consist of *that* followed by an S with an NP gap, or a VP, as in *The man that we saw at the party* and *The man that read the paper.* If you allow *that* to be a relative pronoun with WH feature R, then the above rules also cover these cases. Otherwise, additional rules must be added for *that.*

Finally, there are relative clauses that do not start with an appropriate wh-phrase but otherwise look like normal relative clauses. Examples are

The paper *John read*
The damage *caused by the storm*
The issue *creating the argument*

The latter two examples involve what are often called **reduced relative clauses**. These require two additional rules allowing a relative clause to be a finite S with an NP gap or a VP in a participle form:

REL → (S[fin] **GAP** (NP **AGR** ?a))
REL → (VP **VFORM** {ing pastprt})

Notice that now there are two major uses of gaps: one to handle questions and the other to handle relative clauses. Because of this, you should be careful to examine possible interactions between the two. What happens to relative clauses within questions? They certainly can occur, as in

Which dog$_1$ did the man who$_2$ we saw —$_2$ holding the bone feed —$_1$?

The gaps are shown using dashes, and numbers indicate the fillers for the gaps. The existing grammar does allow this sentence, but it is not obvious how, since the GAP feature can only store one constituent at a time and the sentence seems to require storing two. The answer to this puzzle is that the way the GAP feature is propagated does not allow the initial Q constituent to move into the relative clause. This is because REL is not the head of the rule. In particular, the rule

CNP → *CNP* REL

expands to the rule

(CNP **GAP** ?g) → (CNP **GAP** ?g) (REL **GAP** –)

Thus the gap for the question cannot be found in the relative clause. As a result, when a new gap is proposed within the relative clause, there is no problem.

So the mechanism works in this case, but does it capture the structure of English well? In particular, can a question gap ever appear within a relative clause? The generally accepted answer appears to be no. Otherwise, a question like the following would be acceptable:

*Which dog$_1$ did the man$_2$ we saw —$_2$ petting —$_1$ laughed?

So the mechanism proposed here appears to capture the phenomena well.

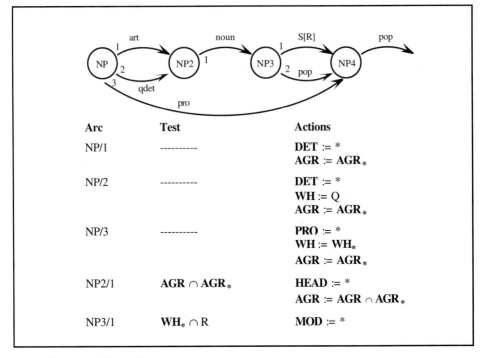

Grammar 5.13 An NP network including wh-words

5.5 The Hold Mechanism in ATNs

Another technique for handling movement was first developed with the ATN framework. A data structure called the **hold list** maintains the constituents that are to be moved. Unlike GAP features, more than one constituent may be on the hold list at a single time. Constituents are added to the hold list by a new action on arcs, the **hold action**, which takes a constituent and places it on the hold list.

The hold action can store a constituent currently in a register (for example, the action HOLD **SUBJ** holds the constituent that is in the **SUBJ** register). To ensure that a held constituent is always used to fill a gap, an ATN system does not allow a pop arc to succeed from a network until any constituent held by an action on an arc in that network has been used. That is, the held constituent must have been used to fill a gap in the current constituent or in one of its subconstituents.

Finally, you need a mechanism to detect and fill gaps. A new arc called VIR (for virtual) that takes a constituent name as an argument can be followed if a constituent of the named category is present on the hold list. If the arc is followed successfully, the constituent is removed from the hold list and returned as the value of the arc in the identical form that a PUSH arc returns a constituent.

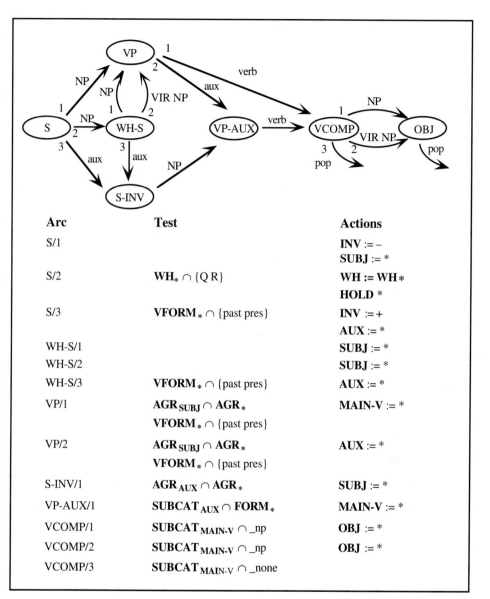

Arc	Test	Actions
S/1		$INV := -$
		$SUBJ := *$
S/2	$WH_* \cap \{Q\ R\}$	$WH := WH*$
		$HOLD *$
S/3	$VFORM_* \cap \{past\ pres\}$	$INV := +$
		$AUX := *$
WH-S/1		$SUBJ := *$
WH-S/2		$SUBJ := *$
WH-S/3	$VFORM_* \cap \{past\ pres\}$	$AUX := *$
VP/1	$AGR_{SUBJ} \cap AGR_*$	$MAIN\text{-}V := *$
	$VFORM_* \cap \{past\ pres\}$	
VP/2	$AGR_{SUBJ} \cap AGR_*$	$AUX := *$
	$VFORM_* \cap \{past\ pres\}$	
S-INV/1	$AGR_{AUX} \cap AGR_*$	$SUBJ := *$
VP-AUX/1	$SUBCAT_{AUX} \cap FORM_*$	$MAIN\text{-}V := *$
VCOMP/1	$SUBCAT_{MAIN\text{-}V} \cap \_np$	$OBJ := *$
VCOMP/2	$SUBCAT_{MAIN\text{-}V} \cap \_np$	$OBJ := *$
VCOMP/3	$SUBCAT_{MAIN\text{-}V} \cap \_none$	

Grammar 5.14   An S network for questions and relative clauses

Grammar 5.13 shows an NP network that recognizes NPs involving wh-words as pronouns or determiners. As with CFGs, the feature WH is set to the value Q to indicate the NP is a wh-NP starting a question. It also accepts relative clauses with a push to the S network, shown in Grammar 5.14. This S network handles yes/no questions, wh-questions, and relative clauses. Wh-questions and relative clauses are processed by putting the initial NP (with a WH feature, Q, or

R) onto the hold list, and later using it in a VIR arc. The network is organized so that all +INV sentences go through node S-INV, while all −INV sentences go through node VP. All wh-questions and relative clauses go through node WH-S and then are redirected back into the standard network based on whether or not the sentence is inverted. The initial NP is put on the hold list when arc S/2 is followed. For noninverted questions, such as *Who ate the pizza?*, and for relative clauses in the NP of form *the man who ate the pizza,* the held NP is immediately used by the VIR arc WH-S/2. For other relative clauses, as in the NP *the man who we saw,* arc WH-S/1 is used to accept the subject in the relative clause, and the held NP is used later on arc VCOMP/2. For inverted questions, such as *Who do I see?*, arc WH-S/3 is followed to accept the auxiliary, and the held NP must be used later.

This network only accepts verbs with SUBCAT values _none and _np but could easily be extended to handle other verb complements. When extended, there would be a much wider range of locations where the held NP might be used. Figure 5.15 shows a trace of the sentence *The man who we saw cried.* In parsing the relative clause, the relative pronoun *who* is held in step 5 and used by a VIR arc in step 8.

Note that this ATN would not accept **Who did the man see the boy?*, as the held constituent *who* is not used by any VIR arc; thus the pop arc from the S network cannot be taken. Similarly, **The man who the boy cried ate the pie* is unacceptable, as the relative pronoun is not used by a VIR arc in the S network that analyzes the relative clause.

Comparing the Methods

You have seen two approaches to handling questions in grammars: the use of the GAP feature and the use of the hold list in ATNs. To decide which is best, we must determine the criteria by which to evaluate them. There are three important considerations: coverage—whether the approach can handle all examples; selectivity—whether it rejects all ill-formed examples; and conciseness—how easily rules can be specified.

Under reasonable assumptions both methods appear to have the necessary coverage, that is, a grammar can be written with either approach that accepts any acceptable sentence. Given that this is the case, the important issues become selectivity and conciseness, and here there are some differences. For instance, one of the underlying assumptions of the GAP feature theory is that a symbol such as NP with an NP gap must be realized as the empty string; that is, you could not have an NP with an NP gap inside it. Such a structure could be parsable using the ATN hold list mechanism. In particular, a sentence such as **Who did the man who saw hit the boy?*, while not comprehensible, would be accepted by the ATN in Grammars 5.13 and 5.14 because the hold list would contain two NPs, one for each occurrence of *who.* In the relative clause, the relative pronoun would be taken as the subject and the initial query NP would be taken as the

Trace of S Network

Step	Node	Position	Arc Followed	Registers
1.	S	1	S/1 (for recursive call see trace below)	**SUBJ** ← (NP **DET** the **HEAD** man **AGR** 3s **MOD** (S who we saw))
11.	VP	6	VP/1	**MAIN-V** ← cried
12.	VCOMP	7	VCOMP/3 succeeds since no words left	returns (S **SUBJ** (NP **DET** the **HEAD** man **AGR** 3p **MOD** (S who we saw)) **MAIN-V** cried)

Trace of First NP Call: Arc S/1

Step	Node	Position	Arc Followed	Registers
2.	NP	1	NP/1	**DET** ← the **AGR** ← {3s 3p}
3.	NP2	2	NP2/1	**HEAD** ← man **AGR** ← 3s
4.	NP3	3	NP3/1 (for recursive call see trace below)	**MOD** ← (S **WH** R **SUBJ** we **MAIN-V** saw **OBJ** who)
10.	NP4	6	NP4/1 pop	returns (NP **DET** the **HEAD** man **AGR** 3s **MOD** (S who we saw))

Trace of Recursive Call to S on Arc NP3/1

Step	Node	Position	Arc Followed	Registers
5.	S	3	S/2 (call to NP network not shown)	**WH** ← {Q R} **HOLDING** (NP **PRO** who **WH** {Q R})
6.	WH-S	4	WH-S/1	**WH** ← R **SUBJ** ← (NP **PRO** we ...)
7.	VP	5	VP/1	**MAIN-V** ← saw
8.	VCOMP	6	VCOMP/2 (uses the NP on the hold list)	**OBJ** ← (NP **PRO** who ...)
9.	OBJ	6	OBJ/1 pop	returns (S **WH** R **SUBJ** we **MAIN-V** saw **OBJ** who)

Figure 5.15 A trace of an ATN parse for $_1$ *The* $_2$ *man* $_3$ *who* $_4$ *we* $_5$ *saw* $_6$ *cried* $_7$

object. This sentence is not acceptable by any grammar using GAP features, however, because the GAP feature cannot be propagated into a relative clause since it is not the head constituent in the rule

CNP → *CNP* REL

Even if it were the head, however, the sentence would still not be acceptable, since the erroneous analysis would require the GAP feature to have two values when it starts analyzing the relative clause.

The hold list mechanism in the ATN framework must be extended to capture these constraints, because there is no obvious way to prevent held constituents from being used anytime they are available. The only possible way to restrict it using the existing mechanism would be to use feature values to keep track of what held constituents are available in each context. This could become quite messy. You can, however, make a simple extension. You can introduce a new action—say, HIDE—that temporarily hides the existing constituents on the hold list until either an explicit action—say, UNHIDE—is executed, or the present constituent is completed. With this extension the ATN grammar to handle relative clauses could be modified to execute a HIDE action just before the hold action that holds the current constituent is performed.

In this case, however, it is not the formalism itself that embodies the constraints. Rather, the formalism is used to state the constraints; it could just as easily describe a language that violates the constraints. The theory based on GAP features, on the other hand, embodies a set of constraints in its definition of how features can propagate. As a result, it would be much more difficult to write a grammar that describes a language that violates the movement constraints.

While a true account of all the movement constraints is still an area of research, this simple analysis makes an important point. If a formalism is too weak, you cannot describe the language at all. If it is too strong, the grammar may become overly complicated in order to eliminate sentence structures that it can describe but that are not possible. The best solution, then, is a formalism that is just powerful enough to describe natural language. In such a language many of the constraints that first appear to be arbitrary restrictions in a language might turn out to be a consequence of the formalism itself and need no further consideration.

While the technique of GAP feature propagation was introduced with context-free grammars, and the hold list mechanism was introduced with ATNs, these techniques are not necessarily restricted to these formalisms. For instance, you could develop an extension to CFGs that incorporates a hold list and uses it for gaps. Likewise, you might be able to develop some rules for GAP feature propagation in an ATN. This would be more difficult, however, since the GAP feature propagation rules depend on the notion of a head subconstituent, which doesn't have a direct correlate in ATN grammars.

5.6　Gap Threading

A third method for handling gaps combines aspects of both the GAP feature approach and the hold list approach. This technique is usually called **gap threading**. It is often used in logic grammars, where two extra argument

1. s(In, Out, FillersIn, FillersOut) :– np(In, In1, FillersIn, Fillers1),
     vp(In1, Out, Fillers1, FillersOut)
2. vp(In, Out, FillersIn, FillersOut) :– v(In, In1)
3. vp(In, Out, FillersIn, FillersOut) :– v(In, In1), np(In1, Out, FillersIn, FillersOut)
4. np(In, Out, Fillers, Fillers) :– art(In, In1), cnp(In1, Out)
5. np(In, Out, Fillers, Fillers) :– pro(In, Out)
6. cnp(In, Out) :– n(In, In1), np-comp(In1, Out)
7. np-comp(In, In) :–
   (This covers the case where there is no NP complement.)
8. np-comp(In, Out) :– rel-intro(In, In1, Filler),
     s(In1, Out, (Filler nil), nil)
   (Here we hold the Rel-Intro constituent, and must use it in the following S.)
9. rel-intro(In, Out, [NP]) :– relpro(In, Out)
   (where relpro accepts any pronoun with WH feature R)
10. np(In, In, [NP | Fillers], Fillers) :–
    (This rule builds an empty np from a filler.)

Grammar 5.16 A logic grammar using gap threading

positions are added to each predicate—one argument for a list of fillers that might be used in the current constituent, and one for the resulting list of fillers that were not used after the constituent is parsed. Thus the predicate

$$s\ (position\text{-}in,\ position\text{-}out,\ fillers\text{-}in,\ fillers\text{-}out)$$

is true only if there is a legal S constituent between *position-in* and *position-out* of the input. If a gap was used to build the S, its filler will be present in *fillers-in,* but not in *fillers-out.* For example, an S constituent with an NP gap would correspond to the predicate s(In, Out, [NP], nil). In cases where there are no gaps in a constituent, the *fillers-in* and *fillers-out* will be identical.

Consider an example dealing with relative clauses. The rules required are shown in Grammar 5.16. The various feature restrictions that would be needed to enforce agreement and subcategorization are not shown so as to keep the example simple.

To see these rules in use, consider the parse of the sentence *The man who we saw cried* in Figure 5.17. The relative clause is analyzed starting with step 7. Using rule 9, the word *who* is recognized as a relative pronoun, and the variable Filler is bound to the list [NP]. This filler is then passed into the embedded S (step 9), to the NP (step 10), and then on to the VP (step 12), since it is not used in the NP. From there it is passed to the NP predicate in step 14, which uses the filler according to rule 10. Note that no other NP rule could have applied at this point, because the filler must be used since the FillersOut variable is nil. Only rules that consume the filler can apply. Once this gap is used, the entire NP from positions 1 to 6 has been found and the rest of the parse is straightforward.

Step	State	Next Operation
1.	s(1, 7, nil, nil)	applying rule 1
2.	np(1, In1,nil, Fillers1) vp(In1, 7, Fillers1, nil)	applying rule 4
3.	art(1, In2) cnp(In2, In1)	proved art(1,2)
4.	cnp(2, In1)	applying rule 6
5.	n(2, In3) np-comp(In3, In1)	proved n(2,3)
6.	np-comp(3, In1)	applying rule 8
7.	rel-intro(3, In4, Filler) s(In4, In1, Filler, nil)	applying rule 9
8.	relpro(3, In4)	proved relpro(3,4)
		proved rel-intro(3,4,[NP])
9.	s(4, In3, [NP], nil)	applying rule 1
10.	np(4, In5, [NP], Fillers1) vp(In5, In1, Fillers1, nil)	
		applying rule 5
11.	pro(4, In5)	proved pro(4,5)
		proved np(4, 5, [NP], [NP])
12.	vp(5, In1,[NP], nil)	applying rule 4
13.	v(5, In6) np(In6, In1, [NP], nil)	proved v(5, 6)
14.	np(6, In1, [NP], nil)	proved np(6, 6, [NP], nil)
		proved vp(5, 6, [NP], nil)
		proved s(4, 6, [NP], nil)
		proved np-comp(3, 6)
		proved cnp(2, 6)
		proved np(1, 6, nil, nil)
15.	vp(6, 7, nil, nil)	applying rule 2
16.	v(6, 7)	proved v(6, 7)
		proved vp(6, 7, nil, nil)
		proved s(1, 7, nil, nil)

Figure 5.17 A trace of the parse of ₁ *The* ₂ *man* ₃ *who* ₄ *we* ₅ *saw* ₆ *cried* ₇

Just as a convenient notation was designed for definite clause grammars, which then could be simply translated into a PROLOG program, a notation has been designed to facilitate the specification of grammars that handle gaps. In particular, there is a formalism called **extraposition grammar**, which, besides allowing normal context-free rules, allows rules of the form

REL-MARK ... TRACE → REL-PRO

which essentially says that the constituent REL-MARK, plus the constituent TRACE later in the sentence, can be rewritten as a REL-PRO. Such a rule violates the tree structure of syntactic forms and allows the analysis shown in Figure 5.18 of the NP *the mouse that the cat ate*. Such rules can be compiled into a logic grammar using the gap-threading technique.

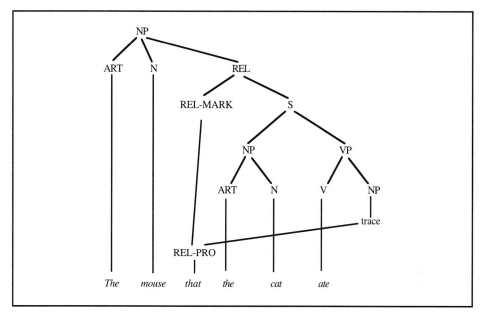

Figure 5.18 A parse tree in extraposition grammar

Consider how gap threading compares with the other approaches. Of course, by using additional arguments on predicates, any of the approaches could be implemented. If viewed as simply an implementation technique, then the gap-threading approach looks like a way to implement a hold list in a logic grammar. Since the grammar designer can decide to propagate the hold list or not in the grammar, it provides the flexibility to avoid some of the problems with the simple hold list mechanism. For instance, Grammar 5.16 does not pass the fillers from outside a noun phrase into its relative clause. So problems like those discussed in the last section can be avoided. It also would be possible to adopt the GAP feature introduction algorithm described in Section 5.3 so that it introduces gap-threading rules into a logic grammar. Thus, the approach provides the grammar writer with great flexibility. Like the hold list approach, however, the propagation constraints must be explicitly enforced rather than being a consequence of the formalism.

Summary

Many of the complex aspects of natural language can be treated as movement phenomena, where a constituent in one position is used to satisfy the constraints at another position. These phenomena are divided into two classes: bounded movement, including yes/no questions and passives; and unbounded movement, including wh-questions and relative clauses. The computational techniques developed for handling movement allow significant generalities to be captured between all of these different sentential forms. By using the feature system carefully, a basic grammar of declarative sentences can be extended to handle the other forms with only a few rules. Three different techniques were introduced to handle such phenomena. The first was the use of the special feature propagation rules using a feature called GAP. The second was the hold list mechanism in ATNs, which involves adding a new action (the hold action) and a new arc type (the VIR arc). The third involved gap threading, with a hold-list-like structure passed from constituent to constituent using features. With suitable care, all of these approaches have been used successfully to build grammars of English with substantial coverage.

Related Work and Further Readings

The phenomena of unbounded dependencies has motivated a significant amount of research into grammatical formalisms. These fall roughly into several categories, depending on how close the grammar remains to the context-free grammars. Theories such as transformational grammar (Chomsky, 1965; Radford, 1981), for example, propose to handle unbounded dependencies completely outside the CFG framework. Theories such as lexical functional grammar (Kaplan and Bresnan, 1982) and generalized phrase structure grammar (GPSG) (Gazdar, 1982; Gazdar et al., 1985) propose methods of capturing the dependencies with the CFG formalism using features. There has also been considerable work in defining new formalisms that are slightly more powerful than context-free grammars and can handle long-distance dependencies such as tree-adjoining grammars (TAGs) (see Box 5.5) and combinatory categorial grammars (Steedman, 1987).

The first reasonably comprehensive computational study of movement phenomena was in the ATN framework by Woods (1970). He went to some length to show that much of the phenomena accounted for by transformational grammar (Chomsky, 1965) could be parsed in ATNs using register testing and setting together with a hold list mechanism. The ATN section of this chapter is a simplified and cleaned-up account of that paper, incorporating later work by Kaplan (1973). Alternative presentations of ATNs can also be found in Bates (1978) and Winograd (1983).

Similar augmentation techniques have been adapted to systems based on CFGs, although in practice many of these systems have accepted many structures that are not reasonable sentences. This is because the grammars are built so that constituents are optional even in contexts where there could be no movement. The parser then depends on some ad hoc feature manipulation to eliminate some of these false positives, or on semantic interpretation to reject the ill-formed sentences that were accepted. A good example of how much can be done with this approach is provided by Robinson (1982).

BOX 5.5 Tree-Adjoining Grammar

Another approach to handling unbounded dependencies is **tree-adjoining grammars** (TAGs) (Joshi, 1985). There are no grammar rules in this formalism. Rather, there is a set of initial tree structures that describe the simplest sentences of the language, and a tree operation, called **adjoining**, that inserts one tree into another to create a more complex structure. For example, a simple initial tree is

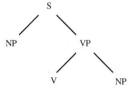

More complex sentences are derived using auxiliary trees, which capture the minimal forms of recursion in the language. For example, an auxiliary tree for allowing an adverbial in a verb phrase could be

The adjunction operation involves inserting an auxiliary tree-capturing recursion of some constituent C into another tree that contains a constituent C. Adjoining the auxiliary tree for VP above into the initial tree for S produces the new tree

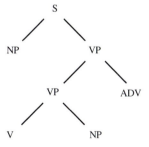

By basing the formalism on trees, enough context is provided to capture long-distance dependencies. In this theory there is no movement. Instead the constituents start off being close to each other, and then additional structure is inserted between them by the adjoining operation. The result is a formalism of slightly greater power than CFGs but definitely weaker than context-sensitive grammars.

The work on handling movement using gap threading and the definition of extraposition grammars can be found in Pereira (1981). Similar techniques can be found in many current parsers (such as Alshawi, 1992).

The section on using GAP feature propagation to handle movement is motivated from GPSG (Gazdar et al., 1985). In GPSG the propagation of features is determined by a set of general principles (see Box 5.4). **Head-driven phrase structure grammar** (Pollard and Sag, 1987; 1993) is a descendant of GPSG that is more oriented toward computational issues. It uses subcategorization information on the heads of phrases extensively and, by so doing, greatly simplifies the context-free grammar at the expense of a more complex lexicon.

Exercises for Chapter 5

1. (*easy*) Distinguish between bounded (local) movement and unbounded (nonlocal) movement. What extensions were added to the augmentation system to enable it to handle unbounded movement? Why is wh-movement called unbounded movement? Give examples to support your claim.

2. (*easy*) Expand the following abbreviated constituents and rules into their full feature structure format.

   (S[–inv, Q] **AGR** ?a)
   NP[R, –gap]
   VP → V[_np_s:inf] NP S[inf]

3. (*medium*) Using the grammar developed in Section 5.3, show the analyses of the following questions in chart form, as shown in Figure 5.12:

   In which town were you born?
   Where were you born?
   When did they leave?
   What town were you born in?

4. (*medium*) GPSG allows certain rules to have multiple head subconstituents. For instance, the rule for a conjunction between two verb phrases would contain two heads:

   VP → *VP* and *VP*

   a   How does the presence of multiple heads affect the algorithm that produces the propagation of the GAP feature? In order to answer this question, consider some examples, such as the following sentences:

   Who did you see and give the book to?
   What man did Mary hate and Sue love?

   Also consider that the following sentences are ill-formed:

   *Who did you see and give the book to John?
   *What man did Mary hate John and Sue love?

   b.   Write out the VP rule showing the GAP features, and then draw the chart for the sentence

Who did Mary see and Sue see?

using Grammar 5.8 augmented with your rule. You need only show the constituents that are used in the final analysis, but be sure to show all the feature values for each constituent.

5. (*medium*) Another phenomenon that requires a movement analysis is topicalization, which allows sentences of the form

John, Mary saw.
To John, Mary told the story.

a. Argue that the same type of constraints that apply to wh-questions apply to topicalization. This establishes that the GAP feature propagation technique can be used.

b. Do you need to introduce a new GAP-like feature to handle topicalization, or can the same GAP feature used for questions and relative clauses be re-used?

c. Extend Grammar 5.8 to accept the forms of topicalization shown in the examples.

6. (*medium*) Consider the following ATN grammar for sentences. On arc NP3/1 there is the action of holding the current noun phrase.

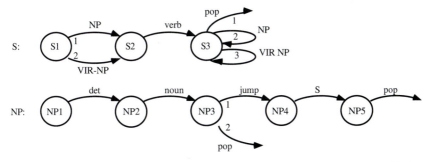

a. Give a sequence of legal sentences that can be made arbitrarily long and still be accepted by this ATN.

b. Which of the following sentences would be accepted by this ATN (assuming appropriate word categories for words)? For those that are accepted, outline the structure of the sentence as parsed by the network (that is, a plausible register value structure).

i. The man Mary hit hit the ball.
ii. The man the man hit the man hit.
iii. The man hit hit.
iv. Hit the man hit the man.

7. (*hard*) The following noun phrases arise in some dialogues between a computer operator and various users of the computer system.

> Could you mount *a magtape* for me?

> *No ring* please.

> I am not exactly sure of *the reason,* but we were given *a list of users we are not supposed to mount magtapes for,* and you are on it.

> Could you possibly retrieve *the following two files*? I think *they* were on *our directory* last night.

> Any chance I can recover from *the most recent system dump*?

Extend the grammar developed in Sections 5.3 and 5.4 so that it accepts these noun phrases. Give lexicon entries for all the new words in the noun phrases, and show the final charts that result from parsing each NP.

8. (*hard*)

   a   The grammar for parsing the auxiliary verb structure in English developed in Section 5.1 cannot handle phrases of the following form:

> Jack *has to see* a doctor.
> The cat *had to be found.*
> Joe *has to be winning* the race.
> The book *would have had to have been found* by Jack.

Extend the grammar such that it accepts the preceding auxiliary sequences yet does not accept unacceptable sentences such as

> *Jack *has to have to see* a doctor.
> *Janet *had to played* the violin.
> *Will *would to go* to the movies.

   b.   Perform a similar analysis, showing examples and counterexamples, of the use of phrases of the form *be going to* within the auxiliary system.

Toward Efficient Parsing

6.1   Human Preferences in Parsing

6.2   Encoding Uncertainty: Shift-Reduce Parsers

6.3   A Deterministic Parser

6.4   Techniques for Efficient Encoding of Ambiguity

6.5   Partial Parsing

All the parsing frameworks discussed so far have depended on complete search techniques to find possible interpretations of a sentence. Such search processes do not correspond well with many people's intuitions about human processing of language. In particular, human parsing seems closer to a **deterministic** process—that is, a process that doesn't extensively search through alternatives but rather uses the information it has at the time to choose the correct interpretation. While intuitions about our own perceptual processes are known to be highly unreliable, experimental evidence also suggests that people do not perform a complete search of a grammar while parsing. This chapter examines some ways of making parsers more efficient, and in some cases, deterministic. If syntactic parsing is not your focus, this entire chapter can be treated as optional material.

There are two different issues that are of concern. The first involves improving the efficiency of parsing algorithms by reducing the search but not changing the final outcome, and the second involves techniques for choosing between different interpretations that the parser might be able to find. Both will be examined in this chapter.

Section 6.1 explores the notion of using preferences in parsers to select certain interpretations, sometimes at the cost of eliminating other possible interpretations. Evidence for this type of model is drawn from psycholinguistic theories concerning the human parsing process. This provides the background for the techniques discussed in the rest of the chapter. Section 6.2 explores one method for improving the efficiency of parsers by pre-compiling much of the search into tables. These techniques are used in shift-reduce parsers, which are used for parsing programming languages. These techniques can be generalized to handle ambiguity and used for natural languages as well. Section 6.3 describes a fully deterministic parsing framework that parses sentences without a recourse to backtracking. This means that the parser might make mistakes and fail to find interpretations for some sentences. If the technique works correctly, however, only sentences that people tend to misparse will be misparsed by the system. Section 6.4 looks at a variety of techniques to efficiently represent ambiguity by "collapsing" interpretations, or by eliminating ambiguity by redefining the goals of syntactic parsing. Section 6.5 looks at techniques of partially parsing the input by analyzing only those aspects of a sentence that can be determined reliably.

6.1   Human Preferences in Parsing

So far this book has discussed parsing in the abstract, without regard to any psychological evidence concerning how people parse sentences. Pycholinguists have conducted many investigations into this issue using a variety of techniques, from intuitions about preferred interpretations to detailed experiments monitoring moment-by-moment processing as subjects read and listen to language. These studies have revealed some general principles concerning how people resolve ambiguity.

1.1	S → NP VP	1.4	NP → ART N
1.2	VP → V NP PP	1.5	NP → NP PP
1.3	VP → V NP	1.6	PP → P NP

Grammar 6.1 A simple CFG

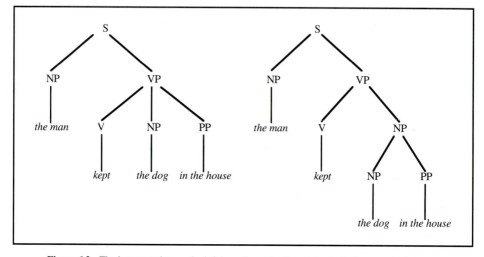

Figure 6.2 The interpretation on the left is preferred by the minimal attachment principle

The most basic result from these studies is that people do not give equal weight to all possible syntactic interpretations. This can be illustrated by sentences that are temporarily ambiguous, which cause a conscious feeling of having pursued the wrong analysis, as in the sentence *The raft floated down the river sank*. When you read the word *sank* you realize that the interpretation you have constructed so far for the sentence is not correct. In the literature, such sentences are often called **garden-path** sentences, based on the expression about leading someone down a garden path. Here are a few of the general principles that appear to predict when garden paths will arise.

Minimal Attachment

The most general principle is called the **minimal attachment** principle, which states that there is a preference for the syntactic analysis that creates the least number of nodes in the parse tree. Thus, given Grammar 6.1, the sentence *The man kept the dog in the house* would be interpreted with the PP *in the house* modifying the verb rather than the NP *the dog*. These two interpretations are shown in Figure 6.2. The interpretation with the PP attached to the VP is derived using rules 1.1, 1.2, and 1.6 and three applications of rule 1.4 for the NPs. The parse tree has a total of 14 nodes. The interpretation with the PP attached to the

NP is derived using rules 1.1, 1.3, 1.5, and 1.6 and three applications of rule 1.4, producing a total of 15 nodes in the parse tree. Thus this principle predicts that the first interpretation is preferred, which probably agrees with your intuition.

This principle appears to be so strong that it can cause certain sentences to be almost impossible to parse correctly. One example is the sentence

We painted all the walls with cracks.

which, against all common sense, is often read as meaning that cracks were painted onto the walls, or that cracks were somehow used as an instrument to paint the walls. Both these anomalous readings arise from the PP being attached to the VP (*paint*) rather than the NP (*the walls*). Another classic example is the sentence

The horse raced past the barn fell.

which has a reasonable interpretation corresponding to the meaning of the sentence *The horse that was raced past the barn fell.* In the initial sentence, however, creating a reduced relative clause when the word *raced* is encountered introduces many more nodes than the simple analysis where *raced* is the main verb of the sentence. Of course, this second interpretation renders the sentence unanalyzable when the word *fell* is encountered.

Right Association

The second principle is called **right association** or **late closure**. This principle states that, all other things being equal, new constituents tend to be interpreted as being part of the current constituent under construction (rather than part of some constituent higher in the parse tree). Thus, given the sentence

George said that Henry left in his car.

the preferred interpretation is that Henry left in the car rather than that George spoke in the car. Both interpretations are, of course, syntactically acceptable analyses. The two interpretations are shown in Figure 6.3. The former attaches the PP to the VP immediately preceding it, whereas the latter attaches the PP to the VP higher in the tree. Thus the right association principle prefers the former. Similarly, the preferred interpretation for the sentence *I thought it would rain yesterday* is that yesterday was when it was thought to rain, rather than the time of the thinking.

Lexical Preferences

In certain cases the two preceding principles seem to conflict with each other. In the sentence *The man kept the dog in the house,* the principle of right association appears to favor the interpretation in which the PP modifies the dog, while the minimal attachment principle appears to favor the PP modifying the VP. You

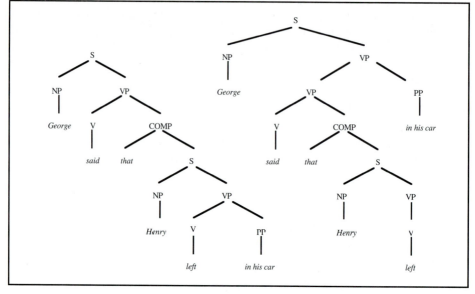

Figure 6.3 Two interpretations of *George said that Henry left in his car.*

might suggest that minimal attachment takes priority over right association in such cases; however, the relationship appears to be more complex than that. Consider the sentences

1. I wanted the dog in the house.
2. I kept the dog in the house.
3. I put the dog in the house.

The PP *in the house* in sentence 1 seems most likely to be modifying *dog* (although the other interpretation is possible, as in the sense *I wanted the dog to be in the house*). In sentence 2, the PP seems most likely to be modifying the VP (although modifying the NP is possible, as in *I kept the dog that was in the house*). Finally, in sentence 3, the PP is definitely attached to the VP, and no alternative reading is possible.

These examples demonstrate that lexical items, in this case the verb used, can influence parsing preferences. In many cases, the **lexical preferences** will override the preferences based on the general principles. For example, if a verb subcategorizes for a prepositional phrase, then some PP must be attached to the VP. Other PPs might also be identified as having a strong preference for attachment within the VP. If neither of these cases holds, the PP will be attached according to the general principles.

Thus, for the preceding verbs, *want* has no preference for any PPs, whereas *keep* might prefer PPs with prepositions *in, on,* or *by* to be attached to the VP. Finally, the verb *put* requires (subcategorizes for) a PP beginning with *in, on, by,* and so on, which must be attached to the VP. This approach has promise but is

2.1 $S \rightarrow NP\ VP$ 2.3 $VP \rightarrow AUX\ V\ NP$
2.2 $NP \rightarrow ART\ N$ 2.4 $VP \rightarrow V\ NP$

Grammar 6.4 A simple grammar with an AUX/V ambiguity

hard to evaluate without developing some formal framework that allows such information to be expressed in a uniform way. Such techniques will be addressed in the next chapter.

6.2 Encoding Uncertainty: Shift-Reduce Parsers

One way to improve the efficiency of parsers is to use techniques that encode uncertainty, so that the parser need not make an arbitrary choice and later backtrack. Rather, the uncertainty is passed forward through the parse to the point where the input eliminates all but one of the possibilities. If you did this explicitly at parse time, you would have an algorithm similar to the breadth-first parser described in Chapter 3. The efficiency of the technique described in this section arises from the fact that all the possibilities are considered in advance, and the information is stored in a table that controls the parser, resulting in parsing algorithms that can be much faster than described thus far.

These techniques were developed for use with unambiguous context-free grammars—grammars for which there is at most one interpretation for any given sentence. While this constraint is reasonable for programming languages, it is clear that there is no unambiguous grammar for natural language. But these techniques can be extended in various ways to make them applicable to natural language parsing.

Specifying the Parser State

Consider using this approach on the small grammar in Grammar 6.4. The technique involves predetermining all possible parser states and determining the transitions from one state to another. A parser state is defined as the complete set of dotted rules (that is, the labels on the active arcs in a chart parser) applicable at that position in the parse. It is complete in the sense that if a state contains a rule of the form $Y \rightarrow \ldots \circ X \ldots$, where X is a nonterminal, then all rules for X are also contained in the state. For instance, the initial state of the parser would include the rule

$$S \rightarrow \circ\ NP\ VP$$

as well as all the rules for NP, which in Grammar 6.4 is only

$$NP \rightarrow \circ\ ART\ N$$

Thus the initial state, S0, could be summarized as follows:

Initial State S0:   S → ° NP VP

NP → ° ART N

In other words, the parser starts in a state where it is looking for an NP to start building an S and looking for an ART to build the NP. What states could follow this initial state? To calculate this, consider advancing the dot over a terminal or a nonterminal and deriving a new state. If you pick the symbol ART, the resulting state is

State S1:   NP → ART ° N

If you pick the symbol NP, the rule is

S → NP ° VP

in the new state. Now if you expand out the VP to find all its possible starting symbols, you get the following:

State S2:   S → NP ° VP

VP → ° AUX V NP

VP → ° V NP

Now, expanding S1, if you have the input N, you get a state consisting of a completed rule:

State S1':   NP → ART N °

Expanding S2, a V would result in the state

State S3:   VP → V ° NP

NP → ° ART N

An AUX from S2 would result in the state

State S4:   VP → AUX ° V NP

and a VP from S2 would result in the state

State S2':   S → NP VP °

Continuing from state S3 with an ART, you find yourself in state S1 again, as you would also if you expand from S0 with an ART. Continuing from S3 with an NP, on the other hand, yields the new state

State S3':   VP → V NP °

Continuing from S4 with a V yields

State S5:   VP → AUX V ° NP

NP → ° ART N

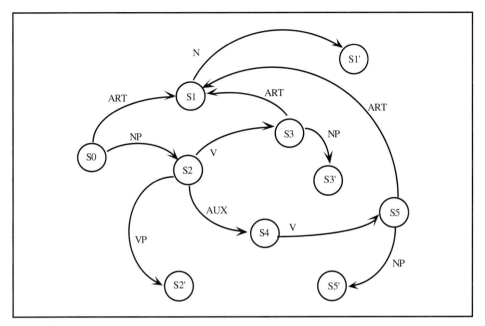

Figure 6.5 A transition graph derived from Grammar 6.1

and continuing from S5 with an ART would produce state S1 again. Finally, continuing from S5 with an NP would produce the state

State S5': VP $\rightarrow$ AUX V NP $\circ$

Now that this process is completed, you can derive a transition graph that can be used to control the parsing of sentences, as is shown in Figure 6.5.

A Shift-Reduce Parser

These states can be used to control a parser that maintains two stacks: the **parse stack**, which contains parse states (that is, the nodes in Figure 6.5) and grammar symbols; and the **input stack**, which contains the input and some grammar symbols. At any time the parser operates using the information specified for the top state on the parse stack.

The states are interpreted as follows. The states that consist of a single rule with the dot at the far right-hand side, such as S2',

S $\rightarrow$ NP VP $\circ$

indicate that the parser should rewrite the top symbols on the parse stack according to this rule. This is called a **reduce action**. The newly derived symbol (S in this case) is pushed onto the top of the input stack.

Any other state not containing any completed rules is interpreted by the transition diagram. If the top input symbol matches an arc, then it and the new

State	Top Input Symbol	Action	GoTo
S0	ART	Shift	S1
S0	NP	Shift	S2
S0	S	Shift	S0'
S0'	ε	Succeed	-----
S1	N	Shift	S1'
S1'	----------	Reduce by rule 2.2	-----
S2	V	Shift	S3
S2	AUX	Shift	S4
S2	VP	Shift	S2'
S2'	----------	Reduce by rule 2.1	-----
S3	ART	Shift	S1
S3	NP	Shift	S3'
S3'	----------	Reduce by rule 2.4	-----
S4	V	Shift	S5
S5	ART	Shift	S1
S5	NP	Shift	S5'
S5'	----------	Reduce by rule 2.3	-----

Figure 6.6 The oracle for Grammar 6.4

state (at the end of the arc) are pushed onto the parse stack. This is called the **shift action**. Using this interpretation of states you can construct a table, called the **oracle**, that tells the parser what to do in every situation. The oracle for Grammar 6.4 is shown in Figure 6.6. For each state and possible input, it specifies the action and the next state. Reduce actions can be applied regardless of the next input, and the accept action only is possible when the input stack is empty (that is, the next symbol is the empty symbol ε). The parsing algorithm for using an oracle is specified in Figure 6.7.

Consider parsing *The man ate the carrot.* The initial state of the parser is

Parse Stack   **Input Stack**

(S0)   (The man ate the carrot)

Looking up the entry in the table in Figure 6.6 for state S0 for the input ART (the category of the word *the*), you see a shift action and a move to state S1:

Parse Stack   **Input Stack**

(S1 ART S0)   (man ate the carrot)

Looking up the entry for state S1 for the input N, you see a shift action and a move to state S1':

This algorithm uses the following information:

- $Action(S, W)$—a function that maps a state and an input constituent to one of the values *shift, reduce i,* or *accept*
- $GoTo(S, W)$—a function that maps a state and an input constituent to a new state
- a parse stack of form $(S_n C_n \ldots S_1 C_1 S_0)$, where S_i are parse states and C_i are constituents
- an input stack of form $(W_1 \ldots W_n)$, where W_i is a constituent symbol or word

The parser operates by continually executing the following steps until success or failure:

1. If $Action(S_n, W_1) = Shift$, and $GoTo(S_n, W_1) = S$, then remove W_1 from the input stack and push it on the parse stack, and then push S onto the parse stack, resulting in the following stacks:

    parse stack: $(S W_1 S_n C_n \ldots S_1 C_1 S_0)$
    input stack: $(W_2 \ldots W_n)$

2. If $Action(S_n, W_1) = Reduce\ i$ and grammar rule i has n constituents on its right-hand side, then remove 2n elements from the parse stack, and push the left-hand side of rule i onto the input stack. For example, if rule i were NP $\rightarrow$ ART N, then the new state would be

    parse stack: $(S_{n-2} C_{n-2} \ldots S_1 C_1 S_0)$
    input stack: $(NP W_1 \ldots W_n)$

3. If $Action(S_n, W_1) = Accept,$ then the parser has succeeded.

4. If $Action(S_n, W_1)$ is not defined, then the parser has failed.

Figure 6.7 The parsing algorithm for a shift-reduce parser

Parse Stack	Input Stack
(S1' N S1 ART S0)	(ate the carrot)

Looking up the entry for state S1', you then reduce by rule 2.2, which removes the S1', N, S1, and ART from the parse stack and adds NP to the input stack:

Parse Stack	Input Stack
(S0)	(NP ate the carrot)

Again, consulting the table for state S0 with input NP, you now do a shift and move to state S2:

Parse Stack	Input Stack
(S2 NP S0)	(ate the carrot)

Next, the three remaining words all cause shifts and a move to a new state, ending up with the parse state:

Parse Stack	Input Stack
(S1' N S1 ART S3 V S2 NP S0)	( )

The reduce action by rule 2.2 specified in state S1' pops the N and ART from the stack (thereby popping S1 and S1' as well), producing the state:

Parse Stack	**Input Stack**
(S3 V S2 NP S0)	(NP)

You are now back at state S3, with an NP in the input, and after a shift to state S3', you reduce by rule 2.4, producing:

Parse Stack	**Input Stack**
(S2 NP S0)	(VP)

Finally, from state S2 you shift to state S2' and reduce by rule 2.1, producing:

Parse Stack	**Input Stack**
(S0)	(S)

From this state you shift to state S0' and are in a position to accept the sentence.

You have parsed the sentence without ever trying a rule in the grammar incorrectly and without ever constructing a constituent that is not part of the final analysis.

Shift-Reduce Parsers and Ambiguity

Shift-reduce parsers are efficient because the algorithm can delay decisions about which rule to apply. For example, if you had the following rules for parsing an NP,

1. NP $\rightarrow$ ART N REL-PRO VP
2. NP $\rightarrow$ ART N PP

a top-down parser would have to generate two new active arcs, both of which would be extended if an ART were found in the input. The shift-reduce parser, on the other hand, represents both using a single state, namely

NP1:   NP $\rightarrow$ ° ART N REL-PRO VP
           NP $\rightarrow$ ° ART N PP

If an ART is found, the next state will be

NP2:   NP $\rightarrow$ ART ° N REL-PRO VP
           NP $\rightarrow$ ART ° N PP

Thus the ART can be recognized and shifted onto the parse stack without committing to which rule it is used in. Similarly, if an N is seen at state NP2, the state is

NP3:   NP $\rightarrow$ ART N ° REL-PRO VP
           NP $\rightarrow$ ART N ° PP
           PP $\rightarrow$ ° P NP

Now from NP3, you finally can distinguish the cases. If a REL-PRO is found next, the state is

NP4:   NP → ART N REL-PRO ° VP
            VP → ° V NP

which leads eventually to a reduction by rule 1. If a P is found, you move to a different state, which eventually builds a PP that is used in the reduction by rule 2. Thus the parser delays the decision until sufficient information is available to choose between rules.

Lexical Ambiguity

This ability to postpone decisions can be used to deal with some lexical ambiguity by a simple extension to the parsing process. Whereas earlier you classified a lexical entry when it was shifted (that is, *carrot* was converted to N during the shift), you now allow ambiguous words to be shifted onto the parse stack as they are, and delay their categorization until a reduction involving them is made.

To accomplish this extension, you must expand the number of states to include states that deal with ambiguities. For instance, if *can* could be a V or an AUX, the oracle cannot determine a unique action to perform from state S2—if it were a V you would shift to state S3 and if it were an AUX you would shift to state S4. Such ambiguities can be encoded, however, by generating a new state from S2 to cover both possibilities simultaneously. This new state will be the union of states S3 and S4:

S3–4:   VP → AUX ° V NP
             VP → V ° NP
             NP → ° ART N

In this case the next input should resolve the ambiguity. If you see a V next, you will move to S5 (just as you would from state S4). If you see an ART next, you will move to S1, and if you see an NP next, you will move to S3' (just as you would from S3). Thus the new state maintains the ambiguity long enough for succeeding words to resolve the problem. Of course, in general, the next word might also be ambiguous, so the number of new states could be quite large. But if the grammar is unambiguous—that is, there is only one possible interpretation of the sentence once it is completely parsed—this technique can be used to delay the decisions as long as necessary. (In fact, for those who know automata theory, this process is simply the construction of a deterministic simulation of a nondeterministic finite automata.)

Ambiguous Parse States

There are, however, other forms of ambiguity that this parser, as it now stands, is not able to handle. The simplest examples involve the ambiguity that arises when one rule is a proper prefix of another, such as the rules

3.   NP → ART N
4.   NP → ART N PP

With these two rules, we will generate a parse state containing the two dotted rules

NP → ART ∘ N
NP → ART ∘ N PP

If the next input in this state is an N, you would move to a state consisting of

NP5:   NP → ART N ∘
            NP → ART N ∘ PP
            PP → ∘ P PP

But now there is a problem. If the next input is a P, eventually a PP will be built and you return to state NP5. But the parser cannot decide whether to reduce by rule 3, leaving the PP to be attached later, or to shift the PP (and then reduce by rule 4). In any reasonable grammar of English, of course, both choices might lead to acceptable parses of the sentence. There are two ways to deal with this problem. The first strategy maintains a deterministic parser and accepts the fact that it may misparse certain sentences. The goal here is to model human parsing performance and fail on only those that would give people trouble. One recent suggestion claims the following heuristics favor more intuitive interpretations over less intuitive ones:

- favor shift operations over reduce operations
- resolve all reduce-reduce conflicts in favor of the longest rule (that is, the one that uses the most symbols from the stack)

Using these strategies, you could build a deterministic parser that picks the most favored rule and ignores the others. It has been claimed that the first heuristic corresponds to the right-association preference and the second to the minimal-attachment preference. While convincing examples can be shown to illustrate this, remember that the strategies themselves, and thus the examples, are highly sensitive to the form of the grammar used.

The second approach to dealing with the ambiguous states is to abandon the deterministic requirement and reintroduce a search. In this case you could consider each alternative by either a depth-first search with backtracking or a breadth-first search maintaining several interpretations in parallel. Both of these approaches can yield efficient parsers. The depth-first approach can be integrated with the preference strategies so that the preferred interpretations are tried first.

6.3   A Deterministic Parser

A deterministic parser can be built that depends entirely on matching parse states to direct its operation. Instead of allowing only shift and reduce actions, however, a richer set of actions is allowed that operates on an input stack called the **buffer**.

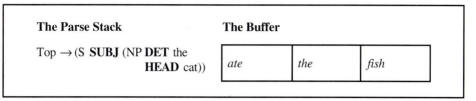

Figure 6.8 A situation during a parse

Rather than shifting constituents onto the parse stack to be later consumed by a reduce action, the parser builds constituents incrementally by **attaching** buffer elements into their parent constituent, an operation similar to feature assignment. Rather than shifting an NP onto the stack to be used later in a reduction S → NP VP, an S constituent is created on the parse stack and the NP is attached to it. Specifically, this parser has the following operations:

- **Create** a new node on the parse stack (to push the symbol onto the stack)
- **Attach** an input constituent to the top node on the parse stack
- **Drop** the top node in the parse stack into the buffer

The drop action allows a completed constituent to be reexamined by the parser, which will then assign it a role in a higher constituent still on the parse stack. This technique makes the limited lookahead technique surprisingly powerful.

To get a feeling for these operations, consider the situation in Figure 6.8, which might occur in parsing the sentence *The cat ate the fish.* Assume that the first NP has been parsed and assigned to the **SUBJ** feature of the S constituent on the parse stack. The operations introduced earlier can be used to complete the analysis. Note that the actual mechanism for deciding what operations to do has not yet been discussed, but the effect of the operations is shown here to provide intuition about the data structure. The operation

Attach to **MAIN-V**

would remove the lexical entry for *ate* from the buffer and assign it to the **MAIN-V** feature in the S on the parse stack. Next the operation

Create NP

would push an empty NP constituent onto the parse stack, creating the situation in Figure 6.9.

Next the two operations

Attach to **DET**
Attach to **HEAD**

would successfully build the NP from the lexical entries for *the* and *fish*. The input buffer would now be empty.

The Parse Stack

Top → (NP)

      (S **SUBJ** (NP **DET** the
              HEAD cat)
     MAIN-V ate)

The Buffer

the	*fish*	

Figure 6.9 After creating an NP

The Parse Stack

Top → (S **SUBJ** (NP **DET** the
              HEAD cat)
     MAIN-V ate)

The Buffer

(NP **DET** the **HEAD** fish)		

Figure 6.10 After the drop action

The operation

Drop

pops the NP from the parse stack and pushes it back onto the buffer, creating the situation in Figure 6.10.

The parser is now in a situation to build the final structure with the operation

Attach to **OBJ**

which takes the NP from the buffer and assigns it to the **OBJ** slot in the S constituent.

Three other operations prove very useful in capturing generalizations in natural languages:

- **Switch** the nodes in the first two buffer positions
- **Insert** a specific lexical item into a specified buffer slot
- **Insert** an empty NP into the first buffer slot

Each rule has a pattern that contains feature checks on the buffer to determine the applicability of the rule. Rules are organized into **packets**, which may be activated or deactivated during the parse. Additional actions are available for changing the parser state by selecting which packets to use. In particular, there are actions to

- **Activate** a packet (that is, all its rules are to be used to interpret the next input)
- **Deactivate** a packet

Pattern	Actions	Priority
Packet BUILD-AUX:		
1. <=AUX, HAVE> <=V, pastprt>	Attach to **PERF**	10
2. <=AUX, BE> <=V, ing>	Attach to **PROG**	10
3. <=AUX, BE> <=V, pastprt>	Attach to **PASSIVE**	10
4. <=AUX, +modal> <=V, inf>	Attach to **MODAL**	10
5. <=AUX, DO> <=V, inf>	Attach to **DO**	10
6. <true>	Drop	15

Grammar 6.11 The rules for packet BUILD-AUX

The active packets are associated with the symbols on the parse stack. If a new constituent is created (that is, pushed on the stack), all the active packets associated with the previous top of the stack become inactive until that constituent is again on the top of the stack. Consequently, the drop action will always deactivate the rules associated with the top node. Packets play a role similar to the states in the shift-reduce parser. Unlike the states in the shift-reduce parser, more than one packet may be active at a time. Thus there would be no need to create packets consisting of the union of packets to deal with word ambiguity, since both can be active simultaneously.

Consider the example rules shown in Grammar 6.11, which deals with parsing the auxiliary structure. The pattern for each rule indicates the feature tests that must succeed on each buffer position for the rule to be applicable. Thus the pattern <=AUX, HAVE> <=V, pastprt> is true only if the first buffer is an AUX structure with ROOT feature value HAVE, and the second is a V structure with the VFORM feature pastprt. The priority associated with each rule is used to decide between conflicting rules. The lower the number, the higher the priority. In particular, rule 6, with the pattern <true>, will always match, but since its priority is low, it will never be used if another one of the rules also matches. It simply covers the case when none of the rules match, and it completes the parsing of the auxiliary and verb structure.

Figure 6.12 shows a parse state in which the state BUILD-AUX is active. It contains an AUXS structure on the top of the stack with packet BUILD-AUX active, and an S structure below with packets PARSE-AUX and CPOOL that will become active once the AUXS constituent is dropped into the buffer.

Given this situation and the rules in Figure 6.11, the parser's next action is determined by seeing which rules match. Rules 1 and 6 succeed, and 1 is chosen because of its higher priority. Applying the actions of rule 1 produces the state in Figure 6.13. Now the rules in BUILD-AUX are applied again. This time only rule 6 succeeds, so the next action is a drop, creating the state in Figure 6.14.

At this stage the rules in packets PARSE-AUX and CPOOL are active; they compete to determine the next move of the parser (which would be to attach the AUXS structure into the S structure).

The Parse Stack

Nodes

Top → (AUXS)

 (S **MOOD** DECL
  SUBJ (NP **NAME** John))

Active Packets

(BUILD-AUX)

(PARSE-AUX CPOOL)

The Input Buffer

(AUX **ROOT** HAVE **FORM** pres **NUM** {3s})	(V **ROOT** SEE **FORM** en)	(ART **ROOT** A **NUM** {3s})

Figure 6.12 A typical state of the parser

The Parse Stack

Nodes

Top → (AUXS **PERF** has)

 (S **MOOD** DECL
 (S **SUBJ** (NP **NAME** John))

Active Packets

(BUILD-AUX)

(PARSE-AUX CPOOL)

The Input Buffer

(V **ROOT** SEE **VFORM** pastprt)	(ART **ROOT** A **NUM** {3s})	(N **ROOT** DAY **NUM** {3s})

Figure 6.13 After rule 1 is applied

The Parse Stack

Nodes

Top → (S **MOOD** DECL
  SUBJ (NP **NAME** John))

Active Packets

(PARSE-AUX CPOOL)

The Input Buffer

(AUXS **PERF** has)	(V **ROOT** SEE **VFORM** pastprt)	(ART **ROOT** A **NUM** {3s})

Figure 6.14 The parse state after a drop action

The lookahead rules are restricted to examining at most the first three buffer elements, with one exception that occurs when an NP subconstituent needs to be constructed. If the NP starts in the second or third buffer position, then while it is being parsed, that position is used as though it were the first buffer. Called **attention shifting**, this circumstance is the only exception to the three-buffer restriction. With this qualification a rule may still inspect only three buffer positions, but the starting position may be shifted. Attention shifting is restricted so that under no circumstances can a rule inspect a position beyond the first five.

One of the more interesting things about this parser is the way it captures many linguistic generalizations in an elegant fashion by manipulating the input buffer. For example, consider what is needed to extend a grammar that parses assertions into one that parses yes/no questions as well. In Chapter 5 you handled yes/no questions by adding a few rules to the grammar that handled the initial AUX and NP, and then connecting back into the grammar for assertions. This present parser actually reuses the rules for the initial subject and auxiliary as well. In particular, it uses the switch action to reorder the subject NP and the AUX in the buffer, directly capturing the intuition of subject-aux inversion.

Psychological Validity

Because of the limits on the lookahead and the deterministic nature of this parser, you can examine in detail its limitations as well as its coverage. Some researchers have argued that the limitations of the mechanism itself account for various constraints on the form of language, such as the complex-NP constraint described in Chapter 5. Rather than having to impose such a constraint in the grammar, this parser, because of its limitations, could not operate in any other way.

Because of the limited lookahead, this mechanism must commit to certain structural analyses before the entire sentence has been examined. In certain cases a sentence may begin in such a way that the wrong decision is made and the sentence becomes unparsable. These examples were referred to earlier as garden-path sentences. The interesting thing about this phenomenon is that it provides a concrete proposal that can be experimentally validated. In particular, you might ask if the sentence structures with which this parser has difficulty are the same ones with which people have trouble. While the answer is not yet clear, the fact that the question can be asked means that this framework can be investigated experimentally.

In essence, the theory is that any sentence that retains an ambiguity over more than a three-constituent window may cause trouble with a reader. Note that the lookahead is three constituents, not words; thus an ambiguity might be retained for quite some time without causing difficulty. For example, the following two sentences are identical for the first seven words:

Have the students who missed the exam take it today.
Have the students who missed the exam taken it today?

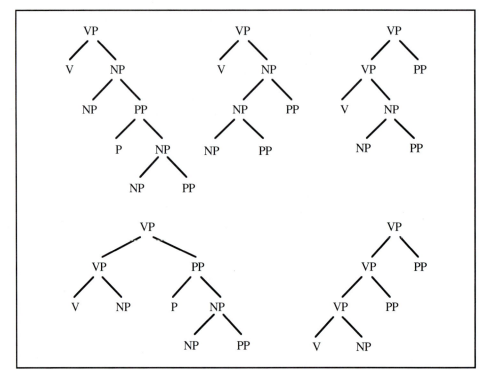

Figure 6.15 Five interpretations of *saw the man in the house with a telescope*

The ambiguity between being an imperative or a sentence versus a yes/no question, however, never extends beyond three constituents, because six of the words are in a single noun phrase. Thus the parser will reach a state where the following two tests can easily distinguish the cases:

<=have> <=NP> <=V, **VFORM**=base> → imperative
<=have> <=NP> <=V, **VFORM**=pastprt> → yes/no question

On the other hand, a sentence such as

Have the soldiers given their medals by their sweethearts.

cannot be disambiguated using only three constituents, and this parser, like most people, will initially misinterpret the sentence as a yes/no question that is ill formed, rather than recognize the appropriate imperative reading corresponding to *Have their sweethearts give the soldiers their medals.*

6.4 Techniques for Efficient Encoding of Ambiguity

Another way to reduce ambiguity is to change the rules of the game by redefining the desired output. For instance, a significant amount of the ambiguity in

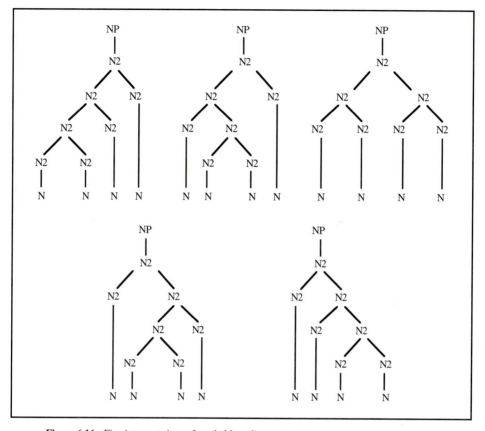

Figure 6.16 Five interpretations of *pot holder adjustment screw*

sentences results from issues like attachment ambiguity and constructs such as coordination that often have many structural interpretations of essentially the same information. Figure 6.15 shows an example of the alternative interpretations that arise from PP attachment ambiguity in the VP *saw the man in the house with a telescope.* There are five interpretations arising from the different attachments, each having a different semantic interpretation. Figure 6.16 shows an example of ambiguities in noun-noun modification, such as *pot holder adjustment screw,* that would arise from a grammar such as

5. $NP \rightarrow N2$
6. $N2 \rightarrow N$
7. $N2 \rightarrow N2\ N2$

These complications of course interact with each other, so a VP with two prepositional phrases and an NP with a sequence of four nouns would have 25 interpretations, and so on. It is not unusual for a moderate-size sentence, say of 12 words, with a reasonable grammar, to have over 1000 different structural

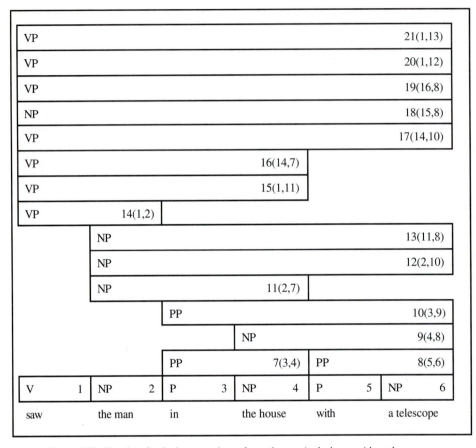

Figure 6.17   The chart for the interpretations of *saw the man in the house with a telescope*

interpretations! Clearly some techniques must be introduced to help manage such complications.

This section briefly examines techniques for representing such large quantities of interpretations efficiently. In fact, the chart data structure used so far is already a significant step towards this goal, as it allows constituents to be shared across interpretations. For example, the PP attachment interpretations shown in Figure 6.15 are represented in the chart shown in Figure 6.17. Each chart entry is numbered, and the subconstituents are listed in parentheses. For example, the NP covering *the man in the house* is constituent 11 and has subconstituents 2 and 7. While Figure 6.15 uses 32 nonlexical nodes, the chart representation of the same five interpretations uses only 21 nonlexical nodes. While the savings are considerable, and grow as the amount of ambiguity grows, they are often not sufficient to handle the problem.

Another technique that is used is called **packing**. This technique takes advantage of a property that may have occurred to you in looking at Figure 6.17,

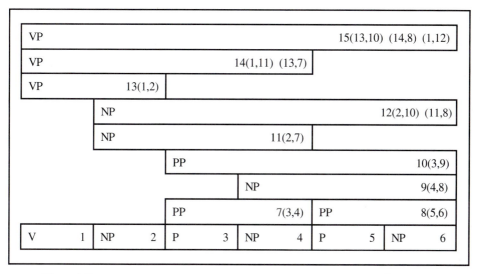

Figure 6.18 A packed chart for the interpretations of *saw the man in the house with a telescope*

namely that there are many constituents of the same type that cover exactly the same input. To a parser without features, each of these constituents would be treated identically by any rule that uses them as a subconstituent. A packed chart representation stores only one constituent of any type over the same input, and any others found are collapsed into the existing one. You can still maintain a record for each derivation found in the single constituent. The chart for the same sentence using the packing technique is shown in Figure 6.18 and uses only 15 nonlexical nodes. Packing produces quite efficient representations of inter-pretations without losing information. With grammars that use feature equations, however, the situation is more complicated. In particular, two VP interpretations covering the same input but having different feature values cannot be merged, because they might differ in how they combine to form larger constituents. You could modify the feature checking to allow success if any one of the possible constituents meets the requirements, but then the chart might overgenerate interpretations, and you would have to reparse the possible solutions at the end to verify that they are valid.

Another way to reduce interpretations is to modify the grammar so that the ambiguities become semantic ambiguities rather than syntactic ambiguities. For example, with noun-noun modification, you might not use rules 5, 6, and 7 mentioned previously, which impose a binary structure onto the noun modifiers, but rather just use a rule that allows a sequence of noun modifiers in a flat structure. In an extended grammar that allows the Kleene + operator, one rule would suffice:

$$N2 \rightarrow N+$$

The N+ notation allows one or more repetitions of the symbol N. Without the + notation, the grammar would need a series of rules, up to some fixed number of modifiers that you would allow, such as

$N2 \rightarrow N$
$N2 \rightarrow N\,N$
$N2 \rightarrow N\,N\,N$
$N2 \rightarrow N\,N\,N\,N$

While such a grammar looks more complicated, it is much more efficient to parse, as the structural ambiguity is eliminated. In particular, there is only one interpretation of the NP *pot holder adjustment screw*.

Similar approaches have been suggested for attachment ambiguity problems. Rather than generating all interpretations, a single interpretation is constructed, say the one where the PP takes the widest scope. This is sometimes called the **canonical interpretation**. The semantic interpreter then needs to be designed so that it can attach the PP lower in the tree, as seems appropriate based on the semantic constraints.

Another approach is called the **D-theory** or description-theory approach. In D-theory, the meaning of the output of the parser is modified. In the traditional view, used throughout this book, constituents are built by defining their immediate subconstituents. The mother constituent **immediately dominates** its subconstituents. D-theory defines a transitive relation **dominates** as follows: A constituent M dominates a constituent C if C is an immediate subconstituent of M, of a subconstituent of a subconstituent of M, and so on. With this new terminology, you can say that the output of a traditional parser is a set of immediate dominance relationships that define the parse tree. In D-theory the output is taken as a set of dominance relationships. Thus, for example, the analysis might say that VP1 dominates PP1. This means that PP1 may be a subconstituent of VP1 but also allows that it might be a subconstituent of a subconstituent of VP1. Thus by changing the nature of the output, many forms of ambiguity can be captured concisely.

6.5 Partial Parsing

The most radical approach to the ambiguity problem is to give up on producing complete parses of sentences and only look for fragments that can be reliably identified. A simple way to approximate such a parser would be to remove rules from a general grammar that lead to ambiguity problems. For instance, if you remove the rules

$VP \rightarrow VP\,PP$
$NP \rightarrow NP\,PP$

from a grammar, the PP attachment problem basically disappears. Of course, you also cannot produce a full parse for most sentences. With this simplified gram-

VP		7(1,2)	PP		8(3,4)	PP		9(5,6)
V	1	NP	2	P	3	NP	4	P	5	NP	6

Figure 6.19 Chart for *saw the man in the house with a telescope* showing partial analysis

mar, a bottom-up chart parser would construct a sequence of syntactic fragments of the sentence that could be useful for later processing. Figure 6.19 shows the final chart for the verb phrase *saw the man in the park with a telescope* using a grammar with the PP modifier rules removed. While much of the global structure is missing, all the local structure is unambiguously identified and the chart contains a lot of useful syntactic information.

Of course, this approach in itself doesn't solve the problem; rather, it delays it until the semantic-interpretation phase. But it may be that the ambiguity problem is easier to solve at the semantic level, as there are more sources of information available. Certainly in limited domain systems this appears to be the case. But a detailed discussion of this must wait until semantic interpretation is introduced. These issues will be developed further in Chapter 10. For the moment, consider how much structure can be identified reliably.

From experience in building such systems, we know that certain structures can be identified quite reliably. These include

the noun group—consisting of noun phrases from the initial determiner through prenominal modifiers to the head noun, but not including postmodifiers such as prepositional phrases

the verb group—consisting of the auxiliary verb sequence, some adverbials, up to the head verb

proper noun phrases—including simple names such as *John* as well as more complex names like the *New York Times*. This is especially easy if the input follows standard capitalization conventions because, with capitalization, names can be parsed even if they are not in the lexicon.

It might appear that other structures could be identified reliably as well, such as prepositional phrases, and verb phrases consisting of obligatory sub-categorized constituents. Such phrases can be generated, but they may not be truly part of the full parse of the sentence because of the limitations in handling noun phrases. In particular, a partial parser might suggest that there is a prepositional phrase *by the leader* in the sentence *We were punished by the leader of the group*. But the full parse of the sentence would not contain such a PP, as it would have a PP with the object of the preposition being *the leader of the group*. Since the partial parser is not able to make attachment decisions, it cannot create the appropriate reading. This leaves you with a choice. Some systems identify the

```
(PRO "We")
(VP   (V "saw")
      (NP "the house boats"))
(PP   (P "near")
      (NP "the lake"))
(V "sink")
(?? "unexpectedly")
(PP   (P "at")
      (NP "dawn"))
```

Figure 6.20   A partial parse of *We saw the house boats near the lake sink unexpectedly at dawn.*

prepositions but leave the PPs unanalyzed, while others construct the incorrect interpretation and depend on the semantic interpretation process to correct it.

Because of the limitations of their coverage, partial parsing systems can be based on regular grammars (or equivalently, finite state machines) rather than using the full power of context-free grammars. They also often depend on a subsystem to accurately predict the correct part of speech for each word. Such part-of-speech tagging systems are discussed in the next chapter. For the moment, you can simply assume that the correct part of speech is given with the input.

The output of such systems is then a sequence of syntactic fragments, some as small as the lexical category of a function word, and others fairly complex verb sequences and NPs. When faced with an unknown word, the partial parser simply leaves it unanalyzed and moves on. Even with a limited grammar there is potential ambiguity, and partial parsers generally use heuristics to reduce the possibilities. One popular technique is to favor longer constituents over shorter ones of the same type. The heuristic would rather interpret *The house boats* as one NP than two (*The house* and *boats*), even though the latter would be possible.

Figure 6.20 shows the sequence of constituents that might be built for such a system given the input *We saw the house boats near the lake sink unexpectedly at dawn.*

Summary

There are several ways to build efficient parsers. Some methods improve the efficiency of search-based parsing models, while others specify models of parsing that are inherently deterministic or only partially analyze the sentences. The methods use several different techniques:

- encoding ambiguity within parse states
- using lookahead techniques to choose appropriate rules
- using efficient encoding techniques for encoding ambiguity
- changing the definition of the output so that it ignores ambiguity

Related Work and Further Readings

There is a large literature in psycholinguistics on parsing preferences, starting with the work by Kimball (1973). Lexical preferences were suggested by Ford, Bresnan, and Kaplan (1982). An excellent collection of recent work in the field is Clifton, Frazier, and Rayner (in press). Some of the articles in this volume focus on exactly the parsing principles and preferences discussed in Section 6.1. The researchers seem to be converging on the conclusion that the human processing system takes into account the frequency with which different words and structures appear in different syntactic environments, and then evaluates the most likely possibilities using semantic information and knowledge of the discourse context. In this view, principles such as minimal attachment and right association provide useful descriptions of the preferences, but the preferences actually arise because of other factors. Computational models that have explicitly involved parsing preferences include Shieber (1984), Pereira (1985), and Schubert (1986). Additional computational models will be discussed in Chapter 7.

As mentioned in the text, shift-reduce parsers have traditionally been used for parsing programming languages with unambiguous grammars. A good text discussing this work is Aho et al. (1986), who would classify the shift-reduce parser described in Section 6.2 as an LR(1) parser (that is, a left-to-right parser using a one-symbol lookahead). These techniques have been generalized to handle ambiguity in natural language by various techniques. Shieber (1984) introduces the techniques, described in Section 6.2, that generalize the treatment of terminal symbols to delay lexical classification of words, and that use parsing preferences to select between rules when more than one rule appears to be applicable. Tomita (1986) reincorporates a full search with an optimized parse-tree representation while taking advantage of the speed of the oracle-driven shift-reduce parsing.

The section on deterministic parsing is based on Marcus (1980). Charniak (1983) developed a variant in which the parse states were automatically generated from a context-free grammar. The most comprehensive grammar within this formalism in the Fidditch parser, of which it is hard to find a description in the literature, but see Hindle (1989) for a brief description. Berwick (1985) used this framework in an investigation of language learning.

The technique of packing is used in many systems. Two recent examples are Tomita (1986) and Alshawi (1992). The extent of ambiguity in natural language is explored systematically by Church and Patil (1982), who discuss techniques such as canonical forms and packing in detail. D-theory is described in Marcus et al. (1983) and has been formalized for use within the TAG formalism by Vijay-Shankar (1992). Fidditch (Hindle, 1989) is one of the best examples of a parser that only analyzes structure that can be reliably identified. Its output is a set of fragments rather than a complete interpretation.

Exercises for Chapter 6

1. (*easy*) Give a trace of the shift-reduce parser using the oracle in Figure 6.6 as it parses the sentence *The dog was eating the bone.*

2. (*medium*) List and define the three parsing strategies that this text says people use. Discuss how the following sentences are ambiguous, and state which reading is preferred in the framework of these parsing strategies.

   a. It flew past the geese over the field.
   b. The artist paints the scene in the park.
   c. He feels the pain in his heart.

3. (*medium*) Build an oracle for the following grammar:

   $S \rightarrow NP\ VP$
   $NP \rightarrow ART\ N$
   $NP \rightarrow ART\ N\ PP$
   $VP \rightarrow V\ NP$
   $VP \rightarrow V\ NP\ PP$

   Identify places where there is an ambiguity that the technique described cannot resolve, and use the heuristics at the end of Section 6.2 to select an unambiguous action for the oracle. Give an example of a sentence that will be incorrectly parsed because of this decision.

4. (*medium*)

   a. Construct the oracle for the following VP grammar involving to-infinitives and prepositions:

   $$VP \rightarrow V\ NP \qquad PP \rightarrow P\ NP$$
   $$VP \rightarrow V\ INF \qquad NP \rightarrow DET\ N$$
   $$VP \rightarrow V\ PP \qquad NP \rightarrow NAME$$
   $$INF \rightarrow to\ VP$$

   b. Can the oracle correctly analyze both of the following VPs without resorting to guessing? Trace the parse for each sentence starting at the word *walked.*

   Jack walked to raise the money.
   Jack walked to the store.

   c. Consider allowing word ambiguity in the grammar. In particular, the word *sand* can be either a noun or a verb. What does your parser do with the VPs

   Jack turned to sand.
   Jack turned to sand the board.

5. (*medium*) Design a deterministic grammar that can successfully parse both

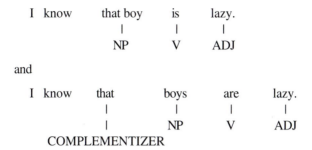

```
    I  know      that boy     is      lazy.
                  |           |        |
                  NP          V       ADJ
```

and

```
    I  know      that         boys     are      lazy.
                  |            |        |         |
                  |            NP       V        ADJ
          COMPLEMENTIZER
```

You may use as much of the grammar presented in this chapter as you wish. Trace the parser on each of these sentences in the style found in this chapter. Describe the important points of your analysis. Discuss how general your solution is in dealing with the various uses of the word *that*. Show at least one further example of a sentence involving *that* and outline how your grammar accounts for it (them).

6. (*medium*) Modify an existing chart parser so that it uses a packed chart, as described in Section 6.4. Perform a set of experiments with a grammar without features and compare the size of the chart with and without packing.

7. (*medium*) Construct an example that shows what problems arise when you use a packed chart with a grammar with features. Devise a strategy for dealing with the problems.

8. (*medium*) Assume a chart parser using a packed representation. Develop an upper limit on the number of operations the parser will have to do to parse a sentence of length S using a grammar that uses N nonterminals and T terminal symbols.

Ambiguity Resolution: Statistical Methods

7.1   Basic Probability Theory

7.2   Estimating Probabilities

7.3   Part-of-Speech Tagging

7.4   Obtaining Lexical Probabilities

7.5   Probabilistic Context-Free Grammars

7.6   Best-First Parsing

7.7   A Simple Context-Dependent Best-First Parser

Chapter 6 suggested employing heuristics to choose between alternate syntactic analyses. Creating such heuristics, however, is difficult and time consuming. Furthermore, there is no systematic method for evaluating how well the heuristic rules work in practice. This section explores some techniques for solving these problems based on probability theory. Such approaches have become very popular in the past few years because large databases, or **corpora**, of natural language data have become available. This data allows you to use statistically based techniques for automatically deriving the probabilities needed. The most commonly available corpus, the Brown corpus, consists of about a million words, all labeled with their parts of speech. More recently, much larger databases have become available in formats ranging from raw text format (as in databases of articles from the AP news wire and the *Wall Street Journal*) to corpora with full syntactic annotation (such as the Penn Treebank). The availability of all this data suggests new analysis techniques that were previously not possible.

Section 7.1 introduces the key ideas in probability theory and explores how they might apply to natural language applications. Section 7.2 considers some techniques for estimating probabilities from corpora, and Section 7.3 develops techniques for part-of-speech tagging. Section 7.4 defines the technique for computing lexical probabilities. Section 7.5 introduces probabilistic context-free grammars, and Section 7.6 explores the issue of building a probabilistically driven best-first parser. The final section introduces a context-dependent probability estimate that has significant advantages over the context-free method.

7.1 Basic Probability Theory

Intuitively, the **probability** of some event is the likelihood that it will occur. A probability of 1 indicates that the event is certain to occur, while a probability of 0 indicates that the event definitely will not occur. Any number between 0 and 1 indicates some degree of uncertainty. This uncertainty can be illuminated by considering the odds of the event occurring, as you would if you were going to bet on whether the event will occur or not. A probability of .5 would indicate that the event is equally likely to occur as not to occur, that is, a "50/50" bet. An event with probability .5 would occur exactly half of the time. An event with probability .1 would occur once in every 10 opportunities (1/10 odds), whereas an event with probability .75 would occur 75 times out of 100 (3/4 odds).

More formally, probability can be defined in terms of a **random variable**, which may range over a predefined set of values. While random variables may range over infinite sets and continuous values, here we will use only random variables that range over a finite set of values. For instance, consider tossing a coin. The random variable TOSS representing the result of a coin toss would range over two possible values: heads (h) or tails (t). One possible event is that the coin comes up heads—TOSS=h; the other is that the coin comes up tails—TOSS=t. No other value for TOSS is possible, reflecting the fact that a tossed coin always comes up either heads or tails. Usually, we will not mention the random variable and will talk of the probability of TOSS=h simply as the probability of the event h.

A probability function, *PROB*, assigns a probability to every possible value of a random variable. Every probability function must have the following properties, where $e_1, ..., e_n$ are the possible distinct values of a random variable E:

1. $PROB(e_i) \geq 0$, for all i
2. $PROB(e_i) \leq 1$, for all i
3. $\Sigma_{i=1,n} PROB(e_i) = 1$

Consider a specific example. A particular horse, Harry, ran 100 races in his career. The result of a race is represented as a random variable R that has one of two values, Win or Lose. Say that Harry won 20 times overall. Thus the probability of Harry winning the race is $PROB(R=Win) = .2$ and the probability of him losing is $PROB(R=Lose) = .8$. Note that these values satisfy the three constraints just defined.

Of course, there may be many different random variables, and we are often interested in how they relate to each other. Continuing the racing example, consider another random variable W representing the state of the weather and ranging over the values Rain and Shine. Let us say that it was raining 30 times out of the 100 times a race was run. Of these 30 races, Harry won 15 times. Intuitively, if you were given the fact that it was raining—that is, that W=Rain— the probability that R=Win would be .5 (15 out of 30). This intuition is captured by the concept of **conditional probability** and is written as $PROB(Win \mid Rain)$, which is often described as the probability of the event Win given the event Rain. Conditional probability is defined by the formula

$$PROB(e \mid e') = PROB(e \,\&\, e') / PROB(e')$$

where $PROB(e \,\&\, e')$ is the probability of the two events e and e' occurring simultaneously.

You know that $PROB(Rain) = .3$ and $PROB(Win \,\&\, Rain) = .15$, and using the definition of conditional probability you can compute $PROB(Win \mid Rain)$ and see that it agrees with your intuition:

$$
\begin{aligned}
PROB(Win \mid Rain) \ &= PROB(Win \,\&\, Rain) / PROB(Rain) \\
&= .15 / .30 \\
&= .5
\end{aligned}
$$

An important theorem relating conditional probabilities is called **Bayes' rule**. This rule relates the conditional probability of an event A given B to the conditional probability of B given A:

$$PROB(A \mid B) = \frac{PROB(B \mid A) * PROB(A)}{PROB(B)}$$

We can illustrate this rule using the race horse example. Using Bayes' rule we can compute the probability that it rained on a day that Harry won a race:

$$PROB(\text{Rain} \mid \text{Win}) = (PROB(\text{Win} \mid \text{Rain}) * PROB(\text{Rain})) / PROB(\text{Win})$$
$$= (.5 * .3) / .2$$
$$= .75$$

which, of course, is the same value as if we calculated the conditional probability directly from its definition:

$$PROB(\text{Rain} \mid \text{Win}) = PROB(\text{Rain \& Win}) / PROB(\text{Win})$$
$$= .15 / .20$$
$$= .75$$

The reason that Bayes' rule is useful is that we usually do not have complete information about a situation and so do not know all the required probabilities. We can, however, often estimate some probabilities reasonably and then use Bayes' rule to calculate the others.

Another important concept in probability theory is the notion of **independence**. Two events are said to be independent of each other if the occurrence of one does not affect the probability of the occurrence of the other. For instance, in the race horse example, consider another random variable, L, that indicates whether I took my lucky rabbit's foot to the race (value Foot) or not (Empty). Say I took my rabbit's foot 60 times, and Harry won 12 races. This means that the probability that Harry won the race on a day that I took the rabbit's foot is PROB(Win | Foot) = 12/60 = .2. Since this is the same as the usual probability of Harry winning, you can conclude that winning the race is independent of taking the rabbit's foot.

More formally, two events A and B are independent of each other if and only if

$$PROB(\text{A} \mid \text{B}) = PROB(\text{A})$$

which, using the definition of conditional probability, is equivalent to saying

$$PROB(\text{A \& B}) = PROB(\text{A}) * PROB(\text{B})$$

Note that the events of winning and raining are not independent, given that $PROB(\text{Win \& Rain}) = .15$ while $PROB(\text{Win}) * PROB(\text{Rain}) = .2 * .3 = .06$. In other words, winning and raining occur together at a rate much greater than random chance.

Consider an application of probability theory related to language, namely part-of-speech identification: Given a sentence with ambiguous words, determine the most likely lexical category for each word. This problem will be examined in detail in Section 7.3. Here we consider a trivial case to illustrate the ideas underlying probability theory. Say you need to identify the correct syntactic category for words that can be either nouns or verbs. This can be formalized using two random variables: one, C, that ranges over the parts of speech (N and V), and another, W, that ranges over all the possible words. Consider an example when W = *flies*. The problem can be stated as determining whether $PROB(\text{C=N} \mid$ W=*flies*) or $PROB(\text{C=V} \mid \text{W=}flies)$ is greater. Note that, as mentioned earlier, the random variables will usually be omitted from the formulas. Thus $PROB(C=N \mid W=flies)$ will usually be abbreviated as $PROB(N \mid flies)$. Given the definition of conditional probability, the probabilities for the categories of the word *flies* are calculated as follows:

$$PROB(N \mid flies) = PROB(flies \ \& \ N) / PROB(flies)$$
$$PROB(V \mid flies) = PROB(flies \ \& \ V) / PROB(flies)$$

So the problem reduces to finding which of $PROB(flies \ \& \ N)$ and $PROB(flies \ \& \ V)$ is greater, since the denominator is the same in each formula.

How might you obtain these probabilities? You clearly cannot determine the true probabilities since you don't have a record of all text ever written, let alone the text that will be processed in the future. But if you have a large enough sample of data, you can estimate the probabilities.

Let's say we have a corpus of simple sentences containing 1,273,000 words. Say we find 1000 uses of the word *flies,* 400 of them in the N sense, and 600 in the V sense. We can approximate the probabilities by looking at the ratios of the frequencies of the words in the corpus. For example, the probability of a randomly selected word being the word *flies* is

$$PROB(flies) \cong 1000 / 1,273,000 = .0008$$

The joint probabilities for *flies* as a noun and *flies* as a verb are

$$PROB(flies \ \& \ N) \cong 400 / 1,273,000 = .0003$$
$$PROB(flies \ \& \ V) \cong 600 / 1,273,000 = .0005$$

Thus our best guess is that each use of *flies* is a verb. We can compute the probability that *flies* is a verb using the formula

$$PROB(V \mid flies) \quad = PROB(V \ \& \ flies) / PROB(flies)$$
$$= .0005 / .0008 = .625$$

Using this method, an algorithm that always asserts *flies* to be a verb will be correct about 60 percent of the time. This is clearly a poor strategy, but better than guessing that it is a noun all the time! To get a better method, you must consider more context, such as the sentence in which *flies* occurs. This idea is developed in Section 7.3.

7.2   Estimating Probabilities

If you have all the data that would ever be relevant to a problem, you can compute exact probabilities for that data. For instance, say Harry, the horse in the last section, ran only 100 races and then was put out to pasture. Now you can compute the exact probability of Harry winning any particular race someone might choose of the 100 possibilities. But, of course, this is not how probability is generally used. Typically, you want to use probability to predict future behavior; that is, you'd use information on Harry's past performance to predict how likely he is

Results	Estimate of *Prob* (H)	Acceptable Estimate?
HH	1.0	NO
HT	.5	YES
TH	.5	YES
TT	0	NO

Figure 7.1　Possible estimates of *Prob*(H) given two flips

to win his 101st race (which you are going to bet on). This is a real-life application of probability theory. You are in the same position when using probabilities to help resolve ambiguity, since you are interested in parsing sentences that have never been seen before. Thus you need to use data on previously occurring sentences to predict the interpretation of the next sentence. We will always be working with estimates of probability rather than the actual probabilities.

As seen in the last section, one method of estimation is to use the ratios from the corpus as the probability to predict the interpretation of the new sentence. Thus, if we have seen the word *flies* 1000 times before, and 600 of them were as a verb, then we assume that *PROB*(V | *flies*) is .6 and use that to guide our guess with the 1001st case. This simple ratio estimate is called the **maximum likelihood estimator (MLE)**. If you have many examples of the events you are estimating, this can be a very reliable estimate of the true probability.

In general, the accuracy of an estimate increases as the amount of data used expands, and there is a theorem of statistics—the law of large numbers—that states that estimates can be made as accurate as desired if you have unlimited data. Estimates can be particularly unreliable, however, when only a small number of samples are involved. Consider trying to estimate the true probability of a fair coin coming up heads when it is flipped. For the sake of discussion, since we know the actual answer is .5, let us say the estimate is accurate enough if it falls between .25 and .75. This range will be called the acceptable **margin of error**. If you only do two trials, there are four possible outcomes, as shown in Figure 7.1: two heads, heads then tails, tails then heads, or two tails. This means that, if you flip a coin twice, half the time you will obtain an estimate of 1/2 or .5. The other half of the time, however, you will estimate that the probability of coming up heads is 1 (the two-heads case) or 0 (the two-tails case). So you have only a 50 percent chance of obtaining an estimate within the desired margin of error. With three flips, the chance of getting a reliable enough estimate jumps to 75 percent, as shown in Figure 7.2. With four flips, there is an 87.5 percent chance of the estimate being accurate enough, with eight flips a 93 percent chance, with 12 flips a 95 percent chance, and so on. No matter how long you flip, there is always a chance that the estimate found is inaccurate, but you can reduce the probability of this occurring to as small a number as you desire if you can do enough trials.

Results	Estimate of *Prob* (H)	Acceptable Estimate?
HHH	1.0	NO
HHT	.66	YES
HTH	.66	YES
HTT	.33	YES
THH	.66	YES
THT	.33	YES
TTH	.33	YES
TTT	0	NO

Figure 7.2   Possible estimates of *Prob*(H) given three flips

Almost any method of estimation works well when there is a lot of data. Unfortunately, there are a vast number of estimates needed for natural language applications, and a large proportion of these events are quite rare. This is the problem of **sparse data**. For instance, the Brown corpus contains about a million words, but due to duplication there are only 49,000 different words. Given this, you might expect each word to occur about 20 times on average. But over 40,000 of the words occur five times or less. With such few numbers, our estimates of the part of speech for such words may be highly inaccurate. The worst case occurs if a low-frequency word does not occur at all in one of its possible categories. Its probability in this category would then be estimated as 0; thus no interpretation using the word in any category would be possible, because the probability of the overall sentence containing the word would be 0 as well. Unfortunately, rare events are common enough in natural language applications that reliable estimates for these low-frequency words are essential for the algorithms.

There are other estimation techniques that attempt to address the problem of estimating probabilities of low-frequency events. To examine them, let's introduce a framework in which they can be compared. For a particular random variable X, all techniques start with a set of values, V_i, computed from the count of the number of times $X = x_i$. The maximum likelihood estimation technique uses $V_i = |x_i|$; that is, V_i is exactly the count of the number of times $X = x_i$. Once V_i is determined for each x_i, the probability estimates are obtained by the formula

$$PROB(X = x_i) \cong V_i / \Sigma_i V_i$$

Note that the denominator guarantees that the estimates obey the three properties of a probability function defined in Section 7.1.

One technique to solve the zero probability problem is to ensure that no V_i has the value 0. We might, for instance, add a small amount, say .5, to every count, such as in $V_i = |x_i| + .5$. This guarantees no zero probabilities yet retains the relative likelihoods for the frequently occurring values. This estimation technique is called the **expected likelihood estimator (ELE)**. To see the difference between this and the MLE, consider a word w that happens not to occur in the corpus, and consider estimating the probability that w occurs in one of 40 word classes L_1, ..., L_{40}. Thus we have a random variable X, where $X = x_i$ only if w appears in word category L_i. The MLE for $PROB(X = x_i)$ will not be defined because the formula has a zero denominator. The ELE, however, gives an equally likely probability to each possible word class. With 40 word classes, for instance, each V_i will be .5, and thus $PROB(L_i \mid w) \cong .5/20 = .025$. This estimate better reflects the fact that we have no information about the word. On the other hand, the ELE is very conservative. If w appears in the corpus five times, once as a verb and four times as a noun, then the MLE estimate of $PROB(N \mid w)$ would be .8, while the ELE estimate would be $4.5/25 = .18$, a very small value compared to intuition.

Evaluation

Once you have a set of estimated probabilities and an algorithm for some particular application, you would like to be able to tell how well your new technique performs compared with other algorithms or variants of your algorithm. The general method for doing this is to divide the corpus into two parts: the **training set** and the **test set**. Typically, the test set consists of 10–20 percent of the total data. The training set is then used to estimate the probabilities, and the algorithm is run on the test set to see how well it does on new data. Running the algorithm on the training set is not considered a reliable method of evaluation because it does not measure the generality of your technique. For instance, you could do well on the training set simply by remembering all the answers and repeating them back in the test! A more thorough method of testing is called **cross-validation**, which involves repeatedly removing different parts of the corpus as the test set, training on the remainder of the corpus, and then evaluating on the new test set. This technique reduces the chance that the test set selected was somehow easier than you might expect.

7.3 Part-of-Speech Tagging

Part-of-speech tagging involves selecting the most likely sequence of syntactic categories for the words in a sentence. A typical set of tags, used in the Penn Treebank project, is shown in Figure 7.3. In Section 7.1 you saw the simplest algorithm for this task: Always choose the interpretation that occurs most frequently in the training set. Surprisingly, this technique often obtains about a 90 percent success rate, primarily because over half the words appearing in most corpora are not ambiguous. So this measure is the starting point from which to evaluate algorithms that use more sophisticated techniques. Unless a method does significantly better than 90 percent, it is not working very well.

1.	CC	Coordinating conjunction	19.	PP\$	Possessive pronoun
2.	CD	Cardinal number	20.	RB	Adverb
3.	DT	Determiner	21.	RBR	Comparative adverb
4.	EX	Existential *there*	22.	RBS	Superlative Adverb
5.	FW	Foreign word	23.	RP	Particle
6.	IN	Preposition / subord. conj	24.	SYM	Symbol (math or scientific)
7.	JJ	Adjective	25.	TO	to
8.	JJR	Comparative adjective	26.	UH	Interjection
9.	JJS	Superlative adjective	27.	VB	Verb, base form
10.	LS	List item marker	28.	VBD	Verb, past tense
11.	MD	Modal	29.	VBG	Verb, gerund/pres. participle
12.	NN	Noun, singular or mass	30.	VBN	Verb, past participle
13.	NNS	Noun, plural	31.	VBP	Verb, non-3s, present
14.	NNP	Proper noun, singular	32.	VBZ	Verb, 3s, present
15.	NNPS	Proper noun, plural	33.	WDT	Wh-determiner
16.	PDT	Predeterminer	34.	WP	Wh-pronoun
17.	POS	Possessive ending	35.	WPZ	Possessive wh-pronoun
18.	PRP	Personal pronoun	36.	WRB	Wh-adverb

Figure 7.3 The Penn Treebank tagset

The general method to improve reliability is to use some of the local context of the sentence in which the word appears. For example, in Section 7.1 you saw that choosing the verb sense of *flies* in the sample corpus was the best choice and would be right about 60 percent of the time. If the word is preceded by the word *the,* on the other hand, it is much more likely to be a noun. The technique developed in this section is able to exploit such information.

Consider the problem in its full generality. Let $w_1, ..., w_T$ be a sequence of words. We want to find the sequence of lexical categories $C_1, ..., C_T$ that maximizes

1. $PROB(C_1, ..., C_T \mid w_1, ..., w_T)$

Unfortunately, it would take far too much data to generate reasonable estimates for such sequences, so direct methods cannot be applied. There are, however, reasonable approximation techniques that produce good results. To develop them, you must restate the problem using Bayes' rule, which says that this conditional probability equals

2. $(PROB(C_1, ..., C_T) * PROB(w_1, ..., w_T \mid C_1, ..., C_T)) / PROB(w_1, ..., w_T)$

As before, since we are interested in finding the $C_1, ..., C_n$ that gives the maximum value, the common denominator in all these cases will not affect the answer. Thus the problem reduces to finding the sequence $C_1, ..., C_n$ that maximizes the formula

3. $PROB(C_1, ..., C_T) * PROB(w_1, ..., w_T | C_1, ..., C_T)$

There are still no effective methods for calculating the probability of these long sequences accurately, as it would require far too much data. But the probabilities can be approximated by probabilities that are simpler to collect by making some independence assumptions. While these independence assumptions are not really valid, the estimates appear to work reasonably well in practice. Each of the two expressions in formula 3 will be approximated. The first expression, the probability of the sequence of categories, can be approximated by a series of probabilities based on a limited number of previous categories. The most common assumptions use either one or two previous categories. The **bigram** model looks at pairs of categories (or words) and uses the conditional probability that a category C_i will follow a category C_{i-1}, written as $PROB(C_i | C_{i-1})$. The **trigram** model uses the conditional probability of one category (or word) given the two preceding categories (or words), that is, $PROB(C_i | C_{i-2} C_{i-1})$. These models are called **n-gram** models, in which n represents the number of words used in the pattern. While the trigram model will produce better results in practice, we will consider the bigram model here for simplicity. Using bigrams, the following approximation can be used:

$$PROB(C_1, ..., C_T) \cong \prod_{i=1,T} PROB(C_i | C_{i-1})$$

To account for the beginning of a sentence, we posit a pseudocategory ø at position 0 as the value of C_0. Thus the first bigram for a sentence beginning with an ART would be $PROB(ART | ø)$. Given this, the approximation of the probability of the sequence ART N V N using bigrams would be

$$PROB(ART\ N\ V\ N) \cong PROB(ART | ø) * PROB(N | ART)$$
$$* PROB(V | N) * PROB(N | V)$$

The second probability in formula 3,

$$PROB(w_1, ..., w_T | C_1, ..., C_T)$$

can be approximated by assuming that a word appears in a category independent of the words in the preceding or succeeding categories. It is approximated by the product of the probability that each word occurs in the indicated part of speech, that is, by

$$PROB(w_1, ..., w_T | C_1, ..., C_T) \cong \prod_{i=1,T} PROB(w_i | C_i)$$

With these two approximations, the problem has changed into finding the sequence $C_1, ..., C_T$ that maximizes the value of

$$\prod_{i=1,T} PROB(C_i | C_{i-1}) * PROB(w_i | C_i)$$

The advantage of this new formula is that the probabilities involved can be readily estimated from a corpus of text labeled with parts of speech. In particular, given a database of text, the bigram probabilities can be estimated simply by counting the number of times each pair of categories occurs compared to the

Category	Count at i	Pair	Count at i,i+1	Bigram	Estimate
ø	300	ø, ART	213	$PROB(\text{ART} \mid ø)$	.71
ø	300	ø, N	87	$PROB(\text{N} \mid ø)$	.29
ART	558	ART, N	558	$PROB(\text{N} \mid \text{ART})$	1
N	833	N, V	358	$PROB(\text{V} \mid \text{N})$	.43
N	833	N, N	108	$PROB(\text{N} \mid \text{N})$	.13
N	833	N, P	366	$PROB(\text{P} \mid \text{N})$	.44
V	300	V, N	75	$PROB(\text{N} \mid \text{V})$	.35
V	300	V, ART	194	$PROB(\text{ART} \mid \text{V})$	.65
P	307	P, ART	226	$PROB(\text{ART} \mid \text{P})$	.74
P	307	P, N	81	$PROB(\text{N} \mid \text{P})$	.26

Figure 7.4 Bigram probabilities from the generated corpus

individual category counts. The probability that a V follows an N would be estimated as follows:

$$PROB(C_i = V \mid C_{i-1} = N) \cong \frac{\text{Count(N at position } i-1 \text{ and V at } i)}{\text{Count(N at position } i-1)}$$

Figure 7.4 gives some bigram frequencies computed from an artificially generated corpus of simple sentences. The corpus consists of 300 sentences but has words in only four categories: N, V, ART, and P. In contrast, a typical real tagset used in the Penn Treebank, shown in Figure 7.3, contains about 40 tags. The artificial corpus contains 1998 words: 833 nouns, 300 verbs, 558 articles, and 307 prepositions. Each bigram is estimated using the previous formula. To deal with the problem of sparse data, any bigram that is not listed here will be assumed to have a token probability of .0001.

The lexical-generation probabilities, $PROB(w_i \mid C_i)$, can be estimated simply by counting the number of occurrences of each word by category. Figure 7.5 gives some counts for individual words from which the lexical-generation probability estimates in Figure 7.6 are computed. Note that the lexical-generation probability is the probability that a given category is realized by a specific word, not the probability that a given word falls in a specific category. For instance, $PROB(the \mid \text{ART})$ is estimated by Count (# times *the* is an ART) / Count (# times an ART occurs). The other probability, $PROB(\text{ART} \mid the)$, would give a very different value.

Given all these probability estimates, how might you find the sequence of categories that has the highest probability of generating a specific sentence? The brute force method would be to generate all possible sequences that could generate the sentence and then estimate the probability of each and pick the best one. The problem with this is that there are an exponential number of sequences—given N categories and T words, there are N^T possible sequences.

	N	V	ART	P	TOTAL
flies	21	23	0	0	44
fruit	49	5	1	0	55
like	10	30	0	21	61
a	1	0	201	0	202
the	1	0	300	2	303
flower	53	15	0	0	68
flowers	42	16	0	0	58
birds	64	1	0	0	65
others	592	210	56	284	1142
TOTAL	833	300	558	307	1998

Figure 7.5   A summary of some of the word counts in the corpus

$PROB(the \mid ART)$	.54	$PROB(a \mid ART)$	.360
$PROB(flies \mid N)$	.025	$PROB(a \mid N)$	.001
$PROB(flies \mid V)$	.076	$PROB(flower \mid N)$	.063
$PROB(like \mid V)$	.1	$PROB(flower \mid V)$	.05
$PROB(like \mid P)$	.068	$PROB(birds \mid N)$	.076
$PROB(like \mid N)$	.012		

Figure 7.6   The lexical-generation probabilities

Luckily, you can do much better than this because of the independence assumptions that were made about the data.

Since we are only dealing with bigram probabilities, the probability that the i'th word is in a category C_i depends only on the category of the $(i-1)$th word, C_{i-1}. Thus the process can be modeled by a special form of probabilistic finite state machine, as shown in Figure 7.7. Each node represents a possible lexical category and the transition probabilities (the bigram probabilities in Figure 7.4) indicate the probability of one category following another.

With such a network you can compute the probability of any sequence of categories simply by finding the path through the network indicated by the sequence and multiplying the transition probabilities together. For instance, the sequence ART N V N would have the probability .71 * 1 * .43 * .35 = .107. This representation, of course, is only accurate if the probability of a category occurring depends only on the one category before it. In probability theory this is often called the **Markov assumption**, and networks like that in Figure 7.7 are called **Markov chains**.

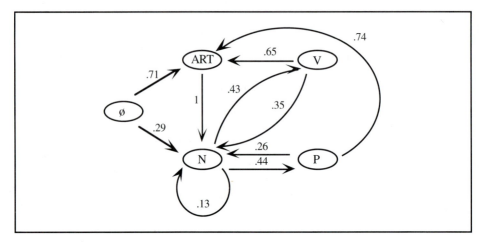

Figure 7.7 A Markov chain capturing the bigram probabilities

The network representation can now be extended to include the lexical-generation probabilities as well. In particular, we allow each node to have an **output probability**, which gives a probability to each possible output that could correspond to the node. For instance, node N in Figure 7.7 would be associated with a probability table that indicates, for each word, how likely that word is to be selected if we randomly select a noun. The output probabilities are exactly the lexical-generation probabilities shown in Figure 7.6. A network like that in Figure 7.7 with output probabilities associated with each node is called a **Hidden Markov Model** (HMM). The word *hidden* in the name indicates that for a specific sequence of words, it is not clear what state the Markov model is in. For instance, the word *flies* could be generated from state N with a probability of .025 (given the values in Figure 7.6), or it could be generated from state V with a probability .076. Because of this ambiguity, it is no longer trivial to compute the probability of a sequence of words from the network. If you are given a parti-cular sequence, however, the probability that it generates a particular output is easily computed by multiplying the probabilities on the path times the probabili-ties for each output. For instance, the probability that the sequence N V ART N generates the output *Flies like a flower* is computed as follows. The probability of the path N V ART N, given the Markov model in Figure 7.7, is .29 * .43 * .65 * 1 = .081. The probability of the output being *Flies like a flower* for this sequence is computed from the output probabilities given in Figure 7.6:

$$PROB(flies \mid N) * PROB(like \mid V) * PROB(a \mid ART) * PROB(flower \mid N)$$
$$= .025 * .1 * .36 * .063$$
$$= 5.4 * 10^{-5}$$

Multiplying these together gives us the likelihood that the HMM would generate the sentence, $4.37 * 10^{-6}$. More generally, the formula for computing the proba-bility of a sentence $w_1, ..., w_T$ given a sequence $C_1, ..., C_T$ is

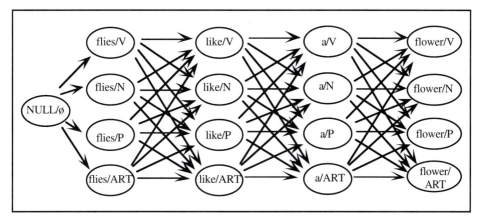

Figure 7.8 Encoding the 256 possible sequences exploiting the Markov assumption

$$\Pi_{i=1,T} \, PROB(C_i \mid C_{i-1}) * PROB(w_i \mid C_i)$$

Now we can resume the discussion of how to find the most likely sequence of categories for a sequence of words. The key insight is that because of the Markov assumption, you do not have to enumerate all the possible sequences. In fact, sequences that end in the same category can be collapsed together since the next category only depends on the one previous category in the sequence. So if you just keep track of the most likely sequence found so far for each possible ending category, you can ignore all the other less likely sequences. For example, consider the problem of finding the most likely categories for the sentence *Flies like a flower,* with the lexical-generation probabilities and bigram probabilities discussed so far. Given that there are four possible categories, there are $4^4 = 256$ different sequences of length four. The brute force algorithm would have to generate all 256 sequences and compare their probabilities in order to find this one. Exploiting the Markov assumption, however, this set of sequences can be collapsed into a representation that considers only the four possibilities for each word. This representation, shown as a transition diagram in Figure 7.8, represents all 256 sequences. To find the most likely sequence, you sweep forward through the words one at a time finding the most likely sequence for each ending category. In other words, you first find the four best sequences for the two words *flies like*: the best ending with *like* as a V, the best as an N, the best as a P, and the best as an ART. You then use this information to find the four best sequences for the three words *flies like a,* each one ending in a different category. This process is repeated until all the words are accounted for. This algorithm is usually called the **Viterbi** algorithm. For a problem involving T words and N lexical categories, it is guaranteed to find the most likely sequence using $k*T*N^2$ steps, for some constant k, significantly better than the N^T steps required by the brute force search! The rest of this section develops the Viterbi algorithm in detail.

Given word sequence $w_1, ..., w_T$, lexical categories $L_1, ..., L_N$, lexical probabilities $PROB(w_t | L_i)$, and bigram probabilities $PROB(L_i | L_j)$, find the most likely sequence of lexical categories $C_1, ..., C_T$ for the word sequence.

Initialization Step

For i = 1 to N do
      SEQSCORE(i, 1) = $PROB(w_1 | L_i)$ * $PROB(L_i | \emptyset)$
      BACKPTR(i, 1) = 0

Iteration Step

For t = 2 to T
   For i = 1 to N
      SEQSCORE(i, t) = $\text{MAX}_{j=1,N}$(SEQSCORE(j, t–1) *
                          $PROB(L_i | L_j))$ * $PROB(w_t | L_i)$
      BACKPTR(i, t) = index of j that gave the max above

Sequence Identification Step

C(T) = i that maximizes SEQSCORE(i, T)
For i = T–1 to 1 do
      C(i) = BACKPTR(C(i+1), i+1)

Figure 7.9 The Viterbi algorithm

○ The Viterbi Algorithm

We will track the probability of the best sequence leading to each possible category at each position using an N×T array, where N is the number of lexical categories ($L_1, ..., L_N$) and T is the number of words in the sentence ($w_1, ..., w_T$). This array, SEQSCORE(n, t), records the probability for the best sequence up to position t that ends with a word in category L_n. To record the actual best sequence for each category at each position, it suffices to record only the one preceding category for each category and position. Another N×T array, BACKPTR, will indicate for each category in each position what the preceding category is in the best sequence at position t–1. The algorithm, shown in Figure 7.9, operates by computing the values for these two arrays.

Let's assume you have analyzed a corpus and obtained the bigram and lexical-generation probabilities in Figures 7.4 and 7.6, and assume that any bigram probability not in Figure 7.4 has a value of .0001. Using these probabilities, the algorithm running on the sentence *Flies like a flower* will operate as follows.

The first row is set in the initialization phase using the formula

SEQSCORE(i, 1) = $PROB(\textit{Flies} | L_i)$ * $PROB(L_i | \emptyset)$

where L_i ranges over V, N, ART, and P. Because of the lexical-generation probabilities in Figure 7.6, only the entries for a noun and a verb are greater than zero.

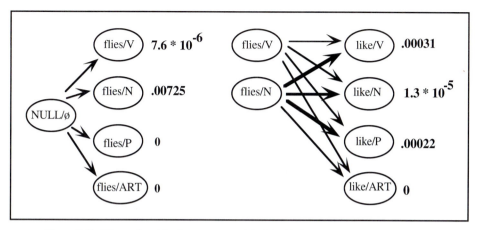

Figure 7.10 The results of the first two steps of the Viterbi algorithm

Thus the most likely sequence of one category ending in a V $(= L_1)$ to generate *flies* has a score of $7.6 * 10^{-6}$, whereas the most likely one ending in an N $(= L_2)$ has a score of .00725.

The result of the first step of the algorithm is shown as the left-hand side network in Figure 7.10. The probability of *flies* in each category has been computed. The second phase of the algorithm extends the sequences one word at a time, keeping track of the best sequence found so far to each category. For instance, the probability of the state like/V is computed as follows:

$$
\begin{aligned}
PROB(\text{like/V}) \ &= \text{MAX}(\ PROB(\text{flies/N}) * PROB(\text{V} \mid \text{N}), \\
&\quad\quad PROB(\text{flies/V}) * PROB(\text{V} \mid \text{V})) * \\
&\quad PROB(\text{like/V}) \\
&= \text{MAX}(.00725 * .43, 7.6 * 10^{-6} * .0001) * .1 \\
&= 3.12 * 10^{-4}
\end{aligned}
$$

The difference in this value from that shown in Figure 7.10 is simply a result of the fact that the calculation here used truncated approximate values for the probabilities. In other words, the most likely sequence of length two generating *Flies like* and ending in a V has a score of $3.1 * 10^{-4}$ (and is the sequence N V), the most likely one ending in a P has a score of $2.2 * 10^{-5}$ (and is the sequence N P), and the most likely one ending in an N has a score of $1.3 * 10^{-5}$ (and is the sequence N N). The heavier arrows indicate the best sequence leading up to each node. The computation continues in the same manner until each word has been processed. Figure 7.11 shows the result after the next iteration, and Figure 7.12 shows the final result. The highest probability sequence ends in state flower/N. It is simple to trace back from this category (using BACKPTR(1, 4) and so on) to find the full sequence N V ART N, agreeing with our intuitions.

Algorithms like this can perform effectively if the probability estimates are computed from a large corpus of data that is of the same style as the input to be classified. Researchers consistently report labeling with 95 percent or better

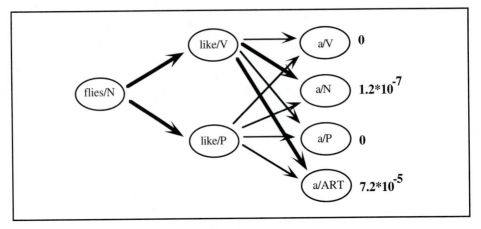

Figure 7.11 The result after the second iteration

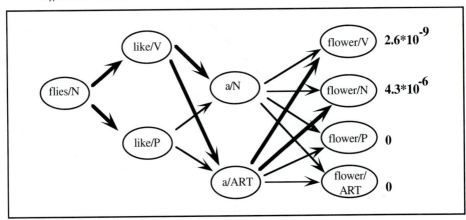

Figure 7.12 The result after the third iteration

accuracy using trigram models. Remember, however, that the naive algorithm picks the most likely category about 90 percent of the time. Still, the error rate is cut in half by introducing these techniques.

7.4 Obtaining Lexical Probabilities

Corpus-based methods suggest some new ways to control parsers. If we had some large corpora of parsed sentences available, we could use statistical methods to identify the common structures in English and favor these in the parsing algorithm. This might allow us to choose the most likely interpretation when a sentence is ambiguous, and might lead to considerably more efficient parsers that are nearly deterministic. Such corpora of parsed sentences are now becoming available.

BOX 7.1 Getting Reliable Statistics

Given that you need to estimate probabilities for lexical items and for n-grams, how much data is needed for these estimates to be reliable? In practice, the amount of data needed depends heavily on the size of the n-grams used, as the number of probabilities that need to be estimated grows rapidly with n. For example, a typical tagset has about 40 different lexical categories. To collect statistics on a unigram (a simple count of the words in each category), you would only need 40 statistics, one for each category. For bigrams, you would need 1600 statistics, one for each pair. For trigrams, you would need 64,000, one for each possible triple. Finally, for four-grams, you would need 2,560,000 statistics. As you can see, even if the corpus is a million words, a four-gram analysis would result in most categories being empty. For trigrams and a million-word corpus, however, there would be an average of 15 examples per category if they were evenly distributed. While the trigrams are definitely not uniformly distributed, this amount of data seems to give good results in practice.

One technique that is very useful for handling sparse data is called **smoothing**. Rather than simply using a trigram to estimate the probability of a category C_i, at position i, you use a formula that combines the trigram, bigram, and unigram statistics. Using this scheme, the probability of category C_i given the preceding categories $C_1, ..., C_{i-1}$ is estimated by the formula

$$PROB(C_i \mid C_1, ..., C_{i-1}) \cong \lambda_1 PROB(C_i) + \lambda_2 PROB(C_i \mid C_{i-1}) + \lambda_3 PROB(C_i \mid C_{i-2} \, C_{i-1})$$

where $\lambda_1 + \lambda_2 + \lambda_3 = 1$. Using this estimate, if the trigram has never been seen before, the bigram or unigram estimates still would guarantee a nonzero estimate in many cases where it is desired. Typically, the best performance will arise if λ_3 is significantly greater than the other parameters so that the trigram information has the most effect on the probabilities. It is also possible to develop algorithms that learn good values for the parameters given a particular training set (for example, see Jelinek (1990)).

The first issue is what the input would be to such a parser. One simple approach would be to use a part-of-speech tagging algorithm from the last section to select a single category for each word and then start the parse with these categories. If the part-of-speech tagging is accurate, this will be an excellent approach, because a considerable amount of lexical ambiguity will be eliminated before the parser even starts. But if the tagging is wrong, it will prevent the parser from ever finding the correct interpretation. Worse, the parser may find a valid but implausible interpretation based on the wrongly tagged word and never realize the error. Consider that even at 95 percent accuracy, the chance that every word is correct in a sentence consisting of only 8 words is .67, and with 12 words it is .46—less than half. Thus the chances of this approach working in general look slim.

$PROB(ART \mid the) \cong$	.99		$PROB(N \mid like) \cong$	.16
$PROB(N \mid flies) \cong$	.48		$PROB(ART \mid a) \cong$	.995
$PROB(V \mid flies) \cong$	.52		$PROB(N \mid a) \cong$	.005
$PROB(V \mid like) \cong$	.49		$PROB(N \mid flower) \cong$	.78
$PROB(P \mid like) \cong$	.34		$PROB(V \mid flower) \cong$	.22

Figure 7.13 Context-independent estimates for the lexical categories

A more appropriate approach would be to compute the probability that each word appears in the possible lexical categories. If we could combine these probabilities with some method of assigning probabilities to rule use in the grammar, then we could develop a parsing algorithm that finds the most probable parse for a given sentence.

You already saw the simplest technique for estimating lexical probability by counting the number of times each word appears in the corpus in each cate-gory. Then the probability that word w appears in a lexical category L_j out of possible categories L_1, ..., L_N could be estimated by the formula

$$PROB(L_j \mid w) \cong count(L_j \& w) / \Sigma_{i=1,N} count(L_i \& w)$$

Using the data shown in Figure 7.5, we could derive the context-independent probabilities for each category and word shown in Figure 7.13.

As we saw earlier, however, such estimates are unreliable because they do not take context into account. A better estimate would be obtained by computing how likely it is that category L_i occurred at position t over all sequences given the input w_1, ..., w_t. In other words, rather than searching for the one sequence that yields the maximum probability for the input, we want to compute the sum of the probabilities for the input from all sequences.

For example, the probability that *flies* is a noun in the sentence *The flies like flowers* would be calculated by summing the probability of all sequences that end with *flies* as a noun. Given the transition and lexical-generation probabilities in Figures 7.4 and 7.6, the sequences that have a nonzero values would be

The/ART flies/N	$9.58 * 10^{-3}$
The/N flies/N	$1.13 * 10^{-6}$
The/P flies/N	$4.55 * 10^{-9}$

which adds up to $9.58 * 10^{-3}$. Likewise, three nonzero sequences end with *flies* as a V, yielding a total sum of $1.13 * 10^{-5}$. Since these are the only sequences that have nonzero scores when the second word is *flies,* the sum of all these sequences will be the probability of the sequence *The flies,* namely $9.591 * 10^{-3}$. We can now compute the probability that *flies* is a noun as follows:

$PROB(flies/N \mid The\ flies)$
$\quad = PROB(flies/N \ \& \ The\ flies) / PROB(The\ flies)$

Initialization Step

For i = 1 to N do

$\quad$ SEQSUM(i, 1) = $PROB(w_1 | L_i) * PROB(L_i | \emptyset)$

Computing the Forward Probabilities

For t = 2 to T do

$\quad$ For i = 1 to N do

$\qquad$ SEQSUM(i, t) = $\Sigma_{j=1,N} (PROB(L_i | L_j) * SEQSUM(j, t-1)) * PROB(w_t | L_i)$

Computing the Lexical Probabilities

For t = 1 to T do

$\quad$ For i = 1 to N do

$\qquad$ $PROB(C_t = L_i)$ = SEQSUM(i, t) / $\Sigma_{j=1,N}$ SEQSUM(j, t)

Figure 7.14 The forward algorithm for computing the lexical probabilities

$$= 9.58 * 10^{-3} / 9.591 * 10^{-3}$$
$$= .9988$$

Likewise, the probability that *flies* is a verb would be .0012.

Of course, it would not be feasible to enumerate all possible sequences in a realistic example. Luckily, however, the same trick used in the Viterbi algorithm can be used here. Rather than selecting the maximum score for each node at each stage of the algorithm, we compute the sum of all scores.

To develop this more precisely, we define the **forward probability**, written as $\alpha_i(t)$, which is the probability of producing the words $w_1, ..., w_t$ and ending in state w_t/L_i:

$$\alpha_i(t) = PROB(w_t/L_i, w_1, ..., w_t)$$

For example, with the sentence *The flies like flowers,* $\alpha_2(3)$ would be the sum of values computed for all sequences ending in V (the second category) in position 3 given the input *The flies like.* Using the definition of conditional probability, you can then derive the probability that word w_t is an instance of lexical category L_i as follows:

$$PROB(w_t/L_i | w_1, ..., w_t) = PROB(w_t/L_i, w_1, ..., w_t) / PROB(w_1, ..., w_t)$$

We estimate the value of $PROB(w_1, ..., w_t)$ by summing over all possible sequences up to any state at position t, which is simply $\Sigma_{j=1,N} \alpha_j(t)$. In other words, we end up with

$$PROB(w_t/L_i | w_1, ..., w_t) \cong \alpha_i(t) / \Sigma_{j=1,N} \alpha_j(t)$$

The first two parts of the algorithm shown in Figure 7.14 compute the forward probabilities using a variant of the Viterbi algorithm. The last step converts the

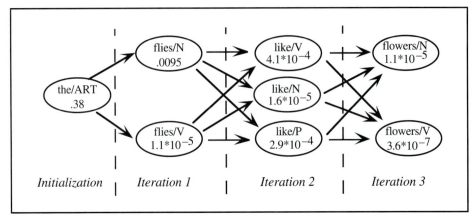

Figure 7.15 Computing the sums of the probabilities of the sequences

$PROB$(the/ART | *the*) = 1.0	$PROB$(like/P | *the flies like*) ≅ .4
$PROB$(flies/N | *the flies*) ≅ .9988	$PROB$(like/N | *the flies like*) ≅ .022
$PROB$(flies/V | *the flies*) ≅ .0011	$PROB$(flowers/N | *the flies like flowers*) ≅ .967
$PROB$(like/V | *the flies like*) ≅ .575	$PROB$(flowers/V | *the flies like flowers*) ≅ .033

Figure 7.16 Context-dependent estimates for lexical categories in the sentence *The flies like flowers*

forward probabilities into lexical probabilities for the given sentence by normalizing the values.

Consider deriving the lexical probabilities for the sentence *The flies like flowers* using the probability estimates in Figures 7.4 and 7.6. The algorithm in Figure 7.14 would produce the sums shown in Figure 7.15 for each category in each position, resulting in the probability estimates shown in Figure 7.16.

Note that while the context-independent approximation in Figure 7.13 slightly favors the verb interpretation of *flies,* the context-dependent approximation virtually eliminates it because the training corpus had no sentences with a verb immediately following an article. These probabilities are significantly different than the context-independent ones and much more in line with intuition.

Note that you could also consider the **backward probability**, $\beta_i(t)$, the probability of producing the sequence $w_t, ..., w_T$ beginning from state w_t/L_j. These values can be computed by an algorithm similar to the forward probability algorithm but starting at the end of the sentence and sweeping backward through the states. Thus a better method of estimating the lexical probabilities for word w_t would be to consider the entire sentence rather than just the words up to t. In this case, the estimate would be

$$PROB(w_t/L_i) = (\alpha_i(t) * \beta_i(t)) / \Sigma_{j=1,N} (\alpha_j(t) * \beta_j(t))$$

Rule		Count for LHS	Count for Rule	Probability
1.	$S \rightarrow NP\ VP$	300	300	1
2.	$VP \rightarrow V$	300	116	.386
3.	$VP \rightarrow V\ NP$	300	118	.393
4.	$VP \rightarrow V\ NP\ PP$	300	66	.22
5.	$NP \rightarrow NP\ PP$	1023	241	.24
6.	$NP \rightarrow N\ N$	1023	92	.09
7.	$NP \rightarrow N$	1023	141	.14
8.	$NP \rightarrow ART\ N$	1023	558	.55
9.	$PP \rightarrow P\ NP$	307	307	1

Grammar 7.17   A simple probabilistic grammar

7.5 Probabilistic Context-Free Grammars

Just as finite state machines could be generalized to the probabilistic case, context-free grammars can also be generalized. To do this, we must have some statistics on rule use. The simplest approach is to count the number of times each rule is used in a corpus containing parsed sentences and use this to estimate the probability of each rule being used. For instance, consider a category C, where the grammar contains m rules, R_1, ..., R_m, with the left-hand side C. You could estimate the probability of using rule R_j to derive C by the formula

$$PROB(R_j \mid C) \cong \text{Count}(\#\ \text{times}\ R_j\ \text{used}) / \Sigma_{i=1,m}\ (\#\ \text{times}\ R_i\ \text{used})$$

Grammar 7.17 shows a probabilistic CFG with the probabilities derived from analyzing a parsed version of the demonstration corpus.

You can then develop algorithms similar in function to the Viterbi algorithm that, given a sentence, will find the most likely parse tree that could have generated that sentence. The technique involves making certain independence assumptions about rule use. In particular, you must assume that the probability of a constituent being derived by a rule R_j is independent of how the constituent is used as a subconstituent. For example, this assumption would imply that the probabilities of NP rules are the same whether the NP is the subject, the object of a verb, or the object of a preposition. We know that this assumption is not valid in most cases. For instance, noun phrases in the subject position are much more likely to be pronouns than noun phrases not in the subject position. But, as before, it might be that useful predictive power can be obtained using these techniques in practice.

With this assumption, a formalism can be developed based on the probability that a constituent C generates a sequence of words w_i, w_{i+1}, ..., w_j,

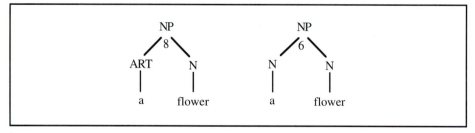

Figure 7.18 The two possible ways that *a flower* could be an NP

written as $w_{i,j}$. This type of probability is called the **inside probability** because it assigns a probability to the word sequence inside the constituent. It is written as

$PROB(w_{i,j} \mid C)$

Consider how to derive inside probabilities. The case for lexical categories is simple. In fact, these are exactly the lexical-generation probabilities derived in Section 7.3. For example, $PROB(flower \mid N)$ is the inside probability that the constituent N is realized as the word *flower*, which for our hypothetical corpus was .06, given in Figure 7.6.

Using such lexical-generation probabilities, we can then derive the probability that the constituent NP generates the sequence *a flower* as follows: There are only two NP rules in Grammar 7.17 that could generate a sequence of two words. The parse trees generated by these two rules are shown in Figure 7.18. You know the likelihood of each rule, estimated from the corpus as shown in Grammar 7.17, so the probability that the constituent NP generates the words *a flower* will be the sum of the probabilities of the two ways it can be derived, as follows:

$PROB(a\ flower \mid NP) =$
$\quad PROB(\text{Rule } 8 \mid NP) * PROB(a \mid ART) * PROB(flower \mid N) +$
$\quad PROB(\text{Rule } 6 \mid NP) * PROB(a \mid N) * PROB(flower \mid N)$
$\quad = .55 * .36 * .06 + .09 * .001 * .06$
$\quad = .012$

This probability can then be used to compute the probability of larger constituents. For instance, the probability of generating the words *A flower wilted* from constituent S could be computed by summing the probabilities generated from each of the possible trees shown in Figure 7.19. Although there are three possible interpretations, the first two differ only in the derivation of *a flower* as an NP. Both these interpretations are already included in the preceding computation of $PROB(a\ flower \mid NP)$. Thus the probability of *a flower blooms* is

$PROB(a\ flower\ blooms \mid S) =$
$\quad PROB(\text{Rule } 1 \mid S) * PROB(a\ flower \mid NP) * PROB(blooms \mid VP) +$
$\quad PROB(\text{Rule } 1 \mid S) * PROB(a \mid NP) * PROB(flower\ blooms \mid VP)$

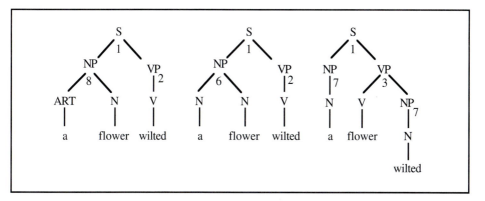

Figure 7.19 The three possible ways to generate *a flower wilted* as an S

Using this method, the probability that a given sentence will be generated by the grammar can be computed efficiently. The method only requires recording the value of each constituent between each two possible positions. In essence, it is using the same optimization that was gained by a packed chart structure, as discussed in Chapter 6.

We will not pursue this development further, however, because in parsing, you are interested in finding the most likely parse rather than the overall probability of a given sentence. In particular, it matters which of the two NP interpretations in Figure 7.19 was used. The probabilities of specific parse trees can be found using a standard chart parsing algorithm, where the probability of each constituent is computed from the probability of its subconstituents and the probability of the rule used. Specifically, when entering an entry E of category C using a rule i with n subconstituents corresponding to entries $E_1, ..., E_n$, then

$$PROB(E) = PROB(\text{Rule i} \mid C) * PROB(E_1) * ... * PROB(E_n)$$

For lexical categories it is better to use the forward probability than the lexical-generation probability. This will produce better estimates, because it accounts for some of the context of the sentence. You can use the standard chart parsing algorithm and add a step that computes the probability of each entry when it is added to the chart. Using the bottom-up algorithm and the probabilities derived from the demonstration corpus, Figure 7.20 shows the complete chart for the input *a flower*. Note that the most intuitive reading, that it is an NP, has the highest probability by far, .54. But there are many other possible interpretations because of the low probability readings of the word *a* as a noun and the reading of *flower* as a verb. Note that the context-independent probabilities for *flower* would favor the verb interpretation, but the forward algorithm strongly favors the noun interpretation in the context where it immediately follows the word *a*. The probabilities for the lexical constituents ART416, N417, V419, and N422 were computed using the forward algorithm. The context-independent lexical probabilities would be much less in line with intuition.

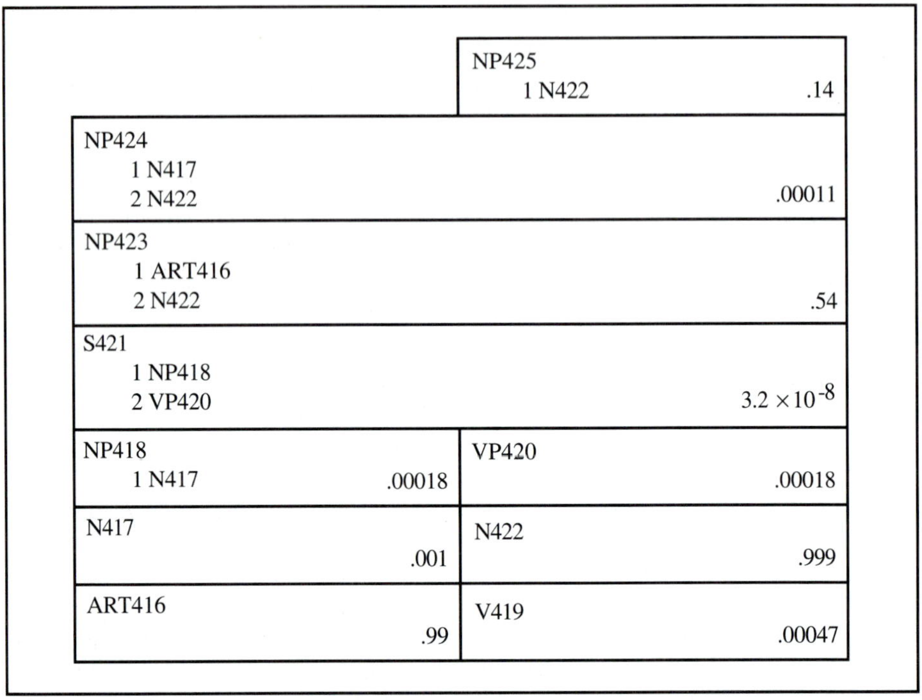

	NP425 1 N422 .14

NP424
   1 N417
   2 N422 .00011	

NP423
   1 ART416
   2 N422 .54	

S421
   1 NP418
   2 VP420 3.2×10^{-8}	

NP418
   1 N417   .00018
	VP420
	                  .00018

N417
              .001
	N422
	                  .999

ART416
               .99
	V419
	                  .00047

Figure 7.20 The full chart for *a flower*

Unfortunately, a parser built using these techniques turns out not to work as well as you might expect, although it does help. Some researchers have found that these techniques identify the correct parse about 50 percent of the time. It doesn't do better because the independence assumptions that need to be made are too radical. Problems arise in many guises, but one critical issue is the handling of lexical items. For instance, the context-free model assumes that the probability of a particular verb being used in a VP rule is independent of which rule is being considered. This means lexical preferences for certain rules cannot be handled within the basic framework. This problem then influences many other issues, such as attachment decisions.

For example, Grammar 7.17 indicates that rule 3 is used 39 percent of the time, rule 4, 22 percent of the time, and rule 5, 24 percent of the time. This means that, independent of whatever words are used, an input sequence of form V NP PP will always be interpreted with the PP attached to the verb. The tree fragments are shown in Figure 7.21: Any structure that attaches the PP to the verb will have a probability of .22 from this fragment, whereas the structure that attaches the PP to the NP will have a probability of .39 * .25, namely .093. So the parser will always attach a PP to the verb phrase independent of what words are used. In fact, there are 23 cases of this situation in the corpus where the PP attaches to an NP, and the probabilistic parser gets every one of them wrong.

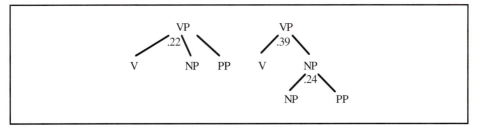

Figure 7.21 The two structures affecting attachment decisions

This is true even with particular verbs that rarely take a _np_pp complement. Because of the context-free assumption made about probabilities, the particular verb used has no effect on the probability of a particular rule being used. Because of this type of problem, a parser based on this approach with a realistic grammar is only a slight improvement over the nonprobabilistic methods.

For example, 84 sentences were selected from the corpus, each involving a PP attachment problem. With the standard bottom-up nonprobabilistic algorithm, using Grammar 7.17, the first complete S structure found was the correct answer on one-third of the sentences. By using probabilistic parsing, the highest probability S structure was correct half of the time. Thus, pure probabilistic parsing is better than guessing but leaves much to be desired. Note also that this test was on the same sentences that were used to compute the probabilities in the first place, so performance on new sentences not in the training corpus would tend to be even worse! Papers in the literature that use real corpora and extensive training report accuracy results similar to those described here.

While the pure probabilistic context-free grammars have their faults, the techniques developed here are important and can be reused in generalizations that attempt to develop more context-dependent probabilistic parsing schemes.

7.6 Best-First Parsing

So far, probabilistic context-free grammars have done nothing to improve the efficiency of the parser. Algorithms can be developed that attempt to explore the high-probability constituents first. These are called **best-first parsing** algorithms. The hope is that the best parse can be found quickly and much of the search space, containing lower-rated possibilities, is never explored.

It turns out that all the chart parsing algorithms in Chapter 3 can be modified fairly easily to consider the most likely constituents first. The central idea is to make the agenda a **priority queue**—a structure where the highest-rated elements are always first in the queue. The parser then operates by always removing the highest-ranked constituent from the agenda and adding it to the chart.

It might seem that this one change in search strategy is all that is needed to modify the algorithms, but there is a complication. The previous chart parsing algorithms all depended on the fact that the parser systematically worked from

To add a constituent C from position p_1 to p_2:

1. Insert C into the chart from position p_1 to p_2.
2. For any active arc of the form $X \rightarrow X_1 \ldots \circ C \ldots X_n$ from position p_0 to p_1, add a new active arc $X \rightarrow X_1 \ldots C \circ \ldots X_n$ from position p_0 to p_2.

To add an active arc $X \rightarrow X_1 \ldots C \circ C' \ldots X_n$ to the chart from p_0 to p_2:

1. If C is the last constituent (that is, the arc is completed), add a new constituent of type X to the agenda.
2. Otherwise, if there is a constituent Y of category C' in the chart from p_2 to p_3, then recursively add an active arc $X \rightarrow X_1 \ldots C C' \circ \ldots X_n$ from p_0 to p_3 (which may of course add further arcs or create further constituents).

Figure 7.22   The new arc extension algorithm

left to right, completely processing constituents occurring earlier in the sentence before considering later ones. With the modified algorithm, this is not the case. If the last word in the sentence has the highest score, it will be added to the chart first. The problem this causes is that you cannot simply add active arcs to the chart (and depend on later steps in the algorithm to extend them). In fact, the constituent needed to extend a particular active arc may already be on the chart. Thus, whenever an active arc is added to the chart, you must check to see if it can be extended immediately, given the current chart. Thus we need to modify the arc extension algorithm. The algorithm is as before (in Section 3.4), except that step 2 is modified to check for constituents that already exist on the chart. The complete algorithm is shown in Figure 7.22.

Adopting a best-first strategy makes a significant improvement in the efficiency of the parser. For instance, using Grammar 7.17 and lexicon trained from the corpus, the sentence *The man put a bird in the house* is parsed correctly after generating 65 constituents with the best-first parser. The standard bottom-up algorithm generates 158 constituents on the same sentence, only to obtain the same result. If the standard algorithm were modified to terminate when the first complete S interpretation is found, it would still generate 106 constituents for the same sentence. So best-first strategies can lead to significant improvements in efficiency.

Even though it does not consider every possible constituent, the best-first parser is guaranteed to find the highest probability interpretation. To see this, assume that the parser finds an interpretation S1 with probability p1. The important property of the probabilistic scoring is that the probability of a constituent must always be lower (or equal) to the probability of any of its subconstituents. So if there were an interpretation S2 that had a score p2, higher than p1, then it would have to be constructed out of subconstituents all with a probability of p2 or higher. This means that all the subconstituents would have been added to the chart before S1 was. But this means that the arc that constructs S2 would be

BOX 7.2 Handling Unknown Words

Another area where statistical methods show great promise is in handling unknown words. In traditional parsing, one unknown word will disrupt the entire parse. The techniques discussed in this chapter, however, suggest some interesting ideas. First, if you have a trigram model of the data, you may already have significant predictive power on the category of the unknown word. For example, consider a sequence $w_1 w_2 w_3$, where the last word is unknown. If the two previous words are in categories C_1 and C_2, respectively, then you could pick the category C for the unknown word that maximizes $PROB(C \mid C_1 \ C_2)$. For instance, if C_2 is the category ART, then the most likely interpretation for C will probably be a noun (or maybe an adjective). Other techniques have been developed that use knowledge of morphology to predict the word class. For instance, if the unknown word ends in *-ing* then it is likely to be a verb; if it ends in *-ly*, then it is likely to be an adverb; and so on. Estimates based on suffixes can be obtained by analyzing a corpus in the standard way to obtain estimates of $PROB$(word is category C | end is -ly) and so on. Techniques for handling unknown words are discussed in Church (1988), de Marcken (1990), and Weischedel et al. (1993).

completed, and hence S2 would be on the agenda. Since S2 has a higher score than S1, it would be considered first.

While the idea of a best-first parser is conceptually simple, there are a few problems that arise when trying to apply this technique in practice. One problem is that if you use a multiplicative method to combine the scores, the scores for constituents tend to fall quickly as they cover more and more input. This might not seem problematic, but in practice, with large grammars, the probabilities drop off so quickly that the search closely resembles a breadth-first search: First build all constituents of length 1, then all constituents of length 2, and so on. Thus the promise of quickly finding the most preferred solution is not realized. To deal with this problem, some systems use a different function to compute the score for constituents. For instance, you could use the minimum score of any subconstituent and the rule used, that is,

$$Score(C) = MIN(Score(C \rightarrow C_1, ..., C_n), Score(C_1), ..., Score(C_n))$$

This gives a higher (or equal) score than the first approach, but a single poorly-rated subconstituent can essentially eliminate any constituent that contains it, no matter how well all the other constituents are rated. Unfortunately, testing the same 84 sentences using the MIN function leads to a significant decrease in accuracy to only 39 percent, not much better than a brute force search. But other researchers have suggested that the technique performs better than this in actual practice. You might also try other means of combining the scores, such as taking the average score of all subconstituents.

Rule	the	house	peaches	flowers
NP → N	0	0	.65	.76
NP → N N	0	.82	0	0
NP → NP PP	.23	.18	.35	.24
NP → ART N	.76	0	0	0
Rule	**ate**	**bloom**	**like**	**put**
VP → V	.28	.84	0	.03
VP → V NP	.57	.1	.9	.03
VP → V NP PP	.14	.05	.1	.93

Figure 7.23 Some rule estimates based on the first word

7.7 A Simple Context-Dependent Best-First Parser

The best-first algorithm leads to improvement in the efficiency of the parser but does not affect the accuracy problem. This section explores a simple alternative method of computing rule probabilities that uses more context-dependent lexical information. The idea exploits the observation that the first word in a constituent is often the head and thus has a dramatic effect on the probabilities of rules that account for its complement. This suggests a new probability measure for rules that is relative to the first word, $PROB(R \mid C, w)$. This is estimated as follows:

$$PROB(R \mid C, w) = \frac{\text{Count(\# times rule R used for cat C starting with w)}}{\text{Count(\# times cat C starts with w)}}$$

The effect of this modification is that probabilities are sensitive to the particular words used. For instance, in the corpus, singular nouns rarely occur alone as a noun phrase (that is, starting rule NP → N), whereas plural nouns rarely are used as a noun modifying (that is, starting rule NP → N N). This can be seen in the difference between the probabilities for these two rules given the words *house* and *peaches,* shown in Figure 7.23. With the context-free probabilities, the rule NP → N had a probability of .14. This underestimates the rule when the input has a plural noun, and overestimates it when the input has a singular noun.

More importantly, the context-sensitive rules encode verb preferences for different subcategorizations. In particular, Figure 7.23 shows that the rule VP → V NP PP is used 93 percent of the time with the verb *put* but only 10 percent of the time with *like.* This difference allows a parser based on these probabilities to do significantly better than the context-free probabilistic parser. In particular, on the same 84 test sentences on which the context-free probabilistic parser had 49 percent accuracy, the context-dependent probabilistic parser has 66 percent accuracy, getting the attachment correct on 14 sentences on which the context-

Strategy	Accuracy on 84 PP Attachment Problems	Size of Chart Generated for *The man put the bird in the house*
Full Parse	33% (taking first S found)	158
Context-Free Probabilities	49%	65
Context-Dependent Probabilities	66%	36

Figure 7.24 A summary of the accuracy and efficiency of different parsing strategies

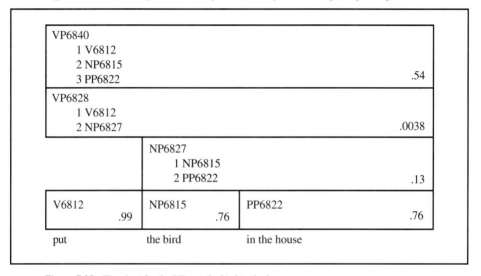

Figure 7.25 The chart for the VP *put the bird in the house*

free parser failed. The context-dependent parser is also more efficient, finding the answer on the sentence *The man put the bird in the house* generating only 36 constituents. The results of the three parsing strategies are summarized in Figure 7.24.

To see why the context-dependent parser does better, consider the attachment decision that has to be made between the trees shown in Figure 7.21 for the verbs *like* and *put,* say in the sentences *The man put the bird in the house* and *The man likes the bird in the house.* The context-free probabilistic parser would assign the same structure to both, getting the example with *put* right and the example with *like* wrong. The relevant parts of the charts are shown in Figures 7.25 and 7.26. In Figure 7.25 the probability of the rule VP → V NP PP, starting with *put,* is .93, yielding a probability of .54 (.93 * .99 * .76 * .76) for constituent VP6840. This is far greater than the probability of .0038 given the alternative VP6828. Changing the verb to *like,* as shown in Figure 7.26, affects the probabilities enough to override the initial bias towards the V-NP-PP interpretation. In this case, the probability of the rule VP → V NP PP, starting with *like,* is only .1,

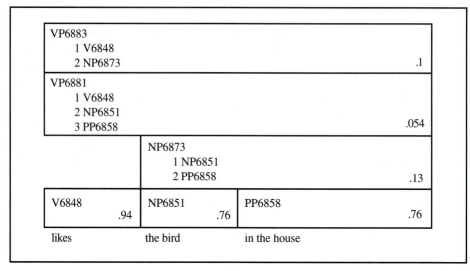

Figure 7.26 The chart for the VP *likes the bird in the house*

whereas the probability of rule VP → V NP is .9. This gives a probability of .1 to VP6883, beating out the alternative.

The question arises as to how accurate a parser can become by using the appropriate contextual information. While 66 percent accuracy was good compared to the alternative strategies, it still leaves a 33 percent error rate on sentences involving a PP attachment decision. What additional information could be added to improve the performance? Clearly, you could make the rule probabilities relative to a larger fragment of the input, using a bigram or trigram at the beginning of the rule. This may help the selectivity if there is enough training data.

Attachment decisions depend not only on the verb but also on the preposition in the PP. You could devise a more complex estimate based on the previous category, the head verb, and the preposition for rule VP → V NP PP. This would require more data to obtain reliable statistics but could lead to a significant increase in reliability. But a complication arises in that you cannot compare across rules as easily now: The VP → V NP PP rule is evaluated using the verb and the preposition, but there is no corresponding preposition with the rule VP → V NP. Thus a more complicated measure would have to be devised.

In general, the more selective the lexical categories, the more predictive the estimates can be, assuming there is enough data. Earlier we claimed that basing the statistics on words would require too much data. But is there a subset of words that could profitably be used individually? Certainly function words such as prepositions seem ideally suited for individual treatment. There is a fixed number of them, and they have a significant impact on the structure of the sentence. Similarly, other closed class words—articles, quantifiers, conjunctions, and so on—could all be treated individually rather than grouped together as a class. It is reasonable to assume we will be able to obtain enough data to obtain reliable estimates with these words.

The complications arise with the open class words. Verbs and nouns, for instance, play a major role in constraining the data, but there are far too many of them to consider individually. One approach is to model the common ones individually, as we did here. Another would be to try to cluster words together into classes based on their similarities. This could be done by hand, based on semantic properties. For instance, all verbs describing motion might have essentially the same behavior and be collapsed into a single class. The other option is to use some automatic technique for learning useful classes by analyzing corpora of sentences with attachment ambiguities.

Summary

Statistically based methods show great promise in addressing the ambiguity resolution problem in natural language processing. Such techniques have been used to good effect for part-of-speech tagging, for estimating lexical probabilities, and for building probabilistically based parsing algorithms. For part-of-speech tagging, the Viterbi algorithm using bigram or trigram probability models can attain accuracy rates of over 95 percent. Context-dependent lexical probabilities can be computed using an algorithm similar to the Viterbi algorithm that computes the forward probabilities. These can then be used as input to a chart parser that uses a context-free probabilistic grammar to find the most likely parse tree. The efficiency of parsers can be dramatically improved by using a best-first search strategy, in which the highest-rated constituents are added to the chart first. Unfortunately, the context-free probabilistic framework often does not identify the intuitively correct parse tree. Context-dependent probability measures can be developed that significantly improve the accuracy of the parser over the context-free methods. This is an area of active research, and significant developments can be expected in the near future.

Related Work and Further Readings

The literature on statistical methods of natural language processing is quite young, with the techniques being developed in the last decade. An excellent source that describes the techniques in detail is Charniak (1993). Many of the basic algorithms were developed in areas outside natural language processing. For instance, the Viterbi algorithm was originally developed on Markov models (Viterbi, 1967) and is in extensive use in a wide range of applications. The technique for developing probability estimates for lexical classes is based on the forward and forward-backward algorithms by Baum (1972). The use of these techniques for speech recognition is described well in an article by Rabiner (1989) and in many of the papers in Waibel and Lee (1990).

The use of these techniques for part-of-speech tagging has been developed by many researchers, including Jelinek (1990), Church (1988), DeRose (1988), and Weischedel et al. (1993), to name a few. Many researchers have also developed parsers based on the context-independent rule probabilities described in Section 7.5, including Jelinek (1990). One of the major attractions for statistically based approaches is the ability to learn effective parameters from processing corpora. These algorithms start with an initial estimate of the probabilities and then process the corpus to compute a better estimate. This can be repeated until further improvement is not found. These techniques are guaranteed to converge but do not necessarily find the optimal values. Rather, they find a local maximum and are thus similar to many hill-climbing algorithms. An example of a technique to learn parameters for a grammar from only partially analyzed data is given in Pereira and Schabes (1992).

Best-first parsing algorithms have been in use for a long time, going back to work such as that by Paxton and Robinson (1973). Only recently have they been explored using data derived from corpora (as in Weischedel et al. (1993) and Chitrao and Grishman (1990)). A good example of a context-dependent method using trigrams is that of Magerman and Weir (1992). In general, an excellent collection of recent work on statistical models can be found in a special issue of *Computational Linguistics* (Volume 19, Issues 1 and 2, 1993).

Prepositional phrase attachment seems to be a problem well suited to statistical techniques. Whittemore et al. (1990) explored the traditional strategies such as right association and minimal attachment and found that they did not have good predictive power, whereas lexical preference models looked promising. Hindle and Rooth (1993) explored some techniques for gathering such data from corpora that is not fully annotated with syntactic analyses.

The Brown corpus is described in Francis and Kucera (1982) and has been widely used as a testbed since its release. A good source for linguistic data is the Linguistic Data Consortium (LDC) housed at the University of Pennsylvania. The LDC has many large databases of language, in written and spoken forms, and in a wide range of styles and formats. It also contains the Penn Treebank data, which is a large corpus of sentences annotated with parses. The Penn Treebank is described in Marcus et al. (1993).

There are many introductory books on probability theory available. One good one, by Ross (1988), introduces the basic concepts and includes brief discussions of Markov chains and information theory.

Exercises for Chapter 7

1. (*easy*) Prove Bayes' rule by using the definition of conditional probability. Also prove that if A and B are independent then $PROB(A \mid B) = PROB(A)$.

2. (*medium*) Say we have an acceptable margin of error of between .4 and .6 for estimating the probability of a fair coin coming up heads. What is the chance of obtaining a reliable estimate for the probability with five flips?

3. (*medium*) Hand-simulate the Viterbi algorithm using the data and probability estimates in Figures 7.4–7.6 on the sentence *Flower flowers like
flowers.* Draw transition networks as in Figures 7.10–7.12 for the problem,
and identify what part of speech the algorithm identifies for each word.

4. (*medium*) Using the bigram and lexical-generation probabilities given in
this chapter, calculate the word probabilities using the forward algorithm
for the sentence *The a flies like flowers* (involving a very rare use of the
word *a* as a noun, as in *the a flies, the b flies,* and so on). Remember to use
.0001 as a probability for any bigram not in the table. Are the results you
get reasonable? If not, what is the problem and how might it be fixed?

5. (*medium*) Using the tagged corpus provided, write code to collect bigram
and lexical statistics, and implement a part-of-speech tagger using the
Viterbi algorithm. Test your algorithm on the same corpus. How many sentences are tagged correctly? How many category errors did this involve?
Would you expect to get better accuracy results on the sentences that
involved an error if you had access to more data?

6. (*medium*) Consider an extended version of Grammar 7.17 with the additional rule

   10. VP $\to$ V PP

   The revised rule probabilities are shown here. (Any not mentioned are the
   same as in Grammar 7.17.)

VP $\to$ V	.32
VP $\to$ V NP	.33
VP $\to$ V NP PP	.20
VP $\to$ V PP	.15

   In addition, the following bigram probabilities differ from those in Figure
   7.4:

   $PROB(N \mid V) = .53$
   $PROB(ART \mid V) = .32$
   $PROB(P \mid V) = .15$

   a. Hand-simulate (or implement) the forward algorithm on *Fruit flies
   like birds* to produce the lexical probabilities.

   b. Draw out the full chart for *Fruit flies like birds,* showing the probabilities of each constituent.

7. (*hard*) Implement an algorithm to derive the forward and backward probabilities for lexical categories. Develop two lexical analysis programs: one
that uses only the forward algorithm, and one that combines both techniques. Give a sentence for which the results differ substantially.

8. (*hard*) Generalize the Viterbi algorithm to operate based on trigram statistics. Since the probability of a state at position t now depends on the two preceding states, this problem does not fit the basic definition of the Markov assumption. It is often called a second-order Markov assumption. The best way to view this is as an HMM in which all the states are labeled by a pair of categories. Thus, the sequence ART N V N could be generated from a sequence of states labeled (ø, ART), (ART, N), (N, V), and (V, N). The transition probabilities between these states would be the trigram probabilities. For example, the probability of the transition from state (ø, ART) to (ART, N) would be the probability of category N following the categories ø and ART. Train your data using the supplied corpus and implement a part-of-speech tagger based on trigrams. Compare its performance on the same data with the performance of the bigram model.

PART II
Semantic Interpretation

As discussed in the introduction, the task of determining the meaning of a sentence will be divided into two steps: first computing a context-independent notion of meaning, called the logical form, and then interpreting the logical form in context to produce the final meaning representation. Part II of the book concerns the first of these steps, which will be called semantic interpretation. Many actual systems do not make this division and use contextual information early in the processing. Nonetheless, the organization is very helpful for classifying the issues and for illustrating the different techniques.

A similar division is often made in linguistics, where the study of context-independent meaning is often called semantics, and the study of language in context is called pragmatics. Using the need for context as the test for dividing up problems, the following are some examples of issues that can be addressed in a context-independent way and hence will be addressed in Part II:

- eliminating possible word senses by exploiting context-independent structural constraints
- identifying the semantic roles that each word and phrase could play in the logical form, specifically identifying the predicate/argument and modification relations
- identifying co-reference restrictions derived from the structure of the sentence

Just as important, the following will *not* be studied in Part II but will be left for the discussion of contextual interpretation in Part III:

- determining the referents of noun phrases and other phrases
- selecting a single interpretation (and set of word senses) from those that are possible
- determining the intended use of each utterance

Chapter 8 discusses the distinction between logical form and the final meaning representation in more detail, and develops a logical form language that is used throughout the rest of the book. Chapter 9 then addresses the issue of how the logical form relates to syntactic structure and shows how the feature system in the grammar can be used to identify the logical form in a rule-by-rule fashion. Chapter 10 discusses the important problem of ambiguity resolution and shows how semantic constraints or preferences can be used to identify the most plausible word senses and semantic structures. Chapter 11 discusses some alternate methods of semantic interpretation that have proven useful in existing systems and applications. Finally, Chapter 12 discusses a selection of more advanced issues in semantic interpretation, including the analysis of scoping dependencies, for the student with strong interests in semantic issues.

CHAPTER

8

Semantics and Logical Form

8.1 Semantics and Logical Form

8.2 Word Senses and Ambiguity

8.3 The Basic Logical Form Language

8.4 Encoding Ambiguity in the Logical Form

8.5 Verbs and States in Logical Form

8.6 Thematic Roles

8.7 Speech Acts and Embedded Sentences

8.8 Defining Semantic Structure: Model Theory

This chapter introduces the basic ideas underlying theories of meaning, or semantics. It introduces a level of context-independent meaning called the logical form, which can be produced directly from the syntactic structure of a sentence. Because it must be context independent, the logical form does not contain the results of any analysis that requires interpretation of the sentence in context.

Section 8.1 introduces the basic notions of meaning and semantics, and describes the role of a logical form in semantic processing. Section 8.2 introduces word senses and the semantic primitives, and discusses the problem of word-sense ambiguity. Section 8.3 then develops the basic logical form language for expressing the context-independent meaning of sentences. This discussion is extended in Section 8.4 with constructs that concisely encode certain common forms of ambiguity. Section 8.5 discusses the representation of verbs and introduces the notion of state and event variables. Section 8.6 then discusses thematic roles, or cases, and shows how they can be used to capture various semantic generalities across verb meanings. Section 8.7 introduces the notion of surface speech acts and discusses the treatment of embedded sentences in the logical form. This completes the description of the logical form language, which is concisely characterized in Figures 8.7 and 8.8. The optional Section 8.8 is for the student interested in defining a model-theoretic semantics for the logical form language itself. It describes a model theory for the logical form language and discusses various semantic relationships among sentences that can be defined in terms of entailment and implicature.

8.1 Semantics and Logical Form

Precisely defining the notions of semantics and meaning is surprisingly difficult because the terms are used for several different purposes in natural and technical usage. For instance, there is a use of the verb *mean* that has nothing to do with language. Say you are walking in the woods and come across a campfire that is just noticeably warm. You might say *This fire means someone camped here last night.* By this you mean that the fire is evidence for the conclusion or implies the conclusion. This is related to, but different from, the notion of meaning that will be the focus of the next few chapters. The meaning we want is closer to the usage when defining a word, such as in the sentence *"Amble" means to walk slowly.* This defines the meaning of a word in terms of other words. To make this more precise, we will have to develop a more formally specified language in which we can specify meaning without having to refer back to natural language itself. But even if we can do this, defining a notion of sentence meaning is difficult. For example, I was at an airport recently and while I was walking towards my departure gate, a guard at the entrance asked, "Do you know what gate you are going to?" I interpreted this as asking whether I knew where I was going and answered yes. But this response was based on a misunderstanding of what the guard meant, as he then asked, "Which gate is it?" He clearly had wanted me to

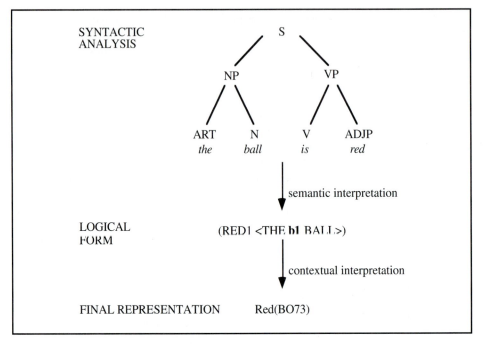

Figure 8.1 Logical form as an intermediate representation

tell him the gate number. Thus the sentence *Do you know what gate you are going to?* appears to mean different things in different contexts.

Can we define a notion of sentence meaning that is independent of context? In other words, is there a level at which the sentence *Do you know what gate you are going to?* has a single meaning, but may be used for different purposes? This is a complex issue, but there are many advantages to trying to make such an approach work. The primary argument is modularity. If such a division can be made, then we can study sentence meaning in detail without all the complications of sentence usage. In particular, if sentences have no context-independent meaning, then we may not be able to separate the study of language from the study of general human reasoning and context. As you will see in the next few chapters, there are many examples of constraints based on the meaning of words that appear to be independent of context. So from now on, we will use the term *meaning* in this context-independent sense, and we will use the term *usage* for the context-dependent aspects. The representation of context-independent meaning is called the **logical form**. The process of mapping a sentence to its logical form is called **semantic interpretation**, and the process of mapping the logical form to the final knowledge representation (KR) language is called **contextual interpretation**. Figure 8.1 shows a simple version of the stages of interpretation. The exact meaning of the notations used will be defined later.

For the moment let us assume the knowledge representation language is the first-order predicate calculus (FOPC). Given that assumption, what is the status of the logical form? In some approaches the logical form is defined as the literal meaning of the utterance, and the logical form language is the same as the final knowledge representation language. If this is to be a viable approach in the long run, however, it would mean that the knowledge representation must be considerably more complex than representations in present use in AI systems. For instance, the logical form language must allow **indexical** terms, that is, terms that are defined by context. The pronouns *I* and *you* are indexical because their interpretation depends on the context of who is speaking and listening. In fact most definite descriptions (such as *the red ball*) are indexical, as the object referred to can only be identified with respect to a context. Many other aspects of language, including the interpretation of tense and determining the scope of quantifiers, depend on context as well and thus cannot be uniquely determined at the logical form level. Of course, all of this could be treated as ambiguity at the logical form level, but this would be impractical, as every sentence would have large numbers of possible logical forms (as in the sentence *The red ball dropped,* which would have a different logical form for every possible object that could be described as a ball that is red).

But if the logical form language is not part of the knowledge representation language, what is its formal status? A promising approach has been developed in linguistics over the last decade that suggests an answer that uses the notion of a **situation**, which is a particular set of circumstances in the world. This corresponds reasonably well to the intuitive notion of the meaning of *situation* in English. For instance, when attending a class, you are in a situation where there are fellow students and an instructor, where certain utterances are made by the lecturer, questions asked, and so on. Also, there will be objects in the lecture hall, say a blackboard and chairs, and so on. More formally, you might think of a situation as a set of objects and relations between those objects. A very simple situation might consist of two objects, a ball B0005 and a person P86, and include the relationship that the person owns the ball. Let us encode this situation as the set {(BALL B0005), (PERSON P86), (OWNS P86 B0005)}.

Language creates special types of situations based on what information is conveyed. These issues will be explored in detail later, but for now consider the following to help your intuition. In any conversation or text, assume there is a discourse situation that records the information conveyed so far. A new sentence is interpreted with respect to this situation and produces a new situation that includes the information conveyed by the new sentence. Given this view, the logical form is a function that maps the discourse situation in which the utterance was made to a new discourse situation that results from the occurrence of the utterance. For example, assume that the situation we just encoded has been created by some preceding sentences describing the ball and who owns it. The utterance *The ball is red* might produce a new situation that consists of the old situation plus the new fact that B0005 has the property RED: {(BALL B0005), (PERSON P86), (OWNS P86 B0005), (RED B0005)}. Figure 8.2 shows this view of the interpretation process, treating the logical form as a function between

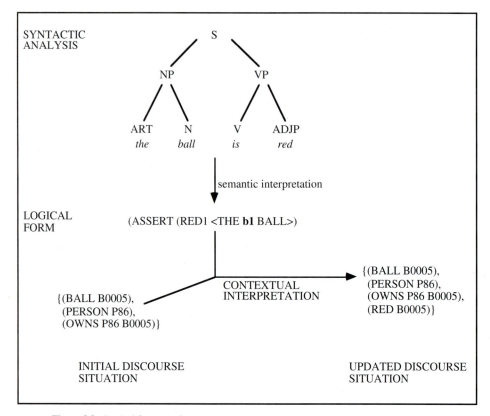

Figure 8.2 Logical form as a function

situations. The two organizations presented in Figures 8.1 and 8.2 differ in that the latter might not include a single identifiable expression in the knowledge representation that fully captures the "meaning" of the sentence. Rather, the logical form might make a variety of changes to produce the updated situation. This allows other implications to be derived from an utterance that are not directly captured in the semantic content of the sentence. Such issues will become important later when we discuss contextual interpretation.

Even though much of language is highly context dependent, there is still considerable semantic structure to language that is context independent and that can be used in the semantic interpretation process to produce the logical form. Much of this semantic knowledge consists of the type of information you can find in dictionaries—the basic semantic properties of words (that is, whether they refer to relations, objects, and so on), what different senses are possible for each word, what senses may combine to form larger semantic structures, and so on. Identifying these forms of information and using this information to compute a logical form are the focus of Part II of the book.

8.2 Word Senses and Ambiguity

To develop a theory of semantics and semantic interpretation, we need to develop a structural model, just as we did for syntax. With syntax we first introduced the notion of the basic syntactic classes and then developed ways to constrain how simple classes combine to form larger structures. We will follow the same basic strategy for semantics. You might think that the basic semantic unit could be the word or the morpheme, but that approach runs into problems because of the presence of ambiguity. For example, it is not unusual for the verb *go* to have more than 40 entries in a typical dictionary. Each one of these definitions reflects a different **sense** of the word. Dictionaries often give synonyms for particular word senses. For *go* you might find synonyms such as *move, depart, pass, vanish, reach, extend,* and *set out.* Many of these highlight a different sense of the verb *go.* Of course, if these are true synonyms of some sense of *go,* then the verbs themselves will share identical senses. For instance, one of the senses of *go* will be identical to one of the senses of *depart.*

If every word has one or more senses then you are looking at a very large number of senses, even given that some words have synonymous senses. Fortunately, the different senses can be organized into a set of broad classes of objects by which we classify the world. The set of different classes of objects in a representation is called its **ontology**. To handle a natural language, we need a much broader ontology than commonly found in work on formal logic. Such classifications of objects have been of interest for a very long time and arise in the writings of Aristotle (384–322 B.C.). The major classes that Aristotle suggested were substance (physical objects), quantity (such as numbers), quality (such as bright red), relation, place, time, position, state, action, and affection. To this list we might add other classes such as events, ideas, concepts, and plans. Two of the most influential classes are **actions** and **events**. Events are things that happen in the world and are important in many semantic theories because they provide a structure for organizing the interpretation of sentences. Actions are things that agents do, thus causing some event. Like all objects in the ontology, actions and events can be referred to by pronouns, as in the discourse fragment

We lifted the box. It was hard work.

Here, the pronoun *it* refers to the action of lifting the box. Another very influential category is the **situation**. As previously mentioned, a situation refers to some particular set of circumstances and can be viewed as subsuming the notion of events. In many cases a situation may act like an abstraction of the world over some location and time. For example, the sentence *We laughed and sang at the football game* describes a set of activities performed at a particular time and location, described as the situation *the football game.*

Not surprisingly, ambiguity is a serious problem during semantic interpretation. We can define a word as being **semantically ambiguous** if it maps to more than one sense. But this is more complex than it might first seem, because we need to have a way to determine what the allowable senses are. For example, intuitively the word *kid* seems to be ambiguous between a baby goat and a human child. But how do we know it doesn't have a single sense that includes both interpretations? The word *horse*, on the other hand, seems not to be ambiguous even though we know that horses may be subdivided into mares, colts, trotters, and so on. Why doesn't the word *horse* seem ambiguous when each time the word is used we might not be able to tell if it refers to a mare or a colt? A few linguistic tests have been suggested to define the notion of semantic ambiguity more precisely. One effective test exploits the property that certain syntactic constructs typically require references to identical classes of objects. For example, the sentence *I have two kids and George has three* could mean that George and I are goat farmers or that we have children, but it can't mean a combination of both (I have goats and George has children). On the other hand you can say *I have one horse and George has two*, even when I have a colt and George has mares. Thus this test provides a way to examine our intuitions about word senses. The word *kid* is ambiguous between two senses, BABY-GOAT1 and BABY-HUMAN1, whereas *horse* is not ambiguous between MARE1 and COLT1 but rather has a sense HORSE1 that includes both. This brings up the important point that some senses are more specific than others. This property is often referred to as **vagueness**. The sense HORSE1 is vague to the extent that it doesn't distinguish between mares and colts. Of course, the sense MARE1 is vague with respect to whether it is a large mare or a small one. Virtually all senses involve some degree of vagueness, as they might always allow some more precise specification.

A similar ambiguity test can be constructed for verb senses as well. For example, the sentence *I ran last year and George did too* could mean that we both were candidates in an election or that we both ran some race, but it would be difficult to read it as a mixture of the two. Thus the word *run* is ambiguous between the senses RUN1 (the exercise sense) and RUN2 (the political sense). In contrast, the verb *kiss* is vague in that it does not specify where one is kissed. You can say *I kissed Sue and George did too*, even though I kissed her on the cheek and George kissed her hand.

In addition to lexical ambiguity, there is considerable structural ambiguity at the semantic level. Some forms of ambiguity are parasitic on the underlying syntactic ambiguity. For instance, the sentence *Happy cats and dogs live on the farm* is ambiguous between whether the dogs are also happy or not (that is, is it happy cats and happy dogs, or happy cats and dogs of any disposition). Although this ambiguity does have semantic consequences, it is actually rooted in the syntactic structure; that is, whether the conjunction involves two noun phrases, (Happy cats) and (dogs), or the single noun phrase (Happy (cats and dogs)). But other forms of structural ambiguity are truly semantic and arise from a single syntactic structure. A very common example involves quantifier scoping. For instance, does the sentence *Every boy loves a dog* mean that there is a single dog that all boys love, or that each boy might love a different dog? The syntactic structure is the same in each case, but the difference lies in how the quantifiers are scoped. For example, the two meanings correspond roughly to the following statements in FOPC:

$$\exists\, d\,.\; Dog(d)\; \&\; \forall\, b\,.\; Boy(b)\supset Loves(b, d)$$
$$\forall\, b\,.\; Boy(b)\supset \exists\, d\,.\; Dog(d)\; \&\; Loves(b, d)$$

Thus, while *Every boy loves a dog* has a single syntactic structure, its semantic structure is ambiguous. Quantifiers also vary with respect to vagueness. The quantifier *all* is precise in specifying every member of some set, but a quantifier such as *many*, as in *Many people saw the accident*, is vague as to how many people were involved.

You might also think that indexical terms such as *you*, *I*, and *here* are ambiguous because their interpretations depend on context. But this is not the sense of ambiguity being discussed here. Note that the word *dog* is not considered ambiguous because there are many dogs to which the noun phrase *the dog* could refer. The semantic meaning of *the dog* is precisely determined. Likewise, the pronoun *I* may be unspecified as to its referent, but it has a single well-defined sense.

While the referents of phrases are context dependent and thus beyond the scope of this discussion, there are context-independent constraints on reference that must be accounted for. Consider the sentence *Jack saw him in the mirror*. While it is not specified who was seen, you know that it wasn't Jack seeing himself. To express this meaning, you would have to use the reflexive pronoun, as in *Jack saw himself in the mirror*. Thus certain reference constraints arise because of the structure of sentences. This topic will be explored in Chapter 12.

A very important aspect of context-independent meaning is the co-occurrence constraints that arise between word senses. Often the correct word sense can be identified because of the structure and meaning of the rest of the sentence. Consider the verb *run*, which has one sense referring to the action you do when jogging and another referring to the action of operating some machine. The first sense is typically realized as an intransitive verb (as in *Jack ran in the park*), whereas the second can only be realized as a transitive verb (as in *Jack ran the printing press for years*). In other cases the syntactic structure remains the same, but the possible senses of the words can only combine in certain ways. For instance, consider *Jack ran in the park* versus *Jack ran in the election*. The syntactic structures of these sentences are identical, but different senses of the verb *run* must be selected because of the possible senses in the modifier. One of the most important tasks of semantic interpretation is to utilize constraints such as this to help reduce the number of possible senses for each word.

8.3   The Basic Logical Form Language

The last section introduced a primitive unit of meaning, namely the word sense. This section defines a language in which you can combine these elements to form meanings for more complex expressions. This language will resemble FOPC,

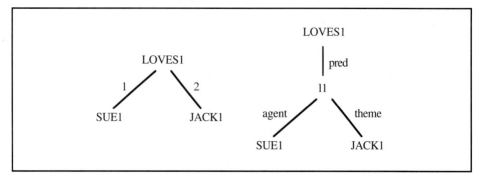

Figure 8.3 Two possible network representations of *Sue loves Jack*

although there are many equivalent forms of representation, such as network-based representations, that use the same basic ideas. The word senses will serve as the **atoms** or **constants** of the representation. These constants can be classified by the types of things they describe. For instance, constants that describe objects in the world, including abstract objects such as events and situations, are called **terms**. Constants that describe relations and properties are called **predicates**. A proposition in the language is formed from a predicate followed by an appropriate number of terms to serve as its arguments. For instance, the proposition corresponding to the sentence *Fido is a dog* would be constructed from the term FIDO1 and the predicate constant DOG1 and is written as

(DOG1 FIDO1)

Predicates that take a single argument are called **unary predicates** or **properties**; those that take two arguments, such as LOVES1, are called **binary predicates**; and those that take n arguments are called ***n*-ary predicates**. The proposition corresponding to the sentence *Sue loves Jack* would involve a binary predicate LOVES1 and would be written as

(LOVES1 SUE1 JACK1)

You can see that different word classes in English correspond to different types of constants in the logical form. Proper names, such as *Jack*, have word senses that are terms; common nouns, such as *dog*, have word senses that are unary predicates; and verbs, such as *run*, *love*, and *put*, have word senses that correspond to n-ary predicates, where n depends on how many terms the verb subcategorizes for.

Note that while the logical forms are presented in a predicate-argument form here, the same distinctions are made in most other meaning representations. For instance, a network representation would have nodes that correspond to the word senses and arcs that indicate the predicate-argument structure. The meaning of the sentence *Sue loves Jack* in a semantic networklike representation might appear in one of the two forms shown in Figure 8.3. For most purposes all of these representation formalisms are equivalent.

More complex propositions are constructed using a new class of constants called **logical operators**. For example, the operator NOT allows you to construct a proposition that says that some proposition is not true. The proposition corresponding to the sentence *Sue does not love Jack* would be

(NOT (LOVES1 SUE1 JACK1))

English also contains operators that combine two or more propositions to form a complex proposition. FOPC contains operators such as disjunction ($\vee$), conjunction (&), what is often called implication ($\supset$), and other forms (there are 16 possible truth functional binary operators in FOPC). English contains many similar operators including *or*, *and*, *if, only if*, and so on. Natural language connectives often involve more complex relationships between sentences. For instance, the conjunction *and* might correspond to the logical operator & but often also involves temporal sequencing, as in *I went home and had a drink*, in which going home preceded having the drink. The connective *but*, on the other hand, is like *and* except that the second argument is something that the hearer might not expect to be true given the first argument. The general form for such a proposition is (*connective proposition proposition*). For example, the logical form of the sentence *Jack loves Sue or Jack loves Mary* would be (OR1 (LOVES1 JACK1 SUE1) (LOVES1 JACK1 MARY1)). The logical form language will allow both operators corresponding to word senses and operators like & directly from FOPC. The logic-based operators will be used to connect propositions not explicitly conjoined in the sentence.

With the simple propositions we just defined, we can define the meaning of only a very limited subset of English, namely sentences consisting of simple verb forms and proper names. To account for more complex sentences, we must define additional semantic constructs. One important construct is the **quantifier**. In first-order predicate calculus, there are only two quantifiers: $\forall$ and $\exists$. English contains a much larger range of quantifiers, including *all*, *some*, *most*, *many*, *a few*, *the*, and so on. To allow quantifiers, variables are introduced as in first-order logic but with an important difference. In first-order logic a variable only retains its significance within the scope of the quantifier. Thus two instances of the same variable x occurring in two different formulas—say in the formulas $\exists x . P(x)$ and $\exists x . Q(x)$—are treated as completely different variables with no relation to each other. Natural languages display a different behavior. For instance, consider the two sentences *A man entered the room. He walked over to the table.* The first sentence introduces a new object to the discussion, namely some man. You might think to treat the meaning of this sentence along the lines of the existential quantifier in logic. But the problem is that the man introduced existentially in the first sentence is referred to by the pronoun *He* in the second sentence. So variables appear to continue their existence after being introduced. To allow this, each time a discourse variable is introduced, it is given a unique name not used before. Under the right circumstances, a subsequent sentence can then refer back to this term.

Quantifier	Use	Example
THE	definite reference	the dog
A	indefinite reference	a dog
BARE	bare singular NP (mass term) or	water, food
BARE	bare plural NP (generics)	dogs

Figure 8.4   Some common quantifiers

Natural language quantifiers have restricted ranges and thus are more complex than those found in FOPC. In FOPC a formula of the form $\forall x \cdot P_x$ is true if and only if P_x is true for every possible object in the domain (that is, x may be any term in the language). Such statements are rare in natural language. Rather, you would say *all dogs bark* or *most people laughed*, which require constructs that are often called **generalized quantifiers**. These quantifiers are used in statements of the general form

(quantifier variable : restriction-proposition body-proposition)

For instance, the sentence *Most dogs bark* would have the logical form

(MOST1 **d1** : (DOG1 **d1**) (BARKS1 **d1**))

This means that most of the objects **d1** that satisfy (DOG1 **d1**) also satisfy (BARKS1 **d1**). Note that this has a very different meaning from the formula

(MOST **d2** : (BARKS1 **d2**) (DOG1 **d2**))

which roughly captures the meaning of the sentence *Most barking things are dogs.*

A very important class of generalized quantifiers corresponds to the articles *the* and *a*. The sentence *The dog barks* would have a logical form

(THE **x** : (DOG1 **x**) (BARKS1 **x**))

which would be true only if there is a uniquely determined dog in context and that dog barks. Clearly, in any natural setting there will be many dogs in the world, so the use of context to identify the correct one is crucial for understanding the sentence. Since this identification process requires context, however, discussion of it is delayed until Part III. Here it suffices to have a way to write the logical form. The special set of quantifiers corresponding to the articles (or the absence of articles in bare noun phrases) is shown in Figure 8.4.

More complex noun phrases will result in more complex restrictions. For instance, the sentence *The happy dog barks* will involve a restriction that is a conjunction, namely (THE **x** : (& (DOG1 **x**) (HAPPY **x**)) (BARKS1 **x**)). This will be true only if there is a contextually unique **x** such that (& (DOG1 **x**) (HAPPY **x**)) is true, and this **x** barks.

Another construct needs to be introduced to handle plural forms, as in a phrase such as *the dogs bark*. A new type of constant called a **predicate operator** is introduced that takes a predicate as an argument and produces a new predicate. For plurals the predicate operator PLUR will be used. If DOG1 is a predicate that is true of any dog, then (PLUR DOG1) is a predicate that is true of any set of dogs. Thus the representation of the meaning of the sentence *The dogs bark* would be

(THE **x** : ((PLUR DOG1) **x**) (BARKS1 **x**))

Plural noun phrases introduce the possibility of a new form of ambiguity. Note that the natural reading of *The dogs bark* is that there is a specific set of dogs, and each one of them barks. This is called the **distributive reading**, since the predicate BARKS1 is distributed over each element of the set. In contrast, consider the sentence *The dogs met at the corner*. In this case, it makes no sense to say that each individual dog met; rather the meeting is true of the entire set of dogs. This is called the **collective reading**. Some sentences allow both interpretations and hence are ambiguous. For instance, the sentence *Two men bought a stereo* can mean that two men each bought a stereo (the distributive reading), or that two men bought a stereo together (the collective reading).

The final constructs to be introduced are the **modal operators**. These are needed to represent the meaning of verbs such as *believe* and *want*, for representing tense, and for many other constructs. Modal operators look similar to logical operators but have some important differences. Specifically, terms within the scope of a modal operator may have an interpretation that differs from the normal one. This affects what conclusions you can draw from a proposition. For example, assume that Jack is also known as John to some people. There are two word senses that are equal; that is, JACK1 = JOHN22. With a simple proposition, it doesn't matter which of these two constants is used: if (HAPPY JOHN22) is true then (HAPPY JACK1) is true, and vice versa. This is true even in complex propositions formed from the logical operators. If (OR (HAPPY JOHN1) (SAD JOHN1)) is true, then so is (OR (HAPPY JACK1) (SAD JACK1)), and vice versa. The same propositions within the scope of a modal operator such as BELIEVE1, however, are not interchangeable. For instance, if Sue believes that Jack is happy, that is,

(BELIEVE SUE1 (HAPPY JACK1))

then it does not necessarily follow that Sue believes John is happy, that is,

(BELIEVE SUE (HAPPY JOHN22))

because Sue might not know that JACK1 and JOHN22 are the same person. Thus you cannot freely substitute equal terms when they occur within the scope of a modal operator. This is often referred to as the **failure of substitutivity** in modal contexts.

An important class of modal operators for natural language are the tense operators, PAST, PRES, and FUT. So far all examples have ignored the effect of tense. With these new operators, however, you can represent the difference in meaning between *John sees Fido*, *John saw Fido*, and *John will see Fido*, namely as the propositions

(PRES (SEES1 JOHN1 FIDO1))
(PAST (SEES1 JOHN1 FIDO1))
(FUT (SEES1 JOHN1 FIDO1))

You can see that these are modal operators because they exhibit the failure of substitutivity. For example, consider the operator PAST, and assume two constants, say JOHN1 and PRESIDENT1, that are equal now, indicating that John is currently the president. But in the past, John was not the president, so JOHN1 did not equal PRESIDENT1. Given this and the fact that John saw Fido in the past, (PAST (SEES1 JOHN1 FIDO1)), you cannot conclude that the president saw Fido in the past, that is, (PAST (SEES1 PRESIDENT1 FIDO1)), since John was not the president at that time. Note also that a proposition and its negation can both be true in the past (but at different times). Thus it is possible for both the sentences *John was happy* and *John was not happy* to be true; that is, (PAST (HAPPY JOHN1)) and (PAST (NOT (HAPPY JOHN1))) are both true.

This completes the specification of the basic logical form language. The next sections discuss various extensions that make the language more convenient for expressing ambiguity and capturing semantic regularities.

8.4 Encoding Ambiguity in the Logical Form

The previous sections defined many of the constructs needed to specify the logical form of a sentence, and if you were interested solely in the nature of logical form, you could be finished. But representations for computational use have another important constraint on them, namely the handling of ambiguity. A typical sentence will have multiple possible syntactic structures, each of which might have multiple possible logical forms. In addition, the words in the sentence will have multiple senses. Simply enumerating the possible logical forms will not be practical. Rather, we will take an approach where certain common ambiguities can be collapsed and locally represented within the logical form, and we will develop techniques to incrementally resolve these ambiguities as additional constraints from the rest of the sentence and from context are brought into play. Many researchers view this ambiguity encoding as a separate level of representation from the logical form, and it is often referred to as the **quasi-logical form**.

Perhaps the greatest source of ambiguity in the logical form comes from the fact that most words have multiple senses. Some of these senses have different structural properties, so they can be eliminated given the context of the surrounding sentence. But often words have different senses that have identical structural constraints. At present, the only way to encode these would be to build

BOX 8.1 The Need for Generalized Quantifiers

For the standard existential and universal quantifiers, there are formulas in standard FOPC equivalent to the generalized quantifier forms. In particular, the formula

$(EXISTS \ x : P_x \ Q_x)$

is equivalent to

$\exists x \ . \ P_x \ \& \ Q_x$

and the universally quantified form

$(ALL \ x : P_x \ Q_x)$

is equivalent to

$\forall x \ . \ P_x \supset Q_x$

These generalized quantifier forms can be thought of simply as abbreviations. But the other quantifiers do not have an equivalent form in standard FOPC. To see this, consider trying to define the meaning of *Most dogs bark* using the standard semantics for quantifiers. Clearly $\forall x \ . \ Dog(x) \supset Bark(x)$ is too strong, and $\exists x \ . \ Dog(x) \ \& \ Bark(x)$ is too weak. Could we define a new quantifier M such that some formula of form $Mx \ . \ P_x$ has the right truth conditions? Say we try to define $Mx \ . \ P_x$ to be true if over half the elements of the domain satisfy P_x. Consider $Mx \ . \ Dog(x) \ \& \ Bark(x)$. This will be true only if over half the objects in the domain satisfy $Dog(x) \ \& \ Bark(x)$. But this is unlikely to be true, even if all dogs bark. Specifically, it requires over half the objects in the domain to be dogs! Maybe $Mx \ . \ Dog(x) \supset Bark(x)$ works. This would be true if more than half the objects in the domain either are not dogs or bark. But this will be true in a model containing 11 objects, 10 seals that bark, and 1 dog that doesn't! You may try other formulas for P_x, but no simple approach will provide a satisfactory account.

a separate logical form for each possible combination of senses for the words in the sentence. To reduce this explosion of logical forms, we can use the same technique used to handle multiple feature values in the syntactic structure. Namely, anywhere an atomic sense is allowed, a set of possible atomic senses can be used. For example, the noun *ball* has at least two senses: BALL1, the object used in games, and BALL2, the social event involving dancing. Thus the sentence *Sue watched the ball* is ambiguous out of context. A single logical form can represent these two possibilities, however:

1. (THE **b1** : ({BALL1 BALL2} **b1**) (PAST (WATCH1 SUE1 **b1**)))

This abbreviates two possible logical forms, namely

2. (THE **b1** : (BALL1 **b1**) (PAST (WATCH1 SUE1 **b1**)))

and

3. (THE **b1** : (BALL2 **b1**) (PAST (WATCH1 SUE1 **b1**)))

One of the most complex forms of ambiguity in logical forms arises from the relative scoping of the quantifiers and operators. You saw in Section 8.1 that a sentence such as *Every boy loves a dog* is ambiguous between two readings depending on the scope of the quantifiers. There is no context-independent method for resolving such issues, so the ambiguity must be represented in the final logical forms for the sentence. Rather than enumerating all possible scopings, which would lead to an exponentially growing number of interpretations based on the number of scoping constructs, we introduce another abbreviation into the logical form language that collapses interpretations together. Specifically, the abbreviated logical form does not contain scoping information at all. Rather, constructs such as generalized quantifiers are treated syntactically like terms and appear in the position indicated by the syntactic structure of the sentence. They are marked using angle brackets to indicate the scoping abbreviation. For example, the logical forms for the sentence *Every boy loves a dog* are captured by a single ambiguous form

(LOVES1 <EVERY **b1** (BOY1 **b1**)> <A **d1** (DOG1 **d1**)>)

This abbreviates an ambiguity between the logical form

(EVERY **b1** : (BOY1 **b1**) (A **d1** : (DOG1 **d1**) (LOVES1 **b1 d1**)))

and

(A **d1** : (DOG1 **d1**) (EVERY **b1** : (BOY1 **b1**) (LOVES1 **b1 d1**)))

While the savings don't amount to much in this example, consider that a sentence with four scoping constructs in it would have 24 (4 factorial) possible orderings, and one with five scoping constructs would have 120 orderings. The abbreviation convention allows all these forms to be collapsed to a single representation. Chapter 12 will explore some heuristic techniques for determining the scope of operators. For the time being, however, it is reasonable to assume that no context-independent scoping constraints need be represented.

If the restriction in a generalized quantifier is a proposition involving a simple unary predicate, a further abbreviation will be used that drops the variable. Thus the form <EVERY **b1** (BOY **b1**)> will often be abbreviated as <EVERY **b1** BOY>.

A large number of constructs in natural language are sensitive to scoping. In particular, all the generalized quantifiers, including *the*, are subject to scoping. For example, in *At every hotel, the receptionist was friendly*, the preferred reading in almost any context has the definite reference *the receptionist* fall within the scope of *every hotel*; that is, there is a different receptionist at each hotel.

In addition, operators such as negation and tense are also scope sensitive. For example, the sentence *Every boy didn't run* is ambiguous between the reading in which some boys didn't run and some did, that is,

(NOT (EVERY **b1** : (BOY1 **b1**) (RUN1 **b1**)))

and the reading where no boys ran, that is,

(EVERY **b1** : (BOY1 **b1**) (NOT (RUN1 **b1**)))

These two readings are captured by the single logical form

(<NOT RUN1> <EVERY **b1** BOY1>)

where unscoped unary operators (for example, NOT, PAST, PRES, and so on) are wrapped around the predicate.

Finally, let us return to two constructs that need to be examined further: proper names and pronouns. So far we have assumed that each proper name identifies a sense that denotes an object in the domain. While this was a useful abstraction to introduce the basic ideas of logical form, it is not a general enough treatment of the phenomena. In fact, proper names must be interpreted in context, and the name *John* will refer to different people in different situations. Our revised treatment resolves these problems by using a discourse variable that has the property of having the specified name. We will introduce this construct as a special function, namely

(NAME <variable> <name>)

which produces the appropriate object with the name in the current context. Thus, the logical form of *John ran* would be (<PAST RUN1> (NAME **j1** "John")).

Arguments similar to those previously given for proper names can be made for pronouns and other indexical words, such as *here* and *yesterday*, and we will treat them using a special function of the form (PRO <variable> <proposition>). For example, the quasi-logical form for *Every man liked him* would be

(<PAST LIKE1> <EVERY **m1** MAN1> (PRO **m2** (HE1 **m2**)))

HE1 is the sense for *he* and *him*, and formally is a predicate true of objects that satisfy the restrictions on any antecedent, that is, being animate-male in this case. As with generalized quantifiers, when the restriction is a simple unary predicate, the pro forms are often abbreviated. For example, the logical form for *he* will often be written as (PRO **m2** HE1).

The constructs described in this chapter dramatically reduce the number of logical forms that must be initially computed for a given sentence. Not all ambiguities can be captured by the abbreviations, however, so there will still be sentences that will require a list of possible logical forms, even for a single syntactic structure.

8.5 Verbs and States in Logical Form

So far, verbs have mapped to appropriate senses acting as predicates in the logical form. This treatment can handle all the different forms but loses some generalities that could be captured. It also has some annoying properties.

Consider the following sentences, all using the verb *break*:

John broke the window with the hammer.
The hammer broke the window.
The window broke.

Intuitively, all these sentences describe the same type of event but in varying detail. Thus it would be nice if the verb *break* mapped to the same sense in each case. But there is a problem, as these three uses of the verb seem to indicate verb senses of differing arity. The first seems to be a ternary relation between John, the window, and the hammer, the second a binary relation between the hammer and the window, and the third a unary relation involving the window. It seems you would need three different senses of break, BREAK1, BREAK2, and BREAK3, that differ in their arity and produce logical forms such as

1. (<PAST BREAK1> (NAME **j1** "John") <THE **w1** WINDOW1>
   <THE **h1** HAMMER1>),
2. (<PAST BREAK2> <THE **h1** HAMMER1 > <THE **w1** WINDOW1>), and
3. (<PAST BREAK3> <THE **w1** WINDOW1>)

Furthermore, to guarantee that each predicate is interpreted appropriately, the representation would need axioms so that whenever 1 is true, 2 is true, and whenever 2 is true, 3 is true. These axioms are often called **meaning postulates**. Having to specify such constraints for every verb seems rather inconvenient.

Davidson (1967) proposed an alternative form of representation to handle such cases as well as more complicated forms of adverbial modification. He suggested introducing events into the ontology, and treating the meaning of a sentence like *John broke it* along the following lines (translated into our notation):

(∃ **e1** : (BREAK **e1** (NAME **j1** "John") (PRO **i1** IT1)))

which asserts that **e1** is an event of John breaking the indicated window. Now the meaning of *John broke it with the hammer* would be

(∃ **e1** : (& (BREAK **e1** (NAME **j1** "John") (PRO **i1** IT1))
   (INSTR **e1** <THE **h1** HAMMER>)))

The advantage is that additional modifiers, such as *with the hammer* or *on Tuesday* or *in the hallway*, can be incrementally added to the basic representation by adding more predications involving the event. Thus only one sense of the verb *break* need be defined to handle all these cases.

Similar intuitions also motivated the development of **case grammar** in the early 1970s. While case grammar has been abandoned as originally proposed, many of its concepts have continued to influence current theories. One claim that remains influential is that there is a limited set of abstract semantic relationships that can hold between a verb and its arguments. These are often called **thematic roles** or **case roles**, and while different researchers have used different sets of roles, the number required has always remained small. The intuition is that *John,* *the hammer*, and *the window* play the same semantic roles in each of these sentences. *John* is the actor (the **agent** role), *the window* is the object (the **theme** role), and *the hammer* is the instrument (the **instrument** role) used in the act of breaking. This suggests a representation of sentence meaning similar to that used in semantic networks, where everything is expressed in terms of unary and binary relations. Specifically, using the three thematic roles just mentioned, the meaning of *John broke the window* would be

$$(\exists \, \mathbf{e} \, (\& \, (BREAK \; \mathbf{e}) \; (AGENT \; \mathbf{e} \, (NAME \; \mathbf{j1} \; \text{``John''}))$$
$$(THEME \; \mathbf{e} \; <THE \; \mathbf{w1} \; WINDOW>)))$$

Because such constructs are so common, we introduce a new notation for them. The abbreviated form for an assertion of the form

$$(\exists \, \mathbf{e} : (\& \, (Event\text{-}p \; \mathbf{e}) \; (Relation_1 \; \mathbf{e} \, obj_1) \, ... \, (Relation_n \; \mathbf{e} \, obj_n)))$$

will be

$$(Event\text{-}p \; \mathbf{e} \; [Relation_1 \; obj_1] \, ... \, [Relation_n \; obj_n])$$

In particular, the quasi-logical form for the sentence *John broke the window* using this abbreviation is

$$(<PAST \; BREAK1> \; \mathbf{e1} \quad [AGENT \; (NAME \; \mathbf{j1} \; \text{``John''})]$$
$$[THEME \; <THE \; \mathbf{w1} \; WINDOW1>])$$

It turns out that similar arguments can be made for verbs other than event verbs. Consider the sentence *Mary was unhappy*. If it is represented using a unary predicate as

$$(<PAST \; UNHAPPY> \; (NAME \; \mathbf{j1} \; \text{``Mary''}))$$

then how can we handle modifiers, as in *Mary was unhappy in the meeting*? Using the previous argument, we can generalize the notion of events to include **states** and use the same technique. For instance, we might make UNHAPPY a predicate that asserts that its argument is a state of unhappiness, and use the THEME role to include John, that is,

$$(\exists \, \mathbf{s} \; <PAST \; UNHAPPY> \; \mathbf{s}) \; (THEME \; \mathbf{s} \, (NAME \; \mathbf{j1} \; \text{``Mary''}))$$

Of course, we could use the same abbreviation convention as previously defined for events and thus represent *Mary was unhappy in the meeting* as

$$(<PAST \; UNHAPPY> \; \mathbf{s} \quad [THEME \; (NAME \; \mathbf{j1} \; \text{``Mary''})]$$
$$[IN\text{-}LOC \; <THE \; \mathbf{m1} \; MEETING>])$$

It has been argued that having event variables as arguments to atomic predicates is still not enough to capture the full expressiveness of natural language. Hwang and Schubert (1993a), for instance, allow events to be defined by arbitrary sentences. For now, having events and states will be sufficient to develop the important ideas in this book.

In many situations using explicit event and state variables in formulas is cumbersome and interferes with the development of other ideas. As a result, we will use different representations depending on what is best for the presentation. For example, the logical form of *Mary sees John* will sometimes be written as

(PRES (SEES1 **l1** [AGENT (NAME **j1** "Mary")]
[THEME (NAME **m1** "John")]))

which of course is equivalent to

(PRES (∃ **l1** (& (SEES1 l1) (AGENT l1 (NAME **j1** "Mary"))
(THEME l1 (NAME **m1** "John")))))

Other times it will be written in predicate argument form:

(PRES (SEES1 (NAME **j1** "Mary") (NAME **m1** "John")))

There has been considerable debate in the literature about whether the thematic role analysis is necessary, or whether all the properties we want from thematic roles can be obtained in other ways from a predicate-argument style representation. While an argument that thematic roles are necessary is hard to construct, the representation is sufficiently helpful to be used in many semantic representation languages.

8.6 Thematic Roles

This section examines theories based on the notion of thematic roles, or cases. One motivating example from the last section included the sentences

John broke the window with the hammer.
The hammer broke the window.
The window broke.

John, the hammer, and *the window* play the same semantic roles in each of these sentences. *John* is the actor, *the window* is the object, and *the hammer* is the instrument used in the act of breaking of the window. We introduced relations such as AGENT, THEME, and INSTR to capture these intuitions. But can we define these relations more precisely, and what other thematic roles have proved useful in natural language systems? These issues are explored in this section.

Perhaps the easiest thematic role to define is the AGENT role. A noun phrase fills the AGENT role if it describes the instigator of the action described by the sentence. Further, this role may attribute intention, volition, or responsibility for the action to the agent described. One test for AGENT-hood involves adding phrases like *intentionally* or *in order to* to active voice sentences. If the resulting sentence is well formed, the subject NP can fill the AGENT role. The following sentences are acceptable:

John intentionally broke the window.
John broke the window in order to let in some air.

But these sentences are not acceptable:

>*The hammer intentionally broke the window.
>*The window broke in order to let in some air.

Thus the NP *John* fills the AGENT role only in the first two sentences.

Not all animate NPs, even in the subject position, fill the AGENT role. For instance, you cannot normally say

>*John intentionally died.
>*Mary remembered her birthday in order to get some presents.

Of course, by adding the phrase *intentionally* to the first sentence, you may construct some plausible reading of the sentence (*John killed himself*), but this is a result of modifying the initial meaning of the sentence *John died*.

NPs that describe something undergoing some change or being acted upon will fill a role called THEME. This usually corresponds to the syntactic OBJECT and, for any transitive verb X, is the answer to the question "What was Xed?" For example, given the sentence *The gray eagle saw the mouse*, the NP *the mouse* is the THEME and is the answer to the question "What was seen?" For intransitive verbs, the THEME role is used for the subject NPs that are not AGENTs. Thus in *The clouds appeared over the horizon*, the NP *the clouds* fills the THEME role. More examples follow, with the THEME NP in italics:

>*The rock* broke.
>John broke *the rock*.
>I gave John *the book*.

A range of roles has to do with locations, or abstract locations. First, we must make the distinction mentioned earlier between relations that indicate a location or place and those that indicate motion or paths. The AT-LOC relation indicates where an object is or where an event takes place, as in

>Harry walked *on the road*.
>The chair is *by the door*.

On the road describes where the walking took place, while *by the door* describes where the chair is located.

Other phrases describe changes in location, direction of motion, or paths:

>I walked *from here to school* yesterday.
>It fell *to the ground*.
>The birds flew *from the lake along the river gorge*.

There are at least three different types of phrases here: those that describe where something came from (the FROM-LOC role), such as *from here*; those that describe the destination (the TO-LOC role), such as *to the ground*; and those that describe the trajectory or path (the PATH-LOC role), such as *along the gorge*.

These location roles can be generalized into roles over arbitrary state values, called the AT role, and roles for arbitrary state change (the FROM, TO, and PATH roles). Thus AT-LOC is a specialization of the AT role, and so on. You can see other specializations of these roles when you consider the abstract relation of possession:

I threw the ball *to John.*   (the TO-LOC role)
I gave a book *to John.*   (the TO-POSS role)
I caught the ball *from John.*   (the FROM-LOC role)
I borrowed a book *from John.*   (the FROM-POSS role)
The box contains a ball.   (the AT-LOC role)
John owns a book.   (the AT-POSS role)

Similarly, you might define AT-TIME, TO-TIME, and FROM-TIME roles, as in

I saw the car at *3 o'clock.*   (the AT-TIME role)
I worked *from one until three.*   (the FROM-TIME and TO-TIME role)

The roles apply to general state change as well, as with temperature in

The temperature remains *at zero.*   (AT-VALUE)
The temperature rose *from zero.*   (FROM-VALUE)

Thus the notion of general value and change of value along many dimensions seems to be supported by the similarity of the ways of realizing these roles in sentences.

Another role is motivated by the problem that, given the present taxonomy, you cannot easily classify the role of the NP in a sentence such as

John believed that it was raining.

The THEME role is filled with the clause *that it was raining*, since this is what is believed. *John* cannot be an AGENT because there is no intentionality in believing something. Thus you must introduce a new role, called EXPERI-ENCER, which is filled by animate objects that are in a described psychological state, or that undergo some psychological process, such as perception, as in the preceding sentence and as in

John saw the unicorn.

Another role is the BENEFICIARY role, which is filled by the animate person for whom a certain event is performed, as in

I rolled on the floor *for Lucy.*
Find *me* the papers!
I gave the book to Jack *for Susan.*

The last example demonstrates the need to distinguish the TO-POSS role (that is, *to Jack*) from the BENEFICIARY role.

The INSTR role describes a tool, material, or force used to perform some event, as in

Harry broke the glass *with the telescope.*
The telescope broke the glass.
I used *some flour* to make a cake.
I made a cake *with some flour.*

Depending on the verb, the INSTR role sometimes can be used as the surface subject when the AGENT role is not specified. Natural forces are also included in the INSTR category here, although you could argue for a different analysis. Thus the following are also examples of the INSTR role:

The sun dried the apples.
Jack used *the sun* to dry the apples.

The AGENT and INSTR roles could be combined into a more general role named CAUSAL-AGENT.

Other roles need to be identified before certain sentences can be analyzed. For example, some sentences describe situations where two people perform an act together:

Henry lifted the piano with Jack.

To handle this, you must introduce a role CO-AGENT to account for the PP *with Jack.*

A more complicated case occurs in sentences involving exchanges or other complex interactions. For example, consider the sentences

Jack paid $1 to the man for the book.
Jack bought the book from the man for $1.

These sentences both describe a situation where Jack gives the man $1 and receives the book in exchange. In the first sentence, however, the *$1* is the THEME and there is no role to account for *the book*. In the second sentence the situation is reversed: *the book* is the THEME and *$1* is unaccounted for. To handle these cases you must add a role CO-THEME for the second object in an exchange.

A more general solution to this problem would be to analyze such sentences as describing two events. The **primary event** is the one you have been considering so far, but a **secondary event** may be present. In this analysis you might analyze the first sentence as follows (the primary event being Jack paying the dollar, and the secondary being Jack receiving the book):

Jack: AGENT of both PRIMARY and SECONDARY event
$1: THEME of PRIMARY event
the man: TO-POSS of PRIMARY, FROM-POSS of SECONDARY
the book: THEME of SECONDARY event

Role and Subroles	Other Common Names	Definition
CAUSAL-AGENT		the object that caused the event
AGENT		intentional causation
INSTR		force/tool used in causing the event
THEME	PATIENT	the thing affected by the event
EXPERIENCER		the person involved in perception or a physical/psychological state
BENEFICIARY		the person for whom an act is done
AT		the state/value on some dimension
AT-LOC	LOCATION	current location
AT-POSS	POSSESSOR	current possessor
AT-VALUE		current value
AT-TIME		current time
TO		final value in a state change
TO-LOC	DESTINATION	final location
TO-POSS	RECIPIENT	final possessor
TO-VALUE		final value
FROM		original value in a state change
FROM-LOC	SOURCE	original location
FROM-POSS		original possessor
FROM-VALUE		original value
PATH		path over which something travels
CO-AGENT		secondary agent in an action
CO-THEME		secondary theme in an exchange

Figure 8.5 Some possible semantic roles

This possibility will not be pursued further, however, since it leads into many issues not relevant to the remainder of this chapter.

Figure 8.5 provides a summary of most of the roles distinguished thus far and the hierarchical relationships between them.

As you've seen, verbs can be classified by the thematic roles that they require. To classify them precisely, however, you must make a distinction between roles that are "intimately" related to the verb and those that are not. For example, almost any past tense verb allows an AT-TIME role realized by the adverb *yesterday*. Thus this role is apparently more a property of verb phrases in general than a property of any individual verb. However, other roles—namely, those realized by constituents for which the verb subcategorizes—seem to be properties of the verb. For example, the verb *put* subcategorizes for a PP, and furthermore, this PP must realize the TO-LOC role. In verb classification this latter type of role is important, and these roles are called the **inner roles** of the verb.

The preceding examples suggest one test for determining whether a given role is an inner role for a given verb: if the role is obligatory, it is an inner role. Other inner roles, however, appear to be optional, so other tests are also needed. Another test is based on the observation that all verbs may take at most one NP in any given inner role. If multiple NPs are needed, they must be related by a conjunction. Thus you can say

John and I ran to the store.

but not

*John I ran to the store.

Similarly, you can say

I ran to the store and to the bank.

but not

*I ran to the store to the bank.

Thus the AGENT and TO-LOC roles for the verb *run* are inner roles.

Verbs typically specify up to three inner roles, at least one of which must always be realized in any sentence using the verb. Sometimes a particular role must always be present (for example, TO-LOC with *put*). Typically, the THEME role is also obligatory, whereas the AGENT role is always optional for any verb that allows the passive form.

There are also syntactic restrictions on how various roles can be realized. Figure 8.6 shows a sample of ways that roles can be realized in different sentences.

The following are some sample sentences with each verb in italics and its argument, whether NP, PP, or embedded S, classified by its role in order of occurrence:

Jack *ran*.	AGENT only
Jack *ran* with a crutch.	AGENT + INSTR
Jack *ran* with a crutch for Susan.	AGENT + INSTR + BENEFICIARY
Jack *destroyed* the car.	AGENT + THEME
Jack *put* the car through the wall.	AGENT + THEME + PATH
Jack *sold* Henry the car.	AGENT + TO-POSS + THEME
Henry *pushed* the car from Jack's house to the junkyard.	AGENT + THEME + FROM-LOC + TO-LOC
Jack *is tall*.	THEME
Henry *believes* that Jack is tall.	EXPERIENCER + THEME
Susan *owns* a car.	AT-POSS + THEME
I *am* in the closet.	THEME + AT-LOC
The ice *melted*.	THEME
Jack *enjoyed* the play.	EXPERIENCER + THEME
The ball *rolled* down the hill to the water.	THEME + PATH + TO-LOC

Role	Realization
AGENT	as subject in active sentences preposition *by* in passive sentences
THEME	as object of transitive verbs as subject of nonaction verbs
INSTR	as subject in active sentences with no agent preposition *with*
EXPERIENCER	as animate subject in active sentences with no agent
BENEFICIARY	as indirect object with transitive verbs preposition *for*
AT-LOC	prepositions *in, on, beyond*, etc.
AT-POSS	possessive NP as subject of sentence if no agent
TO-LOC	prepositions *to, into*
TO-POSS	preposition *to*, indirect object with certain verbs
FROM-LOC	prepositions *from, out of*, etc.
FROM-POSS	preposition *from*

Figure 8.6 Common realizations of the major roles

8.7 Speech Acts and Embedded Sentences

Sentences are used for many different purposes. Each sentential mood indicates a different relation between the speaker and the propositional content of the utterance. These issues will be examined in greater detail in later chapters. For now the logical form language is extended to capture the distinctions. Each of the major sentence types has a corresponding operator that takes the sentence interpretation as an argument and produces what is called a **surface speech act**. These indicate how the proposition described is intended to be used to update the discourse situation. They are indicated by new operators as follows:

ASSERT—the proposition is being asserted.
Y/N-QUERY—the proposition is being queried.
COMMAND—the proposition describes an action to perform.
WH-QUERY—the proposition describes an object to be identified.

For declarative sentences, such as *The man ate a peach*, the complete LF is

(ASSERT (<PAST EAT> **e1**   [AGENT <THE **m1** MAN1>]
                                      [THEME <A **p1** PEACH1>]))

For yes/no questions, such as *Did the man eat a peach?*, the LF is

(Y/N-QUERY (<PAST EAT> **e1**   [AGENT <THE **m1** MAN1>]
                                  [THEME <A **p1** PEACH1>]))

For commands, such as *Eat the peach*, the LF is

(COMMAND (EAT **e1** [THEME <THE **p1** PEACH1>]))

For wh-questions, such as *What did the man eat?*, several additions need to be made to the logical form language. First, you need a way to represent the meaning of noun phrases involving wh-terms. A new quantifier WH is defined that indicates that the term stands for an object or objects under question. Thus a noun phrase such as *what* would be represented <WH **o1** ANYTHING>, *which man* as <WH **m1** MAN1>, and *who* as <WH **p1** PERSON>. Finally, for question forms such as *how many* and *how much*, we introduce the quantifiers HOW-MANY and HOW-MUCH. Note that wh-terms are scope sensitive and thus treating them as quantifiers makes sense. The question *Who is the leader of every group?* is ambiguous between asking for a single person who leads every group, and asking for the leader of each of the groups.

Thus, the logical form of the sentence *What did the man eat?* is

(WH-QUERY (<PAST EAT> **e1** [AGENT <THE **m1** MAN1>]
                            [THEME <WH **w1** PHYSOBJ>]))

Embedded sentences, such as relative clauses, end up as complex restrictions within the noun phrase construction and thus do not need any new notation. For example, the logical form of the sentence *The man who ate a peach left* would be

(ASSERT
    (<PAST LEAVE> **l1**
        [AGENT <THE **m1** (& (MAN1 **m1**)
                               (<PAST EAT1> **e2**
                                   [AGENT **m1**]
                                   [THEME <A **p1** PEACH>]))>]))

Figure 8.7 gives a formal definition of the syntax of the logical form language introduced throughout this chapter. Figure 8.8 gives the additional rules defining the syntax for the quasi-logical form language.

8.8 Defining Semantic Structure: Model Theory

So far, the term semantics has been used to reflect the representation of meanings for sentences. This was expressed in the logical form language. There is another meaning of semantics used in formal language theory that provides a meaning of the logical form language itself. It concentrates on distinguishing the different classes of semantic objects by exploring their model-theoretic properties, that is, by defining semantic units in terms of their mapping to set theory. While these techniques are most commonly used for logics, they can be applied to natural language as well. This section is optional and is not necessary for understanding

$UTTERANCE \rightarrow$ (ASSERT *PROPOSITION*) |
(Y/N-QUERY *PROPOSITION*) |
(COMMAND *PROPOSITION*) |
(WH-QUERY *PROPOSITION*)

$PROPOSITION \rightarrow$ (n-ARY-OPERATOR $PROPOSITION_1$ ... $PROPOSITION_n$) |
(*QUANTIFIER VARIABLE : PROPOSITION PROPOSITION*) |
(n-ARY-PREDICATE $TERM_1$ ... $TERM_n$) |
(*EVENT-STATE-PRED VARIABLE* [*ROLE-NAME TERM*]$_1$ ...
[*ROLE-NAME TERM*]$_n$)

$TERM \rightarrow$ *VARIABLE* |
(NAME *VARIABLE NAME-STRING*) |
(PRO *VARIABLE PROPOSITION*)

$1\text{-}ARY\text{-}OPERATOR \rightarrow$ NOT | PAST | PERF | PROG | ...

$2\text{-}ARY\text{-}OPERATOR \rightarrow$ AND | BUT | IF-THEN | ...

$QUANTIFIER \rightarrow$ THE | SOME | WH | $\exists$ | ..

$VARIABLE \rightarrow$ **b1** | **man3** | ...

$1\text{-}ARY\text{-}PREDICATE \rightarrow$ *TYPE-PREDICATE* | HAPPY1 | RED1 | ...

$TYPE\text{-}PREDICATE \rightarrow$ *EVENT-STATE-PRED* | (PLUR *TYPE-PREDICATE*) | MAN1 | ...

$EVENT\text{-}STATE\text{-}PRED \rightarrow$ RUN1 | LOVE3 | GIVE1 | HAPPY | ...

$2\text{-}ARY\text{-}PREDICATE \rightarrow$ *ROLE-NAME* | ABOVE1 | ...

$ROLE\text{-}NAME \rightarrow$ AGENT | THEME | AT-LOC | INSTR | ...

$NAME\text{-}STRING \rightarrow$ "John" | "The New York Times" | ...

Figure 8.7 A formal definition of the syntax of the logical form language

$TERM \rightarrow$ <*QUANTIFIER VARIABLE PROPOSITION*>
$TERM \rightarrow$ <n-*ARY-OPERATOR* $TERM_1$ ... $TERM_n$>
n-*ARY-PREDICATE*
$\rightarrow$ <m-*ARY-OPERATOR* n-*ARY-PREDICATE*$_1$ ... n-*ARY-PREDICATE*$_m$>
n-*ARY-OPERATOR* $\rightarrow$ {n-*ARY-OPERATOR*$_1$ ... n-*ARY-OPERATOR*$_m$}
$QUANTIFIER \rightarrow$ {$QUANTIFIER_1$ ... $QUANTIFIER_m$}
n-*ARY-PREDICATE* $\rightarrow$ {n-*ARY-PREDICATE*$_1$ ... n-*ARY-PREDICATE*$_m$}
$TYPE$-*PREDICATE* $\rightarrow$ {$TYPE$-*PREDICATE*$_1$ ... $TYPE$-*PREDICATE*$_m$}
$EVENT$-*STATE-PRED* $\rightarrow$ {$EVENT$-*STATE-PRED*$_1$ ... $EVENT$-*STATE-PRED*$_m$}
$ROLE$-*NAME* $\rightarrow$ {$ROLE$-*NAME*$_1$ ... $ROLE$-*NAME*$_m$}

Figure 8.8 Additional rules defining the quasi-logical form

the rest of the book. If you are not familiar with FOPC and its model-theoretic semantics, you should read Appendix B before reading this section.

The basic building block for defining semantic properties is the idea of a **model**, which informally can be thought of as a set of objects and their properties and relationships, together with a specification of how the language being studied relates to those objects and relationships. A model can be thought of as representing a particular context in which a sentence is to be evaluated. You might impose different constraints on what properties a model must have. For instance, the standard models for logic, called Tarskian models, are complete in that they must map every legal term in the language into the domain and assign every statement to be true or false. But various forms of partial models are possible that do not assign all statements to be either true or false. Such models are like the situations described in the last section, and in fact a mathematical theory of situations could be a formal model in the general sense we are using here. These issues will be discussed further as they become relevant to the discussion.

Model theory is an excellent method for studying context-independent meaning, because the meanings of sentences are not defined with respect to one specific model but rather by how they relate to any possible model. In other words, the meaning of a sentence is defined in terms of the properties it has with respect to an arbitrary model.

Formally, a model **m** is a tuple $<D_m, I_m>$, where D_m is the **domain of interpretation** (that is, a set of primitive objects), and I is the **interpretation function**. To handle natural language, the domain of interpretation would have to allow objects of all the different types of things that can be referred to, including physical objects, times, locations, events, and situations. The interpretation function maps senses and larger structures into structures defined on the domain. For example, the following describe how an interpretation function will interpret the senses based on some lexical classes:

Senses of noun phrases—refer to specific objects; the interpretation function maps each to an element of D_m.

Senses of singular common nouns (such as *dog, idea, party*)— identify classes of objects in the domain; the interpretation function maps them to sets of elements from D_m (that is, subsets of D_m).

Senses of verbs—identify sets of *n*-ary relations between objects in D. The arity depends on the verb. For instance, the exercising sense of *run*, RUN1, might map to a set of unary relations ($<X>$, where X runs), and the usual sense of *loves*, LOVES1, to a set of binary relations ($<X, Y>$, where X loves Y), and the usual sense of *put*, PUT1, to a set of ternary relations ($<X, Y, L>$, where X puts Y in location L).

We can now define a notion of **truth** of a proposition in the logical form language, again relative to an arbitrary model **m**. A proposition of the form (V_n $a_1 ... a_n$) is true with respect to a model **m** if and only if the tuple consisting of the interpretations of the a_i's is in the set that is the interpretation of V_n, i.e., the tuple $<I_m(a_1), ..., I_m(a_n)>$ is in the set $I_m(V_n)$. Following conventional notation, we will write the fact that a proposition P is true with respect to a model **m** by

$$\mathbf{m} \models P$$

This is sometimes also read as "**m** supports P." For example, **m** supports (RUN1 JACK1) only if $I_m(JACK1)$ is in the set $I_m(RUN1)$, and **m** supports (LOVES1 JACK1 SUE1) only if $<I_m(JACK1), I_m(SUE1)>$ is in the set $I_m(LOVES1)$.

The semantics of negation depend on the properties of the models used. In standard Tarskian semantics, where the models are complete, negation is defined in terms of the absence of the relation necessary to make the proposition true; that is, a model **m** supports (NOT P) if and only if it doesn't support P. In other models this may be too strong, as a proposition might be neither true nor false. Such models would have to maintain two disjoint sets for every relation name: the tuples for which the relation holds and the tuples for which it is false. Any tuple not in either of these sets would be neither true nor false.

The semantics of the quantifiers in FOPC is fairly simple. For example, the proposition $\forall x . P(x)$ is true with respect to a model **m** if and only if $P(x)$ is true for any value of x in D_m. The proposition $\exists x . P(x)$, on the other hand, is true with respect to a model **m** if and only if $P(x)$ is true for at least one value of x in D_m. For natural languages we have generalized quantifiers. The truth conditions for each quantifier specify the required relationship between the objects satisfying the two propositions. For example, consider the proposition (MOST1 x (P x) (Q x)). This might be defined to be true with respect to a model **m** if and only if over half the objects in $I_m(P)$ are in $I_m(Q)$. For example, (MOST1 x (DOG1 x) (BARKS1 x)) would be true with respect to a model **m** if and only if more than half the elements of the set {x | (DOG1 x)} are also in the set {y | (BARKS1 y)}, that is, only if over half the dogs in **m** bark.

Semantic Relations Among Sentences

With a semantic theory in hand, it is now possible to be more precise about certain inferential relationships among sentences. For instance, when you know that some sentence S is true, then some other sentences must also be true. For instance, if you know *A red box is on the table* then you also know that *A box is on the table*. This relationship between sentences is called **entailment**, and we say the sentence *A red box is on the table* **entails** the sentence *A box is on the table*. Formally, entailment can be defined in terms of the models that support the sentences. In particular, sentence S entails sentence S' if and only if every model that supports S also supports S'; that is,

S entails S' if and only if for any model **m**, if **m** $\models$ S then **m** $\models$ S'

Conversely, if there are no models that support both sentences simultaneously, the sentences are said to **contradict** each other; that is, there is no possible situation in which both statements can be true. Slightly modifying the previous example, we know that the sentences *A red box is on the table* and *There is no box on the table* are contradictory because there is no model that can support these two sentences simultaneously.

Given that entailments must hold in all possible models, it might seem that there won't be very many entailments to be found. This turns out not to be the case as the models share more properties than you might first expect. In particular, all the context-independent properties of language will be shared by every model. Consider the above example. While the set of boxes and the set of red things could vary dramatically from model to model, the above entailment did not rely on the actual objects being referred to. Rather, it depended only on the general interpretation of the senses of *red* and *box*, and the set-theoretic property that given two sets X and Y, then the intersection of X and Y is contained in the set X (and Y for that matter). Thus, as long as the model interprets the NP *A red box* as selecting an object from the set RED1 intersected with the set BOX1, then that same object will be in the set BOX1. This is all that is required. Thus every model will include the entailment. Furthermore, Section 8.2 suggested that word senses could be organized into a hierarchy based on set inclusion. This defines an additional context-independent structure on the senses and thus will be included in all possible models. As a consequence, the sentence *A mare ran away* will entail the sentence *A horse ran away*, because every model must map MARE1 to a subset of HORSE1.

While entailment is a useful property, natural language understanding typically deals in weaker connections between sentences, which we will call **implications**. A sentence S **implies** a sentence S' if S being true suggests or makes it likely that S' is also true. For example, the sentence *I used to walk to school every day* implies that I don't walk to school anymore but doesn't entail it, as I could say *I used to walk to school every day. In fact, I still do!* Given that these two sentences are not anomalous, there must be a model that assigns truth to both of them, and in this model it will not be true that I don't walk to school anymore. However, in a typical context, the models that are relevant to that context might all support that I don't walk to school anymore. One of the difficult problems in language understanding results from the fact that most inferences made are implications rather than entailments, and thus conclusions drawn at one time might need to be reconsidered and retracted at a later time.

Modal Operators and Possible Worlds Semantics

To provide a semantics for modal operators, more structure must be imposed on the model theory. In particular, the truth of a property will be defined with respect to a set of models rather than a single model. In addition, this set of models may have a rich structure and hence is called a **model structure**.

BOX 8.2 Extensional and Intensional Readings

The semantic framework discussed in this chapter almost exclusively concerns what is called the extensional meaning of expressions. This is a way of saying that meaning is defined in terms of what the expressions denote in the world. For example, the word sense DOG1 obtains its meaning from the set of objects that it denotes, namely $I_m(DOG1)$. Likewise, a term such as *the dog* or *John* would derive its meaning from the object in the domain that it denotes. If two terms denote the same object, then they are semantically indistinguishable. The extensional view covers a wide range of language but cannot account for many expressions. Consider a classic example from Montague (1974):

The temperature is rising.

What is the meaning of the NP *the temperature* in this sentence? If it denotes a particular value, say 30°, then it could not be rising, as the sentence *30° is rising* is nonsensical. Rather, the phrase *the temperature* must denote a function over time, say the function *Temp* that, given a time and a location, yields the temperature. Given this meaning, the predicate *is rising* would be true of any function that is increasing in value over time. Thus there seem to be two different meanings for the term *the temperature*. The extensional reading would be the actual value at a particular time and place, say 30°, while the intensional reading would be a function that takes a time and place and yields a value. Some verb phrases, such as *is rising*, require the intensional meaning, while others, such as in the sentence *The temperature is over 90°*, require the extensional meaning, as it would make no sense to say that a function has the property of being over 90°.

Because of the complexities in dealing with intensional readings, we will only deal with extensional readings of expressions throughout this book.

Consider the past tense operator PAST. Let us assume that each individual model **m** represents the state of the world at some point in time. Then a model structure would be the set of models describing one possible history of the world, in which models are related to each other by an operator $<$, where **m1** $<$ **m2** means **m1** describes a state of the world before the state described by **m2**. The truth of propositions is now defined with respect to an arbitrary model structure Ω that has the $<$ relation between models. For example, we can now define a semantics for the expression (PAST P) with respect to a model **m** in a model structure Ω:

$\qquad$ **m** $\models_\Omega$ (PAST P) if and only if there is another model **m'** in Ω such that **m'** $<$ **m** and **m'** $\models_\Omega$ P

In other words, (PAST P) is true in a model **m** if and only if there is another model in the model structure that describes a time previous to **m** in which P is true. This type of analysis is called a **possible worlds semantics**.

Summary

This chapter presented a context-independent semantic representation called the logical form. Such a representation is desirable to simplify the process of computing semantic structures from the syntactic structure, and more generally to modularize the processing of sentences by separating out contextual effects. The logical form language uses many of the concepts from FOPC, including terms, predicates, propositions, and logical operators. The most significant extensions to basic FOPC were the following:

- generalized quantifiers, which indicate a relationship between two sets and correspond to words such as *each, every, some, most, several,* and so on
- modal operators, which identify different modalities in which to consider propositions and correspond to words such as *believe* and *hopes,* as well as the tense operators
- predicate operators, which map one predicate into a new predicate, as with the operator for plural forms that takes a predicate describing individuals with a property P and produces a predicate that describes sets of individuals, each with property P

In addition, the logical form language can encode many common forms of ambiguity in an efficient manner by allowing alternative senses to be listed wherever a single sense is allowed.

An important aspect of the logical form language is its use of event and state variables on predicates. This allows you to represent additional adverbial modifiers without having to introduce different predicates for each possible combination of arguments to the verb. A representation based on thematic roles was also introduced. While the roles may differ from system to system, this style of representation is very common in natural language systems.

Related Work and Further Readings

The logical form language developed here draws from many sources. The most influential early source is the representation language in the LUNAR system (Woods, 1978), which contains initial ideas for many of the details in this representation. More recent strong influences are the logical form languages developed by Schubert and Pelletier (1982), Hwang and Schubert (1993a), and Moore (1981), and the quasi-logical form in the Core Language Engine (Alshawi, 1992).

Like many logical form languages, the one developed here is heavily based on techniques of introducing events into the ontology to handle optional arguments and other verb modifiers. This technique became influential following a landmark paper by Davidson (1967) who presented many arguments for the approach. Moore (1981), Alshawi (1992), and Hobbs et al. (1987) are all good examples of such event-based systems.

Work on thematic roles originates from work on case grammar by Fillmore (1968), who introduced six cases. These ideas have been adapted by many researchers since in linguistics and philosophy (for example, see Jackendoff (1972), Dowty (1989), and Parsons (1990)). Similar techniques can be found in many computational systems. In these systems, thematic roles are often linked to the underlying knowledge representation (for example, Charniak (1981)).

The idea of encoding scoping ambiguity in the logical form has been used by many systems. Woods (1978) and Cooper (1983), for instance, suggested a two-part representation of logical form: one part for the predicate-argument structure and the other for the quantifier information. Encoding the scoped forms using a special syntax has been used in Schubert and Pelletier (1982), McCord (1986), Hobbs and Shieber (1987), and many recent systems such as the Core Language Engine (Alshawi, 1992). This encoding is not only important for encoding ambiguity, but also plays a key role in allowing the definition of compositional semantic interpretation theories, as will be discussed in Chapter 9.

An excellent general source on semantics in linguistics can be found in Chierchia and McConnell-Ginet (1990). This book contains discussions on the nature of semantics and issues such as ambiguity and vagueness, indexicality, denotational semantics, generalized quantifiers, intensionality, and a host of other issues. McCawley (1993) is also an excellent and accessible source on the logical underpinnings of semantics. More detailed presentation of the mathematical underpinnings of semantic representations can be found in Partee et al. (1993). Generalized quantifiers are discussed in Barwise and Cooper (1981). Many of the semantic ideas discussed here were first developed within symbolic logic, for which there are many excellent texts (for example, Thomason (1970); Barwise and Etchemendy (1987)). The current form of semantics for natural language is most heavily influenced by the work of Montague (1974).

Much of the current work in formal semantics is within the framework of situation semantics. The notion of a situation discussed in this chapter is drawn from that work. Situation semantics was developed by Jon Barwise and collaborators, and an initial version of the theory is described in Barwise and Perry (1983). An excellent discussion and formalization of situations in found in Devlin (1991).

Exercises for Chapter 8

1. (*easy*) State why each of the following sentences are ambiguous or not. Specifically, state whether they are ambiguous because of their possible syntactic structures, their word senses, their semantic structures, or a combination of these factors. Give a paraphrase of each reading.

    A man stopped at every truck stop.
    Several people ate the pizza.
    We saw her duck.

2. (*medium*) For each of the following words, argue whether the word is ambiguous or vague. Give at least one linguistic test that supports your answer. Discuss any difficulties that arise in making your decision.

> *face*—as a noun, as in what's on your head, the front of a clock, and the side of a mountain
>
> *bird*—as a noun, as in animals that fly (such as a sparrow) and china figures of such animals
>
> *record*—as a noun, as in where a school keeps your grades or where the FBI writes down your movements

3. (*easy*) Identify the senses of the word *can* used in the following sentences, and specify whether the sense is a term, property (unary predicate), n-ary predicate, logical operator, generalized quantifier, predicate operator, or modal operator. Justify your classification and discuss alternate interpretations that could work just as well. Give an example logical form that uses each sense.

> The yellow can fell to the ground.
>
> He can see it.
>
> He wants to can the tomatoes.

4. (*easy*) Expand out the following ambiguous logical forms, giving a complete list of the full logical forms allowed by the ambiguous form.

> ({RUN1 RUN2} [AGENT (PRO **h1** HE1)])
>
> (SEES1 **s1** [AGENT (PRO **h1** HE1)]
> [<EVERY **b1** {BALL1 BALL2}>])
>
> (GIVES1 **l1** [AGENT <EVERY **m1** MAN1>]
> [THEME <A **g1** GIFT1>])
>
> (<NOT {RUN1 RUN2}>
> [AGENT <EVERY **m1** (& (MAN1 **m1**) (HAPPY **m1**))>])

5. (*medium*) Specify a quasi-logical form for the following sentences. If the sentence is ambiguous, make sure you represent all the possibilities, either using ambiguous logical forms or by listing several logical forms.

> George ate a pizza at every road stop.
>
> Several employees from every company bought a pizza.
>
> We saw John in the park by the beach.

6. (*medium*) Specify the roles for each NP in the following sentences. Give a plausible logical form for each sentence.

> We returned the ring to the store.
>
> We returned to the party.
>
> The owner received a ticket.

7.   (*medium*)

a   Specify a formal semantic model that makes each of the following logical forms true.

(IN1 JOHN1 ROOM1)
(BOY1 JOHN1)
(EVERY **b1** : BOY1 (EAT **b1** PIZZA1))

Specifically, define a set of objects for the domain of the model, and specify the interpretation function that maps each of these symbols into an element or set in the domain. Demonstrate that each of these logical forms is assigned true by specifying their interpretation.

b.   Does your model also assign true to

(EAT JOHN1 PIZZA1)

Could you build a model that does the opposite (assigns false if yours assigns true, or vice versa)? If so, give the model. If not, why not?

8.   (*medium*)   For each of the following lists of sentences, state whether the first sentence entails or implies each of the sentences that follow it or that there is no semantic relationship among them. Justify your answers using some linguistics tests.

a   John didn't manage to find the key.

John didn't find the key.
John looked for the key.
The key is hard to find.

b.   John was disappointed that Fido was last in the dog show.

Fido was last in the dog show.
Fido was entered in the dog show.
John wanted Fido to win.
Fido is a stupid dog.

CHAPTER

9

Linking Syntax and Semantics

9.1 Semantic Interpretation and Compositionality

9.2 A Simple Grammar and Lexicon with Semantic Interpretation

9.3 Prepositional Phrases and Verb Phrases

9.4 Lexicalized Semantic Interpretation and Semantic Roles

9.5 Handling Simple Questions

9.6 Semantic Interpretation Using Feature Unification

9.7 Generating Sentences from Logical Form

This chapter discusses a particular method for linking logical forms with syntactic structures. This will allow logical forms to be computed while parsing, a process called **semantic interpretation**. One version discussed also allows a syntactic tree to be generated from a specified logical form, a process called **semantic realization**. To fully couple syntax and semantics, there must be a well-formed meaning expression for every constituent. The relation between the meaning of a constituent and the meanings of its subconstituents can then be specified in the grammar using features. Because each syntactic rule has a corresponding semantic interpretation rule, this method is often referred to as a **rule-by-rule** style of semantic interpretation.

Section 9.1 discusses the notion of compositionality and introduces the lambda calculus as a tool for building compositional theories. Sections 9.2 and 9.3 then examine some basic constructs in language and develop a grammar for a small fragment of English that computes the logical form of each constituent as it is parsed. The logical form used in Sections 9.2 and 9.3 is a predicate argument structure. Section 9.4 shows how to generate a logical form using semantic roles and briefly discusses the need for hierarchical lexicons to reduce the amount of work required to specify the meanings of lexical items. Section 9.5 discusses how semantic interpretation relates to gaps and shows how to handle simple questions. Section 9.6 develops an alternative method of computing logical forms that uses additional features rather than lambda expressions, thus allowing us to express reversible grammars. Optional Section 9.7 discusses semantic realization, showing how to generate a sentence given a logical form and a reversible grammar.

9.1 Semantic Interpretation and Compositionality

One of the principal assumptions often made about semantic interpretation is that it is a **compositional** process. This means that the meaning of a constituent is derived solely from the meanings of its subconstituents. Compositional theories have some attractive properties. In particular, interpretations can be built incrementally from the interpretations of subphrases. The context-free grammar model of syntax, for example, is a compositional theory of syntax. Rules apply based on the category of the subconstituents, without concern for their internal structure. The rule S → NP VP, for instance, applies no matter what particular form of NP arises. By simply adding another NP rule to the grammar, say NP → PRO, a whole new class of sentences becomes acceptable as well, namely any sentences with a pronoun in an acceptable NP position. This is a very attractive property that we want to have for semantic interpretation.

In linguistics compositionality is often defined in terms of a strict criterion: One subconstituent must have as its meaning a function that maps the meanings of the other subconstituents into the meaning of the new constituent. In computational approaches, the requirement is often more relaxed and requires an incremental process of building meanings constituent by constituent, where the meaning of a constituent is produced by some well-defined computational function (that is, a program), that uses the meanings of the subconstituents as inputs.

Compositional models tend to make grammars easier to extend and maintain. But developing a compositional theory of semantic interpretation is harder than it looks. First, there seems to be a structural inconsistency between syntactic structure and the structure of the logical forms. For instance, a classic problem arises with quantified sentences. Consider the sentence *Jill loves every dog*. The syntactic structure of this sentence clusters the words into phrases in the obvious way: ((Jill) (loves (every dog))). But the unambiguous logical form of the sentence in a predicate-argument form would be something like

(EVERY **d** : (DOG1 **d**) (LOVES1 **l1** (NAME **j1** "Jill") **d**))

This asserts that for every dog **d** there is an event **l1** that consists of Jill loving **d**. There seems to be no simple one-to-one correspondence between parts of the logical form and the constituents in syntactic analysis. The phrase *every dog*, for instance, is a subconstituent of the VP *loves every dog*. Its semantic interpretation, however—the generalized quantified phrase (EVERY **d** : (DOG1 **d**) ...)— seems to have the meaning of the verb phrase as a part of it. Worse than that, the interpretation of *every dog* seems to be split—it produces both the quantifier structure outside the predicate as well as an argument to the predicate. As a result, it is hard to see how the meaning of *every dog* could be represented in isolation and then used to construct the meaning of the sentence. This is one of the most difficult problems to be dealt with if we are to have a compositional theory. Note that introducing the unscoped logical form constructs provides one way around the problem. If we define the goal of semantic interpretation as producing an unscoped logical form, the unscoped version of this sentence would be

(LOVES1 **l1** (NAME **j1** "Jill") <EVERY **d** DOG1>)

which is much closer in structure to the syntactic form.

Another challenge to compositional theories is the presence of idioms. For instance, you may say *Jack kicked the bucket*, meaning that Jack died. This interpretation seems to have no relation to the meanings of the verb *kick* and nothing to do with buckets. Thus the meaning of the sentence does not seem to be constructed out of the meaning of its subconstituents. One way to handle such cases is to allow semantic meanings to be assigned to entire phrases rather than build the meaning compositionally. So far, we have assumed that the primitive unit is the word (or morpheme). Idiomatic expressions suggest that this might be generalized so that complete phrases may have a primitive (that is, nonderived) meaning. In the previous example the verb phrase *kick the bucket* has a primitive meaning similar to the verb *die*. This approach is supported by the observation that certain syntactic paraphrases that are fine for sentences given their compositional meaning do not apply for idiomatic readings. For instance, the passive sentence *The bucket was kicked by Jack* could not mean that Jack died.

Interestingly, *Jack kicked the bucket* is ambiguous. It would have one meaning constructed compositionally from the meanings of each of the words, say (KICK1 **k1** (NAME **j1** "Jack") <THE **b** BUCKET>), and another constructed from the meaning of the word *Jack* and the primitive meaning of the phrase *kick the bucket*, say (DIE1 **d1** (NAME **j1** "Jack")).

Another approach to this problem is to introduce new senses of words that appear in idioms. For example, there might be a sense of *kick* that means DIE1, and that subcategorizes for an object of type BUCKET1. While idioms are a very interesting and important aspect of language, there will not be the space to deal with them in the next few chapters. For the purposes of this book, you can assume that the primitive meanings are always associated with the word.

If the process of semantic interpretation is compositional, then you must be able to assign a semantic structure to any syntactic constituent. For example, you must be able to assign some uniform form of meaning to every verb phrase that can be used in any rule involving a VP as a subconstituent. Consider the simplest case, where the VP consists of an intransitive verb, as in a sentence such as *Jack laughed*. One suggestion is that the meaning of the verb phrase *laughed* is a unary predicate that is true of any object that laughed in the past. Does this approach generalize? In other words, could every VP have a meaning that is a unary predicate? Consider the sentence *Jack kissed Sue*, with the logical form

(KISS1 **k1** (NAME **j1** "Jack") (NAME **s1** "Sue"))

What is the meaning of the VP *kissed Sue*? Again, it could be a unary predicate that is true of any object that kissed Sue. But so far we have no way to express such complex unary predicates. The **lambda calculus** provides a formalism for this. In particular, the expression

(λ x (KISS1 **k1** x (NAME **s1** "Sue")))

is a predicate that takes one argument. You can view x as a parameter, and this predicate is true of any object O, such that substituting O for x in the expression results in a true proposition. Like any other predicate, you can construct a proposition from a lambda expression and an argument. In the logical form language, the following is a proposition:

((λ x (KISS1 **k1** x (NAME **s1** "Sue"))) (NAME **j1** "Jack"))

This proposition is true if and only if (NAME **j1** "Jack") satisfies the predicate (λ x (KISS1 **k1** x (NAME **s1** "Sue"))), which by definition is true if and only if

(KISS1 **k1** (NAME **j1** "Jack") (NAME **s1** "Sue"))

is true. We will often say that this last expression was obtained by **applying** the lambda expression (λ x (KISS1 x (NAME **s1** "Sue"))) to the argument (NAME **j1** "Jack"). This operation is called **lambda reduction**.

Given that we have had to introduce new concepts such as lambda expressions in order to establish a close syntactic-semantic coupling, you might

---

BOX 9.1 The Lambda Calculus and Lambda Reduction

The lambda calculus is a powerful language based on a simple set of primitives. Formulas in the lambda calculus consist of equality assertions of the form

<expression> = <expression>

The most crucial axiom in this system for our purposes is

$((\lambda x\ Px)\ a) = P\{x/a\}$

where Px is an arbitrary formula involving x and P{x/a} is the formula where every instance of x is replaced by a. From this axiom, two principal operations can be defined: lambda reduction (moving from left to right across the axiom) and lambda abstraction (moving from right to left across the axiom). In general, lambda reduc-tion is the principal concern to us because it tends to make formulas simpler. In fact, because lambda reduction simply replaces one formula with a simpler one that is equal to it, the operation is not formally necessary at all to account for semantic interpretation. Without using lambda reduction, however, the answers, though correct, would tend to be unreadable.

---

be tempted to abandon this approach and develop some other method of semantic interpretation. As a grammar becomes larger and handles more complex phenom-ena, however, the compositional theory becomes more attractive. For instance, using this method, verb phrases can easily be conjoined even when they have different syntactic structures, as in the sentence

Sue laughs and opens the door.

There are two VPs here: *laughs*, which has a semantic interpretation as a unary predicate true of someone who laughs, say (λ a (LAUGHS1 l2 a)); and *opens the door*, a unary predicate true of someone who opens the door, namely

(λ a (OPENS1 l2 a <THE **d1** DOOR1>))

These two unary predicates can be combined to form a complex unary predicate that is true of someone who both laughs and opens the door, namely,

(λ a (& (LAUGHS1 l2 a) (OPENS1 o1 a <THE **d1** DOOR1>)))

This is in exactly the right form for a VP and can be combined with other con-stituents like any other VP. For instance, it can be applied to a subject NP with logical form (NAME **s1** "Sue") to form the meaning of the original sentence.

(& (LAUGHS1 l2 (NAME **s1** "Sue"))
    (OPENS1 o1 (NAME **s1** "Sue") <THE **d1** DOOR1>))

Consider another example. Prepositional phrase modifiers in noun phrases could be handled in many different ways. For instance, we might not have an independent meaning for the phrase *in the store* in the noun phrase *The man in the store*. Rather, a special mechanism might be used to look for location modifiers in noun phrases and incorporate them into the interpretation. But this mechanism would then not help in interpreting sentences like *The man is in the store* or *The man was thought to be in the store*. If the prepositional phrase has an independent meaning, in this case the unary predicate

$(\lambda$ o (IN-LOC1 o <THE **s1** STORE1>))

then this same interpretation can be used just as easily as a modifier to a noun phrase (adding a new restriction) or as the predicate of a sentence. The logical form of the noun phrase *the man in the store* would be

<THE **m1** (MAN1 **m1**) (IN-LOC1 **m1** <THE **s1** STORE1>)>

while the logical form of the sentence *The man is in the store* would be

(IN-LOC1 <THE **m1** MAN1> <THE **s1** STORE1>)

These are just two simple examples. There are many other generalities that also arise if you adopt a compositional approach to semantics.

In general, each major syntactic phrase corresponds to a particular semantic construction. VPs and PPs map to unary predicates (possible complex expressions built out of lambda expressions), sentences map to propositions, and NPs map to terms. The minor categories map to expressions that define their role in building the major categories. Since every constituent in the same syntactic category maps to the same sort of semantic construct, these can all be treated uniformly. For example, you don't need to know the specific structure of a VP. As long as its meaning is a unary predicate, you can use it to build the meaning of another larger constituent that contains it.

9.2 A Simple Grammar and Lexicon with Semantic Interpretation

This section constructs a simple grammar and lexicon to illustrate how the logical form can be computed using the features while parsing. To keep the examples simple, the logical form will be the predicate-argument structure used in the last section rather than the thematic role representation. This will allow all verbs with the same subcategorization structure to be treated identically. Section 9.4 will then discuss methods of generalizing the framework to identify thematic roles.

The main extension needed is to add a SEM feature to each lexical entry and grammatical rule. For example, one rule in the grammar might be

(S **SEM** (?semvp ?semnp)) $\rightarrow$ (NP **SEM** ?semnp) (VP **SEM** ?semvp)

Consider what this rule does given the NP subconstituent with SEM (NAME **m1** "Mary") and the VP subconstituent with SEM

$(\lambda$ a (SEES1 **e8** a (NAME **j1** "Jack")))

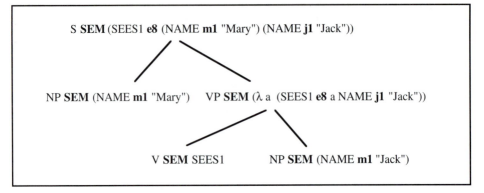

Figure 9.1 A parse tree showing the SEM features

The SEM feature of the new S constituent is simply the expression

$$((\lambda\ a\ (SEES1\ \textbf{e8}\ a\ (NAME\ \textbf{j1}\ ``Jack")))\ (NAME\ \textbf{m1}\ ``Mary"))$$

This expression can be simplified using lambda reduction to the formula

$$(SEES1\ \textbf{e8}\ (NAME\ \textbf{m1}\ ``Mary")\ (NAME\ \textbf{j1}\ ``Jack"))$$

which is the desired logical form for the sentence. Figure 9.1 shows the parse tree for this sentence giving the SEM feature for each constituent.

In the lexicon the SEM feature is used to indicate the possible senses of each word. Generally, a word will have a different word sense for every possible subcategorization it has, since these will be different arity predicates. A sample lexicon is shown in Figure 9.2. When a word has a different SEM form depending on its syntactic features, multiple entries are required. For example, the verb *decide* has two entries: one for the case where the SUBCAT is _none, and one for the case where the SUBCAT is _pp:on, where the verb has an additional argument. Note also that the word *fish* also has two entries because its SEM depends on whether it is singular or plural.

Consider Grammar 9.3, which accepts very simple sentence and verb phrases and computes their logical form. Note that another feature is introduced in addition to the SEM feature. The VAR feature is new and stores the discourse variable that corresponds to the constituent. It will be useful for handling certain forms of modifiers in the development that follows. The VAR feature is automatically generated by the parser when a lexical constituent is constructed from a word, and then it is passed up the tree by treating VAR as a head feature. It guarantees that the discourse variables are always unique.

The lexical rules for morphological derivation must also be modified to handle the SEM feature. For instance, the rule that converts a singular noun into a plural noun takes the SEM of the singular noun and adds the PLUR operators:

(N **AGR** 3p **SEM** (PLUR ?semn)) →
(N **AGR** 3s **IRREG-PL** – **SEM** ?semn) +S

a (art **AGR** 3s **SEM** INDEF1)
can (aux **SUBCAT** base **SEM** CAN1)
car (n **SEM** CAR1 **AGR** 3s)
cry (v **SEM** CRY1 **VFORM** base **SUBCAT** _none)
decide (v **SEM** DECIDES1 **VFORM** base **SUBCAT** _none)
decide (v **SEM** DECIDES-ON1 **VFORM** base **SUBCAT** _pp:on)
dog (n **SEM** DOG1 **AGR** 3s)
fish (n **SEM** FISH1 **AGR** 3s)
fish (n **SEM** (PLUR FISH1) **AGR** 3p)
house (n **SEM** HOUSE1 **AGR** 3s)
has (aux **VFORM** pres **AGR** 3s **SUBCAT** pastprt **SEM** PERF)
he (pro **SEM** HE1 **AGR** 3s)
in (p **PFORM** {LOC MOT} **SEM** IN-LOC1)
Jill (name **AGR** 3s **SEM** "Jill")
man (n **SEM** MAN1 **AGR** 3s)
men (n **SEM** (PLUR MAN1) **AGR** 3p)
on (p **PFORM** LOC **SEM** ON-LOC1)
saw (v **SEM** SEES1 **VFORM** past **SUBCAT** _np **AGR** ?a)
see (v **SEM** SEES1 **VFORM** base **SUBCAT** _np **IRREG-PAST** + **EN-PASTPRT** +)
she (pro **AGR** 3s **SEM** SHE1)
the (art **SEM** THE **AGR** {3s 3p})
to (to **AGR** – **VFORM** inf)

Figure 9.2 A small lexicon showing the SEM features

1. (S **SEM** (?semvp ?semnp) → (NP **SEM** ?semnp) (*VP SEM ?semvp*)

2. (VP **VAR** ?v **SEM** (λ a2 (?semv ?v a2))) → (*V[_none] SEM ?semv*)

3. (VP **VAR** ?v **SEM** (λ a3 (?semv ?v a3 ?semnp))) →
   (*V[_np] SEM ?semv*) (NP **SEM** ?semnp)

4. (NP **WH** – **VAR** ?v **SEM** (PRO ?v ?sempro)) → (*PRO SEM ?sempro*)

5. (NP **VAR** ?v **SEM** (NAME ?v ?semname)) → (*NAME SEM ?semname*)

6. (NP **VAR** ?v **SEM** <?semart ?v (?semcnp ?v)>) →
   (ART **SEM** ?semart) (*CNP SEM ?semcnp*)

7. (CNP **SEM** ?semn) → (*N SEM ?semn*)

Head features for S, VP, NP, CNP: VAR

Grammar 9.3 A simple grammar with SEM features

A similar technique is used to insert unscoped tense operators for the past and present tenses. The revised morphological rules are shown in Grammar 9.4.

L1.　(V **VFORM** pres **AGR** 3s **SEM** <PRES ?semv>) →
　　　(V **VFORM** base **IRREG-PRES – SEM** ?semv) +S

L2.　(V **VFORM** pres **AGR** {1s 2s 1p 2p 3p} **SEM** <PRES ?semv>) →
　　　(V **VFORM** base **IRREG-PRES – SEM** ?semv)

L3.　(V **VFORM** past **AGR** {1s 2s 3s 1p 2p 3p} **SEM** <PAST ?semv>) →
　　　(V **VFORM** base **IRREG-PAST – SEM** ?semv) +ED

L4.　(V **VFORM** pastprt **SEM** ?semv) →
　　　(V **VFORM** base **EN-PASTPRT – SEM** ?semv) +ED

L5.　(V **VFORM** pastprt **SEM** ?semv) →
　　　(V **VFORM** base **EN-PASTPRT + SEM** ?semv) +EN

L6.　(V **VFORM** ing **SEM** ?semv) →
　　　(V **VFORM** base **SEM** ?semv) +ING

L7.　(N **AGR** 3p **SEM** (PLUR ?semn)) →
　　　(V **AGR** 3s **IRREG-PL – SEM** ?semn) +S

Grammar 9.4　The morphological rules with semantic interpretation

These are the same as the original rules given as Grammar 4.5 except for the addition of the SEM feature.

Rule 1 was previously discussed. Rules 2 and 3 handle transitive and intransitive verbs and build the appropriate VP interpretation. Each takes the SEM of the verb, ?semv, and constructs a unary predicate that will apply to the subject. The arguments to the verb sense include an event variable, which is stored in the VAR feature, the subject, and then any additional arguments for subcategorized constituents. Rule 4 constructs the appropriate SEM structure for pronouns given a pronoun sense ?sempro, and rule 5 does the same for proper names. Rule 6 defines an expression that involves an unscoped quantified expression, which consists of the quantifier ?semart, the discourse variable ?v, and a proposition restricting the quantifier, which is constructed by applying the unary predicate ?semcnp to the discourse variable. For example, assuming that the discourse variable ?v is **m1**, the NP *the man* would combine the SEM of *the*, namely the operator THE, with the SEM of *man*, namely MAN1, to form the expression <THE **m1** (MAN1 **m1**)>. Rule 7 builds a simple CNP out of a single N. Since the SEM of a common noun is a unary predicate already, this value simply is used as the SEM of the CNP.

Only two simple modifications need to be made to the standard chart parser to handle semantic interpretation:

- When a lexical rule is instantiated for use, the VAR feature is set to a new discourse variable.
- Whenever a constituent is built, the SEM is simplified by performing any lambda reductions that are possible.

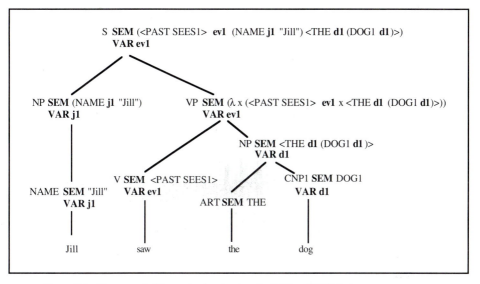

Figure 9.5 The parse of *Jill saw the dog* showing the SEM and VAR features

With these two changes, the existing parser now will compute the logical form as it parses. Consider a trace of the parser on *Jill saw the dog,* whose parse tree is shown in Figure 9.5. The word *Jill* is parsed as a name using the lexical lookup. A new discourse variable, **j1**, is generated and set to the VAR feature. This constituent is used by rule 5 to build an NP. Since VAR is a head feature, the VAR feature of the NP will be **j1** as well, and the SEM is constructed from the equation in the obvious manner. The lexical entry for the word *saw* generates a V constituent with the SEM <PAST SEES1> and a new VAR **ev1**. Rule 6 combines the SEMs of the two entries for *the* and *dog* with the VAR from the noun to build an NP with the SEM <THE **d1** (DOG **d1**)>. This is then combined with the SEM of the verb and its VAR by rule 3 to form a VP with the SEM

$$(\lambda\ x\ (<\text{PAST SEES1}>\ \textbf{ev1}\ x\ <\text{THE}\ \textbf{d1}\ (\text{DOG1}\ \textbf{d1})>))$$

This is then combined with the subject NP to form the final logical form for the sentence.

This completes the description of the basic semantic interpretation process. With the two new features and two minor extensions to the parser described here, a grammar can be specified that builds the logical form as it parses. This technique will work with any of the chart-based parsing strategies that have been discussed in this book.

9.3 Prepositional Phrases and Verb Phrases

While the last section introduced everything needed to semantically interpret sentences, only the simplest interpretation techniques were introduced. This section describes some additional examples of grammatical rules that handle slightly more complicated phenomena. Specifically, it addresses the interpretation of verb phrases and prepositional phrases in more detail. First, consider the rule that is needed for handling auxiliary verbs:

(VP **SEM** (λ a1 (?semaux (?semvp a1)))) $\rightarrow$
    (*AUX* **SUBCAT** *?v* **SEM** *?semaux*)
    (VP **VFORM** ?v **SEM** ?semvp)

This rule inserts a modal operator in the appropriate place for the new VP. The SEM equation for the new VP is a little complicated, so consider it in more detail. If ?semaux is a modal operator such as CAN1, and ?semvp is a lambda expression such as (λ x (LAUGHS1 **e3** x)), then, according to the auxiliary rule, the SEM of the VP *can laugh* will be

(λ a1 (CAN1 ((λ x (LAUGHS1 **e3** x)) a1))

This can be simplified to

(λ a1 (CAN1 (LAUGHS1 **e3** a1)))

It might help to view this type of SEM equation as "lifting" the variable for the subject over the CAN1 operator. Starting with the VP interpretation (λ x (LAUGHS1 **e3** x)), the equation builds a new formula containing the CAN1 operator yet still retaining the lambda variable for the subject on the outside of the formula. Note that, like all VPs, the new SEM is a unary predicate that applies to the subject, so the auxiliary rule could be used recursively to analyze more complex sequences of auxiliary verbs.

To analyze prepositional phrases, it is important to realize that they play two different semantic roles in sentences. In one analysis the PP is a modifier to a noun phrase or verb phrase. In the other use the PP is subcategorized for by a head word, and the preposition acts more as a flag for an argument position than as an independent predicate.

Consider the modification case first. In these cases the SEM of the PP is a unary predicate to be applied to whatever it eventually modifies. Thus the following rule would be appropriate for building a PP modifier:

(PP **SEM** (λ y (?semp y ?semnp))) $\rightarrow$ (*P* **SEM** *?semp*) (NP **SEM** ?semnp)

Given the PP *in the corner*, if the SEM of the P is IN-LOC1, and the SEM of the NP is <THE **c1** (CORNER1 **c1**)>, then the SEM of the PP would be the unary predicate

(λ y (IN-LOC1 y <THE **c1** CORNER1>))

Now you can consider the interpretation of the noun phrase *the man in the corner*. A reasonable rule that incorporates the PP modifier would be

(CNP **SEM** (λ n1 (& (?semcnp n1) (?sempp n1)))) $\rightarrow$
    (*CNP* **SEM** *?semcnp*) (PP **SEM** ?sempp)

Given that the SEM of the CNP *man* is the unary predicate MAN1 and the SEM of the PP *in the corner* is (λ y (IN1 y <THE **c1** CORNER1>)), the new SEM of the CNP, before simplification, would be

(λ n1 (& (MAN1 n1) ((λ y (IN1 y <THE **c1** CORNER1>)) n1)))

The subexpression ((λ y (IN1 y <THE **c1** CORNER1>)) n1) can then be simplified to (IN1 n1 <THE **c1** CORNER1>). Thus the overall expression becomes

(λ n1 (& (MAN1 n1) (IN1 n1 <THE **c1** CORNER1>)))

This is a unary predicate true of any man who is in the corner, the desired interpretation. Combining this with a quantifier such as *the* using rule 6 would form a SEM such as

<THE **m2** ((λ z (& (MAN1 z) (IN1 z <THE **c1** CORNER1>))) **m2**)>

which itself simplifies to

<THE **m2** (& (MAN1 **m2**) (IN1 **m2** <THE **c1** CORNER1>))>

PPs can also modify verb phrases, as in the VP *cry in the corner* in *Jill can cry in the corner.* The syntactic rule that introduces the PP modifier would be

VP $\rightarrow$ VP PP

You might think that the SEM feature equation can be treated in exactly a parallel way as with the noun phrase case, but there is a complication. Consider the desired behavior. The VP subconstituent *cry* has the logical form

(λ x (CRIES1 **e1** x))

and the PP has the logical form shown above. The desired logical form for the entire VP *cry in the corner* is

(λ a (& (CRIES1 **e1** a) (IN-LOC1 **e1** <THE **c1** CORNER1>)))

The problem is that the unary predicate for the VP subconstituent is intended to apply to the subject, where the unary predicate for the PP modifier must apply to the discourse variable generated for the VP. So the technique used for rule 9 does not yield the correct answer. Rather, the SEM constructed from the PP must be applied to the discourse variable instead. In other words, the appropriate rule is

(VP **VAR** ?v **SEM** (λ x (& (?semvp x) (?sempp ?v)))) $\rightarrow$
(VP **VAR** ?v **SEM** ?semvp) (PP **SEM** ?sempp)

The parse tree for the VP *cry in the corner* using this rule is shown in Figure 9.6.

Prepositional phrases also appear as subcategorized constituents in verb phrases, and these cases must be treated differently. Specifically, it is the verb that determines how the prepositional phrase is interpreted. For example, the PP *on a couch* in isolation might indicate the location of some object or event, but with the verb *decide*, it can indicate the object that is being decided about. The

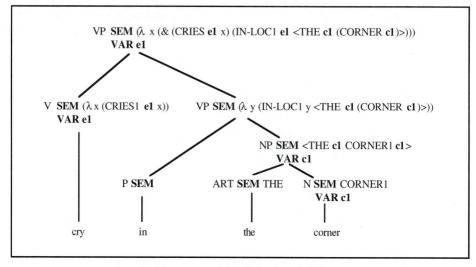

Figure 9.6 Using the VAR feature for PP modifiers of VPs

distinction between the two readings can be illustrated by considering that the sentence *Jill decided on a couch* is ambiguous between two readings:

- Jill made a decision while she was on a couch.
- Jill made a decision about a couch.

The first case results from treating *on a couch* as an adverbial PP, which was discussed above. What is the semantic interpretation equation for the second case? The appropriate syntactic rule is

VP → V[_pp:on] NP PP[on]

and the desired logical form of the final VP is

(λ s (DECIDES-ON1 **d1** s <A **c1** (COUCH **c1**)>))

Note that there appears to be no semantic contribution from the word *on* in this case. Subcategorized PPs are handled in many systems by distinguishing between two different types of prepositional phrases. A new binary feature PRED is introduced, where + indicates that the prepositional phrase should be interpreted as a predicate, and – means it should be interpreted as an argument, that is, a term. This binary distinction allows us to specify two rules for prepositional phrases. These are rules 8 and 9 in Grammar 9.7. Rule 8 is restricted to prepositional phrases with a +PRED value, and the PP acts as a modifier. Rule 9 handles all the subcategorized prepositional phrases, with the –PRED feature, in which case the SEM of the PP is simply the SEM of the object NP. Grammar 9.7 also summarizes all the other rules developed in this section.

Figure 9.8 shows the two readings of the VP *decide on a couch* given the grammar defined by Grammars 9.3 and 9.7. The case in which the decision is

8. (PP **PRED** + **SEM** (λ x (?semp x ?semnp))) $\rightarrow$
   (*P SEM ?semp*) (NP **SEM** ?semnp)

9. (PP **PRED** – **PFORM** ?pf **SEM** ?semnp) $\rightarrow$
   (*P ROOT ?pf*) (NP **SEM** ?semnp)

10. (VP **VAR** **?**v **SEM** (λ ag1 (& (?semvp ag1) (?sempp ?v)))) $\rightarrow$
    (*VP SEM ?semvp*) (PP **PRED** + **SEM** ?sempp)

11. (VP **VAR** ?v **SEM** (λ ag2 (?semv ?v ag2 ?sempp))) $\rightarrow$
    (*V[_np_pp:on SEM ?semv*) (PP **PRED** – **PFORM** on **SEM** ?sempp)

12. (VP **SEM** (λ a1 (?semaux (?semvp a1)))) $\rightarrow$
    (AUX **SUBCAT** ?v **SEM** ?semaux) (VP **VFORM** ?v **SEM** ?semvp)

13. (CNP **SEM** (λ n1 (& (?semcnp n1) (?sempp n1)))) $\rightarrow$
    (*CNP SEM ?semcnp*) (PP **PRED** + **SEM** ?sempp)

Head features for PP: PFORM
Head features for VP, CNP: VAR

Grammar 9.7 Rules to handle PPs in verb phrases

about a couch is shown in the upper half of the figure: the PP has the feature
–PRED, as previously discussed, and its SEM is <A **c1** COUCH1>. The case in
which a decision is made on a couch is shown in the lower half of the figure: the
PP has the feature +PRED and its SEM is (λ x (ON-LOC1 x <A **c1** COUCH1>)).

9.4 Lexicalized Semantic Interpretation and Semantic Roles

So far, the semantic forms of the lexical entries have only consisted of the
possible senses for each word, and all the complexity of the semantic interpretation is encoded in the grammatical rules. While this is a reasonable strategy,
many researchers use a different approach, in which the lexical entries encode the
complexities and the grammatical rules are simpler. Consider the verb *decide*, say
in its intransitive sense, DECIDES1. The SEM of the verb is simply the sense
DECIDES1, and rule 2 builds the lambda expression (λ y (DECIDES1 **e1** y)). An
alternative approach would be to define the SEM of the lexical entry to be (λ y
(DECIDES1 **e1** y)), and then the SEM equation for rule 2 would just use the
SEM of the verb as its SEM. Likewise, the SEM for the lexical entry for the
transitive sense could be the expression (λ o (λ y (DECIDES-ON1 **e1** y o))). The
SEM equation for rule 3 would then apply this predicate to the SEM of the object
to obtain the appropriate SEM, as before.

There is a tradeoff here between the complexity of the grammatical rules
and the complexity of the lexical entries. With the grammar we have developed
so far, it seems better to stay with the simple lexicon. But if the logical forms
become more complex, the alternative approach begins to look attractive. As an

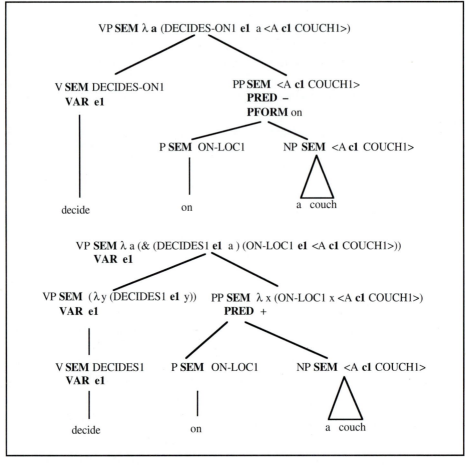

Figure 9.8 Two possible parse trees for the VP *decide on a couch*

example, consider how to specify a grammar that produces a logical form based on thematic roles. Consider first what happens if the lexicon can only store atomic word senses. Whereas the earlier grammar had only one rule that could cover all transitive verbs, the new grammar would have to classify transitive verbs by the thematic roles they use, and a separate rule must be used for each. The verbs *see* and *eat*, for example, both have transitive forms where the subject fills the AGENT role and the object fills the THEME role. The verb *break,* on the other hand, also has a sense where the subject fills the INSTR role and the object fills the THEME role, as in *The hammer broke the window*. To handle these two cases, a new feature, say ROLES, would have to be added to the lexical entries that identifies the appropriate forms, and then a separate grammar rule added for each. These might look as follows:

(VP **VAR** ?v **SEM** (λ a (?semv ?v [AGENT a] [THEME ?semnp]))) $\rightarrow$
    (V **ROLES** AG-THEME **SEM** ?semv) (NP **SEM** ?semnp)
(VP **VAR** ?v **SEM** (λ a (?semv ?v [INSTR a] [THEME ?semnp]))) $\rightarrow$
    (V **ROLES** INSTR-THEME **SEM** ?semv) (NP **SEM** ?semnp)

Additional rules would be added for all the other possible combinations of roles that can be used by the verbs.

Clearly, this approach could be cumbersome. Since it requires adding thematic role information to the lexicon anyway (using the ROLES feature), it might be simpler just to encode the appropriate forms in the lexicon. For instance, if the lexical entries are

see: (V **VAR** ?v **SEM** (λ o (λ a (SEES1 ?v [AGENT a] [THEME ?o]))))
break: (V **VAR** ?v **SEM** (λ o (λ a (BREAKS1 ?v   [INSTR a]
                                                          [THEME ?o]))))

then a single grammar rule, namely,

(VP **SEM** (?semv ?semnp)) $\rightarrow$
    (V **SEM** ?semv) (NP **SEM** ?semnp)

will cover all the cases. Consider the VP *see the book*, where the SEM of *see* is as above and *the book* is <THE **b1** (BOOK1 **b1**)>. The SEM for the VP would be

((λ o (λ a (SEES1 **b1** [AGENT a] [THEME o]))) <THE **b1** (BOOK1 **b1**)>)

which can be simplified using one lambda reduction to

(λ a (SEES1 **b1** [AGENT a] [THEME <THE **b1** (BOOK1 **b1**)>]))

The same rule given the VP *break the book* would apply the SEM of *break* above to the SEM for *the book* to produce the reduced logical form

(λ a (BREAKS1 **b1** [INSTR a] [THEME <THE **b1** (BOOK1 **b1**)>]))

○ Hierarchical Lexicons

The problem with making the lexicon more complex is that there are many words, and specifying a lexicon is difficult even when the entries are simple. Just specifying the semantic interpretation rules for the most common sense is tedious, as there is a different semantic interpretation rule for each complement structure the verb allows. For example, the verb *give* allows the forms

I gave the money.
I gave John the money.
I gave the money to John.

The lexical entries for *give* would include the following:

(V   **SUBCAT** _np
       SEM λ o λ a (GIVE1 * [AGENT a] [THEME o]))

(V   **SUBCAT** _np_np
    SEM λ r λ o λ a (GIVE1 * [AGENT a] [THEME o] [TO-POSS r]))
(V   **SUBCAT** _np_pp:to
    SEM λ o λ r λ a (GIVE1 * [AGENT a] [THEME o] [TO-POSS r]))

This is quite a burden if it must be repeated for every verb. Luckily, we can do much better by exploiting some general regularities across verbs in English. For example, there is a very large class of verbs, including most transitive verbs, that all use the same semantic interpretation rule for the _np SUBCAT form. This class includes verbs such as *give, take, see, find, paint,* and so on—virtually all verbs that describe actions. The idea of a **hierarchical lexicon** is to organize verb senses in such a way that their shared properties can be captured concisely. This depends on a technique called **inheritance**, where word senses inherit or acquire the properties of the abstract classes above them in the hierarchy. For example, a very useful lexical hierarchy can be based on the SUBCAT and SEM properties of verbs. Near the top of the hierarchy are abstract verb senses that define common verb classes. For example, the abstract class INTRANS-ACT defines a class of verbs that allow a SUBCAT _none and have the semantic interpretation rule

λ s (?PREDN * [AGENT s])

where ?PREDN is a predicate name determined by the verb. This fully specifies the semantic interpretation of intransitive verbs such as *run*, *laugh*, *sit*, and so on, except for the actual predicate name that still needs to be specified in the lexical entry for the word. Another common form is the simple transitive verb that describes an action, including the verbs listed above. This form, TRANS-ACT, has a SUBCAT _np and a SEM λ o λ a (?PREDN * [AGENT a] [THEME o]).

We can define similar classes for all the common verb forms and then build an inheritance structure that relates verb senses to the forms they allow. Figure 9.9 shows a lexical hierarchy that encodes the definitions of four different verb senses. It is equivalent to the following entries specified without a hierarchy:

run (in the intransitive exercise sense, RUN1):

(**SUBCAT** _none
  SEM λ a (RUN1 * [AGENT a]))

run (in the transitive "operate" sense, OP1):

(**SUBCAT** _np
  SEM λ o λ a (OP1 * [AGENT a] [THEME o]))

donate (allowing the transitive and "to" form):

(**SUBCAT** _np
  SEM λ o λ a (DONATE1 * [AGENT a] [THEME o]))
(**SUBCAT** _np_pp:to
  SEM λ o λ r λ a (DONATE1 * [AGENT a] [THEME o] [TO-POSS r]))

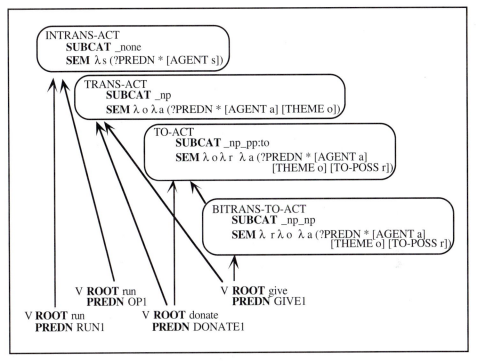

Figure 9.9 Part of a lexical hierarchy for verbs based on SUBCAT and SEM features

and, of course,

give (in all its forms as previously discussed):

(**SUBCAT** _np
SEM λ o λ a (GIVE1 * [AGENT a] [THEME o]))
(**SUBCAT** _np_pp:to
SEM λ o λ r λ a (GIVE1 * [AGENT a] [THEME o] [TO-POSS r]))
(**SUBCAT** _np_np
SEM λ r λ o λ a (GIVE1 * [AGENT a] [THEME o] [TO-POSS r]))

You could implement a lexical hierarchy by adding another feature to each lexical entry called SUP (for superclass), which has as its value a list of abstract categories from which the constituent inherits properties. It is then relatively simple to write a program that searches up this hierarchy to find all the relevant feature values whenever the lexicon is accessed. The entry for the verb *give* might now look like this:

give: (V   **ROOT** give
                PREDN GIVE1
                SUP (BITRANS-TO-ACT TRANS-ACT))

14. (S **INV** – **SEM** (WH-query ?sems)) →
    (NP **WH** Q **AGR** ?a **SEM** ?semnp)
    (S **INV** + **SEM** ?sems **GAP** (NP **AGR** ?a **SEM** ?semnp))

15. (S **INV** + **GAP** ?g **SEM** (?semaux (?semvp ?semnp))) →
    (*AUX AGR ?a SUBCAT ?s SEM ?semaux*)
    (NP **AGR** ?a **GAP** – **SEM** ?sempp)
    (VP **VFORM** ?s **GAP** ?g **SEM** ?semvp)

16. (NP **WH** Q **VAR** ?v **SEM** <WH ?v (?sempro ?v)>) →
    (*PRO WH Q SEM ?sempro*)

Grammar 9.10 Rules to handle simple wh-questions

9.5 Handling Simple Questions

The grammar developed so far deals only with simple declarative sentences. To extend the grammar to handle other sentence types requires adding rules to interpret wh-terms, inverted sentences, and the gap propagation required to handle wh-questions. This can be done quite directly with the mechanisms developed so far and requires no additional extensions to the parser. All you need to do is augment the S rules first developed for questions in Chapter 5 with appropriate SEM feature equations.

The part that may need some explanation is how the SEM feature interacts with the GAP feature. As you recall, many wh-questions use the GAP feature to build the appropriate structures. Examples are

Who did Jill see?
Who did Jill want to see?
Who did Jill want to win the prize?

The rule introduced in Chapter 5 to account for these questions was

(S **INV** –) → (NP **WH** Q **AGR** ?a) (S **INV** + **GAP** (NP **AGR** ?a))

That is, a wh-question consists of an NP with the WH feature Q followed by an inverted sentence with an NP missing that agrees with the first NP. To make the semantic interpretation work, we add the SEM feature to the features of the gap. This way it is passed into the S structure and can be used at the appropriate place when the gap is found. The revised rule is

(S **INV** – **SEM** (WH-query ?sems)) →
(NP **WH** Q **AGR** ?a **SEM** ?semnp)
(S **INV** + **SEM** ?sems **GAP** (NP **AGR** ?a **SEM** ?semnp))

Grammar 9.10 gives the new rules required to handle this type of question. Rule 14 was just discussed. Rule 15 handles inverted sentences and could be used

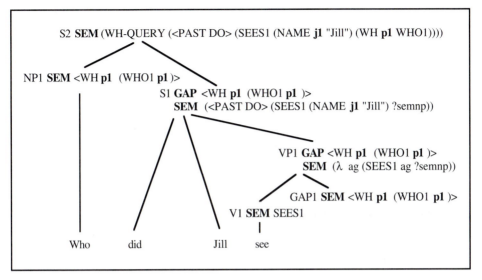

Figure 9.11 The parse tree for *Who did Jill see?*

for yes/no questions as well as for the wh-questions discussed here. Rule 17 allows noun phrases to be built from wh-pronouns, such as *who* and *what*.

The lexical entry for the wh-words would have to be extended with a SEM feature as well. For instance, the word *who* would have the entry

(PRO **WH** {Q R} **SEM** WHO1 **AGR** {3s 3p})

The predicate WHO1 would be true of any objects that are reasonable answers to such questions, including people and possibly other animate agents.

To see how the SEM feature and GAP features interact, consider a derivation of the parse tree for the question *Who did Jill see?,* as shown in Figure 9.11. Using rule 16, the word *who* would be parsed as the noun phrase

(NP **WH** Q **AGR** 3s **SEM** <WH **p1** (WHO1 **p1**)>)

This constituent can be used to start rule 14, and thus we need the following constituent to complete the rule:

(S   **INV** +
      GAP (NP **AGR** 3s **SEM** <WH **p1** (WHO1 **p1**)>)
      SEM ?sems)

Rule 15 can be used to rewrite this, and the words *did* and *Jill* provide the first two subconstituents. The third subconstituent needed is:

(VP   **VFORM** base
      GAP (NP **AGR** 3s **SEM** <WH **p1** (WHO1 **p1**)>)
      SEM ?semvp)

This is a VP with an NP gap. Rule 3 from Grammar 9.3 applies to transitive verbs such as *see*. The GAP feature is used to fill a gap for the object of the verb, instantiating ?semnp to <WH **p1** (WHO **p1**)>. Thus the SEM of the new VP is

$\quad$ (λ a3 (SEES1 **s1** a3 <WH **p1** (WHO1 **p1**)>))

The SEM of the initial word *who* has found its way to the appropriate place in the sentence. The parse can now be completed as usual. This technique of passing in the SEM in the GAP is completely general and can be used to handle all of the question types discussed in Chapter 5.

○ Prepositional Phrase Wh-Questions

Questions can also begin with prepositional phrases, such as *In which box did you put the book?*, *Where did you put the book?*, and *When did he disappear?* The semantic interpretation of these questions will depend on whether the PPs are subcategorized for the verb or are VP modifiers. Many such questions can be handled by a rule virtually identical to rule 14 for NP wh-questions, namely

$\quad$ (S **INV** − **SEM** (WH-query ?sems)) →
$\quad\quad$ (PP **WH** Q **PRED** ?p **PTYPE** ?pt **SEM** ?sempp)
$\quad\quad$ (S **INV** + **SEM** ?sems **GAP** (PP **PRED** ?p **PTYPE** ?pt **SEM** ?sempp))

To handle wh-terms like *where* appropriately, the following rule is also needed:

$\quad$ (PP **PRED** ?pd **PTYPE** ?pt **SEM** ?sem) →
$\quad\quad$ (PP-WRD **PRED** ?pd **PTYPE** ?pt **SEM** ?sem)

The wh-term *where* would have two lexical entries, one for each PRED value:

$\quad$ (PP-WRD $\quad$ **PTYPE** {LOC MOT} **PRED** − **VAR** ?v
$\quad\quad\quad$ **SEM** <WH ?v (LOC1 ?v)>)

$\quad$ (PP **PRED** + **VAR** ?v **SEM** (λ x (AT-LOC x <WH ?v (LOC1 v)>)))

These rules would extend the existing grammar so that many such questions could be answered. Figure 9.12 shows part of the parse tree for the question *Where did Jill go?*

$\quad$ Note that handling questions starting with +PRED prepositional phrases depends on having a solution to the problem concerning gap propagation first mentioned in Chapter 5. Specifically, the rule VP → VP PP, treated in the normal way, would only pass the GAP into the VP subconstituent, namely the nonlexical head. Thus there seems no way to create a PP gap that modifies a verb phrase. But this was a problem with the syntactic grammar as well, and any solution at that level should carry over to the semantic level.

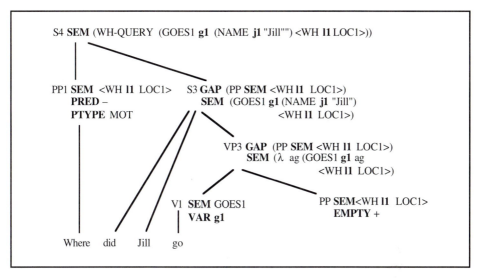

Figure 9.12   The parse tree for *Where did Jill go?*

9.6   Semantic Interpretation Using Feature Unification

So far we have used lambda expressions and lambda reduction to drive the semantic interpretation. This provides a good framework for explaining and comparing techniques for semantic interpretation. However, many systems do not explicitly use lambda expressions and perform semantic interpretation directly using feature values and variables. The basic idea is to introduce new features for the argument positions that earlier would have been filled using lambda reduction. For instance, instead of using rule 1 in Grammar 9.3, namely

(S **SEM** (?semvp ?semnp)) $\rightarrow$ (NP **SEM** ?semnp) (VP **SEM** ?semvp)

a new feature SUBJ is introduced, and the rule becomes

(S **SEM** ?semvp) $\rightarrow$ (NP **SEM** ?semnp) (VP **SUBJ** ?semnp **SEM** ?semvp)

The SEM of the subject is passed into the VP constituent as the SUBJ feature and the SEM equations for the VP insert the subject in the correct position. The new version of rule 3 in Grammar 9.3 that does this is

(VP **VAR** ?v **SUBJ** ?semsubj **SEM** (?semv ?v ?semsubj ?semnp)) $\rightarrow$
(V[_none] **SEM** *?semv*) (NP **SEM** ?semnp)

Figure 9.13 shows how this rule builds the SEM of the sentence *Jill saw the dog*. Compare this to the analysis built using Grammar 9.3 shown in Figure 9.5. The differences appear in the treatment of the VP. Here the SEM is the full proposition with the subject inserted, whereas before the SEM was a lambda expression that would be applied to the subject later in the rule that builds the S.

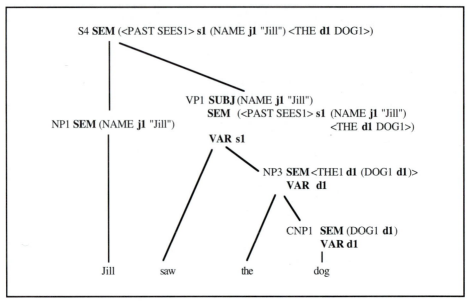

Figure 9.13   The parse tree for *Jill saw the dog* using the SUBJ feature

1. (S **SEM** ?semvp) $\rightarrow$
   (NP **SEM** ?semsubj) (*VP **SUBJ** ?semsubj **SEM** ?semvp*)

2. (VP **VAR** ?v **SUBJ** ?semsubj **SEM** (?semv ?v ?semsubj)) $\rightarrow$
   (*V[_none]* **SEM** *?semv*)

3. (VP **VAR** ?v **SUBJ** ?semsubj **SEM** (?semv ?v ?semsubj ?semnp)) $\rightarrow$
   (*V[_np]* **SEM** *?semv*) (NP **SEM** ?semnp)

4. (NP **VAR** ?v **SEM** (PRO ?v ?sempro)) $\rightarrow$ (*PRO **SEM** ?sempro*)

5. (NP **VAR** ?v **SEM** (NAME ?v ?semname)) $\rightarrow$ (*NAME **SEM** ?semname*)

6. (NP **VAR** ?v **SEM** <?semart ?v ?semcnp>) $\rightarrow$
   (ART **SEM** ?semart) (*CNP **SEM** ?semcnp*)

7. (CNP **VAR** ?v **SEM** (?semn ?v)) $\rightarrow$ (*N **SEM** ?semn*)

Head features for S, VP, NP, CNP: VAR

Grammar 9.14   A simple grammar with SEM features

Grammar 9.14 is a version of Grammar 9.3 reformulated using this technique. Besides the changes to rules 1, 2, and 3, rules 6 and 7 are also modified. Rule 7 uses the VAR value to build a full proposition (as opposed to a unary predicate in the old grammar), and rule 6 is changed appropriately to account for the change to rule 7.

BOX 9.2 Encoding Semantics Entirely in Features

A more radical departure from the approach described in this chapter encodes the entire logical form as a set of features. For instance, rather than the logical form previously developed, the sentence *Jill saw the dog* might have a SEM of

> (**PRED** SEES1
> **VAR s1**
> **TNS** PAST
> **AGENT** (NAME **j1** "Jill")
> **THEME** (**SPEC** THE1
> $\qquad$ **VAR d1**
> $\qquad$ **RESTRICTION** (**PRED** DOG1
> $\qquad\qquad$ **ARG1 d1**)))

Logical forms like this can easily be constructed using additional features for each semantic slot. For instance, here are new versions of the first three rules in Grammar 9.14 that compute this type of logical form:

1. (S **VFORM** past **SEM** ?semvp) $\rightarrow$
   $\qquad$ (NP **SEM** ?semnp) (VP **TNS** past **SUBJ** ?semnp **SEM** ?semvp)
2. (VP **TNS** ?tns **SUBJ** ?semsubj **SEM** ?semv) $\rightarrow$
   $\qquad$ (V[_none] **VAR** ?v **SUBJ** ?semsubj **TNS** ?tns **SEM** ?semv)
3. (VP **TNS** ?tns **SUBJ** ?subj **SEM** ?semv) $\rightarrow$
   $\qquad$ (V[_np] **VAR** ?v **SUBJ** ?subj **OBJVAL** ?obj **TNS** ?tns **SEM** ?semv)
   $\qquad$ (NP **SEM** ?obj)

Note that all the arguments are passed down into the lexical rule, which would assemble the appropriate semantic form. For instance, the lexical entry for *saw* might be

> (V[_np] **SUBJ** ?s **OBJVAL** ?o **VAR** ?v **TNS** past
> $\qquad$ **SEM** (**PRED** SEES1 **VAR** ?v **TNS** PAST **AGENT** ?s **THEME** ?o))

When this entry is unified with the V in rule 3, the appropriate SEM structure would be built and bound to the variable ?semv, as desired.

One advantage of this approach is that no special mechanism need be introduced to handle semantic interpretation. In particular, there is no need to have a lambda reduction step. Everything is accomplished by feature unification. Another significant advantage is that a grammar specified in this form is reversible and hence can be used to generate sentences as well as parse them, as discussed in the next section. Not all lambda expressions can be eliminated using these techniques, however. For instance, to handle conjoined subject phrases as in *Sue and Sam saw Jack*, the meaning of the verb phrase must still be a lambda expression. If the subject were inserted into the VP using a variable for the SUBJ feature, then this variable would have to unify with the SEMs of both *Sue* and *Sam*, which it can't do.

BOX 9.3 Relative Clauses

The syntactic grammar for relative clauses described in Section 5.4 exploits the strong parallels between relative clauses and wh-questions. This similarity continues at the semantic level as well. The logical form of a relative clause will be a unary predicate, and the rule for introducing them is

(CNP **SEM** (λ x (& (?semcnp ?x) (?semrel ?x)))) $\rightarrow$
    (CNP **SEM** ?semcnp) (REL **SEM** ?semrel)

This rule takes two unary predicates (one from the CNP, the other from the REL) and combines them to make a new unary predicate formed by conjoining the two.

Now consider one of the rules for the REL category. The linguistic insight needed here is that the wh-term that introduces a relative clause corresponds to the argument of the unary predicate. Thus, in building the SEM for the REL *who Jill saw,* rather than having <WH **p1** (WHO1 **p1**)> as the SEM of *who,* as in questions, a variable is used. When the embedded sentence is completed, a lambda is wrapped around it to form the SEM of the relative clause, which for this example might be

(λ y (<PAST SEES1> (NAME **j1** "Jill") y))

The wh-term variable is specified in a feature called RVAR in following rule.

(REL **SEM** (λ ?v ?sems)) $\rightarrow$
    (NP **WH** R **RVAR** ?v **AGR** ?a **SEM** ?semnp)
    (S [*fin*] **INV** - **GAP** (*NP AGR ?a* **SEM** *?semnp*) **SEM** *?sems*)

The following parse tree fragment shows the derivation of this relative clause:

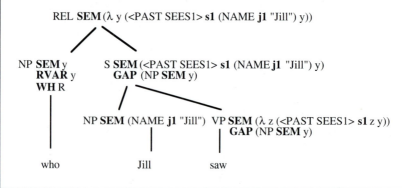

○ 9.7 Generating Sentences from Logical Form

Intuitively, once you have a grammar for parsing, it should be easy to reverse it and use it for generation. Such a sentence generator would be given a constituent with its SEM feature set to a logical form, and then it would use the grammar to decompose this constituent into a series of lexical constituents that would have the appropriate meaning. Not all grammars are reversible, however. In fact, Grammar 9.3 is not reversible because it uses lambda reduction. To see why, consider an example. Say you want to generate a sentence that has the meaning

(<PAST SEES1> **s1** (NAME **j1** "Jill") <THE **d1** (DOG1 **d1**)>)

Grammar 9.3 has only one S rule, and if you try to unify the SEM value in rule 1 with this logical form it will fail. The pattern (?semvp ?semnp) would match any proposition built out of a unary predicate and one argument, but the logical form specified is a proposition with three arguments. The problem is that lambda reduction was used to convert the original logical form, which was

((λ a (<PAST SEES1> **s1** a <THE **d1** (DOG1 **d1**)>)) (NAME **j1** "Jill"))

There is an inverse operation to lambda reduction, called **lambda abstraction**, that could be used to find a match. But the problem is that there are three possible lambda abstractions of the logical form, namely

(λ e (<PAST SEES1> e (NAME **j1** "Jill") <THE **d1** (DOG1 **d1**)>))
(λ a (<PAST SEES1> **s1** a <THE **d1** (DOG1 **d1**)>))
(λ o (<PAST SEES1> **s1** (NAME **j1** "Jill") o))

There is nothing in rule 1 that indicates which is the right abstraction, but only the second will yield an appropriate sentence.

On the other hand, the approach using features, as in Grammar 9.14, is reversible because it retains in the features the information necessary to determine how the logical form was constructed. It is easiest to understand how it does this by considering an example.

In many ways parsing and realization are very similar processes. Both can be viewed as building a syntactic tree. A parser starts with the words and tries to find a tree that accounts for them and hence determine the logical form of the sentence, while a realizer starts with a logical form and tries to find a tree to account for it and hence determine the words to realize it. This analogy suggests that the standard parsing algorithms might be adaptable to realization. For instance, you could imagine using the standard top-down algorithm, where rules are selected from the grammar based on whether they match the intended SEM structure, and the words in the sentence are selected in a left-to-right fashion. The problem is that this approach would be extremely inefficient. For example, consider using Grammar 9.14 to realize an S with the SEM

(<PAST SEES1> **s1** (NAME **j1** "Jill") <THE **d1** (DOG1 **d1**)>)

Rule 1 matches trivially since its SEM feature has a variable as its value, ?semvp. There are no other S rules, so this one is instantiated. The standard top-down algorithm would now attempt to generate the two subconstituents, namely

(NP **SEM** ?semsubj)
(VP **SUBJ** ?semsubj
      SEM (<PAST SEES1> **s1** (NAME **j1** "Jill") <THE **d1** (DOG1 **d1**)>))

Initialization: Set L to a list containing the constituent that you wish to generate.

Do until L contains no nonlexical constituents:

1. If L contains a constituent C that is marked as a nonlexical head,
2. Then use a rule in the grammar to rewrite C. Any variables in C that are bound in the rewrite should be instantiated throughout the entire list.
3. Else choose a nonlexical constituent C, giving preference to one whose SEM feature is bound, if one exists. Use a rule in the grammar to rewrite C. Any variables in C that are bound in the rewrite should be instantiated throughout the entire list.

Figure 9.15 A head-driven realization algorithm

But the SEM of the NP is unconstrained. The realizer could only proceed by randomly generating noun phrases and then attempting to realize the VP with each one and backtracking until an appropriate one is found. Worse than that, with a more general grammar, the algorithm may fall into an infinite loop. Clearly, this is an unworkable strategy.

One method for avoiding these problems is to expand the constituents in a different order. For instance, choosing what term will be the subject depends on decisions made about the verb and the structure of the verb phrase, such as whether the active or passive voice is used, and so on. So it makes sense to expand the verb phrase first and then generate the appropriate subject. In fact, a good general strategy is to expand the head constituents first and then fill in the others. Figure 9.15 gives a simple algorithm to do this. The realization algorithm operates on a list of constituents much like the basic top-down parser described in Chapter 3. It continues to rewrite constituents in this list until the list consists only of lexical constituents, at which point the words can be generated.

This algorithm can easily be generalized so that it searches all possible realizations based on the grammar using a backtracking technique. The reason it works well is that, by expanding the head constituents first, the algorithm moves quickly down to the lexical level and chooses the words that have the most influence on the structure of the overall sentence. Once the lexical head is chosen, most of the structure of the rest of the constituent is determined.

Consider this algorithm operating with Grammar 9.14 and the initial input

(S **SEM** (<PAST SEES1> **s1** (NAME **j1** "Jill") <THE **d1** (DOG1 **d1**)>))

The S constituent is rewritten based on rule 1 in the grammar to produce the following constituent list:

(NP **SEM** ?semsubj)
(*VP **SUBJ** ?semsubj*
    ***SEM** (<PAST SEES1> **s1** (NAME **j1** "Jill") <THE **d1** (DOG1 **d1**)>))*

The nonlexical head constituents are indicated in italics. Thus the VP is expanded next. Only rule 3 will match the SEM structure. As a result of the match, the following variables are bound:

> ?semv ← <PAST SEES1>
> ?v ← **sl**
> ?semsubj ← (NAME **j1** "Jill")
> ?semnp ← <THE **d1** (DOG1 **d1**)>

Thus you obtain the following list of constituents after rewriting the VP and instantiating the variables throughout the list:

> (NP **SEM** (NAME **j1** "Jill"))
> (V[_np] **SEM** <PAST SEES1>)
> (NP **SEM** <THE **d1** (DOG1 **d1**)>)

Since there is no nonlexical head, the algorithm now picks any nonlexical constituent with a bound SEM, say the first NP. Only rule 5 will match, yielding the lexical constituent (NAME **SEM** "Jill") and producing the constituent list

> (NAME **SEM** "Jill")
> (V[_np] **SEM** <PAST SEES1>)
> (NP **SEM** <THE **d1** (DOG1 **d1**)>)

The remaining NP is selected next. Rule 6 matches and the subconstituents (ART **SEM** THE) and (CNP **SEM** DOG1) are generated, producing the constituent list

> (NAME **SEM** "Jill")
> (V[_np] **SEM** <PAST SEES1>)
> (ART **SEM** THE)
> (*CNP SEM DOG1*)

The CNP constituent is selected next and rewritten as a common noun with SEM DOG1, and the algorithm is complete. The constituent list is now a sequence of lexical categories:

> (NAME **SEM** "Jill")
> (V[_np] **SEM** <PAST SEES1>)
> (ART **SEM** THE)
> (N **SEM** DOG1)

It is simple to produce the sentence *Jill saw the dog* from the lexical constituents.

The grammar used in this example was very small, so there is only one possible realization of this sentence. With a larger grammar, a wider range of forms would be possible. For instance, if only the SEM feature is specified, the realization program would randomly pick between active and passive sentences when allowed by the verb. In other cases it might pick between different subcategorization structures. For instance, the same logical form might be realized as *Jill gave the dog to Jack* or *Jill gave Jack the dog*. Depending on the number of word senses used and whether different words have senses in common, the realizer may also randomly pick between various lexical realizations of a logical form. For instance, there could be a logical form that could be realized by the sentence *Jill gave the money to the Humane Society* or *Jack donated the money to the Humane Society.*

Each of these variations may have different effects in context, but these distinctions are not captured in the logical form. To force particular realizations, you would have to specify other features in addition to the SEM feature. For instance, you might set the VOICE feature to active to guarantee an active voice sentence.

Summary

This chapter developed a rule-by-rule model of semantic interpretation by introducing the new features SEM and VAR to encode semantic information. The representation depends on the use of lambda expressions, and every constituent has a well-formed semantic form. With two minor extensions to introduce unique VAR values and to perform lambda reduction, any chart parsing algorithm will compute a logical form as it builds the syntactic structure. A variant of this approach that uses additional features instead of lambda expressions was discussed. This representation produces a reversible grammar, which can be used for semantic realization as well as semantic interpretation. A head-driven realization algorithm was used to generate sentences from a specified logical form. This expands the head constituents first to determine the overall structure of the sentence before filling in the details on the other constituents.

Related Work and Further Readings

Most work in semantics in the last two decades has been influenced by the work of Montague (1974), who proposed that the semantics for natural languages could be defined compositionally in the same way as the semantics for formal languages (1974). He introduced several key concepts, the most influential for our purposes being the adoption of the lambda calculus. A good reference for Montague style semantics is Chierchia and McConnell-Ginet (1990). Dowty et al. (1981) and Partee et al. (1993) give more detailed coverage.

The compositional semantic interpreter described in this chapter draws from a body of work, with key references being Rosenschein and Shieber (1982), Schubert and Pelletier (1982), and GPSG (Gazdar et al., 1985). Other important references on compositional interpretation include Hirst (1987), McCord (1986), Saint-Dizier (1985), and Hwang and Schubert (1993b). The use of feature unification in place of lambda reduction is discussed by Pereira and Shieber (1987) and Moore (1989). A good example of this technique is (Alshawi, 1992).

There is a substantial literature in natural language generation, an area that deals with two main issues: deciding on the content of what should be said, and then realizing that content as a sentence. The algorithm in Section 9.7 addresses the realization part only, as it assumes that a logical form has already been identified. By the time the logical form is identified, many of the most difficult problems in generation—such as deciding on the content and on the main predicates and mode of reference—must have already been resolved. For a good survey of work in generation, see the article by McDonald in Shapiro (1992) under the heading Natural Language Generation. For a good collection of recent work, see the special issue of *Computational Intelligence* 7, 4 (1991) and the papers in Dale et al. (1990). The head-driven algorithm described here is a simplified version of that described by Shieber et al. (1990).

Exercises for Chapter 9

1. (*easy*) Simplify the following formulas using lambda reduction:

    $((\lambda x (P x)) A)$
    $((\lambda x (x A)) (\lambda y (Q y)))$
    $((\lambda x ((\lambda y (P y)) x)) A)$

2. (*easy*) Using the interpretation rules defined in this chapter and defining any others that you need, give a detailed trace of the interpretation of the sentence *The man gave the apple to Bill*. In particular, give the analysis of each constituent and show its SEM feature.

3. (*medium*) This question involves specifying the semantic interpretation rules to analyze the different senses of the verb *roll*, as in

    We rolled the log into the river.
    The log rolled by the house.
    The cook rolled the pastry with a large jar.
    The ball rolled around the room.
    We rolled the piano to the house on a dolly.

    a. Identify the different senses of the verb *roll* in the preceding sentences, and give an informal definition of each meaning. (You may use a dictionary if you wish.) Try to identify how each different sense allows different conclusions to be made from each sentence. Specify the lexical entries for the verb *roll*.

    b. List the VP rules in this chapter that are needed to handle these sentences, and add any new rules as necessary.

    c. Given the rules outlined in Exercise 3b, and assuming appropriate rules exist for the NPs, draw the parse tree with the logical forms shown for each constituent.

4. (*medium*) Draw the parse trees showing the semantic interpretations for the constituents for the following questions. Give the lexical entries showing

the SEM feature for each word used that is not defined in this chapter, and define any additional rules needed that are not specified in this chapter.

Who saw the dog?
Who did John give the book to?

5. (*medium*) Consider the following rules that are designed to handle verbs that take infinitive complements.

1. (VP **VAR** ?v **SEM** (λ ag (?semv ag (?semvp ag)))) $\rightarrow$
   (V *SUBCAT _vp-inf* **SEM** *?semv*)
   (VP **VFORM** inf **SEM** ?semvp)

2. (VP **VAR** ?v **SEM** (λ ag (?semv ag (?semvp ?semnp)))) $\rightarrow$
   (V *SUBCAT _np_vp-inf* **SEM** *?semv*)
   (NP **SEM** ?semnp)
   (VP **VFORM** inf **SEM** ?semvp)

3. (VP **VFORM** inf ?v **SEM** ?semvp) $\rightarrow$
   TO (VP **VFORM** base **SEM** ?semvp)

Note that the semantic structures built identify the subject of the embedded VP. For _vp-inf verbs, rule 1, the implicit subject is the subject of the sentence, whereas for _np_vp-inf verbs, rule 2, the implicit subject is the object of the main verb. Using these rules and the rules described in this chapter, what logical forms are produced for the following sentences?

Jill wants to cry.
Jill wants Jack to cry.
Who does Jill want to see?

6. (*medium*) Consider the following sentences.

John is happy.
John is in the corner.
John is a man with a problem.

Each of these asserts some property of John. This suggests that the phrases *happy*, *in the corner*, and *a man with a problem* all should have similar semantic structures, presumably a unary predicate. In some approaches, the PRED feature is extended to forms other than PPs as a way of capturing the similarities between all three of these cases. Assuming this approach, what should the interpretation of these three phrases be when they have the +PRED feature, as in this context? Write out the necessary rules to add to the grammar described in this chapter so that each sentence is handled appropriately.

CHAPTER

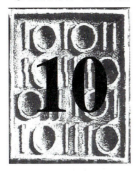

Ambiguity Resolution

10.1   Selectional Restrictions

10.2   Semantic Filtering Using Selectional Restrictions

10.3   Semantic Networks

10.4   Statistical Word Sense Disambiguation

10.5   Statistical Semantic Preferences

10.6   Combining Approaches to Disambiguation

The techniques developed in the last chapter didn't address the issue of resolving ambiguity. The word *bridge*, for example, has at least four distinct senses as a noun: the elevated structure that spans a body of water, the card game, the dental device, and the abstract notion of providing a connection. To distinguish between these different readings, different senses are introduced, say STRUCTURE1, GAME27, DENTAL-DEV37, and CONNECT12. Any given sentence will allow only a subset of the possible senses. For example, the sentence *The bridge crosses the river* only makes sense with the STRUCTURE1 sense. But the mechanism for semantic interpretation in the last chapter allows each of these readings, as there is nothing that defines what combinations of senses are coherent. This chapter develops some ideas and techniques that start to address the ambiguity problem.

Section 10.1 discusses using selectional restrictions and type hierarchies to specify allowable combinations of word senses and develops a constraint propagation algorithm that eliminates impossible word senses. Section 10.2 then uses these techniques during parsing to filter out semantically impossible constituents. Section 10.3 discusses semantic network representations, which generalize the simple type hierarchies. Section 10.4 discusses some statistical methods for word sense identification using word collocations, and Section 10.5 looks at generalizing the notion of selectional restrictions as statistical preferences. Section 10.6 discusses some general issues in combining structurally-based techniques with statistically-based techniques.

10.1 Selectional Restrictions

Word senses can be related in different ways based on the object classes they describe. Some senses are disjoint; that is, no object can be in both classes at the same time. DOG1 (the typical sense of *dog*) and CAT1 (the typical sense of *cat*) are disjoint senses. Other senses are subclasses of other senses. The class DOG1, for instance, would be a subclass of the class MAMMAL1, and a subclass of the class PET1 (house pets). Other senses will overlap, such as MAMMAL1 and PET1. All this general knowledge plays a role in semantic disambiguation.

The subset relation defines an abstraction hierarchy on the word senses. This relation is important as it allows restrictions to be stated in terms of very broad classes of objects in a concise and intuitive way. For instance, an adjective such as *purple* only makes sense if it is modifying a physical object, such as a house or a piece of clothing. It doesn't make sense, for instance, to talk of purple ideas or purple events. This can be stated using one requirement, namely that *purple* must modify a physical object. All senses below physical object would thus be allowed. The modifier *precise*, on the other hand, only makes sense modifying an idea or action (or as a general characteristic of the way a person behaves), and the modifier *unfortunate* only makes sense modifying some event or situation. Figure 10.1 shows a fragment of the top of a type hierarchy that is useful for natural language. This is incomplete, and all the objects in the ontology

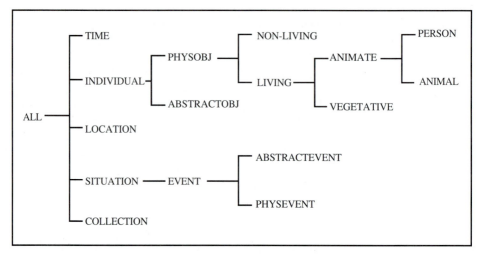

Figure 10.1 A word sense hierarchy

mentioned in the last few chapters would need to find a place here. Also note that hierarchies need not be tree structures; that is, senses may have multiple super-types. The classifications of MALE and FEMALE, for instance, apply at the same level as ANIMATE/VEGETATIVE and combine with all these subclasses across the entire subtree of LIVING individuals. With this, the sense MALE-PERSON would be a subtype of both PERSON and MALE.

Given such a hierarchy, you can start exploring the restrictions that predicates put on their arguments. Consider the verb *read*. It has two principal arguments: the agent, which must be an object capable of reading (for example, something of type PERSON), and the theme, which must be an object that contains text (such as a book, newspaper, label, sign, and so on). To handle such verbs correctly, we might introduce a new type, say TEXTOBJ, under NON-LIVING, which is a superset of BOOK1, ARTICLE/TEXT, and so on. These constraints allow you to select appropriate senses for the words in a sentence. For example, say the noun *dishwasher* has two senses, either a machine (DISH-WASH/MACH1) or a person (DISHWASH/PERS), and the noun *article* can be a paper (ARTICLE/TEXT) or a part of speech (ARTICLE1). These senses fit into the hierarchy as shown in Figure 10.2. Since these two words are ambiguous, the sentence *The dishwasher read the article* might appear to have four distinct semantic meanings, one for each combination of senses. But only one reading makes sense, namely

> (READS1 [AGENT <THE **d1** DISHWASH/PERS>]
> [THEME <THE **p1** ARTICLE/TEXT>])

A semantic interpreter can perform this form of disambiguation by using what are called **selectional restrictions**. These are specifications of the legal combinations of senses that can co-occur and can be applied to eliminate incoherent formulas constructed by the parser.

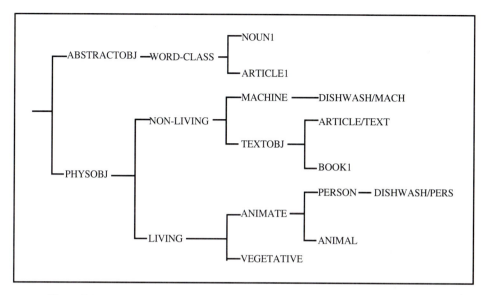

Figure 10.2 A fragment of the hierarchy

To incorporate this technique into the semantic interpreter, you need a mechanism for extracting the type information inherent in the logical form. This is obtained by examining each term in the logical form in terms of the unary and binary predicates that involve it. For instance, consider the logical form of *The dishwasher read the article* before applying any selectional restrictions:

(READS1 **r1** [AGENT <THE **d1** {DISHWASH/MACH1
DISHWASH/PERS}>]
[THEME <THE **p1** {ARTICLE/TEXT ARTICLE1}>])

Unpacking the notation, the following unary and binary relations are found:

(READS1 **r1**)
({DISHWASH/MACH1 DISHWASH/PERS} **d1**)
({ARTICLE/TEXT ARTICLE1} **p1**)
(AGENT **r1 d1**)
(THEME **r1 p1**)

Finding the allowable combinations can be viewed as a **constraint satis-faction problem**. In this case the constraints include the semantic relationships between unary predicates (subclass, disjoint, and so on), which are expressed in type hierarchies such as those in Figures 10.1 and 10.2, and selectional restrictions on the semantic types of the arguments to the binary relations. The selectional restrictions for READS1 are expressed as follows:

(AGENT READS1 PERSON)—the agent must be a person.
(THEME READS1 TEXTOBJ)—the theme must be a TEXTOBJ
object.

If these are the only allowed relations for the READS1 sense, several of the previously mentioned possibilities for the terms in the logical form can be eliminated. For (AGENT **r1 d1**) to be valid, **d1** must be a person. Thus the unary constraints on **d1** can be simplified from ({DISHWASH/MACH1 DISH-WASH/PERS} **d1**) to (DISHWASH/PERS **d1**). Similarly, the interpretation of **p1** is simplified to (ARTICLE/TEXT **p1**). By transferring these constraints back into the logical form, we end up with a single unambiguous reading, as desired.

Of course, in many cases it is more complicated than this. The verb *read*, for instance, might have two senses: READS1, and, say, READS2, as a form of understanding a person's intentions, as in *Jill can read John's mind.* The selec-tional restrictions for READS2 might be

(AGENT READS2 PERSON)
(THEME READS2 MENTAL-STATE)

With this additional sense, the initial logical form of *The dishwasher read the article* is

({READS1 READS2} **r1**
    [AGENT <THE **d1** {DISHWASH/MACH1 DISHWASH/PERS}>]
    [THEME <THE **p1** {ARTICLE/TEXT ARTICLE1}>])

This additional ambiguity does not affect the final result because the READS2 sense requires a MENTAL-STATE as a THEME, and neither of the senses of *article* is a subclass of mental state. Thus, there is no combination of inter-pretations that allows the READS2 sense.

We also need to extend this technique to proper names, pronouns, and adjectives. We will have to assume that we have type information for what proper names may refer to. For example, the type of *John* might be MALE, that is, an animate object that is MALE. Unknown names might just default to having the property INDIVIDUAL. The type of pronominal phrases is defined by the pronoun sense, thus SHE1 should be a subclass of FEMALE, whereas IT1 would be anything but PERSON. Adjectives act like verbs in that they impose restrictions on their arguments. Such modifiers can be handled by introducing the state variable representation for each adjective modifier and a new thematic relation MOD. For example, for the phrase *happy dishwasher,* instead of using the predicate-argument form (HAPPY1 **d1**), we will use the unary relation (HAPPY-STATE **h1**) and the binary relation (MOD **h1 d1**). This way, adjectives are treated the same way as verbs. Thus the set of relations derived from the sentence *The happy dishwasher read the paper* would be

(READS1 **r1**)
({DISHWASH/MACH1 DISHWASH/PERS} **d1**)
({ARTICLE/TEXT ARTICLE1} **p1**)
(HAPPY-STATE **h1**)

Initialization Step

Assign types(variable$_i$) to the list of possible senses for variable i.

Iteration Step

Iterate through each binary relation (rel variable$_1$ variable$_2$):
1. For each sense$_1$ in types(variable$_1$):
   a. find all selectional restrictions (rel sense$_1$ sense$_2$) where sense$_2$ intersects with some sense in types(variable$_2$).
   b. If none found, remove sense$_1$ from types(variable$_1$).
2. Eliminate from types(variable$_2$) any sense that did not match at least one restriction in step 1.

Termination Step

If any changes were made to the types of the variables in the last iteration, then perform the iteration step once again.
Otherwise, if type(variable$_i$) is empty for any i, then fail.

Figure 10.3 A simple constraint satisfaction algorithm

(AGENT **r1 d1**)
(THEME **r1 p1**)
(MOD **h1 d1**)

The selectional restriction for the adjective *happy* would be

(MOD HAPPY-STATE ANIMATE)—HAPPY-STATE must modify an animate object.

Every time a logical form is produced, the set of unary and binary semantic relations it contains can be checked against the selectional constraints. If there is no interpretation that satisfies the constraints, then the interpretation is anomalous and the constituent can be discarded. Otherwise, the simplified logical form, with the impossible senses removed, can be used as the SEM of the constituent. In the remainder of this section, we explore the constraint satisfaction algorithm in a little more detail.

The algorithm is shown in Figure 10.3. To implement the algorithm, you need a procedure that matches senses. A match fails if the two types have no intersection at all. Otherwise, it returns a type that is the intersection of the two. If one is a subtype of the other, the subtype is the result. Given the hierarchy in Figure 10.2, the result of Match(PERSON, DISHWASH/PERS) is DISH-WASH/PERS. In other cases the types might overlap and return a sense that is the subtype of both senses. For example, with appropriate definitions, the result of Match(MALE, PERSON) would be MALE-PERSON1.

The algorithm starts by making a list of all the possible senses of each discourse variable and then iterates through the binary relations to eliminate any unary constraints that cannot satisfy at least one binary constraint. If a change is made, the binary constraints are rechecked again. This continues until no further changes are made.

As an example, consider running this algorithm on the sentence *The dishwasher read the article.* The initialization step produces the following types:

types($r1$) =　READS1, READS2
types($p1$) =　ARTICLE/TEXT, ARTICLE1
types($d1$) =　DISHWASH/PERS, DISHWASH/MACH1

The binary relations for this problem are (AGENT **r1 d1**) and (THEME **r1 p1**). The first iteration step runs as follows:

For (AGENT **r1 d1**), we iterate through the senses of **r1**:

READS1—we find selectional restriction (AGENT READS1 PERSON), and PERSON matches only DISHWASH/PERS (with result DISHWASH/PERS).

READS2—we find selectional restriction (AGENT READS2 PERSON), and PERSON matches only DISHWASH/PERS (with result DISHWASH/PERS).

Thus types(**d1**) becomes (DISHWASH/PERS); that is, DISHWASH/MACH1 has been eliminated because it cannot satisfy any binary constraint.

For (THEME **r1 p1**), we iterate though the senses of **r1**:

READS1—we find selectional restriction (THEME READS2 TEXTOBJ) because TEXTOBJ matches ARTICLE/TEXT (with result ARTICLE/TEXT).

READS2—we find no matching selectional restriction; that is, (THEME READS2 MENTAL-STATE) cannot be satisfied.

Thus types(**r1**) becomes (READS1); that is, READS2 is eliminated, and types(**d1**) becomes (ARTICLE/TEXT) because ARTICLE1 is eliminated.

Since changes were made, we iterate again. The second iteration step runs as follows:

For (AGENT **r1 d1**), only one sense of **r1** remains:

READS1—we find selectional restriction (AGENT READS1 PERSON).

For (THEME **r1 p1**):

READS1—we find selectional restriction (THEME READS2 TEXTOBJ).

Since no changes were made this time, we are done. The final types are

types(**r1**) =   READS1
types(**p1**) =   ARTICLE/TEXT
types(**d1**) =   DISHWASH/PERS

as desired.

Selectional restrictions are also very useful for further refining the type of unknown objects. For instance, the pronoun *it* inherently offers little restriction on the type of object it refers to except that it is not a person. The selectional restrictions on the verb, however, can give a strong indication of the type of the object it refers to. Consider the processing on the sentence *He read it,* assuming just the READS1 sense of the verb:

(READS1 **r3** [AGENT (PRO **i1** HE1)] [THEME (PRO **n1** (IT1 **n1**))])

The unary and binary constraints on the objects are

(READS1 **r3**), (AGENT **r3 i1**), (THEME **r3 n1**), (MALE **i1**), (IT1 **n1**)

After applying the selectional restrictions for the sense READS1, the type of *he* will be constrained to be of type MALE-PERSON1 (the intersection of MALE and PERSON), and the type of *it* will be constrained to be a TEXTOBJ (the intersection of IT1 and TEXTOBJ). This additional information could be extremely useful as you move on to contextual processing, and the referents of these pronouns need to be identified. To maintain this information, it is added to the logical form. Thus, after applying the selectional restrictions, the logical form of the sentence would be

(READS1 **r3** [AGENT (PRO **i1** (& (MALE **i1**) (PERSON **i1**)))]
        [THEME (PRO **n1** (& (IT1 **n1**) (TEXTOBJ **n1**)))])

Selectional restrictions provide an important technique for disambiguation, and are used in some form in almost every computational system. The approach has been criticized, however, and it is worth examining the criticisms and then considering why the methods remain so useful in computational systems despite the problems. The main problem was that semantic well-formedness is a contin-uous scale rather than an all-or-nothing decision. If you are forced to make absolute conditions on well-formedness, either you will eliminate many possible interpretations or you will have so abstract a constraint that it eliminates almost nothing. Consider the following sentences:

1. I ate the pizza.
2. I ate the box.
3. I ate the car.
4. I ate the thought.

Clearly, sentence 1 is good and sentence 4 has some serious problems. But what about the ones in between? If you had been asked to specify the selectional restrictions for the THEME role of eating events, you would probably have suggested a category like FOOD1. This would allow sentence 1 but make 2 ungrammatical. But clearly 2 is not ungrammatical. While not a normal thing to do, I could eat a box, and 2 seems to be a perfectly good sentence. But what category includes FOOD and boxes (and paper, hats, and so on, that one might eat)? We might suggest PHYSOBJ, which would then accept sentences 1, 2, and 3. But in doing so we lose the information that foods are more likely to be eaten than nonfoods, especially metal objects like cars. In particular, a word like *chip* that is ambiguous between a food (potato chips) and some nonfoods (wood chips) would remain ambiguous in *I ate some chips*. This means that selectional restrictions will have little power for disambiguation (in this case distinguishing only between abstract and concrete objects).

Selectional restrictions are also sensitive to the context of the proposition. For instance, in a negated context, restrictions can be violated. The sentence *I could not eat a car,* for example, should be perfectly fine even if the EATS1 event requires a THEME of type FOOD1. Selectional restrictions also will clearly not apply for a sentence such as *My car drinks gasoline* where metaphor is used, although they still could be used to signal places where metaphor-based analysis should be attempted. Despite all these problems, selectional restrictions have turned out to be extremely useful in actual systems. One reason is that if a system operates in a limited domain, then unusual interpretations such as eating boxes often do not arise, and thus the restriction (**THEME EATS1 FOOD**) may function perfectly well. Of course, the technique may start to run into problems as the range of coverage grows and starts to allow such complications.

One way to reconcile the approach with these problems is to view selectional restrictions as **preferences** rather than absolute requirements. In this case an interpretation that satisfies all the selectional restrictions will be preferred over ones that contain a violation, but if all interpretations violate some restrictions, then those that violate the least number are preferred. This type of scheme can be implemented by ranking each interpretation based on how well it satisfies the selectional restrictions and picking the one that violates the fewest restrictions.

10.2 Semantic Filtering Using Selectional Restrictions

There are at least two ways that selectional restrictions can be added to a parser. The sequential model involves simply running the parser and then checking all the complete S interpretations it finds. The incremental model involves checking each constituent as it is suggested by the parser and discarding it if it is semantically ill-formed. The incremental method can be significantly more efficient than the sequential method. This section demonstrates its efficiency using a simple example. In particular, we will assume that the word sense hierarchy is a simple tree. It is not difficult to generalize the model, but it would make the example more complicated and tend to mask the basic issues.

Consider the following sentence, which syntactically has two PP attachment ambiguities:

He booked a flight to the city for me.

1. (S **SEM** ?semvp) → (NP **SEM** ?semsubj) (*VP SUBJ ?semsubj SEM ?semvp*)
2. (VP **SUBJ** ?semsubj **SEM** ?semv) → (*V[_none] SUBJ ?semsubj SEM ?semv*)
3. (VP **SUBJ** ?semsubj **SEM** ?semv) →
   (*V[_np] SUBJ ?semsubj OBJ ?semnp SEM ?semv*) (NP **SEM** ?semnp)
4. (NP **VAR** ?v **SEM** (PRO ?v (?sempro ?v))) → (*PRO SEM ?sempro*)
5. (NP **VAR** ?v **SEM** <?semart ?v ?semcnp>) → (ART **SEM** ?semart) (*CNP SEM ?semcnp*)
6. (CNP **VAR** ?v **SEM** (?semn ?v)) → (*N SEM ?semn*)
7. (CNP **SEM** (& ?semcnp ?sempp)) →
   (*CNP VAR ?v SEM ?semv*) (PP **PRED** + **ARGVAR** ?v **SEM** ?sempp)
8. (VP **SEM** (& ?semvp ?sempp) →
   (*VP VAR ?v SEM ?semv*) (PP **PRED** + **ARGVAR** ?v **SEM** ?sempp)
9. (PP **PRED** + **ARGVAR** ?v1 **SEM** (?semp ?v1 ?semnp) →
   (*P SEM ?semvp*) (NP **SEM** ?semnp)

Head features for S, VP, NP, CNP: VAR

Grammar 10.4   A small grammar allowing PP attachment ambiguity

With a grammar that allows PPs to be attached to either VPs or CNPs, this sentence has five different structures: The PP *to the city* may modify the verb *booked* or the noun *flight,* and the prepositional phrase *for me* may modify the noun *city,* the noun *flight,* or the verb *booked.* There are five ways to combine these possibilities into a legal syntactic structure. If you consider the semantic meaning of the sentence, however, there is only one plausible reading: The flight is to the city and it was booked for me. This intuition can be captured by the selectional restrictions for the verb *book* and the nouns *flight* and *city.*

Grammar 10.4 is a small grammar that allows the different forms of PP attachment. It uses the techniques described in Section 9.6 and does not require the use of lambda reduction. Only the features relevant to semantic interpretation are shown. Rules 7 and 8 introduce the PP modifiers. The feature ARGVAR is used to pass a discourse variable into the PP so that the appropriate proposition can be constructed. Otherwise, this grammar is quite similar to Grammar 9.14.

Figure 10.5 shows some lexical entries and a hierarchy of word senses for use in semantic checking. The predicates HE1 and ME1 encode the semantic restrictions for the pronouns *he* and *me,* respectively, which are approximated for this example by placing them below the sense PERSON. The selectional restrictions relevant for this section are the following:

(**AGENT BOOKS1 PERSON1**)
(**THEME BOOKS1 FLIGHT1**)
(**BENEFICIARY ACTION1 PERSON1**)
(**DESTINATION FLIGHT1 CITY1**)
(**NEARBY PHYSOBJ PHYSOBJ**)
(**NEARBY ACTION PHYSOBJ**)

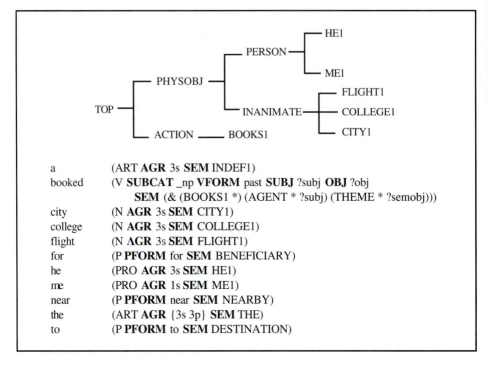

a	(ART **AGR** 3s **SEM** INDEF1)
booked	(V **SUBCAT** _np **VFORM** past **SUBJ** ?subj **OBJ** ?obj
	SEM (& (BOOKS1 *) (AGENT * ?subj) (THEME * ?semobj)))
city	(N **AGR** 3s **SEM** CITY1)
college	(N **AGR** 3s **SEM** COLLEGE1)
flight	(N **AGR** 3s **SEM** FLIGHT1)
for	(P **PFORM** for **SEM** BENEFICIARY)
he	(PRO **AGR** 3s **SEM** HE1)
me	(PRO **AGR** 1s **SEM** ME1)
near	(P **PFORM** near **SEM** NEARBY)
the	(ART **AGR** {3s 3p} **SEM** THE)
to	(P **PFORM** to **SEM** DESTINATION)

Figure 10.5 A small lexicon and word sense hierarchy

These require that the agent of a booking action must be a person, and the theme must be a flight. The third restriction states that the beneficiary relation can hold between any action and a person, and the fourth restriction allows the destination relation to relate flights to cities. The last two restrictions allow the nearby relation to hold between two physical objects and between an action and a physical object, as in *He sighed near the boat.*

This is all the information needed to support the examples. Semantic filtering is added to the chart parser when an entry is to be added to the chart. Before it is added, a check is made to ensure that no relation present in the logical form violates the selectional restrictions. If the SEM value is fully instantiated, then the algorithm specified in the last section can be applied directly. If the SEM value contains variables, then only the relations in the SEM that do not contain variables are checked. If the SEM satisfies the restrictions, then the constituent is added as usual. If it doesn't satisfy the restrictions, the constituent is discarded. Not only does this eliminate the constituent from the chart, but it also means that any larger constituents that would have been built from this constituent will never be considered by the parser. Thus this technique can lead to significant efficiency improvements even with a bottom-up parsing technique.

For example, given Grammar 10.4, consider the bottom-up chart parser on the sentence *He booked the flight to the city for me.* Without semantic filtering, the parser finds five different interpretations and generates 52 constituents on the chart. With semantic filtering, it finds one interpretation and generates only 33 constituents. Consider the first constituent suggested by the parser that is rejected by semantic filtering:

(VP **SEM** (BOOKS1 **v258**
                    [AGENT ?semsubj]
                    [THEME <INDEF1 **v260** (FLIGHT1 **v260**)>]
                    [DESTINATION <THE **v263** (CITY1 **v263**)>])
        VAR v258
        SUBJ ?semsubj)

This constituent is suggested by rule 8, once constituents for the VP *book the flight* and the PP *to the city* are built. It is rejected because it violates the selectional restrictions on the DESTINATION predicate, which cannot relate a booking event to a city; that is, the triple (DESTINATION BOOKS1 CITY1) does not match any selectional restriction. More specifically, the analysis is as follows. The unary constraints on the variables are

v258 BOOKS1
v260 FLIGHT1
v263 CITY1

From these, the relation forms generated from the SEM are (THEME BOOKS1 FLIGHT1) and (DESTINATION BOOKS1 CITY1). The latter form is the one that does not satisfy any selectional restriction. Note that this constituent can be eliminated even though the subject is not yet bound.

The savings become even more significant as more complex sentences are considered. For instance, on the sentence

He booked a flight to the city near the college for me.

the parser using the sequential strategy finds 14 different interpretations and generates 116 constituents on the chart. The parser with incremental semantic filtering finds only 3 interpretations and generates 63 constituents. These 3 readings are all semantically plausible—in the first the city is near the college, in the second the flight to the city is near the college, and in the third the booking event occurred near the college. The first reading is more natural given no information about the context of the sentence, but the others would be plausible in certain contexts. Since we are not considering context until Part III of the book, this is the best that you can expect using context-independent techniques.

10.3 Semantic Networks

In the last section you saw that semantic type hierarchies are very important for ambiguity resolution. This section generalizes these ideas further and develops a representation of lexical knowledge called a semantic network. Semantic networks ease the construction of the lexicon by allowing inheritance of properties,

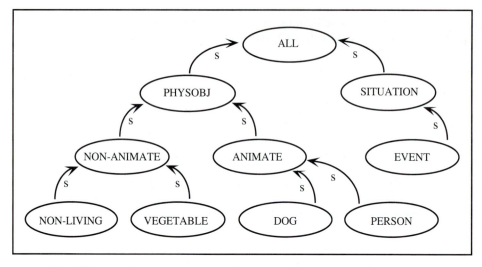

Figure 10.6 Part of a type hierarchy

and they provide a richer set of semantic relationships between word senses to support disambiguation.

A semantic network is a graph with labeled links between labeled nodes. The nodes represent word senses or abstract classes of senses, and the links represent semantic relationships between the senses. The simple abstraction hierarchy shown in Figure 10.6 indicates some semantic relationships between classes of physical and abstract objects. The s arc indicates the subtype relationship. This is just an alternative representation for type hierarchies, as seen in the last two sections.

The selectional restrictions for semantic relations can also be stored in a network form using arcs. Thus you might say that all actions have an agent case filled by an animate object using the network in Figure 10.7. Introduced here is a new node type, an **existential node,** depicted by a square, which represents a particular value. In this case the agent case is restricted to be an object of type ANIMATE. Many such representations allow other information to be stored about case values as well, such as whether they are obligatory or not and whether they represent a single filler or a group of fillers.

An important property of semantic networks is the *inheritance* of properties. For example, given the network shown in Figure 10.8, the action class RUNS1 would inherit the property that every instance has an AGENT role filled by an ANIMATE object. Typically, inheritance is implemented as a graph search starting at the most specific node. To find the restrictions for a certain role R, you first check the most specific node (such as RUNS1) for an R relation, and only if one is not found do you move up the s links (for example, at node ACTION). If an R relation is not found there either, you continue to search up the s hierarchy until either an R relation is found or you hit the top of the s hierarchy.

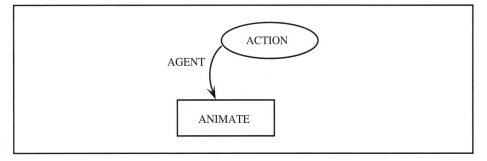

Figure 10.7 All actions have an animate agent

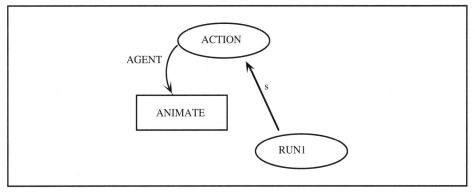

Figure 10.8 A network showing inheritance of roles

Inheritance hierarchies are extremely useful for expressing selectional restrictions across broad classes of verbs. Figure 10.9 shows the selectional restrictions for a set of verb senses that are subclasses of ACTION. Using the inheritance mechanism, you can see that the action class TRANSFER-ACTION allows the semantic relations AGENT, AT-TIME, and AT-LOC, inherited from the class ACTION; the cases THEME and INSTR, inherited from the class OBJ/ACTION; and the case TO-POSS, which is explicitly defined for TRANSFER-ACTION. Note that this representation defines all the allowable semantic relations, not just ones explicitly subcategorized for by the verb.

Often a verb imposes stricter constraints on its arguments than what would be inherited. For example, the sense READS1 fits under the OBJ/ACTION hierarchy and thus could inherit the roles AGENT, AT-TIME, AT-LOC, THEME, and INSTR. But we would like the THEME redefined to be of type TEXTOBJ. The inheritance algorithm sketched above uses the most specific information it has for any verb, since it stops as soon as the first information is found. So this new THEME restriction overrides the more general inherited one.

Semantic networks are also used to represent other forms of general knowledge about the structure of words besides the subtype and argument relationships. Another important hierarchy is the **part-of** hierarchy, in which

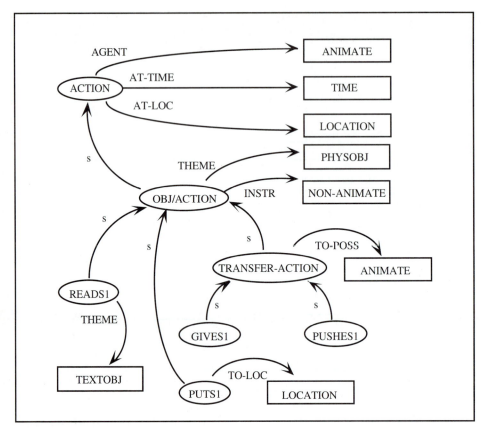

Figure 10.9 Action hierarchy with roles

objects are related to their subparts. This relationship is often expressed in English using the preposition *of,* or in noun-noun modification, or sometimes with the possessive form, as in

The desk drawer   (The drawer that is part of the desk)
The man's head   (The head that is part of the man)
The handle of the drawer   (The handle that is part of the drawer)

To recognize such relationships, and to disambiguate word senses based on these relationships, you need to encode information about the structure of objects in the semantic network. This is done by introducing a new link (the **part-of** link) that encodes this relationship. Thus you can represent that a house has rooms and doors as subparts and that doors have handles, as in Figure 10.10. In this figure, rather than putting the type of the existential node on the node, it is encoded using an **isa** arc, which is found in most semantic network representations.

A complete representation system must be able to indicate whether a subpart is a unique object (the handle on a door) or a set of objects (the rooms in a house). For instance, if a person's body has the subparts head, body, arms, and

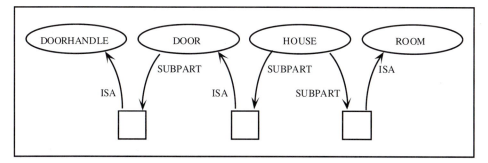

Figure 10.10 Some subpart relationships

legs, then you need to represent that the head is unique and is connected to the body, that there are two arms connected to the body, and so on. All this would be part of the subpart classification of BODY. In addition, the system must be able to represent the spatial and other relationships that hold between subparts. Further details on these issues, though, would lead this book too far afield into knowledge representation.

Besides providing inheritance of properties, semantic networks can also be used for other purposes as well. For instance, one property that will become useful later concerns the semantic closeness of two different word senses. As an initial attack on this problem, we could evaluate the semantic closeness of two objects by finding the distance between the two within the type hierarchy. For instance, with a slightly expanded hierarchy from Figure 10.6, we could find that DOG1 and CAT1 are closely related, as they share the common supertype ANIMATE (only one link away from each). DOG1 and CARROT1, on the other hand, are less closely related, as they share a common supertype PHYSOBJ, several links away from each. DOG1 and EVENT would be even further away. This technique has a few difficulties in that it depends somewhat on the whim of the person who constructed the network, and a different organization might give a different set of answers. As a consequence, a different measure has been suggested that uses the size of the smallest common superset to give a measure of closeness. This way, the individual classification produced by the programmer is not so influential. Basically, the smaller the common set that includes both senses, the more closely related the senses are. In this approach the same results would be obtained for the example above, as the size of the set ANIMATE (the smallest common superset of CAT1 and DOG1) is definitely less that the size of the set PHYSOBJ (the smallest common superset of DOG1 and CARROT1), which in turn is definitely less than the size of the set ALL (the smallest common superset of DOG1 and EVENT).

Of course, using the type hierarchy only captures one notion of semantic closeness. There are many other structures that would have to be encoded to capture the notion more adequately. For instance, you would expect an individual of type DOG1 to be semantically related to the event DOG-SHOW1, but this isn't captured by the type hierarchy. For this sort of association, you would need a closeness measure in terms of what objects typically participate in what events. Given the concepts developed so far, it might work to have a new semantic role, say PARTICIPANT, that relates events to the types of objects they involve. But the hierarchies developed in this section will be sufficient to illustrate the issues that follow.

10.4 Statistical Word Sense Disambiguation

Selectional restrictions provide only a coarse classification of acceptable and nonacceptable forms. As a result, many cases of sense ambiguity cannot be resolved. To better model human processing, more predictive techniques must be developed that give a preference for the common interpretations of senses over the rarer senses. This section explores the use of statistical methods to formalize the notion of common senses. As always, significant effort is necessary to balance the amount of information needed to calculate accurate statistics with the ability to obtain useful information.

The simplest techniques are based on simple unigram statistics. Given a suitably labeled corpus, we can collect information on the usage of the different senses of each word. For instance, we might find 5845 uses of the word *bridge*:

> 5651 uses of STRUCTURE1
> 194 uses of DENTAL-DEV37

Given this data, we would guess that *bridge* occurs in the STRUCTURE1 sense every time. If our training data is representative, this technique would give the right answer 97 percent of the time (5651 times out of 5845 tries). More generally, it has been estimated that this simple strategy would be correct about 70 percent of the time for a broad range of English. Of course, we would like to do much better than this by including some effect of context. Consider the rare sense DENTAL-DEV37. Although it occurs very rarely in the entire corpus, in certain texts (those on dentistry and orthodontics), it will be the most common sense of the word. If you could develop a method to reliably identify such contexts, you could select this sense and perform better than the naive algorithm. It turns out that the actual words used in a text give a good indication of the topic. For instance, in articles on dentistry, there will be many uses of words such as *teeth, dentist, cavity, braces, orthodontics,* and so on. We want to prefer the DENTAL-DEV37 sense when it is found in the presence of such words.

Such information is concerned with word **collocations**, that is, what words tend to appear together. You might consider bigram probabilities, trigrams, or larger groups, say the five surrounding words, the entire sentence, or even larger contexts (some studies have been done using the nearest 100 words). The amount of text examined for each word is called the **window**.

One way to try to do this might be to adapt part-of-speech tagging techniques to use word senses rather than syntactic categories. For this method you need a corpus of words tagged with their senses. Then you could compute unigram statistics (for example, the probability that word w has sense S), bigram statistics, and so on. Of course, building such a corpus requires a considerable effort, but work is underway to make such corpora available. Two factors, however, make directly applying the tagging techniques impractical: First, there are many more senses than syntactic categories; and second, to obtain reasonable results you must use a larger context than simple bigrams or trigrams. Both of these problems mean that it is essentially impossible to obtain sufficient data for training and that a different approach must be used.

The basic idea is to estimate the probability of the senses of a word w relative to a window of words in the text centered on w. Given a window size of n centered on a word w, the words in the window are indicated as follows:

$$w_1 \; w_2 \; ... \; w_{n/2} \; w \; w_{n/2+1} \; ... \; w_{n-1}$$

You want to compute the sense S of a word w that maximizes the formula

$$PROB(w/S \mid w_1 \; w_2 \; ... \; w_{n/2} \; w \; w_{n/2+1} \; ... \; w_{n-1})$$

To estimate these probabilities, we rewrite the formula using Bayes' rule and then make independence assumptions, as we have done several times before. The formula becomes

$$\frac{PROB(w_1 \; ... \; w_{n-1} \mid w/S) * PROB(w/S)}{PROB(w_1 \; ... \; w_{n-1})}$$

Since the denominator doesn't change for each sense, it can be ignored. Furthermore, assuming that each w_i appears independently of the other words in the window, $PROB(w_1 \; ... \; w_{n-1} \mid w/S)$ can be approximated by

$$\Pi_{i=1,n-1} \; PROB_n(w_i \mid w/S)$$

where $PROB_n(w_i \mid w/S)$ is the probability that word w_1 occurs in an n-word window centered on word w in sense S. Putting all this together, the best sense S will be the one that maximizes the formula

$$PROB(w/S) * \Pi_{i=1,n-1} \; PROB_n(w_i \mid w/S)$$

Because of the assumption that each event is independent of all the others, it turns out that the larger the window used the less data is needed, since more data can be collected from each window. Given a corpus, you collect the data by considering the n-word window for each word, counting the number of times the word occurs in each of its senses, and recording all the words in the window. Consider the hypothetical information in Figure 10.11 for the word *bridge,* using a window size of 11 on a corpus of 10 million words.

Based on the definition of $PROB_n(w_i \mid w/S)$, you can estimate its values as follows:

$$PROB_n(w_i \mid w/S) = \frac{Count(\# \text{ times } w_i \text{ occurs in a window centered on } w/S)}{Count(\# \text{ times } w/S \text{ is the center of a window})}$$

	with *bridge/* STRUCTURE1	with *bridge/* DENTAL-DEV37	in any window
teeth	1	10	300
suspension	200	1	2000
the	5500	180	500,000
dentist	2	35	900
total occurrences	5651	194	501,500

Figure 10.11 The counts for the senses for *bridge* in a hypothetical corpus

Given the data in Figure 10.11, you get the following estimates:

$PROB_n$(*teeth* | bridge/STRUCTURE1) = 1/5651 = 1.77 * 10^{-4}
$PROB_n$(*teeth* | bridge/DENTAL-DEV37) = 10/194 = .052
$PROB_n$(*suspension* | bridge/(STRUCTURE1) = 200/5651 = .035
$PROB_n$(*suspension* | bridge/DENTAL-DEV37) = 1/194 = 5.15 * 10^{-3}
$PROB_n$(*the* | bridge/STRUCTURE1) = 5500/5651 = .97
$PROB_n$(*the* | bridge/DENTAL-DEV37) = 180/194 = .93
$PROB_n$(*dentist* | bridge/STRUCTURE1) = 2/5651 = 3.54 * 10^{-4}
$PROB_n$(*dentist* | bridge/DENTAL-DEV37) = 35/194 = .18

The context-independent probabilities of the word senses are easily estimated:

PROB(bridge/STRUCTURE1) = 5651/501500 = .113
PROB(bridge/DENTAL-DEV37) = 194/501500 = 3.87 * 10^{-4}

These two probabilities give the likelihood of each sense without considering any context, that is, using a window of length 1. Note that the probability estimates for the senses in a window that contains just the word *the* are very similar to the no-context estimate:

$PROB_n$(*the* | bridge/STRUCTURE1) * PROB(bridge/STRUCTURE1)
   = .97 * .113 = .109
$PROB_n$(*the* | bridge/DENTAL-DEV37) * PROB(bridge/DENTAL-DEV37)
   = .93 * 3.87 * 10^{-4} = 3.6 * 10^{-4}

This shows that the word *the* has little discrimination power between the two senses, which is what you would expect since *the* is so commonly associated with nouns. In general, function words are so common that they do not help in word sense disambiguation. It is content words, like *teeth* in this example, that have the most dramatic effect. In fact, the probability estimates in a window that contains just the word *dentist* reverse the preference:

$PROB_n$(*dentist* | bridge/STRUCTURE1) * PROB(bridge/STRUCTURE1)
   = 3.54 * 10^{-4} * .113 = 4 * 10^{-5}
$PROB_n$(*dentist* | bridge/DENTAL-DEV37) * PROB(bridge/DENTAL-DEV37) = .18 * 3.87 * 10^{-4} = 6.97 * 10^{-5}

Of course, with a larger window, there are many more chances for content words that strongly affect the decision. For instance, consider the sentence *The dentist put a bridge on my teeth.* All the words except for *dentist* and *teeth* are common words that would co-occur about equally frequently with both senses. Thus they would not affect the relative probabilities for each sense. The words *dentist* and *teeth* together in the same window, however, combine to strongly prefer the rare sense of the word *bridge*. In fact, the estimate for the sense DENTAL-DEV37 would be $3.6 * 10^{-6}$, considerably greater than the estimate of $7.08 * 10^{-7}$ for STRUCTURE1. These values could be used to estimate the actual probabilities by normalizing them. Specifically, if there are only these two senses for the word *bridge*, then the probability that it is used in its DENTAL-DEV37 sense in this window would be $3.6 * 10^{-6} / (3.6 * 10^{-6} + 7.08 * 10^{-7}) = .84$.

○ Collocations and Mutual Information

Much of the work in this area uses collocations, which measure how likely two words are to co-occur in a window of text. One way to compute such a measure is to consider a correlation statistic (where n is the window size)

$$C_n(w/S, w') = \frac{PROB(w/S \ \& \ w' \text{ are in the same window})}{PROB(w/S \text{ in the window}) * PROB(w' \text{ in the window})}$$

Note that this differs from the estimates used above only in the denominator. If K is the number of windows in the corpus, then each of the probabilities above could be estimated as Count(# times event occurs in window) / K. After substituting such estimates in for each probability used in $C_n(w/S, w')$, and simplifying, you get the formula

$$C_n(w/S, w') = \frac{K * \text{Count}(\# \text{ times } w/S \text{ and } w' \text{ co-occur in window})}{\text{Count}(\# \text{ times } w/S \text{ in window}) * \text{Count}(\# \text{ times } w' \text{ in window})}$$

In our sample corpus K is 10^7. Based on the data in Figure 10.11, the estimates for C_n are as follows:

C_n(bridge/STRUCTURE1, teeth) = $(10^7 * 1)/(5651 * 300) = 5.9$
C_n(bridge/DENTAL-DEV37, teeth) = $(10^7 * 10)/(194 * 300) = 171.9$
C_n(bridge/(STRUCTURE1, suspension) = $(10^7 * 200)/(5651 * 2000) = 17.7$
C_n(bridge/DENTAL-DEV37, suspension) = $(10^7 * 1)/(194 * 2000) = 2.5$
C_n(bridge/STRUCTURE1, the) = $(10^7 * 5500)/(5651 * 500,000) = 1.94$
C_n(bridge/DENTAL-DEV37, the) = $(10^7 * 180)/(194 * 500,000) = 1.84$
C_n(bridge/STRUCTURE1, dentist) = $(10^7 * 2)/(5651 * 900) = 3.9$
C_n(bridge/DENTAL-DEV37, dentist) = $(10^7 * 35)/(194 * 900) = 200$

If the ratio is close to one, then the words co-occur at a rate expected by chance. If the ratio is greater than one, then they occur together at a rate better than chance. Note that the correlation figures for the two senses with the word *the* are 1.94 and 1.84. This indicates that both co-occur with *the* at a rate slightly better than chance, but *the* yields no preference for one or the other.

To better distinguish statistics based on ratios, work in this area is often presented in terms of the log of the ratio, which makes the numbers negative if less than one. This more intuitively reflects the preference or dispreference. For word ratios as described in this section, this measure is called the **mutual information** of the two words and is written as $I_n(w_1,w_2)$:

$$I_n(w_1,w_2) = \log C_n(w_1,w_2)$$

For the example involving the two senses of *bridge,* the mutual information statistics are

I_3(bridge/STRUCTURE1, teeth) = 1.77
I_3(bridge/DENTAL-DEV37, teeth) = 5.14
I_3(bridge/STRUCTURE1, the) = .66

Note that words that have no association with each other and co-occur together according to chance will have a mutual information number close to zero. If words are anticorrelated, that is, they co-occur together at a rate less than chance, then the mutual information number will be negative. If you compare different senses using mutual information statistics, you would add the scores together from different words in the window rather than multiplying, in order to account for the fact that they are log values.

10.5 Statistical Semantic Preferences

The first section of this chapter discussed selectional restrictions and their use in disambiguation. One problem with that approach was that the all-or-nothing nature of the restrictions made it impossible to encode semantic preferences. The word *bridge,* for example, was ambiguous between the structure and the dental appliance. In the sentence *I painted the bridge,* however, it seems clear that the structure sense is intended. But the selectional restriction for PAINTS1 would presumably be that the THEME must be a physical object, and both senses of *bridge* fall in that category and satisfy the restriction. So the current model offers no help in selecting the more natural interpretation. Another problem not addressed yet is structural ambiguity, such as with PP attachment. This section develops a model of semantic preference that can help resolve these problems.

The general idea is to collect statistics on the frequency of semantic roles occurring between senses, so that the most common semantic combinations can be preferred when interpreting a sentence. We can start with the selectional restrictions developed in Section 10.1. There, restrictions were stated in terms of unary and binary relations between the discourse variables in the logical form. With a corpus annotated with semantic information, you could collect statistics on the frequency of each of these unary and binary relations. For the moment, let us assume that there is enough data to obtain reliable estimates for every relation. This assumption will be relaxed later in the section.

Consider an example using the sentence *I painted the bridge,* which has the following initial logical form:

(PAINTS1 **p1**   [AGENT (PRO **i1** I1)]
                 [THEME <THE **b1**
                                 {STRUCTURE1 DENTAL-DEV37}>])

The unary and binary relationships are as follows:

(PAINTS1 **p1**), (I1 **i1**), ({STRUCTURE1 DENTAL-DEV37} **b1**),
    (AGENT **p1 i1**), (THEME **p1 b1**)

Let us estimate the semantic likelihood of a particular interpretation by the product of the likelihood of each of its subcomponents; that is, if a logical form LF consists of n relations $R_1, ..., R_n$, then

$$PROB(\text{LF}) = \prod_{i=1,n} PROB(R_i)$$

Of course, this estimate is correct only if all the relations occurred independently of each other; clearly, this is not always a good assumption, but the technique is still useful.

To elaborate on this, a method for computing the probability of the binary relations needs to be developed. We can estimate the probability of some triple (reln head arg) by comparing the number of times it appears to how many times the head appears. The standard maximum likelihood estimation is a reasonable start:

$$PROB((\text{reln head arg}) \mid \text{head}) \approx \frac{\text{Count}((\text{reln head arg}))}{\text{Count}(\text{head})}$$

Consider applying this method. There are two possible readings of *I painted the bridge,* one for each sense of *bridge.* Since the rest of the relations are the same in each case, the difference in probability between the two interpretations will reduce to the difference between the probabilities of (THEME PAINTS1 STRUCTURE1) versus (THEME PAINTS1 DENTAL-DEV37). Given that painting bridges (across bodies of water) is a reasonably common activity and occurs in the database a few times and that painting dental bridges is a very unlikely activity and may not occur in the corpus at all, the former would be preferred.

Of course, sentences that are structurally ambiguous may have significantly different semantic structures to be compared. The same techniques can be used, however, to compare these structures. Consider the sentences *He saw the man with a telescope* and *He saw the man with a hat.* The logical forms for these two sentences are shown in Figure 10.12.

1. He saw the man with a telescope.

   1a. (SEES1 **p1**   [EXPERIENCER (PRO **h1** HE1)]
                   [THEME <THE **w1** MALE-PERSON1>]
                   [INSTR <A **b1** TELESCOPE1>])

   1b. (SEES1 **p1**   [EXPERIENCER (PRO **h1** HE1)]
                   [THEME <THE **w1** MALE-PERSON1
                              ({WITH1 ... WITHn} **w1** <A **b1** TELESCOPE1>)>])

2. He saw the man with a hat.

   2a. (SEES1 **p1**   [EXPERIENCER (PRO **h1** HE1)]
                   [THEME <THE **w1** MALE-PERSON1>]
                   [INSTR <A **w2** HAT1>])

   2b. (SEES1 **p1**   [EXPERIENCER (PRO **h1** HE1)]
                   [THEME <THE **w1** MALE-PERSON1
                              ({WITH1 ... WITHn} **w1** <A **w2** HAT1>)>])

Figure 10.12   The logical forms for two ambiguous sentences

Even though the semantic structures are different, they still share many of the same binary relations. For instance, sentences 1a and 1b share the triples (EXPERIENCER SEES1 MALE1) and (THEME SEES1 MALE-PERSON1). They differ only in that one contains (INSTR SEES1 TELESCOPE1), presumably a commonly occurring pattern, while the other contains (WITHi MAN1 TELESCOPE1), where WITHi ranges over all the semantic relations that can be indicated by *with* (for example, part-of, accompanied-by, wearing, and so on). Since this also probably occurs frequently, both interpretations remain plausible. With sentence 2, comparing the two LFs reduces to comparing the likelihood of the relation (INSTR SEES1 HAT1), presumably a very rare relation if it occurs at all, with (WITHi MAN1 HAT1), which would occur frequently when WITHi is the ACCOMPANY (accompanied by) relation, since men wear hats. Thus, in the second case, interpretation 2b is selected and the interpretation of *with* is disambiguated in the process.

Even though the co-occurrence statistics were not able to favor one interpretation over the other in the first case, the probabilistic model does allow you to quantify the degree of certainty (or ambiguity) in the sentence. In addition, these techniques can be added on as a disambiguation method that is applied to each major constituent as soon as its logical form is constructed. The value returned can be used to contribute to an overall score of the constituent in a best-first parsing strategy.

The principal problem with this approach, however, is obtaining an accurate set of statistics. If you remember, this was a problem even when you were only concerned with the syntactic class of words. When dealing with word senses, the problems are much worse, as there are many different senses per

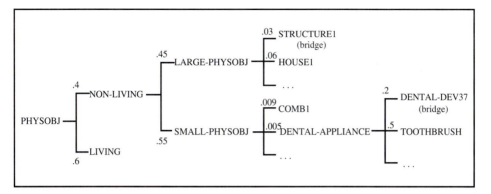

Figure 10.13 A type hierarchy with probabilities

Triple	Number of Occurrences	*PROB*
(THEME PAINTS1 NON-LIVING)	960	.96
(THEME PAINTS1 SMALL-PHYSOBJ)	300	.3
(THEME PAINTS1 LARGE-PHYSOBJ)	650	.65
(THEME PAINTS1 STRUCTURE1)	10	.01

Figure 10.14 Statistics for some semantic relations

word. As a result, techniques for estimating probabilities must be used, because acceptable triples that never occurred in the training corpus will be common.

If there is a predefined abstraction hierarchy, then the hierarchy can be used to provide an estimate for unobserved triples. The basic idea is to collect data on triples not only for the exact senses involved, but also for abstractions of the senses. Consider the hierarchy in Figure 10.13, which also indicates how likely an object of a superclass is to fall into each of the subclasses. According to the figure, the probability of a SMALL-PHYSOBJ being a DENTAL-APPLIANCE, *PROB*(DENTAL-APPLIANCE | SMALL-PHYSOBJ), is .005.

Given such a hierarchy, if we observe a triple (THEME PAINTS1 STRUC-TURE1), we not only record that this triple occurred, but also record an entry for the abstractions for STRUCTURE1, such as (THEME PAINTS1 LARGE-PHYSOBJ) and (THEME PAINTS1 PHYSOBJ). Thus, after analyzing an extensive corpus involving 1000 instances of PAINTS1, you might obtain the data and probability estimates shown in Figure 10.14. There are, of course, many other triples not listed here that were observed. But these four suffice for the example. When a triple not previously observed is found, say (THEME PAINTS1 DENTAL-DEV37), we can use the information about the supertypes to produce an estimate.

Consider again the sentence *I painted the bridge.* Since the DENTAL-DEV37 sense of *bridge* was never seen in the training data, the estimate of the probability of the triple (THEME PAINTS1 DENTAL-DEV37) would be 0, which would indicate that such a reading is impossible, contrary to intuition. But we estimate a probability for this triple by considering abstractions of DENTAL-DEV37. Since DENTAL-DEV37 is a subclass of DENTAL-APPLIANCE, possibly we have an estimate for (THEME PAINTS1 DENTAL-APPLIANCE). If not, consider abstracting again. Since a DENTAL-APPLIANCE is a SMALL-PHYSOBJ, then see if we have an estimate for (THEME PAINTS1 SMALL-PHYSOBJ). We have an estimate for this type of triple, which is .3:

$$PROB((\text{THEME PAINTS1 SMALL-PHYSOBJ}) \mid \text{PAINTS1}) = .3$$

Since DENTAL-DEV37 is a SMALL-PHYSOBJ, this estimate has some relevance. However, the .3 estimate is clearly too optimistic to use directly, given that the set DENTAL-DEV37 is only a small subset of SMALL-PHYSOBJ. We can take this into account by considering the probability that an arbitrary SMALL-PHYSOBJ is a DENTAL-DEV. Using the data from Figure 10.13 we get

$$PROB(\text{DENTAL-DEV37} \mid \text{SMALL-PHYSOBJ}) =$$
$$PROB(\text{DENTAL-DEV37} \mid \text{DENTAL-APPLIANCE}) *$$
$$PROB(\text{DENTAL-APPLIANCE} \mid \text{SMALL-PHYSOBJ})$$
$$= .005 * .2 = .001$$

Thus one estimate for PROB((THEME PAINTS1 DENTAL-DEV37) | PAINTS1) might be

$$PROB((\text{THEME PAINTS1 SMALL-PHYSOBJ}) \mid \text{PAINTS1}) *$$
$$PROB(\text{DENTAL-DEV37} \mid \text{SMALL-PHYSOBJ}) = .0003$$

This is just one example of using smoothing techniques to construct an estimate. You might find other techniques that produce better estimates by introducing additional multiplicative factors or combining other evidence.

10.6 Combining Approaches to Disambiguation

This chapter has considered two different approaches to resolving ambiguity of word senses and semantic relations. The approach based on selectional restrictions assumes a set of hard constraints on what senses of words are allowed as arguments to other senses. These are based on semantic considerations of the meanings of each sense. This approach can then be generalized so that the constraints are indicated as preferences, and the interpretation that violates the fewest constraints is the best interpretation.

The other kind of approach is based on statistical analysis of corpora. Preference is given to combinations of senses that occur most frequently in the data. In a purely statistical approach, the decision has no inherent connection to the underlying meaning of the sentences. Attachment decisions are made based on what patterns of lexical items occur most frequently in what structures.

As such, they seem to be quite different approaches, and many researchers seem to assume that this is an either-or choice. In fact, the two can be viewed as complementary approaches, and we would expect an approach that uses both types of techniques to perform better than an approach based on only one technique. Section 10.5 described a technique that uses both approaches. It used statistical measures from a corpus, but the word senses were organized into a type hierarchy that captures their semantic relationships. This information then allowed statistics to be collected on semantically abstract classes that then could be used to provide estimates for triples that had not been observed before. Thus the semantic knowledge of the type hierarchy enables an interesting approach to handling sparse data.

You might expect that, given enough data, the statistical approach would eventually be able to capture all the information present in the semantically based approach; that is, that the common patterns of usage would generally reveal the semantic relations between words. If this is true, you could then build the equivalent of a type hierarchy based on statistical data alone. One issue that makes this unlikely is the problem of new words (or words new to a particular person). New words are constantly being encountered. If you are given a semantic definition of a word, then you can immediately use the word in appropriate circumstances, even though you have never encountered the word in that context before. As a simple example, say you learn that a *preef* is a type of sailboat. You can then understand the intended interpretation of the sentence *We sailed the lake in my preef yesterday,* namely that *in my preef* modifies the verb phrase rather than the lake. In contrast, if *preef* had been defined as an estate or other large area of land, then the reverse attachment would be preferred. These decisions are made in virtue of the newly acquired semantic knowledge of the word *preef.* A purely statistical approach would not be able to make a reasonable decision, as the PP *in my preef* has never been encountered before and there have not been enough observations of *preef* to associate it with a more abstract class, such as boats or estates, where you might have enough data.

Of course, once you assume the existence of a semantic hierarchy to structure your statistics, as in Section 10.5, statistical methods can be used effectively to determine the appropriate attachment. For example, consider again the word *preef* defined as a kind of boat. In this case you would probably compare the likelihood of a boat being the location of a sailing activity versus the likelihood that a lake is in a boat. But this just supports the point that effective techniques will combine both methods. This combined method could be generalized further by augmenting it with the techniques for PP attachment described in Chapter 7. A simple way would be to assume that the two approaches yield independent results and simply consider the product of the two estimates as the final estimate. Clearly, other ways of combining the results could be developed as well, that attempt to exploit some of the similarities between the methods.

Summary

Ambiguity resolution is a crucial problem facing computational systems. This chapter explored several different methods for handling ambiguity. Disambiguation is typically driven by a hierarchical representation of word senses, often captured in semantic networks. Using these hierarchies, you can define selectional restrictions and use these constraints to reduce the possible word senses. In addition, statistical methods can be used to encode preferences for individual word senses, given the surrounding words, and for particular interpretations, based on the relatively frequencies of semantic relations.

Related Work and Further Readings

Word sense disambiguation has been recognized as one of the most difficult problems facing computational models of language. As early as 1960, Bar-Hillel (1960) argued that it was the major stumbling block to creating natural language applications such as machine translation. Selectional restrictions were proposed in linguistics by Katz and Fodor (1963), and variations on using semantic features have been used in virtually every computational model since. One of the earliest proponents for semantic preferences was Wilks (1975), who created a system that used semantic templates to interpret a representation of the sentence in which the basic phrase structure had been analyzed. This system used heuristic techniques based on minimizing the number of semantic constraint violations.

Systems that have concentrated on the ambiguity problem have usually combined a range of techniques in addition to selectional restrictions. Most of these map directly to the underlying representation rather than to a logical form, but the restrictions specified in the knowledge representation act similarly to selectional restrictions. Hayes (1977) and Hirst (1987) used a combination of selectional restrictions and semantic closeness measures computed from a semantic network of word senses. The BORIS system (Dyer, 1983) used a combination of top-down expectations and selectional restrictions to understand complex text.

Constraint satisfaction was first introduced in AI for interpreting visual scenes by Waltz (1975), and the formal underpinnings of the approach were outlined in detail by Freuder (1982) and MacWorth (1977). Mellish (1985) used constraint satisfaction techniques both to disambiguate word senses and to identify the referents of noun phrases.

Semantic networks for natural language were introduced by Quillian (1968) to represent word meanings and conceptual associations between words. The development of semantic networks sparked much work in network representations (for example, Woods (1975), Findler (1979), Sowa (1984; 1991)). Due to the attractiveness of the representation, semantic networks became general frameworks for representing knowledge and supporting general inference. The system presented here, however, is closer to its origins—the intention is to capture the conceptual associations between words. As a result, we have not tried to define any sort of general inference procedure using these networks, or even stated how to express specific facts about the world. This will be discussed in Chapter 13. A recent effort at building a comprehensive lexical database for English is the WordNet (Miller, 1990), available by ftp from Princeton University.

Only very recently have statistical models been proposed to handle the ambiguity problem. Work on collocations was primarily an area of interest for lexicography. The concept of mutual information is developed in information theory (Fano, 1961), and has been used successfully in word sense disambiguation. A good example of current work is Yarowsky (1992). A good source of recent work in the use of corpora is the special issues of *Computational Linguistics*, Volume 19, Issues 1 and 2, 1993.

Another approach to disambiguation is to use spreading activation methods in semantic networks, in which word senses that are related activate each other. An example of this approach can be found in Hirst (1987). Related to this are connectionist models in which the entire computational process is described in terms of the interactions in neural networks. Examples of this approach are Cottrell and Small (1983) and Pollack and Waltz (1985). A good introduction to distributed connectionist models is Rumelhart and McClelland (1986).

There is a large literature on the attachment problems. Ford, Bresnan, and Kaplan (1982) suggest that lexical preferences on the verb determine likely attachment decisions. Crain and Steedman (1985) suggest filtering interpretations based on whether the noun phrases proposed make sense in the domain. Hirst (1987) describes a system that uses both lexical preferences and semantic plausibility. Jensen and Binot (1987) use an on-line dictionary to find common patterns of prepositional phrase attachment. Dahlgren (1988) develops a set of preference rules based on the different propositions and the semantic class of the object of the preposition. Recent work using statistical techniques similar to those described in Section 10.5 can be found in Grishman and Sterling (1992). Hindle and Rooth (1993) show how to collect statistics about PP attachment from unannotated text. Resnik (1993) has developed techniques for exploiting WordNet to gather statistics to apply to various forms of syntactic ambiguity.

Exercises for Chapter 10

1. (*easy*) List all the selectional restrictions for the verb sense PUTS1 given the hierarchy in Figure 10.9.

2. (*easy*) Using the C_n function described in Section 10.4, compute the score of each of the senses of the word *bridge* in the five-word window *the suspension bridge the construction.*

3. (*easy*) Using the technique for estimating the probability of triples in Section 10.5 and the data given in Figures 10.13 and 10.14, estimate the probability of the triple (THEME PAINTS1 HOUSE1), assuming it has not been seen before.

4. (*medium*) Implement a program to calculate the mutual information statistic between the words *happy* and *dog,* using a window of three words, where windows are allowed to cut across sentences, given the following minuscule corpus:

> I saw a happy dog by the river. I was never happy before I met my dog. It was sad that the dog left. A happy cat is a well-fed cat. Cows sit in pastures all day and eat grass. My dog is happy most of the time.

Do these words occur together at a rate better than chance? Be sure to describe any assumptions you make in calculating your probability estimates and the mutual information value.

5. (*medium*) Define a data structure to represent simple type networks with case value restrictions. Write a program that, given such a hierarchy, computes the complete set of case value restrictions for any given type in the hierarchy. Test this on the network shown in Figure 10.9, and retrieve the case value restrictions for PUTS1. Make sure your data structures and algorithms are well described in your documentation.

6. (*medium*) Implement a system that maintains a type hierarchy and allows you to test whether two types are compatible. In particular, your system should allow type information to be added with the following function:

> (Add-Subtype T1 T2)—asserts that T1 is a proper subtype of T2

This information can then be used in the function

> (Test-Intersection T1 T2)

which returns nil if the two types are not known to intersect and returns the name of the intersection if the types do intersect. In particular, if T1 is a subtype of T2, then T1 would be returned; if T3 is a subtype of both T1 and T2, then T3 is assumed to be the intersection and T3 is returned. Document your data structures and demonstrate the range of input and output that your system can handle.

7. (*medium*) Extend the grammar, lexicon, sense hierarchy, and selectional restrictions given in Section 10.2 as necessary to appropriately interpret the following sentences:

> He gave the book to the college.
> He knows the route to the college.

Describe why the erroneous interpretations would not be produced by the bottom-up chart parser using your data.

8. (*medium*) The technique for disambiguation in Section 10.5 was based only on the probability of the binary relations. How might you extend this

to account for unary relations as well? Describe your algorithm in detail, and show how it would operate given the sentence

He painted the suspension bridge at night.

You may assume that all the words except for *bridge* are unambiguous. Make up any data that you need for your technique that is not present in Sections 10.4 or 10.5.

9. (*hard*) Using your solutions to Questions 5 and 6 as a component, implement the constraint satisfaction algorithm described in Section 10.1, and test it on a range of selectional restrictions generated from ambiguous sentences, including

The dishwasher read the article.
He painted the bridge.

Test your program using a type hierarchy that includes the fragments in Figures 10.1 and 10.2, the verb hierarchy in Figure 10.9, and extensions necessary to include the four different senses of the noun *bridge,* as well as the senses of the other words used in your test sentences. Construct two other sentences with ambiguous words that demonstrate features of your solution not illustrated by the above two sentences. As always, your program should be fully documented and tested.

You do not need to start with the full logical forms for the sentences. Rather, your input may be the unary and binary type relations over the discourse variables. Thus the input for *The dishwasher read the article* would be the list of unary relations

(((DISHWASH1 DISHWASH2) d1) ((READS1 READS2) r1)
  ((ARTICLE1 ARTICLE2) a1))

and the binary relations

((AGENT r1 d1) (THEME r1 a1))

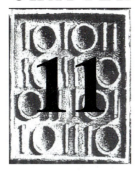

Other Strategies for Semantic Interpretation

11.1   Grammatical Relations

11.2   Semantic Grammars

11.3   Template Matching

11.4   Semantically Driven Parsing Techniques

The previous chapters described methods of semantic interpretation in which the syntactic structure drove semantic interpretation in a rule-by-rule fashion. There are many other ways to organize a system that have other advantages. Some techniques allow for the relatively rapid development of systems for a specific application, whereas others provide interesting approaches to producing more robust systems that do not fail when faced with ungrammaticality. This chapter considers some examples of other ways of organizing semantic interpretation that are found in the literature. These techniques range from loosely coupled syntax and semantics to techniques that are essentially semantically driven and use minimal syntactic information.

The syntax-driven rule-by-rule approach to semantic interpretation discussed in Chapter 9 is attractive on theoretical grounds. It assumes a close linkage between syntax and semantics and allows both to be used simultaneously to build an interpretation of a sentence. It also is the approach most commonly used by researchers interested in formal semantics, because insights from linguistics can be readily incorporated into computational systems. But if you surveyed all the existing computational systems, you would find a wide range of other approaches used, depending on the goals of the project. Is it focusing on long-term research aimed at a comprehensive grammar for a language, or is it focusing on the shorter-term goal of producing a system that will work for a specific application? Generally, you will find that long-term research efforts tend to be based on rule-by-rule syntax-driven approaches, whereas shorter-term applied efforts use other techniques. The practical developer's approach is guided by two important concerns:

- Building a syntax-driven rule-by-rule system is complex, and many theoretical issues arise that will slow the development of the system.
- Purely syntax-driven systems have problems dealing with real language, which is often ungrammatical due to errors, metaphor, and many other phenomena. As a result, a syntax-driven system may not produce any analysis at all for a sentence when it cannot find a parse that covers the entire sentence.

There are many different ways to deal with these problems. One of the most radical is simply to throw out syntax altogether and build a system that produces a semantic interpretation directly from the sentence. The other end of the spectrum would retain the syntax-driven approach but generalize the syntactic processing so that it handles ungrammaticality more robustly. Midway positions include approaches that do a partial syntactic analysis to produce a structured input for subsequent semantic interpretation, and approaches that generalize the notion of a grammar so that it parses based on semantic structure rather than syntactic structure. This chapter gives examples of each of these positions.

The presentation starts with the approaches that retain syntactic processing and then moves to approaches that use less and less syntax. Section 11.1

Jack bought a ticket.	(**s1** PRED BUYS1) (**s1** TNS PAST) (**s1** LSUBJ (NAME **j2** "Jack")) (**s1** LOBJ <A **t1** TICKET1>)
A ticket was bought by Jill.	(**s2** PRED BUYS1) (**s2** TNS PAST) (**s2** LSUBJ (NAME **j2** "Jill")) (**s2** LOBJ <A **t1** TICKET1>)
Jill gave Jack a book.	(**s3** PRED GIVES1) (TNS **s3** PAST) (**s3** LSUBJ (NAME **j1** "Jill")) (**s3** LOBJ <A **b1** BOOK1>) (**s3** IOBJ (NAME **j2** "Jack"))
Jill gave a book to Jack.	(**s4** PRED GIVES1) (TNS **s4** PAST) (**s4** LSUBJ (NAME **j1** "Jill")) (GIVES1 LOBJ <A **b1** BOOK1>) (GIVES1 TO (NAME **j2** "Jack"))
Jill thinks that Jack stole the book.	(**s5** PRED THINKS1) (**s5** LSUBJ (NAME **j1** "Jill")) (**s5** LOBJ s6) (**s6** PRED STEALS1) (**s6** TNS PAST) (**s6** LSUBJ (NAME **j2** "Jack")) (**s6** LOBJ <THE **b1** BOOK1>)

Figure 11.1   A representation based on grammatical relations

describes approaches in which the parser produces a representation that is an abstracted syntactic structure that is then used as input to semantic interpretation. Section 11.2 describes semantic grammars, a method of writing grammars in terms of semantic rather than syntactic concepts. Section 11.3 describes methods that use a partial syntactic analysis and then use a template-driven semantic analysis. Section 11.4 describes an approach that directly semantically interprets the sentences.

11.1 Grammatical Relations

The idea underlying this approach is that the parser produces an output that abstracts away the details of the actual sentence but retains the structure important for semantics as a set of **grammatical relations** or **grammatical dependencies**. The semantic interpreter then produces a meaning representation as a separate interpretation process that uses the grammatical relations as its input.

You have already seen a hint of this type of analysis in the descriptions of ATN-based grammars in earlier chapters. The grammatical relations are often relations like logical subject (LSUBJ), logical object (LOBJ), indirect object (IOBJ), and relations based on prepositional phrases. Figure 11.1 shows some simple sentences and their representations in terms of grammatical relations. Each relation is of the form (*discourse-variable relation value*), where the value may be another discourse variable or a SEM structure.

Pattern		Logical Form
1. (<VAR> PRED <PRED>)	$\rightarrow$	(3 1)
2. (<VERB> AT <LOC>)	$\rightarrow$	(AT-LOC 1 3)
3. (<ACTION-VERB> LSUBJ <ANIMATE>)	$\rightarrow$	(AGENT 1 3)
4. (<ACTION-VERB> LOBJ <PHYSOBJ>)	$\rightarrow$	(THEME 1 3)
5. (<GIVE-VERB> TO <ANIMATE>)	$\rightarrow$	(TO-POSS 1 3)
6. (<GIVE-VERB> IOBJ <ANIMATE>)	$\rightarrow$	(TO-POSS 1 3)
7. (<ATTITUDE-VERB> LSUBJ <ANIMATE>)	$\rightarrow$	(EXPERIENCER 1 3)
8. (<ATTITUDE-VERB> LOBJ <VAR>)	$\rightarrow$	(THEME 1 3)
9. (PAST <VAR>)	$\rightarrow$	(PAST 1)

Figure 11.2 Some patterns for interpreting grammatical relations

Note that the active/passive distinction is removed in the grammatical relation representation because the LSUBJ is always set to the actor of the action, and the LOBJ is the object acted upon, whether it appears as the subject (in passive sentences) or the object (in active sentences).

It is not difficult to augment a context-free grammar to generate this type of representation as it parses. One method is to represent each of the grammatical relations as a feature. The resulting feature structure is easily converted into triples. The features

(PRED BUYS1 **LSUBJ** (NAME **j2** "Jack") **LOBJ** <A t1 TICKET1>)

are easily converted into the triples

(s1 PRED BUYS1) **(s1** LSUBJ (NAME **j2** "Jack"))
     (s1 LOBJ <A **t1** TICKET1>)

The semantic interpreter then may be a separate process that takes the representation of grammatical dependencies and produces a semantic representation. Let's assume that it produces a case-role-based logical form as used in earlier chapters. One common technique for building the representation uses patterns that relate the grammatical roles to the case roles used in the representation. Each verb may define its own mapping. Because the grammatical roles already capture part of the semantic structure, the mapping is often straightforward. For instance, Figure 11.2 shows the patterns needed for the verbs used in Figure 11.1, using the verb hierarchy shown in Figure 11.3.

The rules consist of a pattern in which <T> matches any element of type T. The right side specifies the semantic interpretation, where the number n indicates the value of the n'th element in the pattern. For example, rule 2 contains the pattern (<VERB> AT <LOC>), which will match any triple where the first element is of type VERB, the second is the atom AT, and the third is of type LOC. It produces a SEM structure consisting of the relation AT-LOC with the verb and

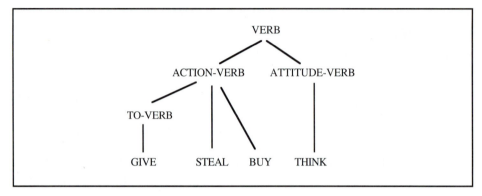

Figure 11.3 A verb hierarchy for pattern matching

the location as its arguments. For the above patterns, verbs must be classified as shown in Figure 11.3. This hierarchy classifies verbs as ACTION-VERB (for example, *give, buy, steal*), ATTITUDE-VERB, which involves verbs describing attitudes (for example, *believes, thinks*), and TO-VERB, which includes verbs involving transferring an object to someone (for example, *give, donate, throw*).

Assuming a mechanism to check the types of terms as the patterns are matched, a set of dependencies generated by a grammar can be interpreted by finding a pattern to match each one and then collecting the set of results into a logical form. For example, consider the sentence *Jack bought a ticket,* which, omitting the tense information, has the structure

> (**s1** PRED BUYS1)
> (**s1** LSUBJ (NAME **j2** "Jack"))
> (**s1** LOBJ <A **t1** TICKET1>)

Rule 1 matches the first triple, rule 3 matches the second, and rule 4 matches the third, producing the three logical form fragments

> (BUYS1 **s1**)
> (AGENT **s1** (NAME **j2** "Jack"))
> (THEME **s1** <A **t1** TICKET1>)

These three fragments conjoined give the full logical form, which in the abbreviated format used throughout this text would be written as

> (BUYS1 **s1** [AGENT (NAME **j2** "Jack")] [THEME <A **t1** TICKET1>])

Similarly, the sentence *Jill thinks that Jack stole the book* would be parsed to the following dependencies, shown with their semantic translation generated by the following patterns:

> (**s5** PRED THINKS1) $\rightarrow$ (THINKS1 **s5**)
> (**s5** LSUBJ (NAME **j1** "Jill")) $\rightarrow$ (EXPERIENCER **s5** (NAME **j1** "Jill"))
> (**s5** LOBJ **s6**) $\rightarrow$ (THEME **s5** **s6**)

(**s6** PRED STEALS1) $\rightarrow$ (STEALS1 **s6**)
(**s6** TNS PAST) $\rightarrow$ (PAST **s6**)
(**s6** LSUBJ (NAME **j2** "Jack")) $\rightarrow$ (AGENT **s6** (NAME **j2** "Jack"))
(**s6** LOBJ <THE **b1** BOOK1>) $\rightarrow$ (THEME **s6** <THE **b1** BOOK1>)

Merging these semantic translations would produce the following logical form in abbreviated form (ignoring tense):

(THINKS1 **s5** [EXPERIENCER (NAME **j1** "Jill")]
            [THEME (STEALS1 **s6**
                    [AGENT (NAME **j2** "Jack")]
                    [THEME **s6** <THE **b1** BOOK1>])])

As presented here, the syntactic and semantic processes are separate and run in sequence. This assumption makes the presentation easier but is not necessary for the approach. It is possible to have the syntactic and semantic analysis occur concurrently as follows. Each time the parser builds a grammatical relation, it is passed to the semantic interpreter, which can then process it. If the grammatical relation has no semantic interpretation, this information is passed back to the parser, which then discards (or downgrades) the syntactic analysis that produced the relation as it is semantically anomalous (or unlikely). Thus you can do semantic filtering on the constituents as they are produced. This technique provides the advantages of a close coupling of syntax and semantics, while retaining separate modules for each.

This section has ignored the issue of how noun phrases are interpreted. In many systems, a special process is used to interpret noun phrases (sometimes identifying the referent in context), and the result of this process is inserted in the dependency relations. It is also possible to extend the general approach to noun phrases, introducing dependency relations between adjectives and the nouns they modify, and so on. The semantic interpreter then must be extended so that it can perform semantic interpretation recursively on subconstituents and then use the results to construct the logical form for the current constituent.

Approaches based on grammatical relations are attractive because the representation provides a convenient interface between the syntactic processing and complex semantic interpretation procedures, allowing them to operate independently. This allows the mapping rules to be considerably more complex than can be easily specified in a rule-by-rule approach. The mapping process could, for instance, involve extensive type checking, inference, and discourse processing in order to disambiguate the intended meaning of the sentence. Of course, the grammatical relations themselves can still be constructed compositionally by the parser using a rule-by-rule approach. One way to view this approach is that the representation based on grammatical relations is an alternative to the logical form used here, and the mapping rules are performing contextual interpretation into the final meaning representation language.

11.2 Semantic Grammars

When building a system for a particular application, there are often techniques that can be used to improve the efficiency and performance of the parsing and semantic interpretation. These techniques take advantage of the predetermined context of the application in order to reduce or eliminate much of the processing required to handle ambiguity in general. This section describes a technique for building a custom-tailored grammar for the application.

A general grammar of English will contain many constructs that are necessary for wide coverage of the language but may not be needed in the application at hand. Certain constructs may appear only with a specific semantic context. In these circumstances the general syntactic rule might be replaced in the grammar with a more specific semantically motivated rule. Consider an application that supports queries to an airline database about flights. The following noun phrases referring to flights occur in this domain:

> the flight to Chicago
> the 8 o'clock flight
> the first flight out
> flight 457 to Chicago

To handle these noun phrases, a general grammar must contain the following rules. (Examples appear in parentheses.)

> $NP \rightarrow DET\ CNP$ (*the flight*)
> $CNP \rightarrow N$ (*flight*)
> $CNP \rightarrow CNP\ PP$ (*flight to Chicago*)
> $CNP \rightarrow N\ PART$ (*flight out*)
> $CNP \rightarrow PRE\text{-}MOD\ CNP$ (*8 o'clock flight*)
> $NP \rightarrow N\ NUMB$ (*flight 457*)

Now, for cities in this domain, we find the following types of noun phrases:

> Chicago
> the nearest city to Dallas

These phrases can be handled by the general grammar we just created, with the addition of one more rule to handle proper names. The problem with this is that now you have to restrict rules to apply to the appropriate categories. For example, the following noun phrases would not occur in this domain (or possibly in any other), even though the rules would suggest that they are legal:

> *the city to Chicago
> *the 8 o'clock city
> *the first city out
> *city 567

To handle such cases in a general grammar, you would need to add selectional restrictions and features on the words to restrict the possible syntactic structures and modifiers. In a limited domain, however, it is often simpler to introduce new specialized lexical categories based on their semantic properties, such as FLIGHT-N (that is, those nouns with senses that indicate flights). With such lexical categories, the general grammar might be rewritten as follows. (Examples are given in parentheses.)

FLIGHT-NP → DET FLIGHT-CNP	(*the flight*)
FLIGHT-CNP → FLIGHT-N	(*flight*)
FLIGHT-CNP → FLIGHT-CNP FLIGHT-DEST	(*flight to Chicago*)
FLIGHT-CNP → FLIGHT-CNP FLIGHT-SOURCE	(*flight from Boston*)
FLIGHT-CNP → FLIGHT-N FLIGHT-PART	(*flight out*)
FLIGHT-CNP → FLIGHT-PRE-MOD FLIGHT-CNP	(*8 o'clock flight*)
FLIGHT-NP → FLIGHT-N NUMB	(*flight 457*)
CITY-NP → CITY-NAME	(*Boston*)
CITY-NP → DET CITY-CNP	(*the city*)
CITY-CNP → CITY-N	(*city*)
CITY-CNP → CITY-MOD CITY-CNP	(*nearest city to*
CITY-MOD-ARG	*Dallas*)

Of course, many other rules are needed, but these use the semantic categories as well. For instance, the FLIGHT-DEST category allows prepositional phrases that specify the destination cities of flights:

FLIGHT-DEST → to CITY-NP
FLIGHT-DEST → for CITY-NP

Higher-level syntactic structures can be similarly tailored to these categories, such as the rule

TIME-QUERY → When does FLIGHT-NP FLIGHT-VP

A grammar that is cast in terms of the major semantic categories of the domain is called a **semantic grammar**. Clearly, there is no precise line between a syntactic grammar and a semantic grammar; rather, there is a continuum between the two extremes. While semantic grammars are considerably larger than their syntactic counterparts, it is generally simpler to define the rules because of the limited context, and complex features are not needed to sort out which forms can go with which semantic categories.

You can augment a semantic grammar to produce a logical form in the normal way. Typically, the interpretation rules will be straightforward because you know most of the semantic information needed directly from the structure of the rule. An alternative method, however, is simply to use the parse tree itself as the logical form. Since it contains the semantic information already, there is little advantage for converting to another notation. For instance, Figure 11.4 shows the parse tree for the query *When does the flight to Chicago leave?*

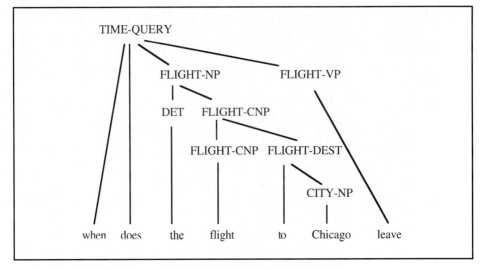

Figure 11.4   The parse tree for *When does the flight to Chicago leave?*

In LISP form this tree might be represented as

```
(TIME-QUERY
    (FLIGHT-NP
        (DET the)
        (FLIGHT-CNP
            (FLIGHT-CNP flight)
            (FLIGHT-DEST to (CITY-NP Chicago))))
    (FLIGHT-EVENT leave))
```

This structure would be at least as easy to convert into a database query as the full logical form for the sentence. So there is no advantage to further semantic analysis. Semantic grammars combine aspects of syntax, semantics, and selectional restrictions in a simple uniform framework. As a result semantic grammars have proven useful for the rapid development of parsers in limited application domains. The down side, however, is that they do not port well to new domains and cannot handle applications in broad domains. Generally, a new domain will require a completely new semantic grammar, whereas most of a syntactic grammar for one domain will apply to another domain.

11.3 Template Matching

In certain applications, the task is specific enough that special-purpose techniques that exploit the domain structure can be used. For example, you might be interested in a system that can create summaries of certain stock transactions described in newspaper stories. The information required might fall into a fixed format, such as who bought what from whom and for what price. Since the

```
TERRORIST INCIDENT
    DATE                        date
    LOCATION                    city/state/country
    TYPE                        e.g., bombing
    STAGE of EXECUTION          e.g., accomplished, planned
    INSTRUMENT                  e.g., bomb, gun
    PERPETRATOR NAME            e.g., "FMLN"
    PHYSICAL TARGET             e.g., car, house
    HUMAN TARGET                e.g., president
    NATIONALITY TARGET          e.g., San Salvador
    EFFECT                      e.g., no injury
```

Figure 11.5 A simplified template for summarizing terrorist attacks

system is not required to understand anything in the text except when it concerns this specific information, techniques that extract information based on local information can be used. Such techniques, while limited to the specific task, often produce a more successful system than one based on general-purpose techniques, where each sentence would have to be completely parsed and interpreted before information can be extracted. This section explores some of these techniques.

The basic idea with such limited domain systems is that you can specify simple patterns that indicate key pieces of information in the domain. These patterns reliably indicate information that can be used to fill in templates that represent the task. In the stock transaction domain, for example, the preposition *to* usually indicates the recipient of the stock. In a different application you would find a different interpretation. In an airline schedule query domain, for example, the preposition *to* usually indicates the destination of the flight.

The task is typically defined as follows: The domain is specified as a set of **templates**, one for each possible class of input. In a domain where the system must generate summaries of articles reporting terrorist attacks in South America, the information desired might be summarized in a template such as that shown in Figure 11.5. The basic idea is to define patterns on the input that identify the different slots in the template. For instance, we might have a pattern such as

> take <HUMAN> hostage $\rightarrow$
>   (TERRORIST-INCIDENT HUMAN-TARGET 1)

which indicates that any sentence containing the sequence consisting of the verb *take* followed by a phrase that describes a human, followed by the word *hostage,* indicates the value of the HUMAN-TARGET slot in a TERRORIST-INCIDENT template.

To make this approach viable, the input must be parsed at least to the extent of identifying noun phrases (for example, a noun phrase that could match

<HUMAN> in our pattern) and producing canonical forms for words (so that all forms of *take* would match in our pattern). The partial parsing techniques described in Chapter 6 can be used here to good effect.

Of course, other patterns may match other parts of the input and suggest other values for slots in the templates. Once all the possible patterns have been matched, the final stage of the analysis would merge the partial templates. The rest of this section explores each component of this approach in more detail.

Consider first the partial parsing. If we are introducing a parser to find a partial parse of the sentence, why not use a full parser and obtain as much information as possible? There are several reasons why this might not be a good idea in these applications. First, a full parser would be computationally very expensive, especially in the text-understanding task where sentences are typically 30 words or longer, and the system needs to process millions of words a day. Second, it is not currently possible to construct a complete grammar for realistic domains, so many sentences will be unparsable. In addition, even if the sentence is parsable, it will likely be ambiguous between many different interpretations.

The partial parser takes advantage of the fact that certain parts of sentences can be parsed fairly reliably. Thus the grammar only handles these parts, and the rest of the sentence remains unanalyzed until the pattern-matching stage. As mentioned in Chapter 6, two major structures can be reasonably detected and parsed: the **verb group**, which consists of those words starting with the first auxiliary verb to the head verb, including adverbial modifiers; and the **noun group**, which consists of the beginning of noun phrases from the initial word up to the head word, including prenominal modifiers but not noun complements. In addition, the parser can reliably identify function words such as prepositions, particles, and conjunctions, and a few other important classes such as proper names, which are often indicated by capitalization. To support pattern matching based on semantic categories, the parser needs to compute the semantic type of the phrases it produces. These are typically taken from features on the head word. Grammars 11.6 and 11.7 give simple grammars for the verb groups and noun groups that compute a feature **TYPE** that is used in the pattern matching. Figure 11.8 gives a small lexicon for use in the examples.

Given these grammars, the partial parsing algorithm described in Chapter 6 could find all possible noun groups and verb groups, filtering out NG and VG constituents that are completely enclosed within a larger constituent of the same type. Words that are unknown or otherwise unanalyzable are ignored. Figure 11.9 shows all the constituents produced for the sentence

> Guerrillas attacked Merino's home in San Salvador five days ago with explosives.

The next stage of analysis uses the semantic patterns on the chart. The simplest form of pattern consists of a sequence of features, typically the TYPE feature, that may match anywhere in the input. If it matches, it produces a fragment of a template.

1. (VG **TYPE** ?typ **LEX** ?l) →
   (VG1 **VFORM** {pres past} **TYPE** ?typ **LEX** ?l)
2. (VG **TYPE** ?typ **LEX** (?l1 ?l2)) →
   (*MODAL* **LEX** *?l1*) (VG1 **VFORM** base **TYPE** ?typ **LEX** ?l2)
3. (VG1 **TYPE** ?typ **LEX** (?l1 ?l2)) →
   (ADV **LEX** ?l1)
   (*VG1* **TYPE** *?typ* **LEX** *?l2*)
4. (VG1 **TYPE** ?typ **LEX** (?l1 ?l2)) →
   (*AUX* **ROOT** *have* **LEX** *?l1*)
   (VG1 **VFORM** pastprt **TYPE** ?typ **LEX** ?l2)
5. (VG1 **TYPE** ?typ **LEX** (?l1 ?l2)) →
   (*AUX* **ROOT** *be* **LEX** *?l1*)
   (VG1 **VFORM** {pastprt ing} **TYPE** ?typ **LEX** ?l1)
6. (VG1 **TYPE** ?typ **LEX** ?l) → (*V* **TYPE** *?typ* **LEX** *?l*)

Head features for VG,VG1: VFORM

Grammar 11.6   A simple grammar for verb groups

7. (NG **LEX** ?l) → (PRO **LEX** ?l)
8. (NG **LEX** ?l) → (N **TYPE** {TIME LOC} **LEX** ?l)
9. (NG **LEX** ?l) → (N **AGR** 3p **LEX** ?l)
10. (NG **LEX** (?l1 ?l2)) → (DETP **AGR** ?a **LEX** ?l) (N **AGR** ?a **LEX** ?l)
11. (NG **LEX** (?l1 ?l2 ?l3)) →
    (DETP **AGR** ?a **LEX** ?l) (ADJP **LEX** ?l) (N **AGR** ?a **LEX** ?l)
12. (NG **LEX** ?l) → (NAMEP **LEX** ?l)
13. (NG **LEX** ?l) → (DATEP **LEX** ?l)
14. (DETP **LEX** ?l) → (ART **LEX** ?l)
15. (DETP **LEX** (?l 's)) → (NG **LEX** ?l) 's
16. ADJP → ADJ
17. ADJP → (V **VFORM** pastprt **SUBCAT** _np)
18. (NAMEP **LEX** ?l) → (NAME **LEX** ?l)
19. (NAMEP **LEX** (?l1 ?l2)) → (N **TITLE** + **LEX** ?l1) (NAMEP **LEX** ?l2)
20. (DATE **LEX** (BEFORE-NOW ?l1 ?l2)) →
    (NUMB **LEX** ?l1) (DATEUNIT **LEX** ?l2) AGO

Head features for (NG LEX ?L): TYPE, LEX
Head features for NAMEP: TYPE

Grammar 11.7   A simple grammar for noun groups and names

ago	(AGO)
attacked	(V **VFORM** past **TYPE** attack)
days	(DATEUNIT **LEX** days)
explosives	(N **AGR** 3p **TYPE** WEAPON **LEX** explosives)
five	(NUMB **LEX** 5)
Guerrillas	(N **AGR** 3p **TYPE** HUMAN-GROUP **LEX** Guerrillas)
home	(N **AGR** 3s **TYPE** LOC **LEX** home)
in	(P **TYPE** IN)
Merino	(NAME **TYPE** person **LEX** Merino)
San-Salvador	(NAME **TYPE** LOC **LEX** San-Salvador)
with	(P **TYPE** WITH)

Figure 11.8   A sample lexicon

(NG **TYPE** HUMAN-GROUP **LEX** Guerrillas)
(VG **TYPE** ATTACK **VFORM** past **LEX** attacked)
(NG **TYPE** LOC **LEX** (Merino home))
(P **TYPE** IN)
(NG **TYPE** LOC **LEX** San-Salvador)
(NG **TYPE** DATE **LEX** (BEFORE-NOW 5 days))
(P **TYPE** WITH)
(NG **TYPE** WEAPON **LEX** explosives)

Figure 11.9   The constituents found by the partial parser

For example, the pattern

<IN> <LOC> → (LOCATION 2)

would match the input anywhere a constituent of type IN is followed by a constituent of type LOC. If found, the input that was analyzed as the LOC constituent is used as the value of the LOCATION slot in the template. The four patterns required to analyze the example sentence are shown in Figure 11.10. These patterns would match against the chart to produce the following partial templates:

(INCIDENT ATTACK
        PERP "Guerrillas"
        TARGET "Merino's home")
(LOCATION "San Salvador")
(DATE "five days ago")
(INSTRUMENT "explosives")

In this case there are no conflicting partial templates, so the final analysis would be a template that includes all the information specified in the partial templates.

```
P1   <HUMAN> <ATTACK> <LOC>        →    (INCIDENT ATTACK
                                          PERP 1
                                          TARGET 2)
P2   <IN> <LOC>                    →    (LOCATION 2)
P3   <DATE>                        →    (DATE 1)
P4   <WITH> <WEAPON>               →    (INSTRUMENT 2)
```

Figure 11.10   A few sample patterns

Of course, sentences are not always this simple to analyze. As domains become more complicated, the patterns must be more selective. For instance, if the system also has to handle articles about weapons trading, then the pattern <WITH> <WEAPON> might not always refer to the instrument of an attack but might refer to the cargo of a shipment, as in *A truck loaded with explosives was stopped at the border.* To handle such cases, we would need more complex patterns that include the verb in the analysis. For instance, we could allow patterns to skip over constituents using rules like

<ATTACK> ... <WITH> <WEAPON> → (INSTRUMENT 3)

which would match any sentence with a verb of type attack, followed sometime later by the prepositional phrase. Then, another pattern such as

<CONVEYER> <LOAD, pastprt> <WITH> <WEAPON> →
   (CARRIER 1 CARGO 4)

would handle the other sense. Note that other features are allowed in patterns in addition to type restrictions. For example, you would not want the same pattern to match the sentences *The guerrillas were attacked by the police* and *The guerrillas attacked the police.* As patterns become more complex, they also can start to make distinctions between information in relative clauses and information in the main clause, since each may describe separate incidents. For example, the sentence *The weapons, which were smuggled in by the guerrillas, were destroyed yesterday* should be analyzed to produce two incidents rather than one combined incident in which the guerrillas both smuggled in and destroyed the weapons. Some systems allow patterns to be specified as arbitrary finite state machines, giving significant power to the programmer to handle such complications. Once this step is made, the system looks quite similar to the semantic grammar approach except that it is operating from preparsed constituents.

Of course, a practical system would have to do additional processing rather than simply filling in the slots with the words. For instance, it might reason about dates, and using the date of the article, calculate exactly what day the phrase *five days ago* refers to. In addition, it might construct richer semantic representations of noun phrases while parsing, and these analyses might be used as the values of

BOX 11.1 Evaluating Message-Understanding Systems

As mentioned at the beginning of this section, one of the principal applications of pattern-based techniques is information extraction from text, where the system has to process large quantities of text (say the AP news wire) and extract templates for any articles that deal with a specific topic, such as stock transactions.

Systems have been evaluated on this task and reported on in a series of annual conferences (the MUC conferences). The systems tested use different combinations of pattern-matching and general-purpose techniques to produce the analyses of the articles. Such systems can be evaluated on several dimensions, including

- system recall—how many articles on the topic it identifies and how much of the template it can fill in
- system precision—how often it produces an incorrect template or an incorrect entry in a template
- system efficiency—how long it takes to process a set of articles

In the 1993 evaluation the systems had 1500 texts to train on, all annotated with a template indicating the best answer. They were then tested on 100 messages not previously seen by the systems. The best systems obtained about 62 percent recall with 53 percent precision. The pattern-based systems are considerably more efficient than the general-purpose systems, being able to process thousands of words per minute. For more information on MUC evaluations, see Chincor et al. (1993).

the slots in the templates. You could also use these same techniques to build logical forms for sentences if templates are organized around verbs and their thematic roles, rather than around incidents.

Systems based on these techniques tend to be robust in that they produce some interpretation for nearly any input. On the other hand, their analyses can be fairly superficial and prone to error. Given the state of research, however, such techniques will probably play a large role in practical systems for the foreseeable future. The big research question to be answered is what happens as the problems scale up. What if information needs to be extracted on a broad range of topics, or if more detailed summaries of the content are required that are not easily expressed as simple templates?

Some systems attempt to gain the best of both worlds: They first use a full parser and semantic interpreter, and only if that fails they use pattern-matching techniques to extract what information they can from the sentence. This has the advantage of handling some sentences in detail but remaining robust when the full parse fails. The disadvantage involves computational efficiency. If you must process millions of sentences a day, partial parsing and template matching may be the only viable techniques.

BOOK.1
    <ANIMATE> "book" → (RESERVING * [AGENT 1])
BOOK.2
    <RESERVING> <TRANSPORT> → 1 ∧ (RESERVING * [THEME 2])
BOOK.3
    <RESERVING> <ANIMATE> → 1 ∧ (RESERVING * [BENEFICIARY 2])
BOOK.4
    <RESERVING> "for" <ANIMATE> → 1 ∧ (RESERVING * [BENEFICIARY 2])
S.end
    <ANYTHING> "." → pop

Figure 11.11   Sample lexicon

11.4 Semantically Driven Parsing Techniques

The last section used a limited syntactic preprocessor to prepare the input for semantic interpretation. It is also possible to eliminate the syntactic processing stage altogether, except for basic morphological analysis, and do everything using semantically driven patterns. This section briefly describes such a technique.

In such systems the grammatical and semantic information is stored in the lexicon entries for the words. In particular, the lexicon will contain essential information such as the different senses possible for the word, including case-frame information for verbs and adjectives, and a specification of a procedure for disambiguating the word and integrating it into larger semantic structures by combining it with other words. Here you will consider a system where this information is stored as a set of pattern-action rules operating on a buffer similar to the deterministic parser described in Chapter 6. The buffer contains the input constituents and is updated by the pattern-action rules. Whenever you enter a new word, the rules in that word's lexicon entry are made active. For example, the rules associated with the word *booked* might be those shown in Figure 11.11. Each rule contains a pattern that tests for semantic categories and individual words in the buffer. When a pattern matches, the buffer elements involved in the match are removed and replaced by the structures specified in the action part. In addition, the action part of the rule may activate and deactivate additional rules. For example, rule BOOK.1 in Figure 11.11 will match a buffer with an entry of type ANIMATE followed by a buffer containing the word *book,* and it will replace these two buffers with an entry of form (RESERVING * [AGENT 1]), where * is instantiated to a new discourse variable. As in the last section, numbers in the interpretation rules are used to refer to the buffer entries that matched the pattern. Thus 1 refers to the value of the first buffer involved in the match.

The operator ($\wedge$) is used to construct a new interpretation by merging two partial descriptions.

Consider how the sentence *John booked me a flight to Chicago* is interpreted using the preceding rules. For the moment, assume that all NPs have been preprocessed before this parse commences. The parser starts with the single rule S.end active (which checks for the end of the sentence) and with the first two buffers filled with the terms (NAME **j1** HUMAN "John") and *booked,* respectively. The rules for *booked* are made active, and BOOK.1 succeeds. This replaces the first two buffers with the value

(RESERVING **r1** [AGENT (NAME **j1** "John")])

The next buffer is filled with the structure (PRO **m1** HUMAN me). This time, rule BOOK.3 succeeds. Its action merges a new structure with the value of the first buffer, producing the following structure as the new value of buffer 1:

(RESERVING **r1** [AGENT (NAME **j1** "John")]
[BENEFICIARY (PRO **m1** ME1)])

The next input is the analysis of the noun phrase *a flight to Chicago,* <INDEF1 **f1** FLIGHT (TO-LOC **f1** (NAME **c1** "Chicago"))>. The rule BOOK.2 matches, and the result is again merged with the first buffer, producing the following analysis:

(RESERVING **r1** [AGENT (NAME **j1** HUMAN "John")]
[BENEFICIARY (PRO **m1** HUMAN "me")]
[THEME <INDEF1 **f1** FLIGHT
(TO-LOC **f1** (NAME **c1** "Chicago"))>])

When the final period is read in, rule S.end fires and signals the completion of the parse with the preceding analysis.

To extend this interpreter to handle the analysis of noun phrases, you need to introduce a mechanism similar to the attention-shifting mechanism in the deterministic parser. In particular, the rule for *a* is

ART.1 "a" $\rightarrow$ INDEF1

In the preceding example, if the noun phrase *a flight to Chicago* had not been preprocessed, the parser would have reached the following position:

Buffer 1: (RESERVING **r1** [AGENT (NAME **j1** "John")]
[BENEFICIARY (PRO **m1** ME1)])
Buffer 2: *a*

None of the currently active rules (BOOK.2, BOOK.4, and ART.1) would match this configuration. However, rule ART.1 could match if patterns are allowed to start matching at positions other than the first. Such matches are allowed and create an attention shift. The rules that were active are temporarily removed from the active list, and the parse continues as though buffer 2 were the first buffer. The parser is now in a position to use the rules for *flight, to,* and

ART.1	"a" → INDEF1 (activate rules NP.end1 and NP.end2)
FLIGHT.1	<DET> "flight" → <1* (FLIGHT *)>
FLIGHT.2	<FLIGHT> "to" <LOC> → <?a ?f (FLIGHT ?f [TO-LOC 3])>
MAN.1	<DET> "man" → <1 * (MAN *)>
CHICAGO.1	"Chicago" → (NAME **c1** "Chicago")
ME.1	"me" → (PRO * HUMAN "me")
NP.end1	"." → pop (a period signals the end of an NP)
NP.end2	<VERB> → pop (a verb signals the end of the subject NP)

Figure 11.12 Some rules for noun phrase analysis

Chicago shown in Figure 11.12 to construct the NP analysis. When the NP is completed, the original state of the parser is restored by a new action called **pop**.

Trace the parse continuing from the point shown earlier where the word *a* enters the second buffer. Rule ART.1 fires and an attention shift is made, result-ing in rules BOOK.2 and BOOK.4 being deactivated temporarily, and buffer 2 is set up as the first buffer for matching. When you enter the word *flight,* you have the following situation:

Buffer 1:   (RESERVING **r1** [AGENT (NAME **j1** "John")]
                                    [BENEFICIARY (PRO **m1** ME1)])
Buffer 2:   INDEF1   **patterns start matching here**
Buffer 3:   *flight*

The active rules are FLIGHT.1 and FLIGHT.2. FLIGHT.1 matches and replaces the contents of buffer 3 with <INDEF1 **f1** FLIGHT). Next the word *to* is entered into buffer 4. No patterns match, however. Next *Chicago* is entered and rule CHICAGO.1 fires, immediately replacing the word with the term (NAME **c1** "Chicago"). Now the buffer looks as follows:

Buffer 1:   (RESERVING **r1** [AGENT (NAME **j1** "John")]
                                    [BENEFICIARY (PRO **m1** ME1)])
Buffer 2:   <INDEF1 **f1** (FLIGHT **f1**)>   **patterns start matching here**
Buffer 3:   *to*
Buffer 4:   (NAME **c1** "Chicago")

Rule FLIGHT.2 matches and replaces buffer 2 with the value <INDEF1 **f1** (FLIGHT **f1** [TO-LOC (NAME **c1** "Chicago")])>. Next a period is entered into buffer 3, and rule NP.end1 fires and executes a pop, resetting the parser to the state before the NP was begun. Rules BOOK.2 and BOOK.4 are reactivated and the parse continues as shown earlier.

While parsers can be built quickly in such a framework to handle some specific set of sentences, problems arise in viewing these systems as a general model of parsing. Since all the rules are indexed by individual words, it is difficult to capture linguistic generalizations in a convenient way. For example, rule BOOK.1 identifies the first noun phrase found as the AGENT of the action RESERVING, one sense of *booked*. But this seems to be an instance of a general rule that applies for all action verbs. When the rules are accessed solely through lexical entries, however, you have no choice but to specify such a rule with each action verb. Thus the extensive grammars can be cumbersome to construct.

More importantly, these systems can use only local syntactic information, because the only state they maintain consists of the current case-frame structure being specified and the current input. Thus, to disambiguate a word, you can at best inspect a word or so before it and a few words after. In practice, as these rules become more complex, they apply to fewer and fewer situations, and more equally complex rules need to be added to handle simple syntactic variants. For example, the definition of the verb *booked* earlier considered only its use as the main verb of a sentence in the simple past. In fact, *booked* is also a past participle and thus can be used in a passive sentence and can introduce a relative clause, as in *The flight booked by the travel agent leaves at three.* Work aimed at remedying these deficiencies often reinstates a syntactic component that can be used to aid the interpretation in complex sentences. You can maintain syntactic context by running a syntactic parser in tandem with this interpreter. The actions of the parser, however, will be suggested by the semantic analyzer. The syntactic parser can simply return whether the syntactic operation identified by the semantic analyzer is a possible next move or not. If it isn't, the semantic interpreter attempts to find a different analysis.

It is not clear, however, whether the semantic analyzer can handle complex sentences involving movement in a clean way. When the syntactic analyzer is controlling the processing, the syntactic component can be used to eliminate these complexities before the semantic analyzer is invoked. With the control scheme suggested here, the semantic analyzer itself would have to be able to handle the complexities, and only then would it have the analysis verified by the syntactic component.

Summary

There are many different strategies for combining syntactic and semantic information beyond the rule-by-rule approach discussed in Chapter 9. These approaches generally use pattern-matching techniques to semantically interpret sentences, and differ on how much explicit syntactic processing is done. One approach is to use a full syntactic processing to compute an intermediate representation between syntax and semantics called the grammatical form. This is then interpreted by a separate semantic interpretation process. Another approach is to use a syntactic preprocessor that produces a partial analysis of the sentence and then perform semantic interpretation on that output. Yet another approach dispenses with any syntactic processing altogether and works by directly matching

---

BOX 11.2 Conceptual Analysis: A Semantically Driven Parser

Many semantically driven parsers have been developed based on work by the Yale natural language understanding group. The analyzer described in Birnbaum and Selfridge (1981) is probably the best reference for an introduction to the approach. The analyzer is driven by a case-based representation called **conceptual dependency**. The key idea is that certain words, especially verbs, identify meaning structures that have cases, and the parser's main job is to identify these words and use the rest of the sentence to fill in the values of these cases. While the details of the parser are different in style from the semantically driven parser described in this section, the type of operations performed are similar. The system is organized as a set of pattern-action rules called **requests** that are associated with lexical items. When a word is read, its requests become active. In general, a request can test for two types of information: It can check for a particular word or phrase in the input, or it can check for certain semantic properties on the structures in the buffer, which is called the C-LIST. The actions allowed include the actions implicit in our presentation. In particular, they may add a new item to the C-LIST, fill in a slot in some structure on the C-LIST (a function performed by merging structures), and activate or deactivate other requests.

---

semantic patterns to the input. A slightly different approach uses a grammar specified directly in terms of semantic constructs, yielding a semantic grammar.

There are advantages to each of these approaches. Generally, the less syntax used, the more domain-specific the system is. This allows you to construct a robust system relatively quickly, but many subtleties may be lost in the interpretation of the sentence. In addition, such systems typically do not generalize well to new domains. In some applications, however, the domain-dependent pattern-matching approach may be the only way to attain reasonable performance for the foreseeable future.

Related Work and Further Readings

The RUS system (Bobrow and Webber, 1980) describes an ATN-based grammar that constructs grammatical relations. It allows actions on the arcs that invoke a semantic interpreter that incrementally constructs a case-frame based semantic representation of the sentence. The semantic interpreter may accept or reject various arcs, thus affecting the behavior of the syntactic parse. Woods (1980) provides a more formal analysis of such interleaved parsers using a formalism called **cascaded ATN grammars**. Another ATN-based system with interleaved semantic processing is described in detail in Ritchie (1980).

Hirst (1987) is a good example of an approach that performs semantic interpretation on a representation based on grammatical relations. It compositionally interprets grammatical relations into a frame-based representation. Another good example is the KERNEL system (Palmer et al., 1993). A linguistic treatment of grammatical relations is lexical functional grammar (Kaplan and Bresnan, 1982). In LFG the syntactic rules use features for grammatical relations, which are then used for semantic interpretation in a rule-by-rule fashion.

Semantic grammars were proposed in the 1970s as a technique to build a fairly robust system that operates in a limited domain. The technique was first used in the SOPHIE system (Brown and Burton, 1975), a tutorial system for debugging electronic circuits. The grammar had terminal types such as REQUEST, TRANSISTOR, JUNCTION/TYPE, and so on. Each rule was associated with a function that would produce LISP code that would perform the appropriate operation. The LIFER system (Hendrix et al., 1978) applied the same techniques to database query applications, constructing a different grammar for each database application using the concepts relevant to that database.

One of the earliest uses of partial understanding techniques for text summarization was the FRUMP system (DeJong, 1982). A considerable literature has developed in the last few years as a result of a focus on message-understanding applications. The specific techniques described in Section 11.3 are based on the FASTUS system (Appelt et al., 1993). This system uses a series of finite state machines to recognize noun and verb groups and to implement the patterns for extracting information. Another good example is the SCISOR system (Jacobs and Rau, 1990).

Wilks (1975) provides a good example of template-driven semantic interpretation with minimal syntactic processing. The semantic information in this system consists of a set of semantic templates defining the possible semantic relationships in the system and a semantic formula for each lexical entry. The essential operation in this system is matching these templates to a representation of the sentence where the basic phrase structure has been extracted. The semantically driven parser in Section 11.4 is modeled after the conceptual analyzer of Birnbaum and Selfridge (1981) (see Box 11.2), which itself is a descendant of the earlier parsers (Schank, 1975; Riesbeck and Schank, 1978). An interesting semantically driven parser that drives a syntactic component to verify the analysis is described by Lytinen (1986).

Exercises for Chapter 11

1. (*easy*) Show the logical form generated from the grammatical dependency representation of the sentence *A ticket was bought at the theater,* using the data shown in Figures 11.1, 11.2, and 11.3.

2. (*easy*) Draw the parse tree produced by the semantic grammar described in Section 11.2 for the query *When does the 8 p.m. train from Boston arrive in Chicago?* Show the additional rules that you have to add to the grammar so that it will accept this sentence.

3. (*medium*) Extend the treatment based on grammatical relations described in Section 11.1 so that it handles the beneficiary case, as in

> Jack bought me a ticket.
> Jack bought a ticket for me.

Give the parser output for each sentence as well as the final logical form produced by your patterns.

4. (*medium*) Complete the semantic grammar sketched in Section 11.2 so that it handles all of the example noun phrases found in that section. Give four other noun phrases (two well-formed and two ill-formed) that are structurally different that your grammar also handles correctly. Design a set of features that can duplicate the restrictions found in your semantic grammar while retaining a purely syntactic grammar. Give a syntactic grammar using these features that is equivalent to your semantic grammar. Which grammar would be easier to construct from scratch for a new domain? Which grammar would be easier to adapt to a new domain?

5. (*medium*) Extend Grammars 11.6 and 11.7 and give a set of pattern-based interpretation rules that can extract the necessary information from each of the following sentences in the terrorist application. You may assume that the templates given in Figure 11.5 specify all the information required for the application. For each, specify the sequence of constituents produced by your grammar in a format similar to that in Figure 11.9. Give the output constructed by your patterns for each of the sentences. Treat each sentence as a separate input, and not as part of the same paragraph.

a Guerrillas used explosives to attack San Salvador yesterday.
b. No one was injured when the guerrillas bombed the government buildings.
c. In San Salvador several terrorists were thwarted in their plan to bomb the home of the president.

Discuss at least one difficult problem that arose in defining these patterns, and describe the strengths and limitations of your solution.

6. (*medium*) Implement the pattern-matching component of a message-understanding system that can interpret sentences such as those in Exercise 5, given an input sequence of preparsed constituents. Test your system on the sentences in Exercise 5 plus three other sentences of your own choosing that demonstrate the scope of your implementation.

7. (*medium*) Design a set of pattern-action rules as described in Section 11.4 that perform the same task as described in Exercise 5 but do not use any syntactic preprocessing. What are the most difficult issues that need to be addressed that are easier with a syntactic preprocessor? Does the approach based on direct semantic interpretation have any advantages?

CHAPTER

Scoping and the Interpretation of Noun Phrases

12.1 Scoping Phenomena

12.2 Definite Descriptions and Scoping

12.3 A Method for Scoping While Parsing

12.4 Co-Reference and Binding Constraints

12.5 Adjective Phrases

12.6 Relational Nouns and Nominalizations

12.7 Other Problems in Semantics

This chapter considers some additional issues in semantic interpretation, mostly those that affect the interpretation of noun phrases. In particular, it considers issues in the scoping of quantifiers and operators, the generation of co-reference constraints based on the structure of the sentence, and assorted issues in interpretation of adjective phrases and other modifiers in noun phrases.

Section 12.1 examines the issues that affect quantifier scoping decisions. Section 12.2 extends this discussion further by examining properties of definite descriptions, which sometimes act like quantified phrases. Section 12.3 then presents a technique for computing likely scope ordering while parsing. Section 12.4 introduces the general issues that affect co-reference constraints between pronouns and other referring noun phrases, and describes a technique for generating such constraints while parsing. Section 12.5 addresses issues in semantically interpreting adjective phrases and other noun modifiers, and Section 12.6 considers special classes of noun phrases involving relational nouns and nominalizations. Finally, Section 12.7 briefly describes some other important issues which have not yet been considered.

12.1 Scoping Phenomena

This section discusses issues that affect scoping in language. Scope ambiguity occurs with quantifiers, logical operators, modal operators, and adverbials in sentences. Speaking loosely, we will refer to each construct that exhibits scoping behavior as an operator. Determining the scope of quantifiers and operators in the logical form is a very complex problem that not only involves using lexical, syntactic, and semantic information but also is strongly influenced by context. There are, however, some constraints and preferences for interpretations that arise without considering context.

Scoping is a pervasive problem in semantic interpretation. Its presence can be illustrated by a series of sentences that are ambiguous due to scope phenomena. Any sentence that contains two or more quantifiers will likely be ambiguous. For example,

A dog entered with every man.

may describe at least three different situations: (1) There are many dogs, each accompanied by a man; (2) a single dog walked in when all the men walked in as a group; and (3) a single dog entered many times, each time with a different man. These readings arise from the relative scoping of the two quantifiers and the implicit existential quantifier associated with the event. Ambiguity also arises from the scoping of logical operators and quantifiers, as in

We didn't see every dog.

which may assert that we didn't see any dog, that is,

(EVERY **d1** : (DOG **d1**) (NOT (SEE1 (PRO **w1** WE1) **d1**))) or that there was at least one dog we didn't see, that is,

(NOT (EVERY : **d1** (DOG **d1**) (SEE1 (PRO **w1** WE1) **d1**)))

An example of an ambiguity with a logical connective is

Everyone thought that Fido or Fifi would win.

which has one reading where either everyone thought Fido would win or everyone thought Fifi would win, and another reading where each person thought that either Fido or Fifi might win. The difference here is the scoping between the universal quantifier and the disjunction.

Ambiguities also arise with tense operators and adverbials, as in

He will feed the hungriest dog tomorrow.

in which it may be that the dog is hungriest now and will be fed later (possibly when it is not hungry), or that the dog will be the hungriest tomorrow when it is fed (and possibly is not hungry now). The sentence

A fat dog always loses the race.

displays a scope ambiguity on the adverbial. It may be a statement that the loser is always a fat dog or that there is a particular fat dog so slow that it loses every race.

Classifying Quantifiers

Noun phrases serve many different functions in language, and it is important to distinguish these functions when considering scoping issues. There are at least three major classes to consider. Those involving **definite** reference indicate that the hearer should in principle be able to identify the object or set. Definite reference occurs with determiners such as *the,* as in *the dog* (an individual) or *the fat men* (a specific set), and with possessive determiners such as *their ideas* or *John's book.* The second class of quantifiers are **existential** or **indefinite**, and they typically introduce new individuals or sets into the discourse. Typical examples of indefinite reference involve determiners such as *a* in *a good book* and indefinite sets constructed with quantifiers such as *some* and *several.* One test for existential quantifiers is whether they can appear in sentences of the form

There are Q men who like golf.

which allows Q to be any existential (plural) quantifier, such as *some, many, a few, several, two, seven, no,* and so on. Note that quantifiers such as *all, each, every,* and *most* would be ill-formed in this context. Such quantifiers form the third class, the **universal** quantifiers, which involve properties of all, or nearly all, members of a set.

Another major distinction in those quantifiers that involve a set is the collective/distributive distinction. **Collective** interpretations treat the set as a unit, as in *The men met at the corner,* in which it is the set of men who met. It makes no sense to say that any individual man in this set met. **Distributive** interpretations range over the members of the set, as in *Each man bought a suit,* in which each man individually bought a suit, rather than them buying one suit as a group, which would be the likely interpretation of *The men bought a suit to give to Harry.* Some quantifiers only support a particular reading (for example, *each* must be distributive), but most are ambiguous as to the distributive/collective distinction. Consider the following four sentences that involve sets:

> Each man lifted the piano.
> Every man lifted the piano.
> All the men lifted the piano.
> The men lifted the piano.

The first sentence only has a distributive reading, in which each man lifted the piano individually. The last strongly prefers a collective reading, in which the set of men lifted the piano together. The other cases fall in between these two readings and might be interpreted either way.

This tendency toward a distributive or collective reading affects the possible scoping decisions, because other quantifiers may depend on a noun phrase only when it is in the distributive reading. For example, consider the sentence

> Each man lifted a piano.

There may be many different pianos that are referred to here, one for each man. We say that the noun phrase *a piano* depends on the noun phrase *each man,* or that *each man* takes wider scope than *a man,* drawing from the way quantifiers are scoped in first-order logic. The dependency is possible only when the wider scoped noun phrase is distributive. If the first noun phrase is collective, as in

> Together, the men lifted a piano.

then there is no dependence and the phrase refers to a single piano. Of course, many constructs are ambiguous, such as in

> A piano was lifted by each man.

which plausibly has a reading in which there are many pianos or a reading in which there is a single piano that is lifted many times. Note that in both cases the noun phrase *each man* is distributive. But the noun phrase *a piano* depends on it only in the first reading. In the second the piano remains the same, but *each* distributes across a set of lifting events (one by each man).

Making Scoping Decisions

The quantifier scoping problem is typically presented as the problem of finding a full scoping of the operators in a nested form as found in FOPC. Note, however, that such a full scoping form does not entail dependence of a variable on the

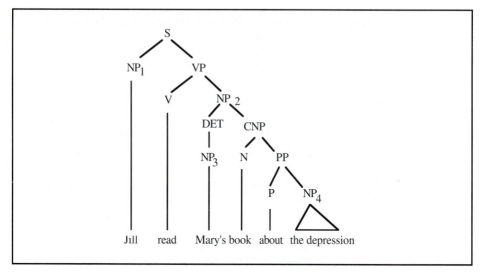

Figure 12.1 A parse tree for demonstrating local domains

variables that outscope it. For instance, a sequence of indefinite noun phrases, as in *a man lifted a piano,* has the same meaning no matter how it is scoped. It is an artifact of the syntax of FOPC that you are forced to pick an ordering. Other representations are possible in which only the dependencies that are necessary are indicated, and variables that are unordered remain independent of each other. Such representations have the advantage of not making a sentence look more ambiguous than it really is. For the sake of maintaining a simple presentation, however, we will assume in the rest of this section that the task of scoping is to construct a full ordering on the quantifiers.

To examine scoping phenomena more closely, it will be useful to define the **local domain** of a constituent. The local domain of a constituent C is the set of constituents contained in the closest S or NP that contains C. Consider the tree in Figure 12.1. The local domain defined by the top S constituent contains NP_1 and NP_2, while the local domain defined by constituent NP_2 contains NP_3 and NP_4. The S or NP constituent defining the domain is called the **dominating constituent** of the constituents it contains.

Two constituents are said to be **horizontally related** if they belong to the same local domain. Two constituents are said to be **vertically related** if the first is the dominating constituent of the local domain of the second. This terminology will be extended to quantifiers as well; that is, two quantifiers are horizontally related if the constituents that contain them are horizontally related.

Horizontal Scoping

One common approach to handling horizontal scoping is to compare each pair of operators and see if there is a pattern where one usually outscopes the other. This tendency is often expressed in terms of quantifier "strength," where the "stronger" quantifier usually outscopes the "weaker." Many researchers have suggested the following hierarchy of quantifier strength:

each > every > all, some, several, a

Of great importance in question answering, wh-terms can also be given a strength. Most question-answering systems place *wh* between *each* and *every,* as shown by the sentences:

Who saw every dog?
Who saw each dog?

The first sentence would be treated as asking for a single person who saw all the dogs; the second would be treated as asking for a list of people—one or more for each dog.

It turns out, however, that such uniform preference schemes are fairly inaccurate in many cases because they do not take into account the structural relationships between the quantifiers. For example, the preferences might change depending on which quantifier occurs as the subject. Consider these sentences:

Every man saw a dog.
A man saw every dog.

The preferred reading of the first sentence allows for a different dog to be seen by each man (that is, *every* outscopes *a*). The preferred reading of the second sentence, however, involves one man (that is, *a* outscopes *every*). Thus the position of quantifiers in the sentence also affects scoping preferences. The following general preferences for wide scope based on position have been suggested, although these preferences may not apply to particular quantifiers:

preposed constituents
> surface subjects
> postposed adverbials
> direct/indirect objects

Resolving Horizontal Scoping Ambiguity

Algorithms that generate fully scoped logical forms are often specified in terms of the operation of **pulling out** a quantifier from its unscoped form to its fully scoped form—a process that involves taking the quantified expression out of the formula, leaving the marker, and wrapping it around a proposition that originally contained the term. By changing the ordering in which quantifiers are pulled out, different scopings are generated. For example, given the unscoped form

(<PRES LOVES1> <EVERY **m1** MAN> <A **d1** DOG>)

you could generate the preferred reading by pulling out **d1** to produce

(A **d1** : (DOG **d1**) (<PRES LOVES1> <EVERY **m1** MAN> **d1**))

and then pulling out **m1** to produce

> (EVERY **m1** : (MAN1 **m1**)
> (A **d1** : (DOG **d1**) <PRES LOVES1> **l1 m1 d1**))

The tense operator could then be pulled out last, producing the fully scoped logical form

> (PRES (EVERY **m1** : (MAN1 **m1**)
> (A **d1** : (DOG1 **d1**) (LOVES1 **l1 m1 d1**))))

If, on the other hand, **m1** were pulled out first and **d1** pulled out next, you would obtain a different reading. The challenge is to develop an algorithm that uses the weights to select the best interpretation.

It will sometimes be easier to work with a different notation that concisely captures the ordering of the quantifiers. Specifically, we will use a list indicating the quantifier ordering that is attached to the unscoped logical form. Thus the scoping order in the fully scoped logical form would be written as [**m1 d1**].

There are many algorithms suggested in the literature that attempt to combine quantifier strength and syntactic role preferences in a heuristic way. For instance, you might first list the quantifiers in the order in which they appear in the sentence to obtain a default order $[V_1 ... V_n]$. Then variables are exchanged when a variable V_{i+1} has a stronger quantifier than the variable V_i. Such exchanges continue until no more exchanges can be made.

Vertical Scoping Relations

The scoping process becomes more complicated when you consider vertical relations. In particular, a quantifier in a nested constituent may be lifted vertically over its dominating operator and then need to be scoped with respect to the other quantifiers at its new level. Thus the vertical scoping algorithm may change the set of quantifiers that need to be scoped with the horizontal scoping algorithm. Whether or not a quantifier is lifted depends on the syntactic structure that leads to the vertical scoping relation. For example, the sentence

> Some man rewarded a boy who gave each dog a bone.

has two finite clauses, as seen in its logical form:

> (<PAST REWARDS1> **r1**
> <SOME **m1** MAN1>
> <A **b1** (& (BOY1 **b1**)
> (<PAST GIVES1> **g1 b1**
> <EACH **d1** DOG1> <A **b2** BONE1>))>)

Based on the syntactic structure, there are two local domains of interest: one containing **m1** and **b1**, and the other containing **d1** and **b2**. Furthermore, **d1** and **b2** are vertically related to the operator in their dominating constituent, **b1**.

Full relative clauses are often called **scope islands** because they tend to prohibit quantifiers from moving out of the clause. In this example, for instance, the most intuitive reading involves one boy, rather than a different boy for each dog. If this constraint always held, then such sentences could be scoped by running the horizontal algorithm twice, once to scope the relative clause and once to scope the main clause.

But relative clauses are not always scope islands, as seen in *The dogs that won each race are hungry,* which has a reading in which there are different dogs in each race (that is, *each* outscopes *the*). In this reading the embedded quantifier must be lifted out of its local domain into the next higher domain, where it is horizontally scoped with the quantifiers at that level. Specifically, ignoring tense for the moment, the unscoped logical form for the sentence is

(HUNGRY1 **h1** <THE **d1** (& ((PLUR DOG1) **d1**)
(RUNS-IN1 **r1 d1** <EACH **r2** RACE1>))>)

The top-level local domain just contains **d1**, and the local domain for the relative clause contains **r2**, which is also vertically related to **d1**. If the quantifier for **r2** is not lifted over the quantifier for **d1**, the most likely fully scoped interpretation is

(THE **d1** : (& ((PLUR DOG1) **d1**)
(EACH **r2** : (RACE1 **r2**) (RUNS-IN1 **r1 d1 r2**))
(HUNGRY **h1 d1**)))

If the quantifier is lifted, then it is horizontally scoped at the top level. In this case it would produce the interpretation

(EACH **r2** : (RACE1 **r2**)
(THE **d1** : (& ((PLUR DOG1) **d1**)
(RUNS-IN1 **r1 d1 r2**))
(HUNGRY1 **h1 d1**)))

Note that if a quantifier is lifted up to the next horizontal level, it must take wider scope than the quantifier that used to dominate it. Otherwise, an ill-formed expression would result. For instance, if the quantifier for **r2** were lifted over the quantifier for **d1** but then horizontally scoped narrower than **d1**, the result would be as follows:

??? (THE **d1** : (& ((PLUR DOG1) **d1**)
(RUNS-IN1 **r1 d1 r2**))
(EACH **r2** : (RACE1 **r2**)
(HUNGRY1 **m1 d1**)))

Note that an instance of the variable **r2** appears outside the scope of its quantifier, creating an uninterpretable expression.

So far, the local domains in the examples have been defined by S consti-tuents, namely the main sentence and relative clauses. Local domains are also defined by NPs, which becomes relevant when they have prepositional phrase modifiers. Consider the sentence

The man in every boat rows.

The unscoped logical form (ignoring tense) for this sentence would be

(ROWS1 **r1**
          <THE **m1** (& (MAN1 **m1**) (IN **m1** <EVERY **b1** BOAT1>))>)

There are two local domains, one just containing **m1** and the other just containing **b1**. Furthermore, **b1** is vertically related to **m1**. If the quantifier for **b1** is not lifted, it remains in the restriction of the definition description, and the final logical form would be

(THE **m1** : (&   (MAN1 **m1**)
            (EVERY **b1** : (BOAT1 **b1**) (IN **m1 b1**)))
    (ROWS1 **r1 m1**))

Here there is one man who somehow is in every boat. If the quantifier is lifted, then it must outscope the quantifier for **m1**, producing the logical form

(EVERY **b1** : (BOAT1 **b1**)
    (THE **m1** : (&   (MAN1 **m1**)
               (IN **m1 b1**))
       (ROWS1 **r1 m1**)))

In this interpretation, there may be different men, one in each boat. This seems to be the preferred reading for this sentence without considering context.

Different vertical embedding relationships have very different preferences with respect to lifting embedded quantifiers to the next higher level. The following ordering on embedding constructs has been suggested, based on the likelihood that embedded quantifiers will be vertically lifted:

possessives > PP modifiers > reduced relative clauses > relative clauses

To analyze vertical relations accurately, however, you have to examine each construct on a case-by-case basis and see how the different operators interact with it. Let's consider PP modification in more detail. When a distributive quantifier, such as *every,* is embedded in a PP modifier, the tendency to be lifted out is quite strong, as in

A man in every boat was singing.

which has a strong preference for the distributive reading in which there are many men singing. But if the embedded quantifier is not distributive, such as *a,* this preference may not hold, as in

Every man in a boat was singing.

which has a strong preference for *every man* to outscope *a boat;* that is, it's not the case that there is one boat in which every man is singing and another boat in which they are not. As with horizontal relations, you could collect data and use probability estimates to represent the tendency for different quantifiers to be lifted out of each of the different embedding constructs.

It is important to also remember that contextual effects can have a strong influence on the preferred interpretation. As a result, any algorithm based on purely structural preferences must be integrated with contextual interpretation. One technique is to generate possible orderings one at a time, starting with the most likely ordering based on structural properties. Only if the interpretation is contextually inappropriate would less likely interpretations be suggested. A more general approach would be to develop some technique to combine the structurally based probabilities with probabilities derived from contextual factors to produce an overall most likely interpretation.

12.2 Definite Descriptions and Scoping

Definite descriptions consist of noun phrases with the quantifier *the.* In some cases, these phrases act like quantified expressions, while in other cases they appear more like names or constructs that are immune to scoping considerations. For example, a sentence such as

The child entered with each dog.

doesn't seem to have a reading in which *each* outscopes *the.* In fact, to understand this sentence, you may need to interpret it in an iterative reading, in which there are many entering events but all involving the same child. There is a single child here, just as in sentences that involve proper names, such as

Jill entered with each dog.

which has no reading where there are many people named Jill. Thus *the* seems to take widest scope in horizontal scoping ambiguities without exception.

But definite descriptions do display scoping ambiguity in certain constructs, as in the sentences

The owner of every house showed us the plumbing.
In every house, the owner showed us the plumbing.

Both these sentences have preferred readings in which there is a different owner for every house. Often world knowledge forces the interpretation in which a quantifier outscopes *the,* as in *The kitchen in every house had a stove,* which only makes sense if there are many different kitchens, one in each house. Thus, with a few constructs, such as universals in PP modifiers and preposed adverbial modifiers, definite descriptions often depend on other quantified variables.

To handle such cases, definite noun phrases will be considered ambiguous between two uses. The first is the referential use, which requires that an object be found in context. The other treats *the* like an existential quantifier (with unique-ness constraints). To see these readings, consider a situation where Jack has a boss, Sam. The sentence *Jack has always been afraid of the boss* would have two interpretations. In the referential reading the sentence is asserting that Jack has always been afraid of Sam (who happens at the moment to be the boss). In the existential reading Jack has always been afraid of the boss, whoever the boss is. These interpretations differ in what they say about a time last year when Jack had a different boss, say Sue. With the referential reading Jack was afraid of Sam last year. With the existential reading he was afraid of Sue last year.

There are only a few cases where the appropriate interpretation can be obtained purely on syntactic and semantic grounds. These cases signal the exis-tential reading. For instance, whenever the definite noun phrase is within the scope of a universal, it should have an existential reading. Similarly, predicative uses, such as in *He seems the best for the job,* indicate the existential reading.

12.3 A Method for Scoping While Parsing

There are many different strategies for determining scoping. You could, for instance, leave the parser as it stands and write a new interpretation procedure that takes an unscoped logical form and produces a fully scoped logical form. Approaches that work directly from the logical form often do not consider the effects of different syntactic structures. Another approach would be to modify the way semantic interpretation is performed in the grammar and have the parser compute the possible (or likely) scoping as the sentence is parsed. This section looks at this second alternative and implements a simple scoping algorithm similar to that used in many database query applications.

The semantic analysis in the grammar is changed so that the quantifier structures and the SEM structure are stored in separate features. For example, whereas in the old method the SEM of a noun phrase such as *the woman* would be <THE **w1** (WOMAN1 **w1**)>, in the new approach a feature QS (for quan-tifiers) is set to <THE **w1** (WOMAN1 **w1**)> and the SEM is set to the discourse variable **w1**. The techniques for constructing SEM forms from subconstituents is exactly as before, and the only extension needed is to define how the QS feature is constructed. Once all the quantifiers in the same local domain have been gathered, they can be sorted and the fully scoped SEM form constructed. You could modify the parser to invoke the scoping algorithm each time an S or NP constituent is constructed. The method here, however, will leave greater flexibility to the grammar designer. A new binary feature SCOPEPOS is defined such that, whenever it is +, the parser invokes a procedure to sort the quantifiers. This procedure decides which quantifiers to lift to a higher horizontal context, and then sorts the remaining quantifiers and inserts them into the SEM.

For example, consider the question *When does each plane fly?* Initially, this question would be parsed to construct an unscoped representation of the form (ignoring tense operators for the moment):

(S **SCOPEPOS** +
   QS (<WH **t1** (TIME **t1**)> <EACH **p1** (PLANE1 **p1**)>)
   SEM (& (FLIES1 **f1 p1**) (AT-TIME **f1 t1**)))

Since this representation has the SCOPEPOS feature, the quantifier scoping algorithm is invoked. This top-level S requires no quantifiers to be lifted, and after sorting, one of the new constituents generated might be

(S **SCOPEPOS** –
   QS nil
   SEM (EACH **f1** : (PLANE1 **p1**)
           (WH **t1** : (TIME **t1**)
              (& (FLIES1 **f1 p1**) (AT-TIME **f1 t1**)))))

If multiple interpretations are possible, then multiple new S constituents could be constructed by the scoping procedure and added to the chart.

As another example, consider the treatment of relative clauses, as in the noun phrase *The flights that each man took*. The embedded sentence that is built as the relative clause might initially have the form

(S **SCOPEPOS** +
   QS (<EACH **m1** MAN1>)
   SEM (TAKES1 **t1 m1** x))

where x is the variable for the relative pronoun. If relative clauses are treated as absolute scope islands, then the only interpretation possible would insert the quantifier into the SEM, producing the constituent

(S **SCOPEPOS** –
   QS nil
   SEM (EACH **m1** : (MAN1 **m1**) (TAKES1 **t1 m1** x)))

If the quantifier is allowed to be lifted, then another constituent is also possible, namely

(S **SCOPEPOS** –
   QS (<EACH **m1** MAN1>)
   SEM (TAKES1 **t1 m1** x))

The same method can be used for scoping quantifiers in NP-dominated local domains. To treat scoping differently depending on the form of the modifier, new features are introduced to collect embedded quantifiers—those that arise in PP modifiers (the feature QSPP) and those that are lifted out of relative clauses (the feature QSREL). This allows different scoping strategies to be used for each case. Note that quantifiers that are not lifted out of an NP context are inserted around the restriction of the quantifier and not into the SEM, as is done for sentences.

For example, consider the NP constituent constructed for *the flights to each city* before scoping:

(NP **SCOPELOC** +
 QS <THE **f1** (& (FLIGHT1 **f1**) (DEST **f1 c1**))>
 QSPP <EACH1 **c1** CITY1>
 SEM f1)

If the quantifier EACH1 is not lifted, the new NP constituent would be

(NP **SCOPELOC** –
 QS <THE **f1** (& (FLIGHT1 **f1**)
                (EACH **c1** (CITY1 **c1**) (DEST **f1 c1**)))>
 SEM f1)

If it is lifted, then the new constituent would be

(NP **SCOPELOC** –
 QS (ORDERED <EACH **c1** CITY1>
                <THE **f1** (& (FLIGHT1 **f1**) (DEST **f1 c1**))>)
 SEM f1)

Note that the QS value contains an additional construct that specifies ordering constraints on constituents that are lifted. In this case EACH must outscope THE.

Unary operators, such as negation and tense, can be treated in the same way. The operator is placed in the QS feature and then assigned its place when the scoping algorithm is invoked. For example, the verb phrase *saw a dog* would be parsed as

(VP **QS** (<PAST> <A **d1** DOG1>)
 SEM (λ ag (SEES1 **s1** ag **d1**)))

These would be passed up to the S structure, which for the sentence *The man saw a dog* would be

(S **SCOPELOC** +
 QS (<THE **m1** MAN1> <PAST> <A **d1** DOG1>)
 SEM (SEES1 **s1 m1 d1**))

This could then be scoped in the normal fashion, inserting the PAST operator wherever the algorithm deems best.

To enable this approach to scoping operators, the lexical entries and morphological rules must be modified to set the QS register appropriately. For example, the rule for regular past-tense verbs would set the QS register, as in

(V **QS** <PAST> **SEM** ?semv) $\rightarrow$
 (V **SEM** ?semv **IRREG-PAST** –) +ED

An Example

Consider using this technique in a simple database query application. Quantifiers are used extensively in questions to databases, so the domain is a good choice as a test case. The preferences for horizontal ordering in S-dominated domains will be indicated using a weighting scheme. Each quantifier is assigned a particular weight that shows its tendency to take wide scope. All horizontally related quantifiers are then sorted according to these weights. The weights used will impose the ordering

tense operators > *the* > *each* > *wh* > other quantifiers > negation

Thus a query such as *When does each plane receive maintenance?* is interpreted as asking for a listing of the maintenance times for each plane individually, whereas *When does every plane receive maintenance?* is interpreted as asking for a time when all planes receive maintenance simultaneously. In a sentence, quantifiers that have the same weight are scoped in the order in which they appear. The tense operators are taken to have the widest scope, because sentences with tense operators with a narrow scope typically do not appear in a database query. The negation operator is taken to have the narrowest scope. This means a form such as

(S   **QS** (<WH **f1** (PLUR FLIGHT1)> <NOT> <A **m1** MEAL1>)
     SEM (SERVES1 **s1 f1 m1**))

will be resolved to the fully scoped form

(WH **f1** : ((PLUR FLIGHT1) **f1**)
     (A **m1** : (MEAL1 **m1**)
         (NOT (SERVES1   **s1 f1 m1**))))

The vertical relationships in NP-dominated domains are handled using simple strategies: All quantifiers within a PP modifier are scoped wider than the quantified phrase they modify, and all quantifiers in relative clauses remain within the clause except for the definite quantifier (that is, relative clauses are strong scope islands).

These heuristics are a little too simple for a real database query system but will serve to illustrate the techniques. They could easily be extended using the same framework.

Grammar 12.2 is a small grammar that can parse some example questions that involve horizontal relationships. You have seen variants of most of these rules before, in Chapter 9. The only real change is the addition of the QS features. Rule 1 is the standard S rule, except that the S is marked +SCOPELOC, so the scoping algorithm will be invoked on all the quantifiers gathered from the NP and the VP. Rule 2 handles questions that begin with wh-phrases such as *when* and *where*. Rule 3 handles inverted S forms needed in wh-questions. Rule 4 is the standard rule of transitive verbs, modified by adding the QS feature. Rule 5 handles noun phrases that start with a determiner. Note the use of the QSPP and

1. (S **SCOPELOC** + **INV** – **QS** (?qsnp ?qss) **SEM** (?semvp ?semnp)) →
   (NP **QS** ?qsnp **SEM** ?semnp) (*VP QS ?qsvp SEM ?semvp*)

2. (S **SCOPELOC** + **QS** (?qspp ?qss) **SEM** (& (?sempp ?v) ?sems)) →
   (PP **WH** Q **QS** ?qspp **SEM** ?sempp)
   (*S INV* + *VAR ?v QS ?qss SEM ?sems*)

3. (S **INV** + **QS** (?qsaux ?qsnp ?qsvp) **SEM** (?semaux (?semvp ?semnp))) →
   (*AUX QS ?qsaux SEM ?semaux*)
   (NP **WH** Q **QS** ?qsnp **SEM** ?semnp)
   (VP **QS** ?qss **SEM** ?semvp)

4. (VP **VAR** ?v **QS** (?qsv ?qs) **SEM** (1 a3 (?semv ?v a3 ?semnp))) →
   (*V[_np] QS ?qsv SEM ?semv*) (NP **QS** ?qs **SEM** ?semnp)

5. (NP **SCOPELOC** + **VAR** ?v **SEM** ?v
   QSPP ?qspp **QSREL** ?qsrel **QS** <?semdet ?v (?semcnp ?v)>) →
   (DET **SEM** ?semart)
   (*CNP QSPP ?qspp QSREL ?qsrel SEM ?semcnp*)

6. (CNP **SEM** ?semn) → (*N SEM ?semn*)

7. (PP **WH** Q **QS** ?qs **SEM** ?sem) → (*PP-WRD WH Q QS ?qs SEM ?sem*)

Head features for S, VP, NP, CNP: VAR

Grammar 12.2   A simple grammar with QS and SEM features

QSREL to store the embedded quantifier, and QS to store the quantifier for the dominating constituent (that is, the new NP). Rule 6 allows unmodified CNP structures, and rule 7 allows the PP-words such as *when* and *where* in questions.

Figure 12.3 shows the parse tree for *When does the flight leave each city?* This sentence contains one nontrivial local domain, which contains all the quantifiers and the tense operator. Note how the operators are passed up the tree to the S structure, where the scoping algorithm produces the fully scoped form.

Grammar 12.4 shows some additional rules that handle PP modification and relative clauses. As previously mentioned, quantifiers in prepositional phrase modifiers are always lifted, whereas quantifiers in relative clauses are never lifted. Rule 8 is the standard rule for predicative prepositional phrases augmented with the QS feature. Rule 9 handles PP modification of CNPs and sets the QSPP feature. Rule 10 handles relative clauses and sets the QSREL feature, while rule 11 handles the actual relative clause.

Using this grammar, the question *When does the flight to each city leave?* would produce the logical form

(EACH **c1** : (CITY1 **c1**)
   (THE **f1** : (& (FLIGHT1 **f1**) (DEST **f1 c1**))
      (WH **t1** : (TIME **t1**)
         (& (<PRES LEAVES1> **l1 f1 c1**) (AT-TIME **f1 t1**))))

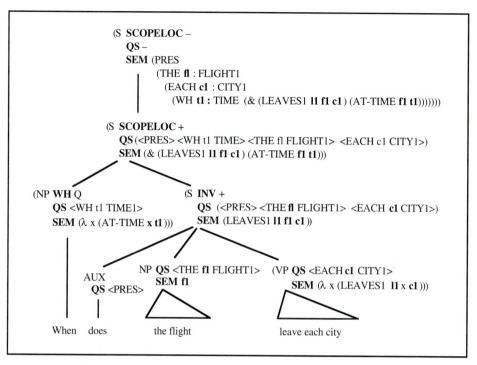

Figure 12.3 The parse tree for *When does the flight leave each city?*

8. (PP **PRED** + **QS** ?qs **SEM** (λ x (?semp x ?semnp)) →
   (*P SEM ?semp*) (NP **QS** ?qs **SEM** ?semnp)

9. (CNP **SEM** (λ n1 (& (?semcnp n1) (?sempp n1)))
          QSPP ?qspp **QS** ?qscnp **QSREL** ?qsrel) →
   (*CNP QS ?qscnp QSREL ?qsrel SEM ?semcnp*)
   (PP **PRED** + **QS** ?qspp **SEM** ?sempp)

10. (CNP **QSPP** ?qs **QSREL** ?qsrel **SEM** (λ n2 (& (?semcnp n2) (?semrel n2)))) →
    (*CNP QSPP ?qs SEM ?semcnp*) (REL **QS** ?qsrel **SEM** ?semrel)

11. (REL **QS** ?qs **RVAR** ?v **SEM** (λ ?v ?sems)) →
    (NP **WH** R **VAR** ?v **SEM** ?semnp)
    (S **QS** ?qs **GAP** (NP **SEM** ?semnp) **SEM** ?sems)

Head features for NP, CNP: VAR

Grammar 12.4 Rules to handle simple PP modification and relative clauses

Specifically, the question is asking about many different flights, one to each city. This scoping is a result of the treatment of PP modifiers. In contrast, the question *When did the flight that each man took leave?* asks about one flight that all the men took. This reading is the result of the treatment of relative clauses.

12.4 Co-Reference and Binding Constraints

There are significant syntactic constraints on how noun phrases may **co-refer**, which to a first approximation means they both refer to the same object. This is an area of active study in linguistics, and only some of the basic results will be discussed here. In particular, consider the following example sentences, where the subscripts on noun phrases indicate that they co-refer, and asterisks indicate ill-formed interpretations, as usual.

1a. *When $Jack_i$ arrived at the party, she_i was drunk.
1b. When $Jill_i$ arrived at the party, she_i was drunk.
2a. *He_i said $Jack_i$ wants to leave.
2b. $Jack_i$ said he_i wants to leave.
3a. *$Jill_i$ saw her_i in the mirror.
3b. $Jill_i$ saw $herself_i$ in the mirror.
3c. *$Jill_i$ thought that Jack saw $herself_i$.
3d. $Jill_i$ thought that Jack saw her_i.
4a. *$Jack_i$ thought the tired man_i was dying.
4b. $Jack_i$ thought he_i was dying.

In case of co-reference, the first phrase is often called the **antecedent** and the second the **anaphor**. These examples illustrate **intrasentential anaphora**—two co-referring expressions occuring in the same sentence. The other major form of anaphora is **discourse anaphora** or **intersentential anaphora**, which will be discussed in Chapter 14. To see the difference, consider the ambiguity in the sentence *Jack found his hat,* in which the pronoun *his* may refer to Jack (intrasentential) or to someone else who was mentioned in a previous sentence (intersentential). Since we are not considering context yet, we only study the intrasentential cases here.

In the next few paragraphs, some preliminary constraints are suggested and problems with them are discussed. This will motivate the development of a better set of constraints in the remainder of the section. Sentences 1a and 1b can be accounted for by an obvious constraint: For two noun phrases to co-refer, they must agree in gender, number, and person. Sentence 1a is ill-formed because *Jack* and *she* disagree in gender.

One tempting constraint to explain sentences 2a and 2b might be that antecedents must precede pronouns that refer to them. Thus 2a is ill-formed because the pronoun occurs first. Unfortunately, this constraint is not valid, as can be seen by the following examples:

In its_i dreams, the goldfish lives in the ocean.
Before she_i went to the party, $Jill_i$ bought some wine.
Most of her_i friends think that $Jill_i$ will win.

A better constraint will be developed later.

Sentences 3a through 3d reveal constraints on the use of the reflexive. It turns out that the notion of local domain defined earlier provides a good start here. A reflexive pronoun must co-refer with a phrase in the same local domain, whereas a nonreflexive pronoun must not co-refer with a phrase in the same local domain. Sentence 3a is ill-formed because *Jill* and *her* are in the same local domain, whereas 3c is ill-formed because *Jill* and *herself* are not in the same local domain. An example of the reflexive use not involving the subject of a sentence is

Jill talked to Jack$_i$ about himself$_i$.

But the constraint as expressed does not explain why the following is ill-formed:

*Jill talked to himself$_i$ about Jack$_i$.

Finally, sentences 4a and 4b indicate that in some circumstances, pronouns must be used. A starting constraint here might be that nonpronominal noun phrases in the same sentence cannot co-refer. But this is too general, as the following sentence shows:

After Jill had been questioned for hours, Sue took the tired witness out to lunch.

A better set of constraints can be obtained by using some additional concepts from linguistics. The definition of local domain from the previous sections is a start. In addition, a new concept called **C-commanding** will be used:

A constituent C C-commands a constituent X if and only if
1. C does not dominate X.
2. The first branching node that dominates C also dominates X.

To understand this definition, consider the syntactic trees in Figure 12.5. The first branching node that dominates NP_1 is the S; thus NP_1 C-commands NP_2 and NP_3. The first branching node dominating NP_2, on the other hand, is the VP node, so NP_2 C-commands NP_3. In the second tree, NP_4 C-commands NP_5, NP_6, and NP_7, while NP_6 C-commands NP_7.

The constraint on reflexivity can now be recast in terms of the C-command relationship:

1. A reflexive pronoun must refer to an NP that C-commands it and is in the same local domain.
2. A nonreflexive pronoun cannot refer to a C-commanding NP within the same local domain.

To explore the implications of these constraints, consider the sentences in Figure 12.5 and some variations. In the sentence on the left, the pronoun *her* cannot refer to either *Jill* or *Mary* because both C-command it and both are in the minimal S that contains the pronoun. In *Jill told Mary about herself,* however, the reflexive pronoun could refer to either *Jill* or *Mary*. In *Jill told herself about Mary,* the reflexive pronoun can only refer to *Mary,* since the pronoun is not C-commanded by *Mary* even though they share the same local domain. In the

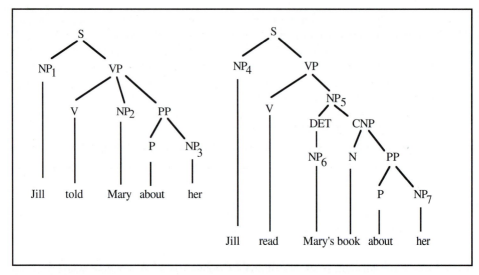

Figure 12.5　Syntactic trees demonstrating the C-command relationships

sentence on the right, the pronoun *her* can refer to *Jill* because, although NP_4 C-commands NP_7, it is not in NP_7's local domain. For NP_7 to co-refer with *Mary,* on the other hand, the pronoun would have to be reflexive.

　　This provides a reasonable account of the problems raised by reflexives, but we still have sentences 2a, 2b, 4a, and 4b to explain. These can be handled by a constraint on nonpronominal noun phrases as follows:

　　3.　A nonpronominal NP cannot co-refer with an NP that C-commands it.

This constraint accounts for all the previous examples. Sentence 2a is ill-formed because the pronoun *He* C-commands *Jack.* Sentence 4a is ill-formed for the same reason: The subject *Jack* C-commands the noun phrase *the tired man.* Note that with the sentence *After Jill$_i$ had been cross-examined for hours, Sue took the tired witness$_i$ out to lunch,* there is no C-command relation between the two noun phrases, so they can co-refer.

Interactions with Universal Quantifiers

Pronouns interact with quantifiers as well. Consider the sentence

　　Every man$_i$ thought he$_i$ would win the race.

in which each man expects to win the race himself. In this case the pronoun *he* falls within the scope of the universal quantifier and refers to each of the individuals being quantified over. This is called the **bound variable** interpretation of the pronoun. Such readings can appear in many constructs, such as

1. A reflexive pronoun must refer to an NP that C-commands it and is in the same local domain.
2. A nonreflexive pronoun cannot refer to a C-commanding NP within the same local domain.
3. A nonpronominal NP cannot co-refer with an NP that C-commands it.
4. Bound variable constraint: a nonreflexive pronoun may be bound to the variable of a universally quantified NP only if the NP C-commands the pronoun.
5. Two co-referential noun phrases must agree in number, gender, and person.

Figure 12.6 A summary of the binding constraints

Every cat$_i$ ate its$_i$ dinner.
Each man$_i$ shot himself$_i$.

Generally, a bound variable interpretation must be C-commanded by the universal quantifier as follows:

4. Bound variable constraint: A nonreflexive pronoun may be bound to the variable of a universally quantified NP only if the NP C-commands the pronoun.

Nonuniversally quantified expressions, such as the existentials, and especially the definite quantifier THE, do not require this constraint and may serve as the antecedent of a pronoun in any situation allowed by names and other referring terms.

Figure 12.6 summarizes the set of principles that have been discussed. There are still some counterexamples to these constraints that indicate that further refinement is necessary to capture all the cases. For instance, the sentence

He saw a book about himself.

appears to violate the reflexive constraint, as the local domain for the reflexive pronoun *himself* would be the noun phrase *the book about himself.* Note that in the sentence

He saw John's book about himself.

the reflexive pronoun would co-refer with John and not the subject of the sentence. One possibility is to refine the definition of the local domain so that it includes only certain noun phrase forms, such as those with possessive determiners, and excludes noun phrases with "simple" determiner structures. Such strategies have been explored extensively in the linguistics literature.

BOX 12.1 Donkey Sentences

Some more complex constructions appear not to follow the general patterns outlined in this chapter. These are often called the "donkey sentences," from a set of examples that was used to illustrate the problem. Consider the sentence

Every man who owns a donkey$_i$ beats it$_i$.

The natural reading here involves *it* being a bound variable co-referring to *a donkey,* which itself ranges over a set of values as it is within the scope of the universally quantified NP *every man.* The problem arises because the pronoun does not seem to fall within the scope of the noun phrase to which it is bound. To see this, consider the unscoped logical form

(PRES (BEAT
    [AGENT <EVERY **m1** MAN1 (OWNS **m1** <A **d1** DONKEY1>)>]
    [THEME **d1**]))

If the quantifier for **d1** is lifted over **m1**, there will only be one donkey that every man owns, not the intended interpretation. But if **d1** stays within the scope of **m1** then the quantifier is trapped within the relative clause and thus shouldn't be available for the bound variable interpretation of *it.* These examples have motivated much work (for example, Kamp (1981) and Heim (1982)).

Computing Co-Reference Constraints

To compute the co-reference constraints, you need to know the set of constituents that C-command each constituent, and of these, which ones are in the local domain. With this information, the co-reference constraints can be generated for the different types of noun phrases. The co-reference constraints will be encoded as additional restrictions in the logical form, using three new predicates. EQ-SET states that the first argument must be equal to one of the terms listed in the second argument. For example,

(EQ-SET **b1** (**g1 d1**))

asserts that **b1** must be equal to either **g1** or **d1**. NEQ-SET, on the other hand, asserts that the first argument cannot be equal to any of the terms listed in the second argument. For example,

(NEQ-SET **b1** (**g1 d1**))

asserts that **b1** cannot be equal to **g1** or to **d1**. Finally, the predicate BV-SET lists the C-commanding noun phrases, which will include all the possible bound variable interpretations for nonreflexive pronominal forms. (The possible bound variable interpretations for reflexive forms will already be included in the EQ-SET for the pronoun.)

These predicates serve to place restrictions in co-reference relations but do not completely define the possibilities. With nonreflexive pronouns, for instance, we only state what noun phrases the pronoun cannot co-refer with based on the syntactic structure. In particular, other intrasentential antecedents may be eliminated because of agreement restrictions. Since the antecedent may follow the pronoun, there is not an easy way to generate all the possible intrasentential referents while parsing. Furthermore, since the agreement check needs to be done for discourse readings as well, it seems best to leave these cases for subsequent contextual processing. But pronouns can take a bound variable reading only when it is explicitly allowed in the restrictions.

For example, the following are the logical forms that should be generated for the noun phrases in the sentence *Every boy thought he saw him*:

Every boy:	<EVERY **b1** (BOY1 **b1**)>
he:	(PRO **h1** (& (HE1 **h1**) (BV-SET **h1** (**b1**))))
him:	(PRO **h2** (& (HE1 **h2**) (NEQ-SET **h2** (**h1**))
	(BV-SET **h2** (**b1**))))

In other words, **h1** may have a bound variable interpretation, co-referring with **b1**, or it may have a discourse intersentential reading. Pronoun **h2** may also take a bound variable reading or a discourse reading, but in no case can it co-refer with **h1**. These restrictions have successfully captured the binding constraints imposed by the syntactic structure of the sentence.

As a final example, consider the sentence *The woman who owns every record bought it for herself.* The reflexive pronoun must refer to *the woman,* but the pronoun *it* cannot have a bound variable reading with *every record* because the quantified phrase does not C-command it. The logical forms are as follows:

every record: <EVERY1 **r1** (RECORD1 **r1**)>
The woman who owns every record:
        <THE **w1** (& (WOMAN1 **w1**)
                (OWNS **o1 w1** <EVERY1 **r1** (RECORD1 **r1**)>))>
it: (PRO **i1** (IT1 **i1**))
herself: (PRO **h1** (& (SHE1 **h1**) (EQ-SET **h1** (**i1 w1**))))

Note that there are no restrictions placed on **i1**. It cannot, however, co-refer with **r1** because this would create a bound variable reading, which is not allowed unless explicitly stated in the restrictions. Note also that **h1** must co-refer with either **i1** or **w1**. If the parser checked agreement restrictions, **i1** could be eliminated here and **h1** would have to co-refer with **w1**.

It is relatively straightforward to modify a grammar to keep track of the C-command relationships and local domains using two new features: CC, the discourse variables of all C-commanding constituents not in the current local domain; and LCC, the variables of the C-commanding constituents in the local domain.

The equations can be derived by considering two observations:

- Since S and NP structures define new local domains, they "reset" the LCC variable. The values in the LCC feature become part of the CC value for the subconstituents.
- No LCC or CC values generated within a subconstituent of an S or NP need to be passed back up outside the constituent.

12.5 Adjective Phrases

Adjectives generally introduce restrictions on the object referred to in the NP, but in many cases the analysis is somewhat complex. Adjectives can be classified into two classes: **intersective** adjectives and **nonintersective** adjectives. Intersective adjectives are so called because they can be analyzed in terms of set intersection. For example, to generate the set of *green balls*, you could intersect the set of balls with the set of green objects. Such adjectives can be treated as predicates that are added as restrictions to the noun phrase. For example, the logical form for *the green ball* would be

<THE **b1** (& (BALL1 **b1**) (GREEN **b1**))>

There are several classes of nonintersective adjectives. Examples of the first class are *large, slow,* and *bright,* which are relative to the noun phrase being modified. For instance, a slow dolphin travels considerably faster than a fast snail. Similarly, a person, when considered as a college professor, might be seen as a fast runner, but when considered as an athlete, might be seen as slow. Thus you cannot simply model *slow* as a one-place predicate true of all objects that are slow in some absolute sense. These constructs will be handled in the logical form by using **predicate modifiers**, which have been used once before to handle plural nouns. A predicate modifier is a function from one predicate to a new predicate. Semantically, these are functions from sets to sets. If DOLPHIN1 is a predicate representing the set of dolphins, then SLOW1 takes a set such as DOLPHIN1 and produces a subset consisting of those dolphins that are slow (relative to the set of dolphins). Because they always produce a subset, these adjectives are often called **subsective** adjectives. Using the notation developed in Chapter 8 for predicate modifiers, the logical form for *the slow dolphin* would be

<THE **d1** ((SLOW1 DOLPHIN1) **d1**)>

A small grammar showing how intersective and subsective adjectives can be treated is shown in Grammar 12.7. The lexical entry for *slow* would be

(ADJ **ROOT** slow **ATYPE** SUBSECTIVE **SEM** SLOW1)

Rule 2 would then produce the following SEM for the CNP *slow dolphin*:

(SLOW1 DOLPHIN1)

which could be used in a standard NP rule to build this SEM for *the slow dolphin.*

1. (CNP **SEM** (λ x (& (?semadjp x) (?semcnp x)))) $\rightarrow$
   (ADJP **ATYPE** INTERSECTIVE **SEM** ?semadjp)
   (CNP **SEM** ?semcnp)

2. (CNP **SEM** (?semadjp ?semcnp)) $\rightarrow$
   (ADJP **ATYPE** SUBSECTIVE **SEM** ?semadjp)
   (CNP **SEM** ?semcnp)

3. (ADJP **ATYPE** ?a **SEM** ?sem) $\rightarrow$ (ADJ **ATYPE** ?a **SEM** ?sem)

Grammar 12.7 Some interpretation rules for adjectival modification

The adjectives in the next class of nonintersective adjectives do not have a simple relation to the sets that they modify. These include adjectives such as *average, toy,* and *alleged.* An average grade may not be an actual grade, a toy gun is not really a gun, and an alleged murderer may not be a murderer. Rather, each of these modifiers relates to the property it modifies in a different way. As another example, the adjective *former,* modifying a property like *astronaut,* would produce a set of individuals who were once astronauts but are not now. The adjective *toy* modifying *gun* would produce a set of objects that are made to look or act like guns. An adequate semantics for these constructs is beyond the scope of this book, but we will consider one class of particular interest for computational applications such as a database query system. These adjectives define a quantity that is the result of a computation over the modified set, like *average.*

To handle such constructs, an explicit set construction operator must be introduced into the logical form. This can be defined as follows:

(SET (λ x P_x)) is the set of all objects that satisfy the predicate (λ x P_x)

Given this, the rule for adjectives like *average* are handled as follows:

(CNP **SEM** (?semadj (SET ?semcnp))) $\rightarrow$
   (ADJ **ATYPE** SET-PROPERTY **SEM** ?semadj) (CNP **SEM** ?semcnp)

Given this rule, the logical form for the NP *the average grade in the class* is

<THE **a1** ((AVERAGE (SET (λ g (& (GRADE1 g)
                                    (IN1 g <THE **c1** CLASS1>))))) **a1**>

Adjective phrases may also have modifiers and complements, although complements to adjectives when used as prenominal modifiers is quite rare. But adjective phrases such as *light red* are common. Such adjectival modifiers can be treated as predicate modifiers and handled without much problem. Thus the rule for simple adjective modifiers would be

(ADJP **SEM** (?semadv ?semadjp)) $\rightarrow$
   (ADV **ATYPE** PREMOD **SEM** ?semadv)
   (ADJP **SEM** ?semadjp)

If the SEM for the adjectival modifier *light* is LIGHT1, then the logical form of the adjective phrase *light red* would be the predicate

(LIGHT1 RED1)

This adjective phrase would then combine with other constituents as usual. For example, the logical form for *the light red bus* would be

<THE **b1** (& (BUS1 **b1**) ((LIGHT1 RED1) **b1**))>

Comparatives

A class of adjective phrases important for computational applications is the comparative forms. These are complex constructions, and only the simple cases will be considered here. Comparative adjective constructions appear in many forms, such as

He is *larger than the boy is.*
He is *larger than the boy.*
The *more brilliant woman* won the prize.
A woman *more brilliant than the first speaker* has won the prize.
I am *happier than I have ever been.*

These cases should be distinguished from constructs such as

I own *more horses than George does.*
Jack gave *as much money as he could.*

which are also called comparative constructs but are noun phrases in which the *more ... than* and *as much ... as* constructs are better treated as quantifiers than adjective phrases. These cases are considered in Box 12.2.

Comparative adjective phrase constructs all implicitly identify some scale by which different objects can be compared. For example, *happier* identifies a scale of happiness, in which the adjective *happy* identifies a range at one end of the scale and *sad* a range at the other end. An object X is happier than an object Y only if X is higher on the scale (that is, closer to *happy*) than Y is. Note that being happier does not entail being happy. Both X and Y might be sad, but X could be happier than Y. Of course, the adjectives may be ambiguous as to the actual scale used. For instance, the sentence *Canada is larger than the U.S.* is true with respect to the area scale but false with respect to the population scale. Different comparatives may identify the same scale. For example, *larger* and *smaller* refer to the same scale but differ in what direction on the scale the objects are being compared.

With this background we define comparative adjectives as being binary predicates that order two objects on a specific scale. Given a scale S, the predicate (MORE S) is a binary predicate that is true when the first argument is greater than the second on scale S. The SEM of *heavier* would be (MORE WEIGHT-

SCALE), the SEM of *higher* would be (MORE HEIGHT-SCALE), and the SEM of *happier* would be (MORE HAPPY-SCALE). Many comparative constructs take a complement that uses the complementizer *than* followed by an S/ADJP or an NP. A rule for the NP case would be

(ADJP **SEM** λ x (?semadjp x ?semnp)) $\rightarrow$
    (ADJP **ATYPE** COMPARATIVE **SEM** ?semadjp)
    (THAN)
    (NP **SEM** ?semnp)

in which (ADJP **ATYPE** COMPARATIVE) would be defined to include constructs such as *more brilliant* and *happier*. Given this, the logical form of the adjective phrase *happier than John* would be

λ x . ((MORE HAPPY-SCALE) x (NAME **j1** "John"))

12.6 Relational Nouns and Nominalizations

Nouns like *sister, boss,* and *author* are quite different from other common nouns like *dog* or *idea.* In particular, they do not refer directly to a type of individual; rather, they are defined in terms of a relationship to other individuals. For example, it makes little sense to talk of the denotation of *sister* as the set of all people who are sisters of someone else. Rather, each time the noun *sister* is used, it is explicitly or implicitly defined in terms of some person whose sister we are considering. Standard constructions indicate this object, such as the possessive, as in *John's sister,* and a PP complement using *of,* as in *the author of this book.* This suggests that a common set of subcategorizations and semantic interpretation rules should be defined for such nouns.

One approach is to define each relational noun by a nonrelational type and a binary relation that uses a subcategorized NP. For example, the meaning of *author* might be

λ b λ p (& (PERSON p) (AUTHOR-OF b p))

where the first variable is bound to the book involved, and the second is the person who is the author. This could be used with a rule like rule 1 in Grammar 12.8 to give the following logical form to the CNP *author of the book*:

λ p (& (PERSON p) (AUTHOR-OF <THE **b1** BOOK1> p))

The possessive form can be treated similarly by a special rule for relational nouns that overrides the standard rule for the possessive described earlier. In this case some feature would have to be introduced to indicate a subcategorized possessive NP, which would then have as its SEM the SEM of the NP embedded in it, just as subcategorized PPs took their SEM from their NP complement. If we use the PRED feature for this, then the rules for the possessive with relational nouns would be rules 2 and 3 in Grammar 12.8. The grammar also needs to

---

BOX 12.2 Numerical Quantifiers and *More*

Numerical quantifiers play an important role in database query applications. For the most part they are straightforward, but there are some complexities that need to be pointed out. Numerical quantifiers fall into the existential class of quantifiers and appear as in the following noun phrases:

> *Three men* rowed the boat.
> *At least three men* rowed the boat.
> *More than three men* rowed the boat.

These are handled by allowing more complex quantifiers such as (EXACTLY 3), (AT-LEAST 3), (MORE-THAN 3), (LESS-THAN 3), and so on. Thus the logical form of the noun phrase *Three men* would be

<(EXACTLY 3) **m1** (PLUR MAN1)>

Noun phrases such as *more men than were at the concert* and *less money than I expected* are more complex. One treatment is to assume that the determiner structure is discontinuous; for example, the quantifier in the first example is *more ... than were at the concert*. The interpretation uses the operator MORE-THAN just defined, but in this case the cardinality of a set is specified as its argument rather than a simple number. Thus the logical form of *more men than were at the concert* would be something like

<(MORE-THAN (SIZE (λ x (& ((PLUR MAN1) x) (AT x <THE **c1** CNC1>))))
m1 (PLUR MAN1))>

---

handle cases where there is no subcategorized constituent present, as in the noun phrase *the author.* To handle this case, we would introduce an anaphoric element to stand for the missing object. This is done in rule 4, where REL-N1 is a new sense for this form of inserted anaphoric element.

Given this grammar and the meaning of *author* above, the noun phrase *the book's author* would have the logical form

<THE **a1** (& (PERSON1 **a1**) (AUTHOR-OF <THE **b1** BOOK1> **a1**))>

whereas the noun phrase *the author* would have the logical form

<THE **a2** (& (PERSON **a2**) (AUTHOR-OF (PRO **b2** REL-N1) **a2**))>

Words like *murderer, actor,* and *thief,* often ending in the suffixes *-er* or *-or,* also fall into this class and identify people by the acts they perform. Thus a murderer performs one or more murders, an actor acts, and a thief steals things. There are other nouns that also identify cases other than the AGENT case. For instance, the noun *recipient* indicates the TO case in transfer acts, *donation* identifies the THEME case in a donating act, and in general words with the suffix *-ee,* such as *addressee* and *rentee,* indicate cases filled by animate objects that are not the AGENT in two-person interactions. These nouns also subcategorize for

1. (CNP **RELATIONAL** – **SEM** (?semcnp ?sempp)) →
   (*CNP RELATIONAL + SEM ?semcnp*)
   (PP **PRED** – **PTYPE** of **SEM** ?sempp)
2. (NP **POSS** + **PRED** – **SEM** ?sem) → (*NP POSS* – *SEM ?semp*) 's
3. (NP **RELATIONAL** – **VAR** ?v **SEM** <THE ?v ((?semcnp ?semnp) ?v)>) →
   (NP **POSS** + **PRED** – **SEM** ?semnp)
   (*CNP RELATIONAL + SEM ?semcnp*)
4. (CNP **RELATIONAL** – **SEM** (?cnp (PRO x REL-N1))) →
   (*CNP RELATIONAL + SEM ?cnp*)

Grammar 12.8   Rules for simple relational noun phrases

constituents that identify other cases in the action. For example, in *the murderer of John,* the NP *John* intuitively fills the THEME case of the murder act. Thus an analysis of *murderer* in terms of the action of murdering seems to capture many generalities.

Specifically, the meaning of words ending in *-er* could be systematically derived from the verb forms. For example, assume that the verb *murder* has the SEM

λ o λ a (MURDER1 * [AGENT a] [THEME o])

This same form can be used for the relational noun *murderer* and, given the rules in Grammar 12.8, the logical form for *the murderer of John* would be

<THE **p1** (MURDER1 **m1** [AGENT **p1**] [THEME (NAME **j1** "John")])>

Not all *-er* forms occur with action verbs with agents. For instance, *owner* would be defined in terms of the verb *own,* which does not have an agent role. The lexical entries for verbs would be extended to define the appropriate inter-pretation of the *-er* form.

Another important class of nouns includes the nominalizations of verbs themselves, such as *destruction,* that can refer to either an act of destroying or to the result of a destroying act. Such nouns also allow PP complements with *of,* as in the noun phrase *the destruction of the city,* which would indicate the THEME role. Similarly, an AGENT case can be introduced using the preposition *by,* as in *the destruction of the city by the Huns,* which has one analysis that refers to a particular destroying act:

<THE **d1** (DESTROY1 **d1**   [AGENT <THE **h1** (PLUR HUN)>]
                            [THEME <THE **c1** CITY>])>

The possessive form can signify either the AGENT case (*the Huns' destruction*) or the THEME case (*the city's destruction*).

12.7 Other Problems in Semantics

This section briefly describes a few additional problems in semantic interpretation that are important but cannot be considered in detail in this book: mass terms, generics, intensional operators, and noun-noun modification. A thorough discussion of these issues would easily take another chapter or two.

Mass Terms

Nearly all the noun phrases used so far in the examples have been count noun phrases, such as *the dog, a few clowns,* and so on. These are called count noun phrases because they refer to specific individuals that can be counted. Thus you can have one dog, three dogs, or more dogs than someone else has. Singular noun phrases involving count nouns refer to individuals, while plural ones refer to sets. In contrast, mass noun phrases such as *some water* and *the hot sand* do not refer to an individual or to sets but rather to substances that occur in quantities. Mass terms are measurable in terms of units of measure, as in the noun phrases *three quarts of water* or *five pounds of sand.* Mass nouns do not occur in the plural form without a change of meaning and cannot be used in noun phrases with the quantifiers *each* and *every.*

It is important to note that, while nouns are classified as either count nouns or mass nouns, most can be coerced into changing forms by the noun phrases in which they appear. For example, since English allows only singular bare noun phrases (such as *sand, very clean water*) in the mass interpretation, if you use a count noun in such a construct, you force a change of meaning into a mass term. If you say *We ate deer for dinner*, then the NP *deer* is a mass term, presumably referring to deer meat. Conversely, while *water* is a mass noun, the NP *many waters* forces a count interpretation, presumably to a set of lakes.

Generics

Another complicated form of sentence involves the generic usage. Sentences involving generics make general claims about the world, as in the following sentences that can all be used to make a claim about lions in general:

> Lions are dangerous.
> The lion is a dangerous animal.
> A lion can be dangerous.

In the generic interpretation the noun phrases neither refer to individuals nor quantify over a set of individuals. The sentence *Lions are dangerous* can be true even if there are some tame lions. In fact, a generic statement may be true even if most objects in the class do not have the property. For instance, Carlson (1979) points out that *Sea turtles lay approximately 100 eggs* may be true even if most sea turtles are male and lay no eggs at all.

Rather, generics seem to make claims about the type or kind of object being described. The discussion of how you may reason with such facts will be delayed until later chapters dealing with knowledge representation and reasoning. For the moment, however, we need to introduce the distinction into the logical form language. Although there are several different theories on how to do this, most involve introducing the notion of a **kind** into the ontology. A kind is separate from an individual or set of individuals and refers to the species, sub-stance, or type of individuals. This allows kinds to have certain properties without committing to whether the individuals of that kind have the properties or not. Of course, it is often the case that if a kind has a property, all or most of the individuals of that kind also have the property. For example, if we know that *Dogs have four legs,* we can infer that most individual dogs have four legs; how-ever, this doesn't exclude the possibility that there is a three-legged dog. Kinds may also have properties that do not hold of their individuals. For instance, say-ing *Dodos are extinct* does not mean that any individual dodo is extinct. Rather, being extinct is a property of the kind (in this case species) denoted by *dodos.*

Note that all bare plural noun phrases are not necessarily treated as generics. A common distinction is found in sentences such as *Large dogs have large noses.* The property being asserted of the kind *large dogs* is not that each one has a number of large noses (a set reading), or that they possess the substance *nose* (the generic reading), but that they have a particular nose (an existential reading). Thus bare plural noun phrases may be interpreted differently depending on their functions.

Many other syntactic factors can indicate generic readings besides the bare plural forms. In fact, as shown at the beginning of this section, generic sentences are possible using singular definite and indefinite noun phrases as well. Another common indicator of generic sentences is the use of the simple present tense. For instance, consider the difference between *Large dogs run over the hill* and *Large dogs ran over the hill.* The first is most likely a generic statement, while the second is most likely a description of a particular event. However, both of these could occur in the generic or nongeneric readings. Temporal modifiers that indi-cate extended duration also indicate the generic, as in *Large dogs ran over the hill in those days,* which is a generic statement about the past. Other adverbials, such as *often* and *rarely,* are also strong indicators of generic readings.

Intensional Operators and Scoping

A verb such as *believe* or *want* that takes a finite clause as a complement will interact with definite and indefinite descriptions in complicated ways. The sen-tence *Jack believes a man found the ring,* for example, is ambiguous between the case in which Jack knows of a particular man whom he believes found the ring and the case in which all Jack believes is that the ring was found by some man. These ambiguities are often captured by scoping differences. To see this, you must examine the logical form of such sentences in more detail.

As described in Chapter 8, the semantics of such verbs is complex because they do not support the normal inference rule of substituting equals. For example, if John is the tallest man, and you are given the fact that John kissed Sue, you can conclude that the tallest man kissed Sue. A similar inference, however, does not work for belief sentences. Given that Sam believes John kissed Sue, you cannot conclude that Sam believes the tallest man kissed Sue, since Sam may not know that John is the tallest man. Worse yet, he may believe that George is the tallest. Because equal terms cannot be substituted for each other in the scope of such operators, they are often called **referentially opaque**, while normal predicates are said to be **referentially transparent**.

Opaque operators introduce a new form of scoping ambiguity: A quantifier can be inside the scope of the operator as well as being outside its scope. This form of scoping can be used to capture the ambiguities in *John believes a man kissed Sue*, which has the unscoped logical form

(PRES (BELIEVE **b1**
    [EXPERIENCER (NAME **j1** "John")]
    [THEME (PAST (KISS **k1** <A **m1** MAN1> (NAME **s1** "Sue")))]))

The first reading involves John knowing who the man is; it could be paraphrased by *There is a particular man whom John believes kissed Sue.* Its form is

(A **m1** : (MAN **m1**)
    (PRES (BELIEVE **b1**
        [EXPERIENCER (NAME **j1** "John")]
        [THEME (PAST (KISS **k1 m1** (NAME **s1** "Sue")))])))

This involves what is often called a **de re** belief, that is, a belief about a particular man. The second case involves John simply believing that some man kissed Sue, though he doesn't know who. It would have the following form:

(PRES (BELIEVE **b1**
    [EXPERIENCER (NAME **j1** "John")]
    [THEME (PAST (A **m1** : (MAN **m1**)
               (KISS **k1 m1** (NAME **s1** "Sue"))))]))

This involves a **de dicto** belief, that is, belief about a proposition.

There are many other examples of this phenomenon, some of which can be quite complicated. For example, some time ago I was at a party and someone walked into the kitchen and said *I'm waiting for a phone call.* This expression later led to some confusion because I had understood it in the usual interpretation that he was waiting for a call from someone in particular. It turned out, however, that the speaker simply wanted to hear the phone ring, so any call would do! Interestingly enough, the intent of the original sentence could have been conveyed unambiguously by the rather unusual sentence *I'm waiting for any phone call.* But this sentence is unusual simply because the contexts in which it is appropriate are very rare.

Noun-Noun Modifiers

NPs with noun-noun modifiers such as *car paint, soup pot handle, water glass,* and *computer evaluation* are notoriously difficult to analyze. The syntactic form provides little guidance, and general semantic constraints like those used for analyzing multiple adjectives do not seem to be present. There are two main problems. One is determining what modifies what, which is similar to the problem with multiple adjectives. The other problem is detecting the semantic relationship between the modifying noun and the modified noun. There are several common patterns on how the nouns are related. Some common relationships for an NP consisting of a sequence of two nouns, X and Y, are

- Y is a subpart of X (*pot handles*).
- Y is used for some activity involving X (*car paint*).
- Y is made out of material X (*stone wall*).

Thus a *pot handle* is a handle that is part of a pot, *car paint* is paint used to paint cars, and a *stone wall* is a wall made out of stone.

Nouns that have associated cases, or that identify the case of a particular verb, can be analyzed in terms of those cases. For example, with the NP *the contest winner,* the noun *winner* identifies the AGENT case of a WIN action, and *contest* can be seen to fit the THEME case. Thus this NP might be analyzed as

<THE **p1** (& (PERSON **p1**) (WIN **w1 p1** <THE **c1** CONTEST>))>

The NP *the car evaluation,* on the other hand, refers to an evaluation event directly, and *car* is seen to fit the THEME case. If the modifier can fill more than one case, the NP will be ambiguous. For example, *the computer evaluation* could be either *the evaluation of the computer* or *the evaluation by the computer.*

In the final analysis many noun-noun modifications appear not to be resolvable by strategies based on reasoning, but rather are learned directly from use in context.

In the logical form, unless there is strong evidence for a more particular relationship, an ambiguous predicate modifier N-N-MOD is used to capture the fact that there is some relationship, but it cannot be determined without context. For example, a noun phrase such as *the smoke box,* which has no obvious modification relation, would have the logical form

<THE **b1** ((N-N-MOD SMOKE1 BOX1) **b1**)>

and it would be left for contextual interpretation to determine the type of the object being described and its other properties.

Summary

This chapter considered many issues that were ignored in the developments in the earlier chapters. Many of these issues concern the scoping of operators and constraints on reference. We showed that the choice of quantifier and syntactic structure can greatly affect the allowed scopings and the preferred interpretation of sentences. In addition, there are significant structural constraints on intra-sentential co-reference between pronouns and other referring expressions. The chapter also considered adjectival modification and showed that you must distinguish between several different classes of adjectives to obtain appropriate interpretations. Finally, we considered nouns that exhibit a complex semantic structure, defining them in terms of relations or in terms of related verb forms.

Related Work and Further Readings

Determining the scoping of quantifiers has been a central concern for those building natural language database query systems, and many of the heuristics described in this book have been used in work by Woods (1978), Pereira (1983), Saint-Dizier (1985), Grosz et al. (1987), and Alshawi (1992). VanLehn (1978) performed a set of experiments to test the preferences that have been suggested in the literature. While humans displayed clear preferences in some cases, many times it appeared that contextual effects dominated the process. Hobbs and Shieber (1987) describe an algorithm for generating all possible scopings, eliminating only those that are linguistically unacceptable in any context. More general treatments of scoping, including adverbs and sentential operators, have been examined by McCord (1986).

One of the first systems to use quantificational structures separate from the semantic form during semantic interpretation was the LUNAR system (Woods, 1978) within the ATN framework, and it has been used in many approaches since. Cooper developed a theory within formal semantics using a technique called quantifier storage that uses the same intuitions. Pereira and Pollack (1991) provide an interesting formalization of this type of approach based on storing and discharge assumptions about the discourse.

There is little computational work specifically aimed at dealing with intrasentential anaphora. One of the few algorithms in the literature is that described by Hobbs (1978). This algorithm effectively uses the constraints in this chapter to eliminate candidates based on reflexivity constraints, and then imposes a heuristic ordering on the remaining candidates, roughly based on the proximity of the antecedent to the pronoun (that is, the closest antecedent is selected).

There is a considerable literature on quantification, anaphora, and binding theory in linguistics. The best place to start is a textbook such as Chierchia and McConnell-Ginet (1990, Chapter 3). May (1985) is a good example of quantifier scoping using syntactic transformations (which he calls quantifier raising). Reinhart (1983) was one of the first to develop an analysis of anaphora based on binding constraints. A more general reference on the underlying linguistic theory, Government and Binding, can be found in Chomsky (1981). Computational work using this approach can be found in Berwick and Weinberg (1984) and Stabler (1992).

A general discussion of the formal semantics of adjective phrases can be found in Chierchia and McConnell-Ginet (1990). More detailed discussions can be found in Kamp (1975) and Klein (1980). There is a good general discussion of comparative adjectives in McCawly (1993). Computational accounts of comparatives can be found in Ballard (1988) and Alshawi (1992).

Relational nouns are discussed in de Bruin and Scha (1988). Noun-noun modification has been considered by Finin (1980). Hobbs et al. (1993) use a vague predicate NN to encode noun-noun modification relationship, which is later resolved using contextual information.

The notion of kinds and their use in generic sentences was introduced by Carlson (1979; 1982), and there has been considerable work in this area since. A good survey of several approaches can be found in Schubert and Pelletier (1987). There is an excellent collection on mass nouns in Pelletier (1979), and a good overview of some of these approaches to mass nouns and generics in McCawley (1993).

Another important area of semantic interpretation not discussed here is the interpretation of phrases (mainly prepositional phrases) describing locations. A good reference for this area is Herskovits (1986).

Exercises for Chapter 12

1. (*easy*) Specify all logically distinct interpretations of each of the following sentences by considering scoping ambiguity. If two different scopings give the same interpretation, however, list only one.

   Each man gave a boy a present.
   Some man from a club stole every present.
   Most people from all companies ate some peaches.

2. (*easy*) Specify all the possible antecedents for the pronouns with indices i or j in the following sentences, considering all the constraints specified in Section 12.4.

   $Jack_1$ realized that he_i would see Sam_2 at the $party_3$.
   After $Jack_1$ left the $room_2$, Sam_3 saw him_i run to his_j car_4.
   Even though Sam_1 apologized, $Jack_2$ wants to kill him_i.

3. (*easy*) Classify each of the following adjectives as intersective, subsective, or neither. Justify your answers. Give a plausible logical form for the object noun phrase in the corresponding sentences.

fake	I bought a fake turtle.
sluggish	I bought a sluggish turtle.
expensive	I bought an expensive turtle.
dead	I bought a dead turtle.
smelly	I bought a smelly turtle.

4. (*medium*) Draw out the parse trees to the level of detail shown in Figure 12.3 for the sentences

> When does the flight to each city leave?
> When did the flight that each man took leave?

using Grammars 12.2 and 12.4 and the scoping strategy described in Section 12.3.

5. (*medium*) Give the semantic analysis of each noun phrase, including co-reference constraints, produced for the following sentences.

> Jack saw the man beside him.
> Sue saw Jill's book about herself.
> Every man gave his book to him.

6. (*medium*)

a Write a program that, given a logical form, generates all possible quantifier scopings consistent with the constraints described in Section 12.1. Thus, given a representation of the following as input,

```
(PRES (SIT s1  [AGENT <A m1 MAN1>]
               [AT-LOC <THE k1 (& (KITCHEN k1)
                                  (IN k1 <(EVERY h1 HOUSE)>))>]))
```

the program would output

```
(m1 (k1 h1))
((k1 h1) m1)
(m1 h1 k1)
(h1 m1 k1)
(h1 k1 m1)
```

Construct a set of test cases that demonstrate your algorithm's capabilities.

b. Extend your program to eliminate logically redundant scopings to produce a smaller set of interpretations. Identify the equivalences you use to identify redundancy and justify that the alternate forms are really logically equivalent.

7. (*medium*) Consider the unscoped logical form for the sentence *In every house, a man fixed his sink.*

```
(PAST (FIX1 f1
      [AGENT <A m1 (MAN1 m1)>]
      [THEME <THE s1 (& (SINK1 s1)(POSS-BY s1 (PRO h1 HE1)))>]
      [AT-LOC <EVERY h2 HOUSE1>]))
```

Draw the syntactic tree for this sentence, and identify the possible ante-cedents for each of the pronominal forms. What are the actual co-reference relations for the most intuitive reading of this sentence? Is the definite description treated referentially or existentially?

8. (*medium*) Section 12.5 discussed the use of adjectives, like *average,* that are functional on some set. *Average* can also be a noun, as in *the class average* or *the average of the best students.* Give an analysis of the proper-ties of such nouns, and develop a set of semantic interpretation rules for them.

PART III

Context and World Knowledge

Part III concerns contextual processing of language. Topics range from knowledge representation and reasoning to discourse structure and pragmatics. The term discourse will be used to refer to any form of multi-sentence or multi-utterance language. The most important forms of discourse in computational applications are text, such as articles and books, and dialogue, which involves a conversation between two or more conversants, whether spoken or by keyboard. Many discourse models apply equally to written and spoken language, so the words sentence and utterance will be used interchangeably and the terms speaker and hearer will be used for writer and reader, respectively.

It will be useful to divide the notion of context into the situational context and the discourse context. Consider a conversation. The situational context consists of the specific setting, which includes the time and location and the objects visible to each conversant, and the general setting, which involves the conversants' background knowledge of the world. The discourse context consists of the local discourse context (or just local context), which is detailed information about the preceding sentence, and the global discourse context, which is information about the overall conversation, including what topics are being addressed. The following table gives an example of some contextual information during a conversation between two agents, John and Mary, just after Mary says *My coffee is cold.*

	Specific/Local Context	General/Global Context
Situational Context	Mary was the speaker. John was the hearer. It is 3 o'clock. They are in the student union. They each have a cup of coffee on the table between them. ...	They are in the USA. The President is Bill Clinton. There is a single moon that rotates around the earth. Birds typically can fly. ...
Discourse Context	The last sentence parse tree is (S (NP my coffee) (VP is cold)). *My coffee* refers to the cup of coffee next to Mary. Mary asserted that the coffee is cold.	John and Mary have been discussing a project for the physics class they are working on. They then began discussing the quality of the food at union.

Chapter 13 provides an introduction to the issues in knowledge representation and reasoning, supplying a foundation for the discussions of how knowledge and reasoning affect the interpretation of language. Chapter 14 addresses a central issue in contextual interpretation, namely the identification of the referent of noun phrases such as pronouns and definite descriptions, primarily using the local discourse context. Chapter 15 addresses issues in the situational context, exploring methods of using knowledge of the world and the specific situation to interpret language. Chapter 16 addresses issues relevant to the global discourse context, focusing on identifying the structure of the discourse itself. Finally, Chapter 17 discusses issues in specifying a conversational agent, looking at how the underlying intentions of speakers can be identified from their utterances, and how intentions can be realized by linguistic means.

CHAPTER

Knowledge Representation and Reasoning

Many problems that arose in earlier chapters were not resolved because they required knowledge of context. Two important aspects of context are general knowledge about the world and specific knowledge about the situation in which the linguistic communication is occurring. To analyze these, you need a formalism for representing knowledge and reasoning. This area of study is called **knowledge representation (KR)**.

Knowledge representation means different things to different researchers. For some, knowledge representation concerns the structure of the language used to express the knowledge—whether it is in logic, semantic networks, frames, or other specially designed representational formalisms. For others, knowledge representation concerns the content of sentences—what predicates are needed and how are they organized. Both of these issues are important. Sometimes, what seems to be a vigorous debate about knowledge representation is actually the result of each of the debaters focusing on one of the aspects of representation without considering the concerns of the other.

There is not the space here for an extended discussion of knowledge representation formalisms. Rather, the central concern is how knowledge and reasoning can be used to facilitate language understanding. Because of this, an abstracted representation based on the first-order predicate calculus will be used. This will enable the discussion of relevant representational issues with the minimum introduction of new material and notation. This does not mean that the underlying knowledge representation used in a system would have to directly represent logical formulas or use theorem-proving techniques as a model of inference. The underlying representation system could be a semantic network, a description logic, a frame-based system, a connectionist model, or any other formalism, as long as the system has at least the expressive power described here. Many modern knowledge representation systems fulfill this requirement.

Section 13.1 discusses some general issues in knowledge representation. The next two sections develop the abstract knowledge representation language that will be used throughout the rest of the book: Section 13.2 discusses a simple representation based on the FOPC, and Section 13.3 discusses a framelike representation as a way of clustering information and representing defaults about stereotypical objects and situations. Section 13.4 discusses an important issue in mapping the logical form language to the knowledge representation language, namely the representation of the complex quantifiers found in natural language. The rest of the chapter is optional but is important if your focus is knowledge representation. Section 13.5 examines the representation of temporal information in language, as revealed by tense and aspectual class. The remaining sections give examples of some different reasoning strategies that are used in knowledge representation systems. Section 13.6 discusses some basic concepts in automated deduction, which are used in systems based on deductive techniques as well as systems based on logic programming. Section 13.7 discusses an approach that uses a procedural semantics and illustrates its use in a question-answering system. Section 13.8 discusses some issues in developing hybrid reasoning systems, which allow different reasoning techniques to be used depending on what sort of information is required.

This chapter assumes that the reader has a basic understanding of the first-order predicate calculus, at least to the level introduced in Appendix A.

13.1 Knowledge Representation

There are two forms of knowledge that are crucial in any knowledge representation system: general knowledge of the world and specific knowledge of the current situation. Some aspects of general world knowledge have already been considered, such as type hierarchies, part/whole relationships, and so on. This consists of information about general constraints on the world and the semantic definition of the terms in the language. For the most part, general knowledge is specified in terms of the **types** or kinds of objects in the world and does not concern information about specific individuals. For instance, it might encode that OWN1 is a relation between people and objects but not that a particular person, say John, owns a particular car. This latter information, knowledge about individuals, is equally important in language understanding and is a major component of what we call the specific setting of the sentence being understood. Virtually all knowledge representation systems support reasoning at both of these levels in one way or another.

General world knowledge is essential for solving many language interpretation problems, one of the most important being disambiguation. For example, the proper attachment of the final PP in the following two sentences depends solely on the reader's background knowledge of the appropriate time needed for reading and for evolution:

> I read a story about evolution in ten minutes.
> I read a story about evolution in the last million years.

Specific knowledge of the situation is important for many issues, including determining the referent of noun phrases and disambiguating word senses based on what makes sense in the current situation.

We will sometimes talk informally of the knowledge representation as encoding the knowledge and beliefs of the understanding system. But since the terms knowledge and belief will be given more precise technical definitions later, more neutral terminology is introduced. A knowledge representation consists of a database of sentences called the **knowledge base** (KB) and a set of **inference techniques** that can be used to derive new sentences given the current KB. A set of inference techniques is **sound** if it only derives true new sentences when the original sentences in the KB are all true. Not all useful inference techniques need be sound, however, as you will see later.

The language in which the sentences in the KB are defined is called the **knowledge representation language** (KRL). The KRL could be the same as the logical form language, but there are practical reasons why they often differ. The two languages are driven by different needs. The logical form language must be very expressive in order to simplify the semantic interpretation process and to allow the effective resolution of ambiguity. The knowledge representation language, on the other hand, must support efficient and predictable reasoning within a specific domain. In other words, it should be relatively easy to define the set of sentences that can be inferred from a particular KB and to build computational models that perform such inferences in a reasonable amount of time.

For example, consider the treatment of quantifiers. In the logical form language a wide range of quantifiers was introduced, closely corresponding to the different word senses of English quantifiers. This allows disambiguation techniques, such as those needed for scoping quantifiers, to use subtle differences between the actual quantifiers (say between *each* and *every*). In most current knowledge representation languages, however, there are usually only a few quantifiers and often only one—a construct allowing universal quantification. Thus inference processes can be easily defined. By keeping the languages separate and defining a mapping function between them, you can have the advantages of both. Of course, the success of this approach will depend on whether or not the mapping function can be effectively defined.

Substantial research will be needed before the best way to satisfy the need for an expressive logical form and an effective knowledge representation can be determined. Given the current state of knowledge, maintaining a separate logical form and knowledge representation languages seems the best compromise.

When a formula P must be true given the formulas in a KB, or given formulas representing the meaning of a sentence, then we say that the KB (or sentence) **entails** P. Many of the conclusions that need to be drawn to understand language are not entailments, however, but are **implications** of the sentence. Implications are conclusions that can typically be drawn from a sentence but that could be explicitly denied in specific circumstances. For instance, the sentence *Jack owns two cars* entails that Jack owns a car (that is, this fact cannot be denied), but only implies that he doesn't own three cars, as you could continue by saying *In fact, he owns three cars.* KR systems must support both these forms of inference.

Types of Inference

Many different forms of inference are necessary to understand natural language. Inference techniques can be classified into **deductive** and **nondeductive** forms. Deductive forms of inference are justified by the logical notion of entailment. Given a set of facts, a deductive inference process will make only conclusions that logically follow from those facts. Nondeductive inference falls into several classes. Examples include inference techniques that involve learning generalities from examples (**inductive inference**) and techniques that involve inferring causes from effects (a form of **abductive inference**).

Abductive inference can be contrasted with deductive inference by considering the axiom

$$A \supset B$$

Deductive inference would use this axiom to infer B when given A. Abductive inference would use it to infer A when given B, since A is a reason that B is true.

Many systems allow the use of default information. A **default rule** is an inference rule to which there may be exceptions; thus it is **defeasible**. If you write default information using the notation $A \Rightarrow B$, then the default inference rule could be stated as follows: If $A \Rightarrow B$, and A is true, and $\neg B$ is not provable, then conclude B. It has been suggested that default rules may provide a good account of generic sentences. For example, the meaning of the sentence *Birds fly* could be represented by the FOPC formula

$$\forall x \, BIRD(x) \Rightarrow FLIES(x)$$

This has the effect that whenever there is a bird B for which it is not provable that $\neg FLIES(B)$, then it can be inferred that $FLIES(B)$. In other words, a specific bird will be assumed to be able to fly unless it is explicitly stated that it cannot.

Defeasible rules introduce a new set of complexities in a representation. Without such rules, most representations are **monotonic**, because adding new assertions only increases the number of formulas entailed. Specifically, in a monotonic representation, if the knowledge base KB1 entails a conclusion C, and if you add an additional formula to KB1 to form a new consistent knowledge base KB2, then KB2 will also entail C. This is not true of a representation that uses default rules, and hence they are called **nonmonotonic** representations. For example, consider a knowledge base K consisting of the formulas

Cat(Sampson)	Sampson is a cat.
TabbyCat(Sampson)	Sampson is a tabby cat.
$\forall c \, . \, Cat(c) \Rightarrow Purrs(c)$	Cats purr.

Given this KB, you can conclude *Purrs(Sampson)* using the default rule because there is no information to contradict *Purrs(S)*. On the other hand, if you add a new fact that no tabby cats purr, then the extended knowledge base would no longer entail that Sampson purrs.

There are other useful techniques for introducing nonmonotonic conclusions besides default rules. For instance, the **closed world assumption (CWA)** asserts that the KB contains complete information about certain predicates. For example, for a predicate P for which the CWA holds, if a proposition involving P cannot be proven from a KB, then its negation is assumed to be true. Consider a database query application for airline schedules. The KB stores information about flights that exist—say, that flight FDG100 flies from Rochester to Boston—but it doesn't explicitly contain negative information—say, that flight FDG100 doesn't fly to Chicago or that there is no flight FDG455. Such information can only be concluded if the inference process makes the closed world assumption on flights.

BOX 13.1 A Semantics for Nonmonotonic Logic

You can develop a model theoretic semantics for many nonmonotonic constructs using the concept of **minimal models**. For example, consider the closed world assumption for a predicate P. We can define an ordering on all the models of the KB as follows:

$$\mathbf{m1} <_P \mathbf{m2} \quad \text{iff } I_{m1}(P) \subseteq I_{m2}(P)$$

In other words, a model **m1** is smaller than a model **m2** with respect to a predicate P if and only if the set of objects x such that P(x) is true in **m1** is a subset of the set of objects x such that P(x) is true in **m2**. With this ordering defined, the minimal models with respect to P consist of the set of models {m | there is no m' $<_P$ m}. Given a suitable knowledge base K, it can be shown that the conclusions derivable from K making the closed world assumption on P are exactly the conclusions that are entailed by the minimal models (with respect to P) of K.

Another way to formalize the closed world assumption is to add an axiom to the KB that specifically entails the closure. This axiom is called the **predicate completion axiom**. Consider a KB containing the propositions

$$P(A), P(B), Q(C), Q(A)$$

The predicate completion axiom for P would be

$$\forall x . P(x) \equiv (x{=}A \vee x{=}B)$$

This axiom would allow you to conclude that P is only true for A and B. Thus you could infer $\neg P(C)$, as desired. It can be shown that the set of models for the KB extended with the predicate completion axioms is exactly the set of minimal models (with respect to P) of the initial KB. Predicate completion axioms can handle more complex KBs as well. For instance, if the KB also included the axiom

$$\forall s . Q(s) \supset P(s),$$

then the predicate completion axiom for P would be

$$\forall x . P(x) \equiv (x{=}A \vee x{=}B \vee Q(x))$$

Predicate completion cannot be applied to all KBs, however, as it can't handle axioms that contain more than one positive occurrence of P. A generalization, called **circumscription** (McCarthy, 1980), can generate an appropriate closure axiom, but may require using a second-order logic (that is, involving quantification over predicates).

Inference Techniques

The two main classes of inference techniques found in knowledge representation systems are **procedural** and **declarative**. Most systems combine these techniques to some extent, forming a continuum from purely declarative

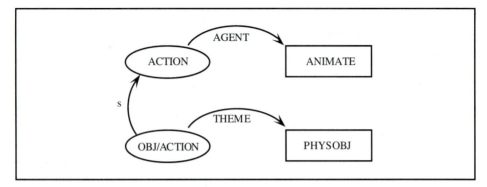

Figure 13.1 An example of simple inheritance

representations to purely procedural ones. The declarative end of the continuum would be a logic-based theorem prover. The KB is represented as a set of axioms, and inference is performed using a deductive theorem-proving algorithm. In a strongly declarative system, the emphasis is on assigning a formal semantics to the expressions of the representation independent of the inference component.

Procedural inference systems, on the other hand, emphasize the inferential aspects of the representation, and in extreme cases the expressions in the KB may be given no meaning independent of how they are manipulated by the program. An example of a procedural representation might be a system that uses the computer's own built-in arithmetic procedures to evaluate arithmetic expressions without any explicit representation of knowledge about mathematics, such as Peano's axioms of arithmetic. In practice, procedural systems can be very effective at specific inference tasks in well-defined domains but are often hard to analyze because they lack formality.

Consider an example. In Chapter 10 the technique of inheritance was introduced for semantic networks. This inference process can be realized procedurally or declaratively. A purely declarative approach would model each fact about subtypes and roles as an axiom and the inheritance properties would result from standard deductive inference. For example, given the simple network in Figure 13.1, the following FOPC axioms might represent this information:

1. $\forall x . ACTION(x) \supset \exists a . AGENT(x, a) \& ANIMATE(a)$
2. $\forall a \exists x . ACTION(x) \& AGENT(x, a) \supset ANIMATE(a)$
3. $\forall x . OBJ/ACTION(x) \supset ACTION(x)$
4. $\forall x . OBJ/ACTION(x) \supset \exists o . THEME(x, o) \& PHYSOBJ(o)$
5. $\forall o \exists x . OBJ/ACTION(x) \& THEME(x, o) \supset PHYSOBJ(o)$

Using these axioms, you can prove that the class OBJ/ACTION "inherits" the AGENT role. In other words, for any object A such that *OBJ/ACTION(A)* is true, you could prove that A has an agent role; that is,

$\exists a . AGENT(A, a) \& ANIMATE(a)$

using axioms 3 and 1.

As described in Chapter 10, a procedural version of this would be a program that starts at the specified node OBJ/ACTION, finds all roles attached at that node, and then follows the S arc up to the supertype ACTION and finds all the roles attached there. The complete set of roles gathered by this procedure is the answer. Thus any OBJ/ACTION has an AGENT role inherited from the class ACTION.

Both these techniques compute the same result, but the first does it by using deduction over logical formulas, while the second uses a program that performs a graph traversal. The first technique seems more rigorously defined, but the second is probably more efficient. In cases like this, in which you can prove that the two techniques obtain the same results, you can have the best of both approaches: a rigorously defined semantics and an efficient procedure to perform that form of inference.

13.2 A Representation Based on FOPC

The KRL used in this book will be an extended version of the first-order predicate calculus. Note that by choosing the language, you are not committed to any particular form of inference. For example, later sections will show how the KRL can be used with both deductive and procedural inference techniques.

The syntax of FOPC was introduced earlier and will not be presented again here. We will focus on the extensions to standard FOPC that are needed to represent the meaning of natural language sentences, and comment on the differences between this language and the logical form language. The terms of the language consist of constants (such as *John1*), functions (such as *father(John1)*), and variables (such as x and y). Note that the logical form language did not use constants. Rather, everything was expressed in terms of discourse variables to keep the representation context independent. In the KB, constants are used to represent the specific individuals. For example, the logical form term (NAME **j1** "John") represents the meaning of a phrase whose referent is named "John." The actual person referred to in a given context might be represented by the constant *John1* in the KB.

It is convenient to use restricted quantification in the KRL, making it similar to the generalized quantifier notation in the logical form language. Restrictions follow the quantified variable separated by a colon. As mentioned in Chapter 8, for the existential and universal quantifiers, this notation can be treated as an abbreviation and does not extend the expressive power of the language. Thus

$\exists x : Man(x) \; Happy(x)$ is equivalent to $\exists x . Man(x) \; \& \; Happy(x)$ and
$\forall x : Man(x) \; Happy(x)$ is equivalent to $\forall x . Man(x) \supset Happy(x)$

We will also need the *equality* predicate, $(a = b)$, which states that terms a and b have the same denotation. Given a simple proposition P_a involving a constant a, if P_a is true and $a = b$, then P_b must be true as well, where P_b is the same as P_a except that a has been replaced by b.

Many knowledge representation systems do not explicitly use quantifiers. They do include variables, however, which act like universally quantified variables with wide scope. For example, a formula such as (P ?x A) in a KB would correspond in meaning to the FOPC formula $\forall x . P(x, A)$. Existentially quantified variables are handled by a technique called **skolemization**, which replaces the variable with a new constant that has not been used before. For example, the formula $\exists y \forall x . P(x, y)$ would be encoded in the KB in a formula such as (P ?x Sk1), where Sk1 is a new constant that has not been used before, that stands for the object that is known to exist. Quantifier scoping dependencies are indicated using new functions, called **Skolem functions**. For example, the formula $\forall y \exists x . P(x, y)$ would be encoded as a formula such as (P (Sk2 ?y) ?y) in the KB, where Sk2 is a new function that produces a (potentially) different object for each value of ?y. Often, formulas will be written in a format merging these two approaches, where the universal quantifiers are still present but the existential variables have been skolemized. For example, the formula $\forall y \exists x . P(x, y)$ may be written as $\forall y P(Sk1(y), y)$. It can be proven that all these different forms of representation are equivalent.

Saying that the basic representation language is FOPC does not place many restrictions on the style of the representation. In particular, it says nothing about what the predicates are. There is a wide range of possibilities in selecting the predicates. At one end you could have a different predicate for each word sense, essentially the strategy used in the logical form language. At the other end you could have a preset set of predicates, called the **primitives**, and every word sense would have to be defined in terms of these primitives. Consider some of the advantages of each position. By allowing a predicate for each word sense, you are able to capture subtle differences between semantically close terms. For example, you might have information in the KB defining SAUNTERS1 as an action that involves walking slowly, using a manner that suggests a carefree state of mind. Thus the sentence *Jack sauntered down the street* might have different implications than *Jack walked down the street.* Of course, you pay for this power by having a wide range of predicates that for the most part have very similar axioms defining them. Specifically, the definitions for SAUNTERS1 and WALKS1 would overlap significantly.

In an approach using primitives, on the other hand, both of these senses would be reduced to the predicate (or set of predicates) that captures the basic action, say MOVE-BY-FOOT. Inference rules are then defined only on the primitive predicates. This approach allows the commonalities between words to be captured very succinctly. Without inference rules on the word senses, however, it is very difficult to capture the subtle distinctions between senses. Of course, you would have to define a new primitive to capture the distinction between sauntering and walking, say a new primitive concerning state-of-mind. Sauntering might then be defined as MOVE-BY-FOOT and CAREFREE-STATE. The more complex the decomposition of the senses, however, the less advantageous the primitive representation becomes, because the number of primitives grows significantly, driven by examples. More crucially, inference rules would have to be based on complex clusters of primitives rather than single predicates, so the inference process is no longer so simply defined.

As with many issues, there is considerable middle ground to be explored. Specifically, many of the advantages of a primitive-based representation can be captured by using type hierarchies. If you assert that SAUNTERS1 and WALKS1 are both subclasses of the more abstract action MOVE-BY-FOOT, then they could inherit most of their common properties from MOVE-BY-FOOTwithout the need for additional axioms. This still leaves you free, however, to add other axioms for SAUNTERS1 to cover its special characteristics.

This approach would also allow you to handle incomplete knowledge. Say the system only knows that SAUNTERS1 is a type of walking. It doesn't know any additional information about the word but can still make most inferences required about it using information inherited from MOVE-BY-FOOT. In addition, it knows that SAUNTERS1 is somehow different from WALKS1, even though if doesn't know why. If, at a later stage, the system acquires additional knowledge about sauntering, this can be added incrementally.

In addition to hierarchical relations, a knowledge representation should also be able to take advantage of other ways to define word senses. Sometimes a complete definition of a term is known. For example, you could define the predicate *father* as a *male parent,* that is,

$$\forall x . FATHER(x) \equiv \exists y \, PARENT(x, y) \, \& \, MALE(x)$$

But most words are not so precisely defined. For instance, there is no set of properties that precisely defines most natural kinds, such as dogs, cats, chairs, and so on. These can be classified into type hierarchies, and axioms stating necessary conditions can be stated, but no absolute definition is possible. Viewed as FOPC axioms, this means that such definitions involve a one-way implication. For instance, an axiom for DOG1 might be

$$\forall x . DOG1(x) \supset CANINE(x) \, \& \, DOMESTIC\text{-}PET(x)$$

where CANINE itself is defined as a type of MAMMAL, and so on. Such axioms capture much of the important properties of being a dog but do not define the concept completely. For instance, someone might have a pet wolf that satisfies all the properties of being a dog but still isn't a dog.

From the point of view of generating sentences, the more the predicates in representation language are abstracted from the words in the language, the harder it is to produce sentences based on meanings. For instance, assume you are given the formula

$$\forall p : ((MaleHuman \, p) \, \& \, \exists c . Parent(p, c)) .$$
$$MoveByCar(p, L1) \, \& \, Building(L1) \, \& \, Used\text{-}for\text{-}teaching(L1)$$

which has a natural realization as the sentence *All fathers drove to the school.* To generate such a sentence, the system would have to be able to realize the formula $((Male\ p)\ \&\ \exists\ c\ .\ Parent(p,\ c))$, which literally might be realized as *male humans who have a child,* as the word *father,* and realize the proposition $MoveByCar(p, L1)\ \&\ Building(L1)\ \&\ Used\text{-}for\text{-}teaching(L1)$, which literally might be realized as *moved by car to a building used for teaching,* as the phrase *drove to school.* Clearly, this would require substantial knowledge about the meanings of the specific words *father* and *drive,* and a complex process of matching formulas in the KRL to these predicates. If there are no predicates corresponding to these word meanings in the KRL, then this process is especially complicated. If such predicates are included, the hierarchical organization would suggest methods for identifying possible realizations of a formula. Specifically, given an abstract predicate, say *MaleHuman,* you could consider all the predicates below it in the abstraction hierarchy to see if any of them more concisely capture the desired meaning. In this case *Father* would be a good choice as it not only entails *MaleHuman* but also another part of the meaning, namely $\exists\ c\ .\ Parent(p,\ c)$.

The trick in designing an effective knowledge representation is to choose the set of predicates so as to make the hierarchical relationships most effective. Often, the best representation will mirror linguistic generalizations that can be made. This aids both in interpreting sentences and in generating sentences from expressions in the KB.

13.3 Frames: Representing Stereotypical Information

Much of the inference required for natural language understanding involves making assumptions about what is typically true of the objects or situations being discussed. Such information is often encoded in structures called **frames**. In its most abstract formulation, a frame is simply a cluster of facts and objects that describe some typical object or situation, together with specific inference strategies for reasoning about the situation. The situations represented could range from visual scenes, to the structure of complex physical objects, to the typical method by which some action is performed. Frame-based systems usually offer facilities such as default reasoning, automatic inheritance of properties through hierarchies, and procedural attachment. In some implementations all reasoning is accomplished by specialized inference procedures attached to the frame; in others the frames are mostly declarative in nature and are interpreted by a more uniform inference procedure. Either way, the key idea is the clustering of information to characterize the properties of commonly occurring objects and situations.

The principal objects in a frame are assigned names, called **slots** or **roles** (similar to the thematic roles in the logical form). For instance, the frame for a house may have slots such as kitchen, living room, hallway, front door, and so on. The frame also specifies the relationships between the slots and the object represented by the frame. For example, the kitchen slot of the house frame has to be physically located within the house, and it contains various appliances needed

BOX 13.2 Conceptual Dependency: A Primitive-Based Representation

Several very influential early semantic representations were based on small sets of primitives that were used to support a set of specialized reasoning techniques. One of the most influential was **conceptual dependency** (Schank, 1975; Schank and Riesbeck, 1981). This representation primarily focused on action verbs and posited a small set of action types. Specifically, the major action types included three notions of transfer:

ATRANS—abstract transfer (as in transfer of ownership)
PTRANS—physical transfer
MTRANS—mental transfer (as in speaking)

There were also primitives based on bodily activity,

PROPEL (applying force)
MOVE (moving a body part)
GRASP
INGEST
EXPEL

as well as the mental actions,

CONC (conceptualize or think)
MBUILD (perform inference)

These primitives, together with a set of case roles and a few causal connectives, essentially completed the representation. In early works, it was claimed that this representation was adequate to express the meaning of all action verbs, but in later work primitives were used as building blocks to construct larger structures to capture the meaning of verbs (for example, see Section 15.5). It was found that inference had to be specified in terms of these larger structures rather than in terms of the primitives. Thus the advantages of the primitive-based representation were lost.

for preparing meals. You can view each of these slots as a function that takes an object described by the frame (an **instance** of the frame) and produces the appropriate slot value. Thus a particular instance of the house frame—say, H1—consists of a particular instance of a kitchen, which can be referred to as "the kitchen-slot of H1," or $kitchen(H1)$, plus particular instances of all the other slots as well.

As an example, the definition of a frame type for personal computers might look as follows:

Define Object Class $PC(e)$:
Roles: $Keyb, Disk1, MainBox$
Constraints: $Keyboard(Keyb), DiskDrive(Disk1), CPU(MainBox)$

This structure means that all objects of type PC have slots of type keyboard, disk drive, and CPU (which are identified by the functions $Keyb, Disk1,$ and $MainBox,$

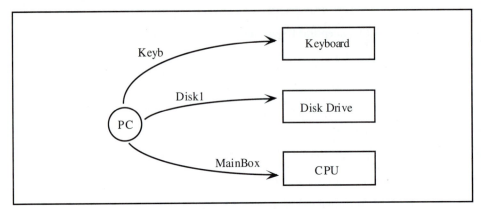

Figure 13.2 A semantic network defining the slots of PC

respectively). This is the same style of representation used in many semantic network systems. In fact, you could easily represent this structure in a semantic network notation as well, as shown in Figure 13.2.

An instance of the type *PC*—say, *PC3*—having the subparts *KEYS13*, *DD11*, and *CPU00023* would be represented in the frame notation as

(*PC3* isa *PC* with *Keyb = KEY13, Disk1 = DD11, MainBox = CPU00023*)

This definition can be viewed as an abbreviation of the FOPC formula *PC(PC3)* & *Keyb(PC3) = KEY13* & *Disk1(PC3) = DD11* & *MainBox(PC3) = CPU00023*.

Slots with Restrictions

In general, you need more than a superficial knowledge of the structural components of a PC. For instance, the PC frame might contain more information about how the slot values typically interrelate. You might want to assert that each slot is a subpart and indicate how the parts are connected: the keyboard, for example, as well as the disk drive, plug into the CPU box at the appropriate connector. To assert this, you would have to define the CPU itself as a frame structure with slots such as *KeyboardPlug, DiskPort, PowerPlug,* and so on. The notation is extended as in the following example that redefines the class of PCs so that the keyboard and disk are subparts and are connected to the CPU.

Define Object Class ***PC(p)***:
Roles: *Keyb, Disk1, MainBox*
Constraints: *Keyboard(Keyb) & PART-OF(Keyb, p) &*
CONNECTED-TO(Keyb, KeyboardPlug(MainBox)) &
DiskDrive(Disk1) & PART-OF(Disk1, p) &
CONNECTED-TO(Disk1, DiskPort(MainBox)) &
CPU(MainBox) & PART-OF(MainBox, p)

With this definition, an instance of PC—say, *PC4*—with slot values *KEY14, DD12,* and *CPU07,* would be written as

(*PC4* isa *PC* with *Keyb* = *KEY14*, *Disk1* = *DD12*, *MainBox* = *CPU07*)

which implies all the following information:

PC(PC4) & *Keyb(PC4)* = *KEY14* & *PART-OF(KEY14, PC4)* &
CONNECTED-TO(KEY14, KeyboardPlug(CPU07)) &
Disk1(PC4) = *DD12* & *PART-OF(DD12, PC4)* &
CONNECTED-TO(DD12, DiskPort(CPU07)) &
MainBox(PC4) = *CPU07* & *PART-OF(CPU07, PC4)*

Since frames are a way of encoding knowledge about classes of objects, it makes sense that frame information should be inherited through the type hierarchy. For example, if you define a subtype of *PCs* called *PC-With-Second-Disk,* this type should inherit all the slots of *PC*. If you define a new slot for this type—say, *Disk2*—then all instances will have four slots: *Keyb, Disk1, MainBox,* and *Disk2.*

Note that the information in a frame should be viewed as default conditions. For instance, it is possible to have a *PC,* say *PC5,* in which the keyboard is not connected to the computer. The fact that this property is violated does not make *PC5* fall out of the class of *PCs*; it just isn't a typical *PC*.

Frame-based representation can be used to encode additional information about situations beyond their subcomponents. One of the most useful examples of this for natural language understanding occurs in representing actions. As you will see in later chapters, knowledge about the usual situations in which actions occur can be very useful in interpreting language. In particular, knowledge about causality—what effects an action typically has and what conditions are typically necessary for the action to occur—are very important. The slot notation is extended to allow relations between the instance of the frame and other propositions or events. For actions, the following relations are useful:

preconditions—properties that typically enable the action,
effects—properties that are typically caused by the action,
decomposition—the way in which an action is typically performed
(usually defined in terms of a sequence of subactions).

For example, Figure 13.3 shows the definition of the action of buying something. The action involves four objects: the buyer, the seller, the object, and an amount of money equal to the price of the object. Furthermore, the definition states that a purchase action can occur only when the buyer has enough money and the seller has the object (the preconditions), and that typically at the end the buyer owns the object and the seller has the money (the effects). Finally, a typical way something is purchased involves the buyer giving the seller the money and the seller giving the buyer the object (the decomposition). While this might seem to be quite mundane everyday information, such knowledge is crucial for understanding the

The Action Class *BUY(b)*:
Roles: *Buyer, Seller, Object, Money*
Constraints: *Human(Buyer), SalesAgent(Seller), IsObject(Object)*
          Value(Money, Price(Object))
Preconditions: *OWNS(Buyer, Money)*
          OWNS(Seller, Object)
Effects: *¬OWNS(Buyer, Money)*
        ¬OWNS(Seller, Object)
        OWNS(Buyer, Object)
        OWNS(Seller, Money)
Decomposition: *GIVE(Buyer, Seller, Money)*
           GIVE(Seller, Buyer, Object)

Figure 13.3   The definition of BUY with its decomposition

connections between actions and states described in sentences, which in turn are crucial for ambiguity resolution.

13. 4 Handling Natural Language Quantification

With the basic KRL defined, you can now consider some issues in mapping the logical form language into the KRL. One of the most obvious differences between the two languages is the treatment of quantifiers. The logical form contains a wide range of quantificational forms corresponding to the English quantifiers, while the KRL allows only universal and existential quantification. Reconciling this difference seems almost hopeless at first glance. Significant progress can be made to reduce the differences, however, by extending the ontology of the KRL to allow sets as objects.

A set is a collection of objects viewed as a unit. While sets in general may be finite (such as the set consisting of John and Mary) or infinite (such as the set of numbers greater than 7), we will only use finite sets in the KRL. A set can be indicated by listing its members in curly brackets; for example, $\{John1\ Mary1\}$ refers to the set consisting of the denotation of *John1* and the denotation of *Mary1*. The order doesn't matter; $\{John1\ Mary1\} = \{Mary1\ John1\}$. We also allow constants to denote sets. Thus *S1* might be a set defined by the formula *S1* $= \{John1\ Mary1\}$. Full set theory would allow sets to be members of other sets. We will not use such sets in the KRL. Sets will usually be defined in terms of some property. This will be written in the form $\{y \mid P_y\}$, which is the set of all objects that satisfy the expression P_y. The set of all men is $\{y \mid Man(y)\}$. In addition, we introduce the following predicates to relate sets and individuals:

$S1 \subset S2$ iff all the elements of *S1* are in *S2*
$x \in S$ iff x is a member of the set S

With setlike objects in the representation, we can produce an interpretation for *Some men met at three,* as follows:

$$\exists\, M : M \subset \{x \mid Man(x)\} \,.\, Meet1(M,\, 3PM)$$

that is, there is a subset of men M that met at three. By convention, we will always use uppercase names for variables ranging over sets. In principle, sets are allowed in all situations where individuals have been allowed. In practice, certain verbs require only sets or only individuals in certain argument positions. For example, the verb *meet* requires its agent to be a set with more than one element, as a single individual cannot meet. Other verbs require individuals and exclude sets, and others allow both sets and individuals as arguments.

Consider the different formulas that arise from the collective/distributive readings. There are two interpretations of the sentence *Some men bought a suit,* which has the following logical form (omitting the tense operator):

(SOME **m1** : (PLUR MAN1)
    (A **s1** : SUIT1
       (BUY1 **m1 s1**)))

The collective reading would map to

$$\exists\, M1 : M1 \subset \{z \mid Man(z)\} \;\; \exists\, s : Suit(s) \,.\, Buy1(M1,\, s)$$

that is, there is a subset of the set of all men who together bought a suit. The distributive reading involves some men individually buying suits and would be represented by

$$\exists\, M2 : M2 \subset \{z \mid Man(z)\} \;\; \forall\, m : m \in M2$$
$$\exists\, s : Suit(s) \,.\, Buy1(m,\, s)$$

Note that the collective and distributive readings both involve a common core meaning involving the subset of men. The only difference is whether you use the set as a unit or quantify over all members of the set.

The set-based representation can also be used to ensure that more than one man bought a suit. To do this we introduce a new function that returns the cardinality of set. For any given set S, let $|S|$ be the number of elements in S. Using arithmetic operators, we can now encode constraints on the size of sets. For example, the meaning of *Three men entered the room* would be as follows, again with tense information omitted,

$$\exists\, M : (M \subset \{y \mid Man(y)\} \;\&\; |M| = 3)$$
$$\forall\, m : m \in M \,.\, Enter1(m,\, Room1)$$

By changing the restriction to $|M| \geq 3$, you get the meaning of *At least three men entered the room,* and so on.

More problematic quantifiers can also be given an approximate meaning using sets. For instance, if we define *most* as being true if more than half of some set has a given property, then *Most men laughed* might have the meaning

$$\exists M : (M \subset \{y \mid Man(y)\} \ \& \ |M| \geq \frac{|\{y \mid Man(y)\}|}{2})$$
$$\forall m : m \in M . Laughed(m)$$

In an actual discourse, the interpretation of the quantified terms will usually be relative to some previously defined set. For example, the sentence *Most men laughed* typically will refer to most of the men in a previously mentioned set rather than to most of the men in the world. In other words, the sentence would not claim that more than half of all men laughed, but that more than half the men in a certain context (say in a given room) laughed. This type of interpretation will be discussed further in Chapter 14.

You have seen that by introducing sets as explicit objects in a representation, a wide range of quantificational constructs can be captured in an intuitively satisfying way. While the development here was in terms of extensions to FOPC, similar capabilities are needed in any representation to capture the same phenomena. For example, assume you are using a semantic network representation. To handle quantification you must be able to have nodes that represent sets, be able to state cardinality restrictions on these nodes, and be able to quantify over these sets to obtain the distributive reading.

13.5 Time and Aspectual Classes of Verbs

One of the central components of any knowledge representation that supports natural language is the treatment of verbs and time. Much of language involves time, including temporal information implicit in the tense and aspect of sentences and explicit temporal information conveyed by a wide range of temporal adverbials (for example, *for five minutes, yesterday, at 3 o'clock, after they had left*).

In the logical form language, temporal information was handled in several ways. There were modal operators to represent tense (for example, PAST, PRES, PROG, FUT) and temporal connectives (for example, BEFORE, DURING), and all predicates could take time arguments. To handle such phenomena, we need to introduce additional extensions to FOPC to represent time.

There are several different types of times. A **time point** is an instantaneous time that is generally associated with some transition in the world, such as a light turning on or someone finding a lost pen. An **interval** of time is an extended stretch of time over which some event occurs. All intervals have **durations** (for example, five minutes long), while points cannot have durations. Many predicates can be defined only over intervals. For example, consider the predicate that asserts that John drove his car to work at a certain time. This can be true only over an interval of time, because driving to a destination necessarily takes time; you cannot drive in a single point.

Points and intervals have to be distinguished because different relationships can hold between them. For example, two intervals may overlap, whereas points cannot overlap. In addition, two intervals may **meet**: One ends where the other begins, but they do not overlap in time or have any time between them. A point or an interval may be contained within another interval, but nothing can be contained within a point. The following predicates are allowed for temporal relations:

$t1 < t2$	point/interval $t1$ is before point/interval $t2$
$t1 : t2$	interval $t1$ meets interval $t2$, or point $t1$ defines the beginning of interval $t2$, or point $t2$ defines the end of interval $t1$
$t1 \subseteq t2$	point/interval $t1$ is contained in interval $t2$

As previously mentioned, some predicates can be true only over intervals of times, whereas others can be true only at points, and others can be true at either. The classification of predicates corresponds with different aspectual classes of verb phrases.

Sentences describe propositions that fall into at least three distinct classes: those that describe states (**stative** propositions), those that define ongoing activities (**activity** propositions), and those that define completed events (**telic** propositions). Stative propositions describe some property of the world that can hold for an instant or extend indefinitely, as in the sentences

Jack is happy.
I believe the world is flat.

Stative propositions describe situations that lack a precisely defined ending point, and cannot appear in certain linguistic contexts. For instance, they do not naturally appear in the progressive form

*Jack is being happy.
*I am believing that the world is flat.

Activity propositions describe activities that occur over an interval of time. Activities are often expressed using the progressive form, as in the sentences

Jack is running.
The door was swinging to and fro.

Sentences describing states and activities do not usually allow temporal modifiers, such as *in five minutes,* but they do allow duration modifiers, such as *for five minutes.*

Telic sentences describe events that are brought to completion, as in

Jack fell asleep.
Jack climbed the mountain.

In both sentences, the event ends at some time (called the **culmination point**), and you know that some resulting property starts at the culmination point. For instance, with the first sentence you know that Jack is asleep at the end of the event, and with the second you know that Jack is at the top of the mountain.

Sentences describing telic propositions can include temporal modifiers such as *in an hour,* as in

> They climbed the mountain in two days.
> Jack fell asleep in an hour.

Telic eventualities are often broken down into two subclasses, depending on whether they essentially describe a transition only (the **achievement** class) or involve some activity leading up to the culmination (the **accomplishment** class). The previous examples describe accomplishments, whereas the following describe achievements:

> Jack recognized the man.
> Helen woke up.

The four types of proposition classes can be distinguished by different types of temporal arguments. In particular, stative propositions can be true at a point or an interval. For example, it makes sense to speak of a ball being red at a particular instant of time or over an extended interval of time. Stative propositions are **homogeneous**—whenever they hold over an interval, they also hold over all subintervals of that interval.

Achievement sentences, such as *Jack reached the summit* or *Helen closed the door,* map to propositions that describe transitions. The first describes a transition after which Jack is at the summit, whereas the second describes a transition after which the door is closed. Such predicates cannot hold over intervals, but their definitions might include information about resulting states, such as

$$\forall\ a1, l1, t1 \ . \ Reach(a1, l1, t1) \supset \exists\ T1 \ . \ t1 : T1 \ \& \ At(a1, l1, T1)$$

that is, if an agent a1 reaches a location l1 at time point t1, then a1 is at l1 for some interval of time that starts at t1.

Propositions that describe processes correspond to activity verbs, such as *Jack ran.* Process predicates can occur only over intervals and tend to be homogeneous, although not in a strict way as with statives. In particular, it could be true that Jack was running between 2 and 3 o'clock, even if he stopped for a five-minute rest sometime during that time. Thus there can be a defeasible implication, but not an entailment, that if a process P occurs over an interval T1, then it is likely to have occurred over an interval T2 within T1.

Accomplishment sentences, such as *Jack ran to the store,* have a more complex structure that seems to combine several forms. We can handle this by mapping the logical form predicates to a more complex sentence in the KRL. In particular, the logical form for *Jack ran to the store* could map to a formula indicating that a process of running occurred that culminated in a state of being at the store, that is,

$$\exists\ T1, T2 \ . \ Running(Jack1, T1) \ \& \ At(Jack1, Store1, T2) \ \& \ T1 : T2$$

Figure 13.4 summarizes some distinguishing properties of the aspectual classes.

Aspectual Class	Can Be True at a Point?	Can Be True at an Interval?	Temporal Modifier *in*
Stative Phrase	YES	YES	NO
Activity	NO	YES	NO
Achievement	YES	NO	YES
Accomplishment	NO	YES	YES

Figure 13.4 Different properties of the aspectual classes

Encoding Tense

Tense operators can also be represented directly in the temporal logic without the need for modal operators. The basic idea is to map tense operators to temporal relations with respect to some indexical term referring to the current time. For the following examples, let us assume that the constant NOW1 denotes the current time. Given this, we could map the PAST operator into a formula that existentially quantifies over a time before now; that is, the sentence *John was happy* would map to the KR expression

$$\exists T1 . T1 < NOW1 . Happy(Jack1, T1)$$

The same sentence in the simple present, *John is happy,* would map to

$$\exists T1 . NOW1 \subseteq T1 . Happy(John1, NOW1)$$

and the simple future, *John will be happy,* would map to

$$\exists T1 . T1 > NOW1 . Happy(Jack1, T1)$$

Note that there is ambiguity in the interpretation of tense, because some simple present sentences refer to the future, as in *The flight arrives at noon,* whereas some simple future sentences refer to the present, as in *Jack will be in class by now.* But we will ignore these complications in this development.

Even without ambiguity, there are some difficult problems. For instance, there are two ways to assert that something was true in the past, corresponding to the simple past and the past perfect, for example,

Helen saw the books.
Helen had seen the books.

What is the difference between these two readings? As isolated sentences, it is hard to tell, but consider these forms in more complex sentences, such as

When Jack opened the door, Helen saw the books.
When Jack opened the door, Helen had seen the books.

In the first sentence the act of seeing is cotemporal with or immediately after the time Jack opened the door, whereas in the second the act of seeing preceded

Jack's opening the door. The generally accepted account of this difference was proposed by Reichenbach (1947), who suggested the notion of **reference time**. In these examples the reference time for the main clause is the time that Jack opened the door. The simple past equates the time of the event (of seeing) with the reference time, whereas the past perfect asserts that the event precedes the reference time. Specifically, Reichenbach developed a theory that tense gives information about three times:

> S — the time of speech
> E — the time of the event/state
> R — the reference time

The reference time can be provided by temporal adverbials, as above, or can often be determined by the discourse context, as will be discussed in Chapter 15.

In the simple tenses the reference time is the same as the event time, that is, $E = R$. The three forms are generated by varying the relationship between R and S:

Jack sings	simple present: $S = R$, $E = R$
Jack sang	simple past: $R < S$, $E = R$
Jack will sing	simple future: $S < R$, $E = R$

The perfect tenses, on the other hand, have the event time preceding the reference time, and differ, as before, in terms of how the reference time and speech time are related. Thus we have

Jack has sung	present perfect: $S = R$, $E < R$
Jack had sung	past perfect: $R < S$, $E < R$
Jack will have sung	future perfect: $S < R$, $E < R$

This analysis also provides an account of the posterior tenses, in which $R < E$:

Jack is going to sing	posterior present: $S = R$, $R < E$
Jack was going to sing	posterior past: $R < S$, $R < E$
Jack will be going to sing	posterior future: $S < R$, $R < E$

These orderings are shown graphically in Figure 13.5.

13.6 Automating Deduction in Logic-Based Representations

The previous sections have developed the abstract knowledge representation language that will be used through the rest of this book. The remaining sections change the focus and look at selected reasoning strategies used in knowledge representation systems. This section describes some techniques for automated reasoning in knowledge representations. As mentioned earlier, reasoning systems fall into two main categories: the declarative techniques based on deductive proof techniques and the procedural approaches. This section considers some purely deductive techniques.

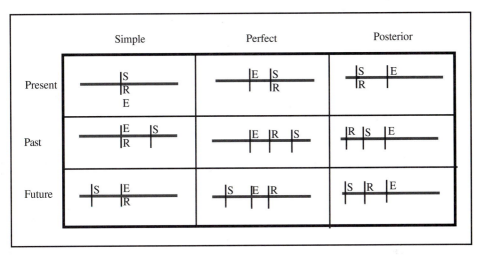

Figure 13.5 Some temporal configurations allowed by the tenses

If you have ever studied proof methods such as natural deduction for FOPC, you know that finding proofs is complicated because there are many different ways to try to prove any given formula. In addition, there are often many syntactic ways to express the same content. Most work in automated reasoning attempts to reduce this complexity before starting the task. In particular, a **normal form** is used for formulas that uses a restricted subset of the full FOPC syntax. Many formulas that are logically equivalent but syntactically different have the same normal form. For example, the formulas

$$\neg P \mathrel{\&} Q$$
$$\neg(P \vee \neg Q)$$
$$\neg(Q \supset P)$$

are all logically equivalent. In a representation based on **conjunctive normal form** (CNF), described later in this section, these all map to the same formula. A second technique concerns the handling of variables. In general, with quantified variables, many particular instantiations of those variables could be used to establish a proof. Thus, when searching for a proof, there is ample opportunity to pick the wrong instantiation and have to reconsider later. The **unification** technique partially avoids this problem by always computing the most general solution possible for a given line of reasoning. If you are not already familiar with unification, see Appendices A and B.

Many different reasoning systems can be viewed with the framework of automatic proof systems, from simple pattern-based retrieval from databases, to Horn clause systems similar to PROLOG, to fully general theorem-proving systems. The differences arise from the form of expressions each system can represent and reason about. To see this, let's first develop a fully general normal form for FOPC. At the level of constants, functions, and atomic propositions,

Formula in FOPC	Clause Form Equivalent
P	$(P \mathrel{<\text{-}})$
$\neg P$	$(\mathrel{<\text{-}} P)$
$P \mathbin{\&} Q$	two clauses: $(P \mathrel{<\text{-}})$ and $(Q \mathrel{<\text{-}})$
$P \vee Q$	$(P\,Q \mathrel{<\text{-}})$
$Q \vee \neg P$	$(Q \mathrel{<\text{-}} P)$
$P \supset Q$	$(Q \mathrel{<\text{-}} P)$
$\neg(P \supset Q)$	two clauses: $(P \mathrel{<\text{-}})$ and $(\mathrel{<\text{-}} Q)$
$(P \mathbin{\&} Q) \vee R$	two clauses: $(P\,R \mathrel{<\text{-}})$ and $(Q\,R \mathrel{<\text{-}})$

Figure 13.6 Formulas in clause form

conjunctive normal form is identical to FOPC. A **literal** corresponds to an atomic proposition, possibly negated, such as the following:

> *Person(John1)*
> *Car(Car1)*
> *Owns(John1, Car1)*
> *¬Happy(John1)*

A **clause** is simply a disjunction of literals such as the following, which asserts that either Helen owns a particular car or she is not happy:

> *Owns(Helen1, Car2)* $\vee$ *¬Happy(Helen1)*

In many systems, clauses are written using a form of the implication operator instead, and the preceding clause would be written as

> *(Owns(Helen1, Car2) <- Happy(Helen1))*

In general, a clause is written as

> *(P1, ..., Pn <- Q1, ..., Qm)*

which states that if *Q1, ..., Qm* are true, then at least one of *P1, ..., Pn* is true. Viewing a clause as a disjunctive formula, the *Qi*'s are all the negated literals, while the *Pi*'s are all the positive literals. It can be shown that all formulas in FOPC have an equivalent clause form. Figure 13.6 gives some examples of some propositional formulas using standard logical operators and their equivalent form in conjunctive normal form. Quantification is handled in clause-based systems using variables and skolemization, as discussed in Section 13.2.

A very useful restriction of this type of expression is the **Horn clause**, which has exactly one literal on the left side, that is, exactly one positive literal. In a KB restricted to Horn clauses, the backward chaining strategy used in PRO-LOG is able to find a proof of any formula that logically follows from the KB.

Reasoning with clauses makes extensive use of the unification algorithm. Consider first a very limited KR that allows only literals in the KB, similar to a relational database that allows quantification. The intuition we want is that a literal P follows from the KB if we can retrieve a formula in the KB that unifies with it. Consider how variables are treated in such a system. The FOPC formula $\forall y \exists x P(x, y)$ would correspond to the literal $P(Sk2(?y), ?y)$. If the KB contains this literal, consider what would happen if you later want to see whether $\forall w \exists z$ $P(w, z)$ follows from the KB. If you convert it to clause form, you would obtain a literal such as $P(Sk3(?w), ?w)$, which will not unify with the literal in the database since the Skolem functions are named differently. In pattern retrieval systems, this is handled by changing the interpretation of quantifiers when they are used as a query. Thus, as a query, $\forall y \exists x P(x, y)$ would map to a literal $P(?z, Sk4)$, which would unify with the literal for the same formula already in the knowledge base.

At first glance, this technique of changing the interpretation of quantifiers for queries may seem rather arbitrary, but it actually follows from the underlying proof strategy being used. In particular, there are always two general methods for proving a formula P. The first is to build a proof of P directly from the KB using the rules of inference. The second is to show that ¬P is inconsistent with the KB (and thus P must follow from the KB). The latter approach is called a **refutation proof** and turns out to be the most useful technique for automatic deduction. It forms the foundation for pattern-matching techniques as previously described, Horn clause proof strategies, and general resolution-based theorem-proving systems. All of these can be viewed as specialized implementations of a single rule of inference called the **resolution rule**. A simple case of the resolution rule resembles modus ponens. In particular, given a clause

$(Q \leftarrow P)$ (that is, P implies Q)

and the clause

$(P \leftarrow)$ (that is, P is true)

the resolution rule allows you to conclude $(Q \leftarrow)$ (that is, Q is true). Another simple case of the resolution rule detects contradictions. Given $(P \leftarrow)$ (that is, P is true) and $(\leftarrow P)$ (that is, P is false), the resolution rule gives the empty clause $(\leftarrow)$, which indicates that the database is inconsistent.

The resolution rule is generalized to FOPC by using unification to instantiate the variables in the two clauses to make the X's identical. For example, consider a KB that includes clauses asserting that all dogs bark and that Fido is a dog:

$(Bark(?x) \leftarrow Dog(?x))$
$(Dog(Fido1) \leftarrow)$

The resolution rule would allow you to conclude that Fido barks, for after substituting $Fido1$ for $?x$ in the two clauses, you can cancel the literal $Dog(Fido1)$ from both clauses to obtain the resulting clause:

$(Bark(Fido1) \leftarrow)$

With the resolution rule in hand, you can now consider the refutation proof strategy. Given a consistent KB in clause form, we can determine whether a formula P follows from the KB by negating P, converting it to clause form and adding it to the KB, and then showing that we can derive the empty clause using the resolution rule. Since this indicates that the KB is now inconsistent, P must follow from the KB. It can be proven that the resolution strategy is complete in the sense that if P does follow from the KB, then a proof can be found. However, the converse is not true in the general case. If P does not follow from the KB, the proof strategy may never be able to tell this fact. By limiting the form of the clauses that can be used, you obtain different properties. For instance, with a KB consisting solely of Horn clauses, you can tell whether a formula P does or does not follow from the KB in every circumstance.

In deductively based systems, a common technique for introducing a default mechanism is called **proof by failure**. A new operator called UNLESS is introduced that recursively calls the theorem prover on the formula that is its argument. If the recursive call to the theorem prover stops without proving the formula true, then the UNLESS formula is true. For example, the default rule that cats purr might be expressed as the following axiom:

$$\forall c . Cat(c) \ \& \ Unless(\neg Purr(c)) \supset Purr(c)$$

That is, you can conclude that a cat purrs except when you can prove it doesn't purr. Because of the potential expense of recursively calling the prover, such techniques are usually used only with restricted proof systems, such as in PROLOG-style Horn-clause representations. Another technique used in many such systems that is closely related to the closed world assumption is the **negation as failure** rule, where a proposition is false if it can't be proven true; that is, for any proposition $P, Unless(P) \supset \neg P$. Of course, you would have to be very careful if using default rules in a system that uses negation as failure. For instance, in a system using negation as failure, the previous default rule would state that you can conclude that cats purr only when you can conclude that cats purr—not a very useful rule!

The notions of clauses, unification, and refutation proofs provide the formal underpinnings of virtually every modern knowledge representation system; that is, any system that uses pattern matching with variables can be seen as a special case of the general technique. Of course, this does not mean that matching covers all the reasoning that a knowledge representation system can do, but it is a crucial part of every system.

○ 13.7 Procedural Semantics and Question Answering

Procedurally based techniques are frequently used in database query applications, where there is a large difference in expressive power between the logical form language and the database language. Cast in terms of the formalism in the last section, the KB (that is, the database) consists only of positive literals, often

```
(FLIGHT F1)              (ATIME F2 CHI 1000HR)
(FLIGHT F2)              (ATIME F3 CHI 900HR)
(FLIGHT F3)              (ATIME F4 BOS 1700HR)
(FLIGHT F4)              (DTIME F1 BOS 1600HR)
(AIRPORT BOS)            (DTIME F2 BOS 900HR)
(AIRPORT CHI)            (DTIME F3 BOS 800HR)
(ATIME F1 CHI 1700HR)    (DTIME F4 CHI 1600HR)
```

Figure 13.7   A simple database of airline schedules

without variables. Rather than convert the logical form language into extended FOPC as described in earlier sections, the logical forms are treated as expressions in a query language. Each logical form language construct corresponds to a particular procedure that performs the appropriate query. For example, the query *Does every flight to Chicago serve breakfast?* with the logical form

(EVERY **f1** : (& (FLIGHT **f1**) (DEST **f1** (NAME **c1** "Chicago")))
    (SERVE-BREAKFAST **f1**))

would be interpreted as a procedure as follows:

1. Find all flights in the database with destination CHI (the database symbol for Chicago).
2. For each flight found, check if it serves breakfast. If all do, return yes; otherwise return no.

This section shows how to interpret logical form expressions as procedures, a method of interpretation often called **procedural semantics**.

To make the development concrete, consider the very simple database retrieval system shown in Figure 13.7. The database consists of a set of positive literals containing no variables. Times are indicated in international notation; for example, 1700HR is 5:00 PM. The relation (ATIME f c t) indicates that flight f arrives at airport c at time t, and (DTIME f c t) indicates that flight f leaves from airport c at time t. The database system provides a simple interface based on pattern matching of literals, where the query may contain variables. Two database query functions are assumed:

(Test <literal>$_1$ ..., <literal>$_n$)—returns true if there is some binding of the variables such that each literal is found in the database.

(Retrieve <var> <literal>$_1$ ..., <literal>$_n$)—like Test, but if it succeeds it returns every instance of the indicated variable that provides a solution.

For example, given the database in Figure 13.7, the query

(Retrieve ?x (FLIGHT ?x) (ATIME ?x CHI 1000HR))

would return the list (F2) because F2 is the only binding of ?x where both these literals are in the database.

All expressions in the logical form language must be interpreted in a way that reduces eventually to these two query forms on the database. The way this is done is by mapping the logical form into a procedure that performs the appropriate queries on the database. Thus answering a question is done in two steps: translating the logical form into a program and then executing that program to compute the answer.

Consider the translation step first. For any logical form expression E, the translation of E in the database query language will be indicated as T(E). The translation of expressions varies depending on the constructs. For instance, expressions such as (NAME **c1** "Chicago") will be translated into the appropriate database constant, in this case CHI. But in addition, the symbol **c1** must be stored with the constant CHI on a structure called the **symbol table**, so that if **c1** is found again in another part of the logical form, it can also be replaced by its value CHI.

Some logical form relations will translate directly into database relations, whereas others will translate into more complex expressions. For instance, the logical form relation DEST is not used in the database; rather, the destination of a flight is encoded in the ATIME relation that includes both the flight's destination and its arrival time. Thus the logical form relation (DEST **f1** (NAME **c1** "Chicago")), where **f1** has already been associated with a variable ?f, would translate into the database relation

(ATIME ?f CHI ?t)

Since the time is not included in the DEST relation, it is interpreted as an unconstrained variable in the translation. In general, the translation of each relation in the logical form must be specified.

The procedural semantics approach gets more interesting as it interprets logical connectives and quantifiers, which of course have no corresponding constructs in the relational database. The logical operators are interpreted as follows:

Conjunctions: (& R_1 ..., R_n)—will translate into a program of the form (CHECK-ALL-TRUE T(R_1) ..., T(R_n)), which when executed will successively query each T(R_i) to make sure it is true and pass on the variable bindings to the queries that follow. If there is a set of variable bindings such that querying each T(R_i) succeeds, then the program succeeds; otherwise it fails.

Disjunctions: (OR R_1 ..., R_n)—will translate into a program of the form (FIND-ONE-TRUE T(R_1) ..., T(R_n)), which when executed will successively query each T(R_i) until one of the R_i succeeds, in which case the program succeeds. If no R_i succeeds, then the program fails.

The procedure for negation assumes the closed world assumption on all relations in the database, and uses proof by failure:

> **(NOT R)**—translates into a program of the form (UNLESS T(R)), which succeeds only if querying T(R) fails.

The most complex translations occur with quantifiers. Each quantifier translates to a program that does the appropriate operations on the database. Because of the limitations of the database language, only the distributive readings of plural quantifiers are usually supported. Consider three quantifiers important in question-answering applications: THE, EACH and WH.

> **(THE x : R_x P_x)**—translates into a program (FIND-THE ?x T($R_{?x}$) T($P_{?x}$)), which first does a retrieval to find all ?x that satisfy T($R_{?x}$), that is, (Retrieve ?x T($R_{?x}$)). If a single answer is found, then that answer is substituted for ?x in the entire expression, and T($P_{?x}$) is executed to provide the answer for the entire expression. If no object is found when querying T($R_{?x}$), then there is a presupposition violation that might be handled by the question-answering system in a special way, say, notifying the user that there is no such object. If multiple answers are found, the designer of the system must decide what is best to do. Some systems allow this situation and execute T(P_x) for each of the values; other systems treat it as a failure.

> **(EACH x : R_x P_x)**—translates to a program (ITERATE ?x T($R_{?x}$) T($P_{?x}$)), which also starts by doing a retrieval to find all ?x that satisfy T($R_{?x}$). It then iteratively executes T($P_{?x}$) for each value found and succeeds only if each of these queries succeeds.

> **(WH x : R_x P_x)**—translates into a program (PRINT-ALL ?x T($R_{?x}$) T($P_{?x}$)), which retrieves all objects that satisfy the translations of R_x and P_x, that is, (Retrieve ?x T($R_{?x}$) T($P_{?x}$)), and then prints out the results. Determining the best format for printing the answers, especially determining whether additional information should be provided, is a complex issue. Here we assume it simply prints the answers found.

This is enough mechanism to show some examples using the database in Figure 13.7. The query *Which flight to Chicago leaves at 4PM?* would have the logical form (after scoping)

> (WH **f1** : (& (FLIGHT **f1**) (DEST **f1** (NAME **c1** "Chicago")))
> (LEAVE **l1** (NAME **t1** "4PM")))

This would translate into a query of the form

> (PRINT-ALL ?f (FLIGHT ?f) (ATIME ?f CHI ?t) (DTIME ?f ?s 1600HR))

Here, the DEST relation maps to an ATIME relation as previously described, and the LEAVE predicate maps into the DTIME relations. Note that the departure location was not specified in the logical form and so is treated as a variable here. In a real application the departure city would be determined by context or by default. With the small database shown in Figure 13.7, however, there is only one flight matching the current description, namely F1, so it works in this case.

Consider a more complex example that involves iteration, as in the request *Give the departure time of each flight to Chicago* with the logical form

$$\text{(EACH } \mathbf{f1} : (\& \text{ (FLIGHT } \mathbf{f1}) \text{ (DEST } \mathbf{f1} \text{ (NAME } \mathbf{c1} \text{ ``Chicago''})))$$
$$\text{(THE } \mathbf{t1} : \text{(DEPART-TIME } \mathbf{f1} \text{ t1})$$
$$\text{(GIVE-SPECIFY1 } \mathbf{g1})))$$

This would translate into the query

$$\text{(ITERATE ?f1 (CHECK-ALL-TRUE (FLIGHT ?f1) (ATIME ?f CHI ?t1))}$$
$$\text{(FIND-THE ?t1 (DTIME ?f1 ?city ?t1)}$$
$$\text{(PRINT ?t1)))}$$

In this case, the interpretation of the verb *give* simply involves printing out its argument, i.e., the departure time. The execution of the expression then proceeds as follows:

1. The first part of the ITERATE step is to find all ?f1 satisfying the restriction. The CHECK-ALL-TRUE procedure succeeds for ?f1 only if both (FLIGHT ?f1) and (ATIME ?f CHI ?t1) are in the database. This step returns the flights F1, F2, and F3.

2. The second part of the step is to execute (FIND-THE ?t1 (DTIME ?f1 ?city ?t1) (PRINT ?t1)) for each of the three values. Consider the execution with the first value, F1. The expression is

$$\text{(FIND-THE ?t1 (DTIME F1 ?city ?t1) (PRINT ?t1))}$$

The program for FIND-THE first performs the query (Retrieve ?t1 (DTIME F1 ?city ?t1)). This returns a unique answer, namely the time 1700HR. The second step of the FIND-THE program executes PRINT on this value, causing 1700HR to be printed. The second and third iterations print the values 1000HR and 900HR, respectively.

Many natural language database query systems use the procedural semantics technique. It provides a convenient way to capture the appropriate behavior for many constructs whose meaning cannot be expressed within the limited language of the database system. Because of the nature of database applications, the limitations of these techniques do not appear to be a problem in practice. For instance, database systems don't typically encode information that would make queries using collective interpretations of quantifiers necessary. In addition, since

BOX 13.3 LUNAR: A Natural Language Database Query System

With the discussion of procedural semantics, you have now seen most of the central components of the LUNAR system. LUNAR, developed in the 1970s, acted as a front-end query system to a database containing information about the rock samples brought back from the Apollo missions to the moon. It was the first natural language system to demonstrate extensive coverage in a realistic application domain, and many of the techniques that are common in the field today either originated or were first developed to an advanced stage in this system. The system used an ATN parser (see Section 4.6) that produced a representation based on grammatical relations, which was then interpreted by a semantic interpretation module that used a recursive pattern-matching technique to produce an expression in a meaning representation, as in Section 11.1. Quantifier information was maintained separately from the rest of the semantic representation and was then ordered using heuristics similar to those described in Section 12.3. The result was a final meaning representation expressed in a meaning representation language similar to our fully scoped logical form. This was then executed using a procedural semantics approach as described in this section. Some examples of queries that LUNAR could handle are

Give me all lunar samples with magnetite.
In which samples has apatite been identified?
What is the specific activity of A126 in soil?
What is the average concentration of olivine in brecchias?
In which brecchias is the average concentration of titanium greater than
    6 percent?

For more information on LUNAR, see Woods (1970; 1977; 1978).

the database does not contain disjunctive information, the limited forms for disjunctive queries also do not pose a problem.

Procedural semantic techniques can also be used with Horn-clause-based databases as well. Most of the procedural definitions of constructs can be defined by Horn clause axioms, with the addition of an ability to recursively invoke the prover to perform tasks such as finding all objects that satisfy some set of literals. With extensions to handle finite sets, such a representation can handle a wide range of quantifiers procedurally using the encoding techniques described in Section 13.4. With their additional expressive power, Horn-clause-based databases are a very attractive generalization to the traditional relational database for supporting natural language query systems.

13.8 Hybrid Knowledge Representations

Even if a knowledge representation language remained first-order, general search strategies in theorem proving would usually be too inefficient for practical systems. The theoretical cleanness of viewing inference as theorem proving,

ANIMAL
↑ s
MAMMAL
↑ s
DOG
↑ isa
Fido1

Figure 13.8 A small type hierarchy

however, has many attractive properties. Hybrid KR systems attempt to gain the advantages of using efficient procedural inference for some tasks while retaining the theoretical framework of theorem-proving systems.

As a start, the ideas of unification and refutation proof can be carried over into most systems. A hybrid system, however, does not depend entirely on these techniques. Rather, certain forms of inference are accomplished using special-purpose techniques that can be considerably more efficient. For example, consider the implementation of type hierarchies in a KR system. You saw earlier that type hierarchies can be encoded as axioms (for example, $\forall x . DOG(x) \supset MAMMAL(x)$), or as graphs, as in semantic networks. These techniques may be formally equivalent, but they can produce radically different computational properties.

One way to combine these techniques is to assume a typed logic resembling the restricted quantification logic developed in Section 13.2. The type hierarchy is predefined in a semantic network structure in which DOG is a subtype of MAMMAL which is a subtype of ANIMAL, and Fido1 is predefined to be a member of the set DOG. Given this general knowledge, the KB encoding the assertion *All animals have a mother* would be

$(MOTHER(?x{:}ANIMAL, Sk1(?x)) <-)$

where the notation *?x:ANIMAL* indicates a variable ranging over type *ANIMAL*. Such expressions could be reasoned about by extending the unification algorithm, so that two terms may unify only if they are of compatible types; that is, *?x:ANIMAL* and *Fido1* will unify only if *Fido1* is a member of the set *ANIMAL*. This constraint can be checked procedurally using the semantic network shown in Figure 13.8. Now the query as to whether Fido has a mother—that is, *MOTHER(Fido1, ?y)*—can be proved using a single unification step.

The procedural approach allows you to write highly optimized procedures that are significantly faster than would be possible doing the same work using axioms. The hybrid representation also allows for a more intuitive encoding of the information, using a semantic network for the type information, and also could permit other nondeductive algorithms to be performed on the semantic network.

Another example of a specialized reasoner that can be put to very effective use concerns equality reasoning. It is very difficult to axiomatize equality directly into a theorem-proving system because it is hard to encode the equivalence of formulas that differ only in using two different names for the same object. Very efficient algorithms exist, however, for maintaining equality information between ground terms based on equivalence classes. If such techniques are built into the unifier, then no explicit axioms about equality need be encoded in the system. Rather, the extended unification algorithm would use the procedures defined for equality to check whether two terms are equal and thus can be unified.

Other forms of specialized reasoning systems can be integrated by defining procedures that establish the truth of particular predicates. The technique is called **procedural attachment**. For instance, consider temporal reasoning. While it is possible to use an axiomatization of time to drive temporal reasoning, the resulting system would be very inefficient. There are, however, specialized reasoning techniques that can manage temporal information quite effectively. Such systems can be integrated into a hybrid system using special predicates. To see this, consider what roles propositions play in a reasoning system. There are generally three different operations applicable to propositions:

Assert that it is true (that is, add it to the KB)
Query whether it is true (that is, invoke the theorem prover on it)
Retract it (that is, remove it from the KB)

While each of these operations was defined in terms of a theorem-proving system, this does not have to be the only way such operations are accomplished. In fact, you could define arbitrary procedures to perform each of the tasks. For instance, consider a specialized temporal reasoning system that maintains a graph of temporal relations and uses graph search techniques to establish temporal relations. Assume that there is a predicate BEFORE in the KB that indicates that one time precedes another. When a proposition such as (BEFORE t1 t2) is to be added to the KB, the specialized temporal reasoner is invoked to add the information to its temporal graph. When the same proposition is queried (either directly by the user, or as a substep of a more complex proof), then the special-ized temporal reasoner is called to establish it. As a result, the specialized temporal reasoner can be fully integrated into the theorem prover, and used whenever temporal information is required. Of course, to be fully integrated, the specialized reasoning would have to be able to handle variables and return results equivalent to unification. For instance, if the theorem prover needed to establish (BEFORE t1 ?x), the temporal reasoner would have to return a binding for ?x. In addition, it would need to be able to handle backtracking when alternate solutions need to be explored.

Hybrid reasoning systems offer an attractive way to integrate specialized reasoning algorithms into a uniform framework.

Summary

Natural language understanding requires a capability to represent and reason about knowledge of the world. While there are many different techniques for representing knowledge, every representation sufficient for general language understanding must at least support the following general capabilities:

- a full range of logical operators and logical quantification, as found in FOPC
- a way to represent default, stereotypical information about the objects and situations that occur in the domain
- a way to explicitly represent and reason about finite sets
- a method of representing and reasoning about temporal information

These are representative but by no means exhaust the areas of concern. In a fully general system, for instance, you would also explore the spatial information in language, and the representation of mental attitudes.

This chapter developed an abstract representation language, combining the techniques of FOPC and frame-based systems, that satisfies the requirements just listed. This abstract representation could be realized within a wide range of knowledge representation systems using different techniques. Any knowledge representation system must support basic capabilities for pattern matching, for which the notion of unification and inference based on refutation provide a formal basis. Many systems also specify specialized procedures for some or all of the reasoning tasks. A system that uses a mix of techniques, including deductive and procedural techniques, is called a hybrid system.

Related Work and Further Readings

Knowledge representation is a highly diverse area in artificial intelligence and is fundamental to many problems beyond language understanding. A good introduction to the field is the collection of papers in Brachman and Levesque (1985). A good sample of current work in the field can be found in the proceedings of the Conferences on Knowledge Representation and Reasoning (for example, Brachman, Levesque, and Reiter (1989); Allen, Fikes, and Sandewall (1991); and Nebel, Rich, and Swartout (1992)). Norvig (1992) has written an excellent text that discusses different implementation techniques for knowledge representation systems.

The introduction of frames by Minsky (1975) produced a large body of subsequent work in representation. One of the first knowledge representation systems based on these ideas was KRL (Bobrow and Winograd, 1977). Hayes (1979) performed an analysis of KRL in terms of FOPC. Most modern representation systems, such as the systems described in Brachman and Levesque (1985), can be seen as combinations of frame systems, semantic networks, and deductive logic. A large class of systems organize knowledge around descriptions of categories of objects and are called **term subsumption languages.** There are good examples in Brachman and Levesque (1985). A good reference for semantic network-based systems is Sowa (1991).

The strongest proponents of knowledge representations based on decompositions into a small set of primitives have been Schank (1975) and Wilks (1975). Most current representation systems, however, use abstraction as the organizational tools in representations, and are often based on semantic networks and frame systems. There have also been many proposals for decomposition in linguistics (such as Dowty (1979) and Jackendoff (1990)).

The treatment of quantifiers by using explicit sets is common in computational systems (for example, Woods (1977); Warren and Pereira (1982); and Alshawi (1992)) and in linguistics (for example, McCawley (1993)).

The study of tense and aspect is a very active area of research in linguistics, philosophy, and computational linguistics. A good reference on tense and aspect in the computational literature is a special issue of *Computational Linguistics* (1988). An excellent place to start in the linguistics literature is with Dowty (1979; 1986) and Bach (1986). More recent work in the area includes Parsons (1990) and Pustejovsky (1991). The classic reference for tense is Reichenbach (1947). There is also a large literature on the treatment of tense as a modal operator (for example, Prior (1967)). McCawley (1993) contains a good introduction to linguistic issues in dealing with tense and aspect. Allen (1984) describes a temporal logic that explicitly involves predicates in three different aspectual categories. Davis (1990) describes a logic-based representation that includes specialized representations for time, space, and many other aspects of the world.

Most deductive techniques have evolved from work in resolution theory proving as introduced by Robinson (1965). Robinson introduced the resolution rule and proved that the resolution refutation proof technique was complete. The technique of proof by failure was used in the early AI programming language PLANNER (Hewitt, 1971), and was formalized by Clark (1978). Much of the work on default logics stems from work by Reiter (1980). Etherington and Reiter (1983) used this formalism to define inheritance formally with exceptions in type hierarchies. There is a large body of literature on representation using semantic techniques based on minimal models. A good general overview can be found in Genesereth and Nilsson (1987).

Procedural semantics was extensively used in early systems, notably Winograd (1973) and Woods (1978), and is still a common technique in database query systems. The CHAT-80 system (Warren and Pereira, 1982) used similar techniques within a PROLOG-based representation to produce an elegant and quite powerful query mechanism. For a brief survey of question-answering techniques, see Webber (1992). A good example of a more current question-answering system is the TEAM system (Grosz et al., 1987). TEAM was aimed at being transportable, which means it can be relatively easily adapted to a different database without having to rewrite the grammar and semantic interpreter. To do this, it uses a context-independent logical form similar to the approach used in Chapter 8.

Exercises for Chapter 13

1. (*easy*) Give a plausible logic-based representation for the meaning of the following sentences, focusing on the interpretation of the quantifiers. If the sentence has a collective/distributive ambiguity, give both interpretations.

   > Several men cried.
   > Seven men in the book met in the park.
   > All but three men bought a suit.

2. (*easy*) For each of the following lists of sentences, state whether the first sentence entails or implies each of the sentences that follow it, or that there is no semantic relationship between them. Justify your answers using some linguistics tests.

   a. John didn't manage to find the key.
   John didn't find the key.
   John looked for the key.
   The key is hard to find.

   b. John was disappointed that Fido was last in the dog show.
   Fido was last in the dog show.
   Fido was entered in the dog show.
   John wanted Fido to win.
   Fido is a stupid dog.

3. (*easy*) Classify the indicated verb phrases in the following sentences as to whether they describe a state, an activity, an achievement, or an accomplishment. Justify your answers with some examples that demonstrate their linguistic behavior. Discuss any problems that arise in your classification.

   > Jack *ran to the store.*
   > Jack *was running to the store.*
   > Jack *hated running.*
   > Jack *runs* every day.
   > Jack *stopped running* when he broke his leg.

4. (*medium*) One of the classic examples of decompositional semantics is the encoding of the verb *kill* using a causation operator and a predicate DIE. In particular, the meaning of the sentence *John killed Sam* would be

   > *CAUSE(John1, DIE1(Sam))*

   Does this decomposition completely capture the meaning of the verb *kill*? Consider whether *John killed Sam* and *John caused Sam to die* are equivalent in all situations. Given your position on this issue, would it be better for a KR to decompose all instances of *kill* to this form, or to use a meaning postulate and retain a predicate KILL in the KR? Justify your answer.

5. (*medium*) Using the translation of inheritance networks into logic described in Section 13.1, give the axioms for the simple network

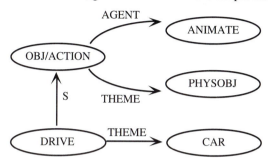

Note that the definition of the drive action places a more restrictive constraint on the type of the THEME role. Does the axiomatization do the right thing, that is, does it show that the resulting axioms are consistent and that, for any drive action D, $\exists o$. THEME(D,o) $\land$ CAR(o)? Did the definition of the THEME role on the general class OBJ/ACTION interfere with this in any way? In answering these questions, explicitly specify any assumptions you need to make about the type hierarchy to do each proof.

6. (*medium*) Using the frame-based representation described in this chapter, define an action class DRIVE that corresponds to a sense of the verb *drive* in

i.   I drove to school today.

In particular, your definition should contain enough detail so that each of the following statements could be concluded from sentence i.

ii.   I was inside the car at some time.
iii.   I had the car keys.
iv.   The car was at school for some time.
v.   I opened the car door.

For each of these sentences, discuss in detail how the necessary knowledge is represented (as a precondition, effect, decomposition, and so on) and what general principle justifies it being a conclusion of sentence i. Identify three other conclusions that can be made from sentence i, and discuss how the required knowledge to make each conclusion is encoded. Should any of the definitions be considered to be default knowledge? If so, why? If not, identify one further conclusion that could be made if some default knowledge were used.

7. (*medium*) Consider a question-answering system on a fixed database restricted to ground literals as shown below and using the closed world assumption:

> TYPE(FORD, COMPANY), TYPE(GM, COMPANY)
> TYPE(CAR1, AUTO), ..., TYPE(CAR9, AUTO)
> MADE-BY(CAR1, FORD), COLOR(CAR1, WHITE)
> MADE-BY(CAR2, FORD), COLOR(CAR2, WHITE)
> MADE-BY(CAR3, FORD), COLOR(CAR3, BLACK)
> MADE-BY(CAR4, FORD), COLOR(CAR4, WHITE)
> MADE-BY(CAR5, GM), COLOR(CAR5, RED)
> MADE-BY(CAR6, GM), COLOR(CAR6, WHITE)
> MADE-BY(CAR7, GM), COLOR(CAR7, BLUE)
> MADE-BY(CAR8, GM), COLOR(CAR8, RED)
> MADE-BY(CAR9, GM), COLOR(CAR9, BLUE)

a. Specify a procedural semantics for the English quantifier *most* appropriate for database queries. Discuss any complications that arise, and any assumptions that you need to make.

b. Give the two different interpretations, due to quantifier scoping, of the sentence *Most cars made by some company are white.* Give an informal trace of the question-answering process in each of the interpretations. What is the answer in each case?

c. What knowledge of the domain could be brought to bear to select the most likely interpretation in part b? Informally describe a disambiguation process that would select the appropriate interpretation in such cases, using the analysis in part b as an example.

Local Discourse Context and Reference

This chapter considers a set of issues related to reference and the local discourse context. This includes the issues of anaphoric reference, ellipsis, VP anaphora, and one-anaphora. In order to explore anaphoric processing in more detail, a simple model of global discourse structure called the history list is introduced. This will allow a range of issues relating to reference to be discussed here, rather than waiting until global discourse context is considered in detail in Chapter 16.

Section 14.1 explores the notion of local context and introduces the idea of discourse entities to serve as the referents for referential expressions. Section 14.2 develops the history list representation and explores its use in the interpretation of definite noun phrases. Section 14.3 looks at pronominal reference in more detail and develops some structural preferences for pronoun reference using a notion of a discourse center. Sections 14.4 and 14.5 explore definite descriptions: The first considers singular definite descriptions and the second considers plural descriptions and sets. Section 14.6 examines ellipsis, where the local context is used to fill in missing information in the current sentence. Finally, Section 14.7 looks at surface anaphora, a phenomena that falls somewhere between pronominal reference and ellipsis.

14.1 Defining Local Discourse Context and Discourse Entities

As a start, think of the local context as including the syntactic and semantic structure of the preceding sentence, together with a list of objects mentioned in the sentence that could be antecedents for subsequent pronouns and other definite noun phrases. The local context is useful for many devices. For instance, it may contain antecedents of pronouns, as in

1a. $Jack_i$ lost his $wallet_j$ in his car.
1b. He_i looked for it_j for several hours.

In addition, the local context defines the structures most useful for interpreting sentences that use verb phrase ellipsis, such as

2a. Jack *forgot his wallet.*
2b. Sam did too.

Such verb phrase ellipsis typically refers to the event described in the previous sentence, as in

3a. Jack forgot his wallet.
3b. He looked for someone to borrow money from.
3c. Sam did too.

In this discourse, sentence 3c cannot mean that Sam forgot his wallet as well.

But there are problems with using the sentence as the unit for local context, due to the presence of conjunctions. For instance, discourse 3 could be modified so that sentences 3a and 3b are conjoined into one sentence, but this doesn't change the possible readings:

4a.　Jack forgot his wallet, so he looked for someone to borrow money from.
4b.　Sam did too.

It is hard to interpret 4b as meaning Sam forgot his wallet. In contrast, a single sentence with a conjunction supports VP ellipsis between the conjuncts, as in

5.　Jack forgot his wallet, and Sam did too.

As a further complication, the following example involving conjunction between verb phrases indicates that some conjunctions do create contexts that support ellipsis, as in

6a.　Jack forgot his wallet and lost his credit cards.
6b.　Sam did too.

In this case, 6b means that Sam also forgot his wallet and lost his credit cards.

Given these examples, a reasonable start is to consider the local context to be derived from the preceding major clause rather than the preceding sentence. For instance, because conjunctions such as *and* can conjoin major clauses, examples like sentence 5 can be accounted for: The first conjunct provides the local context for the second. VP conjunction occurs within a single major clause, so the local context for 6b is all of 6a, as desired. Subordinate clauses are included as part of the major cause they modify so should not create a new local context. This is seen in the following example:

7a.　Jack forgot his wallet when he went out to the movies.
7b.　Sam did too.

Sentence 7b can be interpreted to mean that Sam lost his wallet (or that he lost his wallet when he went out to the movies) but not to mean that he went out to the movies.

An important part of the local context is a list of possible antecedents for pronouns, which we will call the **discourse entity (DE) list**. The DE list is a set of constants defined in the KB that represent the objects that were mentioned in the last major clause and can subsequently be referred to by a pronoun. Some-times a DE is not explicitly mentioned in the previous clause but is implicitly introduced by it. To allow for such cases, we will usually talk of the objects that a sentence **evokes**, which includes those mentioned explicitly as well as the implicit ones, to be discussed later in this chapter.

When we say that a pronoun has a certain antecedent, we really mean that the pronoun and antecedent both refer to the same object; that is, the pronoun and its antecedent **co-refer**. It is important to note that a pronoun and its antecedent may co-refer to the same object X even though neither the speaker nor the hearer could identify X in any concrete way. It simply means that they refer to the same object, no matter what that object is. Consider the discourse fragment

8a.   John bought a car$_i$ yesterday.
8b.   It$_i$ was very expensive.

This can be said and understood without either the speaker or hearer ever having seen the car or having any means to identify it. The indefinite description *a car* asserts the existence of a car and the pronoun *it* is used to add additional information about that car. This discourse is perfectly well understood even though no one knows what car is being talked about in the real world. So how can this referent be represented as a constant in the KB when we don't know which object is referred to? Faced with problems like this, some researchers argue for a completely different level of representation for discourse entities. But we will take a simpler approach and use Skolem functions as the discourse entities. Remember that a Skolem function (or Skolem constant) is simply a new term introduced into the language. When possible, we will use the discourse marker introduced in the logical form as the new Skolem constant. Thus if *a car* had the logical form <A **c1** CAR>, the Skolem constant generated would be C1. Co-reference is indicated by using equality. Thus, if the pronoun *it* has the logical form (PRO **i1** IT1), then the fact that it co-refers with C1 would be captured by asserting (I1 = C1).

Generating Discourse Entities

As a clause is interpreted, a discourse entity is typically generated for each noun phrase. Different NPs place different constraints on the discourse entities they evoke. An indefinite NP typically evokes a new discourse entity, as previously described, and often need not be further identified in the KB. A proper name, on the other hand, generally describes some object already defined in the KB that is associated with the name. A definite NP (including pronouns) typically refers to an object previously mentioned in the discourse, often a discourse entity in the local context. Plural NPs evoke sets of objects. A complex NP involving conjunction evokes a set consisting of all the conjuncts. For example, the NP *John and Mary* evokes three DEs, *John1, Mary1*, and the set {*John1 Mary1*}.

The rest of this section considers the discourse entities evoked by indefinite NPs. This class is very important because indefinite NPs introduce many new discourse entities, and provide much of the background needed for handling definite reference (discussed in later sections). To compute the set of discourse entities, we first convert the logical form into the representation of quantifiers described in Section 12.4, reducing all the natural language quantifiers to universal and existential quantification using explicit sets. Also, for the simple examples here, we assume that all proper names and definite NPs are replaced with KB constants representing their referents.

Plural noun phrases evoke the same set whether interpreted collectively or distributively. In collective readings, the set introduced is used directly in the proposition as an argument, whereas in distributive readings, the set is used as the range of the universal quantifier. To define the set, the modifiers must be

Example	Discourse Entity (DE)	Set Restriction (SR)	Individual Restriction (IR)
a man	MI	none	$MAN1(MI)$
three women	WI	$|WI| = 3$	$WI \subseteq \{w \mid WOMAN1(w)\}$ or equivalently, $\forall w . w \in WI \supset WOMAN1(w)$
some black cats	CI	$|CI| > 1$	$CI \subseteq \{c \mid CAT1(c) \& BLACK1(c)\}$

Figure 14.1   The translation of indefinite noun phrases

divided into two classes in the translation: the restrictions on the set (SR) and the restrictions on each individual in the set (IR). For example, the translation of the noun phrase *Three boys* in the sentence

9.   Three boys lifted Fido.

would involve an SR that states that the set has three elements, and an IR that asserts that each element is a boy. Figure 14.1 summarizes the translation of some indefinite noun phrases.

Indefinite Noun Phrases Within the Scope of Universals

Complications arise when an indefinite noun phrase appears within the scope of a universal quantifier arising from a distributive interpretation. For example, a singular indefinite noun phrase within the scope of a universal evokes a set rather than an individual. Consider the following discourse:

10a.   Three boys$_i$ each bought a pizza$_j$.
10b.   They$_i$ ate them$_j$ in the park.

Note that *They$_i$ ate it$_j$ in the park* is not an allowable continuation to sentence 10a. What properties are needed to define the discourse entity generated from *a pizza* in 10a? The set $\{x \mid Pizza(x)\}$ is far too general, as the *them$_j$* in 10b couldn't refer to the set of all pizzas. A better treatment of *a pizza* is a new discourse entity $P1$ denoting a subset of $\{x \mid Pizza(x)\}$. With this interpretation, *them$_j$* in 10b could refer to the right set of pizzas, namely those introduced in the last sentence. But this treatment would still lose information known about the contents of $P1$, namely that it is the set consisting of the pizzas bought by the boys mentioned in 10a. A representation of $P1$ can be derived by considering the original formula for 10a:

$\forall b : b \in B1$.
   $\exists p : Pizza(p) . Buy(b, p)$ where $|B1| = 3 \& B1 \subseteq \{x \mid Boy(x)\}$

Sentence: Three boys each bought a pizza.

Initial Translation:

$$\exists B : |B| = 3 \ \& \ B \subset \{x \mid Boy(x)\}$$
$$\forall b : b \in B.$$
$$\exists p : Pizza(p) . Buy(b, p)$$

Discourse Entities:

B1: $|B1| = 3 \ \& \ B1 \subset \{x \mid Boy(x)\}$
P1: $P1 = \{x \mid Pizza(x) \ \& \ \exists y : y \in B1 . x = sk4(y)\}$

Semantic Content:

$$\forall b : b \in B1 .$$
$$sk4(b) \in P1 \ \&$$
$$Buy1(b, sk4(b))$$

Figure 14.2 The discourse entities generated from *Three boys each bought a pizza.*

The skolemized form is

$$\forall b : b \in B1 . Pizza(sk4(b)) \ \& \ Buy1(b, sk4(b))$$

where $sk4(b)$ is a new function that yields the pizza that each boy bought. Given this, the set $P1$ could be defined as the set of pizzas generated by this new function:

$$P1 = \{x \mid Pizza(x) \ \& \ \exists y : y \in B1 . x = sk4(y)\}$$

This exactly picks out the pizzas that the boys bought. The entire analysis of this sentence is summarized in Figure 14.2.

14.2 A Simple Model of Anaphora Based on History Lists

This section considers a simple technique used for identifying the antecedents of pronouns. The basic structure idea is the **history list**, which is a list of discourse entities generated by the preceding sentences, with the most recent listed first. Viewed in terms of the previous section, the history list is a sequence of structures corresponding to the discourse entities in the prior local contexts. The entities from the current local context (that is, the entities generated by the previous clause) are listed first, then the entities in local context generated by the sentence before that, and so on.

In Chapter 12 you saw how pronouns may refer to objects within the same sentence, and a set of co-reference constraints were derived that indicated which objects in the same sentence could or could not be the antecedent of each pronoun. These constraints affect the intersentential cases as well. For example, the reflexivity constraint holds even if there is an intersentential occurrence of the same object, as in the discourse

11a. Jack saw Sam at the party.
11b. Sam gave him a drink.

In this discourse the reflexivity constraint indicates that *him* and *Sam* in 11b cannot co-refer. This also prohibits the pronoun *him* from co-referring with the discourse entity evoked by *Sam* in 11a.

The possible antecedents for pronouns are not restricted to appearing in the local context, but the local context is very important for resolving pronominal reference. A large majority of antecedents for pronouns are found in the same sentence or in the local context. The further back in the discourse an antecedent was last mentioned, the less likely it is to be referred to again by a pronoun.

Once the algorithm for producing the discourse entities generated by a sentence is defined, the history list idea is quite simple. The history list consists of all the discourse entities that have been evoked in the reasonably recent past. Some systems allow just the last one or two local contexts, while others let the history list grow unboundedly. Given the history list, the algorithm for finding an antecedent proceeds as follows: Check the most recent local context for an antecedent that matches all the constraints related to the pronoun. Constraints may come from any source. For example, reflexivity constraints will prohibit some objects from being the antecedent, gender and number will eliminate others, and constraints derived from imposing selectional restrictions may introduce further restrictions. If no antecedent is found in the current local context, then move down the history list to the next most recent local context and search there. This algorithm implements what is often called the **recency constraint**, which states that the antecedent should be the most recently mentioned object that satisfies all the constraints. Consider a discourse concerning a sailboat race:

12a. The companies had a lot of money and spent lavishly on their boat.
12b. The boys, in contrast, built their boat on a tight budget.
12c. They knew they would win the race easily.

The *they* in 12c most likely refers to the boys, even though on purely semantic grounds it would be more likely that the companies felt they would win the race.

The history list for sentence 12c might look like that in Figure 14.3. To find the antecedent for the pronoun *they*, you search the history list for the first object that satisfies the pronoun's constraints. In this case it would be an object x satisfying $THEY1(x)$, which would be true on any plural set. The first entity tested, $B2$, would succeed and be selected as the referent. The same basic technique can often be used for definite descriptions as well. For instance, if 12c were *They knew the boat would win easily,* the antecedent of the NP *the boat* would be the first object x that satisfies the constraint $BOAT(x)$, which would be $B3$.

History lists are the basic underpinnings of many computational approaches. The technique must be refined further, however, to capture certain

Sentence	Discourse Entities Generated
Sentence 12b	$B2 : B2 \subseteq \{x \mid Boy(x)\}$
	$B3 : Boat(B3) \And BuiltBy(B3, B2)$
	$B4 : Budget(B4) \And Limited\text{-}Funds(B3)$
Sentence 12a	$C1 : C1 \subseteq \{c \mid Company(c)\}$
	$M1 : Money(M1)$
	$B1 : Boat(B2) \And OwnedBy(B2, C1)$

Figure 14.3 The history list generated by discourse 12

cases. The next two sections look at issues in interpreting pronouns and definite descriptions in more detail. History lists will also be reconsidered in Chapter 16, when issues related to global discourse structure are discussed in more detail.

14.3 Pronouns and Centering

The recency constraint imposes a preference between the local contexts. Are there preferences between DEs within a single local context? The answer is yes. There do seem to be some preferences for the objects playing the central roles in the major clause over the discourse entities generated in adjunct phrases and subordinate clauses. In some cases, these preferences are strong enough to interfere with logically possible interpretations. Consider the discourse (adapted from Wilks (1975))

Jack drank the wine on the table. It was brown and round.

Even though recency and the semantic constraints suggest that *it* refers to the table, most people have trouble finding this interpretation, and many consider the second sentence anomalous, or at least humorous, because *it* appears to refer to the wine.

Preferences between the major arguments in the main clause are more subtle, but consider the discourse

13a. Jack saw Sam at the party.
13b. He went back to the bar to get another drink.

While either Jack or Sam are logically possible antecedents for the *he* in 13b, there seems to be a preference for *he* to be referring to Jack. This preference is not strong enough to override semantic and contextual influences, however, as seen in

14a. Jack saw Sam at the party.
14b. He clearly had drunk too much.

It is hard to interpret *he* in 14b as Jack, for with that interpretation it is not obvious how the two sentences are related to each other.

There seems to be another factor that affects the interpretation as well. It is based on the notion of a **discourse focus** or **center**. The intuition behind these theories is that most discourse is organized around an object that the discourse is about. This object, called the center, tends to remain the same for a few sentences and then shift to a new object. The second key intuition is that the center of a sentence is typically pronominalized. This affects the interpretation of pronouns because once a center is established, there will be a strong preference for subsequent pronouns to continue to refer to the center. For example:

15a. Jack left for the party late.
15b. When he arrived, Sam met him at the door.
15c. He decided to leave early.

Semantically, 15c makes sense with either Jack or Sam as the antecedent, and the structural preferences favor Sam because he plays a central role in the major clause in 15b. Centering theory, however, would predict that Jack is the antecedent because Jack was referred to pronominally in 15b and thus is the center of 15b, and nothing in 15c indicates that the center has changed.

More precisely, two interacting structures are used in the centering theory:

- The discourse entities in the local context, which we will call the **potential next centers** (or **forward-looking centers**). These are listed in an order reflecting structural preferences: subject first, direct object next, indirect object, and then the other discourse entities in the sentence. The first one on the list is called the **preferred next center**, written as **Cp**.
- The center, written as **Cb** (for **backward-looking center**), which is what the current sentence is about. The Cb is one of the potential next centers, and typically it is pronominalized.

The constraints between the center and pronominalization can be stated as follows:

Centering Constraint 1—If any object in the local context is referred to by a pronoun in the current sentence, then the center of that sentence must also be pronominalized.
Centering Constraint 2—The center must be the most preferred discourse entity in the local context that is referred to by a pronoun.
Centering Constraint 3—Continuing with the same center from one sentence to the next is preferred over changing the center.

Note that by constraint 1, if there is only one pronoun in a sentence, then it identifies the center unambiguously. By constraint 2, this means that if the next sentence also contains a single pronoun, and it is contextually reasonable that the two pronouns refer to the same object, then they will co-refer. For example, given the discourse

	$Cb_2 = Cp_2$	$Cb_2 \neq Cp_2$
$Cb_1 = Cb_2$	Continuing	Retaining
$Cb_1 \neq Cb_2$	Shifting to preferred	Shifting to nonpreferred

Figure 14.4   The types of movement for centers

16a. $Jack_1$ saw him_2 in the $park_3$.
16b. He_4 was riding a $bike_5$.

Let DR_1, DR_2, and DR_3 be the three discourse entities produced for *Jack, him,* and *the park* respectively. DR_2 is the center (the Cb) of sentence 16a, and the potential next center list, in order of preference, is DR_1, DR_2, DR_3. The first element of this list, DR_1, is the preferred next center (the Cp). Given this local context, now consider 16b. On purely semantic grounds *he* could refer back to DR_1 or to DR_2. Given the centering constraints, however, there should be a preference that $DR_4 = DR_2$, continuing with the same center. Given this interpretation, DR_4 would be the center of 16b as well as its preferred next center.

A sentence containing multiple pronouns is more complex because there is ambiguity with respect to which pronoun corresponds to the center. For example, the centering constraints given so far would indicate no preferences in the following, where *he* in 17b is interpreted intrasententially, referring to Jack.

17a.   While $Jack_1$ was walking in the $park_2$, he_1 met Sam_3.
17b. He_4 invited him_5 to the $party_6$.

By constraint 1, the center of 17a is unambiguously DR_1, that is, Jack, since there is only one pronoun. Sentence 17b contains two pronouns, however, so the centering constraints can be satisfied with either $DR_4 = DR_1$ or $DR_5 = DR_1$; that is, there is no preference for whether He_4 in 17b refers to Jack or Sam. This may or may not be a problem depending on your intuitions. But for many, there is a preference for He_4 to refer to Jack.

To explore this concept, note that there are four different combinations for how two sentences relate to each other based on the center and preferred next center. These are shown in Figure 14.4, in which Cb_1 and Cb_2 are the centers of the two sentences, and Cp_2 is the preferred next center of the second sentence. When the center remains the same between the two sentences, the transition is either a continuation or a retention, depending on whether or not the center is now the preferred next center as well. If the center shifts, there are two cases, depending on whether or not the new center is the preferred next center.

These distinctions are used in a revised constraint 3:

Centering Constraint 3′—Continuing is preferred over retaining, retaining over shifting to preferred, and shifting to preferred over shifting to nonpreferred.

Sentence 17a: While Jack$_1$ was walking in the park$_2$, he$_1$ met Sam$_3$.
Discourse Entities: Cp: DR$_1$=Jack1, Others: DR$_3$=Sam1, DR$_2$=Park7
Discourse Center: Cb: Jack1

Sentence 17b: He$_4$ invited him$_5$ to the party$_6$.
Interpretation 1: (Continuing)
  Discourse Entities: Cp: DR$_4$=Jack1, Others: DR$_5$=Sam1, DR$_6$=Party1
  Discourse Center: Cb: Jack1
Interpretation 2: (Retaining)
  Discourse Entities: Cp: DR$_4$=Sam1, Others: DR$_5$=Jack1, DR$_6$=Party1
  Discourse Center: Cb: Jack1

Figure 14.5 Continuation versus retention of the center

Consider again the interpretation of discourse 17, which is summarized in Figure 14.5. Since both Jack and Sam are referred to pronominally in 17b, constraint 2 requires that the center be Jack1. But this in itself doesn't determine the referent for *He$_4$* as there are two possible antecedents: DR$_1$, the center in the local context, indicating a continuation of the center, and DR$_3$, indicating a shift to the preferred next center. Constraint 3´ prefers interpretation 1, and *He$_4$* refers to Jack.

How do centering preferences interact with the possibility of intrasentential interpretations? Determining what technique is best must await further development and evaluation of the possible algorithms. Currently, some algorithms always prefer intrasentential referents, while others favor the reverse. An interesting combination is to prefer any interpretation that assigns a pronoun to the center, but failing that, to prefer intrasentential readings over intersentential readings. Whatever the strategy, it is important to remember that it is more general contextual factors that ultimately determine the best interpretation. Any algorithm based solely on structural properties will not be foolproof. This suggests that these structurally based pronoun resolution algorithms will be most useful if they produce a list of possible referents in preferred order for each pronoun and leave the final decision to the general reasoning system.

Finding the Likely Antecedents

What follows is an example algorithm that produces an ordered list of possible referents for each pronoun based on the local discourse context, the co-reference restrictions, and a subset of the centering constraints just discussed. Unfortunately, because of co-reference restrictions, there is no way to independently process each pronoun. For instance, in 17b, if the two pronouns are interpreted independently, the preferred referent for each would be the center in the local context, namely Jack. But we know both cannot refer to Jack because of the reflexivity constraints. There is no way to avoid this problem at this stage of the

For each pronoun (PRO **p** S R) with antecedent constraints CR_x derived from S and R:
1. Create an ordered list L of possible antecedents, consisting of (in order) the Cb and Cp from the local context, the possible referents from intrasentential processing, and the rest of the discourse entities in the local context.
2. Remove any referent R in L that makes CR_R false.
3. Add (REF-LIST **p** L) to the restrictions in the pronoun's logical form.

Figure 14.6 An algorithm for identifying possible antecedent for nonreflexive pronouns

processing except by enumerating each combination of referent assignments to each pronoun. In the following algorithm, we avoid the issue by passing on the problem. The highest-rated referent for both pronouns will be Jack, and we leave it to the reasoning system to apply the co-reference restrictions and the interpretation. Thus centering constraint 3 may need to be considered by the reasoning system when it makes the final choice. There are three steps to the algorithm:

1. Generate a ranked list of possible antecedents for each pronoun.
2. Use general reasoning to select the appropriate antecedents.
3. Use the results of step 2 to define the Cb for the sentence to be used as part of the local context of the next sentence.

Step 2 will be discussed in Chapter 15. Figure 14.6 gives an algorithm for step 1. Consider the algorithm running on discourse 17. The local context generated from 17a was shown in Figure 14.5. The logical form of 17b, *He invited him to the party,* might be

(PAST (INVITE1 i1   [AGENT (PRO **h1** (& (HE1 **h1**) ($\neq$ **h1 h2**)))]
      [THEME (PRO **h2** (& (HE1 **h2**) ($\neq$ **h1 h2**)))]
      [PURPOSE <THE **p1** PARTY1>]))

Consider the pronoun (PRO **h1** (& (HE1 **h1**) ($\neq$ **h1 h2**))). The initial list of candidates consists of the Cb (Jack1), the Cp (Jack1 again), the intrasentential antecedents (none), and the other discourse entities (Sam1, Park3), yielding the list (Jack1 Sam1 Park3). Only the first two of these satisfy the constraints on **h1**, so the logical form is updated to

(PRO **h1** HE1 ($\neq$ **h1 h2**) (REF-LIST **h1** (Jack1 Sam1)))

The second pronoun is handled similarly and is updated to

(PRO **h2** HE1 ($\neq$ **h1 h2**) (REF-LIST **h2** (Jack1 Sam1)))

This information would be passed onto the general reasoning system in step 2, which, if it agrees with intuition, will identify the antecedent of **h1** as Jack1 and **h2** as Sam1. With these results, you can then identify the center of the current sentence, and then use it as part of the local context for the next sentence. The

If the sentence contains no pronouns, then the new Cb is NIL. Otherwise, do the following:
1. Construct a list L consisting of the referents of each pronoun.
2. If the old Cb is in L, the new Cb = the old Cb (a continuation or retention).
3. Otherwise, pick the element of L that was highest ranked in the old discourse entity list and make it the new Cb (a shift).

Figure 14.7 An algorithm for identifying the new Cb

algorithm for step 3, shown in Figure 14.7, implements the centering constraints discussed earlier. In the previous example, this algorithm would identify Jack1 as the new Cb.

14.4 Definite Descriptions

A definite description refers to an object that is usually uniquely determined in the context. To identify the referent, you may have to use information from any of the four types of context. A description may uniquely describe an object in the general or the specific setting, or it may describe an object in the local or global discourse context. There is an important distinction in the use of definite noun phrases, depending on whether they are used existentially or referentially. These readings have been discussed previously, but to remind you, the existential reading asserts the existence of a unique object satisfying the description, and the referential reading uses the description to refer to a previously known object, just as names and pronouns do.

With the referential reading, the hearer must identify the referent, not merely accept that the referent exists. For instance, if we live on a dairy farm and, unbeknownst to me, exactly one of the cows is sick, you cannot simply start a conversation with the sentence *The cow is sick,* unless some preceding context allows me to infer which cow is being talked about. This sentence would be inappropriate as a way of asserting that exactly one cow is sick, as would be suggested by the existential reading. In referential readings, definite descriptions generally must identify objects that already exist in context or the sentence is considered defective.

Note that a definite description does not need to identify an object in some absolute sense, as the discourse context can be used to constrain the possible referents. In fact, a referential noun phrase can successfully refer to an object that is not identifiable in the world by the speaker or hearer. For example, consider the discourse

18a. Helen bought a car$_i$ and a boat yesterday.
18b. She paid too much for the car$_i$.

BOX 14.1 Generating Referring Expressions

Discourse models are crucial for enabling a natural language generation system to appropriately select referring terms. Consider that a generation system starts with a meaning representation that involves constants, without a mode of reference. For instance, consider generating sentences from the following two meanings:

1. *Think(W1, Won(W1)) & Woman(W1)*
2. *Think(W2, Won(W1)) & Woman(W1) & Woman(W2) & W1 $\neq$ W2*

Given no prior discourse context, the generation system might generate something like *A woman thought she won* for the first and *A woman thought a woman won* for the second. Note that the second sentence could not be used to realize meaning 1, because it would violate the co-reference constraints from Section 12.4 that the two instances of the noun phrase *a woman* cannot co-refer.

The centering constraints also affect how a sentence is realized given the context of the previous sentence. Consider what happens if the system must realize meaning 1 after it has just generated the sentence *Jane guessed a number* from the expression

3. *Guess-Number(W1) & Name(W1, "Jane")*

Following this, meaning 1 would best be realized as *She thought she won*. The alternative realization *Jane thought she won* would be acceptable but stilted, while *Jane thought that Jane won* and *Jane thought that the woman won* would suggest incorrect readings. On the other hand, consider the context generated by the discourse

4a. Jane guessed a number.
4b. She picked the one Sue had suggested.

If meaning 2 needs to be realized next, where *W2* represents Sue, then *Sue thought she won* is acceptable but *She thought Jane won* is not, because it violates centering constraints. A good example of a generation system that uses discourse constraints is McKeown (1985).

This is understandable without either the speaker or hearer being able to identify the car in the real world. The definite description *the car* uniquely identifies an object in the KB, namely the car that Helen bought, evoked in the previous sentence. Such examples suggest close parallels between definite descriptions and pronouns, although there are some differences. Definite descriptions, for instance, do not have such a strong tendency to have antecedents in the immediate local context. In addition, as discussed in Chapter 12, they cannot co-refer with many constituents in the same sentence. Rather, they typically refer back to objects introduced earlier in the history list.

Definite descriptions may refer to objects that have not been introduced in an earlier discourse context. These objects are unique within some assumed setting for the discourse. For example, usually the definite description *the moon* refers to the moon that orbits earth, although other moons exist and can be referred to in an appropriate context. But without a specific context that makes some other moon relevant, the description refers to the standard object. Definite descriptions can also be used to refer to objects that are visually present to the participants but have not been mentioned. For example, if I walked up to a house, I could ask someone to open the door (referring to the door in front of us).

We can specify the constraints on successful definite reference by defining the concept of contextual uniqueness. An object O is **contextually unique** with respect to a description D_x, a situation S that includes both the specific and general setting, and a discourse context consisting of a sequence of local discourse contexts $C_1, ..., C_n$, if and only if

1. There is a number k such that
   a. for all $i < k$, there is no object x in C_i such that D_x is true, and
   b. O is the only object in C_k such that D_x is true.
2. Otherwise, there is a unique object O in S such that D_x is true.

This definition suggests an algorithm for handling referential noun phrases that modifies the basic history list search described in Section 14.2. Given a definite description of form $<THE\ x\ D_x>$, where D_x is the formula representing the description, test each discourse entity r in the local context to see if D_r is true. If D_r is true for exactly one r, then that is the referent. If more than one r is found, then the description is faulty in some way. If no discourse entity satisfies D_x, then repeat the same procedure on the previous discourse context. If no referent has been found in any local context, test if D_x is true for exactly one object in S.

As with pronoun interpretation, the final decision on the referent will have to be made by the general reasoning system. Thus, the algorithm just outlined should be used to suggest a list of possible referents in order of preference. This information could be added as an additional restriction in the logical form, as was done for pronouns.

To identify the referents of complex noun phrases, all the referential terms in the noun phrase must be resolved simultaneously. For instance, consider the noun phrase *the cow in the field*. To find the referent of this expression, it might seem that you must first find the referent of the NP *the field*. But if the referents are sought in this order, some problems arise. For instance, consider a situation in which there are two cows, *C1* and *C2*, and two fields, *F1* and *F2*. Furthermore, cow *C1* is in field *F1*, and cow *C2* is in a barn, *B1*. The situation is described by the following formulas:

Cow(C1), Cow(C2), Field(F1), Field(F2), Barn(B1)
In(C1, F1), In(C2, B1)

The NP *the cow in the field* clearly refers to *C1* here, but the NP *the field* is ambiguous between *F1* and *F2*. Thus you would fail to find a unique referent for *the field,* and so the whole NP would not be interpretable. To avoid this problem, you must search for both simultaneously to find an object that satisfies the formula

$$\exists\, c : Cow(c)\ \exists f : Field(f)\ .\ In(c, f)$$

There is only a single solution to this query, namely where c is instantiated with *C1* and f is instantiated with *F1*.

Existential Readings and Indirect Reference

Existential readings typically identify a unique object defined by the description. But being unique is not sufficient, as seen by the example *The cow is sick*, where even if you accept that exactly one cow in your herd is ill, the sentence is defective. Rather, existential readings typically can only introduce an object by defining it in terms of some other object that can be identified referentially. Consider

19.   The winner in the 10K race was American.

Neither the speaker nor hearer need to know who won the 10K race, they only have to agree that there is a single winner of the race, and whoever it was, that person was American. In this case, a general knowledge that races typically have exactly one winner would allow the hearer to verify the uniqueness condition. In other cases, however, the uniqueness can only be inferred from the use of the definite noun phrase. Consider the difference in the interpretations of *The drawer of my dresser is stuck* and *A drawer in my dresser is stuck.* The hearer may know nothing about the dresser before the sentence. To interpret either sentence, the hearer must assume that there is a dresser. Furthermore, the hearer will probably infer that the dresser has exactly one drawer if given the first sentence, and that it has more than one drawer if given the second. These examples show that definite descriptions do not always refer to objects already in the discourse history. They can also introduce objects. This process is often called **accommodation**, because the hearer accommodates the speaker by introducing objects and properties that are required for the sentence to be understood.

A new quantifier is defined for unique existence:

$$\exists!\ x : R_x\ .\ P_x$$

This formula is true only if there is exactly one x that satisfies R_x and if P_x is true of that object. Given this, the translation of sentence 19, assuming *the 10K race* refers to the object *Race10K*, would be

$$\exists!\ w : Win(w, Race10K)\ .$$
$$American(w)$$

The discourse entities evoked by existential definite noun phrases are generated just as with indefinites. The only difference is that the referent is precisely defined by the description. In particular, the discourse entity for *the winner in the 10K race* in sentence 19 would be a discourse entity *W1,* uniquely defined by *Win(W1, Race10K).* Contrast this to an indefinite noun phrase such as in *A runner in the 10K race was American,* in which the discourse entity, *R1,* would be defined by

RunIn(R1, Race10K) & American(R1)

Some existential readings do not explicitly include referential terms that can be used to identify them uniquely. In these cases the object and relationship must be inferred from the discourse context. Consider the discourse

20a. My club held a raffle.
20b. The winner won a car.

There is no complement in the noun phrase *the winner* to indicate what it is defined with respect to. But if the same semantic interpretation is given to the lexical item *winner* as in sentence 19, this suggests that the interpretation of *the winner* should be

$\exists! \, w : Win(w, *PRO*)$

where *PRO* is an anaphoric term that must be contextually determined. Evidence for this analysis can be shown by creating an example where there is no contextually unique contest. For instance, consider

21a. Both my club and John's club held raffles last week.
21b. *The winner won a car.

Sentence 21b is either ill-formed because there is no referent or very awkward because it entails an interpretation where a single individual won both contests.

Examples of indirect reference also arise with words that you might not usually interpret as a function on some other object. For instance, consider

22a. Jack brought a pencil to class.
22b. But he found that the lead was broken.

The NP *the lead* in 22b, which intuitively refers to the lead of the pencil that Jack brought to class, is the problem. This type of reference can be characterized by positing some relation R and an anaphoric term *PRO*. To interpret this noun phrase correctly, an antecedent for the pro-form must be found and the relation *R* identified. The noun phrase *the lead* would then map to an existential reading of the form

$\exists! \, l : Lead(l) \ \& \ *R*(l, *PRO*)$

where *R* and *PRO* need to be identified from the context. In this example, the resolved form would be as follows, where *Pencil1* is the discourse entity generated from *a pencil* in 22a:

$\exists! \, l : Lead(l) \ \& \ SubpartOf(l, Pencil1)$

Note also that since the word *lead* is ambiguous between, say, the lead of a pencil, a fishing lead, or a piece of metal, this relation also needs to be identified in order to identify the correct word sense.

While it is unlikely that there is a fixed set of relationships that can be used for *R*, some relations are quite common. For example, the subpart relation is often seen, as in discourse 22. The subpart relation might also be used to cover cases involving typical contents, such as in the sentence

When we entered the kitchen, we noticed that *the stove* had been left on.

Here you must use information that kitchens generally contain stoves.

Another common class of examples involves events and their roles, as in

The day after we sold our car, *the buyer* returned and wanted his money back.

These can often be identified because the description uses a role noun, which may already have a pro-form included in its logical form from the semantic interpretation.

In systems that use a frame-based knowledge representation, one technique is to allow any slot relation to be used in such cases. To analyze indirect referential forms, the system would check the definitions of the objects on the history list to see if the new noun phrase describes an object that could fill a slot. This representation could handle the range of examples discussed earlier, since subparts could be slots, and case roles would correspond to slots in a frame representing an event described by a verb phrase. This technique provides a way to limit the possible relations that need to be searched, but it is hard to see how it would handle all examples. Consider the sentence *When we entered the kitchen, we saw that the gas had been left on*. In this case the NP *the gas* is presumably the gas used by the stove that is part of the kitchen. It seems that handling a case like this would require some highly sophisticated inference capabilities.

○ 14.5 Definite Reference and Sets

Additional complications arise with descriptions that involve sets, or refer to objects in previously defined sets. You have already seen indefinite descriptions referring to sets such as *three men* and *some men*. Definite versions of these descriptions are *the three men* and *the men* and can be interpreted either as direct or indirect reference.

Consider an example. Remember that modifiers in noun phrases that describe sets may describe either properties of the set itself or properties of individuals in the set. Thus the description *The three men who left the party* describes a set that has a cardinality of 3, in which every member is a man who left the party. The existential reading of this definite noun phrase would be something like

$$\exists! \, M : |M|=3 \, \& \, M = \{ \, m \, | \, Man(m) \, \& \, Leave(m, Party1) \}$$

The fact that this set is unique means that exactly three men left the party; otherwise there would be several possible sets fitting this description. Compare this to the indefinite description, *Three men who left the party,* which would have the reading

$$\exists M : |M|=3 \ \& \ M \subset \{m \mid Man(m) \ \& \ Leave(m, Party1)\}$$

Since this set need not be unique, more than three men may have left the party.

Plural noun phrases without any complement typically involve indirect reference, often to subsets of already introduced sets. For example, consider

23a. Some boys and girls came to the party.
23b. The boys left at 8PM.

The noun phrase *The boys* does not describe a set that is explicitly present in the local context. Rather, it describes a set indirectly, namely the set of all the boys in the previously mentioned set. To allow such interpretations, a translation of 23b could be

$$Left(B1, 8PM) \text{ where } B1 = \{x \mid Boy(x)\} \cap *PROSET*$$

where *PROSET* must be a contextually determined set. If you let S2 be the discourse entity generated from *Some boys and girls* in sentence 23a, this could be resolved to

$$Left(B1, 8PM) \text{ where } B1 = \{x \mid Boy(x)\} \cap S2$$

For another example, consider the discourse

24a. Jack, Mary, Sam and Helen went to the beach.
24b. The boys were too chicken to go in the water.

In sentence 24b, the description *The boys* refers to a set consisting of Jack and Sam, which is a unique set defined by the intersection of the set of boys with the set $\{Jack1 \ Mary1 \ Sam1 \ Helen1\}$ introduced by the conjunctive noun phrase.

This technique will handle many cases, but problematic cases remain where even the referent set is not present in the local context. Consider

25a. Jack met Sam at the beach.
25b. The two boys then went to the store.

Here there is no explicit set mentioned in 25a. One proposal is that the set $\{Jack \ Sam\}$ becomes relevant via reasoning about the situation. In this case we might use general knowledge that when two people meet, they are together and naturally form a new set. But this technique won't work for other examples, such as

26a. Jack lived in San Francisco, while Sam lived in New York.
26b. The two boys never met.

Handling such cases in a general way remains problematic.

BOX 14.2 Planning Definite Descriptions

An important problem in natural language generation is planning definite noun phrases. The generation system must first decide whether it is best to use a pronominal form, a proper name if available, or a definite description. Some issues relating to this decision were described in Box 14.1. If the decision is to generate a definite description, however, many problems remain, as there are many different ways to describe objects. Some possible descriptions can be eliminated by considering whether the description provides sufficient information to make the referent contextually unique given the discourse context. But even with this constraint, many possibilities remain. Another constraint is conciseness. A generation strategy that simply includes everything known about an object in the description would likely produce an incomprehensible sentence. A good description is one that is short yet still contextually unique. For instance, given a context with two red boxes, one large and one small, a good description for the small box is *the small box*. The description *the small red box* also uniquely identifies its referent, but contains unnecessary information. The description *the red box,* on the other hand, is not a good description as it does not uniquely describe its referent.

In many cases, there will still be many ways to describe an object that satisfy the two properties above. Consider a KB that includes the following information:

$SellEvent(s1)$ & $Agent(s1) = M1$ & $Recip(s1) = J1$ & $Theme(s1) = P1$ &
$Person(M1)$ & $Named(M1, "Mary")$ & $LivesIn(M1, CITY1)$ &
$Person(J1)$ & $Named(J1, "John")$ & $President(J1, COMP1)$ &
$Plans(P1)$ & $Secret(P1)$ & $Named(COMP1, "XTRA Corp")$

Consider the context in which the sentence *Mary sold the secret plans* has already been generated to realize event *s1*, and consider the following possible realizations of the proposition $Recip(s1) = J1$:

1. *John is the president of XTRA Corp.*
2. *The buyer was the president of XTRA Corp.*
3. *The buyer was John.*

Logically, all three realize the content and uniquely identify the terms. Sentence 1, for instance, uses the uniquely identifying name *John* to realize the term $Recip(s1)$ and the uniquely identifying description *the president of XTRA Corp* to realize the term *J1*. It does not, however, provide necessary information on how to link the sentence into the context. Thus it is not a good realization. Sentences 2 and 3 fare better because they provide a connection to the discourse context via the description *the buyer,* identifying a role in the selling event. Since the noun phrases *John* and *the president of XTRA Corp* both uniquely describe *J1*, they might seem equivalent, but they are not. Which of these two is appropriate depends on the overall goals of the speaker. If, for instance, the speaker is attempting to reveal some act of industrial espionage, then sentence 3 is not a good realization as it does not provide the key information that Mary sold the plans to another company. A good example of a system that generates definite descriptions is Dale (1992).

Reference to Elements of Sets

When a set is in the discourse context, descriptions can also refer to elements of the set. Many of these examples use specific devices that signal the behavior. For instance, the word *one* can be used for indirect reference to a set, as in NPs like *one* and *a large one,* which are indefinite descriptions, and *the one I saw* and *the large one,* which are definite descriptions. Consider

27a.   At the zoo, a monkey scampered between two elephants.
27b.   One snorted at it.
27b´.   The large one snorted at it.

The appropriate behavior of *one* can be obtained if we assume it translates to

$$\exists\, x: x \in \text{*}PROSET\text{*} \dots$$

where **PROSET** is referentially determined. In 27b the antecedent would be the set of elephants described in 27a, say ELS1, and the form for 27b is

$$\exists\, x: x \in ELS1 \,.$$
$$SnortAt(x, monkey1)$$

The definite reference case shown in 27b´ is an indirect reference with the form

$$\exists!\, x : x \in ELS1 \ \& \ Large(x)\,.$$
$$SnortAt(x, monkey1)$$

More complex examples arise in which there is no explicit signal that the referent is defined contextually by a set. Consider

28a.   Jack used two scuba tanks on his trip.
28b.   He preferred the 1600psi tank.

In this case there may be no object in the discourse context that has the property of being a tank rated at 1600psi. Rather, this noun phrase has selected one element from the previously mentioned set and asserted additional properties of it (that presumably make it unique). Thus, assuming the discourse entity for *two scuba tanks* is TNKS1, then the representation of sentence 28b would be

$$\exists!\, t : t \in TNKS1 \ \& \ Rated(t, 1600psi)\,.$$
$$Prefer(Jack1, t)$$

Because such cases contain properties that are not known to the hearer before the utterance, they are often difficult to detect.

Universal Quantification and Sets

Universal quantifiers such as *each* and *every* display an interesting behavior. They are syntactically singular, and support intrasentential singular pronouns, as in *When each boy$_i$ saw Helen, he$_i$ was angry.* Intersententially, however, they evoke a set as a discourse entity, as in

29a.   Each boy$_i$ in the park saw Helen.
29b.   *He$_i$ was angry at her.
29b′.   They$_i$ were angry at her.

Note that *He* in sentence 29b cannot refer to one of the boys introduced in 29a, whereas *They* in sentence 29b′ can refer to the boys in 29a. So the discourse entity evoked by *Each boy in the park* is the set $\{x \mid Boy(x) \& In(x, Park1)\}$.

These noun phrases often involve an implicit definite reference to a set that limits the range of the quantifier. For example, in isolation the discourse entity generated for *each girl* in the sentence *Each girl saw Helen* would be simply the set $\{x \mid Girl(x)\}$. This is a very unlikely interpretation, though, as it claims that every girl who exists saw Helen. Rather, the range of *each girl* is contextually defined, as in the discourse

30a.   Several girls arrived at the party.
30b.   Each girl saw Helen.

When processing 30a, the noun phrase *several girls* would cause the creation of a constant, say G1, that is a set of girls. With G1 in the local context for sentence 30b, the interpretation of *each girl* is most naturally interpreted as ranging over all girls in G1, and the initial translation of 30b is

$$\forall\, g: g \in G1 \,.\, See1\,(g, Helen1\,)$$

This analysis essentially treats the noun phrase *each girl* as a paraphrase of *each of the girls,* and *every girl* as *every one of the girls.* The set of girls must be determined referentially, and then is used as the scope of the quantifier. In other examples the set is defined using indirect reference. For example, consider 30b in the context created by the sentence *Several boys and girls arrived at the party,* where a discourse entity BG1 was created for the set of boys and girls evoked. In this case, the range is created by intersection, as seen before with 23b. The initial translation of 30b would be

$$\exists!\; G3 : G3 = \{x \mid Girl(x)\} \cap BG1$$
$$\forall\, g : g \in G3 \,.\, See1\,(g, Helen1\,)$$

14.6 Ellipsis

As described in Section 14.1, ellipsis involves the use of clauses that are not syntactically complete sentences. Often the parts that are missing can be recovered from the previous major clause. Ellipsis occurs across conjunctions, as in

31.   Helen saw the movie and Mary did too.

BOX 14.3 Reference to Objects Not Evoked by NPs

All the examples of referential readings in this chapter have involved antecedents evoked by noun phrases. There are many examples of reference to other objects evoked in the sentence. In most of these cases, the content of the referring expression or the selectional restrictions explicitly identify that the referent is of a special type. In general, the referent for these constructions is found in the local context. Consider some example continuations following the sentence

Jack went to New Orleans last year.

You can refer to the event described, as in the sentences

The trip changed his life.
It changed his life.

You can refer to the action that Jack did, as in the sentences

He does *that* every year.
Sam did *it* last year as well.

You can refer to the fact that Jack went to New Orleans, as in

That really surprised Helen.

You can also refer to the event's time and location with the special pronouns *then* and *there:*

Mardi Gras was on *then.*
He loves to go *there.*

There are two ways to handle these. The set of discourse entities generated can be extended to include any action, event, time, location, or proposition implicitly described in the clause, or techniques can be developed to derive the referents from the local context when needed. Usually the surface form and selectional restrictions signal the use of such referring expressions, so both methods work equally well.

where it is understood that Mary saw the movie. Other cases involve sentence pairs, as in

32a. Some think that Jack will win the race next week.
32b. But he never will.

Of importance in question-answering applications, ellipsis may occur in a series of questions, such as the following dialogue between two conversants A and B:

33a. A: Did Sam find the bananas?
33b. B: Yes.
33c. A: The peach?

Here speaker A's second utterance can be understood only in the context of A's first question and is understood as an elliptical form of *Did Sam find the peach?*

Contextual Clause: Helen saw the movie.
Syntactic Structure: (S (NP Helen)
        (VP saw
           (NP the movie)))
Semantic Form: *See1 (Helen1 , Movie24)*

Elliptical Clause: Mary did too.
Syntactic Structure: (S (NP Mary)
        (VP did))

Figure 14.8 A simple example of VP ellipsis

Syntactic Constraints on Ellipsis

The hypothesis underlying most analyses of ellipsis is that the completed phrase structure of the elliptical clause corresponds to the structure of the previous clause. Once the structural correspondence between the two clauses is identified, the semantic interpretation of the previous clause can be updated with the new information in the elliptical clause to produce the new interpretation. Consider sentence 31, whose initial analysis is shown in Figure 14.8. Matching the syntactic structures, a correspondence would be found between the two subject noun phrases, *Helen* and *Mary*. These determine the transformations required on the semantic form as follows. First, *Helen1* is abstracted out of the semantic form of the first clause to produce

$\lambda\, p\; See1\,(p,\, Movie24)$

This form is then applied to the new information, namely the interpretation of *Mary* to produce the semantic form of the elliptical clause:

See1 (Mary1, Movie24)

This technique works with more complex examples as well. For instance, a classic problem in the literature (often called the sloppy identity problem) involves accounting for the ambiguity in discourses such as

34a. Jack kissed his wife.
34b. Sam did too.

Sentence 34b can mean that Sam kissed Jack's wife (called the sloppy reading) or that Sam kissed his own wife. The syntactic structure matching would proceed as before and find a correspondence between Jack and Sam. Assume that the semantic form of 34a is

Kiss1(Jack1, wifeOf(Jack1))

To generate the semantic form of 34b, this form needed to be abstracted. But there are two possible ways to abstract Jack1 from the expression, producing the two forms

λp *Kiss1* $(p, wifeOf(Jack1))$ and
λp *Kiss1* $(p, wifeOf(p))$

Applying the first to Sam1 produces *Kiss1* (*Sam1*, *wifeOf*(*Jack1*)) while applying the second produces *Kiss1*(*Sam1*, *wifeOf*(*Sam1*)). Thus two readings can be derived, as required by intuition.

An Algorithm Based on Syntax

The crux of this technique is clearly finding the structural correspondence between the two clauses. This process is most strongly influenced by syntactic factors. The input for the algorithm is the syntactic structure in the local context, and a partial syntactic structure generated for the elliptical clause. Note that a bottom-up chart parser can produce this analysis despite the fact that a full sentential analysis may not be derivable.

With some constructs such as VP ellipsis, the correspondence is unambiguously signaled. A verb phrase consisting of the auxiliary *do* with no complement and the presence of modifiers such as *too, as well,* and *also* indicate VP ellipsis, and the correspondence is between the two subjects. In others, finding the correspondence is more problematic. For instance, consider dialogue 33, in which the NP in the elliptical clause corresponds to the object NP in the previous clause.

Potential correspondences can be found by a search using a pattern derived from the input fragment. To find fragments that are as syntactically parallel in structure as possible, start with a pattern that contains all the information in the input fragment except for the content words such as nouns and adjectives. Function words (such as prepositions and articles) will be retained. If this match fails to produce any potential target fragments, you can try again using a less specific pattern (for example, by deleting the number restrictions, removing specific articles and prepositions, removing modifiers, and so on). Consider processing dialogue 33. The input to the algorithm is shown in Figure 14.9.

The initial pattern will be (NP[3s] (DET the) (CNP)). The syntactic structure of the contextual clause is searched for a constituent that matches, and none is found. If the number restriction in the pattern is relaxed, yielding (NP (DET the) (CNP)), a match is found between *the bananas* and *the peach,* and the semantic form can be derived as described before. If this pattern had not matched, you could continue to relax constraints, trying (NP (DET) (CNP)), and if that failed, finally trying (NP). You would want to define the series of relaxations in a way such that the first pattern to match would capture the most important structural properties.

Elliptical forms that consist of a sequence of constituents are more complicated. Consider the example

Contextual Clause: Did Sam find the bananas?
Syntactic Structure: (S   (AUX did)
                   (S   (NP$_1$ Sam1)
                       (VP   find)
                          (NP$_2$[3p]   (DET the)
                                      (CNP bananas))))
Semantic Form: ? *Find1*(*Sam1*, *Bananas2*)

Elliptical Clause: The peach?
Syntactic Structure: (NP[3s]   (DET the)
                            (CNP peach))

Figure 14.9   A simple example of ellipsis

35a. A: Did the clerk put the bananas on the shelf?
35b. B: Yes.
35c. A: The ice cream in the refrigerator?

The correct interpretation of 35c involves two independent constituents rather than a single constituent, namely the NP *the ice cream* and the PP *in the refrigerator* (which will match as part of the complement of the verb *put*). The pattern matcher can be extended to search for each fragment individually with the additional constraint that the order of the constituents in the input fragment should be the same as the order of the target constituents in the initial question. Furthermore, the sequence of target fragments should all be subparts of the same constituent. For example, consider dialogue 35. The syntactic forms of A's initial utterance and the input fragment are shown in Figure 14.10, together with the pattern sequence generated from the input fragment.

    The pattern generated from NP$_6$ would successfully match NP$_3$, NP$_4$, and NP$_5$, whereas the pattern from PP$_3$ would initially fail, but after relaxing the constraint that the preposition be *in,* it would successfully match PP$_2$. Only the pair NP$_4$ and PP$_2$ occur within a single constituent (VP$_1$) and appear in the original sentence in the appropriate order. Thus NP$_6$ corresponds to NP$_4$ and PP$_3$ corresponds to PP$_2$ when constructing the new interpretation. The semantic form would then have to be abstracted at the argument positions for NP$_4$ and PP$_2$, and the result applied to the interpretation of the new constituents NP$_6$ and PP$_3$.

Semantic Preferences

The algorithm given earlier will sometimes not uniquely identify the appropriate target fragment. For example, consider the dialogue

A: Did the clerk put the ice cream in the refrigerator?
B: No.
A: The TV dinners?

Contextual Clause: Did the clerk put the bananas on the shelf?
Syntactic Structure:

$$
\begin{aligned}
&\text{(S} \quad \text{(AUX did)} \\
&\qquad (\text{NP}_3 \quad \text{(DET the)} \\
&\qquad\qquad \text{(CNP clerk))} \\
&\qquad (\text{VP}_1 \quad \text{(V put)} \\
&\qquad\qquad (\text{NP}_4 \quad \text{(DET the)} \\
&\qquad\qquad\qquad \text{(CNP bananas))} \\
&\qquad\qquad (\text{PP}_2 \quad \text{(P on)} \\
&\qquad\qquad\qquad (\text{NP}_5 \quad \text{(DET the)} \\
&\qquad\qquad\qquad\qquad \text{(CNP shelf)))))}
\end{aligned}
$$

Elliptical Clause: The ice cream in the refrigerator?
Syntactic Structure: two constituents

$$
\begin{aligned}
&(\text{NP}_6 \quad \text{(DET the)} \qquad\qquad (\text{PP}_3 \quad \text{(P in)} \\
&\qquad \text{(CNP ice-cream))} \qquad\qquad\qquad (\text{NP}_7 \quad \text{(DET the))} \\
&\qquad\qquad\qquad\qquad\qquad\qquad\qquad\qquad \text{(CNP refrigerator))}
\end{aligned}
$$

Figure 14.10 An example with multiple constituents

In this case the pattern generated from the input fragment will match the NPs *the clerk, the ice cream,* and *the refrigerator* equally well. Semantic information has to be used to select *the ice cream* as the appropriate target fragment. Similarly, a continuation of *The manager?* should identify *the clerk* as the appropriate target fragment, and a continuation of *The freezer?* should identify *the refrigerator* as the target fragment.

A technique that can account for each of the preceding examples is to compute a semantic similarity measure between the input fragment and the potential target fragments and then select the closest one. The techniques introduced in Chapter 10 when considering word-sense disambiguation will work well. For example, assume the system has a taxonomic hierarchy as shown in Figure 14.11.

Let us use the simplest measure of similarity: the graph distance between each sense. Consider the case where the input fragment is *The TV dinners?* and the possible target fragments are *the clerk, the ice cream,* and *the refrigerator.* You can compute a semantic closeness measure between these by counting the number of steps between the nodes in the hierarchy. The results are

TV-DINNER and CLERK: 7 (via PHYSOBJ)
TV-DINNER and ICE-CREAM: 4 (via FOOD)
TV-DINNER and REFRIG: 6 (via INANIMATE)

Thus the preferred target fragment is *the ice cream,* and the appropriate analysis is generated.

Of course, semantic closeness is not foolproof, and it may select a target that turns out to be inappropriate. If the semantic interpreter is unable to analyze

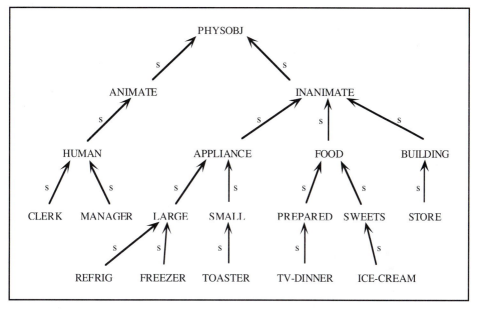

Figure 14.11   A type hierarchy

the resulting structure successfully, then other possible target choices can be attempted. Consider the following dialogue:

A: Did you see the clerk in the store?
B: Yes.
A: The toaster oven?

This case would have the following semantic closeness checks:

> TOASTER and CLERK: 7 (via PHYSOBJ)
> TOASTER and STORE: 5 (via INANIMATE)

Thus the semantic closeness check would select *the store* as the target fragment and construct a new interpretation corresponding to the sentence *Did you see the clerk in the toaster oven?* Hopefully, the semantic interpretation rules are rich enough to suggest that this reading is unlikely. The ellipsis algorithm then would suggest the next alternative, with *the clerk* being the target fragment, and construct an interpretation corresponding to the sentence *Did you see the toaster oven in the store?*, as desired.

14.7 Surface Anaphora

There is a whole class of referring expressions that introduce new objects related to objects in the discourse context. These cases are often called **surface anaphora** because many theories account for them in terms of the surface form of the previous sentence. In contrast, all the cases you have seen so far refer to objects in the discourse context and are called **deep anaphora**. Consider some typical examples of surface anaphora:

36a.   Tell me John's grade in CSC271.
36b′.   Give me *it in MTH444* as well.
36b′′. Give me *Mike's in MTH444* too.

The objects referred to in 36b′ and 36b′′ are not mentioned in 36a. But the context created by 36a allows you to interpret each one as referring to some other grade (John's grade in MTH444 and Mike's grade in MTH444, respectively).

Note that there are specific syntactic devices that signal surface anaphora. One large class involve noun phrases with a missing head word, such as *Mike's — in MTH444.* Others involve a pronoun, but with a complement phrase, as *it in MTH444.* Furthermore, many cases involve the use of adverbials like *too, also,* and *as well,* which explicitly indicate a comparison to something in the discourse context.

There are several methods proposed for dealing with surface anaphora. The first approach uses syntactic/semantic structure matching as used for handling ellipsis. The idea is that the surface anaphoric phrase is an incomplete constituent. The phrase is processed by searching the syntactic tree of the previous sentence for a constituent whose structure matches and then merging that information with the new information to build a new phrase that can then be parsed as usual to produce the interpretation. Consider this technique using example 36b′′, a phrase with a missing head noun. The phrase *Mike's in MTH444* might produce an NP constituent as follows:

```
(NP  (DET  (NP (NAME m1 "Mike"))
            ('s))
     (CNP (CNP *missing*)
          (PP   (P in)
                (NP (NAME m2 "MTH444")))))
```

This constituent is used to generate a pattern as described in the last section. The pattern is then matched against all the subconstituents of the previous sentence. In discourse 36, there is only one constituent that matches, namely the NP *John's grade in CSC271.* This constituent is then copied, replacing old information with new whenever it is specified. The new NP would be

```
(NP  (DET  (NP (NAME m1 "Mike"))
            ('s))
     (CNP (CNP GRADE1)
          (PP   (P in)
                (NP (NAME m2 "MTH444")))))
```

This new NP can be inserted into the current tree and will produce the correct interpretation. Examples that utilize pronouns are treated similarly, and the pronoun simply fills a missing constituent.

The problem with structural approaches is that they are very sensitive to exactly the way things are phrased. For example, given the context generated by 36a, the technique just described would not work for *Give me it for Mike as well,* as it couldn't detect the parallelism between the possessive determiner *John's* and the PP complement *for Mike.*

The other approach is semantically based. It assumes that the missing information is characterized by some set previously mentioned. To make this work, you must allow the abstractions of the sets mentioned. Sentence 36a would evoke the singleton set of John's grades in CSC271, that is, $\{g \mid Grade(g, John, CSC271)\}$. An abstraction of this might be the set of anyone's grades, $\{g \mid \exists\, p : Person(p) : Grade(g, p, CSC271)\}$, or the set of John's grades in any course, $\{g \mid \exists\, c : Course(c) . Grade(g, John, c)\}$, or the set of anyone's grades in any course, $\{g \mid \exists\, p : Person(p) \,\exists\, c : Course(c) . Grade(g, p, c)\}$. The surface anaphora would then pick out one of these sets and add back in the necessary properties based on the new information in the phrase. To make this work, however, you would need a way to incorporate additional modifiers into the set. For instance, consider *Give me it for Mike as well* again. The appropriate abstraction would be the set of grades in CSC271, that is, $\{g \mid \exists\, p : Person(p)\ Grade(g, p, CSC271)\}$. You now would have to interpret the modifier *for Mike* as restricting the person to be Mike. But if you do not use the lexical information that the head word in 36a was *grade,* it is not clear how this could be done. Thus an approach based purely on the set abstractions is difficult to make work in such cases.

Summary

In discourse the preceding major clause has a substantial effect on the interpretation of the next major clause. The information in the preceding clause defines the local discourse context of the next clause. One important component of the local context is the set of discourse entities evoked by the clause. These serve as the most likely antecedents of pronouns in the next clause. Discourse entities evoked by singular noun phrases represent individuals, whereas those evoked by plural noun phrases are sets. A singular noun phrase within the scope of a universal quantifier also evokes a set, namely the set of all objects generated for each value of the universally quantified variable.

The history list is a sequence of local contexts generated by the preceding clauses. The simplest algorithms for finding antecedents for definite NPs (including pronouns) simply scan back through the history list looking for the first (most recent) discourse entity that satisfies the restrictions. Preferences for the antecedents of pronouns within the local discourse context are affected by the discourse focus or center. If a sentence contains at least one pronoun, then one of the pronouns must refer to the center. Constraints on how the center can change from sentence to sentence determine the preferred interpretations of pronouns.

The local context also contains the syntactic and semantic structure of the previous clause, which is crucial for interpreting ellipsis and surface anaphora.

These phenomena are typically handled using pattern-matching techniques to find syntactic similarities between the previous clause and the fragments in the current clause. Once a correspondence is found, the new interpretation can be constructed by substituting the information in the elliptical sentence into the structure of the previous clause and then reinterpreting the revised structure.

Related Work and Further Readings

Early natural language systems used linear history lists with heuristic techniques to handle common pronouns and verb phrase ellipsis (for example, Winograd (1972) and Woods (1977)). These systems depended strongly on semantic filtering to identify the most appropriate referent. Webber (1983) produced the first computationally motivated study of the range of discourse entities a sentence evokes, with special emphasis on definite and indefinite phrases within the scope of universals. The material in Section 14.1 is based on this work and subsequent improvements by Ayuso (1989).

Most work on anaphora in linguistics has focused on constraints on intra-sentential cases. There is some work on intersentential cases, which introduced the notion of discourse entities (for example, Kartunnen (1976) called them discourse referents). The most influential works in formal linguistic models that use these ideas are by Kamp (1981) and Heim (1982). Kamp's discourse representation theory (DRT) uses discourse entities to provide a uniform account of pronouns, whether they appear as bound anaphora, intrasentential, or inter-sentential anaphora. This work has influenced much subsequent work in linguistics and computational linguistics (for example, Harper (1992)).

Sidner (1983) developed a computational model of focus and its effect on pronoun interpretation. Her hypothesis was that the focus is selected according to preference heuristics based on thematic roles. The most preferred discourse entity was selected as the antecedent for a pronoun unless some semantic or pragmatic contradiction prevented it. This model evolved into the centering model for definite noun phrases proposed by Grosz, Joshi, and Weinstein (1983). The centering model has sparked considerable work. The material in Section 14.3 adapts an algorithm based on centering constraints developed by Brennan, Friedman, and Pollard (1987). Walker (1989) compared the Brennan et al. algorithm with the Hobbs algorithm (Hobbs, 1978), an algorithm based on syntactic structure and recency. The comparison is interesting since the Hobbs algorithm always prefers an intrasentential reading if possible, whereas centering always prefers an intersentential center-based reading. Both algorithms performed about the same, correctly identifying the antecedents about 90 percent of the time in written text, but only about 50 percent of the time in dialogue.

In linguistics, many different theories have been proposed that capture notions related to discourse focusing behavior. These theories typically divide the information in a sentence into two parts, often indicating what part of the sentence is conveying new information and what is providing background information. Influential theories have involved distinctions between topic and comment, theme and rheme, and given and new (for example, see Halliday (1967), Chafe (1975), Clark and Haviland (1977), and Prince (1981)). But there is an important distinction to remember when looking at different theories. Computational models are usually based on a cognitive model of the speaker; that is, the center is a focus of attention that affects inference. In linguistics the same terms may be used to refer to structural properties of a sentence. While these may coincide much of the time, they also could be quite different.

Definite descriptions have been the focus of extensive study in philosophy and linguistics. Russell and Whitehead (1925) introduced the notion of definite descriptions as special existential operators. Donellan (1966) introduced the distinction between referential and attributive uses of definite descriptions. Lewis (1979) and Stalnaker (1974) developed the concept of accommodation. This is a central component in the work by Kamp (1981) and Heim (1982). For more information, consult McCawley (1993) or Chierchia and McConnell-Ginet (1990). Most computational systems handle definite descriptions using a linear history list as described in this chapter, allowing also for reference to uniquely described objects in the KB (for example, Winograd (1972) and Woods (1977)). Grosz (1977) showed that in extended discourse, a linear history list is insufficient to handle many cases. These issues will be considered in Chapter 16.

Many computational models have used syntactically based analyses of ellipsis, where once a structural correspondence is found, a new syntactic structure is built that then is semantically interpreted from scratch. Techniques based on semantic closeness are used in a wide range of systems, especially those providing natural language interfaces to databases, where ellipsis is very common (for example, Hendrix et al. (1978), Bates et al. (1986), and Grosz et al. (1987)). The analysis of ellipsis in Section 14.6 draws on this work but follows the approach described in Dalrymple, Shieber, and Pereira (1991).

Surface anaphora was first addressed in a computational system in the LUNAR system (Woods, 1977). These techniques are important for question-answering applications where such cases arise frequently. Webber (1983) provides a detailed analysis of the phenomena and how it can be handled. Hankamer and Sag (1976) draw the distinction between deep and surface anaphora for linguistic analysis, and argue that making the distinction is essential for handling a wide range of linguistic phenomena.

Exercises for Chapter 14

1. (*medium*) Identify the discourse entities evoked by the following two sentences and give their semantic form. For each, assume a set of races R1 was introduced by the previous discourse.

   In every race, the winner was American.
   In every race, some runner was American.

2. (*medium*) Consider the sentence *Two boys ate three pizzas,* which has at least two readings: The two boys together ate three pizzas, or the two boys each ate three pizzas. For each of these readings, specify the discourse entities generated and the sentence meaning. Discuss any problems that arise.

3. (*medium*) Use the centering theory to explain why discourse a is coherent but discourse b seems awkward:

   a1. Sue got up late.
   a2. Helen didn't have time to drive her to school.
   a3. She had to walk.

   b1. Helen had to be at work early.
   b2. She didn't have to time drive Sue to school.
   b3. She had to walk.

4. (*medium*) For each sentence in the following discourse, give its center and preferred next center. State what centering theory predicts as the antecedent for each pronoun based on the four constraints and the preferences described in Section 14.3. Based on your analysis, classify each transition as a center continuation, retention, or one of the shifts. Discuss whether the predicted interpretations agree with your intuitions. If they don't, which constraint or preference seems to cause the problem?

   a. Sue got up late the day that Helen was supposed to drive her to school.
   b. So she had to walk.
   c. Mary saw her walking down the street.
   d. She stopped to pick her up.

5. (*medium*) In Section 12.6, a treatment of relational nouns was suggested for semantic analysis. Show how such a representation can be used with the history list mechanism to identify the referent of NPs involving such nouns. In particular, for each NP in the following text, give a reasonable logical form and the current state of the history list, and discuss the process of identifying the referent.

   The museum received a large grant from a local corporation.
   The donation will allow the recipient to stay open through the summer.

6. (*medium*) One suggestion for handling reference to subsets of sets created from NP conjunctions would be that every subset of the set is introduced as a discourse entity. For example, the sentence

   Jack, Sam, and Helen went to the beach.

would generate the sets {*Jack1*}, {*Sam1*}, {*Helen1*}, {*Jack1 Sam1*}, {*Jack1 Helen1*}, {*Sam1 Helen1*}, and {*Jack1 Sam1 Helen1*}. Now, given the sentence

The boys were too chicken to go in the water.

the appropriate referent is already defined as a discourse entity. Is this a reasonable general approach to the problem? Compare it to the methods described in Section 14.5, and give arguments for why it is worse or better than that approach.

7. (*medium*) Give the syntactic structures for each of these sentences and show in detail how the one-anaphora in the second sentence is resolved.

I bought a ticket for the early show on Tuesday.
Jack bought one for the late show.

8. (*medium*) Using the semantic preference technique with the hierarchy in Figure 14.11, show in detail how the interpretation is constructed for the third sentence. Discuss the result.

A: Did Jack give the toaster to the manager?
B: No.
C: The clerk?

Using World Knowledge

15.1 Using World Knowledge: Establishing Coherence

15.2 Matching Against Expectations

15.3 Reference and Matching Expectations

15.4 Using Knowledge About Action and Causality

15.5 Scripts: Understanding Stereotypical Situations

15.6 Using Hierarchical Plans

○ 15.7 Action-Effect-Based Reasoning

○ 15.8 Using Knowledge About Rational Behavior

Language cannot be understood without considering the everyday knowledge that all speakers share about the world. Some general world knowledge has been used in previous chapters. For instance, knowledge about type restrictions on predicate argument relations was used to support word sense disambiguation in Chapter 11. But these techniques were limited and did not try to relate what was said to some evolving situation in the world that was being described. This chapter considers how general knowledge of the world is used to interpret language.

Section 15.1 discusses the notion of coherence, which provides the motivation and justification for all the techniques in the chapter. A general framework for using knowledge of the world is developed in Section 15.2, which develops the notion of expectations produced from the previous discourse. If a sentence matches an expectation, then the result of the match produces the connections that make the discourse appear coherent. This idea is further developed in Section 15.3, where it is shown that some problems in definite reference can be treated within the same framework. The remainder of the chapter explores different ways of producing expectations. Section 15.4 discusses the use of knowledge about action and causality to generate expectations. Section 15.5 discusses script-based processing, in which the system is driven by large-scale action descriptions that characterize the different situations that the discourse may be about. Sections 15.6 and 15.7 discuss plan-based techniques, where knowledge of causality and intentions is used to generate the expectations. Section 15.8 looks at more complex issues in using knowledge of an agent's problem-solving behavior to generate expectations.

15.1 Using World Knowledge: Establishing Coherence

In many examples considered so far in this book, the final decision about the interpretation of a sentence has been left to contextual processing. This chapter attempts to define some techniques that automate this process. Doing this, however, will require a better understanding of what it means for a sentence to make sense in a context. There is clearly a relationship between logical consistency and making sense. A reading that is inconsistent will not make sense in any context. But more often than not, there are many logically consistent readings, only some of which make sense. So making sense is more a notion of **coherence** than logical consistency. Certain readings seem coherent, whereas others are not coherent at all.

A discourse is coherent if you can easily determine how the sentences in the discourse are related to each other. A discourse consisting of unrelated sentences would be very unnatural. To understand a discourse, you must identify how each sentence relates to the others and to the discourse as a whole. It is this assumption of coherence that drives the interpretation process. Consider the following discourse:

1a.   Jack took out a match.
1b.   He lit a candle.

There are several conclusions about sentence 1b, motivated by the assumption of coherence between 1a and 1b, that can be classified into several categories:

> **reference**—*He* refers to Jack1 (as suggested by centering)
> **disambiguation**—*lit* refers to igniting rather than illuminating the candle
> **implicature**—the instrument of the lighting is the match introduced in 1a

Note that to identify how sentences 1a and 1b are related, you must know that a typical way to light a candle involves using a match. This general knowledge about the world allows you to draw connections between the sentences. In other cases there may be almost no apparent relationship between two sentences, but assumptions of coherence still impose some relationship. For example, consider

2a. John took out a match.
2b. The sun set.

While it might seem that there is no identifiable relationship between 2a and 2b, in fact you assume a temporal relationship, that is, that Jack took out the match before (or while) the sun set. While only a minimal connection, it is still enough to construct a coherent situation that 2a and 2b describe.

Note that many conclusions drawn from the coherence assumption are implications, not entailments. They can be overridden by later discussion and thus are defeasible. As a result, the inference process of drawing such conclusions will be complex. The techniques considered in this chapter will all be cast in terms of matching possible interpretations against expectations generated from the previous discourse. This is discussed in detail in the next section.

15.2 Matching Against Expectations

We assume that the specific setting created by a discourse is represented by the content of the previous sentences and any inferences made when interpreting those sentences. This information is used to generate a set of **expectations** about plausible eventualities that may be described next. Later sections will explore different techniques for generating expectations. This section examines the problem of matching possible interpretations to expectations, assuming the expectations have already been generated.

More formally, the problem is the following: Given a set of possible expectations $E_1, ..., E_n$, and a set of possible interpretations for the sentence $I_1, ..., I_k$, determine the set of pairs E_i, I_j such that E_i and I_j **match**. If there is a unique expectation/interpretation pair that match, then the interpretation of the sentence would be the result of matching the two. If there are multiple possible matches, then some other process must determine which is the best match.

Consider the example of discourse 1. By methods to be discussed later, sentence 1a would sanction an expectation that Jack is going to use the match to light something. Using our event-based logic, this expectation might be written as an event E1 defined as:

Expectation 1:
$LIGHT1(E1) \& Agent(E1) = Jack1 \& Instrument(E1) = Match33$

where *Match33* would be a new constant introduced by the indefinite NP *a match* in sentence 1a. Sentence 1b is ambiguous between two readings: One in which someone ignites a candle and the other in which someone illuminates a candle (as in *He lit the room with a lamp*). For the moment, assume that *he* has already been resolved to *Jack1*. The two interpretations are captured by two different events, E2 and E3:

Interpretation 1:
$LIGHT1(E2) \& Agent(E2) = Jack1 \& Theme(E2) = Candle1$
Interpretation 2:
$ILLUMINATE1(E3) \& Agent(E3) = Jack1 \& Theme(E3) = Candle1$

The constant *Candle1* is introduced for the indefinite noun phrase *a candle*.

The matching process must somehow use the expectation to select the first interpretation and conclude that Jack lit the candle with the match. The remainder of this section explores two methods for defining the matching process. First, however, we should make sure that a simple deductive solution will not suffice. There are two ways deduction could be used to select an interpretation. We could see whether an interpretation could be proved from an expectation, or we could see whether an interpretation could be used to prove an expectation. Neither will work for discourse 1.

Attempt 1: Proving an Interpretation from an Expectation

This technique would involve finding an expectation E_i that entails one of the interpretations I_j. This technique is too weak to handle discourse 1 because expectation 1 entails neither interpretation. In particular, the expectation makes no claims about the theme being *Candle1*. In fact, since *Candle1* is a Skolem introduced by sentence 1b, no expectation could possibly anticipate its use.

Attempt 2: Proving an Expectation from an Interpretation

This approach is the mirror image of the first one. The goal is to select an interpretation I_j such that there is an E_i where I_j entails E_i. This technique is also too weak to be useful. It requires the input sentence to fully anticipate all the information in an expectation; thus the expectation would not contribute any information not already present in the sentence. This technique fails on discourse 1 as well. Specifically, interpretation 1 does not entail expectation 1 since it doesn't entail that the instrument used was the match in sentence 1a.

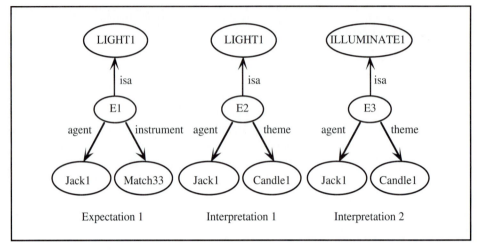

Figure 15.1 The expectation and two interpretations

Equality-Based Techniques

The problem with attempts 1 and 2 is that both the interpretation and the expectation contain information that is not contained in the other, and thus neither will entail the other. The intuition behind the nonmonotonic equality techniques is that two formulas match if there is a consistent set of equality assumptions that can be made such that an E_i then entails an I_j. For example, with discourse 1, the expectation and two equality assumptions entail interpretation 1:

> Expectation: *LIGHT1(E1) & Agent(E1) = Jack1 & Instrument(E1) = Match33*
> Assumptions: *Theme(E1) = Candle1 & E1 = E2*

In contrast, there is no set of equality assertions that allows expectation 1 to entail interpretation 2.

This technique can be implemented as a graph-matching process as follows. Each formula is encoded as a semantic network graph rooted at a node representing the eventuality. The expectation and two interpretations for discourse 1 are represented as graphs in Figure 15.1. The graph matching algorithm is specified as follows: For any node N, let Label(N) be the term that labels the node, T(N) be the type of the node (found by following the isa link), and LL(N) be the set of outgoing links from N. For any arc A, let END(A) be the node to which the arc points. Then two nodes N1 and N2 match if and only if the following three conditions hold:

1. T(N1) and T(N2) are the same, or one is a subtype of the other.
2. Label(N1) and Label(N2) are not known to refer to distinct objects.

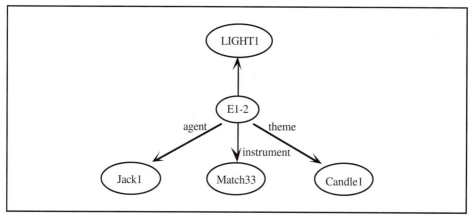

Figure 15.2 The result of matching E1 and E2

3. For all links L1 in LL(N1)
   a. there is no link with the same label leaving N2, or
   b. there is a link L2 with same label leaving N2, and
      END(L1) and END(L2) match recursively.

This is the same general algorithm used with graph-based unification except that nodes match based on the type and equality information rather than by unifying feature lists. If two graphs match, then the result is a graph constructed by collapsing together all the nodes that match. For example, nodes E1 and E3 will not match since their types are not compatible. Nodes E1 and E2, on the other hand, will match, and produce the resulting merged graph shown in Figure 15.2. This is the desired interpretation for sentence 1b.

Note that this method is still not foolproof, however, as it may be that each pair of nodes matched are not known to be distinct, but as a whole the entire new graph is inconsistent. Consider a KB with three constants, *Jack1, Sam1,* and *Person1,* where *Jack1* ≠ *Sam1*. Figure 15.3 shows two graphs corresponding to an expectation that someone will shave himself, and the interpretation that Jack shaved Sam. The matching algorithm will succeed in matching E4 and E5, because *Person1* and *Jack1* are not known to be distinct, and *Person1* and *Sam1* are not known to be distinct. The overall result, however, would entail that *Jack1* = *Sam1,* which is known not to be the case. To handle this case, the algorithm would need to verify the global consistency of the resulting graph.

In essence, what the graph algorithm does is a heuristic verification of whether two eventualities can be equal; for example, matching E1 and E2 was a way to verify whether it was consistent that E1 = E2, using heuristics based on typing and explicit distinctness information. By checking all the outgoing arcs, case relations involving E1 and E2 were also checked. This procedure does not guarantee consistency given a match, but it does detect most common cases of inconsistency. In fact, since determining consistency of a set of formulas in

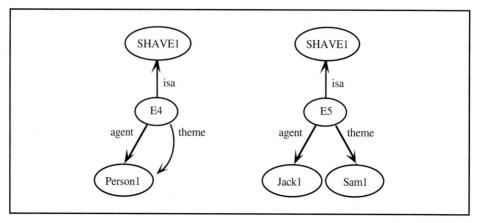

Figure 15.3 A problem case

FOPC is not decidable, there can be no general algorithm that will give guaranteed results. But most knowledge representations provide a heuristic facility for checking consistency of facts. Given such a KR system, you can check whether it is consistent that two constants C1 and C2 are equal by doing the following:

1. Find all propositions in the KB that involve C2.
2. For each, add a new proposition with C2 replaced by C1 throughout.
3. If the resulting KB appears consistent given the limits of the KR, then allow C1 = C2.

Of course, this could be a very expensive operation in principle. In practice, however, remember that many of the constants being matched will be new Skolem constants, so very little will be known about them. In such cases there are only a few propositions that need to be tested to check consistency.

Abduction-Based Techniques

The abductive approach is based on the intuition that we must find an explanation for why the current sentence is true. In other words, we must use the specific situation and expectations to construct an argument that proves the current sentence. Assumptions must be made that do not follow from the KB in order to construct the proof.

More formally, the approach is as follows. Given a specific situation S (including expectations) and possible interpretations $I_1, ..., I_k$, then consider what assumptions A_j must be added to S such that

1. $S \& A_j$ entails I_j.
2. $S \& A_j$ are consistent.

for each I_j. Choose the interpretation I_j that requires the minimum set of assumptions A_j. Of course, this requires having some metric on assumptions so that the minimal set can be defined. Simply counting the number of different atomic propositions in each A_j will not work in general, as some propositions are much less likely than others.

Abductive theories are very general and thus do not make very specific claims until some measure on assumptions has been defined. The method subsumes more specialized techniques like the equality-based technique previously defined. To see this, you can reformulate the equality-based method above as an abductive method with the following restrictions:

3. The only assumptions allowed are equality assumptions together with exactly one expectation.

4. The A_i with the least number of equality assumptions is preferred.

For sentence 1b, the minimal set of assumptions added to expectation 1 would be simply that E1 = E2 and Theme(E1) = Candle1. These two assumptions and expectation 1 entail interpretation 1.

Clearly, much more can be done with the abductive technique if additional types of assumptions are allowed, but this is sufficient mechanism to formalize matching.

15.3 Reference and Matching Expectations

In the last section, the matching algorithm assumed that all definite NPs had been resolved to their referents in the KB. This section relaxes this assumption and uses expectation matching to identify referents. The technique is simple. If you generate a new Skolem constant for every definite NP, then when the interpretation is matched against an expectation, an equality assumption will be needed to enable the match. In this case the equality assumption identifies the referent.

Consider sentence 1b again, this time without the referent of the pronoun *he* being resolved. A Skolem constant, H1, is generated, and the first interpretation is

Interpretation 1: *LIGHT1(E2) & Agent(E2) = H1 & Theme(E2) = Candle1*

Matching interpretation 1 against the expectation will proceed as before. But now there are three nodes that are merged, corresponding to the equality assumptions *E1 = E2, Theme(E1) = Candle1,* and *H1 = Jack1.* Thus the referent of the pronoun is identified during the match. In this case the referent is identical to the preferred interpretation given the centering constraints.

Consider two examples that show how general reasoning can augment the centering technique:

3a. Jack poisoned Sam.
3b. He died within a week.

In this case the most natural reading of 3b has Sam dying. On the other hand, consider sentence 3a followed by a different continuation:

4a. Jack poisoned Sam.
4b. He was arrested within a week.

The most natural reading of 4b has Jack being convicted. Centering theory would either predict the same antecedent in 3b and 4b, or not choose between them in either case. The expectation-matching approach can readily identify the correct referent, however. For example, assume that the following expectations are generated given the assertion that Jack poisoned Sam:

> Expectation 1: $DIE(E4)$ & $Theme(E4) = Sam1$
> Expectation 2: $IS\text{-}ILL(E5)$ & $Theme(E5) = Sam1$
> Expectation 3: $ARREST(E6)$ & $Theme(E6) = Jack1$

The interpretation of 3b (with the temporal expression ignored) would be

> $DIE(E7)$ & $Theme(E7) = H1$

$E7$ will clearly match $E4$, expectation 1, and thus $H1$ will equal $Sam1$. The interpretation of 4b, on the other hand, would be

> $ARREST(E8)$ & $Theme(E8) = H2$

$E8$ will match $E6$, expectation 3, and $H2$ will equal $Jack1$.
    The same technique works for definite noun phrases. For instance, consider

5a. Jack poisoned Sam.
5b. The villain was arrested within a week.

Even though it was not known previously that Jack was a villain, the same techniques will work. The interpretation of 5b would be

> $ARREST(E9)$ & $Theme(E9) = V1$ & $Villain(V1)$

Given suitable knowledge that a villain is a type of person, and that Jack is a person, this will match expectation 3 with the assumption that $V1 = Jack1,$ as desired. A consequence of this is that Jack is claimed to be a villain.
    Thus, expectation matching can be a powerful tool for resolving reference, but it does not replace the other techniques as described earlier. For instance, constraints from local context may be important even when there would seem to be an unambiguous referent using only semantic information. Recall the example

6. Jack walked over to the table and drank the wine. It was brown and round.

Even though the table is the only object that could be brown and round, this discourse is awkward and defective. Preferences from local context are also important in other cases where there appears to be an ambiguity given the expectations. Consider

7a. Jack poisoned the man from whom George stole the jewels.
7b. He was arrested within a week.

In this case there could be expectations about being arrested for both Jack and George, since both were involved in illegal activity. Based on expectation matching, $H3 = Jack1$ and $H3 = George1$ would be equally preferred. Preferences based on centering, however, would strongly prefer the former reading, which agrees with intuition. Further evidence that this is a structural preference rather than something to do with expectations can be seen by considering a paraphrase of 7a, which changes the preferred reading:

8a. George stole the jewels from the man that Jack poisoned.
8b. He was arrested within a week.

In this case it is George who is arrested, in agreement with the centering constraints.

To incorporate these constraints into the expectation-matching procedure, you simply need to add the condition that if multiple interpretations match into the expectations, then the interpretation that agrees with the preferences from local context will be preferred.

Expectation matching is a very powerful technique, but it is only as good as the process that generates the expectations in the first place. This issue is discussed in the rest of this chapter.

15.4 Using Knowledge About Action and Causality

Much discourse involves action and causality. This section examines some of the issues involving representing actions and how this information can be used to generate expectations.

Before getting to the details, consider how you might define action. This issue has occupied philosophers for thousands of years, so do not expect to find a simple answer. But you can make some distinctions. First, there is a distinction between the sense of action performed by intentional agents and the sense of action that arises in physics, where concepts such as force and inertia provide a reasonable theory. We will be concerned primarily with the former sense here.

While actions have been discussed earlier as separate from events, what is of interest here are the events that consist of actions being performed. We will loosely refer to such an event as an action, where more precisely we should refer to it as the event of the action's performance.

For current purposes, knowing about actions is important in order to identify causal relationships that can be used to generate expectations. For instance, if you are told that Jack walked to the store, you would next expect him to be at the store (a direct effect of the action), and probably to buy something (an activity suggested by knowledge about normal intentional behavior). Many forms of causality are needed to understand discourse. These include the following two classes relating actions to states:

Effect causality—Every action has a set of effects that are typically caused by the action and usually hold after the action is completed (or while the action is in execution). Effects can be divided into intended effects—those that the action is performed for—and side effects—those that are caused by the action but not intended. If an action is attempted but fails, it still may have side effects. An action **fails** when the intended effects are not caused.

Precondition causality—Every action has a set of conditions that typically must hold just before the action starts (or during the action) in order for there to be a reasonable chance that the action will succeed.

There are also important relationships between two actions that generate expectations. These include the following:

Enablement—One action enables another if the effects of the first establish the preconditions of the second. More usually, the first action establishes only a subset of the preconditions, and the others are established by other means.

Decomposition—One action is a subpart (or substep) of another action if the first is one of a sequence of substeps that constitute the execution of the other action. For example, to perform the action of entering my car, I might unlock the door, open the door, and then get inside. Each one of these actions is a substep of entering my car, and if all three are performed correctly, then the action of entering my car is accomplished.

Generation—One action generates another if executing the first under a certain set of conditions counts as executing the second. For instance, assuming I have a working electrical system and light bulb in my room, then the action of flipping the switch generates the action of turning on the light. Some researchers treat generation as a degenerate case of decomposition where there is a single substep.

There are natural language constructs that explicitly identify each of these relationships. For instance, the connective *by* typically indicates a generation relationship, as in *I turned on the light by flipping the switch,* or sometimes an enablement relation, as in *I bought some milk by going to the store.* The connective *in order to* indicates the same relationships, as in *I flipped the switch in order to turn on the light,* and *I went to the store in order to buy some milk.* Of course, verbs such as *enable* and *cause* explicitly indicate relationships, as in *The*

BOX 15.1 Defining Causality

There are several commonsense notions concerning how actions relate to each other and the world around them. Many of these fall under the notion of causality. One action causes another to occur, or causes some effect, if the performance of that action somehow leads to that effect. Intuitively, you might want to say that the effect would not have arisen if the action had not occurred. While this seems straightforward, it is extremely difficult to define causality in terms of some simpler concepts. For example, you might try to model that the action of dropping the glass caused the glass to break in FOPC by an axiom of the form

   $DROP(Sam, Glass) \supset BROKEN(Glass)$

But this formula would be trivially true if Sam did not drop the glass because, given the definition of logical implication, a false antecedent trivially makes the implication true. If you then augment this condition by adding that the antecedent is true (that is, Sam did drop the glass), then this is logically equivalent to the conjunction

   $DROP(Sam, Glass) \& BROKEN(Glass)$

which doesn't capture the notion of causality either. You might augment this further by saying that if Sam had not dropped the glass, it would not have broken. This gets closer to a definition but introduces further problems. First, the preceding statement is called a **counterfactual** statement; that is, it makes a claim about how the world would be if something that is actually true were not true. Such statements cannot be modeled in simple FOPC but require the introduction of modal operators and an appropriately more complex semantic model (Lewis, 1973). Even if this were done, however, it still wouldn't precisely define the notion of causality, because if Sam had not dropped the glass, some other event could have occurred causing the glass to break (maybe Sam dropped the glass because someone had thrown a stone at him, and if he had not dropped the glass, it would have been hit by the stone). Given all these difficulties, many theories usually take the notion of causality as primitive and do not try to decompose it further.

explosion caused the window to break, and *Being at the store earlier enabled me to buy many items on sale.*

In order to identify and use such relationships, the KR system must be able to represent general knowledge about actions and causality. Most representations organize such information around each predicate defining an action occurrence. Figure 15.4 shows the definitions of two actions, *BUY* and *PURCHASE-TICKET*. The definition of *BUY* is the same as presented in Chapter 13. The roles define the important objects involved in an action, and the constraints indicate the typical properties of the role values. As usual, the preconditions indicate what typically is true before the action can occur, and the effects indicate how the world changes after it occurs. The decomposition indicates a typical way to accomplish the action in terms of a sequence of subactions. The actions in the

The Action Class *BUY(e)*:
Roles: *Buyer, Seller, Object, Money*
Constraints: *Human(Buyer), SalesAgent(Seller), IsObject(Object),*
Value(Money, Price(Object))
Preconditions: *AT(Buyer, Loc(Seller))*
OWNS(Buyer, Money)
OWNS(Seller, Object)
Effects: $\neg OWNS(Buyer, Money)$
$\neg OWNS(Seller, Object)$
OWNS(Buyer, Object)
OWNS(Seller, Money)
Decomposition: *GIVE(Buyer, Seller, Money)*
GIVE(Seller, Buyer, Object)

The Action Class *PURCHASE-TICKET(e)*:
Roles: *Agent, Clerk, Ticket, Booth, Money, Station*
Constraints: *Human(Agent), Clerk(Clerk), IsTicket(Ticket),*
TicketBooth(Booth), At(Clerk, Booth),
Value(Money, Price(Ticket)), In(Booth, Station)
Preconditions: *OWNS(Agent, Money)*
Effects: *OWNS(Agent, Ticket)*
Decomposition: *GOTO(Agent, Booth)*
BUY(Agent, Clerk, Ticket)

Figure 15.4 The definitions of *BUY* and *PURCHASE-TICKET*

figure display differing levels of detail. *BUY* is a general action allowing almost any object to be bought and giving the details of the exchange of money and the object. It has preconditions that the buyer has the money and the seller has the object, and effects that change the possession of the money and object. It is accomplished by two GIVE actions. *PURCHASE-TICKET* is restricted to a particular setting of buying tickets at a ticket booth, and only the important details of the transaction, such as the agent having a ticket afterwards, are provided. *PURCHASE-TICKET* uses *BUY* as one of its substeps.

This information can be used in several ways. First, given a sentence that asserts the occurrence of such an action, the preconditions and effects suggest some implications of the sentence. Given *Jack bought a stereo at the mall,* a system could conclude that Jack now owns a stereo, that he no longer has the money, and that there was a store (at the mall) that once owned the stereo but no longer does. These implicatures could also be used as expectations, as the speaker might refer to one of these conditions next. But expectations based on effects or preconditions are usually too obvious to be very useful for interpreting the following sentences. The discourse

9a. Jack bought a stereo at the mall.
9b. He now owns it.

while understandable, is boring because 9b is such an obvious consequence of 9a that there seems no point in saying it.

Other more interesting expectations arise from actions that are enabled by the buying action or that the buying action is part of. Potentially, any action in the KB with a precondition that matches an effect of the buy action is a possible expectation. For instance, consider

10a. Jack bought a stereo at the mall.
10b. Now he can disturb his neighbors late at night.

The connection is that buying a stereo enables Jack playing the stereo loudly, which in turn can generate the action of annoying Jack's neighbors. Clearly, there is a vast range of actions that could be enabled by buying a stereo, so in practice it is not feasible to generate all the expectations in advance. The next few sections describe some techniques for controlling the generation of expectations.

15.5 Scripts: Understanding Stereotypical Situations

One way to control the generation of expectations is to store larger units of information, often called **scripts**, that identify common situations and scenarios in the domain of interest. Then, rather than generating expectations from first principles using causality reasoning, the expectations are encoded in the script. To be useful in controlling inference, scripts must involve many different actions, possibly by different agents, and specify a specific commonly occurring chain of causality between them. The representation of actions developed so far is general enough to be used to represent scripts as well. Figure 15.5 shows a *TRAVEL-BY-TRAIN* action (or script) that describes a typical scenario in which a passenger takes a train trip. It includes the steps of going to the station and buying the ticket, and then going to the appropriate departure location and boarding the train, and so on. The script also contains a large number of constraints detailing how the objects involved relate to each other.

Two main problems arise when you use script-based knowledge in language understanding. The first problem is script selection: How can the system tell which script is relevant? The second problem is keeping track of what part of the script is currently being described. You can make an analogy between this problem and that of trying to follow a play using a playwright's script. You would first have to identify which play is in progress; then you would have to find the place in the script for that play that corresponds to what is currently being performed. This place is called the **now point**, since it indicates the present time from the perspective of the script.

You match sentences into the script structures in different ways depending on what the sentence describes. For instance, sentences describing goals are used to identify the relevant scripts. Sentences describing actions are used to update

TRAVEL-BY-TRAIN (e):
Roles: *Actor, Clerk, SourceCity, DestCity, Train, Station, Booth, Ticket, Money*
Constraints: *Person(Actor), Person(Clerk), City(SourceCity), City(DestCity),*
    TrainStation(Station), TicketBooth(Booth), In(Station, SourceCity),
    In(Booth, Station), At(Clerk, Booth), DepartCity(Train, SourceCity),
    Destination(Train, DestCity), TicketFor(Ticket, SourceCity, DestCity)
    Value(Money, Price(Ticket))
Preconditions: *Owns(Actor, Money)*
                 At(Actor, SourceCity)
Effects: *¬Owns(Actor, Money)*
         ¬At(Actor, SourceCity)
         At(Actor, DestCity)
Decomposition: *GoTo(Actor, Station)*
               Purchase-Ticket(Actor, Clerk, Ticket, Station)
               GoTo(Actor, Loc(Train))
               GetOn(Actor, Train)
               Travel(Train, SourceCity, DestCity)
               Arrive(Train, DestCity)
               GetOff(Actor, Train)

Figure 15.5 A script to travel by train

the progress of a script. More specifically, there are three ways to introduce a script if none is currently in progress:

1. Describe an action as a goal, as in *Jack wanted to take the train to Rochester;* in these cases the desired action serves to name the script.

2. Describe a state as a goal, as in *Jack needed to be in Rochester;* in these cases the content is matched against the effects of the scripts to find ones that could achieve the desired state.

3. Describe an action in execution, as in *Jack walked up to the ticket booth;* in these cases the content is matched against the decompositions of the scripts to find ones that could have this action as a step.

Once a script is selected, it is updated when descriptions of actions, such as in *Jack walked up to the ticket booth,* are given. In these cases the now point of the script is updated to be just after the described action.

Script and Role Instantiation

Consider how the simple *TRAVEL-BY-TRAIN* script could be used to analyze the following story fragment:

$$
\begin{array}{l}
GoTo(Sam1, Station(T1)) \\
PurchaseTicket(Sam1, Clerk(T1), Ticket(T1), Station(T1)) \\
GoTo(Sam1, Loc(TR1)) \\
GetOn(Sam1, TR1) \\
Travel(TR1, SourceCity(T1), ROC) \\
Arrive(TR1, ROC) \\
GetOff(Sam1, TR1)
\end{array}
$$

Figure 15.6 The instantiated decomposition of T1 given sentence 11a

11a. Sam wanted to take a train to Rochester.
11b. He purchased a ticket at the station.

To handle 11a, the system has to recognize that a sentence of the form "agent wants action" is a statement of a goal to perform an action—in this case taking the train. Assuming that the verb *take* with appropriate arguments can be used to identify *TRAVEL-BY-TRAIN* as the relevant script, an instantiation of the script, *T1*, is created to describe the current situation. Consider this in detail. The goal described in 11a could be

$$
\begin{array}{l}
Travel(E1) \,\&\, Agent(E1) = Sam1 \,\&\, Instrument(E1) = TR1 \,\& \\
\quad IsTrain(TR1) \,\&\, Dest(TR1, ROC)
\end{array}
$$

Matching this to *T1*, an instantiation of the *TRAVEL-BY-TRAIN* action, using appropriate translations between the verb case roles and the script roles, would produce the following equality assumptions:

$$
\begin{array}{l}
Actor(T1) = Agent(E1) = Sam1 \\
Train(T1) = Instrument(E1) = TR1 \\
DestCity(T1) = ROC
\end{array}
$$

The instantiated decomposition of *T1* using these assumptions is shown in Figure 15.6. The system now uses this instantiated script to interpret 11b. You need to find a set of equality assumptions such that some substep matches the semantic content of the new sentence, which in this case might be

$$
\begin{array}{l}
PurchaseTicket(E2) \,\&\, Agent(E2) = H1 \,\&\, Theme(E2) = TIC3 \,\& \\
\quad At\text{-}Loc(E2) = STAT3 \,\&\, Ticket(TIC3) \,\&\, Station(STAT3)
\end{array}
$$

where *TIC3* is a new constant generated for *a ticket*, and *H1* is the constant generated for the pronoun *he*. This will match the second step in the decomposition of *T1*, which looks as follows in the event-based form:

$$
\begin{array}{l}
PurchaseTicket(P1) \,\&\, Agent(P1) = Sam1 \,\&\, Clerk(P1) = Clerk(T1) \,\& \\
\quad Ticket(P1) = Ticket(T1) \,\&\, Station(P1) = Station(T1)
\end{array}
$$

The match would produce the following equality assumptions:

$H1 = Sam1$
$TIC3 = Ticket(P1) = Ticket(T1)$
$STAT3 = Station(P1) = Station(T1)$

As a result of this match, the pronoun *he* is resolved to *Sam1* as desired, and a unique referent for the definite description *the station* is identified as the train station *Station(T1)* even though it has not been mentioned previously in the discourse. In addition, there are a large number of implicatures that can be drawn from the constraints defined for the script. We can infer that the station is in the city that Sam is leaving from, that the ticket introduced in 11b is a train ticket to Rochester, and that Sam went to the station. Also, we have expectations about Sam boarding the train, as well as the other actions involved in taking the trip.

Several fairly obvious generalizations of the script structure would be needed to handle more realistic examples. The decomposition structure would need to be extended to allow a partial ordering on the subactions. Another important extension would be to allow the representation of choices between actions in a script. This would allow a script to follow different paths depending on the state of the world when the actions are executed. Some stories explicitly refer to choices in giving explanations of why some action was performed or was successful. For instance, a script for entering a house may have a different action sequence depending on whether the doors are locked. If they are locked, the agent must have a key and use it to unlock the door. Even with such generalizations, however, script-based techniques only work in limited domains where the actions that can be described in the discourses can be enumerated in advance.

15.6 Using Hierarchical Plans

A script can successfully model the content of a discourse only if it proceeds along lines anticipated by the script. A richer framework is needed to model the content of a discourse in which unexpected connections need to be made between actions. Plan-based models were developed to address this deficiency. The same representation of actions is used, but the actions defined tend to be smaller-scale than those in scripts. A **plan** is a set of actions, related by equality assertions and causal relations, that if executed would achieve some goal. A **goal** is a state that an agent wants to make true or an action that an agent wants to execute. The classic planning problem in AI takes a goal and a set of possible actions as input and produces a plan, typically a sequence of actions, that will achieve the goal. The reasoning needed in language understanding is different: It involves inferring the plans of other agents based on their actions. This process is generally called **plan recognition** or **plan inference**. The input to a plan inference process is a list of the goals that an agent might plausibly be pursuing and a set of actions that have been described or observed. The task is to construct a plan involving all the actions in a way that contributes toward achieving one of the goals. By forcing all

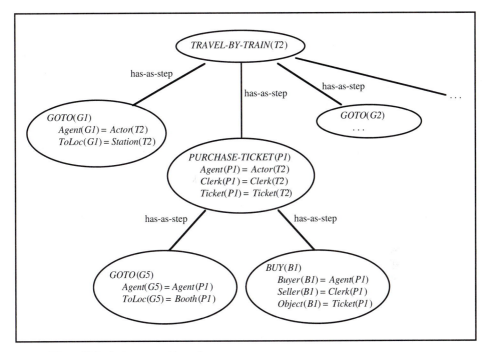

Figure 15.7 A plan to travel by train

the actions to relate to a limited number of goals, or to a single goal, the plan-based model constrains the set of possible expectations that can be generated.

The script-based system can be seen as a simple plan-based system. Each script defines both a plausible goal and the way to achieve it. The plan inference task involves selecting the appropriate plan that matches the input. A plan-based system, however, is not limited to selecting from a predetermined set of plans. It can use causal reasoning to construct new plans out of any of the actions defined in the domain. Thus the plan inference framework has the potential to model much richer discourse.

Let us start with a simple case of plans called **hierarchical plans**. Hierarchical plans are built out of a set of actions defined in the KB, called the **action library**. The most important aspect of each action definition is its decomposition relation, as this defines a hierarchical relationship between actions. A subset of the actions in the library are identified as plausible goals. A hierarchical plan is defined as a tree of actions, rooted by an action that is a plausible goal, where the mother/daughter relation indicates a decomposition relationship. The entailments of a plan are the consequences of each action definition in the tree, together with the equality relations resulting from the matches to the input, and matches of actions into decompositions of other actions. Figure 15.7 shows a simple hierarchical plan constructed by combining the *TRAVEL-BY-TRAIN* and *PURCHASE-TICKET* actions defined previously, and assuming that the *TRAVEL-BY-TRAIN* action is identified as a plausible goal.

> *PURCHASE-TICKET (P1):*
> **Roles:** *Agent = S1, Clerk = C1, Booth = LOC1*
> **Constraints:** *At (C1, LOC1)*
> **Decomposition:** *GOTO(Sue1, LOC1)*
>   *BUY (Sue1, C1, Ticket(P1))*

Figure 15.8   The parts of the instantiated action P1 that entail sentence 12b

Assume for the moment that the plan in Figure 15.7 is already constructed. It then can be used to account for the coherence of the following discourse:

12a.   Sue wanted to take a train to Rochester.
12b.   She walked up to the ticket clerk.

Sentence 12a serves to identify Sue's goal as traveling to Rochester by train. Utterances that describe goals must match an action that is the root node of the plan. This would match the root of the plan in the same way described with scripts in the last section and produce the equality assumptions

$Actor(T2) = Sue1$
$Train(T2) = TR37$
$DestCity(T2) = ROC$

Sentence 12b, with the content

$GoTo(E3) \& Agent(E3) = PRO1 \& ToLoc(E3) =$
$\quad LOC1 \& At(C1, LOC1) \& TicketClerk(C1)$

matches the first step of the decomposition of P1, given the equality assumptions

$G5 = E3$
$Agent(G5) = PRO1 (= Agent(P1) = Actor(T2) = Sue1)$
$ToLoc(G5) = LOC1 (= Booth(P1))$
$Clerk(P1) = C1$

With these equality assumptions, the plan entails the contents of 12b. You can see this by considering part of the definition of P1 after the roles are instantiated, as shown in Figure 15.8. Only the formulas used to entail the contents of 12b are shown.

Of course, the success of this method depends on having an algorithm that can construct such a plan given the input. A technique called **decomposition chaining** can be used here, which involves searching through decomposition relations until a chain of actions is found where the first matches the input and the last matches a plausible goal. When the goal is already defined, top-down methods usually prove to be most effective. For example, after processing 12a, the plan would consist of the single node *TRAVEL-BY-TRAIN(T2)*. A top-down breadth-first search through the decompositions could be used to generate expectations to match against the content of 12b. This strategy would generate the following expectations (in the order listed):

> First check all the immediate substeps of *T2:*
> $GOTO(G1)$—fails to match as $LOC1 \neq Station(T2)$
> $PURCHASE(P1)$—fails to match because of type incompatibility
> $GOTO(G2)$—fails to match because $LOC1 \neq Loc(TR37)$
> $GET\text{-}ON(G3)$, $TRAVEL(T3)$, $ARRIVE(A1)$, $GET\text{-}OFF(G4)$—
> all fail to match because of type incompatibility
> Next check the substeps of *G1:* assume there is no decomposition
> Next check the substeps of *P1:*
> $GOTO(G5)$—matches with equalities defined above.

Several difficult problems were skipped over in this example, however, regarding how this particular set of matches was found. For example, why doesn't 12b match step 1 of *T2, GoTo(Actor, Station)*, as shown in Figure 15.5? The answer must lie in the subsystem that reasons about locations. It would have to conclude that the location of the clerk, *LOC1*, does not equal the location of the station. Such issues are typically handled heuristically, and a thorough study of how location reasoning integrates with plan-based matching remains to be done.

The other issue is what to do when the goal is not defined. You can either search top-down from all plausible goals looking for a match, or use a bottom-up technique, matching into the substeps of any action, and then use the actions found to match into the substeps of other actions. Complications arise either way, as there will often be many possible matches. For instance, assume the first sentence was 12b. How might the goal be identified? There will likely be many actions in the KB that involve a *GOTO* step. Perhaps the KB has a *GO-FOR-A-WALK* action that is a plausible goal in addition to *TRAVEL-BY-TRAIN* and that probably contains a *GOTO* action. How might a system decide between the two? There is no foolproof answer. Some systems use heuristic preferences for one reading over another. Another strategy is to not decide yet, but wait for additional input that might affect the decision.

○ 15.7 Action-Effect-Based Reasoning

While decomposition chaining on hierarchical plans is an effective technique that constrains the search space, it is often not powerful enough to interpret many discourses. The problem is that not all causal relations are easily encoded as decomposition relationships. This section considers other methods for inferring more general plans that greatly expand the range of situations a system can interpret, at the price of expanding the search space.

Consider a simple example involving the action-effect relationship. The discourse

13a. Jack needed to be in Rochester by noon.
13b. He bought a ticket at the station.

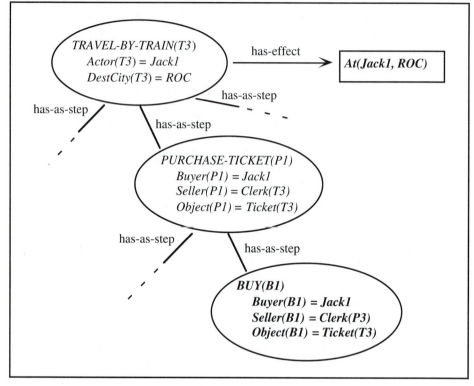

Figure 15.9 The plan recognized from discourse 13

can be interpreted only if the system realizes that the first sentence describes the effect of performing the action *TRAVEL-BY-TRAIN* to Rochester, and the second is a substep of that plan. To do this, states must be allowed as goals as well as actions, and the plan inference algorithm must search not only from actions to other actions via decompositions but also from actions to states via the actions' effects, and vice versa.

For example, sentence 13a would be analyzed initially as a goal state *At(Jack1, ROC)*. The logical form of 13b would not match directly into the expectation. To find the connection, the system would first have to match the appropriate effect of the *TRAVEL-BY-TRAIN* action to this goal state and then use decomposition chaining to find the match to the *PURCHASE* action described in 13b. The resulting plan is shown in Figure 15.9. Nodes representing actions are drawn as ovals, and those representing states as rectangles. Three types of causal links are used:

> **has-as-step**—relates an action to an act in its decomposition
> **enables**—relates a state to an action that has it as a precondition
> **has-effect**—relates an action to one of its effects

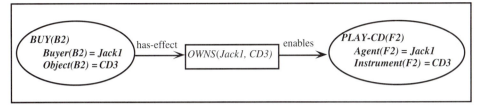

Figure 15.10   The plan involving an enablement relation from discourse 14

Furthermore, nodes that have matched the logical form of a sentences are labeled in boldface, whereas the others are labeled in plain text. For example, the graph in Figure 15.9 indicates that an effect of the *TRAVEL-BY-TRAIN* action is the state *At(Jack1, ROC)*.

More complex examples of action-effect-based reasoning arise when two actions are related, not by both being steps of some other action, but by one action enabling the other to occur (that is, one action's effects satisfy the precon-ditions of the other). For example, consider the discourse

14a.   Jack bought a CD player.
14b.   He played his favorite CDs all night long.

Let's assume that there is no pre-existing action in the library that involves buying a CD player and then using it to play CDs, but there are definitions of the individual actions. Then the action of playing a CD could have a precondition that the agent owns a CD player, and the action of buying something could have an effect that the agent now owns the thing bought. This precondition and effect can match to identify an enabling relation between the two actions. The resulting plan is shown in Figure 15.10.

A Plan Inference Algorithm

This section formulates a plan inference algorithm in a more precise manner. The plan structure that serves to generate expectations will be called the E-plan. In general the system might have to maintain many different E-plans to handle ambiguity, though here the algorithm will assume that it always starts with a single E-plan. Generalizing to a set of E-plans is straightforward. The new algorithm will still involve decomposition chaining, but it also will check for immediate action-effect and action-precondition connections.

In stating the algorithm, some additional definitions will be helpful. In particular, the nodes in an E-plan P that have matched a logical form are called the **realized nodes**, whereas those not yet matched directly to a logical form are called **expectation nodes**. Expectation nodes are further classified into the following sets:

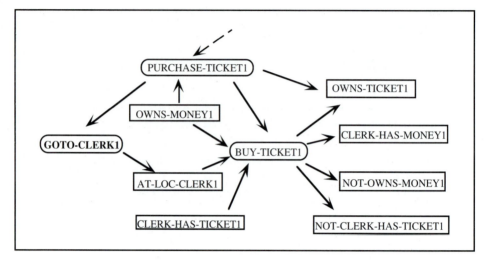

Figure 15.11 A fragment of the E-plan for discourse 12

A-set(P)—the expectation nodes that describe actions
P-set(P)—the expectation nodes that describe states that enable an action
E-set(P)—the expectation nodes that describe an effect of an action

These sets are useful as they contain the nodes in the plan most likely to match a new sentence. Note that the P-set and E-set usually overlap, as one state may be the effect of one action and enable another.

For example, consider the plan shown in Figure 15.11, which is part of the plan that might be inferred from discourse 12, discussed earlier. Because the arc labels can be determined by context, they are not shown. In other words, an arc between two actions is a has-as-step arc, an arc from a state to an action is an enables arc, and an arc from an action to a state is a has-effect arc. Nodes are labeled to suggest their content, but details on the role values and equalities are not shown. The node labeled GOTO-CLERK1 matched the logical form of sentence 12b, *She walked up to the ticket clerk*. Given this plan, the A-set consists of the nodes describing the actions PURCHASE-TICKET1 and BUY-TICKET1, the P-set consists of the nodes describing the states OWNS-MONEY1, AT-LOC-CLERK1, and CLERK-HAS-TICKET1, while the E-set consists of the nodes describing the states AT-LOC-CLERK1, OWNS-TICKET1, CLERK-HAS-MONEY1, NOT-OWNS-MONEY1, and NOT-CLERK-HAS-TICKET1.

Given a plan P, **expanding** the plan involves taking all the actions in its A-set and adding their decompositions to the plan. This action is used to perform the decomposition chaining inference described earlier in a breadth-first manner. Expanding the plan in Figure 15.11, for example, would add the decomposition BUY-TICKET1, adding the actions GIVE-CLERK-MONEY1 and GIVE-SUE-TICKET1, together with their precondition and effect states. The action

To incorporate a goal G into an E-plan E:
1. If E is the empty plan, then
    1.1. If G describes an action, add the action and its preconditions and effects to the E-plan, and mark the action as the goal.
    1.2. If G describes a state, then find all actions $A_1, ..., A_n$ that could have G as an effect. Create a new E-plan for each A_i as described in step 1.1.
2. If E is not empty, then
    2.1. Try to incorporate G into E (using the incorporate-action or incorporate-state yet to be described).
    2.2. If 2.1 failed, then let OLDG be the goal of E. Build the possible new E-plans with G as the goal (as in step 1). Then try to incorporate OLDG into the new E-plans. For those that match successfully, add OLDG and the old E-plan into the new E-plan.

Figure 15.12 The algorithm for incorporating goals

PURCHASE-TICKET1 is also in the A-set but has already been decomposed, so it is not expanded again.

With these concepts, the algorithm can be described. Whenever an action is added to a plan, all its preconditions and effects must be included with the appropriate arcs linking them to the actions. In addition, the A-set, P-set, and E-set must be updated with the new information. There are three classes of input, depending on whether the new sentence describes an action occurrence, a state, or a goal. The algorithm considers each case separately.

First consider when the input describes a goal. If the current E-plan is empty and the goal is an action, then you add the action to the empty plan and mark it as the goal. If the current E-plan is empty and the goal described is a state, then you find all actions that have this state as a goal and create a new possible E-plan for each one found. Now consider the cases when the initial E-plan is not empty. There are two possible interpretations. Either the new goal is a subgoal of the current E-plan, which means it should describe an action or effect in the E-plan, or the new goal is a higher level goal than that in the current E-plan, and the goal in the E-plan should be updated. Since this is a little complicated, a more precise formulation of the algorithm is shown in Figure 15.12.

Now consider the algorithm for incorporating an action A. First, if the E-plan is empty, then incorporate the action using the incorporate-goal algorithm. If the E-plan is not empty, then you can check for matches into the plan in three different ways:

- the action matches an action in the A-set
- the action has an effect that matches a state in the P-set
- the action has a precondition that matches a state in the E-set

For each match found, a new E-plan can be generated by adding the action and links appropriate to the part of the E-plan matched. As usual, whenever an action is added, all its preconditions and effects are added as well. If no match is found using these techniques, then you may expand the actions in the E-plan and try again. Generally, you will need to limit the number of times an E-plan can be expanded before giving up. Otherwise, there may be a combinatorial explosion of possible E-plans. The strategy assumed here is that you can only expand the actions in the A-set once before failing.

Discourse 14 can be handled by the algorithm specified so far. Sentence 14a, *Jack bought a CD player,* describes a buying action, *B1,* and since the E-plan is empty, it is added as the goal of the E-plan. Sentence 14b, *He played his favorite CDs all night long,* describes an action of playing CDs. Trying to directly match the action *PLAY-CD* into the A-set fails. Also, none of the effects of *PLAY-CD* match a precondition of *B1.* But a precondition of *PLAY-CD* will match an effect of *B1,* namely owning a CD player. Thus the *PLAY-CD* action can be integrated into the plan, creating an E-plan similar to that already shown in Figure 15.10.

The following is an example of a discourse that introduces a goal after some actions have been described. Sentence 15a introduces an action, and then 15b describes why it was performed:

15a. Jack bought a new stereo.
15b. He wants to play music at his party.

Sentence 15b is handled in step 2.2 of the algorithm in Figure 15.12. Specifically, 15b suggests a new E-plan with the action of playing music as the goal, and the action described in 15a can be interpreted as enabling this action, again resulting in a plan like that shown in Figure 15.10.

Finally, consider discourse 13, repeated here:

13a. Jack needed to be in Rochester by noon.
13b. He bought a ticket at the station.

Sentence 13a introduces a goal, and 13b describes a step that requires decomposition chaining. To incorporate the goal described in 13a, the system would find all actions that could have *At(Jack1, ROC)* as an effect (step 2.1). The *TRAVEL-BY-TRAIN* action is one of these, so an E-plan is constructed that contains an instance of *TRAVEL-BY-TRAIN*, connected to the effect and with its decomposition. The E-plan created is shown in Figure 15.13. To incorporate 13b, the *BUY* action would be matched into the E-plan, and no match found. After failing to match the effects or preconditions of the actions in the E-plan as well, the plan would be expanded. After expansion, a match would be found to the second step of the *PURCHASE-TICKET* action, and the resulting plan would be similar to that already shown in Figure 15.9.

The final class of input to be handled involves sentences that describe states but are not goal statements. Such statements are typically used to provide

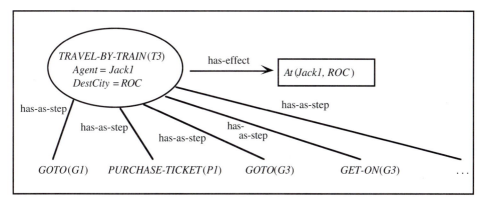

Figure 15.13 The E-plan after incorporation of sentence 13a

background or to describe the effects of actions in the plan. If the current E-plan is empty, then the state should be interpreted as background information. This is done by adding the state to the E-set and P-set of the plan. While it is not an effect or precondition of an action currently in the plan, this allows the state to be connected to actions that are incorporated later. For example, consider the discourse

16a. Sue had twenty dollars.
16b. She bought a ticket to Rochester.

In this case the incorporate action algorithm operating on 16b would find the connection that having money enables buying the ticket. If the E-plan is not empty, then you attempt to match the state into the E-set and the P-set. For each match found, the plan is updated with the new equality assumptions derived, and the state is removed from the E-set or P-set it was in as it has now been realized. If no match is found, the state is added to the E-set so it can be used later.

Limitations of the Algorithm

While the algorithm described can find connections between sentences in many cases, there are many other cases that it cannot handle. For example, it does not perform any bottom-up decomposition chaining, which would allow you to predict superactions for which the current action is a subpart. Thus it would not be able to find the connection between the two sentences in the discourse

17a. Sue bought a ticket to Rochester.
17b. She boarded the train at 4PM.

To find the connection between these two sentences, you must recognize that both are part of the decomposition of the TRAVEL-BY-TRAIN action: Buying a ticket is a subpart of purchasing a ticket, which is a subpart of traveling by train, and boarding the train is a direct subpart of traveling by train. Because of this failure, some obvious connection, such as that the train mentioned is going to

Rochester, will be missed. Many plan recognition algorithms use bottom-up decomposition chaining extensively and could find the connections here. With any large library of actions, however, such techniques will generate a very large number of possible E-plans, and search becomes a major problem. You could, however, add a limited strategy, say by looking for actions that could include an action in the E-plan and the new action as part of its immediate decomposition, and if found, adding the actions to make the connection.

Another important class of cases that are not handled here but should be are statements that describe undesirable states and suggest goals. For instance, if a discourse contained the sentence *Jack was hungry,* you might want to interpret this as a statement of a goal to eat. To handle such cases, the KB would need to represent knowledge about desirable and undesirable states and how they may lead to new goals for the agents. Some of these issues are considered in the next section.

15.8 Using Knowledge About Rational Behavior

The preceding representation of plans still can represent the content of only quite simple situations. Most actual stories and conversations rapidly move beyond the range of this formalism. This section considers areas in which extensions need to be made to handle more realistic text.

Perhaps the most obvious deficiency is that the discourses that can be modeled still all involve the unimpeded execution of some plan, that is, with no problems encountered. In actual situations, however, much time is spent dealing with and describing the problem-solving process itself. Many stories describe people's attempts at achieving some goal, including how they failed, how they thought they might succeed, what reaction they had to failure, how they compensated, and ultimately, how they overcame the problem. With multiple agents, there also is the possibility of competition and interacting plans. If you are to model such stories, you need to make the process of planning and acting more explicit. Given the present state of research in this area, no concrete answers can be given, but a few ideas can be described.

Consider a sketch of how an intelligent planning agent might behave. While still a simplification, this model provides enough intuition to motivate some techniques. The model describes an intelligent agent in a constant cycle involving the following steps (which may occur concurrently):

1. Observe the current situation (including monitoring whether or not the action the agent has just attempted has succeeded).
2. Select a goal, or set of goals, on which to focus.
3. Start to develop a plan to achieve these goals.
4. Execute actions in the plan when appropriate.

Different planning architectures operate at different granularities of planning and execution. The classical planning systems in the literature generally start with a

---

BOX 15.2 A Formal Analysis of Plan Inference

It should be clear that plan inference is a nonmonotonic process because the conclusions it draws are assumptions rather than entailments. As a result, it is difficult to give a precise formalization of the process, as can be done for deductive theories. Kautz (1990) solved this problem for the class of decomposition-chaining plan inference algorithms. He showed how to transform a knowledge base, KB, on which plan recognition would be performed, into a new KB, KB', such that any nonmonotonic conclusion based on plan inference from the first KB is a logical consequence of the KB'. The transformation is based on adding the effects of three basic assumptions that underlie the plan inference process. These assumptions are

1. The action library is complete; that is, the plan you are trying to recognize is a plan that you know about, or can construct.
2. Every action observed is intentional; that is, all observed actions are part of some plan.
3. As few top-level goals are being pursued as possible; that is, the explanation should be as concise as possible.

Kautz showed how to generate a new KB that incorporates these assumptions. Plan inference can then be performed by means of deduction from the observations using the new KB. In other words, in the revised KB, the observations will entail the set of possible plans that could be inferred.

---

high-level goal and fully construct a plan before any execution is considered. This model is not appropriate for our purposes. An opportunistic or reactive planner selects smaller-scale goals, often in response to the current world state, and generally executes actions as soon as they have been planned. This architecture allows the agent to respond "reactively" to the environment as it performs actions and is a more appropriate model for understanding discourse about an agent's planning behavior.

To instantiate such a model, there are some new distinctions that need to be made. First, goals must be divided into a hierarchy: At the top are the agent's most general goals, which provide the ultimate explanation for the agent's behavior. Below that are more specific goals (or subgoals) that are adopted as a means of achieving the top-level goals. Finally, at the finest level of detail, there is the goal regarding the actions that the agent is currently executing, which we will call the **active goal**. To achieve this active goal, the agent plans one or more actions. The action in this sequence that is being executed is called the **current action**.

Consider how an agent might behave given this model. If it has an active goal, say to open a door, it might plan an action that involves turning the door handle and pulling on the door. If it then discovers that the door is locked, it might abandon the current action and plan a different sequence to achieve the same active goal. For instance, it might plan to knock on the door and wait for a response. Alternatively, it might decide to abandon the goal of entering the house and pursue some other goal. Note that there is no single plan that would involve actions the agent performed, but there is a perfectly good explanation of the sequence given the above model of an intelligent agent.

Since an agent's behavior does not necessarily follow a well-formed plan in the sense developed earlier, the plan recognition component must be able to recognize actions based on this more general model of intentional behavior. To make this more precise, let us define a new structure called an **iplan** (for inten-tional plan). An iplan consists of

- a tree hierarchy of goals, with one leaf goal marked the **active goal**
- a sequence of actions, where the final action achieves the active goal, and one action is marked the **current action**

The previous plan inference algorithms can be adapted to model the decompo-sition chaining, and other reasoning is used to fill out the goal hierarchy and plan the sequence of actions to achieve the active goal. The agent's behavior is defined in terms of a set of **rational updates** (or just **updates**) to the iplan, which is formally a relation between two iplans. Intuitively, two iplans IP_1 and IP_2 are related by the update relation if an intelligent agent with iplan IP_1 and possibly with some new observation O from the world might adopt the set of goals described by IP_2.

Consider some examples of reasonable updates. They are organized into three classes that give a feel for the type of behavior, although the taxonomy is not intended to be complete. In each case, IP_1 is the old iplan, and IP_2 is a legal update that is specified in terms of modifications to IP_1.

Planning Updates

These updates result from the planning behavior of the agent and do not involve any observations on the part of the agent.

1. **goal/action**—If an agent has a goal G in IP_1 and there is no action in IP_1 that achieves G, then IP_2 may be constructed by adding an action, or tree of actions, whose root achieves G.

2. **decomposition**—If an agent has an action hierarchy with current action C in IP_1, but C is not directly executable, then IP_2 may be constructed by decomposing C into subactions.

3. **precondition failure**—If the current action C has a precondition that is not believed to be true, then either the action hierarchy is extended in IP_2 with a new current action to achieve the precondition, or action C is abandoned and a new action is introduced to achieve the active goal.

Execution-Based Updates

These updates arise from observations by the agent that concern the success or failure of the actions it executes.

4. **successful execution**—If the agent has observation O that indicates that the current action C was successfully executed, then the new current action of IP_2 will be the next action in the sequence (if there is one), or if not, a new active goal is selected since the old one is accomplished.

5. **unsuccessful execution**—If the agent has observation O that indicates that the current action C failed, then IP_2 marks the current action as failed.

6. **action failure 1**—If the current action failed, the IP_2 might involve trying the same action again, or it might involve a new action that also could achieve the active goal.

Goal Updates

These updates arise from observations on the part of the agent that cause it to change its goal structure.

7. **undesirable state**—If the agent observes state O, and O suggests an undesirable condition U, then IP_2 may be constructed by adding ¬U into the existing goal structure of IP_1. This might require abandoning goals already in IP_1.

8. **action failure 2**—If the current action failed, then the active goal is removed in IP_2 and a new goal is made active.

Consider the following discourse:

18a. When Jack got home, he tried the door
18b.   but found it was locked.
18c. He knocked,
18d.   but there was no one home.
18e. He walked around the house to the back door.

The analysis is summarized in Figure 15.14, where the active goals and current actions are shown in bold. To handle this, the KB would have to contain knowledge about getting home, which would include knowledge about getting into the house through a door. Let us assume that the initial iplan is recognized from clause 18a in IPLAN-18a, which has the goal hierarchy *Inside-House(Jack1)* and the subgoal *EnterViaDoor(Jack1, Door1)*, which is the active goal. The sequence of actions planned to achieve the active goal consists of *OpenDoor(Jack1, Door1)* and *WalkThrough(Jack1, Door1)*, with the first one being the current action. Clause 18b indicates that the action failed by stating a precondition failure, producing IPLAN-18b. This, of course, assumes the appropriate action

IPLAN-18a
  Goal Hierarchy: *Inside-House* (*Jack1*), ***EnterViaDoor***(***Jack1***, ***Door1***)
  Actions: ***OpenDoor*** (***Jack1, Door1***), *WalkThrough* (*Jack1, Door1*)

via update 5, on observation *Locked* (*Door1*), to

IPLAN-18b
  Goal Hierarchy: *Inside-House* (*Jack1*), ***EnterViaDoor***(***Jack1, Door1***)
  Actions: ***OpenDoor*** (***Jack1, Door1***), *WalkThrough* (*Jack1, Door1*) ** FAILED

via update 6, precondition failure, to

IPLAN-18c
  Goal Hierarchy: *Inside-House* (*Jack1*), ***EnterViaDoor***(***Jack1, Door1***)
  Actions: ***Knock***(***Jack1***), $\exists p$ *UnlockDoor*(*p*)

via update 5, observation $\neg \exists\ p\ .\ AtHome(p)$, to

IPLAN-18d
  Goal Hierarchy: *Inside-House* (*Jack1*), ***EnterViaDoor***(***Jack1, Door1***)
  Actions: ***Knock***(***Jack1***), $\exists p$ *UnlockDoor*(*p*) ** FAILED

via update 8, precondition failure, to

IPLAN-18e
  Goal Hierarchy: *Inside-House* (*Jack1*), *EnterViaDoor*(*Jack1, BackDoor1*),
            At (***Jack1, BackDoor1***)
  Actions: *GoTo*(*Jack1, BackDoor1*)

Figure 15.14   A trace of the iplans for discourse 18

definition for the *OpenDoor* action, which requires the door to be unlocked. Clause 18c is then interpreted as a response to a failed action, which in this case is an alternate way to achieve the active goal. Clause 18d indicates that this attempt also failed due to precondition failure, producing IPLAN-18d. Finally, 18e is interpreted as indicating an abandonment of the active goal and the development of a new way to achieve the higher level goal of *Inside-House*(*Jack1*).

There are many constructs in language that explicitly refer to concepts and actions that need to be defined by such a model. For example, discourse 18 showed two uses of the connective *but,* in each case treated as having a sense indicating a precondition failure. Other expressions are easy to find. Consider the discourse

19a. Sue had to find a way to get enough money for the ticket.
19b. She tried to use the automatic teller machine, but it was broken.
19c. She eventually gave up and walked to the bus station and took a bus.

The phrases *find a way, try,* and *give up* all directly relate to activities that can be defined within the iplan model.

The iplan model is just a start, however, and many other complications arise that indicate a need for still more general models. For instance, plans that involve repetition of some activity, such as pounding in a nail with a hammer, or cyclic events, such as walking to school each day, cannot be represented in any general fashion. For instance, the system might need to recognize that an agent bought a bus pass so that he or she could take the bus into work each day. The one action of buying the pass serves as an enabling condition for a whole series of bus trips. Important aspects of a story could be missed if the action of buying a bus pass was linked only to a single occurrence of the *TAKE-BUS* action. Other goals are difficult to represent even though they don't involve repetition. For instance, what is the goal of the action of going to the theater? Intuitively you know it is to see the play and ultimately to enjoy yourself. You would have to represent this goal explicitly to understand a story in which an evening out at the theater was ruined because your wallet was stolen. To handle this, you would need a theory of what makes activities worthwhile and enjoyable.

Complications also arise because people usually don't have a single goal, and when considering situations where multiple goals are described, the system needs to understand situations where these goals conflict or are in concord. For example, a discourse might describe a person's dilemma in deciding between studying for an exam tomorrow (and thus passing) or going out to see a movie. The system would need to be able to represent this dilemma and reason about such things as why the goals conflict. It would also have to understand descriptions of how the person attempts to avoid the conflict and achieve both goals. Another discourse might describe a situation where two people have conflicting goals (say both want to own a particular race horse) and their respective actions would need to be interpreted in light of this conflict. Similar cases occur when goals complement each other and when people are cooperating toward mutually compatible goals.

Summary

Knowledge about causality and everyday activities is essential for understanding much discourse. Indeed, you cannot correctly handle many word ambiguities and examples of reference without using such knowledge. This knowledge is used to generate expectations that are matched into possible interpretations of the input. Significant effort has been made to find ways to control the generation of expectations. Techniques in this area range from the fairly large-scale script structures to more flexible plan inference systems that use general knowledge about actions and goals. Significant work remains to be done before these techniques can be applied successfully in realistic domains.

Related Work and Further Readings

The notion of coherence is crucial to motivate techniques for understanding discourse. It is important to realize that this involves finding semantic connections between sentences rather than finding structural properties. For instance, Halliday and Hasan (1976) claim that discourse **coheres** as a result of certain linguistic devices, such as

> **reference**—using pronouns and definite descriptions to refer back to objects mentioned in other sentences (deep and surface forms, one-anaphora, and so on)
>
> **ellipsis**—using the structure of one sentence to "fill in" another
>
> **conjunction**—connecting sentences by *and, further, but,* and so on
>
> **lexical connections**—using words that are related to each other, such as opposites, paraphrase, repetition, and so on

This approach is dramatically different from the computational theories presented in this chapter. Halliday and Hasan claim that these phenomena cause cohesion, whereas the computational approaches say that the content and topic flow of a discourse make it coherent and the phenomena listed above arise because of coherence. In other words, referential connections do not make a text coherent; rather, a coherent text enables referential connections. This distinction is considered at length in Hobbs (1979).

Almost every language understanding system that uses knowledge of the world to interpret sentences uses some form of matching. Often, the formal properties of the matching algorithm are not explored, though it seems clear that the formulation in Section 15.2 captures the essential parts of most of the algorithms used. The formalization of equality-based matching mostly follows Charniak (1988), who also discusses using the technique for handling definite reference. Kautz (1990) presents a similar analysis within a general framework for plan recognition. One of the strongest proponents of general abductive techniques for natural language understanding is Hobbs (Hobbs et al., 1993).

One of the earliest works that used general world knowledge to identify the connections between sentences was by Schank and Rieger (1974). They identified 16 different classes of connections, most of which have since been reformulated into the plan-based reasoning systems. Rieger's system involved searching through all possible inferences from each sentence, and thus was quite inefficient. Much of the work that has followed has been aimed at removing the inefficiencies by using more specialized representations of knowledge about actions.

Schank and Abelson (1977) introduced the idea of scripts, and Cullingford (1981) built the first script-based system. Section 15.5 describes this work in some detail but recasts it in a more conventional action representation. DeJong (1979) used scripts to extract partial information from newspaper stories. These systems all used forms of matching and inference to resolve anaphoric reference.

The work on representing action draws from the large literature in AI dealing with planning. Two classic foundational papers are McCarthy and Hayes (1969) and Fikes and Nilsson (1971). A good overview of planning can be found in the articles in Allen, Hendler, and Tate (1990). These representations were adapted for use in plan inference systems by Allen and Perrault (1980). The formalism used here is similar to that proposed by Litman and Allen (1987;

1990). Precisely defining the causal relationships between actions is quite tricky. A good reference from philosophy is that of Goldman (1970), who introduced the generation relation and distinguished it from enablement and decomposition. The work was adapted and extended for computational systems by Pollack (1990).

Plan recognition has been studied as a problem in AI for some time (for example, Schmidt et al. (1978)), and has similarities to work in automatic diagnosis and automatic tutoring. It was applied to language understanding by Wilensky (1983) and Allen and Perrault (1980). Hierarchical plans were developed by Sacerdoti (1977). Plan recognition techniques can be used both for understanding the content of language, as in this chapter, and for understanding the speaker's purpose in speaking, as will be described in Chapters 16 and 17. Carberry (1991) contains a good survey of the use of plan recognition in language understanding. Charniak and Goldman (1993) describe techniques for building a probabilistic plan recognition system. The algorithms described in Sections 15.6 and 15.7 draw ideas from Allen and Perrault (1980), Kautz (1990), and Ferguson and Allen (1993).

Wilensky (1983) was the first to extensively explore the use of knowledge about intentional behavior for interpreting stories. Section 15.8 describes some of these techniques in terms of the iplan construct. Wilensky covers a wide range of other problems as well, including goal conflict and subsumption, not covered here. The other influence on Section 15.8 is the development of reactive planning and intelligent agent architectures in the planning literature. A few papers on these topics can be found in Allen, Hendler, and Tate (1990). These issues will be explored again in more detail in Chapter 17.

Exercises for Chapter 15

1. (*easy*) For each of the following sentences, state some facts about typical behavior that could be used to justify them as expectations generated from the sentence *Jack walked to school.*

   a. He is going to attend class.
   b. His car is broken.
   c. He will be tired at school.

2. (*easy*) Express the following two formulas in graph form. What knowledge about types, equality, and inequality is needed to allow the two to match? What equality assumptions are generated by the match? State the entailments resulting from the match.

   $$Acquire(E1) \ \& \ Agent(E1) = Jack1 \ \& \ Theme(E1) =$$
   $$Book1 \ \& \ AtLoc(E1) = Store34$$

   $$Buy(E2) \ \& \ Agent(E2) = He1 \ \& \ Theme(E2) = It1 \ \& \ Price(E2) = \$10$$

3.   (*easy*) State the most likely causal relationship (if any) and the temporal relationship between each of the following sentences if said after the sentence *Jack went to the store.*

a.   He took his car from the garage.
b.   He had taken the money from Sue's room.
c.   He bought some peaches.
d.   Now he has plenty of beer.
e.   His car broke down along the way.

4.   (*medium*) Consider the following discourse:

a.   Jack bought some roses at Honest John's Flower Mart.
b.   He paid thirty dollars for them
c.   and Honest John swore that they were fresh.
d.   But they wilted as soon as he left the store.

For each sentence give the following:

- a representation of the meaning using the event-based KRL
- the equality assumptions needed to match an expectation generated earlier (except for first sentence)
- the expectation that would have to be generated from the sentence in order to account for the later sentences
- a commonsense rule that could be used to generated the expectation from the sentence

5.   (*medium*) Implement a version of the matching algorithm described in Section 15.2. You will need to implement a subsystem to reason about type hierarchies, as described in Chapter 13, and another subsystem to keep track of what constants are not equal. Given the type hierarchy and inequality information, your program should take two graphs and return a set of equality assumptions if the two graphs match. Demonstrate your system on the examples shown in Section 15.2, as well as some additional examples that show the different capabilities of your program.

6.   (*medium*) Assuming the action definitions in Figures 15.4 and 15.5, give a definition of the *GetOn* action that includes an interaction with the train conductor. With these definitions, describe in detail the steps taken by a plan inference algorithm that uses decomposition chaining to recognize the following sentence, given that the goal is known to be the action *TRAVEL-BY-TRAIN*. List each expectation in the order that it is generated and state why the input matches or fails to match.

Jack gave the conductor a ticket.

Draw the resulting decomposition chain showing the values of each role.

7. (*medium*) Trace the full plan inference algorithm, as described in Section 15.7, as it processes the following two sentences:

> Jack needed to have a ticket.
> He walked to the ticket clerk.

In particular, define a meaning for each sentence, and trace each step of the plan inference algorithm as it searches for a solution. Discuss any problems you have with ambiguity and suggest ways to decide on the appropriate interpretation. Draw the final plan constructed to connect the two sentences.

8. (*hard*) Implement a plan recognition system that uses the technique of decomposition chaining. It should use definitions of actions with decompositions, but need not explicitly represent role values. In other words, each action is represented as an atom, like the example shown in Figure 15.11. Test your system on some sample discourses, where each sentence has been converted to your representation by hand.

Discourse Structure

16.1 The Need for Discourse Structure

16.2 Segmentation and Cue Phrases

16.3 Discourse Structure and Reference

16.4 Relating Discourse Structure and Inference

16.5 Discourse Structure, Tense, and Aspect

16.6 Managing the Attentional Stack

16.7 An Example

This chapter examines techniques for representing and reasoning about extended discourse beyond finding local connections between sentences as seen in Chapter 14. Extended discourse cannot be viewed simply as a linear sequence of sentences. Rather, in many cases the utterances cluster together into units, called segments, that have a hierarchical structure. Section 16.1 discusses the problems in viewing discourse as a linear sequence of sentences. Section 16.2 then defines the notions of discourse segments and cue phrases that signal segmental structure. Section 16.3 shows how the segment structure affects the interpretation of referential expressions, especially pronouns. Section 16.4 discusses how segments interact with inference to facilitate an understanding of the content of the discourse. Section 16.5 discusses tense and aspect, and shows how the interpretation of the temporal and causal connections between eventualities requires the use of segmental structure. Section 16.6 puts all the different components discussed earlier together to specify a model of discourse understanding. Section 16.7 presents an example that illustrates the issues discussed in the chapter.

16.1 The Need for Discourse Structure

The reference mechanisms presented in Chapter 14 were based on the structure of the previous sentence and on recency constraints. In dialogues where the topic may shift and change, however, you can see that these techniques are inadequate. Consider the following fragment, which could occur near the end of a dialogue between two persons, E and A, while E helps A assemble a lawn mower:

1a.	E:	So you have the engine assembly finished.
1b.		Now attach the rope to the top of the engine.
1c.		By the way, did you buy gasoline today?
1d.	A:	Yes. I got some when I bought the new lawn mower wheel.
1e.		I forgot to take my gas can with me, so I bought a new one.
1f.	E:	Did it cost much?
1g.	A:	No, and I could use another anyway to keep with the tractor.
1h.	E:	OK.
1i.		Have you got it attached yet?

The antecedent of *it* in sentence 1i is the rope last mentioned seven sentences earlier in 1b, even though objects mentioned since then, such as the gas can in sentence 1e, would satisfy any of the selectional restrictions that would be derived for *it*. Thus the history list mechanism fails to make the correct predictions in this dialogue. In fact, no simple generalization based on a linear ordering of discourse entities can provide a satisfactory solution. Intuitively, though, it is clear what is going on. Sentences 1c through 1g are a subdialogue incidental to the interaction involving attaching the rope. In 1h, E indicates that the current topic is completed by using the phrase *OK*. Thus in the interpretation of 1i, the relevant previous context is based on 1b. An account of this structure requires a notion of **discourse segments**—stretches of discourse in which the sentences are addressing the same topic—and a generalization of the history list structure that takes the segments into account.

You might think that a generalization of the plan inference models derived in the last chapter might be useful for identifying the segments. Using such techniques, the system might be able to recognize that 1c is not a possible continuation of the plan to attach the rope, and thus represents a digression. Once the digression is completed, the plan recognizer could analyze 1i as querying the status of the action introduced in 1b. But trying to do all the work within the plan recognizer would be difficult. Whenever there is a shift of topic, such as at 1c and 1h, the plan reasoner would have to fail to find a connection between the old sentence and the new, and on the basis of this failure, initiate a new topic. This could be quite expensive, and might not be possible in some cases, since there might be an obscure interpretation that would allow a sentence such as 1c to be viewed as a continuation of the action described in 1b (for instance, the gasoline might be used to clean the engine before attaching the rope). Furthermore, you no doubt recognize that E explicitly told A that the topic had changed in 1c by using the phrase *By the way*. Such phrases, known as **cue phrases**, play an important role in signaling topic changes in discourse.

In addition, a plan-based model may not be appropriate in other conversational settings, such as debates, where intersentential relationships such as "sentence X supports the claim in sentence Y" or "sentence X contradicts the claim in sentence Y" may be relevant. Yet the same cue phrases could be used in this setting. These arguments lead to the conclusion that a theory of discourse structure cannot be explained solely in terms of action reasoning.

This chapter examines a model of discourse structure that allows each of the techniques discussed in the last two chapters to be generalized and integrated. The key idea is that a discourse can be broken down into discourse segments, each of which is a coherent unit and analyzable using techniques similar to those already presented.

16.2 Segmentation and Cue Phrases

While the need for segmentation of discourse is almost universally agreed upon, there is no consensus on what the segments of a particular discourse should be or how segmentation could be accomplished. One reason for this lack of consensus is that there is no precise definition of what a segment is beyond the intuition that certain sentences naturally group together. Notwithstanding these difficulties, a good model of segmentation is essential to understanding discourse. It divides the problem into two major subproblems: (1) What techniques are needed to analyze the sentences within a segment, and (2) how segments can be related to each other.

For practical purposes, a discourse segment consists of a sequence of clauses that display local coherence. The following properties should hold within a segment:

Event Described	Informational Relation	Communicative Goal
E1: Jack goes to store		Describe E1 as start of story
E2: Jack drives car	E2 part of E1	Elaborate on E1
E3: Jack buys lobsters	E2 before E3, E3 part of E1	Elaborate on E1
E4: Jack gets home	E4 provides temporal setting for E5	Elaborate story after E1
E5: Jack prepares for feast	E5 follows E4, E4 enables E5	Elaborate story after E4

Figure 16.1 Informational relations versus communicative goals

- Some technique based on recency (for example, a history list) should be usable for referential analysis and the handling of ellipsis.
- A fixed time and location characterize the clauses, or there is a simple progression of time and location (as in simple narratives).
- A fixed set of speakers and hearers are participating.
- A fixed set of background assumptions is relevant.

The last property requires that the modality of the text remains constant. For example, the text cannot switch from describing a sequence of actual events to describing a hypothetical event within a single segment.

These are the structural requirements on a segment. There are two approaches to characterizing what defines a segment. The **intentional** view is that all the sentences in a segment contribute to a common discourse purpose; that is, the same communicative goal motivates the speaker to say each sentence in the segment. The **informational** view is that all the sentences in a segment are related to each other by some temporal, causal, or rhetorical relations. For example, in narratives the sentences in a single segment should combine together to describe a coherent event or situation.

There is often a close correspondence between these two definitions. For instance, in most narratives, the writer's discourse intentions closely correspond to the informational level analysis. Consider the following start of a story:

2a. Jack shopped early in the day.
2b. He took his car
2c. and he bought a dozen live lobsters.
2d. When he got home,
2e. he spent the day preparing the feast.

Figure 16.1 shows an analysis at both the informational level and the intentional level. The informational relations tend to describe the "fine structure" of the discourse, primarily how the events are causally and temporally related. The intentional level tends to address more global structural issues in terms of the communicative goal of relating the story.

While it seems that there is always an intentional level analysis, there are discourse situations where there is no informational analysis. In discourse 1, for example, sentence 1c does not have any informational relationship to the content of 1a and 1b. Rather, it is introducing a new topic for discussion. This can be analyzed at the intentional level as a change to a new topic. Examples like this motivate some researchers to argue that the intentional analysis is primary. But both levels are essential, and which approach seems more important will depend on the form of the discourse studied. In dialogues and debates, the intentional analysis seems most informative. In narratives and descriptive essays, on the other hand, the informational view seems most informative. Each view provides a useful analysis of the discourse, and neither can replace the other.

With this background, the issue of segmentation can be explored in more detail. We define a segment as a sequence of clauses, possibly interrupted by subsegments, forming a hierarchical structure. In some views, each clause forms its own primitive segment, and these segments combine to form larger segments. For reasons to be seen later, we will not take this view. A clause does not necessarily form a segment by itself, although it can do so under the right circumstances.

The most important aspect of segments is that they have a hierarchical structure. The explanation of why the pronoun *it* in sentence 1i cannot refer to the gas can mentioned in 1e depended on this fact. Since 1i is not in the segment defined by sentences 1c–1h, the gas can is not available as a discourse entity for 1i. Rather, sentences 1a, 1b, and 1i define a segment. The history list generated from these four sentences correctly predicts the antecedent for *it* in 1i.

This example shows an important function of discourse segments: They define the local context for the interpretation of referential expressions. The hierarchical structure then controls the availability of various different local contexts that might be used to process the current sentence.

The second important function of segments is to organize the information conveyed in a way that facilitates the identification of the relationship between a new sentence and the prior discourse. To support this identification process there must be some representation of the semantic content of each segment constructed by inferential processing.

Each segment is associated with a **local discourse state** (or simply discourse state), which consists of (at least) the following:

- the sentences that are in the segment
- the local discourse context, generated from the sentences in the segment, using techniques described in Chapter 14
- the semantic content of the sentences in the segment together with the semantic relationships that make the segment coherent

SEG1
a) Jack and Sue went to buy a new lawn mower
b)   since their old one was stolen.

> SEG2
> c) Sue had seen the men who took it and
> d)   she had chased them down the street,
> e)   but they'd driven away in a truck.

f) After looking in the store,
g)   they realized they couldn't afford a new one.

> SEG3
> h) By the way, Jack lost his job last month
> i)   so he's been short of cash recently.
> j) He has been looking for a new one,
> k)   but so far hasn't had any luck.

l) Anyway, they finally found a used one at a garage sale.

Figure 16.2   The segment hierarchy represented by boxing

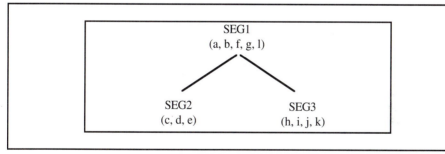

Figure 16.3   The same segment hierarchy represented as a tree

A complete discourse will typically involve many segments. Figure 16.2 shows the segmental structure of a dialogue represented by boxing of text. A segment is said to **contain** the segments that appear within it. The same information can be represented in tree form, as shown in Figure 16.3.

Additional concerns need to be addressed when considering on-line algorithms that understand discourse on a sentence-by-sentence basis. Such a processing model must be described in terms of extending an agent's representation of the discourse so far with a new sentence to create an updated representation of the discourse. This representation is called the **attentional stack** (or discourse stack) because it reflects what the agent is attending to in order to understand the next sentence.

The attentional stack consists of the discourse states reflecting the current structure of the ongoing discourse. The states on the discourse stack correspond

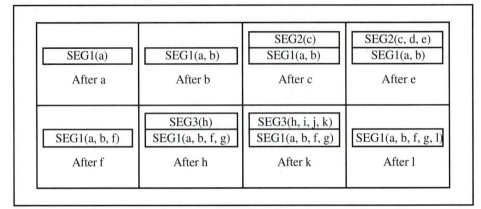

Figure 16.4   Part of the sequence of discourse stacks for the same discourse

to the set of segments that could be extended by the next clause. The top state on the stack corresponds to the most deeply embedded segment that can be extended. Each state on the stack corresponds to a segment that contains the segments of the states above it. To begin a new segment in the discourse, a new state must be pushed on the stack. To extend a segment corresponding to a state lower on the stack, all the states above it must be popped from the stack. This might sound complicated, but the stack model is quite simply related to the hierarchical segment structure. In particular, if you consider the sequence of discourse stacks, one after each clause, the sequence resembles a depth-first traversal through the tree of discourse segments. Figure 16.4 shows snapshots from the sequence of discourse stacks for the discourse shown in Figures 16.2 and 16.3. To show the relationship between the discourse states and their corresponding segments, the discourse states are labeled with the segment name followed by a list of the clauses seen so far in the segment. This provides a unique name for each of the discourse states produced during a discourse. For example, discourse state SEG1(a, b) is the discourse state corresponding to segment SEG1 at the point when clauses a and b have been processed. While not shown in the figure to save space, segment names will also need to include the completed subsegments so that the state of a segment can be tracked over multiple subsegments. Thus the full name for the state after clause f would be SEG1(a, b, seg2, f).

One of the more important indicators of the structure of a discourse is the use of cue phrases to signal the relationship of the next clause to the preceding discourse. Depending on the goals of their research, different researchers use different sets of cue phrases, but they can all be divided into two broad classes depending on what they signal. The first class identifies semantic relationships between clauses or states, and the second class indicates discourse structure directly without identifying a semantic relationship.

To introduce the first class, consider the two sentences

Jack went to the store. Sam stayed home.

Cue Phrases for Structure	Typical Use	Cue Phrases for Semantic Relations	Typical Use
anyway	end digression	and	continuation
by the way	start digression	because	causation/reason
bye	end dialogue	but	contrast
first	intro. subtopic (itemization)	furthermore	new subtopic
		however	contrast
incidentally	start digression	meanwhile	new topic
last	new subtopic (itemization)		(at same time)
		so	conclusion
next	new subtopic (itemization)	then	causal/ temporal
		therefore	summary
now	intro. subtopic	though	contrast
OK	close topic		

Figure 16.5 Some cue phrases and their uses

Taken as presented, there is no obvious relationship between the two sentences except an implied temporal overlap. But many words could be added to explicitly indicate the intended relationship between the events. For instance, you could indicate that the reason that Jack went to the store was because Sam stayed home,

> Jack went to the store because Sam stayed home.

or that Sam stayed home because Jack went to the store,

> Jack went to the store. So Sam stayed home.
> Jack went to the store. Therefore, Sam stayed home.

or that Sam stayed home even though you would have expected him not to,

> Jack went to the store but Sam stayed home.
> Jack went to the store. However, Sam stayed home.

or that these two events are both evidence for some other conclusion,

> Jack went to the store. Furthermore, Sam stayed home.

or finally, that a certain temporal relationship holds,

> Jack went to the store. Meanwhile, Sam stayed home.

The second class of cue phrases signals the discourse structure directly without necessarily indicating a semantic relationship. Typically, they indicate segment boundaries. They include phrases used to end the current topic under discussion (such as *OK, fine*), to end the discourse itself (such as *bye, thanks*), to signal a digression (such as *by the way, incidentally*), to signal the end of a digression (such as *anyway*), or to indicate a particular discourse organization, such as itemization (for example, *first, second, next, last*). Figure 16.5 lists some cue phrases in these two broad classes together with some of their typical uses.

SEG1(1a, 1b):
Center: Ø, **Cp**: R1, **Others**: T1, E1
Content: PullRope(R1), TopOf(T1, E1), Engine(E1)

Figure 16.6   The discourse stack after sentence 1b

16.3 Discourse Structure and Reference

The example at the beginning of this chapter used a reference problem to motivate the need for a hierarchical discourse structure. The attentional stacks described in the last section provide the mechanism to account for this problem. The digression creates a new discourse state that temporarily hides the original discourse state when it is pushed on the stack. When the digression ends, its state is popped off the stack, and the original state becomes available. Consider this example in more detail. Figure 16.6 shows the discourse stack at the end of sentence 1b, *Now attach the rope to the top of the engine.* The current discourse entities and their properties are shown as part of the local discourse state for the segment. In particular, entities R1 (the rope), T1 (the top), and E1 (the engine) are available for subsequent reference, and R1 is the preferred next center. In sentence 1c, the cue phrase *By the way* signals a digression, so a new discourse state is pushed on the stack. This top state is then extended by utterances 1d through 1g, resulting in the stack shown in Figure 16.7. The discourse entities available for reference describe the new gas can, G3, and the tractor, T2. The clue word *OK* in 1h indicates the end of the digression, and the discourse state for SEG2 is popped off the stack, resulting in the discourse stack shown in Figure 16.8. Note that this state is the same as the one in Figure 16.6 that arose after sentence 1b. Thus when utterance 1i is processed, the pronoun *it* will refer to R1, as expected. It is not possible for it to refer to the gas can, G3, because that discourse entity is no longer available in the discourse state.

Pronouns play an important role in most arguments about discourse structure because, as you saw in Chapter 14, there are strong constraints on where the antecedent can appear. In particular, in most cases the antecedent is in the previous sentence and is subject to recency constraints. That is why examples such as the pronoun *it* in sentence 1i pose such a problem. The hierarchical discourse model provides an elegant solution to the problem that retains intuitions about the importance of recency.

The analysis for digressions is fairly straightforward because cue phrases typically signal the segment boundaries. Some other forms of discourse also have a clearly defined segment structure. For example, itemization constructs often use cue phrases to explicitly indicate their structure, as in the discourse

SEG2(1c, 1d, 1e, 1f, 1g):
Center: Ø, Cp: G3, **Others**: T2
Content: GasCan(G3), Tractor(T2), GasCan(G2), Old(G2), Wheel(W1), Gasoline(G1)

SEG1(1a, 1b):
Center: Ø, **Cp**: R1, **Others**: T1, E1
Content: PullRope(R1), TopOf(T1, E1), Engine(E1)

Figure 16.7 The discourse stack after sentence 1g

SEG1(1a, 1b):
Center: Ø, **Cp**: R1, **Others**: T1, E1
Content: PullRope(R1), TopOf(T1, E1), Engine(E1)

Figure 16.8 The discourse stack after sentence 1h

3a. There are many ways to identify a silver maple leaf.
3b. First, it has a silvery sheen on the back.
3c. If you hold it in your hand and move it,
3d.   you will see the sun reflect off the back.
3e. Second, it has deep, pronounced notches between the points.
3f. The shape is quite similar to a red maple leaf.
3g. And third, if you break its stem, the sap will be milky.
3h. Break the stem and wait about 20 seconds and the sap should be visible.

This discourse has three subsegments. The beginning of each subsegment is explicitly marked by the cue phrases *first, second,* and *and third,* respectively. As each subsegment is popped and a new one begun, the discourse state for the segment consisting of 3a is used to identify the appropriate antecedent for the pronoun *it*. The discourse entities introduced in the previous subsegment are not available. For example, the pronoun *it* in 3g can't refer to the red maple leaf described in 3f, even though it is in the previous sentence. The segment structure of this discourse is shown in tree form in Figure 16.9.

Segmentation becomes more difficult to detect when a discourse has no explicit signal, but the topic slowly changes. It is sometimes difficult to distinguish between the case of a sentence that introduces a new segment and the case of a sentence that involves a natural progression of a topic occurring within a single segment. Such problems arise very frequently in narratives and stories, in which there is a continual progression of topic throughout. The story might describe a sequence of events over a long stretch of time and yet never show evidence of any hierarchical structure. If there is never an instance of popping

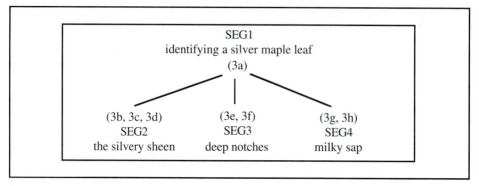

Figure 16.9 The structure of discourse 3

back to a previous segment, then you could argue that the entire story consists of a single segment.

The referential analysis itself can also suggest segmentation. In particular, if a referring expression is used that requires a discourse state lower on the stack in order to succeed, then this might force the completion of the segments corresponding to the states above it on the stack. Consider discourse 3 extended with the utterance

3i.   These three tests are all you need to know.

Before processing 3i, the attentional stack contains the discourse states SEG1(3a, seg2, seg3) and SEG4(3g, 3h). Thus 3i could extend state SEG4(3g, 3h), or SEG4(3g, 3h) could be popped and 3i could extend SEG1(3a, seg2, seg3, seg4). There are no cue phrases in 3i to indicate a pop, but to successfully analyze the referring expression, SEG4(3g, 3h) must be popped. In particular, SEG1(3a, seg2, seg3, seg4) provides the discourse entities for the expression *These three tests,* which refers to the three methods described in SEG2, SEG3, and SEG4. The only context where all three tests could exist would be in the context SEG1(3a). Thus, in this case, it would be referential analysis that indicates a segment pop, based on the failure to produce a reasonable analysis of the referring expressions in the context SEG4.

This example also motivates another argument for segment structure. Consider what phrases evoke the discourse entities referred to in 3i by the NP *these three tests.* Interestingly, none are evoked by a single phrase. For instance, the first test is described by utterances 3b, 3c, and 3d. It is the combination of the content of all three utterances that evokes the discourse entity. This shows that segments themselves evoke discourse entities, presumably situations, that can be available for subsequent reference.

16.4 Relating Discourse Structure and Inference

As stated earlier, sentences within a segment must display local coherence. Depending on the form of the discourse, coherence may arise from causal

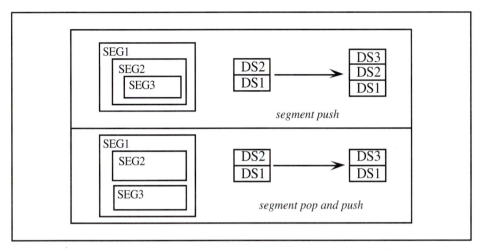

Figure 16.10 Two different ways a new segment can start

connections (as explored in detail in Chapter 15), or it may arise from other relationships such as evidence and counterevidence, as in a debate or argument. Whatever the mechanism for establishing local coherence, it is clear that this process will be strongly interrelated with the discourse structure. On the one hand, the segmentation of the discourse should be used to focus and direct the search for connections, and on the other hand, finding connections (or failing to find connections) can affect decisions about segmental structure. This section explores the relationship between discourse structure and inference.

You have seen several examples of segmentation so far. When considering inferential processing, these examples fall into two very different classes. Discourse 1 shows an example of a subsegment that is a digression. In this case there is no inferential connection between the segments. Each segment is treated independently and has its own coherent structure. Discourse 3 shows the opposite extreme. Here there would be a one-to-one correspondence between the discourse structure and a representation of the task of identifying silver maple leaves using the three tests.

Given this range of behavior, it might seem that there is little to say about how discourse structure and inferential structure relate. There is, however, an important constraint between the two that helps decide what segmentation structures are possible. Specifically, whenever a sentence begins a new segment, there is an ambiguity between whether the new segment ends the prior segment or is a subsegment of the prior segment. Figure 16.10 shows this choice in terms of its effect on both the segmental structure and the change in the discourse stack. The discourse state for each segment SEG_i is written as DS_i. The decision affects what discourse entities are available for reference and how the discourse could continue once the new segment ends.

The noncommittal approach would be to always push new segments, thereby allowing any previous topic to be resumed later. This approach certainly seems to work for digressions and interruptions, but it goes against intuition for the structure of discourses such as 3. If SEG3 was a subsegment of SEG2 in discourse 3, the sun mentioned in 3d would still be available for later pronominal reference. In this discourse, the cue phrases explicitly signal the desired structure, so this interpretation is not possible.

Unfortunately, in many cases there are no explicit signals to indicate which interpretation is intended. In these cases the distinction is made based on inferential grounds. Specifically, if an inferential connection can be identified, we may know that a segment is completed because the discourse has moved on to the logical next topic. For instance, in a discourse that is describing some event, segment pushes might correspond to a decomposition relationship between the events, while a segment pop and push might correspond to moving to the next event in a sequence.

While all discourses clearly are not descriptions of events, the hierarchical structure is useful for many different forms of discourse. To unify these approaches across domains, the notion of the **discourse purpose** of a segment is introduced. While defining this notion precisely is difficult, the intuitions are clear. The idea is that the constraints between segments arise because of why the speaker is saying the sentences in each segment. The claim is that a segment push occurs when the new segment (corresponding to DS3) is said to accomplish a subgoal of the goal of the current segment (corresponding to DS2). A pop and push, on the other hand, occurs when the goal of the new segment is not a subgoal of the goal of the previous segment, but is a subgoal of the goal of the segment embedding the previous segment. The specification of what goals are suitable as discourse purposes is defined by the type of discourse.

For instance, in a discourse in which the conversational goal is to describe a (possibly complex) event, the discourse purpose hierarchy might correspond to the event decomposition hierarchy. In particular, the discourse purposes would all be of the form "describe event X." If event X is part of event Y, the discourse purpose "describe event X" would be a subgoal of the discourse purpose "describe event Y."

Consider another form of discourse, namely debates. The discourse purpose is to establish some claim and the subgoal relationship corresponds to evidential support. For example, if you have a goal to establish claim X, then a subgoal might be to establish claim Y, where Y would tend to make the other person believe X, that is, where Y provides evidence for X. With this correspondence a segment push may correspond to the case where the new segment has a discourse purpose of establishing a claim made in the prior segment.

As one final example, consider a discourse whose purpose is to describe all the rooms in a house. The discourse purpose hierarchy could reflect the physical layout of the house, for example, describing the living room is a subgoal of describing the house, and describing the alcove in the living room is a subgoal of describing the living room.

With this abstraction away from the specific inference process underlying the discourse, we can now state the constraint between discourse structure and inference in general terms. We say that a discourse purpose DP1 **dominates** another discourse purpose DP2 if and only if DP2 is viewed as a subgoal of DP1. A discourse purpose DP1 **immediately dominates** a discourse purpose DP2 if and only if DP1 dominates DP2 and there is no discourse purpose DP3 such that DP2 is a subgoal of DP3 and DP3 is a subgoal of DP1.

It is important to remember that not all segments must be related to each other in these ways. In fact, segments may be unrelated to each other, as seen in interruptions and digressions. So the fact that a segment is contained within another segment does not mean that the discourse purpose of the first must dominate the discourse purpose of the second. Rather, the constraints work in the opposite direction. When the inferential component identifies a dominance relationship, this imposes a constraint on the possible attentional stacks (and hence segmental structure). In particular, the following constraint holds:

> **Domination Constraint**—If the discourse purpose of the segment associated with discourse state DS1 immediately dominates the discourse purpose of the segment associated with DS2, then if DS2 is on the attentional stack, DS1 must be immediately below it on the stack.

This constraint forces attentional stack updates that agree with intuition. For example, consider the following discourse, which is a revised version of discourse 3 with the cue phrases removed:

4a. There are many ways to identify a silver maple leaf.
4b. It has a silvery sheen on the back.
4c. If you hold it in your hand and move it,
4d.   you will see the sun reflect off the back.
4e. It also has deep, pronounced notches between the points.
4f. It is quite similar to a red maple leaf.
4g. If you break its stem, the sap will be milky.
4h. Break the stem and wait about 20 seconds and the sap should be visible.

Removing the cue phrases makes the discourse a bit more difficult to understand, but it is still comprehensible. The desired segment structure is still as shown in Figure 16.9; that is, the top level segment for the discourse is SEG1, and there are three subsegments, SEG2, consisting of 4b, 4c, and 4d, SEG3 with 4e and 4f, and SEG4 with 4g and 4h. In this setting the discourse purpose is to convey how to perform the task of identifying silver maple leaves, and the domination relationship is defined by the task/subtask relationship. Assuming the appropriate domain reasoner, the discourse purpose of SEG1 immediately dominates the discourse purposes of all three of SEG2, SEG3, and SEG4. Thus the domination constraint uniquely determines the progression of discourse stacks. Figure 16.11 shows the discourse stack update given sentence 4b. Given the domination constraint, there

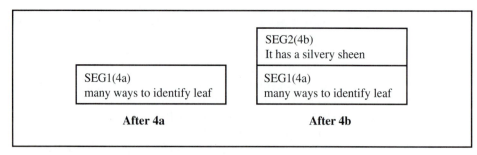

Figure 16.11 The attentional stack update given sentence 4b

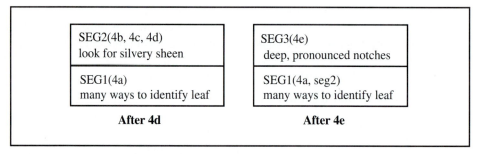

Figure 16.12 The attentional stack update given sentence 4e

is no other possibility. In particular, the discourse state SEG1(4a) could not have been popped off the stack because its purpose dominates the purpose of the new segment started by 4b.

Figure 16.12 shows the attentional stack update for (4e). Again, if the domain reasoner identifies that SEG1 immediately dominates the new segment SEG3, then exactly one transition satisfies the domination constraint. The state SEG2(4b, 4c, 4e) must be popped off the stack so that SEG3(4e) can be immediately above SEG1(4a, seg2).

Thus, to use this model in a particular application, you must determine what inferential connections in your domain induce the immediate dominance relationship between discourse segment purposes. Once this is determined, the domination constraint will allow you to use the inferential processing to restrict the possible discourse structure and attentional stack updates.

Another important advantage to the discourse purpose approach is that it allows the analysis of discourses that may be defective in some way. For instance, it might be that silver maple leaves do not have a silvery sheen on the back, and the speaker is mistaken. However, the analysis of the discourse remains the same because the discourse purposes are the same, even if they are based on erroneous beliefs. Of course, to recognize the structure of such dialogues, you must be able to identify the intended purpose even when it is based on an erroneous belief. This is a very difficult problem in general, but the theory leaves the door open for future research. Note that in discourse 3, with the structure made explicit by cue phrases, the constraints could be used in reverse. A system could use the domination constraint to infer from the discourse structure that the speaker believes that silver maple leaves have a silvery sheen on the back, since this is the most plausible explanation for the way the discourse is structured.

16.5 Discourse Structure, Tense, and Aspect

Tense and aspect provide a rich source of information relating events within a discourse segment as well as providing constraints that can be used to identify segment boundaries. This section considers how tense and aspect affect both segmentation and the inferential processes used to derive the connections required to establish coherence.

Consider first the effect of tense and aspect within a single segment. In simple narratives within a single segment, if a sequence of sentences describes a series of events, then the events occurred in the same order as they are described. This is sometimes called the **narrative convention**. Consider the discourse

5a. Jack went to the store.
5b. He bought some roses.

The intuitive reading is that Jack bought the roses after going to the store. Some researchers have suggested using this constraint to improve their inference algorithms by only considering expectations that involve events after the last described event. Unfortunately, this hope is unfounded except in the simplest domains. Consider the discourse

6a. Jack went to the store.
6b. He walked there along the river.

In the most natural interpretation, the event of walking along the river occurs as part of going to the store. Or consider the discourse

7a. Jack showed us his new car.
7b. He bought it at Honest John's Auto Mart.

In this case the event described in 7b clearly precedes the event described in 7a.

It might appear that any relationship can hold between the events in two simple past tense sentences, but this is not the case. The relationships seem to be limited to a few specific causal relationships plus a default temporal reading. We capture this fact with a new relation called the **orients relation**. Any two consecutive eventualities in the same segment will have an orients relation between them. A reasonable first attempt at defining the orients relation is as follows:

If an event E_1 orients an event E_2, then
1. If E_2 is part of E_1, then $E_2 \subseteq E_1$ (i.e., E_2 occurs during E_1).
2. If E_2 enables E_1, then $E_2 <: E_1$ (i.e., E_2 precedes E_1).
3. Otherwise, $E_1 <: E_2$ (i.e., E_1 precedes E_2).

Condition 3 gives the default case, encoding the narrative convention.

BOX 16.1 Explicit Signals of Intentional Structure

There is quite a range of cue phrases that explicitly signal the intentional structure of a discourse, and thus determine the segmentation. You saw one example already, called itemization, in which the words *first, second,* and so on explicitly identify a sequence of subsegments whose purpose is to elaborate on the general purpose of the containing segment. Here are some other examples:

Elaboration/Expansion Constructions: A new subsegment is created that serves to better define the purpose of the embedding segment. Some cue phrases that signal particular types of elaboration are

> *In particular*—the subsegment supports the embedding segment's purpose by a more specific discussion.
> *In addition*—the subsegment supports the embedding segment's purpose using a supplemental point.
> *For example*—the subsegment supports the embedding segment's purpose with a specific illustration.
> *In general*—the subsegment supports the embedding segment's purpose with a generalization.

Parallel Constructions: These organize a set of segments that address the same point, sometimes expressing different points of view. Some cue phrases are

> *On one hand ... on the other hand*—the subsegments give both sides of an argument or opinion.
> *In contrast*—the subsegment describes some contrasting information to the previous subsegment.
> *Similarly*—the subsegment describes some correspondence with the previous subsegment.

Some approaches to discourse take relations such as elaborate, exemplify, contrast, and so on as the primitive building blocks of discourse structure, and define a discourse as coherent only if such relations can be found between every segment. Two examples are the **coherence relations** approach of Hobbs (1979) and **Rhetorical Structure Theory**, described by Mann and Thompson (1986).

But discourses do more than describe events, and the orients relation must be extended to handle other eventualities such as states. For instance, if a sentence that describes a state is followed by one that describes an event, then the event typically occurs while the state holds. This is seen in the most intuitive reading of the discourse

8a.   Jack was at the store.
8b.   He bought some roses.

Here, Jack bought the roses while he was at the store. But the following examples show that there are other possibilities when given appropriate causal connections.

BOX 16.2 The Progressive Aspect

The progressive aspect introduces some additional complications. Consider the discourse

a1. Jack was going to the store.
a2. He bought some roses.

It appears that the interpretation in which Jack bought the roses after arriving at the store is not possible. Rather, he must have bought the roses while on his way to the store. This is the same as the default interpretation for states. The progressive aspect describes an event in progress, and thus the event time of the sentence is actually a subinterval of time of the event described. Thus, the event time, E_1, for sentence a1 is a subinterval of the time of the event E_{go} in which Jack went to the store. Therefore, there is a strong preference for the event time of the next sentence to also be within E_{go}, because it will be related to E_1.

As usual, specific causal information can produce other interpretations:

b1. Jack was walking home.
b2. His car broke down at work.

Here, the event described in b2 is a cause of the event in a2. As another example, the event described in c2 below describes the ending of the event in c1:

c1. Jack was walking home.
c2. He arrived home with blisters on his feet.

For instance, the state might enable the event, as in

9a. Jack had five dollars.
9b. He bought some roses.

In this case the event follows the state. In other cases the event precedes the state, as in

10a. Jack had some roses.
10b. He bought them at the store.

This interpretation arises since 10a describes an effect of the event in 10b. As with events, we assume a default reading when no causal connection can be found between the state and event, but otherwise the interpretation is determined by the causal relationships found. More precisely, we define the orients relation between a state and an event as follows:

If a state S_1 orients an event E_2, then
1. If S_1 enables E_2, then $S_1 <: E_2$;
2. If E_2 causes S_1, then $E_2 <: S_1$;
3. Otherwise, $E_2 \subseteq S_1$.

X_1 orients X_2	Event E_1	State S_1
Event E_2	Default: $E_1 < E_2$ Other Possibilities: $E_2 \subseteq E_1$ (decomp) $E_2 < E_1$ (enablement)	Default: $E_2 \subseteq S_1$ Other Possibilities: $S_1 <: E_2$ (enablement) $E_2 <: S_1$ (causation)
State S_2	same as S_1, E_2	Default: $S_1 = S_2$

Figure 16.13 A summary of the consequences of the orients relation

For the most part, switching sentence order within a state/event pair of sentences does not change the interpretation. Consider discourse 11, which has the same interpretation as discourse 8:

11a. Jack bought some roses.
11b. He was at the store.

With few exceptions, when two consecutive sentences both describe states, the two states hold simultaneously, as in the discourse

12a. Jack had some roses.
12b. He was happy.

where Jack has roses and is happy simultaneously. Figure 16.13 summarizes the consequences of the orients relation between all possible combinations of states and events.

So far, the interpretation of tense seems to have contributed little in the way of constraints on segment boundaries, although it has provided some information that might help focus the search of expectations to find inferential connections. When considering the interaction of more complex tenses, however, some constraints do seem to be forced by the tenses, rather than the causal knowledge. For example, consider the discourse

13a. Jack went to the store.
13b. He had bought some roses.

Only interpretations in which buying the roses precedes going to the store can be considered. Alhough the same causal knowledge as used in discourse 7 would suggest that the roses could have been bought at the store, the use of the past perfect tense in 13b excludes this interpretation and forces a jump back in time.

Many accounts of tense interpretation in discourse assume a Reichenbachian representation of tense, as described in Section 13.5. Remember that in this representation every tensed clause C_i defines three times: its speech time, S_i, its event time, E_i, and its reference time, T_i. The tense of the clause determines the temporal relationships between these three times. In a discourse consisting of n clauses $C_1, ..., C_n$, we also know that the speech times form a sequence, that is,

$$S_1 < S_2 < ... < S_n$$

Unfortunately, this information by itself doesn't provide any clue to the temporal relationships between times of events described in sequence. In particular, consider discourse 13. The first clause is in the simple past, so we know that $E_1 = R_1 < S_1$; the second is in the past perfect, so $E_2 < R_2 < S_2$ and we know that $S_1 < S_2$. Putting all the constraints together, we have

$$E_1 = R_1 < S_1 \ \& \ E_2 < R_2 < S_2 \ \& \ S_1 < S_2$$

These constraints do not entail any relationship between E_1 and E_2.

To solve this problem, additional constraints are proposed that arise from the discourse. One proposal is that the reference time is anaphoric and must refer back to a time evoked by the previous utterance. The preferred time for the antecedent is sometimes called the **temporal focus** to draw a parallel to the discourse focus or center. In particular, if you add the constraint $R_2 = R_1$ to the constraints developed for discourse 13, then this entails $E_2 < E_1$ as desired. So far, this looks good. But if the previous sentence is in the past perfect tense as well, then there is still a problem. Consider a continuation of discourse 13:

13c. He had wrapped them in fancy paper.

The temporal constraints from 13c would be $E_3 < R_3 < S_3$, and the discourse constraint is $R_3 = R_2$. Combining this with the constraints from 13b, $E_2 < R_2 < S_2$ entails no relation between E_2 and E_3 (although both are before E_1, as desired). Thus the intuitive reading that E_2 precedes E_3 is not obtained. It seems that this intuition arises from the default narrative interpretation, just as with two events described in the simple past. If this is the case, can causal knowledge override this assumption, just as before? The answer is yes, and thus it appears that the desired constraint is that E_2 orients E_3. Consider the discourse

14a. Jack took Helen on a date.
14b. He had impressed her with his new car the day before.
14c. He had bought it at Honest John's Auto Mart.

Here, causal knowledge leads you to infer that the event in 14c precedes (in fact enables) the event in 14b.

What structure can account for this behavior of the past perfect? One solution to this problem uses a construct called **tense trees**. A tense tree encodes the sequence of tense operators in a sentence. Each node on the tree represents a different possible modality based on tense. Figure 16.14 shows a tense tree fully expanded to show the common tense modalities. The root of the tree is the simple present. Descendants in the tree indicate the addition of the past, perfect, or future operators. Since these operators can be nested, the tree can be expanded downward several times.

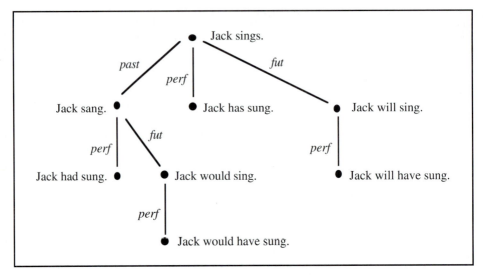

Figure 16.14 Different tense modalities shown as a tense tree

The relationships between the eventualities in a discourse can be obtained by placing each at the appropriate node in the tree depending on its tense. Whenever two eventualities are placed at the same node, the earlier one orients the new one. Events at different nodes are related by the constraints produced by the operator linking them. For example, the tense trees for discourses 5 and 13 are shown in Figure 16.15.

In discourse 5, the two events map to the same node, as they are both in the simple past. Thus, the first event orients the second. Given that there is no causal relationship to the contrary, this implies that going to the store preceded buying the roses. In discourse 13, the three events are arranged as shown. Because of the *perf* link, you know that buying the roses and wrapping them both precede going to the store. Also, the event of buying the roses orients the event of having them wrapped, since these two events are at the same node. As a result, this implies that buying the roses precedes having them wrapped.

Given this framework, we can now explore the relationship between tense across segment boundaries. The starting hypothesis is that the discourse state representing a segment will contain a tense tree that is used to relate the different states and events described within that segment. Note that this mechanism allows you to relate sentences using different tenses, so a change in tense would not necessitate a change in segment. But there is a problem with this approach. Consider discourse 15, which uses the past perfect tense in two different locations:

15a. Jack went to Helen's house.
15b. He had bought some roses.
15c. He dropped them on the carpet when he gave them to her.
15d. Helen had had the carpet cleaned, so she was upset.

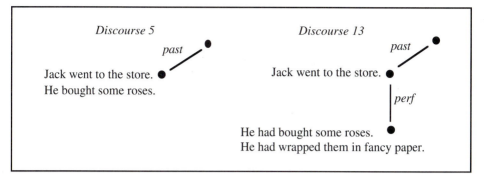

Figure 16.15 The tense trees for discourses 5 and 13

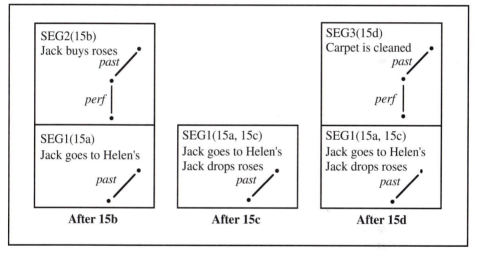

Figure 16.16 Tense trees and segmentation for discourse 15

If these utterances all fall in the same segment and thus fit into the same tense tree, the events in 15b and 15d will both be assigned to the same node in the tense tree, with the consequence that the event of buying the roses will orient the event of Helen cleaning the carpet—clearly an unintuitive analysis, as they seem unrelated.

This analysis is avoided if each segment can be associated with exactly one node in the tense tree. A sentence that shifts to a tense below the tense of the present segment signals a push, and a sentence that uses a tense above the tense of the current segment signals a pop and resumption. With this, the analysis of 15 appears as shown in Figure 16.16. Sentence 15b signals a push as it moves to the past perfect tense. Sentence 15c, on the other hand, resumes the simple past, signaling a pop and resumption of segment SEG1. Sentence 15d, also in the past perfect, signals a segment push, creating a new segment not related to SEG2. This produces the desired interpretation.

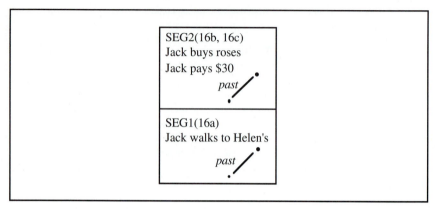

Figure 16.17 The attentional stack after sentence 16c

Unfortunately, tracking tense is not always so simple. Sometimes a speaker uses the past perfect tense to signal a shift to an event back in time, but then elaborates on that event using the simple past, as in the following discourse:

16a. Jack was walking over to Helen's house.
16b. He had bought some roses at Honest John's Flower Mart.
16c. He paid thirty dollars for them
16d.   and Honest John swore they were fresh.
16e. But they wilted before he got to Helen's.

Here, 16b signals a new segment in the past of the event in 16a, and 16c and 16d further elaborate on the event in 16b. But these two sentences are in the simple past. What has happened is that there has been a shift in temporal perspective. This might be handled by allowing a modification of the tense tree associated with the segment. The attentional stack after sentence 16c would be as shown in Figure 16.17. Given this context, if the next sentence is in the simple past, it will be ambiguous as to whether it continues the top segment or resumes the lower segment. Such issues would have to be decided based on inferential processing, as they cannot be determined by the tense information.

16.6 Managing the Attentional Stack

The previous sections have explored different issues affecting discourse structure. This section brings these issues together to specify a simple model for the on-line processing of discourse. In order to be specific, it will concentrate on a particular form of discourse, namely that which describes events and situations in the world. This includes much narrative, instructional text, and dialogues about specific tasks—essentially any discourse where the inferential component is based on causal and temporal reasoning. These forms of discourse will be referred to as causally related discourse.

With the form of inference defined, the discourse purposes of a segment can be explored in more detail. In particular, each segment is motivated by the

Local Discourse Context:
   Center: Jack1,   **Cp**: Jack1, **Others**: Roses1
Last Eventuality: Eb (Jack1 buys Roses1)
Situation Es:
   Events: Ea (Jack1 goes to Store1), Ea $\subseteq$ Es
            Eb (Jack1 buys Roses1), Eb $\subseteq$ Es
   Relations: Ea <: Eb
               Ea enables Eb

Figure 16.18   SEG1(17a, 17b): the discourse state after sentence 17b

goal to describe some situation. The situation might be an event that happened or a state that holds, and it might be arbitrarily complex. For example, it might describe an interacting set of actions by different agents. As long as the actions are causally or temporally connected, they can be grouped together into a single situation. We will assume that each clause describes an eventuality (event, process, or state, depending on what the clause describes). These eventualities are actually simple situations, and are incorporated into larger situations by finding a causal or temporal connection to the other eventualities already in the situation. We say that a situation S dominates a situation S' if S' represents a subpart of the situation represented by S.

Given this background, a local discourse state associated with a segment will contain the following information:

- the current local discourse context (derived primarily from the last sentence in the segment, as described in Chapter 14)
- a history list generated from earlier sentences in the segment
- the tense tree for the segment, labeled with all the eventualities in the segment
- the eventuality last described in the segment
- a situation that captures all that has been described in the segment so far

Figure 16.18 shows the discourse state after processing 17b in discourse 17:

17a. Jack went to the store.
17b. He bought some roses.
17c. He wanted to surprise Helen.

The local discourse context and last eventuality reflect the last sentence in the segment. Here you see that the center is Jack1, the preferred next center is also Jack1, and the other possible next center is Roses1. The last eventuality is Eb, described by sentence 17b. The situation being built for the segment is Es, and it currently consists of Ea and Eb, where Ea enables (and precedes) Eb. Both Ea and Eb occur within Es. The tense tree encodes that the two events mentioned were described in the simple past tense, and Ea orients Eb.

Local Discourse Context:
  Center: Jack1, **Cp**: Jack1, **Others**: Helen1
Last Eventuality: Ec (Jack1 wants to surprise Helen1)
Situation Es:
  Events: Ea (Jack1 goes to Store1), Ea $\subseteq$ Es
    Eb (Jack1 buys Roses1), Eb $\subseteq$ Es
    Ec (Jack1 wants to surprise Helen1), Ec $\subseteq$ Es
  Relations: Ea <: Eb
    Ea enables Eb
    Eb $\subseteq$ Ec

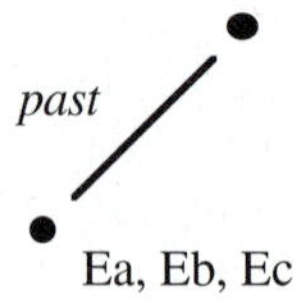

past

Ea, Eb, Ec

Figure 16.19 The discourse state after being extended with sentence 17c

Manipulating Discourse States

There are two ways in which a new sentence may affect the discourse states. It may extend an existing state (continuing an existing segment) or it may create a new state (starting a new segment). When a sentence S describing an eventuality E extends a state, it does the following:

- It updates the local discourse state with the structure derived from S.
- It updates the history list.
- It adds E to the tense tree, and derives the appropriate orients relations and other temporal constraints.
- It sets the last eventuality of the state to E.
- It invokes the inference component to derive the appropriate consequences to extend the contents of the situation described so far.

Consider an example. Figure 16.19 shows the new discourse state after the state in Figure 16.18 has been extended with sentence 17c.

  There are three different circumstances in which a new discourse state is created, depending on how it relates to the discourse state on the top of the discourse stack. Specifically, these are

  digression—the new state is unrelated to the old state.
  temporal shift—the new state is temporally related to the old state.
  expansion—the new state is expanding the last eventuality in the old state.

  In a digression, the new state is based on the new sentence and is unrelated to the prior discourse. Thus the new state is built solely from the analysis of the new sentence.

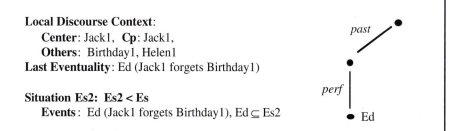

Local Discourse Context:
   Center: Jack1, **Cp**: Jack1,
   Others: Birthday1, Helen1
Last Eventuality: Ed (Jack1 forgets Birthday1)

Situation Es2: Es2 < Es
   Events: Ed (Jack1 forgets Birthday1), Ed $\subseteq$ Es2

Figure 16.20   The new discourse state created for sentence 17d

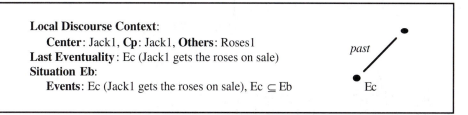

Local Discourse Context:
   Center: Jack1, **Cp**: Jack1, **Others**: Roses1
Last Eventuality: Ec (Jack1 gets the roses on sale)
Situation Eb:
   Events: Ec (Jack1 gets the roses on sale), Ec $\subseteq$ Eb

Figure 16.21   The new discourse state created by sentence 18c

In a temporal shift the new state includes a temporal constraint relating the new situation to the previous situation. Consider an extension to discourse 17:

17d. He had forgotten her birthday the day before.
17e. He had been busy at work and hadn't noticed the date.

Sentence 17d introduces a new subsegment describing a situation in the past of the events described so far. The new state pushed on the stack above the state shown in Figure 16.19 is shown in Figure 16.20. Note the temporal constraint that the new situation Es2 is before Es, the situation of the state below it on the stack. With this context, 17e will be temporally located not only because it is oriented by Ed, but also because it is in the past of Es.

     The third case, an expansion, introduces a new segment that is expanding detail about the last eventuality. This case is handled by using the last eventuality as the situation to be constructed in the new segment. Consider a variant of discourse 17:

18a. Jack went to the store.
18b. He bought some roses.
18c. He got ones that were on sale
18d.   and paid cash for them.

Sentence 18c starts a new segment that elaborates on the purchasing action in 18b. The discourse state at this point was shown in Figure 16.18. The new state created for 18c is shown in Figure 16.21. Note that the situation being described in this segment is Eb, rather than a new situation. This entails the desired implication that Ec is during Eb.

Determining Stack Updates

So far this section has considered the different operations that can be done to update the attentional stack, but it has not considered how to decide what updates to make in a certain situation. This problem can be broken into two main sub-problems characterized by the two questions

- Can the new sentence extend the top state?
- Can the new sentence create a new segment to be pushed onto the stack above the current top state?

You could find a complete set of possible interpretations by asking these two questions for each discourse state on the stack. In the previous sections several constraints were developed based on discourse segment purposes, tense analysis, and cue phrases, all making demands on the inference component. These constraints suggest some methods for answering the questions. While they are too simple in some ways, they give a feel for the mode of processing.

Constraints on Extending a Discourse State

Reference Constraint—a sentence S can extend a state only if its anaphoric components can be resolved to discourse entities in the state.

Tense Constraint—a sentence S can extend a state only if its tense is identical to the tense defined for the state, or is the same tense except that the perfect aspect has been dropped, signaling a shift in temporal perspective.

Inference Constraint—a sentence can extend a state only if the eventuality described by the sentence can be part of the situation that the state describes.

The constraints on pushing a new state above an existing state (called the **originating state**) will be different depending on whether the push represents a digression, temporal shift, or expansion. But in all cases the originating state typically provides the local discourse context for resolving the anaphoric terms in the new sentence. Beyond that, each type of push has its own constraints, such as the following:

Constraints on Pushes

Reference Constraint on all Pushes—a sentence S may push a new state only if its anaphoric components can be resolved to discourse entities in the originating state.

Constraint on Temporal Shifting—either the tense of S extends the tense tree in the originating state, or an explicit temporal phrase is used to locate the new state.

Input Parameters: STACK—the discourse stack
S—the new sentence
POP, PUSH, CONTINUE—the flags for cue phrases

Algorithm:

1. If POP is set to true, then pop STACK once and continue.
2. If PUSH is not set, then search STACK for a state that can be extended by S. The first one found is the answer.
3. If step 2 failed to produce an answer, and CONTINUE is not set to true, then search STACK for a state from which S can push a new state.

Figure 16.22 Algorithm for incorporating the next sentence into the discourse stack

> **Constraint of Expansion**—a new sentence S must describe part of the situation marked as the last eventuality in the originating state.
>
> **Constraint on Digressions**—digressions must be explicitly marked by a cue phrase or other linguistic device.

Because of ambiguity, there often will be many different interpretations of how a sentence might update the attentional stack. For these cases we will need some preferences on interpretations, such as the following:

- A continuation is preferred over a push of a subsegment.
- The interpretation that involves the least number of pops of the stack is preferred.

Structural Cue Phrases

The final consideration is the effect of structural cue phrases on the model. Each cue phrase can be classified in terms of three factors: whether it indicates a termination of a segment (a **POP**), the start of a new segment (a **PUSH**), or the continuation of a segment (a **CONTINUE**). An individual cue phrase may indicate one or more of these functions. The word *anyway,* for instance, signals both a POP and a CONTINUE. Of course, these phrases may have effects on inferential processing as well, but this is the only information needed for our present purposes.

Figure 16.22 shows an algorithm that uses cue phrases. It takes as input the discourse stack, the analysis of the new sentence, and three variables—POP, PUSH, and CONTINUE—that are set to true if a corresponding cue phrase is present in the sentence. The first step is a check for an explicit POP; if it is found, the top state is popped. Then the algorithm checks repeatedly for possible extensions of states on the stack and then for possible pushes of new states onto the stack.

BOX 16.3 Reference to Situations Created by Discourse Segments

Further evidence for segmentational structure can be found in examining the events or situations that can be referred to anaphorically in a discourse. Consider the following discourse:

a. When Jack entered the room, everyone threw balloons at him.
b. In retaliation, he picked up the ladle and started throwing punch at everyone.
c. Just then, the chairman walked into the room.
d. Jack hit him with a ladleful, right in the face.
e. Everyone talked about it for years afterwards.

In e, the pronoun *it* may refer to the situation described by a through d. These utterances form a segment that describes a complex situation, which is referred to anaphorically in e. Which of the other events described in the discourse could also be anaphoric antecedents at position e? It appears that only the event described in d is also available for reference, as in the alternate continuation

e'. It was a foolish thing to do.

It is not possible to construct a sentence at position e with a pronoun that refers to the event of the chairman walking in, however. Webber (1991) argues that the events/situations available for anaphoric reference at any given time consist of the last mentioned eventuality and the situations constructed in each of the discourse states lower on the discourse stack.

16.7 An Example

Consider how the model described in the last section could be used to account for the discourse in Figure 16.2, repeated here as discourse 19:

19a. Jack and Sue went to buy a new lawn mower
19b.   since their old one was stolen.
19c. Sue had seen the men who took it and
19d.   she had chased them down the street,
19e.   but they'd driven away in a truck.
19f. After looking in the store,
19g.   they realized they couldn't afford a new one.
19h. By the way, Jack lost his job last month
19i.   so he's been short of cash recently.
19j. He has been looking for a new one,
19k.   but so far hasn't had any luck.
19l. Anyway, they finally found a used one at a garage sale.

Clause 19a creates a new discourse state SEG1(19a), as expected, and 19b extends this state. The connective *since* should help the inference component identify that the eventuality in 19b is the motivation for the eventuality in 19a.

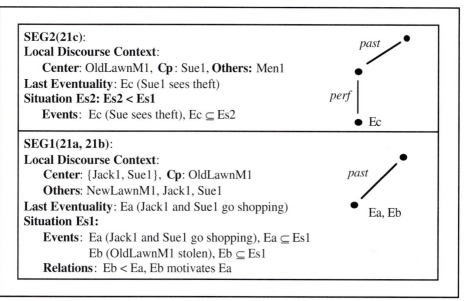

Figure 16.23   The discourse stack after clause 19c

Clause 19c, in the past perfect tense, signals a temporal shift, and a new discourse state SEG2(19c) is pushed on the stack above SEG1(19a, 19b). Figure 16.23 shows the discourse stack after 19c. The next clause, 19d, is an acceptable extension of SEG2(19c), as is 19e.

Clause 19f is untensed and subordinate to 19g, so its interpretation is determined by 19g. Clause 19g is in the simple past, so either it is resuming SEG1(19b) or there has been a perspective shift and it is continuing SEG2(19c, 19d, 19e). The inference component has to decide whether it is more likely that Ee (driving in truck) orients Eg (can't afford lawn mower), or Eb (old one stolen) orients Eg. It is very unlikely that the men who stole the lawn mower would be considering buying new lawn mowers, so Ee orienting Eg is implausible. That Jack and Sue are considering buying a lawn mower is much more likely—in fact, expected—given the context in state SEG1(19a, 19b). Thus 19g is interpreted as an extension of SEG1(19a, 19b) after a pop. Note that the interpretation of the pronoun *they* is affected by this decision. If 19g had extended SEG2(19c, 19d, 19e), it would have referred to the men rather than Jack and Sue. This new discourse stack is shown in Figure 16.24.

Now that SEG2(19c, 19d, 19e) is popped from the state, what has happened to all the information it encoded? It clearly shouldn't be completely forgotten, since it forms part of the understanding of the discourse. In fact, later in the discourse, the events it contains could be referred to again. So what is the significance of it being popped off the stack? The answer is that this discourse state cannot be resumed later in the discourse as SEG1 was resumed; in other words, you couldn't just start talking as though the context it defined were still

SEG1(21a, 21b, 21f, 21g):
Local Discourse Context:
   Center: {Jack1, Sue1}, **Cp**: {Jack1, Sue1}
   Others: NewLawnM1, Jack1, Sue1
Last Eventuality: Eg (J&S can't afford new one)
Situation Es1:
   Events: Ea (J&S go shopping), Ea $\subseteq$ Es1
          Eb (OldLawnM1 stolen), Eb $\subseteq$ Es1
          Ef (J&S look in store), Ef $\subseteq$ Es1
          Eg (J&S realize can't afford new one)
   Relations: Eb < Ea, Eb motivates Ea
           Ef ends Ea, Ef < Eg

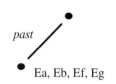

Figure 16.24 The discourse stack after clause 19g

active. But you can always explicitly reactivate the context of a prior segment, perhaps by saying, *Remember when I told you about the men stealing the lawn mower?* Once this was done, you could resume talking about this episode. This type of reference to a prior subpart of a discussion is sometimes called a **semantic return** in the literature. In the model here it would be treated as creating a new segment (discussing old context), rather than returning to a prior discourse state.

Returning to the example, 19h contains the cue phrase *By the way,* signaling the start of a digression. This pushes a new state, SEG2(19h) onto the discourse stack, which is extended by 19i, 19j, and 19k. In clause 19l, the cue phrase *Anyway* signals a pop and a continue, so SEG3(19h, 19i, 19j, 19k) is popped off the stack, and 19l is successfully analyzed as a continuation of SEG1(19a, 19b, 19f, 19g), as desired. As a result, the one-anaphor is appropriately identified as a lawn mower. Note that if the cue phrase *Anyway* had not been present, it might be possible to interpret 19l as an extension of SEG3(19h, 19i, 19j, 19k), in which case the interpretation of the pronoun *one* would have been a new job.

This example shows that by using information from tense analysis, inference, reference, and cue phrases, the intended structure can be identified. Each of these forms of analysis is crucial, and none is sufficient to do the task alone.

Summary

To interpret extended discourse, many researchers view discourse as a hierarchically organized set of segments. Each segment displays local coherence, which means that a reference resolution strategy based on recency is effective and that the sentences can be viewed as all addressing the same general point, or describing the same situation. As such, the algorithms developed in Chapters 14 and 15 are effective within a segment. The hierarchical structure of segments motivates a stack-based organization of discourse states, each capturing the state of a single segment. It allows a segment to be temporarily suspended and then later resumed when its interrupting subsegment is completed. Three important aspects of discourse were discussed within this model, and an example was presented showing how the segment-based model provided the framework to integrate the different processing techniques. These were reference resolution, tense and aspect, and general reasoning in the domain. In addition, the structure provided a framework for interpreting cue phrases in discourse that explicitly signal changes in the discourse structure.

Related Work and Further Readings

The diverse area of discourse analysis has mainly consisted of work that focuses on only one aspect, such as anaphoric reference, tense analysis, and so on. Few researchers have attempted to integrate the different aspects of discourse processing into a comprehensive theory of discourse, but some work has been done on overall frameworks. Grosz and Sidner (1986) outlined a model that motivated the organization of this chapter. They distinguished between the discourse structure as revealed by segmentation, the attentional stack, and the intentional structure of discourse as encoded in discourse segment purposes. The terms informational level and intentional level come from Moore and Pollack (1992).

The idea that sentences can be related by some analysis of the speaker's purpose has a long history. In recent times, however, a major influence on the approach comes from Grimes (1975). He identifies three general classes of functions that can be used in discourse: a sentence may support or supplement what has come before (elaborate); it may create a setting (identify time and location of an event); and it may identify an object (introduce a new object for discussion or revert to an old object). A fair number of computationally oriented frameworks have since been developed, each one introducing a different set of relations. A good survey of these models and their use in the analysis of anaphora can be found in Hirst (1981b).

Linde (1979) and Grosz (1977) both observed that the flow of the topic of conversation in task-oriented conversations could be explained in terms of the hierarchical structure of the task being discussed. Studying descriptions of apartments, Linde showed that rooms were not randomly chosen, but that the discourse topics progressed according to a hypothetical "walk" through the apartment. Grosz studied dialogues in which an expert aids an apprentice in assembling a water pump. Again, the flow of topics followed the actual execution of the plan to assemble the pump. Grosz defined the notion of **global focus** for reference, which would correspond here to the plan reasoner being constrained by the discourse stack mechanism. She used a mechanism called **focus spaces**, which identified the parts of the plan that were under discussion. These focus spaces were maintained in a stack structure, which gave the appropriate objects for determining the referents of definite descriptions. This corresponds to the organization of the history list by segments that was discussed earlier. She showed that after the focus stack is "popped," objects in the resumed focus space could be immediately pronominalized without explicit reintroduction.

Reichman (1978; 1985) proposes a theory of discourse that is an important influence on the on-line processing model in Section 16.6. Her work points out the importance of incorporating cue phrases (**clue words** in her model). The model uses an explicit representation of the state of the discourse based on **context spaces**, which correspond roughly to our discourse states. In Reichman's model, there can be up to three context spaces relevant to the discourse at any time: the active one, which corresponds to the top of our discourse stack; the controlling one, directly below on the stack; and the generating space, which has no correlate in the model described in this chapter. The generating space contains some claim by a speaker that has not yet been resolved and may be returned to later, but it does not allow the immediate pronominalization of the focused elements when resumed. Reichman uses this space for an analysis of some forms of deictic reference (for example, the use of *this* and *that*).

Many researchers have found cue phrases to be an important structuring device for discourse (for example, Grosz and Sidner (1986), Cohen (1987), and Litman and Allen (1987; 1990)). Hirschberg and Litman (1993) provide a list of cue phrases used by other researchers and show that in spoken discourse, some cue phrases have distinctive intonational characteristics.

There is a vast literature on tense and aspect, some of which was already discussed at the end of Chapter 13. The idea that tense interpretation involves anaphoric relations has been suggested by many researchers, including Leech (1987) and Partee (1984). The idea of the reference time as the anaphoric element has been suggested many times. Two good examples are Steedman (1982) and Hinrichs (1986). Many of the theories concerning tense have been developed only in the context of simple narratives, where the narrative convention is assumed. Song and Cohen (1991) is a good example of a computational model that relates tense and aspect to plan inference, but only for simple narratives.

Section 16.5 is based on work by Webber (1988) and Hwang and Schubert (1992). Webber argues for the anaphoric nature of tense interpretation and introduces a notion of temporal focus. She then explores how segment boundaries affect the range of possible interpretations. Our model for building situations in Section 16.6 is similar to the model she proposes that views discourse interpretation as building an event structure. Hwang and Schubert (1992) develop the notion of tense trees and formalize the orients relation. They also discuss some issues relating tense trees and discourse segmentation. Although not discussed here, tense trees also provide a good analysis of sentences of embedded tensed clauses that are problematic for other approaches. The specific definition of the orients relation is influenced by the approach to tense interpretation in Lascarides et al. (1992), in which the narrative convention arises as a default in the absence of any contradictory information from the causal reasoning. An issue not addressed in this chapter, but crucial for the temporal analysis of discourse, is the analysis of temporal connectives and temporal adverbials that specifically iden-tify the time of an event. A good paper examining the complexities of analyzing temporal connectives such as *when* and *while* is Steedman (1982).

An approach to discourse that has influenced many of the ideas in this chapter is the work on defining coherence relations, discussed briefly in Box 16.1. For example, Hobbs (1979) defines a set of **coherence relations**, and con-siders discourse interpretation a process of abductively assuming a set of coherence relations that allows him to prove that the input is true (Hobbs et al., 1993). Lascarides and Asher (1993) pursue a similar approach. Rather than using abductive inference, however, they use a deductive technique that employs defeasible reasoning. Hovy (1993) presents an excellent discussion of the use of discourse structure relations in natural language generation systems. Mann and Thompson (1986) define **Rhetorical Structure Theory (RST)**, which includes a large taxonomy of different relations that can hold between sentences and segments. Fox (1987) contains an excellent survey of RST. Moore and Pollack (1992) argue that RST blurs the intentional and informational levels of analysis, which creates significant problems. RST-like models, however, turn out to very useful for natural language generation.

Another approach to modeling discourse structure is to develop a discourse grammar. Some discourse grammars address the semantic connections between sentences and others addresses topic flow, interruption, and resumption. Rumel-hart (1975) proposes modeling the structure of simple stories using a grammar. Scha and Polanyi (1988) present a grammar that models the flow of topic.

Exercises for Chapter 16

1. (*easy*) Draw the sequence of attentional stacks in a format like that in Figure 16.4 for a discourse whose segmental structure is as follows (each number represents a clause):

2. (*medium*) Draw the discourse stack, showing the tense trees and the situation description for each state, after each sentence in discourse 16:

16a. Jack was walking over to Helen's house.
16b. He had bought some roses at Honest John's Flower Mart.
16c. He paid thirty dollars for them
16d.   and Honest John swore they were fresh.
16e. But they wilted before he got to Helen's.

3. (*medium*) Trace the algorithm in Figure 16.22 as the following sentences are analyzed. Show the resulting discourse state after each clause, and identify the inferential connections between the eventualities and the ante-cedents of each referring expression. The discourse is part of a conversation between two people getting ready for a garage sale. You can assume that the garage is uniquely identified from the setting of the discourse.

a. An old lawn mower is next to the TV set in the garage.
b. Last summer, the engine stalled frequently,
c.   so no one really used it.
d. But I still hope to sell it.

Did the model suggest the intuitively correct interpretation of the pronoun *it* in the third sentence? If not, can you suggest an extension to the model so that it can produce the correct answer?

4. (*medium*) For every occurrence of the pronoun *it* in discourse 3, show the discourse stack at the time the pronoun is interpreted. Does the structure predict the appropriate reference in each case? If not, discuss why not.

5. (*medium*) Find about half a page of text somewhere and use the techniques described in this chapter, and your intuitions, to produce a segmentation of it. Define what the overall discourse purpose is of the text, and define what corresponds to the goal/subgoal relationship between discourse purposes. Describe your reasons for selecting each segment boundary location.

6. (*medium*) For each of the cue phrases mentioned in Box 16.1, discuss whether the cue phrase signals a segment push or a segment push and pop. Give examples of discourse fragments that illustrate the use of two of the cue phrases of your choice: one that signals a push, and the other that signals a pop and push. For each discourse, identify its segment structure as indicated by the cue phrase.

7. (*medium*) Consider the following discourse:

a. Jack went to the music store.
b. He bought a new CD player.
c. His old one had stopped working.

Each clause defines an event time, reference time, and speech time. If you add a discourse constraint that the three reference times are equal, what conclusions can you draw about the temporal relationships between each event? Does this give the desired results? If not, how might you modify this approach so that it does? Show the same analysis using the tense tree and the orients relation. Does this give the desired results? If not, how might you modify this approach so it does?

8. (*hard*) In some situations, the simple past and present perfect seem interchangeable. A person who has been shopping can say either *I went shopping* or *I have gone shopping,* with little if any difference between the two. But they can have quite different effects. You can say *I went shopping yesterday* but not **I have gone shopping yesterday.* Consider a situation in which Jack won a million dollars in a lottery, but has since lost it all gambling. To tell someone that he won the lottery, you could say *Jack won the lottery,* but *Jack has won the lottery* is awkward at best. What seems to be the difference in these meanings? Support your argument with additional examples. What implications does this distinction have for finding the temporal relations between clauses in extended discourse?

Defining a Conversational Agent

This chapter discusses some concepts that are necessary to define a conversational agent, that is, an agent that can participate fully in natural dialogue. A system implementing such an agent could be used in any application that requires human-machine interaction using language. This includes applications as simple as question-answering systems and applications as complex as a computer planning-assistant that helps make plans, assists in their execution, and otherwise provides reasoning and information retrieval services. Section 17.1 considers what is necessary to construct such an agent, specifically to enable its conversational abilities. Section 17.2 discusses the nature of language as a multi-agent, social interaction. Section 17.3 explores an important issue in representing the cognitive state required in such an agent, namely the representation of beliefs. Section 17.4 explores issues in the representation of desires, intentions, and plans. Section 17.5 explores the view of language as action and develops the notion of speech acts. Section 17.6 explores how to use speech acts in planning. Section 17.7 examines the problems of recognizing intentions, and Section 17.8 explores the issue of how the agent's intentions arise. Section 17.9 examines techniques for recognizing illocutionary acts. Finally, Section 17.10 discusses using plan-based techniques to reason about discourse structure.

17.1 What's Necessary to Build a Conversational Agent?

The big question to answer in defining a conversational agent is, why should the agent ever speak? What motivates it to say anything or to attempt to comprehend the utterances that are said to it? One answer could be that it is simply programmed to behave in this way. For instance, the behavior of a database question-answering agent might be defined by a program that alternately performs two steps:

1. Parse and interpret an input question into a logical form representing a query.
2. Execute the query on the database and generate output based on the answer returned.

But you would not consider such a program very intelligent or conversational. For instance, it wouldn't be able to do anything appropriate if you gave it an utterance that is not a question about the database. Furthermore, it would display no independent behavior that might lead you to think that it was intelligent.

Of course, at some level, even the most sophisticated system is driven by a top-level program with not much more sophistication than that just specified. But we can instill some intelligence into a system's behavior by basing it on a representation that more closely reflects the things that motivate human behavior. Specifically, people act because they have goals that they want to achieve. In addition, people are aware of the situation they are in and have various positive and negative feelings towards the situation. Often they act in a way to get into a better situation. For example, if you find yourself standing on a highway, you will probably move off it. This behavior, simple as it seems, is best accounted for by positing a complex cognitive structure. Based on your visual perception, you believe that you are on the highway. You know this is dangerous, so you acquire a desire to get off the road. Say you reason that moving backward will get you off the road more quickly than trying to move forward across the road. Thus you move back off the road. This example reveals several important components of an intelligent agent:

> **perception**—the agent must be able to perceive the world around it.
>
> **beliefs**—the agent must have a representation of the present state of the world.
>
> **desires/wants**—the agent should have positive or negative responses to various states of the world, creating a way to compare the desirability of states.
>
> **planning/reasoning**—the agent must be able to reason about ways to attain other states.
>
> **commitment**—the agent must be able to decide to act to get to a different state.
>
> **intentions**—the agent must be able to maintain the course of action decided on.
>
> **acting**—the agent must be able to act and thus change its state.

Our conversational agent lives in the somewhat impoverished world of language and thought. Its only perceptions are utterances said to it, and its only actions are generating utterances. Of course, in many applications the agent might have other perceptual and acting abilities, but the linguistic ones are the focus of this chapter.

Of the seven aspects of intelligent behavior just mentioned, four—perception, planning, commitment, and acting—are processes, and three—beliefs, desires, and intentions—are part of the agent's cognitive state. Such models are sometimes called **BDI** (belief, desire, and intention) models. All of these terms will be defined more precisely later. For the moment consider the overall model based simply on an intuitive understanding of the terms. An architecture of an intelligent agent is shown in Figure 17.1. The boxes represent aspects of its cognitive state, and the other labels indicate ongoing processes that operate concurrently. The agent is continually updating its beliefs based on perceptions, using its beliefs to reason about possible plans, committing to certain intentions based on its beliefs and desires, and realizing these intentions by acting.

To apply such a model to language, the act of uttering a sentence must be made explicit. Such actions involving language are called **speech acts** and will play a crucial role in the development of the conversational agent. Like any other actions that have been discussed, there are English verbs that name the speech acts. Examples are *ask, request, inform, deny, congratulate, confirm,* and *promise.* Like other actions, we should be able to define and reason about speech acts. They turn out to be more complicated to define than other actions, however,

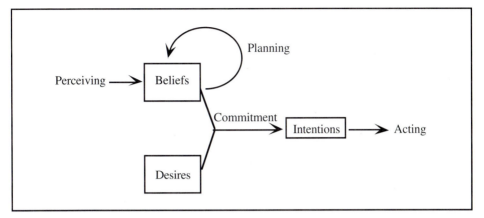

Figure 17.1 A BDI model of an intelligent agent

because they involve more than one agent, that is, they are communicative actions. In addition, they are defined in terms of the agent's cognitive state rather than in terms of physical properties of the world.

17.2 Language as a Multi-Agent Activity

Language and all other forms of communication necessarily involve multiple agents. You cannot communicate by speaking in a room with no one else present. Other forms of communication, such as writing, can extend the communication act out over time. You may write something now to be read in 10 year's time. But in all cases the purpose of communication is for one person to affect the cognitive state of the other.

In addition, communication cannot occur if one of the agents does not recognize the other's attempt to communicate. For example, say that Jack and Sue are involved in industrial espionage and have worked out a scheme where Jack leaves his window open when it is safe for Sue to visit him. With this system established, Jack can communicate with Sue using the window. He opens the window, and when Sue sees it she understands that it is safe to visit. Now say that one day Jack opens the window because it is hot, and Sue comes by and decides it is safe to visit. This is a mistake, as the open window does not indicate that it is safe, because Jack didn't open the window with this intention. Conversely, say that even though it is hot, Jack does open the window to signal to Sue. But when Sue comes by, she decides that it is so hot that Jack opened the window to cool off. In this case Jack's attempt to communicate failed because Sue didn't recognize his intention in opening the window.

So communication can occur only when one agent intends to communicate and the other agent recognizes that intention. The other crucial requirement for communication is that there be an agreed-upon set of conventions with agreed-upon meanings. In the previous example, only two conventional symbols are required—the window being open (meaning it is safe) and the window being shut (meaning it is not safe). Jack and Sue have defined their own private language that functions perfectly well, as long as Jack is careful on hot days.

These same requirements underlie linguistic communication. But they are so ingrained in language that we often don't notice them. In fact, just seeing a sequence of words spelling out a sentence is enough for us to decide that it is an attempt to communicate. This is because, unlike in the window example, the physical acts performed to speak and write are seldom used for purposes other than communication. When someone starts uttering some words, we assume they are trying to communicate, because the act of uttering words is rarely used for any other purpose. Note that the window example made its points by exploiting this ambiguity. The act of opening the window could be used for two different purposes—to communicate with Sue and to get some fresh air. This illustrates an important distinction between the physical act performed and the communicative act. Austin (1962) made this point for language and observed that there are three acts performed whenever something is said:

> **the locutionary act**—the act of uttering a sequence of words.
> **the illocutionary act**—the act that the speaker performs in saying the words.
> **the perlocutionary act**—the act that actually occurs as a result of the utterance.

The window language example illustrates these different acts. Jack opening the window is the locutionary act, and as we saw it can be performed with or without communicative intent. When Jack opens the window with the intention to signal that all is clear, he is also performing an illocutionary act, that of signaling that all is clear. If Sue sees the open window and recognizes Jack's intention, and thus knows that all is clear, then a perlocutionary act, convincing Sue that all is clear, has also occurred.

Some verbs may describe illocutionary acts while others describe perlocutionary acts. Illocutionary acts can be used in sentences that explicitly name the act being performed. These uses are called **explicit performatives**. Thus I may promise to mow the lawn by saying *I hereby promise to mow the lawn.* Likewise, *inform* describes an illocutionary act, as in *I hereby inform you that your bank account is overdrawn.* The verb *convince,* on the other hand, describes a perlocutionary act. It is something you might intend to occur when you inform someone of something, but its occurrence is beyond your control. As a result, you cannot say **I hereby convince you that your bank account is overdrawn.* Note also that you may achieve perlocutionary acts without the other agent recognizing any intention to communicate. For instance, Sue might convince Jack that his bank account is overdrawn by leaving his bank statement out on a table where he will see it when she is not around.

A difficult problem in language understanding is identifying the illocutionary act intended by the speaker. The same locutionary act—say, uttering the sentence

Do you know the time?

might generate the illocutionary act of asking a yes/no question, or the act of asking for the time, or the act of offering to tell the hearer the time, depending on the speaker's intention. Identifying the appropriate intention underlying a locutionary act is the key problem in speech act theory. Of course, there are ways in language to signal intentions explicitly. Using explicit performatives is one way to do that, although it results in very formal, stilted language. Another is the use of the word *please*. If we add *please* to this sentence, it would not be possible to interpret it as a yes/no question or an offer. Unfortunately, such explicit signals are relatively rare in English, and the recognition of intention from context is a crucial problem in the process of identifying the correct interpretation.

The final consequence of language being a multi-agent activity is that it requires some means for the agents to coordinate their communicative acts and to monitor whether they are being understood. In dialogue, agents use various mechanisms to signal that they understand each other. This includes explicit statements such as *I understand,* simple acknowledgments such as *OK,* and other devices such as repeating back certain parts of the previous utterance. A common example of this occurs when people communicate telephone numbers. Typically, the first agent says the number, and then the other agent says it back, and the first confirms it. These are all methods for two agents to establish that they agree on what was communicated. Confirming this mutual agreement is a crucial aspect of any dialogue.

17.3 Representing Cognitive States: Beliefs

There are many ways to represent the beliefs of the agent, varying in how introspective and aware you want the agent to be. For instance, we have been using a knowledge base (KB) of facts throughout the last few chapters. You could simply say that anything in the KB is believed by the agent and leave it at that. But this will produce a limited agent. It can't, for instance, represent information about the beliefs of other agents, so it is unlikely that it can be motivated to communicate. In addition, it has no self awareness—it can't distinguish between what it believes and what it observes to be true in the world. Thus it would be hard to give a good account of using perception to learn more about the world.

The simplest extension is to divide the KB up into different areas, called **belief spaces**. A space is simply a set of propositions and thus specifies a KB in its own right. Each one could be used to represent some agent's beliefs. For a two-party conversation, we might need two spaces: one capturing one agent's beliefs and the other representing the other agent's beliefs. But this isn't a very intuitive model of the beliefs of a single agent, as it appears to give the agent direct access to the other agent's beliefs. Rather, it would be better if all beliefs were relative to the agent we are modeling. To capture this, we will allow a predicate *BEL,* which relates an agent and a space and is true if the space

Left side:

$Bel(Jack1, Dog(Fido1))$

$Bel(Jack1, \forall x : Dog(x) . Bark(x))$

$Bel(Jack1, BEL(Sue1, Dog(Fido1)))$

$Bel(Jack1, BEL(Sue1,$
$\quad \forall x : Dog(x) . Bark(x)))$

$Bel(Jack1, BEL(Sue1,$
$\quad \forall x : Dog(x) . Bark(x) \supset Fierce(x))$

Statements in Modal Logic

Right side:

$BEL(Jack1, BS1)$

BS1: Jack's beliefs
$Dog(Fido1)$
$\forall x : Dog(x) . Bark(x)$
$BEL(Sue1, BS2)$

BS2: Jack's beliefs about Sue's beliefs
$Dog(Fido1)$
$\forall x : Dog(x) . Bark(x)$
$\forall x : Dog(x) . Bark(x) \supset Fierce(x)$

Statements Using Belief Spaces

Figure 17.2   Representing beliefs in belief spaces

characterizes beliefs of the agent. Since propositions using this predicate can occur in other spaces, it allows us to define a hierarchy of nested belief spaces. A simple example is shown in Figure 17.2. The two sides of the figure show the same set of propositions, first using a modal operator *Bel* for belief as described in Section 8.3, and then using the belief space approach. This KB asserts that Jack's beliefs are characterized by space BS1, which contains the propositions that Fido is a dog, that dogs bark, and that Sue's beliefs are described in space BS2. Space BS2 describes what Jack believes that Sue believes: that Fido is a dog, that dogs bark, and that all dogs that bark are fierce.

In such a model, inference is always done with respect to a space. For example, with respect to space BS2, we could infer that Fido is fierce, concluding that Jack believes that Sue believes that Fido is fierce. A similar conclusion could not be drawn in space BS1, so Jack doesn't believe that Fido is fierce.

This brings out an important distinction about what it means to believe something. An agent's **explicit beliefs** are the propositions that are listed in the appropriate space. An agent's **implicit beliefs** are those propositions that can be derived from the explicit ones by some inference process. When we say that someone believes something, say that Jack believes the world is flat, we usually mean something most similar to the notion of explicit belief, possibly with some very limited forms of inference allowed. But consider the case in which Jack has a set of beliefs that logically entail that the world is flat, although Jack has never realized this connection by making these inferences. In this case, although he has an implicit belief that the world is flat, we probably wouldn't usually say that Jack believes the world is flat.

Maintaining the distinction between what you believe and what you believe others believe is crucial for understanding communication. This can be seen most clearly when the two conversants have different beliefs. Suppose Jack believes that there is a combination lock on his locker but believes that Sue thinks the locker has a key lock. When she asks for his key, he should be able to recognize

BOX 17.1 Sentential Models of Belief

There are two general approaches to defining a semantics for the belief operator. The first treats *Bel* as a modal operator and gives a possible worlds semantics as described in Section 8.8. The only difference between *Bel* and *Know* is that the accessibility relation for *Bel* is not reflexive. As a consequence, while

$$Know(P) \supset P$$

is a valid axiom for *know*, it is not a reasonable axiom for *Bel*. Just because an agent believes something doesn't mean that it must be true.

The other approach is closer to the intuitions of the belief space representation. The *Bel* operator relates an agent to a proposition, which requires us to extend the logical framework to allow propositions as objects. This is often done by introducing a **quotation** operator. While *Happy(Jack1)* is a proposition, the expression $\lceil Happy(Jack1) \rceil$ is a term that denotes the proposition. With this, you would now write the formula for *Jack believes that he is happy* as $Bel(Jack1, \lceil Happy(Jack1) \rceil)$ Once this step has been taken, you then need to rebuild any axioms that you desire for reasoning about an agent's beliefs, as the usual axioms do not apply to quoted expressions. Examples of such representations can be found in Haas (1986) and Konolige (1986).

that Sue's plan is to open the locker, even though opening his locker with a key is an incoherent plan from his point of view.

As another example, belief models are crucial for determining the intended referent of a noun phrase. For example, suppose Sue knows that a certain book—say, *The Revenge of Mrs. Smith*—is in Jack's office, but she believes that Jack believes it is on a table in the lounge. Then if he asks her, *Have you read the book on the table in the lounge?*, she should recognize that he means *The Revenge of Mrs. Smith,* even though the description Jack used to refer to it is inaccurate.

Thus one agent's beliefs about another's beliefs play an important role in language understanding. The natural question to ask is how deep a nesting of beliefs is required to understand all language. It is easy to see a need for a third level of nesting. Suppose Jack believes that Sue thinks she just successfully lied to him when she said it was raining outside. In this case Jack believes the following:

Jack believes: It is not raining.
Jack believes that Sue believes: It is not raining.
Jack believes that Sue believes that Jack believes: It is raining.

Both Jack and Sue believe it is not raining, but Jack also believes that Sue believes that he thinks it is raining, since he thinks that she thinks her lie was successful.

Similar examples can be constructed that require ever deeper levels of nested beliefs. A way out of this problem is to introduce the notion of **shared knowledge**, which is the knowledge that both agents know and know that the other knows. Shared knowledge arises from the common background and situation that the agents find themselves in and includes general knowledge about the world (such as how common actions are done, the standard type hierarchy classifications of objects, general facts about the society we live in, and so on). Agents that know each other or share a common profession will also have considerable shared knowledge as a result of their previous interactions and their education in that field. If agents construct their plans using only shared knowledge, they can be reasonably sure that the plan can be successfully recognized. Thus shared knowledge plays a crucial role in successful communication. While individual beliefs may play a central role in the content of a conversation, most of the knowledge brought to bear to interpret the other's actions will be shared knowledge.

Knowledge About Another's Beliefs

Perhaps the most tricky problem in building belief models is that much knowledge is of the form that you know that some other agent knows something, yet you do not know what they know. For instance, Jack can believe that Sue knows her mother's name even though Jack does not know the name. You cannot represent this situation simply by adding a fact into the appropriate belief space, because there is no formula of the form $NameOf(Mother(Sue1), xxx)$ that can be in the appropriate belief space since Jack does not know Sue's mother's name. If we use a Skolem constant—say, $Sk33$—and add $NameOf(Mother(Sue1), Sk33)$ to Sue's belief space, it simply asserts that Sue believes that her mother has a name, not the right fact at all. In modal logic this is equivalent to the formula

1.　$Bel(Sue, \exists! \, x \, . \, NameOf(Mother(Sue1), x))$

The common solution to this problem in modal logic approaches is to allow quantifiers to outscope the belief operator. Thus formula 1 means that Sue believes that her mother has a name, whereas

2.　$\exists! \, x \, . \, Bel(Sue1, NameOf(Mother(Sue1), x))$

means that she actually knows what the name is. Unfortunately, most knowledge representations handle existential quantification by skolemization, and quantifier scoping with modal operators is not preserved by a simple skolemization scheme. We can capture this scoping distinction, however, by indexing every Skolem and variable by the belief space in which it is created. Thus adding a fact corresponding to formula 1 to the KB would create a Skolem dependent on the belief space BS2 (that is, what Jack believes Sue believes), and the resulting fact

3.　$NameOf(Mother(Sue1), Sk1_{BS2})$

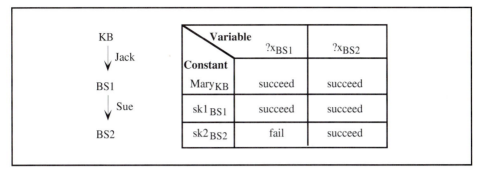

Figure 17.3 Matching variables and constants indexed by belief spaces

is added to space BS2. Adding a fact corresponding to formula 2 would create a Skolem dependent on BS1 (that is, what Jack believes), and would add

4. $NameOf(Mother(Sue1), Sk2_{BS1})$

to the space BS1.

This method of retaining the scoping of existentials must have a corresponding proof method for testing existential statements and be able to make a distinction between a query such as *Does Sue believe that her mother has a name?* and one such as *Does Sue know her mother's name?* To do this, the inference system must be able to restrict variables so that they only match objects defined in appropriate belief spaces. Say formula 1 is asserted, resulting in formula 3 being added to space BS2. Now suppose formula 2 is queried. Using the standard methods, formula 2 would translate into a query of the form

5. $Bel(Sue1, NameOf(Mother(Sue1), ?x))$

which would result in querying the formula $NameOf(Mother(Sue1), ?x)$ in belief space BS2. But this would unify with formula 3 (corresponding to assertion 1). The problem arises because the variable $?x$ should only match objects defined in space BS1, and Sk1 was defined in BS2. If variables are indexed by spaces as well, the problem can be avoided. In particular, unification would be extended so that a variable defined in space X can only match objects that are defined in spaces accessible to X. The accessibility relation would be defined by the nesting hierarchy of belief spaces. Thus a constant defined in BS1 would be accessible in BS2, but not vice versa. Figure 17.3 shows the hierarchy of belief spaces and specifies a chart showing what variables can match what constants.

For convenience, we can define a new operator *KnowRef* that states that an agent knows a unique object satisfying some description, represented as a lambda expression. In particular,

6. $KnowRef(A, \lambda x\, P_x) \equiv \exists!\, y\,.\, Bel(A, ((\lambda x\, P_x)y)) \equiv \exists!\, y\,.\, Bel(A, P_y)$

Given this, formula 2 is equivalent to

$KnowRef(Sue1, \lambda x\, NameOf(Mother(Sue1), x))$

Another important form of knowledge involves knowing that someone else knows whether a certain fact is true (yet the original agent doesn't know whether it's true or not). For example, Jack may believe that Sue knows whether or not she owns Fido. This is represented as a disjunction of beliefs in modal logic — that is, Jack believes that either Sue believes she owns Fido, or Sue believes she doesn't own Fido. Thus there is a distinction similar to quantifier scoping previously discussed. If a disjunction is within the belief operator

7. $Bel(Sue1, Own(Sue1, Fido) \lor \neg Own(Sue1, Fido))$

then Sue believes that either she owns Fido or she doesn't. This is almost certainly believed by Sue or by any other rational agent. The case with the disjunction outside the belief operator

8. $Bel(Sue1, Own(Sue1, Fido)) \lor Bel(Sue1, \neg Own(Sue1, Fido))$

represents that Sue knows whether she owns Fido or not. This is more difficult to express in terms of belief spaces. Here we introduce a new operator, *KnowIf*, which captures the meaning expressed in formula 8:

9. $KnowIf(A, P) \equiv Bel(A, P) \lor Bel(A, \neg P)$

Reducing this to an expression using belief spaces would require introducing additional mechanisms that allow you to explicitly assert that a particular formula is in a belief space. Then *know* would be defined in terms of a disjunction of this relation. We will use the *KnowIf* operator directly in the representation, however, and not decompose into a more primitive form.

One final aspect is the most difficult to deal with but ultimately is far more important than the two forms of knowing discussed thus far. In fact, the two preceding forms could be viewed as limited special cases of knowledge about what others know. In particular, what if your stereo is not working and you want to get help fixing it? You have knowledge that someone, such as Joe of Joe's Stereo Repair, can help you. Joe knows about fixing stereos and can tell you what you need to know. But you don't know enough to know what propositions it is that Joe must know about in order to fix stereos. You may not even know the vocabulary to express those propositions. Yet you do have some beliefs about Joe's beliefs and knowledge that enable you to reason that Joe is the person to ask about your stereo.

Only very specialized and limited techniques have been developed so far to address this question. Typically, this knowledge is embedded in heuristics that are hand-tailored to the expected user of the system. For example, for each action class, a system might explicitly represent what users know enough to be able to execute the action. Then the system could introduce action classes that are only partially described. For example, a (possibly partial) set of preconditions and effects could be defined for an action class *FixStereo*, and yet the system may have no decomposition for such actions. It would then be asserted that Joe knows how to execute actions of the type *FixStereo*. Thus, given a goal *Working(S1)*, where $S1$ is a stereo, the system might find that *FixStereo* is relevant because its effects match the goal, but it would not be able to decompose the action. It could then look up which agent it believes knows how to perform the action. You might call this relation *KnowingHow*.

17.4 Representing Cognitive States: Desires, Intentions, and Plans

There are many terms used in the literature that seem related to desires and intentions, including plans, goals, wants, and purposes. This section attempts to provide definitions for these terms that capture the range of concepts needed to model a conversational agent. Of course, not all researchers will use these terms in the way defined here, but these are some common interpretations.

First consider the distinction between desires and intentions. Desires reflect what states of the world the agent finds pleasant or unpleasant. Typically, an agent has many desires, often conflicting with each other. For instance, you might desire to take the day off and go to the beach. On the other hand, you might also desire to do well on your final exam, and to do this, you should stay home and study. These two desires conflict, and your behavior will result from some compromise between the two. In contrast, your intentions generally do not conflict. You can't simultaneously intend to go to the beach today and intend to stay home and study. Intentions are strongly related to behavior, and you can only do one of these things at a time.

So while both desires and intentions affect your behavior, they are quite different. Desires seem to arise subconsciously and allow you to evaluate the attractiveness of certain states. Intentions, on the other hand, arise from rational deliberation about what course of action you should follow. Looking again at Figure 17.1, you see that desires and beliefs are considered as input to some deliberation process that eventually commits to a course of actions, captured by your intentions.

There are two notions of intention. The first is often called **intention in action** and refers to the property of acting intentionally. For instance, much importance is given to the distinction between a situation where you run into someone on your bicycle unintentionally and a situation where you run into someone intentionally. For the latter you could be charged with assault, but the former is an unfortunate accident. The second notion of intention is called **future-directed intention** and reflects decisions you have made about your future action. For example, if after some deliberation you decide to forget about the exam and go to the beach, then you have adopted a future-directed intention to go to the beach.

Of course, having a future-directed intention often leads to intentional action. Because you intend to go the beach, you may then ride your bicycle there intentionally (avoiding pedestrians, we hope). But future-directed intentions are not necessarily realized. On your way out to the bike rack, you might meet friends on their way to study and feel so guilty that you change your mind. In this case you still had the intention to go to the beach, but you abandoned it and now have the intention to study.

For our purposes, the notion of future-directed intention is the most critical concept. We introduce an operator *Intend* that relates an agent to an action that the agent intends to perform. There are several requirements on having intentions that capture part of what it means to be a rational agent:

Rationality Constraint 1—An agent can't intend to do two actions that it believes are mutually exclusive.

Rationality Constraint 2—An agent can't intend an action it believes it can't perform.

Expressing these constraints in a formal logic is complex. Rather, we will depend on the processes of planning and plan adoption to procedurally guarantee that our agent doesn't adopt intentions unless it believes it can perform them.

Clearly, plans, goals, and planning are intimately related to intentions. But the relationship is more complicated than it might seem. First, note that if you say

Jack has a plan for robbing the bank.

you may mean one of two very different things:

- Jack intends to rob the bank.
- Jack has worked out a scheme by which someone could rob the bank.

In the first reading, having the plan seems to be a way of describing one of Jack's future-directed intentions, whereas in the second, having the plan seems to say that Jack knows, in principle, how to rob the bank. In this latter sense, a plan specifies a set of actions that could achieve a specific effect, like a recipe. A recipe gives a set of actions (steps in cooking) that will cause some effect (a meal). Having a recipe does not mean that you intend to make the meal.

The plans-as-recipes sense seems to correspond to the notion of plans in the AI literature, as described in Chapter 15. When a planning system constructs a plan, there is no commitment by any agent to execute the plan. Rather, the task is simply to find a "recipe" that would achieve the goal statement. Note that, corresponding to the two notions of "having a plan," there are two notions of the term *goal*. In one sense a goal seems much like an intention. In the other a goal is simply the name for the resulting state of a plan-as-recipe.

Given this, pick some readings for the different terms. The term **plan** will always be used in the plan-as-recipe sense. In other words, a plan is a set of actions with a specified effect, called the **plan's goal**. A goal can be either a proposition that will be attained by the actions in the plan or an action that will be performed by the actions in the plan. Thus the term **plan recognition** refers to the task of constructing a plan-as-recipe that could account for a set of observed actions.

$Bel(Jack1,$ $\quad Generates(RideBike(Jack1),$ $\qquad GoToBeach(Jack1)))$	$Intends(Jack1, RideBike(Jack1)) \&$ $Intends(Jack1, GoToBeach(Jack1)) \&$ $Intends(Jack1,$ $\qquad Generates(RideBike(Jack1),$ $\qquad\quad GoToBeach(Jack1)))$
Knowing a plan to go to the beach	**Intending to go to the beach**

Figure 17.4 The two readings of *Jack has a plan to go the beach.*

What about the other sense of having a plan related to intention? To avoid confusion, the term *plan* will never be used in this sense. Rather, we will talk about the **intentional structure** of an agent. The intentional structure of an agent is part of its mental state, like its beliefs and desires. The intentional structure arises when the agent commits to performing a plan. Not surprisingly, there will be a strong correspondence between the structure of the plan and the resulting intentional structure. Consider the simplest case. Say that Jack knows a very simple plan to go to the beach, namely riding his bike there. This plan is simply a set of beliefs that assert that if Jack rides his bike in the right direction, he will get to the beach. Later, Jack has a desire to go to the beach. Knowing the plan to get there by bike, he might adopt this plan. He now has the intention to go to the beach by riding his bike. Jack's beliefs about the plan and the intentional structure from adopting the plan are shown in Figure 17.4. Note that the intentions must include both of the actions and the generation relationship between them. If you omitted the action of bike riding, then Jack would intend to go to the beach but not have a way specified to get there. If you omitted the action of going to the beach, then Jack would intend to ride his bike but not necessarily end up at the beach. If you omitted the generation relation, Jack might accomplish each action separately, say by first riding his bike and then walking to the beach.

The distinction between knowing a plan and having a set of intentions is sometimes lost in the literature because one natural way to represent the two situations in a knowledge representation uses a very similar representation for each. Figure 17.5 contrasts the representations of Jack knowing about the plan-as-recipe and Jack having an intention. It uses the graph representation developed in Chapter 15 and places the graph in a space that represents the plan Jack believes will work. A natural way to represent the intentional structure, on the other hand, is to also use a new type of space that acts as an argument to the *Intend* operator. The confusion arises because, except for the difference in the interpretation of the spaces, the same plan graph is used in both cases.

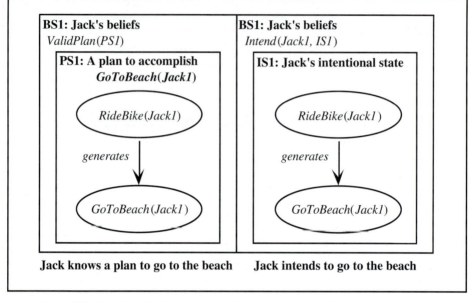

Figure 17.5 Knowing of a plan versus intending to perform a plan using spaces

To summarize, here's a list of all the concepts discussed in this section and their correlates in our BDI model.

belief—the operator *Bel* and belief spaces.

future-directed intention—the operator *Intend* and intentional state spaces.

intention-in-action—performing an action because it is in the intentional space.

plan-as-recipe—a plan, typically represented as a plan graph in a plan space.

having a plan in the intentional sense—same as future-directed intention.

goal (of an agent)—a future-directed intention.

goal (of a plan)—an end effect in a plan graph.

desires—unanalyzed; realized in the decision-making process that creates goals and evaluates plans.

wants—another word for desires.

17.5 Speech Acts and Communicative Acts

As previously stated, speech acts are actions that are performed by speaking, and we hope to be able to represent them using the model of action developed in Chapter 15. In order to do this, however, several complications must be

BOX 17.2 Intention and Action Generation

In many theories of intention, you can only intend actions. This might call into question whether the intentions expressed in Figures 17.4 and 17.5 are well formed. In particular, they seem to imply intending a generation relation between actions. If this bothers you, then the intentions can be recast as complex actions. In this case the complex action would be going to the beach by riding a bike. To do this, a suitable action constructor would have to be defined to create such actions. Pollack (1990) introduces an operator By, such that given any two actions α and β, $By(\alpha, \beta)$ is the complex action of doing α by doing β. Given this, the third intention in Figure 17.4 would be

$$Intend(Jack1, By(GoToBeach(Jack1), RideBike(Jack1)))$$

This way, all intentions are stated in terms of actions.

addressed because of the multi-agent nature of communicative acts, and because their effects will be defined in terms of changes of the agents' cognitive states.

For planning purposes, it is the intended perlocutionary acts that are the most important, because these capture the intended effects that agents have when they speak. For example, an agent would construct a plan in terms of convincing the other agent that some fact is true or that the other agent should perform some act. To accomplish such an action, the agent would perform an illocutionary act (such as asserting or requesting) and hope for the other agent to do the right thing so that the perlocutionary act is accomplished. And, of course, to accomplish the illocutionary act, the agent would perform a locutionary act that would involve uttering an appropriate sentence.

The model developed here involves **communicative acts,** which correspond to perlocutionary acts that are generated by illocutionary acts. For example, the communicative act *ConvinceByInform* involves getting another agent to believe some proposition by saying it is true. It is instructive to consider what is involved in the successful performance of such a communicative act. Consider what must be true for Sam to successfully *ConvinceByInform* Helen that it is raining:

1. Sam says the words *It's raining* with the intention to inform Helen of this fact.
2. Helen hears the sentence *It's raining* and recognizes Sam's intention to inform her of this fact. Because of this, Helen decides that Sam intends to get her to believe that it is raining.
3. Helen considers the evidence for the fact that it is raining, including the fact that Sam said that it is raining.
4. Helen comes to believe that it is raining.

All of these steps are essential. To convince yourself of this, consider removing any of the steps. If you remove step 1, then Sam didn't say anything so certainly

The Action Class *ConvinceByInform(e)*:
Roles: *Speaker, Hearer, Prop*
Constraints: *Agent(Speaker), Agent(Hearer), Proposition(Prop),*
$\qquad\qquad$ *Bel(Speaker, Prop)*
Preconditions: *At(Speaker, Loc(Hearer))*
Effects: *Bel(Hearer, Prop)*

The Action Class *MotivateByRequest(e)*:
Roles: *Speaker, Hearer, Act*
Constraints: *Agent(Speaker), Agent(Hearer), Action(Act)*
Preconditions: *At(Speaker, Loc(Hearer))*
Effects: *Intend(Hearer, Act)*

Figure 17.6 The definitions of two communicative acts

didn't inform Helen that it was raining. You have removed the locutionary act. If you remove just the intention condition, then you get the implausible scenario of Sam just randomly uttering sounds (say, Sam is under hypnosis). Even if Helen is fooled and performs all the rest of the steps, Sam could later deny that he informed her that it was raining. He could claim that he didn't know what he was saying so she couldn't attach any significance to it.

If you remove step 2, then Helen didn't hear the sentence. If you remove just the condition that Helen recognize Sam's intention, then Helen heard Sam speak but has no idea why he spoke to her; that is, she has failed to recognize the illocutionary act. Even if she did the rest of steps that are possible in this scenario and comes to believe that it is raining, she would deny that Sam informed her of this fact.

If you remove step 3, then Helen, while recognizing that Sam tried to inform her of something, completely ignores the information he told her. This would be impolite to say the least, but assuming it is the case, even if she then comes to believe that it is raining, this belief will have nothing to do with what Sam said.

If you remove step 4, then Sam told Helen that it is raining, but failed to convince her. In this case the illocutionary act *Inform* succeeded, but the communicative act *ConvinceByInform* failed.

While you can develop action representations for all three levels of the speech act, it is the communicative actions that provide the principal connection to the agent's general reasoning. Figure 17.6 shows the definitions of two basic communicative acts needed in any model of communication, corresponding to simple informing and requesting. These definitions build in the assumption that agents are sincere. For instance, a constraint on *ConvinceByInform* is that the speaker believes the proposition asserted. This condition, of course, would need to be dropped to handle acts like lying, but such complicated acts are beyond what is needed for most conversational agents we might be able to build. The decomposition, which would include the illocutionary act, is not shown for the

> **BOX 17.3 Classifying Speech Acts**
>
> An interesting question is how many different kinds of speech acts are there? Searle (1979) argues that there are only five classes of illocutionary acts, each class capturing a different general point or purpose. Each act in the class is then distinguished by additional conditions. The classes are as follows:
>
> > **representative class**—the speaker commits to the truth of what is expressed, including the acts described by the verbs *inform, deny, affirm,* and *confirm.*
> >
> > **directive class**—the speaker attempts to influence the intentions and behavior of another agent, including the acts described by the verbs *request, command, invite, ask,* and *beg.*
> >
> > **commissive class**—the speaker commits to some future action, including the acts described by the verbs *promise* and *commit*.
> >
> > **expressive class**—the speaker expresses a psychological state or reaction, including acts described by the verbs *apologize, congratulate, thank,* and *welcome.*
> >
> > **declarative class**—the speaker performs some conventional or ritual action by the speech act, including acts described by the verbs *christen, fire, resign,* and *appoint.*

moment. Issues related to interpreting illocutionary acts will be delayed until Section 17.9.

The next section considers a model that allows an agent to plan communicative acts, just like any other acts, to accomplish goals in its world. This sets the stage for modeling the understanding of other agents' communicative acts.

17.6 Planning Communicative Acts

Consider a situation in which Jack tries to buy a ticket for a train. Assume that he doesn't know the exact price of the ticket. Also assume that he knows a plan for buying, which involves the following two substeps (from the definition of *Buy* in Figure 15.4):

10. *Give(Jack1, Clerk1, Price(Ticket1))*
11. *Give(Clerk1, Jack1, Ticket1)*

Jack cannot simply adopt this plan directly as a set of intentions. For one thing, 11 involves action by another agent, which Jack can't directly intend. This step is a crucial part of Jack's plan, so it can't simply be ignored.

In fact, there is something Jack must do as part of 11, because giving is a multi-agent action. It takes two agents to give: one to provide and the other to receive. Thus we might replace 11 by the action that is Jack's part in the giving action. In fact, there is a verb for this in English, namely *receive,* but to make the analysis more general we will not use it. Rather, we define an action operator *MyPartOf,* which takes an agent and a multi-agent action A and produces an action that is the agent's role or part in A. Thus, the action *MyPartOf(Jack1, Give(Clerk1, Jack1, Ticket1))* might involve Jack putting out his hand, waiting for the ticket, and then grasping the ticket. The action *MyPartOf(Clerk1, Give(Clerk1, Jack1, Ticket1))* would involve putting the ticket into Jack's hand and letting go of it. Note that this function can apply to single agent actions as well. If the agent specified is the agent of the action, then it is the identity function, for example, *MyPartOf(Jack1, Grasp(Jack1, Ticket1)) = Grasp(Jack1, Ticket1)*. On the other hand, if the agent is different, then the function denotes some action of not interfering while the other agent does it.

The intentions adopted from this plan might be to do the following actions

12. *MyPartOf(Jack1, Give(Jack1, Clerk1, Price(Ticket1)))*
13. *MyPartOf(Jack1, Give(Clerk1, Jack1, Ticket1))*

These actions are at least things that Jack can intend to do, but it probably is not a very useful set of intentions. In particular, it will do no good for Jack to do his part if the clerk doesn't do his or her part. So far, nothing in Jack's intentions addresses the issue of getting the clerk to cooperate in his plan! For this, Jack will have to communicate with the clerk and get the clerk to have the right intentions.

Before developing this, however, consider one more problem. Jack may not even be able to execute the first action because he doesn't know the price of the ticket. This reveals a general constraint on action that has been ignored until now. To execute any action, an agent must know the values of the parameters. One way of viewing this constraint is that there is a set of implicit preconditions on every action that the agent must know the value of the parameters. These are sometimes called the **knowledge preconditions**. In this example, the implicit precondition would be

14. *KnowRef(Jack1, $\lambda x(Price(Ticket1) = x)$)*

This then becomes a new goal for Jack. Intuitively, he could achieve this goal in several ways. He could look up the price on a fare schedule, or he could ask someone who knows the price. This latter method involves language and so will be used for the example. Suppose Jack has reason to believe that a *ConvinceBy-Inform* act by the clerk will achieve his goal. To get the clerk to do this action, Jack might plan to ask the clerk to perform the *Inform* act. But what is the act that he is asking the clerk to perform? Because Jack doesn't know the price of the ticket, he can't represent the action that the clerk must perform. This is the same problem as when we needed to represent the fact that someone knows something, but we didn't know what it was. The solution is to introduce two additional *Inform* acts used for planning that use the *KnowRef* and *KnowIf* operators introduced earlier, as shown in Figure 17.7.

To summarize the situation so far, there are two problems with Jack's plan: There's no reason to expect that the clerk will perform his or her part of the plan as required, and Jack doesn't have enough information to perform his own part of the plan. Both of these problems can be overcome if Jack can affect the clerk's

The Action Class **_ConvinceByInformRef(e)_**:
Roles: _Speaker, Hearer, Pred_$_x$
Constraints: _Agent_(_Speaker_), _Agent_(_Hearer_), _UnaryPred_(_Pred_$_x$),
KnowRef(_Speaker_, _Pred_$_x$)
Preconditions: _At_(_Speaker, Loc_(_Hearer_))
Effects: _KnowRef_(_Hearer_, _Pred_$_x$)

The Action Class **_ConvinceByInformIf(e)_**:
Roles: _Speaker, Hearer, Prop_
Constraints: _Agent_(_Speaker_), _Agent_(_Hearer_), _Proposition_(_Prop_),
KnowIf(_Speaker, Prop_)
Preconditions: _At_(_Speaker, Loc_(_Hearer_))
Effects: _KnowIf_(_Hearer, Prop_)

Figure 17.7 Variants of _ConvinceByInform_ for acquiring information

intentional structure so that he or she tells him the price of the ticket and participates in the buying action. Specifically, he needs the clerk to do the following:

15. _MyPartOf(Clerk1,_
$\quad$ _ConvinceByInformRef(Clerk1, Jack1 , λ x(Price (Ticket1) = x)))_
16. _MyPartOf(Clerk1, Give(Jack1, Clerk1, Price(Ticket1)))_
17. _MyPartOf(Clerk1,Give(Clerk1, Jack1, Ticket1))_

Jack cannot make these actions happen by willing them, but he can act in a way to attempt to get the clerk to acquire the intentions to perform these acts. Specifically, he may perform _MotivateByRequest_ acts for each of these acts. For the first, he may plan to perform the act

18. _MotivateByRequest (Jack1, Clerk1,_
$\quad$ _ConvinceByInformRef(Clerk1, Jack1, λ x(Price (Ticket1) = x)))_ ·

which, if successful, will achieve the effect

19. _Intend (Clerk1, ConvinceByInformRef(Clerk1, Jack1, λ x(Price(Ticket1)_
$\quad$ _= x)))_

Note that these acts really should all have a _MyPartOf_ operator around them to indicate who is doing what, but we will drop this from now on when it is clear what is intended. The request act, 18, might get realized by a locutionary act such as the question _What is the price of a ticket to Toronto?_

Similarly, Jack might attempt to motivate the clerk to do actions 16 and 17 by issuing two more requests. But this would produce very stilted dialogue, such as the following:

What is the price of a ticket to Toronto?
Please take this money I am offering you.
Please give me a ticket.

If this were what was required every time two agents interacted, very little would ever get accomplished. But how does Jack know he can get away with saying any less? The answer lies in the belief that the clerk is an intelligent agent as well and will use general knowledge about the world to interpret actions. Furthermore, from the actions the clerk observes, he or she will be able to recognize what Jack is trying to do. This will be explored in more detail in the next section. But let's consider some possible lines of inference that Jack might depend on the clerk to explore in this situation.

Assuming they have a shared knowledge about common actions like buying things, Jack could depend on the clerk using this information to interpret his actions. For instance, assume after finding out the price he says *OK, please give me a ticket.* This is a request for action 17. Jack would depend on the clerk using their shared knowledge about buying things so that the clerk also expects 16 to happen and forms the appropriate intentions. Alternatively, Jack might just say *OK* and hand over the money. In this case, he is depending on the clerk observing that he is doing his part of the buying plan, and he expects that the clerk will be motivated to perform his or her part. This type of example takes us away from language, however, so will not be pursued further. As a final example, Jack might simply identify the more abstract goal of buying a ticket, depending on the clerk to know the details. He might say *OK, I'd like to buy one.* This sentence identifies Jack's intention to perform the joint action and depends on the clerk adopting the complementary intentions so that it is successful.

In summary, the final set of actions that Jack might intend after all this reasoning might be as follows:

20. *MotivateByRequest(Jack1, Clerk1,*
     ConvinceByInformRef(Clerk1, Jack1, $\lambda x(Price(Ticket1) = x)$))
21. *MyPartOf(Jack1, ConvinceByInformRef(Clerk1, Jack1, $\lambda x(Price(Ticket1)$*
     $= x$)))
22. *MotivateByRequest(Jack1, Clerk1, Buy(Jack1, Clerk1, Ticket1))*
23. *Give(Jack1, Clerk1, Price(Ticket1))*
24. *MyPartOf(Jack1, Give(Clerk1, Jack1, Ticket1))*

Intention 20 involves asking for the price of the ticket, 21 involves listening to the answer, 22 involves the request to buy a ticket, and 23 and 24 are the steps involved in buying the ticket. This set of intentions, together with those adopted by the clerk, might result in the following dialogue:

25a. Jack: Hi. How much is a ticket to Toronto?
25b. Clerk: Twenty five dollars.
25c. Jack: OK. I'd like one.   <Jack hands the clerk the money>
25d. Clerk: OK. Here.   <The clerk hands Jack the ticket>

The plan that might have motivated these intentions is shown in Figure 17.8, where *Jack1* and *Clerk1* have been shortened to *J1* and *C1* to save space. The details of the decomposition of the *Buy* action are also not shown.

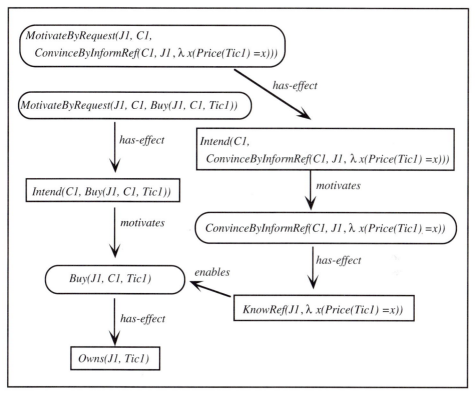

Figure 17.8 Jack's final plan for buying the ticket

17.7 Communicative Acts and the Recognition of Intention

The example in the last section showed that without an ability to recognize another agent's intentions, multi-agent action would be extremely difficult, if not impossible. In particular, it would be almost impossible to understand and act appropriately in a dialogue. This section considers the recognition-of-intention problem and how it relates to speech act interpretation.

Chapter 15 discussed the use of plan recognition to find the causal and intentional connections between eventualities described in sentences. It would seem that the same techniques could be applied here to recognize the intentions of the speaker. For the most part, this will be true, but there are some complications. In this section we will refer to the agent who performs the action as the acting agent, and the agent who observes the action as the observing agent. The issue is how the observing agent can recognize the intentions of the acting agent.

First, just because you can identify a plan that includes all the observed actions doesn't mean that this plan describes the agent's intentions. There may be many possible plans that account for the observed actions, and the acting agent is only performing one of these. So finding a plan using some plan recognition algorithm only suggests a possible set of intentions that the acting agent might have. In fact, determining whether this is the correct plan may be theoretically impossible, but we seem to survive by attributing intentions to agents based on the most likely plan we can recognize.

Also, as mentioned in Section 17.3, the plan recognized must be plausible, given the acting agent's beliefs, and might seem wrong or inefficient from the observing agent's point of view. In practice, this means that plan recognition can only be based on shared knowledge, although a few particular facts about the other agent's beliefs can be used if available. Consider the locker example from Section 17.3 again. Jack knows he has a combination lock on his locker, while Sue believes he has a key lock. They share knowledge about the need to unlock lockers to open them, knowledge about the effects of different communicative acts, and other knowledge of the situation. They must both know, for instance, that it is reasonable for Sue to want to get into Jack's locker. Given this, what can Jack recognize from the question

Sue: Can I have the key to your locker?

Skipping over the details as to how Jack identifies this locutionary act as a request for the key, he can infer a plausible plan including this action as follows. First, the utterance is identified as part of the action

$MotivateByRequest(Sue1, Jack1, Give(Jack1, Sue1, KeyTo(Locker1)))$

Using their shared knowledge about communicative acts, Jack knows that Sue believes that an effect of this act is

$Intend(Jack1, Give(Jack1, Sue1, KeyTo(Locker1)))$

which in turn, using shared knowledge about intentional behavior, would motivate the action

$Give(Jack1, Sue1, KeyTo(Locker1))$

which, given their shared knowledge about giving actions, would have the effect

$Have(Sue1, KeyTo(Locker1))$

Now the crucial step. Jack believes that Sue thinks he has a key lock on his locker. Thus he knows that Sue believes that having the key would enable the action

$Open(Sue1, Locker1)$

Assuming Jack finds this action to be a reasonable intention in this domain, he would have constructed a plausible explanation of why Sue asked him for the key. Of course, the plan constructed will not work, but this doesn't matter for the purposes of recognizing the plan. What matters is that Sue thinks it will work. Assuming this is the only plan that seems plausible, he would assume that it defines Sue's intentional structure. The plan recognized is shown in Figure 17.9.

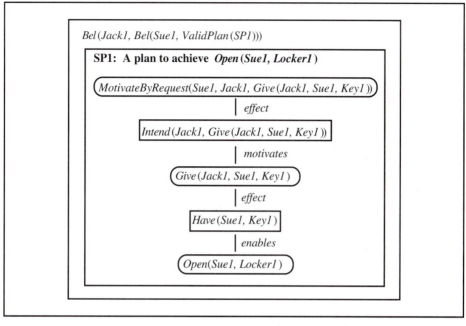

Figure 17.9 A plausible plan recognized from *Can I have the key to your locker?*

Given this plan, the primary intentions that Jack would attribute to Sue would include

> *Intend(Sue1, MotivateByRequest(Sue1, Jack1, Give(Jack1, Sue1, KeyTo(Locker1))))*
> *Intend(Sue1, Achieve(Have(Sue1, KeyTo(Locker1))))*
> *Intend(Sue1, Open(Sue1, Locker1))*

In practice, a computational system that used an algorithm such as this would have to be given a list of possible intentions that would serve as its expectations. In the example, *Intend(Sue1, Open(Sue1, Locker1))* would be one of the expectations. Given an input, the system would then use plan recognition to suggest some plausible plans, and hope that only one of them "matches" an expected intention.

Of course, you do not need to recognize the ultimate intention behind every utterance. As long as there are plausible intentions that could motivate the utterance, identifying the exact one is often not necessary. For instance, let us assume that there is no expectation that Sue might intend to open John's locker. This, after all, is a rather specific intention that was convenient to make this example simple. But let's say it is not an expected intention. Rather, the expected intentions are more global things like studying for classes and going to the beach. Now, let's assume it is shared knowledge that Jack's locker contains both the textbooks for a course Jack and Sue are taking and also some beach towels. Now, when Sue asks for the key to the locker, Jack cannot identify Sue's intention—she might be intending to study or to go to the beach. The plan shown in Figure 17.9, however, is a subpart of either one. The plans diverge at the next action: whether Sue takes out the books or the towels. Now Jack might have some interest in exactly what Sue's intention is, but he does not need to identify her intention in order to understand her request. He has identified sufficient motivation for the request based on what's in Figure 17.9 and the knowledge that opening the locker is a reasonable thing to do for several expected intentions. Thus, the analysis may be fine as it stands.

In addition, the depth to which you need to recognize intentions in order to feel you have understood depends on your own goals in the interaction. In some conversations—say, when negotiating a peace plan—it is very important to know exactly what other people intend when they are speaking. In other conversations—say, when someone stops you on the street and asks for the time—you have almost no interest in the other person's intentions beyond the obvious one of wanting to know the time. In a computational system operating in a specific domain, the required level of detail will need to be specified based on the range of tasks the system is supposed to accomplish.

Once the intentions are recognized, the next thing to explain is what the observing agent does with the information about the acting agent's intentions. For example, what will Jack do now that Sue has asked him for the key? This question leads us again to agents' planning and reasoning processes, which are discussed in the next section.

17.8 The Source of Intentions in Dialogue

If you look back at Figure 17.1, you will see that the intentions arise from a combination of the agent's beliefs and desires. It believes it is in a certain state, or will be in a certain state in the future, and this state is evaluated with respect to the agent's desires. New intentions arise from the decision to do something to change the way things will be if the agent continues on its present course. We will represent desires as a function on states that evaluates the attractiveness of different states. With this formalization, the decision-making process can be viewed as a continual striving to attain, or remain in, the more attractive states.

A particular conversational agent will have its desires specified as part of the domain. For instance, a simple database question-answering agent might have only one desire, to answer all questions put to it. Thus it prefers states where there are no unanswered questions, and when it finds itself in a state where a question is unanswered, it would act to put itself in a more attractive state by answering the question. But even this simple agent must be more complex if you consider it carefully.

If all the agent cares about is not having unanswered questions, then why not simply not process any input at all? Then it will never know it is in a state with an unanswered question because there will be no questions. So there needs to be a constraint on the agent's behavior that we might call the **attentiveness constraint**. When a question is asked, it will attempt to understand it. Now this behavior might not arise from a desire—it might be built into the system as an automatic process that occurs whenever a question arises. This is a quite plausible approach, even for modeling humans. If someone speaks to you, it is almost impossible not to interpret what that person is saying. You may decide to do nothing about what was said or to ignore the speaker, but it is very hard to not interpret the sentences that you hear. So, moving back to our conversational agent, we will assume that the language-understanding process occurs automatically on any input.

Given that it cannot ignore its input, what prevents the system from simply making up answers? If the system is to useful, then there must be some reason why it should give accurate answers. Using the BDI model, this means that the agent should believe what it says. This is often called the **sincerity condition**, and it plays an important role in many approaches to speech act theory. Thus we would want to make sure that the desirability function evaluates states such that, all other things being equal, states resulting from sincere responses are preferred over states resulting from insincere ones. We will say that a desirability function that has this property has a **sincerity preference**. Note that sincerity was built into the definition of the *ConvinceByInform* act previously defined, so that if the agent never performs an action unless its constraints are satisfied, it will have to be sincere.

With the addition of the attentiveness constraint and a desire to be sincere, there are enough constraints to drive the behavior of a simple question-answering agent. But this agent will still not be considered very helpful. Consider the example of Jack's locker again. Assume the question-answering agent is playing the role of Jack. Say that Sue asks Jack whether he has the key to the locker. Jack inspects his beliefs and, finding that he has no key to the locker (since one doesn't exist), can sincerely answer no! If you knew the background and overheard this conversation, you would consider Jack's answer misleading and uncooperative. The problem is that by answering no, Jack has implicitly indicated that the question was well-formed, thereby confirming a presupposition in the question that the locker opens with a key. As a result, what Sue believes is shared knowledge is now diverging from what Jack believes to be the case. Although an agent might have some purpose that makes it want to allow such a misconception, typically conversants attempt to remedy misconceptions immediately in the dialogue. Thus we add a **shared knowledge preference** to the desirability function. An agent prefers states that minimize the difference between what each agent believes is shared knowledge. If the other agent says something that implies something that our agent believes is false, then our agent will prefer states that involve resolving the contradiction to states that do not. Thus, an answer such as *No, the locker has a combination lock* would be preferred over a simple *No*. Both responses are sincere, but only the first also obeys the shared knowledge preference.

BOX 17.4 Conversational Maxims

One of the most influential proponents of the view that language can be explained by examining general rational behavior and multi-agent cooperation is Grice (1975). He proposes that implicatures in conversation can be analyzed by assuming a set of conversational maxims that all agents will follow unless there is some reason not to. As a result, these maxims sanction assumptions that are crucial for understanding discourse. Grice's four main maxims are as follows:

Maxim of Quantity—Make your contribution as informative as is required, but not overly informative. This maxim would prevent withholding key information, such as a violated presupposition, on the one hand, and excessive verbosity, on the other.

Maxim of Quality—Do not say things for which you lack evidence. This maxim is reflected in our sincerity preference discussed in Section 17.8.

Maxim of Relation—What you say should be relevant to the current topic. This maxim sanctions the coherence assumptions discussed in Chapter 15.

Maxim of Manner—Avoid obscurity of expression and ambiguity.

The maxims are not fixed rules, but rather are preferences and default assumptions. A speaker may choose to violate a maxim for any number of reasons: to mislead the hearer, for example, or to communicate something by explicitly violating one. For instance, you might reply to one question by answering a different question, thereby indicating that you wish to avoid answering the original question.

The sincerity and shared knowledge preferences apply in almost any conversational situation and so can be taken as quite fundamental properties of dialogue itself. Additional preferences arise in more limited classes of situations. One that is particularly relevant for most applications is the **helpfulness preference**. This is a preference for responses that allow the other agent to achieve their intentions more efficiently. Consider a conversational agent whose task is to answer queries about train schedules. It knows that in order for agents to board trains, they have to get to the appropriate locations at the appropriate times. Knowing this, if a person asks *When does the train to Windsor leave?*, it might answer by giving both the departure time and its location, saying something like *Four o'clock from gate seven.* This answer is preferred over a simple *Four o'clock* because it eliminates the need for another act by the person to find out where the train leaves from. Of course, if the conversational agent believes that the person already knows where the train leaves from, then this second answer is not more helpful, it's just more verbose. To satisfy this preference, our agent should consider as much of the other agent's plan as can be reliably recognized and identify what information is needed.

Of course, there must be a limit to how much is said as a response. Suppose in a certain situation the agent recognizes the other agent's plan in detail, and finds a wealth of information that the agent may require during the course of the plan. Clearly, providing too much information can be as bad as not providing enough. This could be encoded as a **conciseness preference**: If all other things are equal, prefer the response that is more concise. (Don't you wish more people used this constraint?) Of course, it might be that the helpfulness preference and the conciseness preference do not agree on the most preferred state. In this case some mechanism must be developed to adjudicate between conflicting choices.

17.9 Recognizing Illocutionary Acts

As discussed earlier, linguistic communication doesn't occur unless the relevant intentions are recognized. Unfortunately, there is no simple mapping between a set of words and a particular intention. For example, you already saw that the sentence *Do you know the time?* can be a question, a request, or an offer, depending on what the speaker intended. Thus it seems that the connection between the actual language and what is communicated is quite remote. But, if this is the case, how can one agent recognize what another agent intends based on what is said? This section explores this issue.

The most common approach to this problem is based on the **literal meaning hypothesis**. This approach assumes that all sentences have a literal meaning that is based purely on the conventions of language. For example, the sentence *Do you know the time?* has a literal meaning in which it is a yes/no question asking about whether the hearer knows the time. This will be called the **surface speech act** and is identified from the syntactic mood of the sentence (that is, it is an interrogative sentence). Given the literal meaning, the **intended speech act** is then derived by an inference process, in our case using plan recognition techniques.

There are two ways to view the surface speech act. In the first, the surface speech act is an illocutionary act but may be faulty in some way. For example, to sincerely ask a question, the speaker must want to know the answer. Consider a situation in which Helen knows that Jack is unaware of the time, and she says *Do you know the time?* as an offer. The surface speech act is a yes/no question about whether Jack knows the time and is faulty because Helen does not want to know the answer. The realization that the surface speech act is faulty initiates the search for an alternative intended reading. One problem with this approach is that the literal act need not always be faulty for the utterance to have an indirect meaning. For instance, Helen might not know whether Jack knows the time or not. In this case, Helen might say *Do you know the time?* and intend both the yes/no-question interpretation and the offer interpretation.

In the other approach the surface speech act is not an illocutionary act but an act at another level of analysis, and inference must be used to identify the intended speech act. In this case the surface speech act is part of the semantic analysis of the sentence. For instance, *Do you know the time?* might be an *Interrog* act with propositional content *Know(Jack1, the time)*. Then, each of the illocutionary acts would specify which surface forms can be used to realize it. Figure 17.10 shows the definitions of the illocutionary act *RequestRef* with

The Action Class *MotivateInformRef(e)*:
Roles: *Speaker, Hearer, Pred$_x$*
Constraints: *Agent(Speaker), Agent(Hearer), UnaryPred(Pred$_x$), ¬KnowRef(Speaker, Pred$_x$) KnowRef(Hearer, Pred$_x$)*
Preconditions: *At(Speaker, Loc(Hearer))*
Effects: *Intend(Hearer, InformRef(Hearer, Speaker, Pred$_x$))*
Decomposition: *RequestRef(Speaker, Hearer, Pred$_x$) DecideTo(Hearer, InformRef(Hearer, Speaker, Pred$_x$))*

The Illocutionary Act *RequestRef(e)*:
Decomp1: *WhQuestion(Speaker, Hearer, Pred$_x$)*
Decomp 2: *Interrog(Speaker, Hearer, KnowRef(Hearer, Pred$_x$))*
Decomp 3: *Imper(Speaker, Hearer, InformRef(Hearer, Speaker, Pred$_x$))*

Figure 17.10   Speech act definitions for wh-requests

multiple decompositions, each corresponding to a particular surface speech act form. Also shown is the communicative act *MotivateInformRef*, which is a specialized version of the *MotivateByRequest* act.

The three decompositions identify three different surface forms that are commonly used to convey a *RequestRef* act. These forms correspond to the sentences *What is the time?*, *Do you know the time?*, and *Tell me the time*, respectively. If we make the reasonable assumption that these action definitions are shared knowledge between the conversing agents, then it is simple to see how an agent may plan an appropriate form of utterance to realize a *MotivateInformRef* action. Similarly, a simple decomposition chaining technique could be used to recognize a particular surface form as a particular communicative act. Of course, each surface form may appear in many different illocutionary acts, so there is still an ambiguity problem. For instance, Figure 17.11 shows definitions of the acts for yes/no questions.

The question *Do you know the time?* now matches decompositions in both *InformRef* and *InformIf*. Specifically, the literal meaning produced by the semantic interpreter would be

Interrog(Helen1, Jack1, KnowRef(Jack1, λ t . NowTime(t)))

This will match decomposition 2 of *RequestRef* and decomposition 1 of *RequestIf*, producing two possible interpretations:

RequestRef(Helen1, Jack1, λ t . NowTime(t))
RequestIf(Helen1, Jack1, KnowRef(Jack1, λ t . NowTime(t)))

To choose between these, the system can check whether each makes sense in the context. To adopt a particular reading means that the constraints defined for the reading must be presupposed by the utterance. Thus if a constraint in one interpretation is not satisfiable, that reading is unlikely. If we assume that it is shared

The Action Class *MotivateInformIf(e)*:
Roles: *Speaker, Hearer, Prop*
Constraints: *Agent (Speaker), Agent(Hearer), Proposition (Prop)*
                  ¬KnowIf(Speaker, Prop)
                  KnowIf(Hearer, Prop)
Preconditions: *At (Speaker, Loc (Hearer))*
Effects: *Intend (Hearer, InformIf(Hearer, Speaker, Prop))*
Decomposition: *RequestIf (Speaker, Hearer, Prop)*
                   DecideTo (Hearer, InformIf(Hearer, Speaker, Prop))

The Illocutionary Act *RequestIf (e)*:
Decomp1: *Interrog (Speaker, Hearer, Prop)*
Decomp 2: *Interrog (Speaker, Hearer, KnowIf(Hearer, Prop))*
Decomp 3: *Imper(Speaker, Hearer, InformIf(Hearer, Speaker, Prop))*

Figure 17.11 Speech act definitions for yes/no questions

knowledge that Helen already knows the time, that is, *KnowRef(Helen1, λ t . NowTime(t))*, then the *RequestRef* reading would be eliminated and the utterance would be interpreted as a yes/no question (or some other act, such as an offer). If, on the other hand, it is shared knowledge that Helen does not know the time but Jack does, then only the *RequestRef* interpretation is plausible. If none of this information is shared knowledge, then both interpretations remain plausible.

The interpretations that are left after filtering based on the constraints can then be used to initiate further plan recognition to attempt to determine which interpretations best fit into the current situation.

Note that even if the literal reading is eliminated and an indirect reading is taken, the original form of the utterance affects what responses are allowed. This suggests that at least the form of the literal meaning must be retained somehow in the final analysis. For instance, consider the following as responses to the utterances *Do you know the time?* and *Tell me the time,* both intended as requests for the time:

26a. Yes, it's three o'clock.
26b. No, I'm afraid not.
26c. Three o'clock.
26d. OK. It's three o'clock.
26e. No. I can't.

Responses 26a, 26b, and 26c are fine for *Do you know the time?*, but 26d and 26e seem quite unnatural. On the other hand, in response to the direct request *Tell me the time,* responses 26a and 26b seem very unnatural, but the other three are fine.

Not all indirect speech acts occur in conventional forms. For instance, the sentence *It's cold in here* could be uttered as a request that the hearer shut the window, but there is nothing in the structure of the sentence that might suggest such an interpretation. Rather, this sentence can only be interpreted by using the

---

BOX 17.5 Recognizing Intentions and Defining Illocutionary Acts

Not all communication results from recognition of intention, and not all intentions that are recognized contribute to the definition of what speech act was performed. This makes the definition of illocutionary acts extremely difficult. Here is a series of examples that bring up the problems.

Assume that Jack lisps slightly, and thus when he introduces himself to Sue, she might come to believe that he lisps. This fact is communicated to Sue but has nothing to do with what he is trying to say, that is, his illocutionary act. Since Jack didn't intend to convey that he lisps but merely intended to tell Sue his name, you would not say that Jack informed Sue that he lisps. To perform an illocutionary act, the speaker must intend to perform the act. But this is not enough: Say that Jack doesn't really lisp at all but imitates a lisp when he introduces himself to Sue. In this case Jack does intend Sue to believe that he lisps, but you still wouldn't say that Jack informed Sue that he lisps, because Sue doesn't recognize his intention to get her to believe that he lisps. But even if Sue did recognize Jack's intention, it still isn't an *Inform* act. Say that a friend told Sue that Jack often plays tricks like this on people he meets. Then the situation is as before, but now Sue recognizes that Jack has an intention to make her believe that he lisps. Despite this, Jack still didn't inform Sue that he lisps. What's missing is that Jack didn't intend Sue to recognize his intention to get her to believe that he lisps. So, to perform an illocutionary act, the speaker must intend for the intention to be recognized. You might think this solves the problem, but there are further counterexamples in which all these conditions are satisfied yet which wouldn't be considered *Inform* acts. What seems to be required is shared knowledge between the agents of what intentions the speaker intended to be recognized. A computational model for recognizing speech acts using such criterion can be found in Perrault and Allen (1980) and Allen (1983).

---

general knowledge that being cold may be undesirable, and the specific knowledge that the window is currently open and causes it to be cold. Such interpretation can only be recognized by some form of reasoning about an agent's beliefs and intentions. Such a system would need to recognize that the utterance was said with the intention of getting the hearer to close the window (and the intention that this intention be recognized). Due to this intention, the utterance is interpreted as a request. See Box 17.5 for more details on this problem.

17.10 Discourse-Level Planning

The conversational agent model described so far attempts to account for the intentions underlying single utterances but has not addressed any larger-scale coherence of discourse. This section explores plan-based models at the discourse level, in which the relationships between utterances can be used to plan utterances and recognize the structure of utterances the other agent makes.

The Communicative Action *DefineClass* (*e*):
Roles: *Speaker, Hearer, Class*
Decomposition: *IdentifySuperClass(Speaker, Hearer, Class)*
IdentifyProperties(Speaker, Hearer, Class)
GiveExample(Speaker, Hearer, Class)

The Communicative Action *IdentifySuperClass (Speaker, Hearer, Class)*:
Roles: *Speaker, Hearer, Class, SuperClass*
Constraints: *Agent(Speaker), Agent(Hearer), SubType(Class, SuperClass)*
Decomposition: *ConvinceByInform(Speaker, Hearer, SubType(Class, SuperClass))*

Figure 17.12 Some discourse-level actions used to define a class of objects

Many theories of discourse involve the use of a fixed set of relationships between utterances. Different researchers call these relations different names, such as discourse relations, rhetorical relations, conversational games, and discourse moves, but they all view these relations as defining the structure of well-formed discourse. As a result, identifying these relationships is essential to understanding utterances in discourse. There is some debate about whether such explicit relations are necessary. For instance, consider whether an explicit question-answer relation is necessary in a theory of discourse. Given the model developed in this chapter, if a *MotivateInformIf* action is performed successfully, the receiving agent will then have an intention to perform a *ConvinceByInformIf* action. Thus an answer will typically follow a question because of the preferences that define each agent's behavior. The observation that discourse is often organized as question-answer pairs can be explained without requiring an explicit question-answer relationship to be recognized. Hence the debate. One group argues for the existence of a set of discourse relations that structure discourse, while the other argues that such relations are epiphenomenal and arise as a consequence of a more basic model of multi-agent behavior.

No matter who ends up winning this argument, it is true that for any given application, having some set of discourse relations appropriate for the domain is of great benefit. This is especially true on the language-generation side, where the system may need to convey large amounts of information using multiple utterances. In such cases, the organization of the information into utterance-size units is often viewed as a planning process using a set of discourse relations. For example, consider an application where the system provides an interface to an encyclopedia database. One of the tasks the system might have to perform is to define different classes of objects. Typically, a definition might take several utterances. By defining a set of discourse-level acts that involve different ways to define classes, this can be made into a planning problem. For instance, an action to define a class might be defined as shown in Figure 17.12.

Each of the substeps of *DefineClass* would be defined in the system in terms of other actions or speech acts, just as *IdentifySuperClass* is in the figure.

The discourse script *TakeOrder(e)*:
Roles: *System, User, Name, Address, CreditCardInfo, Items*
Decomposition: *Greetings(System, User)*
GetAddress(System, User, Address)
GetCreditInfo(System, User, CreditCardInfo)
GetOrder(System, User, Items)
VerifyDeliveryStatus(System, User, Items)
Closings(System, User)

The discourse script *GetCreditInfo(e)*:
Roles: *System, User, CreditCardInfo*
Decomposition: *MotivateInformRef(System, User, λx CreditCardInfo $= x$)*
ConvinceByInformRef(User, System, λx CreditCardInfo $= x$)
VerifyNumber(System, User, CreditCardInfo)

Figure 17.13 Parts of the discourse-level scripts for an automated ordering application

The system would then use these definitions to help plan a series of utterances that define the object. Given an appropriate database, the system might plan the following speech acts given a query *What is a dog?*:

ConvinceByInform(Speaker, Hearer, SubType(Dog, Animal))
ConvinceByInform(Speaker, Hearer, Property(Dog, CommonPet))
ConvinceByInform(Speaker, Hearer, ExampleOf(Fido1, Dog))

which might produce the output

Dogs are animals. They are common pets. For example, Fido is a dog.

To be useful, even in limited applications, there would need to be many different strategies for defining classes and constraints on each class that would help determine which strategy is best to use for any particular task. For instance, some classes of objects might better be defined in terms of contrast and comparison with another class that the user already knows about.

In other applications, large discourse-level scripts might be used to determine the structure of dialogue. For instance, consider an automated ordering system that engages in a dialogue with a user to order items from a catalog. In this case there are several stages of the dialogue, involving obtaining the address and credit card number of the user, obtaining the order, and then giving the user information on delivery. Such a system might be driven by a top-level discourse script, as shown in Figure 17.13.

Of course, there may be many different actions defined to handle a wide range of circumstances. For instance, the *VerifyNumber* action would involve at least two scripts. One, when the number is valid, would simply involve the system acknowledging the information. The other, when the number is not valid, would involve further dialogue to reconfirm the number and possibly to obtain an alternative number. The use of the scripts allows the user to rapidly define and modify the behavior of the agent. The penalty paid is in generality. The system can only continue to behave appropriately as long as the user is in accordance with the script. For instance, if the user tries to order the items first and give the card afterwards, the system will not be able to understand the interaction (unless, of course, there is another script to cover this case). In other words, the system must control the development of the dialogue, and there is no possibility for mixed-initiative interaction where the user can control the flow of topics. But in some applications, like catalog ordering, such limitations are reasonable.

In more general dialogue applications, discourse-level plans become important for another reason. If the user is allowed to control the flow of the dialogue, then the system must be able to recognize what the user is doing. For instance, it must be able to recognize when the user is changing topics as opposed to continuing to talk about the current topic. And it must be able to identify when the user requires additional detail on a particular aspect of the previous dialogue. Such a system must be able to perform plan recognition at the discourse level to identify such behavior, and to relate this level of analysis to the recognition that is performed at the domain level.

Summary

To model a participant in a dialogue, you need to define a conversational agent. To do this requires defining the notions of belief, desire, and intention and relating these notions to planning models. Communication is a multi-agent activity and requires each agent to recognize the intentions of the other, especially those intentions relating to the communication process itself. A speech act can be defined as a form of communicative act. To identify the intended speech act, a system must take into account the structure of the utterance as well as the immediate context, especially what is shared knowledge about what the speaker and hearer know and want. Speech act models can be generalized to define a level of discourse plan that is useful for controlling dialogue systems in a wide range of applications.

Related Work and Further Readings

BDI models of agents have been studied primarily in the context of planning and acting systems (for example, Bratman, Israel, and Pollack (1988)). This work arose from a desire to clarify the nature of intentions, which had previously been ignored in planning work. Bratman (1987) argues that intentions are a primitive construct not reducible to beliefs and desires and that future-directed intentions are of primary importance in explaining rational behavior.

There is a considerable literature formalizing operators such as *Believe* and *Intend*. Most formal models of belief in the computational literature are derived from Hintikka (1969), who defined belief within a possible world semantics

(Kripke, 1963). A good example of a computational model of knowledge is that developed by Moore (1977). Two good examples of work formalizing intention and belief are Cohen and Levesque (1990a) and Rao and Georgeff (1991).

The database belief model described uses the techniques suggested by Moore (1973) and developed in detail by Cohen (1978). The resulting system was further refined and used in a system for recognizing speech acts by Allen and Perrault (1980). Konolige (1986) presents a formalization that generalizes the development here. The distinction between explicit beliefs and implicit beliefs is made by Levesque (1984). He develops a logic of explicit beliefs (the propositions you actually believe) based on a weakened set of inference rules, where the implicit beliefs (the propositions you could consistently believe) would be the deductive closure of the beliefs given their normal first-order semantics.

Austin (1962) introduced the concept of speech acts. He considered only explicit performatives for the most part. Searle (1975) used a theory of communication developed by Grice (1957) to develop a speech act theory for everyday acts such as informs, requests, and promises. Grice argued that the essential requirement for communication to occur is the speaker's intention to communicate and the hearer's recognition of that intention. Grice (1975) also introduced a set of guiding principles that underlie all communication (see Box 17.4). The necessity for mutual beliefs or shared knowledge is discussed in detail by Schiffer (1972) and Strawson (1964) in philosophy and is used for problems of reference by Perrault and Cohen (1981) and Clark and Marshall (1981).

A plan-based model of speech acts was suggested by Bruce (1975) and developed in a series of papers, starting with one by Cohen and Perrault (1979). This paper lays out the general principles of the approach and shows how speech acts can be planned in order to achieve goals using standard planning techniques. Cohen and Perrault did not, however, consider details of generating actual text from speech acts. Appelt (1985) extended this work to generate actual text. He developed techniques for eliminating unnecessary sentences by combining the information in multiple inform acts into a single sentence, and modeled the generation of referring phrases as a planning process.

Pollack (1990) emphasizes the difference between recognizing plans and recognizing intentions. She defines a model of intention recognition based on the inference of mental states, although the model of action is limited to the generation relation. Grosz and Sidner (1990) extend this work and use a notion of shared plans to account for discourse intentions.

Perrault and Allen (1980) developed a computational model of indirect speech acts using plan recognition from a literal meaning, drawing on the work by Searle (1975). They also showed how the same model could be used for planning helpful responses. Cohen and Levesque (1990b) develop a model of rational behavior in which indirect speech acts are not explicitly represented, but their properties fall out of the general model. Perrault (1990) describes a model of speech act interpretation that uses default logic. All practical systems, however, use explicit representations of indirect acts to enable effective recognition techniques (for example, Sidner (1985), Litman and Allen (1987; 1990), Carberry (1990), and Traum and Hinkelman (1992)). These systems encode common forms of indirect acts as part of the decomposition of discourse acts and recognize indirect interpretations using decomposition chaining. Litman and Allen (1987; 1990) also introduce a multi-level model of plans that uses discourse-level and domain-level plans simultaneously to interpret utterances.

Exercises for Chapter 17

1. (*easy*) Consider a situation where Jack is driving his car in one direction while Sue is driving her car in the other. Jack signals a left turn by sticking his hand out the window, and Sue understands the action. Analyze this communicative situation as done in Section 17.2. What is the locutionary act, the illocutionary act, and the perlocutionary act? What are the communicative conventions that allow this act to succeed?

2. (*easy*) For each of the following sentences, state whether it describes a desire, intention, plan-as-recipe, or is ambiguous. Justify your answer. Can you come up with linguistic tests that distinguish these three readings?

   a. Sue wants to pass with honors this year, but she also wants to leave town all through March to ski.
   b. Sue knows how to get good grades on her exams.
   c. Sue intends to study all night for her exam.
   d. Jack plans to go to the concert tonight.
   e. Jack has a plan to get into the concert tonight.
   f. Jack knows a plan to get into the concert tonight.

3. (*easy*) Many multi-agent action verbs allow a reading in which a sentence that normally would describe the entire action can be used to describe one agent's part. Thus you can say

   Jack gave Sue the money, but she wouldn't take it.

   which might be paraphrased as *Jack tried to give Sue the money, but she wouldn't take it.* In contrast, sentences describing single-agent actions are hard to interpret this way:

   *Jack ate the pizza, but it was too hot.

   The only readings of this would involve Jack eating the pizza (and possibly burning his mouth). It is difficult to read it as *Jack tried to eat the pizza, but it was too hot.* Use this argument to show that communicative acts described by verbs such as *inform* and *warn* are multi-agent actions. What does this test say about perlocutionary verbs such as *convince* and *scare*?

4. (*medium*) Draw out the representation of the following formulas using belief spaces:

a. $Bel(Jack1, Happy(Sue1))$
b. $Bel(Jack1, Owns(Jack1, Fido1))$
c. $Bel(Jack1, Bel(Sue1, \neg Happy(Sue1)))$
d. $Bel(Jack1, \exists x . Bel(Sue1, Age(Sue1, x)))$
e. $Bel(Jack1, Bel(Sue1, \exists x . Owns(Jack1, x)))$

Given this database, what would be the result of each of the following queries?

f. $Bel(Jack1, \exists x . Happy(x))$
g. $Bel(Jack1, \exists x . Bel(Sue1, \neg Happy(x)))$
h. $\exists x . Bel(Jack1, Bel(Sue1, Age(Sue1, x)))$
i. $Bel(Jack1, Bel(Sue1, \exists x . Age(Sue1, x)))$
j. $Bel(Jack1, \exists x . Bel(Sue1, Owns(Jack1, x)))$

5. (*medium*) Consider the speech act *Promise*. Can this communicative act be defined in terms of the modalities presented in this chapter, namely beliefs, desires, and intentions? If not, what additional modalities are needed? Give a definition of this action in the style used in Section 17.5. Why would a conversational agent need to plan promises in order to achieve its goals? Describe a situation in which a plan using a promise would be useful.

6. (*medium*) Does the definition of the *ConvinceByInform* act allow for a case in which an agent plans to lie? In particular, consider whether the constraint that the speaker believes the proposition should be removed from the definition of the communicative act. What would the hearer believe about the speaker's beliefs if the condition is kept? What would the hearer believe about the speaker's beliefs if it were removed? Which is a better analysis of the act of lying? Using the version you prefer, draw out a plan in which Jack lies about his age. In addition to the plan, show all of Jack's beliefs that are relevant, and show the beliefs that Sue would have if the lie were successful.

7. (*medium*) Complete the definitions of the actions needed to refine the *TakeOrder* action in Figure 17.13 down to the level of speech acts. Make up a dialogue that might occur over the telephone for ordering an item, and show how the dialogue follows your dialogue script. Do you need to extend the language for defining action decompositions in order to handle a wide range of dialogues?

8. (*hard*) Write a program for adding and testing simple propositional beliefs (allowing existentials), based on the algorithm descriptions in Section 17.3. Trace its operation in adding and testing the formulas corresponding to the facts in Exercise 4.

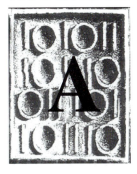

An Introduction to Logic and Model-Theoretic Semantics

A.1 Logic and Natural Language

A.2 Model-Theoretic Semantics

A.3 A Semantics for FOPC: Set-Theoretic Models

Logic has a long history, beginning before Aristotle. Modern logic, however, takes its form from the work of Frege in the late 19th century. The set-theoretic semantics for logic was developed by Tarski (1944). It is important to keep in mind here that there are many possible different notations for a logic, but the principles remain the same. In particular, many of the notations used in AI are expressively equivalent to the first-order predicate calculus (FOPC), or a subset of it. Section A.1 introduces the first-order predicate calculus, and Sections A.2 and A.3 develop a semantics for FOPC that defines the notion of truth.

A.1 Logic and Natural Language

Logic was developed as a formal notation to capture the essential properties of natural language and reasoning. As a consequence, many of the structural properties have a parallel in natural language. For instance, an important distinction is made between expressions that identify objects and expressions that assert properties of objects and identify relationships between objects. Noun phrases perform the first task in language, and sentences and clauses perform the second. In FOPC the same distinction is made between **terms**, which denote individuals or objects in the world, and **propositions**, which make claims about objects in the world.

There are two major classes of terms: **constants** and **functions**. The constants, which correspond most closely to proper names in language, will be written in italics, usually with one or more digits following, e.g., *John1, John2, C1,* and so on. Constants do not have any inherent meaning by themselves. Rather, their properties arise solely from the formulas in which they are used. There is an important difference between names in natural language and constants in FOPC: While natural language is ambiguous, each symbol in FOPC has a single meaning. The name *John* can be used in natural language to refer to many different people. This cannot happen in logic, which would require a unique constant to represent each different person.

Functions in FOPC correspond to noun phrases that refer to an object in terms of some property or relationship to other objects, such as *John's father* or *the king of Prussia.* They are written in FOPC as an expression consisting of a function name, which is a new sort of constant, followed by a list of arguments (other terms) enclosed in parentheses. For example, the function corresponding to *John's father* might be *father(John1).*

Simple propositions in FOPC consist of a predicate name, which is another sort of constant, and a list of arguments, which are terms, enclosed in parentheses. These correspond to simple sentences in natural language, where the predicate names correspond to the verbs. For example, the sentence *John likes his father* might correspond to the formula *Likes(John1, father(John1)).* More complex propositions are built out of simple ones using a set of logical operators, which have correlates in natural language. The simplest logical operator is the negation operator, written as ¬, which corresponds to one common use of negation in natural language. The sentence *John doesn't like his father* would correspond to the following formula:

$\neg Likes(John1, father(John1))$

Other logical operators correspond to some of the connectives found in language. For example, the connective *and* in language corresponds to a conjunction operator, written as &, in FOPC. The connective *or* in language is ambiguous between two logical operators. The first, called disjunction and written as $\vee$, corresponds to the interpretation of the sentence *John likes Sue or John likes Mary,* where it is allowed that he might like both of them. The second, called exclusive-or and written as $\oplus$, corresponds to the interpretation where he may like only one or the other, not both. Another important logical operator is the implication operator, written as $\supset$, which corresponds roughly to the language connective *if... then* in sentences such as *If John has no money, then he will not be able to buy a car.* Finally, the logical equivalence operator, written as $\equiv$, corresponds to the phrase *if and only if* in sentences such as *John will come to the party if and only if Sue comes.* In other words, either they both will come to the party, or neither of them will.

The final construct in FOPC involves quantified variables. A new term, known as a **logical variable**, is allowed in the logic, and two new operators are introduced to identify the way the variable is to be interpreted. The **existential quantifier**, written as $\exists$, is used for variables in sentences such as *There is a man who likes John,* which could be represented by the following formula:

$\exists x . MAN(x) \& Likes(x, John1)$

The **universal quantifier**, written as $\forall$, is used for variables in sentences such as *All men like John*, which could be represented by the following formula:

$\forall y . MAN(y) \supset Likes(y, John1)$

(that is, for all objects y, if y is a man then y likes John).

Since logical operators can be nested within each other, a potential ambiguity arises in formulas depending on what operator is within the scope of what other operator. For example, the formula

$\neg P \& Q$

could be read as the conjunction of two formulas ($\neg P$ and Q), or as the negation of the formula $P\&Q$. To eliminate this possible ambiguity, a convention is used where the negation operator always takes the smallest possible scope. If a wider scope is desired, then parentheses can be introduced. Thus the preceding formula takes the first interpretation described, whereas the second would be written as

$\neg(P \& Q)$

One other convenient notation was introduced earlier with the logical quantifiers. A dot (.) in a formula is used to indicate that the scope of the

Phrase	FOPC Equivalent
John	$John1$
John's father, the father of John	$father(John1)$
John likes his father	$Likes(John1, father(John1))$
John doesn't like his father	$\neg Likes(John1, father(John1))$
Either Sue is happy, or she is rich (or both)	$Happy(Sue1) \vee Rich(Sue1)$
Either Sue is rich, or she is poor	$Rich(Sue1) \oplus Poor(Sue1)$
Sue is happy and rich	$Happy(Sue1) \,\&\, Rich(Sue1)$
If Sue is rich, then she is happy	$Rich(Sue1) \supset Happy(Sue1)$
John is rich if and only if Sue is	$Rich(John1) \equiv Rich(Sue1)$
There is a fish in the pond	$\exists f. Fish(f) \,\&\, In(f, Pond44)$
All fish are in the pond	$\forall f. Fish(f) \supset In(f, Pond44)$

Figure A.1   The FOPC correlates of some natural language phrases

preceding operator extends to the end of the entire formula. This is a convenient way to eliminate deep nesting of parentheses. Consider the following formula, which corresponds to a reading of the sentence *Every boy likes some girl*:

$$\forall b . BOY(b) \supset \exists g . GIRL(g) \,\&\, Likes(b, g)$$

Without the dot convention this would be written as follows:

$$\forall b (BOY(b) \supset \exists g (GIRL(g) \,\&\, Likes(b, g)))$$

The notation is summarized in Figure A.1.

Inference: Logic as a Model of Thought

A primary motivation for developing FOPC is that it allows a precise formulation of the notions of inference and valid argument. For instance, you will recognize the following as an acceptable line of reasoning:

All dogs love bones and Fido is a dog. Thus Fido must love bones.

On the other hand, you will probably find the following argument faulty:

Some dogs have fleas and Fido is a dog. Thus Fido must have fleas.

Acceptable lines of reasoning can be stated in an abstract form called an **inference rule**. For example, the first argument just cited could be stated in FOPC as the following rule, where D is a predicate true only of dogs, and LB is a predicate true only of objects that like bones:

$$\forall x . D(x) \supset LB(x)$$
$$\underline{D(FIDO1)}$$
$$LB(FIDO1)$$

Implication-Elimination Rule
(or Modus Ponens)

$$p \supset q$$
$$\underline{p}$$
$$q$$

Universal-Elimination Rule

$$\forall x . px$$
$$\overline{}$$
$$pa$$

Figure A.2 Two inference rules

Step	Formula	Justification
1.	$\forall x . D(x) \supset LB(x)$	*premise*
2.	$D(FIDO1)$	*premise*
3.	$D(FIDO1) \supset LB(FIDO1)$	*univ-elim from step 1*
		(x replaced by FIDO1)
4.	$LB(FIDO1)$	*implication-elim from steps 2 and 3*

Figure A.3 A proof that Fido likes bones

This is read as follows: If the formula $\forall x . D(x) \supset LB(x)$ and the formula $D(FIDO1)$ are true, then the formula $LB(FIDO1)$ also must be true. An alternative way to read this, stated in computational terms, is as follows: To prove $LB(FIDO1)$, prove $D(FIDO1)$ and $\forall x . D(x) \supset LB(x)$.

In practice, inference rules are not specific to a particular predicate name; they are expressed using schemas in which parameters of the form p, q, r, s stand for arbitrary propositions, a, b, c stand for arbitrary terms, and x, y, z stand for arbitrary logical variables. If an index is added, as in p_x, then the parameter stands for an arbitrary proposition involving a term x. Two inference rules of FOPC that account for the earlier argument are shown in Figure A.2.

Multiple inference rules may be combined to derive conclusions by constructing a **proof**. A proof consists of a set of **premises** and a sequence of formulas, each derived from the previous formulas and the premises using some inference rule. For example, the simple argument about Fido loving bones can now be formally justified by the proof in Figure A.3.

In general, two inference rules are defined for every logical operator in the logic—the **elimination rule** and the **introduction rule**. Elimination rules take a formula that contains the connective as a premise and have a conclusion that does not contain the operator, while introduction rules take one or more premises that do not contain the operator and have a conclusion that contains the operator. While many of the rules can be expressed in the notation developed so far, some require an extension. These typically involve making some assumption and then showing that some other formula can then be proved or that a contradiction can be proved. A **contradiction** arises in a proof if there is a formula P such that the proof establishes both P and ¬P. For example, the rule of neg-introduction

Step	Formula	Justification
1.	$\neg LB(JACK1)$	*premise*
2.	$\forall x . D(x) \supset LB(x)$	*premise*
2.1.	$D(JACK1)$	*assumption for subproof*
2.2.	$D(JACK1) \supset LB(JACK1)$	*univ-elim from step 2*
2.3.	$LB(JACK1)$	*modus ponens from steps 2.1, 2.2*
2.4.	$\neg LB(JACK1)$	*reiterating step 1, revealing a contradiction*
3.	$\neg D(JACK1)$	*neg-introduction, steps 2.1, 2.3, 2.4*

Figure A.4 A proof deriving a negation via a contradiction

intuitively is as follows: To prove $\neg p$, assume p is true and show that this results in a contradiction. Suppose you are given that Jack does not love bones, and you want to prove that Jack is not a dog, given that all dogs love bones. You assume that Jack is a dog and show that this allows you to conclude that Jack loves bones, which contradicts your original premises. This proof is shown in Figure A.4, where the subproof based on the assumption is indented to separate it from the main proof. In step 2.1, the assumption is made, and a contradiction is derived in steps 2.3 and 2.4. Step 2.4 is simply copied from step 1 using a simple inference rule called **reiteration**, which allows a formula previously derived to be copied later in the proof. While not formally necessary, it allows for more intuitively clear proofs. In this case it allows us to point out the contradiction by placing steps 2.3 and 2.4 together.

A similar inference rule based on making assumptions is needed to formulate implication introduction, which is stated informally as follows: Assume p, and then, if you can derive q in the subproof, then you can conclude $p \supset q$. Another is needed for the rule of universal introduction. Some additional inference rules are shown in Figure A.5.

Given a set of inference rules, there will be formulas that can be proven starting with no premises. These are called **tautologies** or, more simply, **theorems** and reflect inherent properties of the logic itself. One fundamental theorem, given the system of inference rules, is the law of the excluded middle, which states that every proposition is either true or false (it can't be "undetermined"). This law states that any formula of the form

$$p \vee \neg p$$

must be true. It is very important to realize that this law does not say that a particular reasoning system can prove p or prove $\neg p$; all it says is that p is either true or false in actual fact.

Two important theorems are called De Morgan's Laws:

1. $\neg(p \,\&\, q) \equiv \neg p \vee \neg q$
2. $\neg(p \vee q) \equiv \neg p \,\&\, \neg q$

And-Introduction Rule

$$\frac{p}{q}$$
$$\frac{}{p \,\&\, q}$$

And-Elimination Rules

$$\frac{p \,\&\, q}{p} \qquad \frac{p \,\&\, q}{q}$$

Or-Introduction Rule

$$\frac{p}{p \lor q}$$

∃-Introduction Rule

$$\frac{p_a}{\exists x . Px}$$

Neg-Elimination Rule

$$\frac{\neg\neg p}{p}$$

Neg-Introduction Rule

$$\frac{\textit{assume } p}{\underline{\textit{derive } q \textit{ and } \neg q}}$$
$$\neg p$$

Figure A.5 Some additional inference rules

Using theorem 1, you can see that the law of the excluded middle, $p \lor \neg p$, is equivalent to $\neg(\neg p \,\&\, p)$; that is, any proposition p cannot simultaneously be true and false.

The syntactic description of legal formulas and the set of inference rules defines a rich framework in which many things can be proven. But this is not the most important point of logic for the present purposes. For these applications, the most important aspect of logic is that you can independently specify a notion of truth and assign a "meaning" to arbitrary formulas. This is the role of logical semantics, and it is the topic of the rest of this appendix.

A.2 Model-Theoretic Semantics

The aim of a formal semantics for logic is to be able to answer the following sorts of questions. Is there a definition of truth independent of what is provable from a set of axioms? How can you tell if a system contains enough inference rules? How can you tell if the set of inference rules proposed is reasonable—that they can't be used to "prove" things that are false? How can you tell if a set of axioms is coherent and could describe an actual situation? These questions can be answered by formalizing the notion of what an actual situation could be and showing how formulas in the logic map to assertions about that situation. Such situations will be called **models** of the logic, and the approach to semantics described here is called **model theory**.

First consider a subset of FOPC consisting solely of propositions and the logical connectives. In other words, there are no terms, no variables, and no quantifiers. This subset is usually called the **propositional calculus**. A model for the propositional calculus will map every propositional formula to the values T (for true) and F (for false). Such a model is constructed by specifying the mapping for all atomic propositions and then deriving the values for compound formulas using definitions of the logical operators. In other words, the logical operators are mapped to functions from truth values to a single truth value. As such, this method embodies the assumption that the meaning of the logical operators can be defined solely in terms of the truth values of their arguments and is independent of the actual propositions themselves. For example, suppose the propositions P and Q are true (both are mapped to T). Then if $P \& R$ is true for some proposition R, $Q \& R$ must also be true. The operator & is not affected by whether P or Q is its first argument, since both have identical truth values.

To define a model, you define a function V, called the **valuation function**, that maps formulas to the values T or F. For instance, given a logic containing one proposition P, there are only two possible distinct valuation functions, V_1 and V_2, such that $V_1(P) = T$, and $V_2(P) = F$. Given a logic with two propositions, P and Q, there are four possible valuation functions, and in general, given n propositions, there are 2^n possible valuation functions. Each valuation function defines a possible model of the logic.

Every valuation function has the following properties that recursively define the meaning of the logical operators:

V.1. $V_m(p \& q) = T$ if $V_m(p) = T$ and $V_m(q) = T$, and is F otherwise.
V.2. $V_m(\neg p) = T$ if $V_m(p) = F$, and is F otherwise.
V.3. $V_m(p \vee q) = T$ if $V_m(p) = T$ or if $V_m(q) = T$, and is F otherwise.
V.4. $V_m(p \supset q) = T$ if $V_m(p) = F$ or if $V_m(q) = T$, and is F otherwise.
V.5. $V_m(p \equiv q) = T$ if $V_m(p) = V_m(q)$, and is F otherwise.

The definitions V.1 through V.3 should agree readily with your initial intuitions when the operators were first defined using their natural language analogs. For instance, a conjunction $p \& q$ is true only if both p and q are true, which is exactly what rule V.1 says. The definition for implication in V.4, however, requires some explanation. Consider the sentence *If John was in the room, then he saw the murder.* If in fact John was not in the room, what is the truth value of this sentence? Stated more generally, what is the truth value of the formula $p \supset q$ when p is false? While there are several options available, each one defining a possible operator, the interpretation in common use, and the one assumed in constructing the inference rules for implication, is that $p \supset q$ is true in such cases. This is captured in rule V.4.

Given a model (that is, a valuation function), you can determine the truth values for any formulas in the propositional calculus with respect to that model. Consider the case of a logic with two propositions, P and Q. Exactly four models are possible, each capturing one of the possible ways to assign T or F to each of the propositions. These models are summarized in tabular form in Figure A.6, in which each row of truth values represents a single model. The truth values for simple formulas built from a single application of a logical connective are shown as well. All of these values are derived using rules V.1 through V.5. Inspecting the table, you can see a new way to demonstrate logical equivalence between

Model	P	Q	$\neg P$	$P\&Q$	$P \lor Q$	$P \supset Q$	$P \equiv Q$	$\neg P \lor Q$
1.	T	T	F	T	T	T	T	T
2.	T	F	F	F	T	F	F	F
3.	F	T	T	F	T	T	F	T
4.	F	F	T	F	F	T	T	T

Figure A.6   The possible models for P and Q

formulas. Rather than constructing a proof that the formula $P \supset Q$ is equivalent to the formula $\neg P \lor Q$, you can show that they have the same truth value in all possible models. Consider determining the truth value for these two formulas with respect to model 2 in Figure A.6. Using rule V.4, you see that the value for $P \supset Q$ is F. Using rule V.2, you see that the value of $\neg P$ is F, and via V.3 you see that the value of $\neg P \lor Q$ is F. Thus the two formulas have the same truth value in model 2. Similarly, they have the same truth values in all the other models as well. No matter what the valuation function, the two formulas have the same true value. Thus the formulas are logically equivalent.

So you now have two independent definitions of the logical operators: one using inference rules and the other using valuation functions. Can you show that both methods agree on all formulas? If so, you have gone a long way toward answering the questions posed at the beginning of this section.

The Relationship Between Logics and Semantics

Start by examining whether the inference rules are **sound**—that is, they can never be used to prove something unless it is true in all possible models. For example, consider the rule of modus ponens (implication elimination):

$$p \supset q$$
$$\underline{p}$$
$$q$$

While the inference rule is stated in terms of parameters ranging over propositions, you can instead consider the single case involving the propositions P and Q, since you are considering all possible combinations of truth values anyway. To show that this inference rule is sound, you need to show that in any possible model where the premises are true, the conclusion must hold as well. In this case, using P and Q for p and q, respectively, you see that $P \supset Q$ and P are true only in model 1 in Figure A.6, in which Q is also assigned T as well. The only model in which the premises are true also makes the conclusion true. Thus the rule is sound, at least in logics with only two propositions. It turns out, however, that additional propositions will not affect this argument one way or another, so the rule is sound given any number of propositions.

Model	P	Q	R	$\neg Q$	$Q\&R$	$P \supset (Q\&R)$
1.	T	T	T	F	T	T
2.	T	T	F	F	F	F
3.	T	F	T	T	F	F
4.	T	F	F	T	F	F
5.	F	T	T	F	T	T
6.	F	T	F	F	F	T
7.	F	F	T	T	F	T
8.	F	F	F	T	F	T

Figure A.7 The possible models for P, Q, and R

Another problem described earlier can now be solved. You can show that a given set of formulas is **consistent**—that is, that they could describe an actual situation—by finding a model that assigns every formula in the set to T. Such a model is said to **satisfy** the set of formulas. For example, you can show that the set of formulas

$$\{\neg P, P \vee Q, Q\}$$

is consistent because model 3 in Figure A.6 assigns each one of them to T. Conversely, you can show that the set of formulas

$$\{P \supset (Q \& R), P, \neg Q\}$$

is **inconsistent** because no model exists that assigns each of them to T simultaneously. The complete truth table for this example is shown in Figure A.7. As you can see, no model simultaneously assigns T to all three formulas.

We can now define the notion of a tautology:

A formula f is a tautology if every model assigns f to T.

As a simple example, consider the formula $P \vee \neg P$. Since it involves only one proposition, you need only consider two possible models: one in which P is assigned T and one in which P is assigned F. In either model the formula $P \vee \neg P$ is assigned T: if P is assigned T, then by rule V.3, $P \vee \neg P$ is assigned T; if, on the other hand, P is assigned F then $\neg P$ is assigned T and hence by rule V.3, $P \vee \neg P$ is assigned T. Thus $P \vee \neg P$ is a tautology.

There are two useful relationships that can be defined between formulas. The notion of **entailment** is defined as follows:

s entails p (written as $s \models p$) if and only if p is assigned T in all models that satisfy s

The notion of **provability** is defined as follows:

p can be proven from s (written as $s \vdash p$) if and only if there is a proof of p with s as its only premise

The final question to consider is whether you can show that a given set of inference rules is sufficient to allow all true formulas to be proven. In other words, if, by using the model theory, you can show that some formula p is true in all models, then you want to show that p is provable using the inference rules defined for the logic. Using the previously defined notation of entailment, this would mean that whenever s entails p (that is, $s \models p$), then p can be proven from s (that is, $s \vdash p$). Such a proof system is said to be **complete**. Completeness can be shown for a wide variety of different sets of inference rules. Of most importance to computational approaches, the resolution method specifies a single inference rule that can be proven to be complete. That is, every true formula can be proven using repeated applications of the resolution rule.

A.3 A Semantics for FOPC: Set-Theoretic Models

A semantics for the first-order predicate calculus requires an extension of the notion of a model and is most conveniently expressed in terms of set theory. The complications arise because the meanings of other expressions besides propositions must be defined. The terms in FOPC do not represent truth values but rather physical objects, events, times, locations, and so on. All these objects are considered to be members of a set of objects called the **domain**. In general, every model can have a different domain. To simplify the presentation here, however, we will assume that all models have the same domain, written as Σ.

In the propositional calculus, the valuation function mapped propositional symbols to T or F. In FOPC, propositions themselves have a structure, and the valuation function must define the interpretation of constants, functions, and predicate names. In particular, the valuation function maps each term into some element in the domain. Consider a domain Σ consisting of the three elements α, σ, and δ, and a model in which the valuation function V_1 is defined as follows for three terms $A1$, $B1$, and $C1$:

$$V_1(A1) = \alpha; \ V_1(B1) = \sigma; \ \text{and } V_1(C1) = \delta$$

The valuation function also maps predicate names to different types of sets depending on the number of arguments it takes. For the moment, consider only unary predicates, such as RED, which map to a subset of Σ (that is, those objects specified to be red). For instance, let us assume that the model defines the predicate RED as the set $\{\alpha, \sigma\}$:

$$V_1(RED) = \{\alpha, \sigma\}$$

The truth value of simple propositions built from a unary predicate name and an argument can now be defined by the following rule (where P is any unary predicate name and a is any term):

$$V_m(P(a)) = T \text{ if } V_m(a) \text{ is a member of } V_m(P), \text{ and F otherwise}$$

Model	$A1$	$B1$	$C1$	RED	$RED(A1)$	$RED(B1)$	$RED(C1)$
1.	α	σ	δ	$\{\alpha\}$	T	F	F
2.	α	α	σ	$\{\alpha\}$	T	T	F
3.	α	σ	δ	$\{\alpha\}$	T	F	F
4.	α	α	α	$\{\alpha, \delta\}$	T	T	T
5.	α	α	σ	$\{\alpha, \delta\}$	T	T	F
6.	α	α	α	$\{\alpha, \delta\}$	T	T	T
7.	α	α	α	$\{\delta, \sigma\}$	F	F	F
8.	α	α	σ	$\{\delta, \sigma\}$	F	F	F
9.	α	σ	δ	$\{\delta, \sigma\}$	F	F	F

Figure A.8 Some possible models assuming the domain $\Sigma = \{\alpha, \delta, \sigma\}$

Given the definition of V_1 and the rule defining the truth value of propositions constructed from unary predicate names, it is easy to see that

$$V_1(P(A1)) = T; V_1(P(B1)) = T; \text{ and } V_1(P(C1)) = F$$

Just as in the propositional case, you could construct truth tables for all possible models. Figure A.8 shows some of the possible models for the logic with the three constants and the one predicate name RED, assuming the domain Σ. As you can see, the truth table method is unwieldy for the predicate calculus because there are so many possible models. The full table would have 216 entries.

A valuation function maps a predicate name P that takes n arguments to a set of lists of elements of length n. For example, the binary predicate $Loves$ might be defined in V_1 as follows (where α loves δ and σ loves δ):

$$V_1(Loves) = \{(\alpha\ \delta), (\sigma\ \alpha)\}$$

The rule defining the truth value of simple propositions built out of n-ary predicates is defined as follows (where P is any n-argument predicate name, and $a_1, ..., a_n$ are any terms):

$V(P(a_1, ..., a_n)) = T$ if $(V(a_1)... V(a_n))$ is a member of $V(P)$,
     and F otherwise

We can now determine the truth of formulas with respect to model 1, for example:

$$V_1(Loves(A1, B1)) = F; V_1(Loves(B1, A1)) = T; V_1(Loves(A1, C1)) = T$$

Once the different valuation function for propositions has been defined, the rules for defining the logical operators are identical to those defined for the propositional calculus. Thus we can calculate the assignment that V_1 gives to formulas such as $\neg(Red(A1) \vee Loves(A1, B1))$, as shown in Figure A.9.

Expression e	$V_1(e)$
$A1$	α
$B1$	σ
Red	$\{\alpha\}$
$Loves$	$\{(\alpha\delta),(\sigma\alpha)\}$
$Red(A1)$	T
$Loves(A1, B1)$	F
$Red(A1) \vee Loves(A1, B1)$	T
$\neg(Red(A1) \vee Loves(A1, B1))$	F

Figure A.9   Computing the valuation of $\neg(Red(A1) \vee Loves(A1, B1))$ for model 1

The Semantics for Quantifiers

To define the semantics of formulas with quantified variables, we need the ability to make substitutions for variables in formulas. This can be done by augmenting the notion of a valuation function with what is called a variable substitution. Let us define $V_i\{x/\alpha\}$ to be an extended valuation function that is identical to V_i except that it defines the valuation of variable x to the domain constant α. For example, given the previously defined valuation function V_1,

$$V_{1\{x/\alpha\}}(x) = \alpha$$
$$V_{1\{x/\alpha\}}(Red) = V_1(Red) = \{\alpha\}$$

Thus $V_{1\{x/\alpha\}}(Red(x)) = T$, since $V_{1\{x/\alpha\}}(x)$ is a member of $V_{1\{x/\alpha\}}(Red)$.

With the notion of variable substitutions, the semantics of formulas involving quantifiers is defined by the following rules on valuation functions:

$$V_m(\forall x . P) = T \text{ if for every element } \alpha \text{ in } \Sigma, V_{m\{x/\alpha\}}(P) = T$$
$$V_m(\exists x . P) = T \text{ if there is at least one } \alpha \text{ in } \Sigma \text{ such that } V_{m\{x/\alpha\}}(P) = T$$

Intuitively, this is saying that a formula such as $\forall x . P$ is true if and only if the formula P is true no matter what value the variable x takes, and a formula such as $\exists x . P$ is true if and only if there is at least one value of x that makes P true.

All of the preceding definitions of soundness, consistency, completeness, and so on carry over to the semantics for FOPC without change. For instance, you can show that a set of formulas is consistent by constructing a model that makes each one true. For example, consider the following set of formulas:

$$\{\forall x . Q(x) \supset R(x), Q(A1), Q(B1), \neg Q(C1)\}$$

A model can be constructed for these formulas as follows: Let Σ be the set $\{\sigma, \delta, \phi\}$ where $V(A1) = \sigma$, $V(B1) = \delta$, and $V(C1) = \phi$. Let $V(Q) = \{\sigma, \delta\}$ and $V(R) = \{\sigma, \delta, \phi\}$. Now you see that each of the preceding formulas evaluates to T given this model.

Related Work and Further Readings

A good text on logic and its relevance to linguistics is McCawley (1993). An excellent comprehensive source on logic and the use of other formal models in linguistics is Partee et al. (1990). Many introductory AI texts also discuss logic. Good examples are Luger and Stubblefield (1993), Winston (1992), Rich and Knight (1992), and Genesereth and Nilsson (1987). There are many good introductory texts in logic, although many emphasize proof theory and do not deal with semantics. Barwise and Etchemendy (1987) give an excellent introduction, complete with an interactive program that allows you to explore issues in logic.

Exercises for Appendix A

1. (*easy*) Assume *Sam is Bill's father* is represented by *FatherOf(Bill, Sam)*, and *Harry is one of Bill's ancestors* is represented by *Ancestor(Bill, Harry)*. Define the other predicates necessary, and then write a formula to represent the meaning of the sentence *Every ancestor of Bill is either his father, his mother, or one of their ancestors.*

2. (*easy*) Give two English sentences that seem difficult to express in predicate calculus and discuss why you think this is so.

3. (*easy*) Define the valuation function that defines the semantics of the exclusive-or operator as defined in this appendix, and then show that the following rules of inference are sound.

$$\frac{\begin{array}{c} p \oplus q \\ p \end{array}}{\neg q} \qquad \frac{\begin{array}{c} p \oplus q \\ \neg p \end{array}}{q}$$

4. (*easy*) For each of the following sets of formulas, determine whether or not the formulas are consistent by constructing a truth table.

$$S1 = \{P, \neg P\}$$
$$S2 = \{P \supset Q, \neg P, \neg Q\}$$
$$S3 = \{P \supset Q, Q \supset R, \neg P, R, \neg Q\}$$
$$S4 = \{P \vee Q, \neg P \& \neg Q\}$$

5. (*medium*) Express the following facts in FOPC and give a proof of the conclusion. If necessary, add common-sense axioms so that the conclusion follows from the given assumptions.

   a. Assumptions: Tomorrow it will either be warm and sunny or cold and rainy. Tomorrow it will be sunny.
   Conclusion: Tomorrow it will be warm.

   b. Assumptions: Tweety is a bird. Tweety eats all good food. Sunflower seeds are good food.
   Conclusion: There is a bird that eats sunflower seeds.

Symbolic Computation

This appendix introduces some of the basic techniques of symbolic computation. The text assumes familiarity with some programming language but not necessarily one that deals with symbolic data. If you are familiar with the languages LISP or PROLOG, Section B.1 may be safely skipped. If, in addition, you have some background in AI and know the unification algorithm, you may be able to skip the entire appendix. Section B.2 deals with matching and unification. Section B.3 describes basic ideas of search techniques, and Section B.4 combines the techniques of matching and search in discussing PROLOG. Finally, Section B.5 presents the unification algorithm in detail.

B.1 Symbolic Data Structures

This text uses many different data structures to represent the results of different forms of analyses. All of these structures are built from a simple data structure called a **list**, on which the programming language LISP is based. A simple list is built of a sequence of expressions called **atoms**, which are simply sequences of characters. For example,

(A Happy TOAD)

is a list consisting of three atoms—A, Happy, and TOAD. The only property that atoms have is that they can be distinguished by their names. Thus we know that the atom Happy and the atom TOAD are distinct atoms because they are constructed out of different characters. Atoms do not have to be English words; the following is also a valid list of five atoms:

(R3 forty XX3Y7 AAA1 ?X3)

A list in general may contain not only atoms but also other lists. The following is a valid list consisting of four **elements**: the atom NP, the list (DET the), the list (ADJ happy), and the list (HEAD toad):

(NP (DET the) (ADJ happy) (HEAD toad))

You will see many structures like this later. This one could be a syntactic representation of the English noun phrase *the happy toad*.

There is no limit to how many times a list may be embedded in another list. Thus

(((A TWO) (B THREE)) (((D)) E))

is a valid list. Taking it apart, you can see that it is a list consisting of two elements: the list ((A TWO) (B THREE)) and the list (((D)) E). The second element is itself a list consisting of two elements: the list ((D)) and the atom E. The element ((D)) is also a list, consisting of one element, the list (D), which consists of one element, the atom D.

The list containing one atom, such as (D), is very different from the atom—that is, D. These might have completely different interpretations by a program.

First((A B C))	equals	A
First(((A B) C))	equals	(A B)
First(((A B C)))	equals	(A B C)
Rest((A B C))	equals	(B C)
Rest(((A B) C))	equals	(C)
Rest(((A B C)))	equals	( ), the empty list

Figure B.1 Examples of list operations

Insert(A, (B C))	equals	(A B C)
Insert((A B), (C))	equals	((A B) C)
Insert((A B C), ( ))	equals	((A B C))
Append((A), (B C))	equals	(B C A)
Append(((A B)), (C))	equals	(C (A B))
Append((A B C), ( ))	equals	(A B C)

Figure B.2 Examples of list constructors

The list containing no elements, written as ( ), is a valid list and may itself be an element of another list. It is called the **null** or **empty list**, and is often written as NIL or nil.

There are two basic operations used for taking a list apart: First and Rest. Figure B.1 shows the results of applying these functions to various lists.

First(<list>)—takes any list and returns its first element. It is undefined on the empty list and on atoms.

Rest(<list>)—takes a list and produces the list consisting of all elements but the first one. It is also not defined on atoms or on the empty list.

There are two basic functions for constructing lists: Insert and Append. Figure B.2 shows these functions used in various situations.

Insert(<atom>, <list>)—returns a new list with <atom> as the first element, followed by the elements in <list>.

Append(<list1>, <list2>)—returns a new list consisting of the elements of <list2> followed by <list1>.

Finally, some tests are useful for examining lists. These tests return a value of TRUE or FALSE depending on the structure of their arguments, and are usable in **if-then-else** type statements:

Null(<list>)—TRUE only if the <list> is the empty list.

Member(<atom>, <list>)—TRUE only if <atom> is an element of the <list>.

Member(A, (A B C))	is	TRUE
Member(A, ((A) B C))	is	FALSE
Member((A), (A B C))	is	FALSE
Member((A), ((A) B C))	is	TRUE
Member(B, (A B C))	is	TRUE
Member(B, (A B C B))	is	TRUE
Member(B, ((A B) C))	is	FALSE

Figure B.3 Examples of the Member predicate

Operation	**LISP Equivalent**
First((A B C))	(CAR '(A B C))
Rest((A B C))	(CDR '(A B C))
Insert(A, (B C))	(CONS 'A '(B C))
Append((A), (B C))	(APPEND '(B C) '(A))
Null((A))	(NULL '(A))
Member(A, (A B C))	(MEMBER 'A '(A B C))

Figure B.4 LISP equivalents

Multiple occurrences of an atom in a list are allowed, and the Member predicate will return TRUE in such situations. Member succeeds only if the atom is an element of the list, not if the atom occurs within an embedded sublist. Figure B.3 shows examples.

While this book can be understood without a knowledge of the LISP language, the LISP equivalents to these functions and predicates are shown in Figure B.4 for those who are interested. Further details on LISP can be found in textbooks such as Wilensky (1986) and Winston and Horn (1989).

Stacks and Queues

In the algorithms outlined in this text you will often use data structures named **stacks** and **queues**. These can be built simply from list structures but are important enough to consider separately. A stack is a list in which all adding and removing of elements takes place at one end, called the **top** of the stack. This is analogous to a stack of trays in a cafeteria: When a tray is returned, it is put on the top; when a tray is taken, it is removed from the top. So at any time, the tray just removed is always the last one that was added. For this reason, stacks are also often called LIFO (last in/first out) lists.

Stacks will be used in algorithms to keep track of items that need considering by the program. The general organization of such a program looks as follows:

1. Initialize the stack with one or more items.
2. Repeat the following until the answer is found:

2.1. Remove the top item of stack.
2.2. Consider the item.
2.3. Add any new items to be considered onto the stack.

In general, the operation of adding an item to the stack is called **pushing** the item onto the stack, while removing an item is called **popping** the stack.

A more concrete example of a stack organization is the "in" tray in an office. The person in the office might operate as follows:

1. Letters are added to tray overnight.
2. Repeat until no letters:
   2.1. Remove top letter.
   2.2. Read it and reply.
   2.3. If new letters arrive in the meantime, add them to the tray.

Of course, if more letters are arriving than the person can read, some letters that arrived overnight might never get read. Thus sometimes a different data structure is needed.

A queue is a list in which all adding is done at one end, and all removing is done at the other end. This is analogous to a queue in a bank. People enter at the end of the line, while the people at the front get served. This scheme is often called a FIFO queue (first in/first out), since the first person to arrive is the first one served.

If the harried office worker above used a queue instead of a stack to organize the letters, he or she would eventually get to all the letters that arrived overnight, even though new letters arrived at an ever-increasing rate. Similar considerations will arise later in algorithms when you have to decide whether to use a stack or a queue structure.

B.2 Matching

Most of the techniques discussed throughout will involve some notion of matching lists together. The simplest match between two lists is whether they are identical. To obtain more general forms of matching, you need to allow **variables** in lists, which can match any element. Variables will be indicated by atoms with a ? prefix.

A variable may match any atom, sublist, or another variable. Thus a list with a variable, such as (A ?x C), could match (A B C), (A (B C) C), or (A ?z C), but could not match (A B D C), since ?x can take the place only of a single element.

It is often useful to know what a variable matched against. We say that a variable is **bound** to the value that it matched. Thus, in the preceding examples, ?x would have been bound to B, (B C), and ?z, respectively, on the three successful matches. These results are summarized in Figure B.5.

Given this background, you can now define the concept of matching more precisely as follows:

List 1	List 2	Match Result	Bindings
(A ?x C)	(A B C)	success	?x ← B
(A ?x C)	(A (B C) C)	success	?x ← (B C)
(A ?x C)	(A ?z C)	success	?x ← ?z
(A ?x C)	(A B D C)	failure	-------

Figure B.5 Some simple examples of matching with variables

	Bindings	Result
1.	?x ← ?z	(A ?z C)
2.	?x ← B, ?z ← B	(A B C)
3.	?x ← C, ?z ← C	(A C C)

Figure B.6 Three possible unifications of (A ?x C) and (A ?z C)

Two lists are said to **unify** if there is a set of bindings for the variables in the lists such that, if you replace the variables with their bindings, the two lists are identical.

Given that two lists unify, there may be many possible bindings that make them identical. For example, in unifying (A ?x C) with (A ?z C), there are many possible bindings for ?x and ?z, as shown in Figure B.6. When this arises, there is always one set of bindings that produces a new list that could unify with all the other solutions. This one is called the **most general unifier**. In Figure B.6, result 1 is the most general unifier because it could unify with results 2 and 3. Neither 2 nor 3 can be most general because they do not match with each other. If two lists unify, there is always a most general unifier, and it can be found reasonably efficiently using an algorithm called the **unification algorithm**.

Consider some more complex cases of unification. These arise when the same variable is used more than once in a list. In such cases some possible matches that look like they might succeed don't, because there is no single value for the variable that will make the two lists identical. The list (A ?x ?x), for example, does not unify with (A B C) because ?x would have to match both B and C. If ?x was bound to B, the first list would become (A B B), which is not identical to (A B C). Similarly, if ?x was bound to C, the first list would become (A C C), which is not identical to (A B C).

More complex examples can occur with sublists. For example, (A ?x C) will match (A (f ?y) C), since you can bind ?x to (f ?y) and the lists are identical. Furthermore, (A ?x C) would match (A (f ?y) ?y), since if you let ?x ← (f C) and ?y ← C, both lists become (A (f C) C).

Informally, you can match two lists by going through each list element by element. Every time a variable must be bound, rewrite each formula with every

To match (A ?x C ?x) with (A (f ?y) ?y ?z):

1. First elements are: A and A

2. Second elements are: ?x and (f ?y)
   Bind ?x to (f ?y), rewrite the two formulas to
   (A (f ?y) C (f ?y)) and (A (f ?y) ?y ?z)

3. Continue with third elements: C and ?y
   Bind ?y to C, rewrite the two formulas to
   (A (f C) C (f C)) and (A (f C) C ?z)

4. Continue with fourth elements: (f C) and ?z
   Bind ?z to (f C), rewrite the two formulas to
   (A (f C) C (f C)) and (A (f C) C (f C))

The lists are identical, so they unify.

Figure B.7   An informal trace of a unification procedure

To match (A ?x C ?x) with (A (f ?y) ?y ?y):

1. First elements are: A and A

2. Second elements are: ?x and (f ?y)
   Bind ?x to (f ?y), rewrite the formulas to
   (A (f ?y) C (f ?y)) and (A (f ?y) ?y ?y)

3. Third elements are: C and ?y
   Bind ?y to C, rewrite the formulas to
   (A (f C) C (f C)) and (A (f C) C C)

4. Fourth elements are: (f C) and C

Failure, since these cannot be made identical.

Figure B.8   An informal trace of a failure to unify

occurrence of the variable replaced by its new binding, and continue matching. If you are careful not to bind a variable unnecessarily, you will produce a most general unifier. Figures B.7 and B.8 contain a trace of this process on two situations: one a success and one a failure. The unification algorithm is presented in detail in Section B.5.

B.3 Search Algorithms

Virtually all AI programs use some form of search to find the desired solution. In fact, one area of research in AI expressly studies different search algorithms. This section describes some of the basic ideas underlying search algorithms.

Viewed abstractly, all search algorithms operate by exploring a space of different possible **states** to find some state that satisfies the **goal** of the search. For instance, in a program that plays chess, a state would represent a board

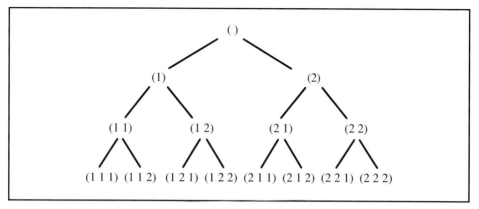

Figure B.9 The search space for a simple combination lock

position in the game. The goal would be to find a state where the program has checkmated the opponent. To search for a winning state, the program applies a transition function that takes one state and produces another. In a chess-playing program the transition function would be defined by the moves of chess. Given one state, the program computes a new state that results from a particular move. Typically, a program will consider the set of states that would result from every possible move. These states are called the **successor states**.

Chess is a very complex game and produces a correspondingly complex search space, so let's consider a much simpler example. Say you want to find the combination to a friend's locker. You could randomly try combinations and hope to get lucky, but if you want to systematically consider all possibilities, you must decide on a particular search strategy. We can formalize the problem as a state space search as follows. A state is a list representing the numbers you have dialed so far. A move is accomplished by dialing another number, producing a new state that is represented by appending the new number onto the original state. Assume that we don't know how many numbers need to be dialed. To make the example manageable, also assume that the combination only has two numbers, 1 and 2, on the dial. Figure B.9 shows the space of states involving up to three numbers. From the initial state ( ), you can dial either a 1 or a 2. Thus there are two successor states, (1) and (2), shown in the figure. From each of these, you can try a second number. Thus each has two successor states, and so on. Many different search strategies can be explored within a single general scheme that maintains a list of the states that still remain to be explored. The general algorithm is as follows. Let TODO be a list of the states that you need to consider.

1. Initialize TODO to a list containing only the initial state (( )).
2. Repeat until the goal state is found:
   2.1. Remove a state from the TODO list.
   2.2. Check if it is the goal state (does it open the locker?).
   2.3. If not, generate all successors and add them to the TODO list.

Depending on the different strategies used for selecting the next state to be processed, different search strategies are produced. There are two basic strategies. The first, **depth-first search**, uses a stack for the TODO list. Thus it always selects the last state to be added to the stack for further processing. Consider this strategy in operation on the combination lock problem, where the actual combination is (2 1 1). Initially, TODO contains only the initial state ( ). Two successors are generated and added to the list, namely (1) and (2). After adding them, TODO has the value ((1) (2)). State (1) is selected next. It is found not to be the goal state (that is, it does not open the locker), so two successor states, (1 1) and (1 2), are generated and added to the TODO list, which is now ((1 1) (1 2) (2)). The state (1 1) is selected next, and after failing to open the locker, two successor states, (1 1 1) and (1 1 2), are generated and added to the TODO list, which is now ((1 1 1) (1 1 2) (1 2) (2)). Given that (1 1 1) is not the combination, the successor states (1 1 1 1) and (1 1 1 2) are added to the TODO list. By now you may have noticed that unless the algorithm places an upper limit on how many numbers need to be dialed, this strategy will never find the solution.

The other basic strategy, called **breadth-first search**, treats TODO as a queue rather than a stack. Thus successor states are added to the end of the TODO list. Starting again from the state ( ), the TODO list takes the following values as the algorithm operates:

((1) (2))
((2) (1 1) (1 2))
((1 1) (1 2) (2 1) (2 2))
((1 2) (2 1) (2 2) (1 1 1) (1 1 2))
((2 1) (2 2) (1 1 1) (1 1 2) (1 2 1) (1 2 2))
and so on

You can see that the two strategies explore the space in quite different orders. If you follow the search strategies by tracing the states considered on the tree representing the search space in Figure B.9, you will see that the depth-first strategy quickly moves down the tree exploring states at ever deeper levels. The breadth-first strategy, on the other hand, systematically explores each possibility at one level of the tree before considering the states at the next level.

With a finite search space (for example, we might specify that the combination has at most four digits, so a state such as (1 1 1 1) has no successors), the depth-first strategy will often find a solution faster. With infinite search spaces, however, as in the unconstrained combination lock problem, the depth-first strategy is not guaranteed to find a solution, as it might search down an infinite chain of successor states that does not contain a solution. The breadth-first strategy is guaranteed to find a solution if one exists.

Many other search strategies are possible. A strategy called **iterative deepening** acts like a depth-first strategy except that it stops when it reaches a certain depth in the tree. If no solution is found at that depth, it increases the depth and repeats. While this involves duplication of work, it turns out to be better overall than either the pure depth-first or breadth-first strategies. Alternatively, you might use a heuristic search, in which the next state is chosen based on some heuristic information. For instance, if you believe that the combination most likely involves a sequence that does not repeat digits consecutively, you might always choose a state without a repetition if possible, and only consider the others if there are no other possibilities. You might add states involving repetitions to the end of the TODO list, and the others to the front.

```
((1) (2))
((1 2) (2) (1 1))
((1 2 1) (2) (1 1) (1 2 2))
and so on
```

A general formulation for heuristic search is often called **best-first search**. This strategy uses a function that returns a heuristic value for each state. At any iteration of the search, you select the state that has the highest value.

B.4 Logic Programming

Many natural language applications are implemented in the programming language PROLOG, or in extensions built on top of PROLOG. PROLOG turns out to be a useful tool, as it builds in the notions of unification and search. Thus it provides the basic building blocks necessary for many AI applications.

PROLOG is built on the notion of a **Horn clause**, which can be defined as a logical implication in which the left side of the implication is a single simple proposition. Thus the expression

```
friendly(fido1) :- dog(fido1) well-fed(fido1)
```

in PROLOG corresponds to the assertion that Fido is friendly if he is a dog and is well fed. This would be expressed in FOPC as

$$(Dog(Fido1) \ \& \ Well\text{-}Fed(Fido1)) \supset Friendly(Fido1)$$

Of course, more useful rules would use variables to apply to a range of objects. The general statement that dogs that are well fed are friendly would be expressed as follows, where variables are indicated by symbols beginning with an upper-case letter:

1.   friendly(X) :- dog(X) well-fed(X)

This is equivalent to the FOPC assertion $\forall x \ (DOG(x) \ \& \ WELL\text{-}FED(x)) \supset FRIENDLY(x)$. In PROLOG it is interpreted procedurally: For any object x, to prove that x is friendly, prove that x is a dog and that x is well fed.

Horn clauses without a right side are called **facts**. To assert that Fifi is a dog that is well fed, you would add the facts

2.   dog(fifi) :-
3.   well-fed(fifi) :-

Using clauses 1, 2, and 3, PROLOG can now prove that Fifi is friendly as follows:

Goal: Friendly(fifi)

Using the unification algorithm, clause 1 is specialized to apply to the goal (that is, the variable X is bound to fifi)

4.　friendly(fifi) :- dog(fifi) well-fed(fifi)

To prove the goal in light of this rule, it must prove the subgoals

5.　Goal: dog(fifi)
6.　Goal: well-fed(fifi)

Since these subgoals are asserted in clauses 2 and 3, the proof of each is trivial, and the original goal is proved.

In general, many different rules might apply to a goal. They will be tried in turn until one succeeds. As another example, consider the following axioms:

All fish live in the sea.
7.　live-in-sea(X) :- fish(X)
All cod are fish.
8.　fish(X) :- cod(X)
All mackerel are fish.
9.　fish(X) :- mackerel(X)
Whales live in the sea.
10.　live-in-sea(X) :- whale(X)
Homer is a cod.
11.　mackerel(homer) :-
Willie is a whale.
12.　whale(willie) :-

Given these axioms, a system can prove that Willie lives in the sea as follows, using what is called a **backtracking** search. It uses a depth-first search strategy to systematically search through every possible sequence of applying clauses to see if the goal can be established. Figure B.10 shows a trace of a typical PROLOG search given the previously given clauses and the goal

live-in-sea(willie)

The best way to get a feeling for PROLOG is to play with the system and use the tracing facility to explore exactly how it operates. PROLOG systems are readily available for most types of workstations and personal computers.

B.5　The Unification Algorithm

This section presents the unification algorithm in detail. Remember that two arbitrary lists containing constants and variables unify if there is a set of bindings for the variables that make the lists identical.

G1: live-in-sea(willie)
    Trying clause 7, which after unification with G1 is
        live-in-sea(willie) :- fish(willie)
    This creates a new subgoal G2.
        G2: fish(willie)
            Rule 8 applies, giving
                fish(willie) :- cod(willie)
            so there is a new subgoal
                G3: cod(willie)
                × No rule applies, try other ways to prove G2
            Rule 9 applies, giving
                fish(willie) :- mackerel(willie)
            so there is a new subgoal
                G4: mackerel(willie)
                × No rule applies, try other ways to prove G2
            × No other rules apply to G2, try other ways to prove G1
    Rule 10 applies giving
        live-in-sea(willie) := whale(willie)
    So there is a new subgoal
    G5: whale(willie)
        Fact 12 unifies with G5
        √ Thus Goal G5 is Proved.
  √ Goal G1 is Proved.

Figure B.10 A proof of live-in-sea(willie)

The values of variables can be stored in a data structure called the **symbol table**, or ST. Suppose you have an ST as follows:

variable	value
?x	A
?y	?z
?z	B

This would mean that ?x has the value A and ?y has the value ?z, and ?z has the value B (thus ?y has the value B). Two functions need to be defined:

ADD-TO-ST(varname, value)—adds a new entry onto the ST.
GET-VALUE(varname)—returns the value for a variable.

GET-VALUE should check the symbol table repeatedly to find the most specific value for a variable. For example, GET-VALUE(?y) with the preceding ST should return B. If the variable has no entry on the ST, the variable name is returned. Thus, given the preceding table, GET-VALUE(?t) should return ?t.

With these tools the matching algorithm between two formulas T1 and T2 is defined in Figure B.11. Rather than rewriting the formulas each time a variable

To MATCH T1 and T2

1. **If** T1 is a variable,
    then assign T1 to GET-VALUE(T1)

2. **If** T2 is a variable
    then assign T2 to GET-VALUE(T2)

3. **If** T1 = T2
    then return SUCCESS
    else if T1 is a variable
        then ADD-TO-ST(T1, T2) and **return** SUCCESS
        else if T2 is a variable
            then ADD-TO-ST(T2, T1) and **return** SUCCESS
            else if T1 and T2 are both lists
                then if MATCH(First(T1), First(T2)) succeeds
                    then return result from MATCH(Rest(T1), Rest(T2))
                    else return FAIL
                else return FAIL

Figure B.11 A preliminary matching algorithm

binding is found, the information is stored in the symbol table. If MATCH succeeds, it returns SUCCESS and the symbol table contains the variable values.

Steps 1 and 2 in Figure B.11 find the values of variables if they are already known. Step 3 does the actual matching. If one of the formulas is still a variable, that variable can be bound to the value of the other formula. Finally, if T1 and T2 are both list structures, it checks each element to make sure each list matches. As an example, consider the trace of the algorithm in Figure B.12, matching the formula (A ?y ?z) with the formula (?x (B ?x) ?x), starting with an empty ST.

The final result is SUCCESS, and the ST is set to the following:

variable	value
?x	A
?y	(B ?x)
?z	A

If you **instantiate** the variables in one of the formulas with the values in the ST, you will get the answer, which is (A (B A) A). Note that ?y is bound to (B ?x), but ?x is bound to A, so ?y is actually bound to the value (B A).

One minor problem is left to resolve. If you were to try to match the formula (P ?x ?x) with (P (f ?y) ?y) with the present algorithm, it would succeed with the following ST:

variable	value
?x	(f ?y)
?y	(f ?y)

MATCHING (A ?y ?z) with (?x (B ?x) ?x)

Both are lists, so
    MATCHING A with ?x
    ← returns SUCCESS, and the ST now has the value A for ?x
    MATCHING (?y ?z) with ((B ?x) ?x)
        Both are lists, so
            MATCHING ?y with (B ?x)
            ← returns SUCCESS, and ST now has value (B ?x) for ?y
            MATCHING (?z) with (?x)
                Both are lists, so
                    MATCHING ?z with ?x
                        Step 2: ?x has value A
                        ← returns SUCCESS, and ST now has value A for ?z
                ← returns SUCCESS
← returns SUCCESS

Figure B.12   Trace of the matching algorithm

To MATCH T1 and T2

1.   **If** T1 is a variable,
    then replace T1 with value of GET-VALUE(T1)

2.   **If** T2 is a variable
    then replace T2 with value of GET-VALUE(T2)

3.   **If** T1 = T2
    then return SUCCESS
    else if T1 is a variable and T2 does not contain T1
        then ADD-TO-ST(T1, T2) and **return** SUCCESS
        else if T2 is a variable and T1 does not contain T2
            then ADD-TO-ST(T2, T1) and **return** SUCCESS
            else if both T1 and T2 are lists
                then if MATCH(First(T1), First(T2)) succeeds
                    then return result from MATCH(Rest(T1), Rest(T2))
                else return FAIL
            else return FAIL

Figure B.13   The unification algorithm

The problem is that now there is no instantiation of the variables that makes the two formulas identical. This is because ?y has the value (f ?y), which is actually (f (f ?y)), which is actually (f (f (f ?y))), and so on. Each time you replace ?y with its value, another ?y is introduced that needs replacing. These cases can be eliminated by preventing a variable from matching a value that contains the same variable. The final algorithm is as shown in Figure B.13. In practice, however, most PROLOG systems use the simpler version for efficiency reasons.

Related Work and Further Readings

The best sources for additional reading in this area are textbooks on programming techniques in AI, including sections on pattern matching, such as Winston and Horn (1989) and Wilensky (1986). Gazdar and Mellish (1989b) show how to use PROLOG for a wide range of natural language applications. An excellent source for AI programming techniques is Norvig (1992).

Exercises for Appendix B

1. (*easy*) Using the list functions First, Rest, Insert, and Append, write a function to transform

    a.   (B A) into (A B)
    b.   (A B) into (A B C)
    c.   (D B C) into (A B C) and D

2. (*easy*) Unify the following pairs of lists, if possible. If not, show why they cannot be unified. Show the final symbol table and the most general unifier.

    a.   ((A ?X) ?X), (?Y (B c))
    b.   (?X ?Y), ((A ?Y) (B ?X))
    c.   ((A ?X) ?X), (?Y ?Z)

3. (*easy*) Find the most general unifier for the following clauses, or explain why they do not unify (x, y, and z are variables):

    a. $P(f(x), y)$, $P(z, g(z))$
    b. $P(f(x, x), A)$, $P(f(y, f(y, A)), A)$
    c. $P(f(A), x)$, $P(x, A)$

4. (*easy*) Assume that Figure B.9 is the complete search space for the combination lock problem (that is, you know the combination has three or less numbers). Redraw the tree showing all the states that would be considered by a depth-first search to find the solution at (1 2 2). Number each state indicating the order in which it was considered. Now do the same for the breadth-first strategy. Which strategy found the solution faster? Which would find the solution faster if the solution were (2 2)?

5. (*easy*) Using the format in Figure B.10, give a trace of a proof of

    live-in-sea(homer)

APPENDIX C

Speech Recognition and Spoken Language

C.1 Issues in Speech Recognition

C.2 The Sound Structure of Language

C.3 Signal Processing

C.4 Speech Recognition

C.5 Speech Recognition and Natural Language Understanding

C.6 Prosody and Intonation

While most of this book concerns written language, the techniques developed are applicable to spoken language understanding as well. Because of recent advances in speech recognition technology, you will see many speech-driven applications arising in the next few years. This appendix provides an introduction to speech recognition technology and its application in spoken language understanding systems. Section C.1 discusses various general characteristics of speech recognition systems. Section C.2 outlines the basic sound structure of language and Section C.3 discusses signal processing algorithms. Section C.4 then describes how speech recognition systems work, and Section C.5 discusses how these systems are used for spoken language understanding. Finally, Section C.6 discusses prosody and intonation and their role in speech.

C.1 Issues in Speech Recognition

Speech is the predominant mode of human communication. Certainly written language is very important, and much of the knowledge that is passed from generation to generation is in written form, but speech is our preferred mode for everyday interaction. It is natural to assume that speech will also be the preferred mode for human-machine interaction as well. Speech is very efficient and convenient, and allows your hands to be free for performing other tasks. Until recently, however, speech recognition systems have not been accurate or fast enough to support useful applications. This is changing rapidly as new recognition techniques and faster machines appear.

Speech recognition systems fall into two classes. An **isolated word recognition** system recognizes one word at a time. To use such a system, you must pause between each word. A **continuous speech recognition** system recognizes speech as we normally speak it, with words flowing together in a continuous stream. Most systems currently on the market use isolated word recognition techniques. Continuous speech recognition systems are under active development, however, and are nearing practical use. Other major factors that distinguish different systems are vocabulary size and the range of speakers that can be handled. Systems range from low-end recognizers that can recognize 30 or so words from a single speaker to high-end systems that can recognize 20,000 words from multiple speakers. When comparing different recognition rates, it is important to remember that it is much more difficult to attain high accuracy rates with large-vocabulary, multiple-speaker continuous speech recognition.

While the same basic techniques for parsing, semantic interpretation, and contextual interpretation can be used for spoken or written language, there are some significant differences that affect system design. For instance, with spoken input the system has to deal with uncertainty. In written language the system knows exactly what words are to be processed. With spoken language it only has a guess at what was said. In addition, spoken language is structurally quite different than written language. In fact, sometimes a transcript of perfectly understandable speech is not comprehensible when read. Spoken language occurs more

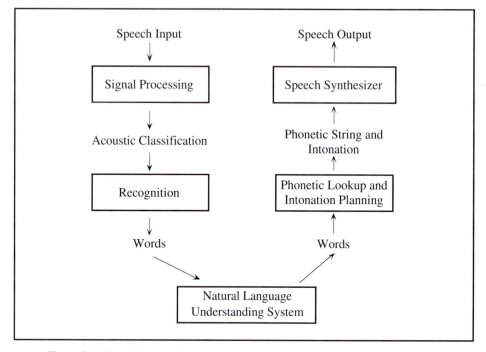

Figure C.1 The architecture of a speech understanding system

incrementally, a phrase at a time, and contains considerable intonational information that is not captured in written form. It also contains many **repairs**, in which the speaker corrects or rephrases something that was just said. In addition, spoken dialogue has a rich interaction of acknowledgment and confirmation that maintains the conversation, which doesn't appear in written forms.

The basic architecture of a spoken language understanding system is shown in Figure C.1, which shows the entire natural language system compressed into a single box. The sounds produced by the speaker are converted into digital form by an analog-to-digital converter. This signal is then processed to extract various features, such as the intensity of sound at different frequencies and the change in intensity over time. These features serve as the input to the speech recognition system, which generally uses Hidden Markov Model (HMM) techniques (see Chapter 7) to identify the most likely sequence of words that could have produced the output. The speech recognizer then outputs the most likely sequence of words to serve as input to the natural language understanding system. When the natural language system needs to generate an utterance, it passes a sentence to a module that translates the words into a phonemic sequence and determines an intonational contour, and then passes this information on to a speech synthesis system, which produces the spoken output.

Phoneme	Example	Phoneme	Example	Phoneme	Example
/ee/	beat	/p/	pin	/s/	sin
/I/	bit	/t/	tin	/z/	zoo
/e/	bait	/k/	kin	/zh/	pleasure
/ε/	bet	/b/	bin	/jh/	jail
/ae/	bat	/d/	din	/m/	mail
/a/	bought	/g/	go	/n/	nail
/o/	boat	/f/	fin	/ng/	sing
/u/	book	/th/	thin	/l/	line
/oo/	boot	/sh/	shin	/r/	rib
/uh/	but	/ch/	chin	/w/	will
/er/	bird	/h/	honk	/y/	yes
/ai/	bite	/v/	verb		
/au/	bough				
/oi/	boil				

Figure C.2   The phonemes of American English

C.2 The Sound Structure of Language

The structure of the sounds in spoken language can be accounted for at two different levels: The phonemic level classifies sound in terms of its use in language, and the acoustic level classifies sound in terms of its physical properties.

The phonemic level divides speech into primitive components of meaning, much as morphology divides words into primitive components of meaning. To do this, you must consider all the different sounds used in words in a language and cluster them together so that two sounds that are never used to distinguish one word from another are put into the same group. For example, there are two different sounds that appear to be associated with *th* in English. One is quite breathy and is found in the word *thin,* while the other is more substantial and is found in the word *then.* These could be different phonemes, but it turns out that in English there is no pair of words that are identical except that one uses the first *th* sound while the other uses the second. Thus we may group these two sounds together as different variations (or **allophones**) of the same phoneme. If you do this for English, you will end up with about 40 different categories, which are shown in Figure C.2. Other languages would have a different set, making some of the same distinctions here, while also making additional distinctions or collapsing categories used in English. For example, Japanese would not make the distinction between /r/ and /l/.

Phonemes can be classified into common groups based on certain distinctive features that they share. For instance, all vowels and some consonants involve the use of the vocal chords to produce a sound, while other consonants, such as /s/ and /sh/, do not involve the vocal chords. The former are called the

voiced phonemes, while the latter are unvoiced. Some consonants, such as /p/ and /k/, involve stopping the flow of air momentarily and then releasing the air quickly. These are called **stops** or **plosives**. Other consonants, such as /n/ and /m/, involve using the nasal passage to change the sound and are called **nasal** phonemes. There are many different ways to classify the phonemes depending on how they are produced, and the phoneme set can be represented as a set of features that uniquely identify each phoneme.

The other level of analysis important for speech recognition is the acoustic level. At this level sounds are classified by the physical characteristics of the speech signal. Essentially, a speech recognition system must identify a way of matching various templates of sounds against the new input in order to identify what words have been spoken. Unfortunately, the speech signal itself is far too complicated to represent directly, and the signals arising from two occurrences of the same word may differ dramatically, even within a single speaker. The signal is affected greatly by the rate of speech, background noise, and emotional state of the speaker, all factors not directly related to the words uttered. The trick is to identify a set of acoustic features that capture those aspects of the signal that appear consistently across many instances of the same sound. These issues will be explored in the next section. Before that, consider some general properties of the speech signal.

One of the principal techniques for identifying significant features is to use a **spectral analysis**, a frequency analysis of the signal. This information can be obtained using analog filters on the input, or using digital methods such as the **Fast Fourier Transform.** This information is very useful for distinguishing the different sound patterns. For example, any voiced sounds will tend to have con- siderable intensity in the lower frequency ranges, while unvoiced consonants will tend to have their intensity more evenly spread across all frequencies. To see this, consider Figure C.3, which shows a spectrogram that indicates the signal inten- sity at different frequency ranges during the word *sad*. The frequency varies on the vertical axis, from 0 to 4000 Hz (cycles per second). Time is indicated on the horizontal axis. In this example the word occurred 3.9 to 4.6 seconds from the start of the utterance. Black indicates silence at that frequency, and white indi- cates a strong intensity at that frequency. The word *sad* consists of three phonemes: /s/, /ae/, and /d/. You can see the /s/ between times 3.9 and 4.1, with intensity over a broad range of the higher frequencies, especially between 2000 and 4000 Hz. The vowel starts just after 4.1 with a marked increase in intensity in the lower frequency range. Notice that there are three strong peaks: at approxi- mately 660 Hz, 1700 Hz, and 2400 Hz. These are characteristic of voiced phonemes and are called the **formants**. This combination of formant frequencies is typical of the vowel /ae/. The third formant loses intensity as the vowel continues, and the first formant rises and drops slightly. At 4.4 there is an abrupt stop of the sound, essentially yielding a silence. This is typical of stop consonants, including /d/. Shortly before 4.5 the sound resumes. Notice some weak formant peaks around 4.5. These arise because /d/ is a voiced consonant. If

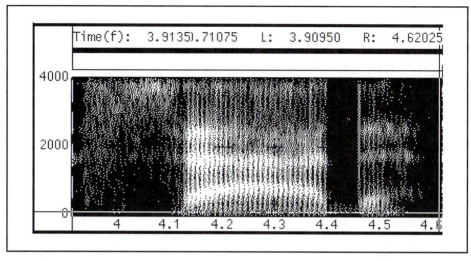

Figure C.3 A spectogram for the word *sad*

Vowel	ee	I	e	ɛ	ae	a
first formant	270	390	500	530	660	730
second formant	2290	1990	1880	1840	1720	1100
third formant	3010	2550	2520	2410	2410	2440

Figure C.4 The average formant frequencies for some vowels

the word had been *sat* instead of *sad,* then this last section of the signal would look similar to the /s/ sound at the beginning, as /t/ would be unvoiced.

The first three formants are quite reliable indicators of the vowel. Figure C.4 shows some data on the average frequency of the first three formants for some English vowels, taken from Denes (1993). The formants reflect the reso-nances from shape of the vocal tract and are distinct from the frequency produced by the vocal chords, which is called the **pitch** or the **fundamental frequency**. The fundamental frequency varies considerably in most speech as part of natural intonation to convey questions, make assertions, express surprise, and so on. But even as it varies, the formants for vowels remain relatively constant, as they reflect the shape of the vocal tract.

Unfortunately, there is not a one-to-one correspondence between phonemes and the acoustic features. For instance, the phoneme /t/ is part of the phonemic spelling of the words *time, sting, stripe,* and *fit.* But listen carefully to each sound as you say the words. In each case the /t/ contributes quite a different sound to the word as it combines with the surrounding phonemes. If you look at a spectrogram for each, the distinctions are even more prominent. Even with the same word the sounds corresponding to phonemes will differ considerably depending on whether the words are stressed or reduced in the utterance. While stressed vowels can generally be recognized reliably, when reduced in unstressed words or rapid speech, they are often so degraded that different vowels are completely indistinguishable from each other. These properties make speech recognition considerably more difficult than you might expect.

C.3 Signal Processing

A microphone converts sound into a varying electric current that corresponds to the complex sound wave. The existence of stereo systems demonstrates that this electric signal contains all the relevant information present in the sound since, using a loudspeaker, it can be converted back into sound that is virtually indistinguishable from the original. To use such a signal as input to a computer, it must be digitized. This is performed by an analog-to-digital (A/D) converter, a standard component of virtually all modern personal computers. There are two important factors in digitizing a signal. The first is the sampling rate, how often the current is measured, and the second is the quantization factor, the number of different levels of intensity that can be distinguished. The sampling rate determines how high a frequency in the signal can be accurately recorded. A theorem in information theory states that the signal must be sampled at twice the rate of the highest frequency required in the analysis. As a point of reference, perceptual studies generally indicate that frequencies up to about 10 kHz (10,000 cycles per second) occur in speech, but speech remains intelligible within a considerably narrower range. Telephone speech, for instance, has traditionally only transmitted frequencies up to 3 kHz (although modern telephone technology uses an expanded range). In general, a sampling rate between 8 and 20 kHz is used for speech recognition applications.

The second important factor is the quantization factor, which determines what scale is used to represent the signal intensity. For instance, a 1-bit quantization would only be able to indicate whether a signal is higher or lower than some mid-range intensity. A 2-bit measurement would distinguish four different levels, and so on. Generally, it appears that 11-bit numbers capture sufficient information, although by using a log scale, you can get by with 8-bit numbers.

So a typical representation of a speech signal is a stream of 8-bit numbers arriving at the rate of 10,000 numbers per second—clearly a large amount of data. The challenge for speech recognition is to reduce this data to a manageable representation. In fact, most current speech recognition systems end up classifying each segment of signal into only one of 256 distinct categories. Clearly, we must be very careful in choosing these categories to ensure that they capture the important distinctions in the signal and ignore the variations that do not matter. The rest of this section describes how this task can be accomplished.

The first technique is to represent the signal as a sequence of segments. There is a tradeoff in how much signal to capture in a single segment. The larger the segment, the more data is available to make a classification, but the less sensitive the classification will be for representing the rapid transitions that are

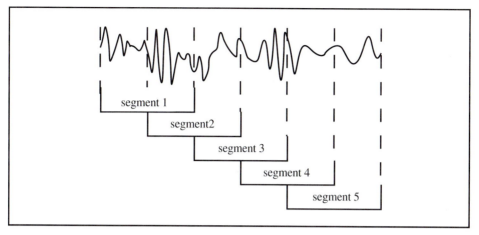

Figure C.5 20 ms segments at 10 ms intervals

necessary to reliably recognize stops and other transient consonants. A typical segment size would be 20 ms (containing 200 samples when using a 10 kHz sampling rate). Rather than divide the signal into discrete segments, most systems use overlapping segments to make sure that segment boundaries don't accidentally mask important rapid transitions. A typical increment might be 10 ms, yielding a sequence of segments as shown in Figure C.5.

Now the task is to characterize the signal within each segment in a way that captures the information that most reliably identifies particular speech sounds over a wide range of conditions. Two simple measures on a segment are:

overall intensity—intensity can be measured by the sum of the squares of the numbers in the segment, and it is a good indicator of whether the segment is part of a voiced phoneme, an unvoiced phoneme, or silence.

peak measurements—the average time between significant intensity peaks in the signal will tend to reflect the fundamental frequency in voiced speech.

Other measures on a segment can be obtained from performing a spectral analysis, using a technique such as the Fast Fourier Transform to produce an analysis of the intensity of the signal at different frequencies. The spectral analysis can be used for many purposes. You might identify the peaks in the spectrum that tend to reflect the formants in voiced speech, and different spectral patterns will reflect different sorts of consonants. Often the spectral analysis is used as an intermediate stage for additional processing to extract the key aspects of the spectrum. For instance, you might try to fit a polynomial curve to the frequency spectrum, and use the roots of the polynomial as an abstract representation of the spectrum. A large number of techniques are used in the literature to reduce this information to a few key features.

The other major set of techniques for classifying a segment characterize how it relates to the preceding segment. In particular, because of the overlap in segments and their relatively short duration, many adjacent segments are very similar to each other. For instance, if a vowel sound lasts 100 ms, there would be 10 segments during that period. The changes between the segments would be gradual. With consonants such as stops, however, there is dramatic change over a short period. One segment might be characteristic of silence and the next of a voiced consonant.

A technique used in many systems is **linear predictive coding (LPC)**. This operates directly on the actual sample values, which we denote by $x(1)$, $x(2)$, and so on. At a 10 kHz sampling rate, there are 10,000 of these values a second. The technique involves finding a set of parameters α_k, such that the current sample value, $x(k)$, is predicted by the following formula in terms of the previous n samples:

$$x(k) = \Sigma_{i=1,n} \; \alpha_i \; x(k-i)$$

The idea is that patterns in the speech signal will be reflected in the coefficients found. To use the technique, a uniform set of coefficients must be used to estimate all the sample values within a single segment. Of course, this means that there will be errors in the prediction of some samples. The coefficients that minimize the error over the samples in a segment are used to characterize the segment. The error term will tend to be small when the signal is periodic, as with voiced segments, and large when the signal is not periodic, as with unvoiced segments. For voiced segments, the coefficients can be used to produce quite reliable estimates of the formants in the signal.

In summary, segments can be classified by features based on information such as

- the overall intensity of the signal
- the overall intensity in various frequency ranges
- the formants
- the rate of change of the above measures between segments

The simplest signal processing system might just measure the intensity in 5 to 10 different frequency ranges, while the most complex might use sophisticated algorithms to represent the shape of the frequency spectrum and how it changes over time. In all cases the end result is a small set of values that forms the input to the speech recognition system.

The actual recognition process is driven by methods of comparing templates of segments constructed from training data to the segments constructed from the new input. To do this matching, some measure of similarity must be defined based on the features extracted for each segment. To explore this, consider a very simple system that attempts to classify each segment as a voiced phoneme, an unvoiced phoneme, or silence. Say that each segment is represented by a vector of three numbers (from 0 to 256) that represent the overall intensity of the signal and the intensity in two frequency ranges, 100–600 Hz and 600–1500 Hz. For example, a segment represented by the vector (210 140 60) would have an overall intensity of 210 with an intensity of 140 between 100 and 600 Hz and 60 between 600 and 1500. After training on a sample of labeled data, assume the following templates are produced based on the average values for each type of segment:

voiced segments: (180 120 50)
unvoiced segments: (50 10 10)
silences: (30 15 10)

We will measure the similarity between an input segment and a template by measuring least squared difference. The smaller the number, the more similar the patterns. The input vector (210 140 60), would produce the following measures:

Difference from voiced: $(210-180)^2 + (140-120)^2 + (60-50)^2 = 1,400$
Difference from unvoiced: $(210-50)^2 + (140-10)^2 + (60-10)^2 = 45,000$
Difference from silence: $(210-30)^2 + (140-15)^2 + (60-10)^2 = 50,525$

Thus this segment would be classified as a voiced phoneme. An input segment represented as (40 10 12), on the other hand, would be classified as an unvoiced phoneme (with score of 104 versus 129 for silence versus 33,144 for voiced).

Of course, a speech recognition system will need a much more sophisticated representation of segments than this. A typical vector size consists of 24 numbers, capturing various measures such as intensity, formants, and changes from the previous segment, as discussed earlier. In addition, the similarity measures can be considerably more complicated, reflecting the fact that some measures are more important than others, or reflecting interdependencies between the measures. A typical system uses 256 templates for classifying segments. These templates define a set of symbols called the **codebook**. There are automatic techniques for designing a codebook that optimizes recognition performance on a given set of training data.

C.4 Speech Recognition

Once the signal processing has reduced the signal to a sequence of symbols from the codebook, the speech recognition task looks more like a traditional parsing problem. Specifically, it is given a sequence of symbols and must identify the most likely sequence of words that could have generated that input. This is similar to the problem of determining the best parts of speech for words in a sentence and suggests that HMM models can be used effectively. This is in fact the case, and the most successful speech recognition systems today are based on HMM techniques.

An important issue to consider is at what level the HMM should be based. One obvious possibility is the word. For each word in the lexicon, we could define an HMM network that defines the likely sequences of codebook symbols that could realize the word. For limited-vocabulary applications, this is a viable technique. It is possible to obtain enough training examples for each word to define the networks. The result is a robust recognition system. But if you are considering large-vocabulary applications, it is difficult to find enough training data. For instance, some speech recognition systems now have vocabulary sizes of 20,000 words or more. Finding enough training data for such a vocabulary size is near to impossible.

Another problem arises in continuous speech applications. A word may be realized differently depending on what words surround it. These **co-articulation** effects can have a significant effect on the realization of the word. This is especially true with functions words such as *the,* which are highly influenced by the words that follow it. To account for this data, you would need to train the models not only on individual words but also on pairs of words, making the training problem even more difficult.

Because of these difficulties, large-vocabulary speech recognition systems are typically based on subword units. The phoneme would seem to be a natural unit. In a phoneme-based system, there would be an HMM network that defines the likely codebook sequences that realize each phoneme. Even with a liberal set of phonemes that included common allophones, there would be less than 100 units that require training, making training of even five minutes of speech data feasible. The problem, as mentioned earlier, is that the realization of phonemes is highly dependent on the surrounding context. Remember that the phoneme /t/ will look very different depending on its context. One successful solution to this problem is to use **triphones**, or **phonemes in context (PIC)**. In this model there would be no HMM for the phoneme /d/, but there would be an HMM defined for the phoneme /d/ when preceded by a silence and followed by the vowel /ee/, written as sil/d/ee, and another for the combinations sil/d/I, I/d/sil, and so on. Of course, the full set of triphones would consist of at least 40^3 (64,000) PICs, so training would become unmanageable again. Luckily, many combinations never occur in a given language, so the actual number is not nearly so big. In addition, it is possible to collapse the preceding and following phonemes into more general classes that all affect the central phoneme in the same way. By using these techniques, the number of phonemes in context that need to be modeled can be kept to a manageable size (on the order of 1000). In addition, with this model there is a possibility of using smoothing techniques. For instance, if a particular phoneme-in-context triple has never been observed, you might estimate its characteristics based on phoneme pair models, or a general model of the context-independent phoneme.

Each PIC is represented as an HMM that encodes likely sequences of code-book symbols that realize the signal. A simplified HMM model for a phoneme is shown in Figure C.6. The state labeled S is the start state. The states capture the normal progression through symbols typical of the beginning part of the PIC (state B), then the middle part (state M), and finally the ending part (state E), and

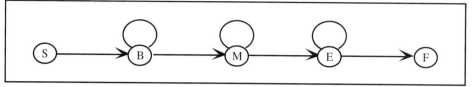

Figure C.6 A simplified HMM template for a phoneme in context

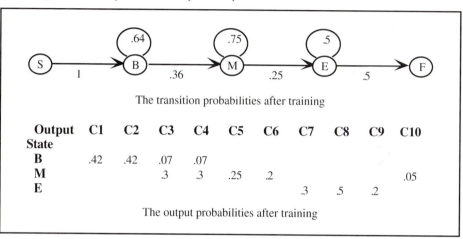

The transition probabilities after training

Output State	C1	C2	C3	C4	C5	C6	C7	C8	C9	C10
B	.42	.42	.07	.07						
M			.3	.3	.25	.2				.05
E							.3	.5	.2	

The output probabilities after training

Figure C.7 The HMM model for sil/p/l after training

the phoneme is completed when it reaches state F. Each node is associated with a different probability distribution for the codebook symbols (C1, ..., C256).

Consider an example of how such an HMM model is trained. For each PIC, a set of training instances are selected from the data. Each of these is represented by a sequence of codebook symbols produced by the signal processing component. For instance, for the PIC sil/p/l, we might find examples such as the following in the training data:

C1 C1 C2 C1 C3 C3 C9 C3 C4 C7 C8
C1 C2 C2 C4 C4 C3 C5 C9
C2 C2 C3 C5 C5 C6 C3 C8 C7 C7
C3 C4 C3 C3 C5 C6 C6 C6 C8 C9
C1 C2 C1 C4 C4 C4 C5 C8 C8

Using standard HMM training techniques, the system might then produce the model shown in Figure C.7, where the transition probabilities and the output probabilities have been chosen to locally optimize the probability that the network would generate the five observed sequences. Note that the HMM model provides a solution to a difficult problem that arises because words are often said at quite different speech rates. Thus a phoneme might sometimes be realized by 10 codebook symbols (100 ms) and other times by only 3 or 4 symbols (30 to 40 ms). The arcs that return to the same state that they left allow the model to assign a probability of staying in the same state for multiple input symbols. Many

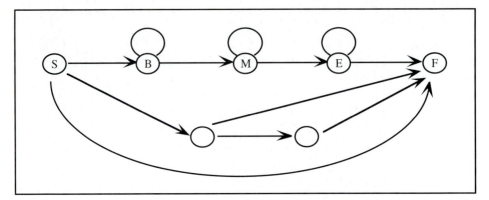

Figure C.8 The HMM model for phonemes used in the SPHINX system

systems, however, find this model still too crude and augment the recognition system with additional mechanisms that explicitly model the expectation durations of various syllables.

In general, HMMs for phonemes must be more complicated in order to handle variations based on whether the phoneme is in a stressed or reduced syllable and other variations such as in very rapid speech. For example, the basic HMM model used in the SPHINX system (Lee, 1990) is shown in Figure C.8.

Given a sequence of observations (expressed as symbols from the code-book), O1, ..., On, and a set of trained HMM models for each PIC, the Viterbi algorithm described in Chapter 7 can be used to calculate the best path through each HMM representing a phoneme in context. From this, we can calculate the probability of the sequence given each HMM, and hence identify the PIC with the highest probability of generating the sequence.

But this simple scheme would only work if the input was segmented into phonetic units that could be analyzed one at a time. This is not possible in practice, so the recognition system must solve two problems at once: phoneme segmentation and phoneme recognition. To constrain this task, you can use word definitions to predict what phoneme sequences are likely. For example, the word *please* could be spelled phonetically as /p/ /l/ /ee/ /z/. To recognize this word in the input, you would need to recognize the sequence of PICs

sil/p/l p/l/ee l/ee/z ee/z/sil

Each of these is defined by an HMM, so we have a sequence of HMMs to account for the set of observations. We can construct an HMM for the word *please* by concatenating the PIC HMMs together, creating a new network as shown in Figure C.9. The Viterbi algorithm using this network will then segment the observations into the best PIC boundaries as it finds the most likely state sequence.

Of course, there may be multiple pronunciations of the word *please,* so alternative phonetic spellings must be allowed as well. If you wish to account for the different frequencies of alternate pronunciations, then an HMM network can

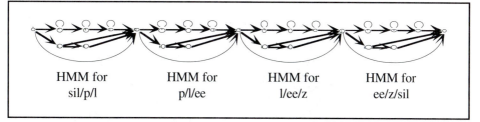

| HMM for | HMM for | HMM for | HMM for |
| sil/p/l | p/l/ee | l/ee/z | ee/z/sil |

Figure C.9 Concatenated PIC HMMs to form an HMM for the word *please*

	No Grammar	**Bigram Word Grammar**
Simple phone model	50%	90%
Triphone model	70%	95%

Figure C.10 Effect of triphone models and bigram word grammars on performance

be defined for each word that specifies the likelihood of various phoneme sequences in the realization of the word.

This scheme will work for isolated words but will be inadequate for continuous speech. In particular, two adjacent words might not have a silence between them. This can be handled by constructing a network that allows two different PIC sequences, one that includes a silence and one that doesn't. The two possible phoneme sequences to model the word sequence *please send* might be

sil/p/l p/l/ee l/ee/z ee/z/sil sil/s/ε s/ε/n ε/n/d n/d/sil
sil/p/l p/l/ee l/ee/z ee/z/s z/s/ε s/ε/n ε/n/d n/d/sil

To model likely word sequences, speech recognition systems typically use a bigram model of syntax, such as discussed in Chapter 7. This model defines another level of HMMs, which can be used to model the category transitions, yielding probabilities of word sequences. The use of a bigram model can greatly increase the accuracy of the speech recognition system, as it eliminates many possibilities that would otherwise be considered. For instance, in one experiment, adding a bigram word grammar increased the accuracy of the SPHINX system from 70 percent to 95 percent (on the resource management task used for evaluating ARPA-sponsored systems). The same system using simple phone models rather than triphones has an accuracy rate of only 50 percent with no word grammar but 90 percent with a bigram grammar. These results are summarized in Figure C.10. Clearly, the word grammar is an extremely important component contributing to the success of current speech recognition systems.

C.5 Speech Recognition and Natural Language Understanding

As you have just seen, augmenting a speech recognition system with a bigram word model significantly improves the performance of the system. This suggests that a more comprehensive model would produce even better performance. In practice, however, this is difficult to accomplish. Word trigrams could be used, but this would require significantly more data. Directly integrating a probabilistic context-free grammar also poses difficulties. First, speech systems currently achieve an elegant integration of the bigram models, word models, and phoneme models because all can be represented within the same framework, namely HMMs. Introducing a context-free grammar formalism for the syntactic component would cause a lack of integration that could adversely affect the recognition accuracy or the efficiency of recognition. As a result, all current spoken language understanding systems maintain a strict separation between the speech recognizer and the natural language understanding system, as shown in Figure C.1.

Accepting this division, there are still many options for designing the interface. The simplest interface, and the one in common use, is one in which the speech recognizer outputs the single best sequence of words it can find. The language system then processes this and hopes that there are no serious recognition errors. A generalization of this scheme is called **N-best**, where the speech recognizer outputs the N best sequences it can find. This allows the parser to attempt other interpretations if the first one fails. While many systems have a capability for using an N-best interface, it has proven to yield only a slight improvement in accuracy, and so far has not been worth the extra processing cost. One reason for this is that the N-best sequences often are substantially the same, with differences of only a word or two. Thus, if the speech recognizer has made an error in recognition on a particular word, it is likely that the same error occurs in all the N-best alternatives.

An interesting alternative to N-best is a word-lattice output. In this approach the speech recognition system would output a lattice of the most likely words in the input. A word lattice provides a compact representation of a large number of possible sentences, creating a substantially richer environment for error recovery based on parser and semantic interpretation. Note that you can view a word lattice as an initial chart for a chart parser. The fact that there are multiple alternatives for what words appear at what positions does not affect the basic parsing algorithm.

Such general techniques have not been pursued extensively, as the current-generation systems use highly domain-specific techniques to optimize their short-term performance. For instance, several different spoken language understanding systems have been built in the Air Travel Information System (ATIS) domain, in which the system answers queries based on a database of airline schedules. Because of the narrow focus of the application, the domain-specific techniques for interpretation described in Chapter 11 can be used to correctly interpret a query even when portions of it are misrecognized. Researchers have found it more effective in the short term to improve the domain-specific interpretation heuristics than to explore more general and robust interfaces between the speech recognizer and the natural language system. This should change as the applications become more complex.

Even given the limited domain, the performance of the systems in the ATIS domain is impressive. To give you an idea, the ATIS systems typically involve about a 2000-word vocabulary, are speaker independent, and accomplish the speech recognition task with little noticeable delay using standard workstations with no special signal processing hardware. The systems are tested on a set of several hundred queries that have not been seen before. In 1993, the best speech recognition systems had a word accuracy rate of about 95 percent. The best overall systems produced an appropriate answer for about 88 percent of the queries.

C.6 Prosody and Intonation

There is one further aspect of speech that is extremely important for language understanding. This is prosody: a collection of phenomena relating to how sentences are spoken rather than what is spoken. It consists of a wide variety of perceptual cues, including

the intonation contour—the fundamental frequency (or pitch) rises and falls throughout an utterance.

the speech rate—a speaker continually varies the speech rate, elongating some syllables, shortening others, adding pauses between words, and so on.

the intensity—a speaker varies the intensity during an utterance, emphasizing certain words and de-emphasizing others.

Prosody is critically important for spoken language understanding because it conveys how the speaker relates to what is being said. In some cases it plays the role that punctuation plays in written language. Actually, though, it's the other way around: Punctuation plays the role in written language that prosody plays in spoken language. For instance, in a common intonational pattern in English questions, the pitch rises at the end of the sentence. In assertions the pitch falls. The intonational pattern tends to override other factors, such as syntax, in determining what is a question. For instance, the sentence *You are coming to the party* can be used as a question with a rising intonation, corresponding to the written form

You are coming to the party?

Intonation, however, is much richer than punctuation. Based on different intonational patterns, this sentence could be identified as an invitation, a true question, or an indication of surprise. In written language all of these interpretations would be indicated with the question mark.

Another important aspect of spoken language is stress. All sentences have a typical stress pattern that is normally used, but the speaker can vary the stress in order to indicate what is being focused on or to indicate contrasts and corrections. Stress in speech is signaled by increased intensity and by factors such as a lengthening of the word and the use of intonational patterns, such as a temporary rise in pitch at the stressed word. In written language, stress is sometimes indicated by putting the word in all uppercase letters, as in

> I only took TWO candies. (that is, not three)
> I only took two CANDIES. (that is, no cookies)

Consider possible answers to the question *Do you own a red car?*

> No, but I own a red BIKE.
> No, but I own a BLUE car.

It would be very strange to answer the question with the sentences

> *No, but I own a RED bike.
> *No, but I own a blue CAR.

The reason is that the stress emphasizes new and contrastive information. It makes no sense to stress words that are already expected given the context.

The intonational contour and speech rate are also important in phrasing, indicating where one phrase or sentence ends and another begins. Here is a sequence of words uttered by a single person in a dialogue. Without prosodic information, you cannot tell where the phrase and sentence boundaries are:

> Not at the same time OK we're gonna hook up engine E2 to the boxcar at Elmira and send that off to Corning now while we're loading that boxcar with oranges at Corning we're gonna take engine E3 and send it over to Corning hook it up to the tanker car and send it back to Elmira.

Without prosodic information, this sequence of words is highly ambiguous as to where the utterance boundaries are located. Consider the word *now* in the second line. It might be a temporal adverbial, part of the utterance

> Send that off to Corning now while we're loading the boxcar

Alternatively, it might be a discourse cue word and its own separate utterance, yielding this sequence of utterances:

> Send that off to Corning
> Now
> While we're loading the boxcar, ...

The different utterance segmentations yield radically different interpretations, yet you cannot tell from the words which one is intended. If you could listen to this in its original spoken form, however, it would be obvious that its structure is the latter interpretation.

While prosody clearly plays a crucial role in spoken dialogue, computational methods have not been extensively studied. One reason for this is that current speech recognition systems are designed to handle a single utterance at a time (that is, the sentence boundaries are determined externally) and have very limited dialogue capabilities. As a result, most of the information conveyed by prosody is not relevant for current applications. Some work has indicated that prosodic analysis can improve the accuracy of speech recognition, but no system has yet integrated prosodic processing in any significant way.

One place where prosody is of crucial importance is in speech synthesis. A system that synthesizes speech with no prosodic phrasing sounds extremely artificial and is difficult to understand. So the best speech synthesis systems all use heuristic techniques for determining a prosodic contour, typically based on statistical methods for determining phrase boundaries for written text. It is important that these methods work well, as a synthesizer using inappropriate prosody would be much worse than one that doesn't use prosody at all.

Related Work and Further Readings

An excellent introduction to human speech production and perception is Denes (1993), which provides a good description of how speech is produced, its general characteristics, and a summary of results from the active research area in psychology of speech perception. A good text on speech recognition is Rabiner and Juang (1993).

The best source of papers on speech recognition is the collection in Waibel and Lee (1990). This contains many good tutorial papers. For instance, Rabiner (1989) is an excellent introduction to Hidden Markov Models and their use in speech recognition. Schafer and Rabiner (1975) is a good survey of the different signal processing techniques used to represent speech signals. Lee (1990) contains an excellent discussion of the use of triphone representations for speech recognition. The collection also contains many other papers that illustrate important techniques and describe sample systems.

Primary sources of information on current research in the area are found in the *IEEE Transactions on Acoustics, Speech and Signal Processing,* in *Computer Speech and Language,* and in the proceedings of the DARPA Workshops on Speech and Natural Language Processing, distributed by Morgan Kaufmann.

There is a large literature on prosody in general, but little of it is computational. The paper by Pierrehumbert and Hirschberg (1990) describes a particular theory of prosodic structure and discusses how it might affect various aspects of discourse processing. A good example of work on automatically recognizing intonational phrase boundaries is Wang and Hirshberg (1992).

Exercises for Appendix C

1. (*easy*) Say you are given a spectrogram of an unknown vowel, and you estimate the first three formants to be at 600 Hz, 1800 Hz, and 2400 Hz. Given the data on formants specified in Figure C.4, devise a numerical test

for classifying the unknown vowel. Which are the two most likely inter-pretations, and which of these two is preferred by your measure?

2.   (*easy*) Classify the phonemes of English given in Figure C.2 using the following features:

> **+/–voiced**—whether or not the vocal chords are used (as in /e/, /n/, and /d/).
>
> **+/–stop**—whether or not the phoneme involves a stopping of sound followed by a quick release (as in /d/ and /t/).
>
> **+/–fricative**—whether or not the phoneme involves a high frequency "hissing" sound (as in /s/).

3.   (*medium*) Using the Viterbi algorithm described in Chapter 7 on the HMM defined in Figure C.7, determine which of the following inputs is most likely to be the PIC sil/p/l:

> C1 C1 C2 C4 C5 C6 C5 C8 C8
> C1 C2 C3 C4 C5 C6 C7 C8

Bibliography

Abbreviations are used for many of the references from conference proceedings and journals. In particular, AAAI is the American Association for Artificial Intelligence, and proceedings are distributed by MIT Press. IJCAI is the International Joint Conference on Artificial Intelligence, and proceedings are distributed by Morgan Kaufmann Publishers.

ACL is the Association of Computational Linguistics, COLING is the International Conference on Computational Linguistics, and AJCL is the *American Journal of Computational Linguistics,* the old name of the journal currently named *Computational Linguistics.* These conference proceedings and the journal can be obtained from the Association for Computational Linguistics; Walker; C. N. 925; Bernardsville, New Jersey, USA, 07924-0925.

An excellent collection of papers is *Readings in Natural Language Processing,* edited by B. Grosz, K. Jones, and B. Webber and published by Morgan Kaufmann Publishers, Inc., in 1986. Papers reprinted in that volume are indicated here by the abbreviation RNLP.

Aho, A. V., and J. D. Ullman. 1972. *The Theory of Parsing, Translation and Compiling.* Englewood Cliffs, NJ: Prentice-Hall.

Aho, A. V., R. Sethi, and J. D. Ullman. 1986. *Compilers: Principles, Techniques, and Tools.* Reading, MA: Addison-Wesley.

Allen, J. F. 1983. "Recognizing intentions from natural language utterances." In M. Brady and R. C. Berwick (eds.), *Computational Models of Discourse,* 107–166. Cambridge, MA: MIT Press.

Allen, J. F. 1984. "Towards a general theory of action and time," *Artificial Intelligence* 23, 2:123–154.

Allen, J. F., and C. R. Perrault. 1980. "Analyzing intention in utterances," *Artificial Intelligence* 15, 3:143–178. Reprinted in RNLP.

Allen, J. F., R. Fikes, and E. Sandewall (eds.). 1991. *Proc. 2nd Conf. on Principles of Knowledge Representation and Reasoning* (Cambridge, MA, April 1991). San Mateo, CA: Morgan Kaufmann.

Allen, J. F., J. Hendler, and A. Tate. 1990. *Readings in Planning.* San Mateo, CA: Morgan Kaufmann.

Alshawi, H. (ed.). 1992. *The Core Language Engine.* Cambridge, MA: MIT Press.

Appelt, D. E. 1985. *Studies in Natural Language Processing: Planning English Sentences.* Cambridge, U.K.: Cambridge U. Press.

Appelt, D. E., J. R. Hobbs, J. Bear, D. Israel, and M. Tyson. 1993. "FASTUS: A finite-state processor for information extraction from real-world text," *Proc. IJCAI.*

Austin, J. L. 1962. *How to Do Things with Words.* New York: Oxford U. Press.

629

Ayuso, D. 1989. "Discourse entities in Janus," *Proc. ACL.*

Bach, E. 1986. "The algebra of events," *Linguistics and Philosophy* 9, 1:5–16.

Baker, C. L. 1989. *English Syntax.* Cambridge, MA: MIT Press.

Ballard, B. 1988. "A general treatment of comparatives for natural language question answering," *Proc. ACL,* 41–48.

Bar-Hillel, Y. 1960. "The present status of automatic translation of languages." In F. L. Alt (ed.), *Advances in Computers.* Vol. 1. New York: Academic Press, 91–163.

Barwise, J., and R. Cooper. 1981. "Generalized quantifiers and natural language," *Linguistics and Philosophy* 4:159–219.

Barwise, J., and J. Etchemendy. 1987. *Tarski's World.* Chicago, IL: Chicago U. Press.

Barwise, J., and J. Perry. 1983. *Situations and Attitudes.* Cambridge, MA: Bradford Books, MIT Press.

Bates, M. 1978. "The theory and practice of augmented transition networks." In L. Bloc (ed.), *Natural Language Communication with Computers.* New York: Springer-Verlag.

Bates, M., M. G. Moser, and D. Stallard. 1986. "The IRUS transportable natural language database interface." In L. Kerschberg (ed.), *Expert Database Systems.* Redwood City, CA: Benjamin/Cummings.

Baum, L. E. 1972. "An inequality and associated maximization technique in statistical estimation for probabilistic functions of a Markov process," *Inequalities* 3:1–8.

Berwick, R. C. 1985. *The Acquisition of Syntactic Knowledge.* Cambridge, MA: MIT Press.

Berwick, R. C., and A. Weinberg. 1984. *The Grammatical Basis of Linguistic Performance: Language Use and Acquisition.* Cambridge, MA: MIT Press.

Birnbaum, L., and M. Selfridge. 1981. "Conceptual analysis of natural language." In R. Schank and C. Riesbeck (eds.), *Inside Computer Understanding.* Hillsdale, NJ: Lawrence Erlbaum.

Blank, G. D. 1989. "A finite and real-time processor for natural language," *Commun. of the ACM* 32, 10, 1174–1189.

Bobrow, R. J., and B. L. Webber. 1980. "Knowledge representation for syntactic/semantic processing," *Proc. AAAI,* 316–323.

Bobrow, D. G., and T. Winograd. 1977. "An overview of KRL, a knowledge representation language," *Cognitive Science* 1, 3:3–46.

Brachman, R. J., and H. Levesque (eds.). 1985. *Readings in Knowledge Representation.* San Mateo, CA: Morgan Kaufmann.

Brachman, R. J., H. Levesque, and R. Reiter (eds.). 1989. *Proc. 1st Conf. on Principles of Knowledge Representation and Reasoning.* San Mateo, CA: Morgan Kaufmann.

Bratman, M. E. 1987. *Intentions, Plans and Practical Reasoning.* Cambridge, MA: Harvard U. Press.

Bratman, M. E., D. Israel, and M. Pollack. 1988. "Plans and resource-bounded practical reasoning," *Computational Intelligence* 4:349–355.

Brennan, S., L. Friedman, and C. Pollard. 1987. "A centering approach to pronouns," *Proc. ACL.*

Brown, J. S., and R. R. Burton. 1975. "Multiple representations of knowledge for tutorial reasoning." In D. G. Bobrow and A. Collins (eds.), *Representation and Understanding.* New York: Academic Press.

Bruce, B. C. 1975. "Generation as a social action," *Proc. Theoretical Issues in Natural Language Processing (ACL),* 64–67. Reprinted in RNLP.

de Bruin, J., and R. Scha. 1988. "The interpretation of relational nouns," *Proc. ACL,* 25–32.

Carberry, S. 1991. *Plan Recognition in Natural Language Dialogue.* Cambridge, MA: MIT Press.

Carlson, G. 1979. "Generics and atemporal when," *Linguistics and Philosophy* 3:49–98.

Carlson, G. 1982. "Generic terms and generic sentences," *J. Philosophical Logic* 11:145–181.

Chafe, W. L. 1975. "Givenness, contrastiveness, definiteness, subjects, topics, and points of view," *Linguistic Inquiry,* 25–55.

Charniak, E. 1981. "The case-slot identity theory," *Cognitive Science* 5, 3:285–292.

Charniak, E. 1983. "A parser with something for everyone." In M. King (ed.), *Parsing Natural Language.* New York: Academic Press.

Charniak, E. 1988. "Motivation analysis, abductive unification, and nonmonotonic equality," *Artificial Intelligence* 34, 3:275–296.

Charniak, E. 1993. *Statistical Language Learning.* Cambridge, MA: MIT Press.

Charniak, E., and R. Goldman. 1993. "A Bayesian model of plan recognition," *Artificial Intelligence* 64, 1:53–80.

Charniak, E., and D. McDermott. 1985. *An Introduction to Artificial Intelligence.* Reading, MA: Addison-Wesley.

Chierchia, G., and S. McConnell-Ginet. 1990. *Meaning and Grammar.* Cambridge, MA: MIT Press.

Chincor, N., L. Hirschman, and D. Lewis. 1993. "Evaluating message understanding systems," *Computational Linguistics* 19, 3:409–450.

Chitrao, M., and R. Grishman. 1990. "Statistical parsing of messages," *Proc. DARPA SNLP Workshop,* San Mateo, CA: Morgan Kaufmann.

Chomsky, N. 1956. "Three models for the description of language," *IRE Transactions PGIT,* 2, 113–124.

Chomsky, N. 1965. *Aspects of the Theory of Syntax.* Cambridge, MA: MIT Press.

Chomsky, N. 1981. *Lectures on Government and Binding.* Cinnaminson, NJ: Foris Publications.

Church, K. 1988. "A stochastic parts program and noun phrase parser for unrestricted text," *Proc. 2nd Conf. Applied Natural Language Processing,* 136–143.

Church, K., and R. Patil. 1982. "Coping with syntactic ambiguity, or how to put the block on the box on the table," *AJCL* 8, 3–4:139–149.

Clark, H. H., and S. Haviland. 1977. "Comprehension and the given-new contract." In R. O. Freedle (ed.), *Discourse Production and Comprehension.* Norwood, NJ: Ablex.

Clark, H. H., and C. R. Marshall. 1981. "Definite reference and mutual knowledge." In A. Joshi, B. Webber, and I. Sag (eds.), *Elements of Discourse Understanding*. New York: Cambridge U. Press.

Clark, K. 1978. "Negation as failure." In H. Gallaire and J. Minker (eds.), *Logic and Data Bases*. New York: Plenum Press, 293–322.

Clifton, C., L. Frazier, and K. Rayner. In press. *Perspectives on Sentence Processing*. Hillsdale, NJ: Lawrence Erlbaum.

Clocksin, W., and C. Mellish. 1981. *Programming in PROLOG*. New York: Springer-Verlag.

Cohen, P. R. 1978. "On knowing what to say: Planning speech acts," Ph.D. thesis and TR 118, Computer Science Dept., U. Toronto.

Cohen, P. R., and H. J. Levesque. 1990a. "Intention is choice with commitment," *Artificial Intelligence* 42, 3.

Cohen, P. R., and H. J. Levesque. 1990b. "Rational interaction as the basis for communication." In Cohen et al. (1990), 221–256.

Cohen, P. R., and C. R. Perrault. 1979. "Elements of a plan-based theory of speech acts," *Cognitive Science* 3:177–212. Reprinted in RNLP.

Cohen, P. R., J. Morgan, and M. Pollack. 1990. *Intentions in Communication*. Cambridge, MA: MIT Press.

Cohen, R. 1987. "Analyzing the structure of argumentative discourse," *Computational Linguistics* 13, 1–2:11–24.

Colmerauer, A. 1978. "Metamorphosis grammars." In L. Bloc (ed.), *Natural Language Communication with Computers*. Berlin: Springer-Verlag.

Computational Linguistics 9, 3–4 (special issue on ill-formed input), 1983.

Computational Linguistics 14, 2 (special issue on tense and aspect), 1988.

Computational Linguistics 19, 1–2 (special issue on large corpora), 1993.

Cooper, R. 1983. *Quantification and Syntactic Theory*. Dordrecht: D. Reidel.

Cottrell, G. W., and S. L. Small. 1983. "A connectionist scheme for modelling word sense disambiguation," *Cognition and Brain Theory* 6:89–120.

Crain, S., and M. Steedman. 1985. "On not being led up the garden path." In D. R. Dowty, L. Kartunnen, and A. Zwicky (eds), *Natural Language Parsing*. New York: Cambridge U. Press.

Cullingford, R. 1981. "SAM." In R. Schank and C. Riesbeck (eds.), *Inside Computer Understanding*. Hillsdale, NJ: Lawrence Erlbaum, 75–119.

Dahlgren, K. 1988. *Naive Semantics for Natural Language Understanding*. Boston, MA: Kluwer Academic Publishers.

Dale, R. 1992. *Generating Referring Expressions*. Cambridge, MA: MIT Press.

Dale, R., C. Mellish, and M. Zock (eds.). 1990. *Current Research in Natural Language Generation*. New York: Academic Press.

Dalrymple, M., S. Shieber, and F. Pereira. 1991. "Ellipsis and higher-order unification," *Linguistics and Philosophy* 14, 4.

Davidson, D. 1967. "The logical form of action sentences." In N. Rescher (ed.), *The Logic of Decision and Action.* Pittsburgh, PA: U. Pittsburgh Press.

Davis, E. 1990. *Representations of Commonsense Reasoning.* San Mateo, CA: Morgan Kaufmann.

DeJong, G. 1979. "Prediction and substantiation: A new approach to natural language processing," *Cognitive Science* 3:251–273.

DeJong, G. 1982. "An overview of the FRUMP system." In W. Lehnert and M. Ringle (eds.), *Strategies for Natural Language Processing.* Hillsdale, NJ: Lawrence Erlbaum, 149–176.

Denes, P. 1993. *The Speech Chain (2nd ed.).* San Francisco, CA: Freeman.

DeRose, S. 1988. "Grammatical category disambiguation by statistical optimization," *Computational Linguistics* 14, 1:31–39.

Devlin, K. 1991. *Logic and Information.* Cambridge, U.K.: Cambridge U. Press.

Donnellan, K. 1966. "Reference and definite descriptions," *Philosophical Review* 75:281–304. Reprinted in S. Schwartz (ed.). 1977. *Naming, Necessity, and Natural Kinds.* Ithaca, NY: Cornell U. Press.

Dowty, D. R. 1979. *Word Meaning and Montague Grammar.* Dordrecht: D. Reidel.

Dowty, D. R. (ed.). 1986. "Tense and aspect in discourse," *Linguistics and Philosophy* 9, 1 (special issue).

Dowty, D. R. 1989. "On the semantic content of the notion 'thematic role'." In G. Chierchia, B. Partee, and R. Turner (eds.), *Properties, Types and Meaning.* Vol. 2. Dordrecht: Kluwer Academic Publishers, 69–130.

Dowty, D. R., L. Karttunen, and A. Zwicky (eds.). 1985. *Natural Language Parsing.* New York: Cambridge U. Press.

Dowty, D. R., R. E. Wall, and S. Peters. 1981. *Introduction to Montague Semantics.* Dordrecht: D. Reidel.

Dyer, M. 1983. *In-Depth Understanding: A Computer Model of Integrated Processing for Narrative Comprehension.* Cambridge, MA: MIT Press.

Earley, J. 1970. "An efficient context-free parsing algorithm," *Commun. of the ACM* 13, 2:94–102. Reprinted in RNLP.

Etherington, D., and R. Reiter. 1983. "On inheritance hierarchies with exceptions," *Proc. AAAI,* 104–108.

Fano, R. 1961. *Transmission of Information.* Cambridge, MA: MIT Press.

Ferguson, G. M., and J. F. Allen. 1993. "Generic plan recognition for dialogue," *Proc. ARPA Human Language Technology Workshop,* San Mateo, CA: Morgan Kaufmann.

Fikes, R. E., and N. J. Nilsson. 1971. "STRIPS: A new approach to the application of theorem proving to problem solving," *Artificial Intelligence* 2, 3/4:189–208.

Fillmore, C. J. 1968. "The case for case." In E. Bach and R. Harms (eds.), *Universals in Linguistic Theory.* New York: Holt, Rinehart, and Winston, 1–90.

Fillmore, C. J. 1977. "The case for case reopened." In P. Cole and J. Sadock (eds.), *Syntax and Semantics.* Vol. 8: *Grammatical Relations.* New York: Academic Press, 59–81.

Findler, N. 1979. *Associative Networks.* New York: Academic Press.

Finin, T. 1980. "The semantic interpretation of nominal compounds," *Proc. AAAI,* 310–312.

Ford, M., J. W. Bresnan, and R. M. Kaplan. 1982. "A competence based theory of syntactic closure." In J. W. Bresnan (ed.), *The Mental Representation of Grammatical Relationss.* Cambridge, MA: MIT Press.

Fox, B. 1987. *Discourse Structure and Anaphora: Written and Conversational English.* New York: Cambridge U. Press.

Francis, W., and H. Kucera. 1982. *Frequency Analysis of English Usage: Lexicon and Grammar.* Boston: Houghton Mifflin.

Freuder, E. C. 1982. "A sufficient condition for backtrack-free search," *JACM* 29, 1.

Gazdar, G. 1982. "Phrase structure grammar." In P. Jacobson and G. K. Pullum (eds.), *The Nature of Syntactic Representation.* Dordrecht: D. Reidel, 131–186.

Gazdar, G., and C. Mellish. 1989a. *Natural Language Processing in LISP.* Reading, MA: Addison-Wesley.

Gazdar, G., and C. Mellish. 1989b. *Natural Language Processing in PROLOG.* Reading, MA: Addison-Wesley.

Gazdar, G., E. Klein, G. K. Pullum, and I. Sag. 1985. *Generalized Phrase Structure Grammar.* Oxford: Basil Blackwell.

Genesereth, M., and N. Nilsson. 1987. *Logical Foundations of Artificial Intelligence.* San Mateo, CA: Morgan Kaufmann.

Goldman, A. 1970. *A Theory of Human Action.* Princeton, NJ: Princeton U. Press.

Goodman, B. 1986. "Reference identification and reference identification failures," *Computational Linguistics* 12, 4.

Grice, H. P. 1957. "Meaning," *Philosophical Review* 66, 377–388. Reprinted in D. Steinburg and L. Jakobovits (eds.). 1971. *Semantics.* New York: Cambridge U. Press.

Grice, H. P. 1975. "Logic and conversation." In P. Cole and J. Morgan (eds.), *Syntax and Semantics.* Vol. 3: *Speech Acts.* New York: Academic Press, 41–58.

Grimes, J. E. 1975. *The Thread of Discourse.* The Hague: Moulton Press.

Grishman, R., and J. Sterling. 1992. "Acquisition of selectional patterns," *Proc. 14th COLING,* 658–664.

Grosz, B. J. 1974. "The structure of task oriented dialog," *IEEE Symp. on Speech Recognition.* Reprinted in L. Polanyi (ed.). 1986. *The Structure of Discourse.* Norwood, NJ: Ablex.

Grosz, B. J. 1977. "The representation and use of focus in a system for understanding dialogs," *Proc. IJCAI,* 67–76. Reprinted in RNLP.

Grosz, B. J., and C. Sidner. 1986. "Attention, intention, and the structure of discourse," *Computational Linguistics* 12, 3.

Grosz, B. J., and C. Sidner. 1990. "Plans for discourse." In Cohen et al. (1990), 417–444.

Grosz, B. J., A. K. Joshi, and S. Weinstein. 1983. "Providing a unified account of definite noun phrases in discourse," *Proc. ACL,* 44–50.

Grosz, B. J., D. Appelt, P. Martin, and F. Pereira. 1987. "TEAM: An experiment in the design of transportable natural-language interfaces," *Artificial Intelligence* 32, 2:173–244.

Haas, A. R. 1986. "A syntactic theory of belief and action," *Artificial Intelligence* 28, 3:245–292.

Halliday, M. A. K. 1967. "Notes on transitivity and theme in English," *Journal of Linguistics* 3:199–244.

Halliday, M. A. K. 1985. *A Short Introduction to Functional Grammar.* London: Arnold.

Halliday, M. A. K., and R. Hasan. 1976. *Cohesion in English.* London: Longman.

Hankamer, J., and I. Sag. 1976. "Deep and surface anaphora," *Linguistic Inquiry* 7, 3:391–426.

Harper, M. 1992. "Ambiguous noun phrases in logical form," *Computational Linguistics* 18, 4, 419–466.

Hayes, P. J. 1977. "On semantic nets, frames, and associations," *Proc. IJCAI*, 99–107.

Hayes, P. J. 1979. "The logic of frames." In D. Metzing (ed.), *Frame Conceptions and Text Understanding.* New York: de Gruyter.

Heim, I. 1982. "The semantics of definite and indefinite noun phrases," Ph.D. dissertation, U. Massachusetts.

Hendrix, G. G., E. Sacerdoti, D. Sagalowicz, and J. Slocum. 1978. "Developing a natural language interface to complex data," *ACM Trans. on Database Systems* 3, 2:105–147.

Herskovits, A. 1986. *Language and Spatial Cognition.* New York: Cambridge U. Press.

Hewitt, C. 1971. "PLANNER: A language for proving theorems in robots," *Proc. IJCAI.*

Hindle, D. 1989. "Acquiring disambiguation rules from text," *Proc. ACL,* 118–125.

Hindle, D., and M. Rooth. 1993. "Structural ambiguity and lexical relations," *Computational Linguistics* 19, 1.

Hinrichs, E. 1986. "Temporal anaphora in discourse of English," *Linguistics and Philosophy* 9, 1:63–82.

Hirschberg, J., and D. J. Litman. 1993. "Empirical studies on the disambiguation of cue phrases," *Computational Linguistics* 19, 3, 501–530.

Hintikka, J. 1969. "Semantics for propositional attitudes." In J. W. Davis, D. J. Hockney, and K. W. Wilson (eds.), *Philosophical Logic.* Dordrecht: D. Reidel. Also appeared in L. Linsky (ed.). 1971. *Reference and Modality.* New York: Oxford U. Press.

Hirst, G. 1981a. *Anaphora in Natural Language Understanding.* Berlin: Springer-Verlag.

Hirst, G. 1981b. "Discourse oriented anaphora resolution in natural language understanding: A review," *AJCL* 7, 2:85–98.

Hirst, G. 1987. *Semantic Interpretation Against Ambiguity.* New York: Cambridge U. Press.

Hobbs, J. R. 1978. "Resolving pronoun references," *Lingua* 44, B11–338. Reprinted in RNLP.

Hobbs, J. R. 1979. "Coherence and co-reference," *Cognitive Science* 3, 1:67–82.

Hobbs, J. R., and S. M. Shieber. 1987. "An algorithm for generating quantifier scopings," *Computational Linguistics* 13:1–2.

Hobbs, J. R., M. Stickel, D. Appelt, and P. Martin. 1993. "Interpretation as abduction," *Artificial Intelligence* 63, 1–2:69–142.

Hobbs, J. R., W. Croft, T. Davies, D. Edwards, and K. Laws. 1987. "Commonsense metaphysics and lexical semantics," *Computational Linguistics* 13, 3–4:241–250.

Hovy, E. 1993. "Automated discourse generation using discourse structure relations," *Artificial Intelligence* 63, 1–2:341–386.

Huddleston, R. 1988. *English Grammar: An Outline.* New York: Cambridge U. Press.

Hwang, C. H., and L. K. Schubert. 1992. "Tense trees as the 'fine structure' of discourse," *Proc. 30th Annual Meeting, Assoc. for Computational Linguistics,* 232–240.

Hwang, C. H., and L. K. Schubert. 1993a. "Episodic logic: A situational logic for natural language processing." In P. Aczel, D. Israel, Y. Katagiri, and S. Peters (eds.), *Situation Theory and its Applications,* Vol. 3, CSLI Series (Center for the Study of Language and Information, Stanford U.). Chicago: Chicago U. Press.

Hwang, C. H., and L. K. Schubert. 1993b. "Meeting the interlocking needs of LF-computation, deindexing and inference: An organic approach to natural language understanding," *Proc. IJCAI,* 1297–1302.

Jackendoff, R. S. 1972. *Semantic Interpretation in Generative Grammar.* Cambridge, MA: MIT Press.

Jackendoff, R. S. 1990. *Semantic Structures.* Cambridge, MA: MIT Press.

Jacobs, P., and L. Rau. 1990. "SCISOR: A system for extracting information from on-line news," *Commun. of the ACM* 33, 11, 88–97.

Jelinek, F. 1990. "Self-organized language modeling for speech recognition." In A. Waibel and K. F. Lee (eds.), *Readings in Speech Recognition.* San Mateo, CA: Morgan Kaufmann, 450–506.

Jensen, K., and J. Binot. 1987. "Disambiguating prepositional phrase attachments by using on-line dictionary definitions," *Computational Linguistics* 13:3–4.

Johnson, M. 1991. "Features and formulae," *Computational Linguistics* 17, 2:131–153.

Joshi, A. 1985. "Tree-adjoining grammars: How much context sensitivity is required to provide reasonable structural descriptions." In D. R. Dowty, L. Karttunen, and A. Zwicky (eds.), *Natural Language Parsing.* New York: Cambridge U. Press.

Kamp, H. 1975. "Two theories about adjectives." In E. Keenan (ed.), *Formal Semantics of Natural Language.* Cambridge, U.K.: Cambridge U. Press.

Kamp, H. 1981. "A theory of truth and semantic representation." In J. Groenendijk, T. Janssen, and M. Stokhof (eds.), *Formal Methods in the Study of Language.* Amsterdam: Amsterdam Press.

Kaplan, R. M. 1973. "A general syntactic processor." In R. Rustin (ed.), *Natural Language Processing.* New York: Algorithmics Press.

Kaplan, R. M., and J. Bresnan. 1982. "Lexical-functional grammar: A formal system for grammatical representation." In J. Bresnan (ed.), *The Mental Representation of Grammatical Relations.* Cambridge, MA: MIT Press.

Kartunnen, L. 1976. "Discourse referents." In J. McCawley (ed.), *Syntax and Semantics.* Vol. 7. New York: Academic Press, 363–386.

Katz, J. J., and J. A. Fodor. 1963. "The structure of semantic theory," *Language* 39, 170–210. Reprinted in J. A. Fodor et al. (eds.). 1984. *The Structure of Language: Readings in the Philosophy of Language.* Englewood Cliffs, NJ: Prentice-Hall.

Kautz, H. 1990. "A circumscriptive theory of plan recognition." In Cohen et al. (1990), 105–134.

Kay, M. 1973. "The MIND system." In R. Rustin (ed.), *Natural Language Processing.* New York: Algorithmics Press, 155–188.

Kay, M. 1980. "Algorithm schemata and data structures in syntactic processing," CSL-80-12, Xerox Corporation. Reprinted in RNLP.

Kay, M. 1982. "Parsing in functional unification grammar." In D. R. Dowty, L. Karttunen, and A. Zwicky (eds.), *Natural Language Parsing.* New York: Cambridge U. Press, 251–278. Reprinted in RNLP.

Kimball, J. 1973. "Seven principles of surface structure parsing in natural language," *Cognition* 2, 1:15–47.

Klein, E. 1980. "A semantics for positive and comparative adjectives," *Linguistics and Philosophy* 4, 1–45.

Knuth, D. E. 1968. "Semantics for context-free languages," *Mathematical Systems Theory* 2, 127–145.

Konolige, K. 1985. "A computational theory of belief introspection," *Proc. IJCAI,* 502–508.

Konolige, K. 1986. *A Deduction Model of Belief.* San Mateo, CA: Morgan Kaufmann.

Koskenniemi, K. 1983. "Two-level model for morphological analysis," *Proc. IJCAI,* 683–685.

Kripke, S. 1963. "Semantical consideration on modal logic," *Acta Philosophica Fennica* 16:83–94.

Lascarides, A., and N. Asher. 1993. "Temporal interpretation, discourse relations, and commonsense entailment," *Linguistics and Philosophy* 16, 5.

Lascarides, A., N. Asher, and J. Oberlander. 1992. "Inferring discourse relations in context," *Proc. ACL,* 1–8.

Lee, K. 1990. "Context dependent phonetic hidden Markov models for continuous speech recognition," *IEEE Trans. on Acoustics, Speech and Signal Processing.* Reprinted in Waibel and Lee (1990).

Leech, G. 1987. *Meaning and the English Verb (2nd ed.).* London: Longman.

Leech, G., and J. Svartvik. 1975. *A Communicative Grammar of English.* Singapore: Longman Singapore Publishers Ltd.

Levesque, H. J. 1984. "A logic of implicit and explicit belief," *Proc. AAAI.*

Levin, J., and J. Moore. 1977. "Dialogue-games: Metacommunication structures for natural language interaction," *Cognitive Science* 1, 4:395–421.

Lewis, D. K. 1973. *Counterfactuals.* Oxford: Basil Blackwell.

Lewis, D. K. 1979. "Scorekeeping in a language game." In R. Bäuerle, U. Egli, and A. von Stechow (eds.), *Semantics from Different Points of View.* Berlin: Springer-Verlag.

Linde, C. 1979. "Focus of attention and the choice of pronouns in discourse." In T. Given (ed.), *Syntax and Semantics.* Vol. 12. New York: Academic Press.

Litman, D. J., and J. F. Allen. 1987. "A plan recognition model for subdialogues in conversations," *Cognitive Science* 11, 2:163–200.

Litman, D. J., and J. F. Allen. 1990. "Discourse processing and commonsense plans." In Cohen et al. (1990), 365–388.

Luger, G., and W. Stubblefield. 1993. *Artificial Intelligence (2nd ed.).* Redwood City, CA: Benjamin/Cummings.

Lytinen, S. L. 1986. "Dynamically combining syntax and semantics in natural language processing," *Proc. AAAI,* 574–578.

MacWorth, A. K. 1977. "Consistency in networks of relations," *Artificial Intelligence* 8, 1.

Magerman, D., and C. Weir. 1992. "Efficiency, robustness and accuracy in picky chart parsing," *Proc. ACL.*

Mann, W. C., and C. Mathiesson. 1985. "Nigel: A systemic grammar for text generation." In R. O. Freedle (ed.), *Systemic Perspectives on Discourse.* Norwood, NJ: Ablex.

Mann, W. C., and S. Thompson. 1986. "Rhetorical structure theory: Description and construction of text structures." In G. Kempen (ed.), *Natural Language Generation.* Boston, MA: Kluwer Academic Publishers, 279–300.

de Marcken, C. 1990. "Parsing the LOB corpus," *Proc. ACL,* 243–251.

Marcus, M. 1980. *A Theory of Syntactic Recognition for Natural Language.* Cambridge, MA: MIT Press.

Marcus, M., D. Hindle, and M. Fleck. 1983. "D-Theory: Talking about talking about trees," *Proc. ACL.*

Marcus, M., B. Santorini, and M. Marcinkiewicz. 1993. "Building a large annotated corpus of English: The Penn Treebank," *Computational Linguistics* 19, 2.

May, R. 1985. *Logical Form.* Cambridge, MA: MIT Press.

McCarthy, J. 1980. "Circumscription: A form of non-monotonic reasoning," *Artificial Intelligence* 13:27–39.

McCarthy, J. and P. J. Hayes. 1969. "Some philosophical problems from the standpoint of artificial intelligence." In B. Meltzer and D. Michie (eds.), *Machine Intelligence 4.* Edinburgh: Edinburgh U. Press.

McCawley, J. D. 1993. *Everything That Linguists Have Always Wanted to Know about Logic (2nd ed.).* Chicago: Chicago U. Press.

McCord, M. C. 1980. "Slot grammars," *AJCL* 6, 1:31–43.

McCord, M. C. 1986. "Focalizers, the scoping problem, and semantic interpretation rules in logic grammars." In D. H. Warren and M. van Canegham (eds.), *Logic Programming and its Applications.* Norwood, NJ: Ablex.

McKeown, K. R. 1985. *Text Generation.* New York: Cambridge U. Press.

Mellish, C. 1985. *Computer Interpretation of Natural Language Descriptions.* New York: Wiley.

Miller, G. 1990. "WordNet: An online lexical database," *International Journal of Lexicography* 3, 4.

Minsky, M. 1975. "A framework for representing knowledge." In P. H. Winston (ed.), *The Psychology of Computer Vision.* New York: McGraw-Hill, 211–277.

Montague, R. 1974. *Formal Philosophy.* New Haven: Yale U. Press.

Moore, J., and M. Pollack. 1992. "A problem for RST: The need for multi-level discourse analysis," *Computational Linguistics* 18, 4:537–544.

Moore, R. C. 1973. "D-SCRIPT: A computational theory of description," *Proc. IJCAI,* 223–229.

Moore, R. C. 1977. "Reasoning about knowledge and action," *Proc. IJCAI,* 223–227. Extended version in J. R. Hobbs and J. Moore (eds.). 1985. *Formal Theories of the Common Sense World.* Vol. 1. Norwood, NJ: Ablex.

Moore, R. C. 1981. "Problems in logical form," *Proc. 19th ACL,* 117–124. Reprinted in RNLP.

Moore, R. C. 1989. "Unification-based semantic interpretation," *Proc. ACL.*

Nebel, B., C. Rich, and W. Swartout (eds.) 1992. *Proc. 3rd Int'l. Conf. on Principles of Knowledge Representation and Reasoning.* San Mateo, CA: Morgan Kaufmann.

Norvig, P. 1992. *Paradigms of Artificial Intelligence Programming.* San Mateo, CA: Morgan Kaufmann.

Palmer, M., R. Passonneau, C. Wier, and T. Finin. 1993. "The KERNEL text understanding system," *Artificial Intelligence* 63:17–68.

Parsons, T. 1990. *Events in the Semantics of English.* Cambridge, MA: MIT Press.

Partee, B. 1984. "Nominal and temporal anaphora," *Linguistics and Philosophy* 7:243–286.

Partee, B., A. ter Meulen, and R. Wall. 1993. *Mathematical Methods in Linguistics (corrected 1st ed.).* Boston: Kluwer Academic Publishers.

Patten, T. 1988. *Systemic Text Generation as Problem Solving.* Cambridge U. Press.

Paxton, W., and A. Robinson. 1973. "A parser for a speech understanding system," *Proc. IJCAI.*

Pelletier, J. 1979. *Mass Terms: Some Philosophical Problems.* Dordrecht: D. Reidel.

Pereira, F. C. N. 1981. "Extraposition grammars," *AJCL* 7, 4:243–256.

Pereira, F. C. N. 1983. "Logic for natural language analysis," SRI Technical Note 275, SRI International, Menlo Park, California.

Pereira, F. C. N. 1985. "Characterization of attachment preferences." In D. R. Dowty, L. Karttunen, and A. Zwicky (eds.), *Natural Language Parsing.* New York: Cambridge U. Press, 307–319.

Pereira, F. C. N., and M. Pollack. 1991. "Incremental interpretation," *Artificial Intelligence* 50:37–82.

Pereira, F. C. N., and Y. Schabes. 1992. "Inside-outside re-estimation from partially bracketed corpora," *Proc. ACL,* 128–135.

Pereira, F. C. N., and S. M. Shieber. 1987. *Prolog and Natural Language Analysis.* Chicago: Chicago U. Press.

Pereira, F. C. N., and D. H. D. Warren. 1980. "Definite clause grammars for language analysis— A survey of the formalism and a comparison with augmented transition networks," *Artificial Intelligence* 13, 3:231–278. Reprinted in RNLP.

Perrault, C. R. 1984. "On the mathematical properties of linguistic theories," *Computational Linguistics* 10, 3–4:165–176. Reprinted in RNLP.

Perrault, C. R. 1990. "An application of default logic to speech act theory." In Cohen et al. (1990), 161–186.

Perrault, C. R., and J. F. Allen. 1980. "A plan-based analysis of indirect speech acts," *AJCL* 6, 3–4:167–182.

Perrault, C. R., and P. R. Cohen. 1981. "It's for your own good: A note on inaccurate reference." In A. Joshi, B. Webber, and I. Sag (eds.), *Elements of Discourse Understanding.* New York: Cambridge U. Press.

Perrault, C. R., and B. J. Grosz. 1986. "Natural language interfaces," *Annual Review of Computer Science* 1:47–82.

Pierrehumbert, J., and J. Hirschberg. 1990. "The meaning of intonational contours in the interpretation of discourse." In Cohen et al. (1990), 271–312.

Pollack, J., and D. Waltz. 1985. "Massively parallel parsing: A strongly interactive model of natural language interpretation," *Cognitive Science* 9:51–74.

Pollack, M. 1990. "Plans as complex mental attitudes." In Cohen et al. (1990), 77–104.

Pollard, C., and I. Sag. 1987. *Information-Based Syntax and Semantics.* Vol. I: *Fundamentals.* CSLI Lecture Notes 13. Chicago: Chicago U. Press.

Pollard, C., and I. Sag. 1993. *Head-Driven Phrase Structure Grammar.* Chicago, IL: Chicago U. Press.

Prince, E. 1981. "Towards a taxonomy of given-new information." In P. Cole (ed.), *Radical Pragmatics.* New York: Academic Press, 236–256.

Prior, A. N. 1967. *Past, Present, and Future.* Oxford: Oxford U. Press.

Pustejovsky, J. 1991. "The syntax of event structures," *Cognition* 41:47–81.

Quillian, M. R. 1968. "Semantic memory." In M. Minsky (ed.), *Semantic Information Processing.* Cambridge, MA: MIT Press.

Quirk, R., S. Greenbaum, G. Leech, and J. Svartik. 1972. *A Grammar of Contemporary English.* New York: Seminar Press.

Rabiner, L. R. 1989. "A tutorial on hidden Markov models and selected applications in speech recognition," *Proc. IEEE.* Reprinted in Waibel and Lee (1990).

Rabiner, L. R., and B.-H. Juang. 1993. *Fundamentals of Speech Recognition.* Englewoods Cliffs, NJ: Prentice-Hall, Inc.

Radford, A. 1981. *Transformational Syntax.* New York: Cambridge U. Press.

Rao, A., and M. Georgeff. 1991. "Modeling rational agents within a BDI architecture." In J. F. Allen, R. Fikes, and E. Sandewall (eds.), *Proc. 2nd Conf. on Principles of Knowledge Representation and Reasoning.* San Mateo, CA: Morgan Kaufmann, 473–484.

Reichenbach, H. 1947. *Elements of Symbolic Logic.* New York: Macmillan.

Reichman, R. 1978. "Conversational coherency," *Cognitive Science* 2, 4:283–328.

Reichman, R. 1985. *Getting Computers to Talk Like You and Me.* Cambridge, MA: MIT Press.

Reinhart, T. 1983. "Co-reference and bound anaphora: A restatement of the anaphora question," *Linguistics and Philosophy* 6:47–88.

Reiter, R. 1980. "A logic for default reasoning," *Artificial Intelligence* 13:81–132.

Resnik, P. 1993. "Semantic classes and syntactic ambiguity," *Proc. ARPA Human Language Technology Workshop,* San Mateo, CA: Morgan Kaufmann.

Rich, E., and K. Knight. 1992. *Artificial Intelligence (2nd ed.).* McGraw-Hill.

Riesbeck, C., and R. C. Schank. 1978. "Comprehension by computer." In W. Levelt and G. B. Flores d'Arcais (eds.), *Studies in the Perception of Language.* Chichester, U.K.: Wiley.

Ritchie, G. D. 1980. *Computational Grammar.* New York: Barnes and Noble.

Ritchie, G. D., G. Russell, A. Black, and S. Pulman. 1992. *Computational Morphology.* Cambridge, MA: MIT Press.

Robinson, J. A. 1965. "A machine-oriented logic based on the resolution principle," *Journal of the ACM* 12, 1.

Robinson, J. J. 1982. "DIAGRAM: A grammar for dialogues," *Commun. of the ACM* 25, 1:27–47. Reprinted in RNLP.

Rosenschein, S. J., and S. M. Shieber. 1982. "Translating English into logical form," *Proc. ACL,* 1–8.

Ross, S. 1988. *A First Course in Probability (3rd ed.).* New York: Macmillan.

Rounds, W. C. 1988. "LFP: A logic for linguistic description and an analysis of its complexity," *Computational Linguistics* 14, 4:1–10.

Rumelhart, D. E. 1975. "Notes on schema for stories." In D. Bobrow and A. Collins (eds.), *Representation and Understanding.* New York: Academic Press.

Rumelhart, D. E., and J. McClelland. 1986. *Parallel Distributive Processing.* Cambridge, MA: MIT Press.

Russell, B., and A. N. Whitehead. 1925. *Principia Mathematica (2nd ed.).* Vol. 1. New York: Cambridge U. Press.

Sacerdoti, E. 1977. *A Structure for Plans and Behavior.* New York: Elsevier North-Holland.

Sager, N. 1981. *Natural Language Information Processing: A Computer Grammar of English and its Applications.* Reading, MA: Addison-Wesley.

Saint-Dizier, P. 1985. "Handling quantifier scoping ambiguities in a semantic representation of natural language sentences." In V. Dahl and P. Saint-Dizier (eds.), *Natural Language Understanding and Logic Programming.* Amsterdam: North-Holland.

Saint-Dizier, P. 1986. "An approach to natural language semantics in logic programming," *Journal of Logic Programming* 3, 4:329–356.

Scha, R., and L. Polanyi. 1988. "An augmented context free grammar for discourse," *Proc. COLING.*

Schafer, R. W., and L. R. Rabiner. 1975. "Digital representations of speech," *Proc. IEEE* 63, 4:662–667. Reprinted in Waibel and Lee (1990).

Schank, R. C. (ed.). 1975. *Conceptual Information Processing.* Amsterdam: North-Holland.

Schank, R. C., and R. Abelson. 1977. *Scripts, Plans, Goals and Understanding.* Hillsdale, NJ: Lawrence Erlbaum.

Schank, R. C., and K. M. Colby. 1973. *Computer Models of Thought and Language.* San Francisco, CA: Freeman.

Schank, R. C., and C. J. Rieger. 1974. "Inference and the computer understanding of natural language," *Artificial Intelligence* 5:373–412.

Schank, R. C., and C. K. Riesbeck. 1981. *Inside Computer Understanding.* Hillsdale, NJ: Lawrence Erlbaum.

Schiffer, S. R. 1972. *Meaning.* London: Oxford U. Press.

Schmidt, C., N. Sridharan, and J. Goodson. 1978. "The plan recognition problem: An intersection of psychology and artificial intelligence," *Artificial Intelligence* 11:45–83.

Schubert, L. K. 1986. "Are there preference tradeoffs in attachment decision?," *Proc. AAAI,* 601–605.

Schubert, L. K., and F. J. Pelletier. 1982. "From English to logic: Context-free computation of conventional logical translation," *AJCL* 8, 1:165–176. Reprinted in RNLP.

Schubert, L. K., and F. J. Pelletier. 1987. "Problems in the representation of the logical form of generics, plurals, and mass nouns." In E. LePore (ed.), *New Directions in Semantics.* New York: Academic Press, 385–451.

Searle, J. R. 1975. "Indirect speech acts." In P. Cole and J. Morgan (eds.), *Syntax and Semantics.* Vol. 3: *Speech Acts.* New York: Academic Press, 59–82.

Searle, J. R. 1979. "A taxonomy of speech acts." In J. Searle (ed.), *Expression and Meaning.* Cambridge, U.K.: Cambridge U. Press, 1–29.

Sells, P. 1985. *Lectures on Contemporary Syntactic Theories.* Chicago: Chicago U. Press.

Shapiro, S. C. 1982. "Generalized augmented transition network grammars for generation from semantic networks," *AJCL* 8, 1:12–25.

Shapiro, S. C. (ed.). 1992. *Encyclopedia of Artificial Intelligence (2nd ed.).* New York: Wiley.

Shieber, S. M. 1984. "The design of a computer language for linguistic information," *Proc. COLING,* 362–366.

Shieber, S. M. 1986. *An Introduction to Unification-Based Approaches to Grammar.* CSLI Lecture Notes 4. Chicago: Chicago U. Press.

Shieber, S. M., G. van Noord, F. C. N. Pereira, and R. C. Moore. 1990. "Semantic-head-driven generation," *Computational Linguistics* 16, 1:30–42.

Sidner, C. 1983. "Focusing in the comprehension of definite anaphora." In M. Brady and R. C. Berwick (eds.), *Computational Models of Discourse.* Cambridge, MA: MIT Press, 267–330. Reprinted in RNLP.

Sidner, C. 1985. "Plan parsing for intended response recognition in discourse," *Computational Intelligence* 1, 1:1–10.

Slocum, J. 1985. "A survey of machine translation," *Comput'l. Linguistics* 11, 1:1–17.

Small, S. L., and C. Rieger. 1982. "Parsing and comprehending with word experts." In W. Lehnert and M. Ringle (eds.), *Strategies for Natural Language Processing.* Hillsdale, NJ: Lawrence Erlbaum.

Song, F., and R. Cohen. 1991. "Tense interpretation in the context of narrative," *Proc. AAAI,* 131–136.

Sowa, J. 1984. *Conceptual Structures.* Reading, MA: Addison-Wesley.

Sowa, J. (ed.). 1991. *Principles of Semantic Networks.* San Mateo, CA: Morgan Kaufmann.

Sproat, R. 1992. *Morphology and Computation.* Cambridge, MA: MIT Press.

Stabler, E. 1992. *The Logical Approach to Syntax.* Cambridge, MA: MIT Press.

Stalnaker, R. 1974. "Pragmatic presuppositions." In M. Munitz and P. Unger (eds.), *Semantics and Philosophy.* New York: New York University Press.

Steedman, M. 1982. "Reference to past time." In R. J. Jarvella and W. Klein (eds.), *Speech, Place and Action.* New York: Wiley.

Steedman, M. 1987. "Combinatory grammars and parasitic gaps," *Natural Language and Linguistic Theory* 5, 403–439.

Strawson, P. F. 1964. "Intention and convention in speech acts," *Philosophical Review* 73, 4:439–460. Reprinted in J. R. Searle (ed.). 1971. *The Philosophy of Language.* New York: Oxford U. Press.

Tarski, A. 1944. "The semantic conception of truth and the foundations of semantics," *Philosophy and Phenomenological Research* 4:341–375.

Tedesci, P and A. Zaenen (eds.). 1981. *Syntax and Semantics.* Vol. 14: *Tense and Aspect.* New York: Academic Press.

Thomason, R. 1970. *Symbolic Logic.* New York: Macmillan.

Tomita, M. 1986. *Efficient Parsing for Natural Language.* Boston: Kluwer Academic Publishers.

Traum, D. R., and E. A. Hinkelman. 1992. "Conversation acts in task-oriented spoken dialogue," *Computational Intelligence* 8, 3 (special issue on computational approaches to non-literal language).

VanLehn, K. 1978. "Determining the scope of English quantifiers," TR AI-TR-483, AI Lab, Massachusetts Inst. of Technology.

Vendler, Z. 1967. *Linguistics in Philosophy.* Ithaca, NY: Cornell U. Press.

Vijay-Shankar, K. 1992. "Using descriptions of trees in tree adjoining grammar," *Computational Linguistics* 18, 4.

Viterbi, A. J. 1967. "Error bounds for convolution codes and an asymptotically optimal decoding algorithm," *IEEE Trans. on Information Theory* 13:260–269.

Waibel, A., and K. F. Lee (eds.). 1990. *Readings in Speech Recognition.* San Mateo, CA: Morgan Kaufmann.

Walker, M. 1989. "Evaluating discourse processing algorithms," *Proc. ACL,* 251–261.

Waltz, D. L. 1975. "Understanding line drawings of scenes with shadows." In P. H. Winston (ed.), *Psychology of Computer Vision.* Cambridge, MA: MIT Press.

Wang, M., and J. Hirschberg. 1992. "Automatic classification of intonational phrase boundaries," *Speech and Language* 6:175–196.

Warren, D. H. D., and F. C. N. Pereira. 1982. "An efficient easily adaptable system for interpreting natural language queries," *Computational Linguistics* 8, 3–4:110–122.

Webber, B. L. 1983. "So what can we talk about now." In M. Brady and B. Berwick (eds.), *Computational Models of Discourse.* Cambridge, MA: MIT Press, 331–370. Reprinted in RNLP.

Webber, B. L. 1988. "Tense as discourse anaphora," *Comput'l. Linguistics* 14, 2:61–73.

Webber, B. L. 1991. "Structure and ostension in the interpretation of discourse diexis," *Language and Cognitive Processes* 6:107–135.

Webber, B. L. 1992. "Question answering." In S. C. Shapiro (ed.), *Encyclopedia of Artificial Intelligence.* New York: Wiley, 814–822.

Weischedel, R. M. 1979. "A new semantic computation while parsing: Presupposition and entailment." In C. Oh and D. Dineen (eds.), *Syntax and Semantics.* Vol. II: *Presupposition.* New York: Academic Press, 155–182. Reprinted in RNLP.

Weischedel, R. M., M. Meteer, R. Schwartz, L. Ramshaw, and J. Palmucci. 1993. "Coping with ambiguity and unknown words through probabilistic models," *Computational Linguistics* 19, 2 (special issue on using corpora).

Weizenbaum, J. 1966. "ELIZA," *Commun. of the ACM* 9:36–45.

Whittemore, G., K. Ferrara, and H. Bruner. 1990. "Empirical study of predictive powers of simple prepositional attachment schemes for post-modifier prepositional phrases," *Proc. ACL,* 23–30.

Wilensky, R. 1983. *Planning and Understanding.* Reading, MA: Addison-Wesley.

Wilensky, R. 1986. *Common LISPcraft.* New York: W. W. Norton.

Wilks, Y. 1975. "An intelligent analyzer and understander of English," *Commun. of the ACM* 18, 5:264–274. Reprinted in RNLP.

Winograd, T. 1972. *Understanding Natural Language.* New York: Academic Press.

Winograd, T. 1973. "A procedural model of language understanding." In R. C. Schank and K. M. Colby (eds.), *Computer Models of Thought and Language.* San Francisco, CA: Freeman, 152–186.

Winograd, T. 1983. *Language as a Cognitive Process.* Vol. 1: *Syntax.* Reading, MA: Addison-Wesley.

Winston, P. H. 1992. *Artificial Intelligence (3rd ed.).* Reading, MA: Addison-Wesley.

Winston, P. H., and B. K. P. Horn. 1989. *LISP (3rd ed.).* Reading, MA: Addison-Wesley.

Woods, W. A. 1970. "Transition network grammars for natural language analysis," *Commun. of the ACM* 13:591–606. Reprinted in RNLP.

Woods, W. A. 1973. "An experimental parsing system for transition network grammars." In R. Rustin (ed.), *Natural Language Processing.* New York: Algorithmics Press.

Woods, W. A. 1975. "What's in a link: Foundations for semantic networks." In D. G. Bobrow and A. Collins (eds.), *Representation and Understanding: Studies in Cognitive Science.* New York: Academic Press.

Woods, W. A. 1977. "Lunar rocks in natural English: Explorations in natural language question answering." In A. Zampoli (ed.), *Linguistic Structures Processing.* New York: Elsevier North-Holland.

Woods, W. A. 1978. "Semantics and quantification in natural language question answering." In M. Yovitz (ed.), *Advances in Computers.* Vol. 17. New York: Academic Press. Reprinted in RNLP.

Woods, W. A. 1980. "Cascaded ATN grammars," *AJCL* 6, 1:1–12.

Yarowsky, D. 1992. "Word-sense disambiguation using statistical models of Roget's categories trained on large corpora," *Proc. COLING,* 454–460.

Index